OXFORD STUDIES IN ANCIE

OXFORD STUDIES IN ANCIENT PHILOSOPHY

EDITOR: DAVID SEDLEY

VOLUME XXXIV

SUMMER 2008

OXFORD
UNIVERSITY PRESS

OXFORD
UNIVERSITY PRESS

Great Clarendon Street, Oxford OX2 6DP

Oxford University Press is a department of the University of Oxford.
It furthers the University's objective of excellence in research, scholarship,
and education by publishing worldwide in

Oxford New York

Auckland Cape Town Dar es Salaam Hong Kong Karachi
Kuala Lumpur Madrid Melbourne Mexico City Nairobi
New Delhi Shanghai Taipei Toronto

With offices in

Argentina Austria Brazil Chile Czech Republic France Greece
Guatemala Hungary Italy Japan Poland Portugal Singapore
South Korea Switzerland Thailand Turkey Ukraine Vietnam

Oxford is a registered trade mark of Oxford University Press
in the UK and in certain other countries

Published in the United States
by Oxford University Press Inc., New York

British Library Cataloguing in Publication Data
Data available

Library of Congress Cataloging in Publication Data
Oxford studies in ancient philosophy.—
Vol. xxxiv (2008).—Oxford: Clarendon Press;
New York: Oxford University Press, 1983–
v.; 22 cm. Annual.
1. Philosophy, Ancient—Periodicals.
B1.O9   180.'5—dc.19   84-645022
AACR 2   MARC-S

Typeset by John Waś, Oxford
Printed in Great Britain
on acid-free paper by
Biddles Ltd, King's Lynn, Norfolk

ISBN 978-0-19-954487-5
ISBN 978-0-19-954489-9 (Pbk.)

1 3 5 7 9 10 8 6 4 2

ADVISORY BOARD

Contributions and books for review should be sent to the Editor, Professor Brad Inwood, Department of Classics, University of Toronto, 125 Queen's Park, Toronto M5S 2C7, Canada (e-mail brad.inwood@utoronto.ca).

Contributors are asked to observe the 'Notes for Contributors to Oxford Studies in Ancient Philosophy', printed at the end of this volume.

Up-to-date contact details, the latest version of Notes to Contributors, and publication schedules can be checked on the *Oxford Studies in Ancient Philosophy* website:

www.oup.co.uk/philosophy/series/osap

CONTENTS

Socratic Irony as Pretence   1
G. R. F. FERRARI

Appearances and Calculations: Plato's Division of the Soul   35
JESSICA MOSS

Glaucon's Challenge and Thrasymacheanism   69
C. D. C. REEVE

The Copula and Semantic Continuity in Plato's *Sophist*   105
FIONA LEIGH

'What's the Matter with Prime Matter?'   123
FRANK A. LEWIS

Elemental Teleology in Aristotle's *Physics* 2. 8   147
MARGARET SCHARLE

Alteration and Aristotle's Theory of Change in *Physics* 6   185
DAMIAN MURPHY

Kinēsis vs. *Energeia*: A Much-Read Passage in (but not of)
Aristotle's *Metaphysics*   219
M. F. BURNYEAT

Aristotle's Argument for a Human Function   293
RACHEL BARNEY

Nicomachean Ethics 7. 3 on Akratic Ignorance   323
MARTIN PICKAVÉ AND JENNIFER WHITING

Automatic Action in Plotinus   373
JAMES WILBERDING

Index Locorum   409

SOCRATIC IRONY AS PRETENCE

G. R. F. FERRARI

THERE is a very obvious feature of Socratic irony that has never-theless not received the discussion it merits, despite the fact that Socratic irony has been much discussed in recent years by specia-lists in ancient philosophy. The likely reason that its significance has been missed is that specialists in ancient philosophy are not in the habit of approaching irony as it is approached by contempo-rary linguists, psychologists, and philosophers of language—or if they are, have not at any rate applied the results of their study to their own field. So they have not paused to consider how the irony that Socrates employs in Plato's aporetic dialogues should best be analysed when treated as what it appears within the fiction to be: everyday language. Instead their tendency has been to turn imme-diately to what Socrates' irony can tell us, at the deepest level, about Socrates as a philosopher. The linguistic technicians, for their part, are not in the habit of including Socratic irony within their range of targets for analysis, preferring to direct their attention to less exotic-seeming data.

In what follows I attempt to remedy this situation, addressing it from both sides. In the opening section of this article I describe the pretence theory of irony, which I believe offers the most satisfying

© G. R. F. Ferrari 2008

The seeds of this article were sown some years ago in a talk I gave at a conference on 'Context and Interpretation' at the University of California, Berkeley, in 1993. I was fortunate to have Dan Sperber and Bernard Williams as my formal commentators at the time. For general comment on that early version I am grateful also to Herbert Clark, Tony Long, Alexander Nehamas, Stephen Neale, and Deirdre Wilson. The remains of that version are to be found mostly in the first section of this article, and in the opening of the second section. The ideas in the present version met with useful critique at a meeting of the Faculty Forum of the College of Letters and Science of the University of California, Berkeley, in September 2006. David Sedley helped me streamline the final result.

and intuitive account of what ironists are actually doing when they ironize; and I attempt to show that my version of this theory is proof against the criticisms that have been directed against earlier versions. This is followed in Section 2 by a discussion of Socratic irony as pretence, in which I consider first what is quite ordinary about it, then use the results of this investigation to say what makes Socratic irony peculiar. It is in this section that I point to the obvious feature of Socratic irony that has escaped due attention among specialists in ancient philosophy; but the section also distinguishes a form of everyday irony—which I call the 'solipsistic'—that may be of independent interest to the linguists, psychologists, and philosophers. Finally, in Section 3 I turn to the implications of my analysis of Socratic irony for our understanding of Plato as a writer. Here I resist the temptation to equate the effect that the character Socrates aims to have on his interlocutors with that which Plato as writer aims to have on his readers. When we linger over the analysis of Socratic irony as a phenomenon of everyday language, we are better able to appreciate how Plato's philosophic fictions differ from the philosopher Socrates' pretences.

If the approach adopted in this article is distinctive, its distinctiveness would lie in the fact that it pursues both the study of irony in general and the study of Socratic irony in particular for their own sakes, exhibiting an equal interest in both; it can therefore attempt to illuminate each in the light of the other.

1. Irony as pretence

Gregory Vlastos's account of Socratic irony swiftly became a classic, and like all classics has attracted a good deal of criticism since it first appeared. Much of that criticism seems to me to be justified.[1]

---

[1] G. Vlastos, 'Socratic Irony', in G. Vlastos, *Socrates, Ironist and Moral Philosopher* (Cambridge, 1991), 21–44. For criticism see A. Nehamas, 'Voices of Silence: On Gregory Vlastos' Socrates' ['Silence'], *Arion*, 2/1 (1992), 157–86, and *The Art of Living: Socratic Reflections from Plato to Foucault* [*Art*] (Sather Classical Lectures, 61; Berkeley, 1998), 62–9; P. Gottlieb, 'The Complexity of Socratic Irony: A Note on Professor Vlastos' Account', *Classical Quarterly*, NS 42 (1992), 278–9; J. Gordon, 'Against Vlastos on Complex Irony', *Classical Quarterly*, NS 46 (1996), 131–7; C. L. Griswold, Jr., 'Irony in the Platonic Dialogues', *Philosophy and Literature*, 26 (2001), 84–106 at n. 16; T. C. Brickhouse and N. D. Smith, *The Philosophy of Socrates* (Boulder, 2002), 58–68; M. Lane, 'The Evolution of *Eirōneia* in Classical Greek Texts: Why Socratic *Eirōneia* is Not Socratic Irony', *Oxford Studies in*

But one of Vlastos's ideas that is well worth building upon is the claim that irony can be understood as a kind of pretence.

Surveying the ancient usage of the Greek term *eirōneia*—the word from which our term 'irony' is derived, and which Plato uses on occasion to describe what we now know as Socratic irony— Vlastos notes that it gets applied not only to the utterances of the ironist who intends his irony to be appreciated for what it is but also to the smooth talk of the con artist who intends simply to deceive.[2] In other words, it gets applied to a broader range of utterances than we would now wish to call ironic. Vlastos accounts for the semantic spread of the term by comparing that of the word 'pretence' in English. If a child pretends to his mother that he has finished his homework he is trying to deceive her; but if he goes back to his room, starts up a computer game, and pretends to be saving the earth from alien invaders, he is not deceiving anyone, and does not intend to deceive anyone. Vlastos suggests that this second sense of 'pretending', in which pretence is equivalent to make-believe or role-playing, could be used to explain verbal irony (27).

And so it could; but Vlastos himself does not develop the idea. The account of Socratic irony that he does develop is based instead on a theory traditional since the codification of ancient rhetoric, which claims that we understand an ironical utterance by replacing the literal meaning with a figurative meaning that contradicts it or, more vaguely, is its opposite. It is Vlastos's developed theory that has come in for criticism.

The traditional theory of irony has in any case been jettisoned by linguists, philosophers, and psychologists in recent decades, although this fact seems to have gone unremarked by specialists in ancient philosophy.[3] While the traditional theory superficially fits

Ancient Philosophy, 31 (2006), 49–83. (Works by authors with a single entry in the bibliography will be cited hereafter by author's name alone.)

[2] Vlastos's history of the term *eirōneia* is not a topic I shall address (although see n. 20). For criticism see Nehamas, *Art*, 54–6; Gottlieb; M. C. Stokes (ed.), *Plato: Apology* (Warminster, 1997), 177 ad 38 A 1; Lane. This article is premissed on the belief that, interesting though the history of the term *eirōneia* is, and genuine though the differences are between its semantic field and that of the term 'irony', none of this alters the fact that what Socrates employs in the dialogues is recognizably a form of irony. To identify it we need not rely on those few places in Plato where the term *eirōneia* is used; indeed, given the differences between the Greek and English terms, we should not.

[3] Nehamas is aware that the traditional theory is inadequate (see *Art*, 55); but he makes use instead of a different proposal from the ancient rhetorical tradition,

many cases of irony, there are many other cases that it does not
fit. Dan Sperber and Deirdre Wilson unearth an elegant example
from Voltaire's *Candide*: 'When all was over and the rival kings
were celebrating their victory with Te Deums in their respective
camps . . .'. Here the narrator is clearly being ironic but equally
clearly does not mean the opposite of what he says—whether that
the kings were *not* celebrating, or that they were bemoaning their
defeat.[4] Ironic questions, indeed any type of expression other than
a declarative assertion, can be similarly problematic for the traditional view, for they seem not to have opposites.[5] Moreover, declarative assertions can be literally true and yet ironic: an example
in the literature is 'You sure know a lot', addressed to someone who
is making a pretentious display of his knowledge.[6]

It is rather the idea that Vlastos chose not to develop for the
analysis of Socratic irony that has in recent years made a significant contribution to our understanding of irony. Irony is a form
of pretence. The seminal discussion here is that of Herbert Clark
and Richard Gerrig.[7] They propose that in order for an audience
to appreciate an ironic utterance, it must recognize that the ironist
is pretending to be an injudicious or uninformed speaker addressing an audience that shares his ignorance. So there would be two

namely that to speak ironically is to mean, not the opposite of what you say, but only
something different from what you say. (Nehamas's view is followed by Griswold,
n. 16. Lane, n. 3, has it both ways: irony, she stipulates, aims to convey a meaning
opposite to or otherwise different from what is said.) This proposal, however, is
far too broad to capture what is special about irony. It would, for example, include
all indirect speech-acts (discussed below in the main text), ironic or otherwise.
Jonathan Lear, for his part, in 'The Socratic Method and Psychoanalysis', in S. A.
Rappe and R. Kamtekar (eds.), *A Companion to Socrates* (Oxford, 2006), 442–62 at
448, moves directly from the traditional theory, which he brackets as the 'popular'
conception of irony, to a Kierkegaardian conception of irony in its most profound
manifestations. He does not stop to consider more adequate theories of common-
or-garden irony.

   [4] D. Sperber and D. Wilson, *Relevance: Communication and Cognition* [*Relevance*]
(Cambridge, Mass., 1988), 241.
   [5] D. Sperber and D. Wilson, 'Irony and the Use–Mention Distinction', in S. Davis
(ed.), *Pragmatics: A Reader* (Oxford, 1991), 550–63 at 554; S. Kumon-Nakamura,
S. Glucksberg, and M. Brown, 'How about another piece of pie: The Allusional-
Pretence Theory of Discourse Irony', *Journal of Experimental Psychology: General*,
124/1 (1995), 3–21 at 4.　　　　　　　　　　[6] Kumon-Nakamura *et al.*, 4.
   [7] H. H. Clark and R. J. Gerrig, 'On the Pretense Theory of Irony', *Journal of
Experimental Psychology: General*, 113/1 (1984), 121–6. Clark and Gerrig claim Paul
Grice as father of their theory (121); but the attribution has been rightly questioned
(see D. Sperber, 'Verbal Irony: Pretense or Echoic Mention?' ['Verbal Irony'],
Journal of Experimental Psychology: General, 113/1 (1984), 130–6 at 136).

audiences: one that is in on the irony, and another that is not. This uninitiated audience may be actually present or merely imagined. For example: you are caught in an unforecast downpour, turn to your neighbour, and exclaim, 'Trust the Weather Bureau! See what lovely weather it is: rain, rain, rain.' Here, according to Clark and Gerrig (122), with the words 'See what lovely weather it is' you are 'pretending to be an unseeing person . . . exclaiming to an unknowing audience how beautiful the weather is'. You intend your neighbour to see through this pretence, and to understand that what you are therefore doing is 'ridiculing the sort of person who would make such an exclamation (e.g. the weather forecaster), the sort of person who would accept it, and the exclamation itself'.

Clark and Gerrig are right to treat ironic communication as the acting out of a little scene; but they give the actor an unnecessarily complicated role to play. The ironist in the rain shower is not pretending to be someone so unseeing as to think the weather is fine; he is pretending something simpler than that: he is pretending that the weather is fine. Faced with your acting someone so unseeing as to think a rainstorm fine weather, I could be forgiven for asking: Why are you doing something so silly as to act someone so silly? In order to ridicule and so dissociate yourself from such a person? But what is the point of that? I never thought you were such a person in the first place. Nor did I think, *pace* Clark and Gerrig, that the weather forecaster—or anyone else for that matter—was such a person. (Weather forecasters may be fallible, but they do not deny reality.)

A more faithful account of what you are trying to communicate, and how you do it, is the following. I recognize that you are only pretending that the weather is fine, and that you want me to recognize your pretence. I ask myself why you are doing this, and this time there is a ready answer: in order to show that only pretence is possible in the current lousy weather. You are dissociating yourself, not from someone silly enough to think the weather fine, but from the judgement that the weather is fine.

Certainly, to pretend that the weather is fine is equally to pretend to be someone finding the weather fine. This is a trivial consequence of the non-trivial fact that the pretence which makes for ironic communication has the ironist acting out a little scene. And it is also true that irony may involve the ironist in pretending to be a particular person or type of person (as when irony is parodic).

Typically, however, the 'someone' is simply oneself, in imaginary circumstances. Thus, whereas Clark and Gerrig claim that the ironist is pretending to be someone enjoying the weather in a rainstorm, in fact the ironist is, more simply, pretending to be someone (that is, himself) enjoying the weather, and pretending this in a rainstorm. Or, to change the example to Socratic irony: Clark and Gerrig would have to claim that Socrates is pretending to be someone asking advice of those he believes are unqualified to give it; but in fact Socrates is pretending to be someone (that is, himself) asking advice, and pretending this among people whom he believes are unqualified to give it. In neither case is the ironist attempting to play the role of nincompoop, as Clark and Gerrig require.[8]

In general, then, to communicate ironically is to engage in a pretence before an audience with the intention of eliciting a response from that audience by means of their recognition of two things: one, that the pretence would be in some way inappropriate if it were actual rather than just a pretence; and the other, that the ironist intended them to recognize this fact.[9]

By specifying that the audience's response must arise from the recognition of the inappropriateness of the pretence if more than just a pretence, this account keeps irony distinct from other forms of communicative pretence. Consider the case of an actor's utterances while performing. The audience recognizes that the actor is engaging in a pretence that would be inappropriate if actual rather

[8] This way of framing the matter protects pretence theory against Sperber's counter-examples of ironic utterances for which no plausible speaker or audience can be imagined, so rendering pretence impossible (see 'Verbal Irony', 133). The ironist who makes a self-contradictory statement such as 'Jones, this murderer, this thief, this crook, is indeed an honourable fellow!' does not, according to my account, have to pretend to be someone who finds murderers virtuous (as he does according to Clark and Gerrig). Rather, he pretends to compliment someone on his virtue, and that someone is in fact Jones, of all people.

[9] By dispensing with Clark and Gerrig's apparatus of imaginary and clueless speaker and equally clueless (and potentially imaginary) audience, this version of pretence theory sidesteps those who suppose that the problems with this apparatus disqualify pretence theory as a whole: Sperber, 'Verbal Irony', 134–5; R. J. Kreuz and S. Glucksberg, 'How to be Sarcastic', *Journal of Experimental Psychology: General*, 118/4 (1989), 375–86 at 384; A. Utsumi, 'Verbal Irony as Implicit Display of Ironic Environment: Distinguishing Ironic Utterances from Nonirony', *Journal of Pragmatics*, 32 (2000), 1777–1806 at 1782. Clark himself drops the apparatus (without discussion) in the version of pretence theory included in his *Using Language* [*Using*] (Cambridge, 1996), 369–74; but his new theory unnecessarily insists that the pretence must be a joint performance (see Utsumi, 1782), and it continues to depend on the notion of the ironic victim (see n. 12).

than a pretence, and that the actor intended them to recognize this; but the audience response that the actor intends to elicit with each utterance derives from their understanding the utterance in character rather than from their recognizing its inappropriateness if not part of a pretence. Live ironic communication makes use of acting, but it should not be confused with acting.[10] Or consider indirect speech-acts. You ask me 'Do you know the time?' and I respond simply 'It's 6:30', rather than 'Yes I do; it's 6:30'. That is, I ignore your question about the state of my knowledge because I take it as entirely pro forma. I recognize that you were only pretending to enquire whether I know the time and were in fact requesting that I tell you the time. Assume for the sake of the example that I would also regard an enquiry about whether I know the time as inappropriate if seriously meant (inappropriately pernickety, say). Finally, I recognize that you intended me to recognize all this. What still distinguishes such a case from irony is that my response is not the result of recognizing the inappropriateness of the pretence if meant seriously but simply the result of recognizing it as a pretence. The fact that I would find the enquiry about whether I know the time inappropriate if taken seriously helps me identify it as a pretence. But suppose I thought the enquiry appropriate enough if meant seriously, and recognized it as a pretence only because of its conventionality: my response would be no different. This shows that my response is not in either case the result of recognizing the inappropriateness of the pretence if seriously meant.[11]

Finally, consider communication by secret code. You and I are partners cheating at cards. We have arranged in advance that when I ask you whether you remembered to lock the car, you will know that I have drawn a certain hand. You appreciate that I am only

---

[10] This is a response to the challenge at p. 129 of J. Williams, 'Does Mention (or Pretense) Exhaust the Concept of Irony?' *Journal of Experimental Psychology: General*, 113/1 (1984), 127–9, that pretence theory cannot distinguish the ironic utterances of ordinary conversation from those of actors speaking their lines. Another reason to avoid equating irony with acting is that ironic utterances can range from being spoken deadpan, to being spoken in an ironic tone of voice, a tone which belies one's pretence, to being outright parodic—for example, if I were to respond to your peremptory demand with a 'Jawohl, mein Führer!' (The fact that pretence theory makes parody a type of irony rather than a related but distinct type of utterance does not seem to me to be a count against it—*pace* Sperber, 'Verbal Irony', 135, who is followed on this point by Utsumi, 1782–3.)

[11] It is a mistake, then, to think that indirect speech-acts are a problem for the pretence theory of irony, as do Kreuz and Glucksberg, 384, seconded by Utsumi, 1782.

pretending to enquire about the car, that the pretence would be inappropriate if more than just a pretence (you know that I have no reason to believe that you failed to lock the car), and that I intended you to appreciate all this. Nevertheless (and as with the previous case), my response is not the result of recognizing the inappropriateness of the pretence if meant seriously. It would not matter, for example, if after we sat down to cards you and I both realize, and realize that we both realize, that we have in fact forgotten to lock the car. Your response is simply the result of recognizing the prearranged signal. No one who was not in on the prearrangement could understand my meaning.

Not only does this version of pretence theory do without the imaginary victim who fails to appreciate the pretence (at least as a component of its core account of irony); it also recognizes that some ironies need have no victim at all, whether imaginary or actual. (This fact will prove important when we come to consider Socratic irony—a type of irony for which a victim is essential.[12])

The irony about the lovely weather is itself an example of victimless irony. The weather forecaster may indeed be the intended butt of the ironist's joke (although in the case of an irony about bad weather that did not mention the Weather Bureau even this much need not be conceded); but he is not its victim, since neither he nor anyone else could fail to appreciate so obvious an irony—that is, fail to penetrate the pretence involved. It is an irony that does not depend on a victim for its effect. The only real 'victims' here are the rueful ironist and his audience, whose picnic has been spoilt; and they are victims of the weather, not of the irony.

A more subtle example of victimless irony is the quotation from Voltaire considered at the outset: 'When all was over and the rival kings were celebrating their victory with Te Deums in their respective camps . . .'. Sperber and Wilson point out, correctly, that in the following version of this statement the irony is lost: 'When all was over and the rival kings were celebrating *what they described as* their victory with Te Deums in their respective camps' (emphasis added). They explain the difference as follows. The ironic version

---

[12] On this point I disagree with Clark, who continues, despite having modified his theory (see n. 9), to endorse the pivotal role supposedly played in irony by an 'uninitiated audience' (*Using*, 372). Likewise, although independently, Nehamas, *Art*, 49, insists that a victim, whether actual or implied, is 'essential to irony in all its forms' (see further 51, 58). He correlates this feature with the 'element of boastfulness' that he also detects in all irony.

implies that author and reader share a cynical vision and require no explicit prompt in order to recognize that 'after a battle both sides invariably claim victory, that this behaviour is always absurd, that the author and reader are not the sort of people to be fooled, and so on' (*Relevance*, 242). The problem with this analysis is that *no one* is the sort of person to be fooled when two sides both claim victory; no one can be expected to accept an obvious contradiction. A more satisfactory analysis would dispense with the appeal to a victim.

Voltaire pretends, deadpan, to report the kings' victories (and not, as he ought on pain of contradiction, their alleged victories), and he does so when those victories are claimed for the very same battle (and this is what alerts us to the pretence). The kings are the butt of the ironic joke, but not its victims—they know as well as anyone that there has to be a winner and loser.

Finally, let us consider whether the pretence theory of irony is a mere variant of the influential 'echoic mention' theory introduced by Sperber and Wilson, as some have suggested.[13] According to Sperber and Wilson, what makes an utterance ironic is that it expresses the speaker's attitude to the thought conveyed by the utterance taken literally—an attitude of dissociation—and does so by means of presenting that thought as an echo rather than as the speaker's own. One reason not to think this theory the equivalent of pretence theory (in addition to those already current in the literature)[14] is that it depends on the figure of a hypothetical victim in order to explain why ironic echoes must remain implicit; for only if the echo is implicit can the speaker and the appreciative audience feel superior to the victims of the irony, just by virtue of their ability to appreciate what is left implicit.[15]

But if there can be victimless ironies, then we cannot use the notion of the ironic victim to explain the fact that all ironic echoes are implicit. Pretence theory, however, can provide a general explanation of why ironic echoes must be implicit—one that applies to all ironies, with and without victims. According to pretence theory you bring off an irony by maintaining a pretence while some feature of the situation permits the inference that you are only pretending. Make an echo explicit and it remains an echo none the less; make a pretence explicit and it ceases to be a pretence. That is why an echo

---

[13] e.g. Kreuz and Glucksberg, 384.   [14] See e.g. Clark, *Using*, 371.
[15] See *Relevance*, 239, 242; 'Verbal Irony', 132.

that makes for an ironic pretence must remain implicit; because to make the echo explicit is to destroy the pretence.

2. Who is the audience for Socratic irony?

We have seen that Vlastos did not capitalize on his insight that irony is a kind of pretence. But this is not to say that he is a complete traditionalist about irony. Vlastos follows tradition when he defines irony as 'expressing what we mean by saying something contrary to it' (43). But he calls this 'simple irony', to distinguish it from a special form of irony, 'complex irony', which he sees as peculiarly Socratic (31) and as characterizing many of Socrates' most important and self-defining assertions. When Socrates claims not to be wise, or not to be a teacher, an appreciative audience would understand his claim to be true in the ordinary sense of 'wise' and 'teacher', but false in a special and deeper sense which Socrates gives to these terms (32).

If Socrates' characteristic disavowals were indeed complex ironies, he would be spending his time letting those who have ears to hear learn something about himself. What the aporetic dialogues seem rather to put before us, however, is an ironist who spends his time letting those who have ears to hear learn something, not about Socrates, but about the person whom Socrates is questioning. And there is no need to appeal to so complex a thing as complex irony in order to explain the behaviour of such an ironist as this; Vlastos's own insight about pretence can do the job. (This is not, of course, to claim that we learn nothing of Socrates' beliefs about himself from the aporetic dialogues; only that it is not the function of his typical ironies—including Vlastos's star examples—to offer information about himself.)

It is important to see that the Socratic claim to be ignorant of the matter at hand, or his denial that he is a teacher, does not typically take the underlying form 'I am not a teacher', 'I am ignorant of these matters'. It is more usually of the underlying form '*I* am not a teacher', '*I* do not know about these matters'. In other words, Socrates typically implies that, although he does not know and cannot teach the truth about the matter at hand, perhaps someone else in the company does and can. This implication—which Socrates usually proceeds to make explicit—is what constitutes Socrates' pretence; it is from this that Socrates ironically dissociates himself. Take, for example, a classic piece of entrapment from the *Laches* (186 B ff.). Socrates claims never to have had a teacher in the care of the soul—for all that he has long wanted one—being unable to afford the fees of the only people who profess to teach it, the sophists. And he remains incapable of discovering the art for himself. He would not be surprised, however, if his interlocutors Nicias and Laches had been taught it, since they have the money to pay for classes; or if they had discovered it for themselves, since they are older than he. And presumably they *are* competent in the art, since they would not so fearlessly have passed judgement earlier on what pursuits a young man should engage in if they were not sure of their own knowledge of these matters. So he is generally confident in them. But the fact that they disagreed with each other—this he finds surprising.

Notice that this heavily ironic passage begins with a series of utterances in which either what is said happens to be true, or else the truth or falsity of what is said is unclear, and ends with a series of utterances in which what is said happens to be false. On the one hand, Socrates has indeed had no teacher in these matters, and is indeed too poor to pay sophists; these are mundane facts about the character portrayed in the dialogues. (Diotima in the *Symposium* he claims at 201 D for his teacher in matters of love, not in the care of the soul.) Whether he has or has not discovered the art of making people virtuous is unclear; what is clear is only that he does not go around professing to make people virtuous. On the other hand, he clearly *would* be surprised if Nicias or Laches had discovered it, he *does not* think they are competent in it, he is *not* surprised that they have contradicted each other. (These things we are entitled to infer both from the standard scenario of an aporetic dialogue and from the characterization of Laches and Nicias.)

Pretence theory treats these differences as superficial. In all cases the irony consists in Socrates' pretending to treat Nicias, Laches, and the sophists as his superiors, when in fact he believes that they are merely less self-critical than he. When Socrates says that he could not afford the classes of the only professors who claimed to teach virtue, and has not been able to discover the art for himself, he implies that had he been able to afford the classes he might now know the art; but the Socrates known to the reader from the dialogues does not believe this. When he says that, to begin with himself, he has never been taught the art, he implies that Laches and Nicias may well have; but this too he does not believe. These implications are then made explicit in the series of false statements that follow. Nevertheless, the utterances in which what is said is true would be ironic even if unaccompanied by those in which what is said is false. The crucial matter is that, true or false, they abet the pretence.[16]

That each of these ironies is equally a pretence means that we cannot use the ironies themselves as evidence of the truth or falsity of the claims by which Socrates perpetrates the irony. In the absence of other indications, therefore, we must allow the truth-status of those claims whose truth or falsity is unclear to remain unclear. These, of course, will include all the most interesting and controversial claims that Socrates makes about himself when he is being ironic, such as his professions of ignorance about crucial matters.[17]

If we believe ourselves to have found a non-ironic source of true assertions about Socrates—Socrates' defence of his way of life in the *Apology*, perhaps—well and good; but we should not attempt, as Vlastos does, to uncover these assertions in the irony itself, in the guise of complex irony, with its deep but unequivocal meanings. As ironist, Socrates remains more private than that.

I agree, then, with Alexander Nehamas when he urges that

[16] A list of passages in which Socrates declares his ignorance in order to entice his interlocutor into attempting to provide the answer that Socrates claims he cannot would include *Chrm.* 169 B; *Lys.* 212 A; *H.Ma.* 286 D; *H.Min.* 369 D; and *Meno* 71 B. Sometimes we find only the request to be taught, the declaration of ignorance being left implicit: *Euthph.* 5 A; *Euthd.* 273 E–274 A. Typically there is a reprise of the declaration of ignorance at the end of the dialogue, now with the sting of reproach that the interlocutor has not yet been able to supply the answer, and coupled with an invitation to try again in the future: *Chrm.* 175 A–end; *Lys.* 223 B; *H.Ma.* 304 D–E; *H.Min.* 376 C; *Euthphr.* 15 D–end. Other dialogues have this conclusion without having begun with a declaration of ignorance: *Gorg.* 509 A; *Prot.* 361 C–D; *Rep.* book I (if treated as an aporetic dialogue in its own right), 337 D. In all these cases, then, Plato presents Socratic ignorance as a stimulus to others rather than dwelling on it in its own terms.

[17] Brickhouse and Smith, for example, recognize that what they call Socrates' 'mocking irony' is in effect 'mock praise' of the interlocutors; but they make the mistake of thinking that if they confine the irony to the mock praise they are entitled to assert that Socrates' demonstration of modesty is not mock modesty but genuine, on the grounds that 'the mockery does not work by his own disclaimer of such things'; the irony would lie only in his mocking compliments of others (63). What I have tried to show is that the mockery does indeed work by Socrates' own disclaimer of wisdom, which is part of his pretence and therefore part of the irony, despite the fact that the point of the disclaimer is to imply a compliment of others.

Socrates is stranger than Vlastos allows (*Art*, 67). Nehamas successfully demonstrates Socrates' mysteriousness. In the remainder of this section, however, it is Socrates' solitariness that I wish to bring to the fore.

Anyone who cares to apply the analysis of ironic communication in the first section of this article to Socratic irony as just described will immediately notice that something is missing from Socratic conversation: an audience for the irony. Socrates by his ironies lets those who have ears to hear, it was proposed, learn something about the person he is questioning. But who are 'those who have ears to hear'? Victims of Socratic irony there are in plenty; but where is the audience? Although Socrates is speaking ironically to his interlocutors, he is not engaging in ironic communication with them; his irony goes over their heads.

Could Socrates' irony instead be intended within the fiction for an audience of onlookers familiar with his procedure? Plato could very easily have made such an audience a feature of the aporetic dialogues; yet he does not. He assigns no equivalent to Socrates of the admiring claque he grants to the sophists and showmen Euthydemus and Dionysodorus (*Euthd.* 276 c). Given the explicit mention by Socrates in the *Apology* (33 c) of a band of followers who trail after him for the pleasure of watching as pretensions are punctured, the fact that Plato does not make such a band thematic to the very dialogues in which the puncturing occurs is significant.

The tendency among those who discuss this issue is to regard the absence of an audience for Socratic irony as a lacuna that must be filled post-haste; and the audience they rely upon to fill the empty stands is not an audience of onlookers within the fiction but the one made up of Plato's readers. Charles Griswold's reaction may be taken as emblematic. Discussing an irony deployed by Socrates in conversation with an interlocutor, in this case Phaedrus, he remarks that 'we must presume that [Socrates] has grounds for hoping that Phaedrus will understand the irony; for otherwise Socrates is in the (impossible) situation of a man alone on a mountain top ironizing for his own amusement'. Phaedrus, however, as Griswold duly notes, gives no sign of appreciating this irony, or even of being capable of appreciating it. Griswold's recourse is to imagine a studio audience: 'Socrates thus acts as though he were—*per impossibile*—addressing himself to the reader, an act which can be intended only by Plato' (98–9).

The second of the two impossibilities declared by Griswold truly is impossible: Socrates is not an actor performing in front of a live audience, one that he could address directly by breaking the dramatic frame; he is a character in a book. Only Plato can address the reader, whether directly, by breaking the fictional frame (something Plato opts never to do), or indirectly, via the words and actions of his fictional characters.

The first of these two supposed impossibilities, however, is far from impossible. In fact the image of Socrates alone on a mountain top is as good an image as any to capture the poignancy of Socrates' situation as ironist. By not pausing to consider that poignancy but instead moving immediately to give Socrates the comfort of an appreciative audience, commentators have missed an important aspect of Socratic irony; they have therefore also missed the chance to consider what Plato was up to in making him that sort of ironist.[18]

People do, after all, sometimes choose to aim their irony over the heads of its victim even though no audience but only the victim is present; and among the possible situations in which they will do so, two in particular seem relevant to Socratic irony. To a person who feels in some respect powerless, inferior, weak, or marginalized, solipsistic irony offers consolation and goes some way to restore the balance of power. True, it is a weapon that does not dent its victim's armour; but the victim's very obliviousness gives the ironist a heady freedom—that of sticking his tongue out at his superior and getting away with it. Punctilious courtesy, deference, or obedience is often the ironist's tool here. Rudely cut off at a revolving door by a mean-looking person twice his size, the ironist quietly remarks as he steps aside: 'Sorry; you seem to be in a hurry.' Although he is only pretending to excuse himself and to be considerate rather than disapproving of the other's haste, and although the apology would be inappropriate if genuine (for *he* is the one who deserves the apology), he does not want the pretence to be recognized; this might lead to a confrontation. The audience for his irony is only himself. Still, he thinks, at least one party to this transaction is acting politely and maintaining self-control; that is something.

This little scene belongs to a type that is not uncommon. No

[18] Views similar to Griswold's can be found in W. Boder, *Die Sokratische Ironie in den Platonischen Frühdialogen* (Amsterdam, 1973), 166; Nehamas, *Art*, 41; M. Gifford, 'Dramatic Dialectic in *Republic* Book 1', *Oxford Studies in Ancient Philosophy*, 20 (2001), 35–106 at 39 n. 3.

customer is so often called 'sir' by a sales assistant as the customer who is being obstreperous. In all such cases, however, the deference must be nicely calculated if the irony is to pass unnoticed. Hyper-politeness is an inherently risky strategy for the ironist; indeed, it is typically discussed in the literature as a tool of choice for open sarcasm.[19] In our scene at the revolving door, a minimal escalation of rhetoric might tip the balance from solipsism to communication: for example, if the ironist loudly called out his remark to the bully's disappearing back, or if the remark was 'Please don't let me stand in your way, you're obviously in a great hurry!'—let alone something so blatant as 'Pardon me for existing!'

A second context that may give rise to solipsistic irony aimed over the victim's head is one in which we hold authority over those who cannot fully understand us. Here the technical term 'victim' can mislead; one might suppose that such irony is always patronizing or mocking. A stereotypical case of the patronizing type would be that of the lonely, live-in daughter of a senile parent who vents frus-tration by making ironic fun of her oblivious charge. Or imagine a teacher of small children who, resigned to their continuing dis-obedience and inattention, soliloquizes: 'That's right, by all means ignore me; you might actually learn something otherwise.'

But it is important to understand that solipsistic irony can equally well express solidarity with its 'victim'. Take the case of a mother who wants to get her toddler into the car, but finds he has turned aside to stare at a child walking by with an ice cream in hand. She waits till he is done, then greets his restored attention with a big smile and an ecstatic 'Melvyn, you're back!' If the toddler reacts by laughing along with his mother, this is only the contagion of hilarity; he is too young to appreciate the irony. (The case would be quite different if a slightly older child had initiated the game by running ahead to 'surprise' his mother at each street corner.) His mother, for her part, has helped ensure an amiable re-entry into the car, and has had some fun into the bargain. Quite similar is the banter that dog-owners engage in when alone with their dogs; at least ninety per cent of it surpasses the animal's understanding and is so much solipsistic irony. (Owner to dog wagging its tail: 'I'll take that as a yes.') What the dog appreciates throughout, of course, is the affection that rides on those ironic wings.

Although these two species of solipsistic irony are at home in

[19] See e.g. Kumon-Nakamura *et al.*, 4; Utsumi, 1786.

apparently opposite environments—in the one, irony is the recourse of the weak, in the other, of the strong—it is not difficult to see that even in the former case the irony derives from the ironist's sense of superiority. The courteous fellow at the revolving door thinks his addressee a brute; weak he may be, but right is on his side.

The character Socrates' situation partakes of both these stimuli to private irony. His conversational goal, as is apparent from his activity in the aporetic dialogues, is to challenge those around him to justify their apparent confidence about what makes for a truly good life. But his social position is marginal: he is relatively poor, neglects his family for the sake of philosophy, shows none of the enthusiasm for participating in the business of running the city that was expected of a democratic Athenian; he is eccentric; he even *looks* odd. And the conversational goal itself could seem importunate, no matter who was taking it upon himself to put his fellow citizens to such a test. Anytus' bristling at Socrates in the *Meno* (94 E) is a case in point: it makes a theme of the disrespect for authority inherent in Socratic questioning. But by calibrating his challenge with a judicious balance of courtesy, amiability, and self-effacement, Socrates generally avoids so overt a confrontation as this—one that a person in his position would be wise to avoid. His interlocutors often do not recognize the seriousness of the challenge until it is too late—until they are too caught up in the business of question and answer to recognize the irony that entrapped them.

Notice, then, that Socrates does not rest content with the some-what tepid satisfaction that solipsistic irony affords the weak; in this he differs from the man left behind at the revolving door. By dialogue's end the tables are turned, and if the irony itself remains concealed, at least one thing has become clear: the interlocutor's inability to hold his own under questioning from Socrates. It is as if the ironist at the revolving door topped his remark with a sur-reptitious push that spun the bully, apparently of his own impetus, right back out of the building again.

But to apply only the parallel of this first kind of solipsistic irony to the dialogues would be to cast an unnecessary pall over Socrates' practice. Not only would it fail to capture the variety of Socrates' interlocutors and of their treatment at his hands (he is a lot gentler, for example, with youngsters like Lysis and Charmides; a good deal warmer with Gorgias than with Polus), it would ill accord with Socrates' claim in the *Apology* to have been urging his fellow citizens towards virtue 'like a father or an older brother' (31 B). Socrates' efforts to bestir his interlocutors to self-awareness, at some cost to his public standing and to his material circumstances, have about them the selflessness and solidarity that one finds among kin. At *Apology* 30 A he offers as a reason for devoting himself more to examining his fellow Athenians than foreign visitors the fact that they are closer kin to him.

His irony, however, he does not share with them; if they show themselves oblivious of it, he does not disabuse them. Like the mother of the distracted child, he can be content to let his pretence serve a public purpose by enticing the addressee, while it privately acknowledges the gulf in understanding that makes pretence a suitable recourse in the first place. Yet by choosing to play this asymmetrical game rather than to leave the table he also accepts that a bond of responsibility ties the manipulator to the one he manipulates. This would remain true even if we take Socrates' claims of parental concern for his fellow citizens in the *Apology* to be less than completely sincere.

The point of these comparisons is not, however, to map Socratic irony precisely onto either of these two types of solipsistic irony; the point is to show, first, that solipsistic irony is nothing strange, and then that the character Socrates' situation in society makes him likely to employ it. The natural opacity of irony, combined with Plato's reticence about his character's inner feelings, makes it difficult to gauge just how much civic solidarity and *bonhomie* lies behind Socrates' prodding of his interlocutor and how much it smacks of indignation, even contempt. The difficulty is exacerbated by the fact that it is quite possible to blend these pairs—to be indignant at those one holds in affection, or to acknowledge solidarity with those one looks down upon. What is clear is that Socrates is ironizing to himself.[20]

[20] Solipsistic irony therefore transcends the distinction around which Melissa Lane builds her challenge to the traditional picture of the ironic Socrates as a self-effacing praiser of others: the distinction between 'the purpose of someone called an *eirōn*', which is 'to *conceal* what is not said', and that of 'someone called an ironist', which is 'to *convey* what is not said' (51). While I agree with Lane that our conception of Socratic irony should not base itself on Plato's use of the term *eirōneia* and its cognates (see n. 2), it would seem to follow that by the same token one should not base an assault against a conception of Socratic irony, as Lane does, on Plato's use of the term *eirōneia* and its cognates. In general, whereas Lane assumes that the element of pretence in *eirōneia* (construed by her as 'concealing by feigning') serves to dissociate it from irony, I assume the opposite. That is because I subscribe to a

The rare occasions on which Plato pierces the veil of Socrates' solipsistic irony serve only to emphasize for the reader how constant a background it is to Socratic conversation. Not every character in a Platonic dialogue is as oblivious as Laches, for example, to what Socrates' amiable approach typically portends. In fact the *Laches* itself contains a paragon of alertness in the character Nicias. Early in the dialogue he warns old Lysimachus not to imagine that Socrates is joining their discussion simply in order to advise him about whether his son should study martial arts. Socrates, he reveals, has as usual been manipulating the conversation. The topic will not be their sons but themselves. They are being led to give account of themselves—an account that is unlikely to be flattering (187 E–188 C).

Nicias, then, is alive to Socrates' irony; he is its internal audience rather than its victim. This does not prevent him from succumbing to defeat under questioning from Socrates later in the dialogue (199 E). It is one thing to be able to see through Socrates' conversational ploys, quite another to see a sufficient number of moves ahead to avoid being led into self-contradiction in the chess game of question and answer at which Socrates is a grand master.[21]

Alcibiades in the *Symposium*, who like Nicias (see *La.* 188 A–B) is sympathetic to Socrates, is another who has learnt from experience to be no mere victim of Socratic irony. He has learnt, for example, not to suppose on the basis of Socrates' protestations of passion for good-looking boys that he can use his own spectacular beauty to secure Socrates' favour (*Sym.* 218 C–219 D). In his frustration he declares Socrates' whole life a game of *eirōneia* (216 E).

Others are sceptical of Socrates' gambits from the outset and do not require personal experience to alert them: Thrasymachus in the *Republic*; Callicles in the *Gorgias*. Deeply involved with rhetoric themselves—Thrasymachus is a professional (*Phdr.* 267 C), while the eloquent Callicles is happy to play host to a professional, Gor-

pretence theory of irony, while Lane cleaves to tradition on this score (see n. 3). If I were to hazard a translation of *eirōneia* that could adapt to the range of its usage, as found in Aristophanes no less than in Plato, I would opt for the phrase 'putting on an act'. To put on an act is not the same thing as to deceive. Hence *eirōneia*—as with politeness, which it resembles—sometimes does and sometimes does not appear in contexts of outright trickery.

[21] The metaphor is Plato's, voiced by Adeimantus in the *Republic* at 487 B–D. 'Chess', that is to say, is the modern equivalent of Plato's term *petteia*, although only at the level of metaphor.

gias (*Gorg.* 447 b)—both treat Socrates as an opponent in a speaking contest and assume he is out to trick them (*Rep.* 341 A–C; *Gorg.* 482 C–E). Ironic dissimulation is just one item in the orator's bag of tricks; but it is no accident that these two should refuse to take at face value what seems to them typical Socratic unctuousness, instead accusing Socrates directly of *eirōneia* (*Rep.* 337 A; *Gorg.* 489 E).

But none of this alters the solipsistic nature of Socratic irony. These characters assume that the pretence they are penetrating is one that Socrates did not intend them to penetrate. Unlike ironic communication, his is not a game that two must play. And although his banter is often sharper with hostile characters, and on occasion comes close to open mockery (e.g. *Rep.* 341 C; *Gorg.* 475 D), Socrates never confesses to the irony that either they or the more sympathetic characters uncover. He either denies it, or responds with further irony, or else another speaker intervenes, allowing Socrates to avoid a response.

Nor is it clear how successfully these characters have in fact penetrated Socrates' pretence. Their declarations reveal more about themselves than about Socrates. Socrates' line of questioning in the *Laches* will not after all require the participants to give a chastening account of their past and present conduct, as Nicias suggests; it will simply require them to say what courage is and to defend their definition. What emerges of themselves and of their conduct in the course of this discussion emerges indirectly. It seems, then, that Nicias' interpretation of Socratic practice is that of a cautious man seeking a cautionary tale (*La.* 188 B). Likewise, Alcibiades all too evidently speaks from wounded pride; Thrasymachus from ambitious distrust of a rival; Callicles from contemptuous distrust of a hair-splitting intellectual. Socrates remains throughout a *provocateur* who is all the more provoking for refusing to reveal himself.

These stabs at the Socratic veil, then, are Plato's way of ensuring that the reader appreciates the ubiquity of Socrates' solipsistic irony, and its importance as a theme. What makes Socratic irony special, what gives it title to its special name, is not that the irony Socrates employs is of a type peculiar to him; for solipsistic irony is quite normal. What makes Socrates' solipsistic irony special is that he uses it so constantly. It has become who he is. As Plato makes

Alcibiades say, and as Quintilian later emphasized: Socrates' whole life is a game of irony.[22]

Never in the aporetic dialogues does Socrates take interlocutors into his confidence. Nor does Plato ever give him the opportunity to have a philosophic discussion with intimates who are also his equals. His conversations in the aporetic dialogues are most often with obvious intellectual inferiors—young men like Charmides or Lysias or Alcibiades, buffoons like Euthyphro or Ion or Hippias. On his dying day, the company (in the *Phaedo*) consists of younger acolytes and Crito—a childhood friend, but hardly bright. Socrates in Plato's dialogues is rarely unaccompanied, yet seems always alone.

The fact that Socrates never breaks cover but always retains his ironic mask is a clue to what distinguishes his stance from, say, the false humility of a Uriah Heep. Dickens's character is set on deceiving those around him in order to make his way in the world. His pretence is a stratagem for self-advancement; he longs for the day when he can throw off his mask and hold in subjection those to whom he was compelled to make a show of humility. For him, true power can only be unfeigned power; the contentment he feigns over his own humility is something he finds genuinely humiliating.

Socrates, however, is not looking to remove his mask, for he has no conversational goal deeper than that of putting his fellows to the philosophic test, and seems for all the world to have no goal in life other than to engage in philosophic conversation. Far from humiliating him, his ironic, self-effacing pretence gives him his consciousness of superiority; it gives him the only power over others that he seeks to hold. The characteristic utterances of a Uriah Heep, by contrast, are not ironic, not even solipsistically ironic; they are contributions to a cynical and deceptive performance that has become his habitual ruse.

What makes the difference between Heep's utterances and solipsistic irony in general is this: solipsistic irony depends for its value to the solipsist on the contrast between the victim's ignorance and the response the victim might make if he were instead an audience in the know. The satisfaction that our man at the revolving door derives from his polite remark to the bully—the point of his irony—depends on his imagining (or on his being able to imagine) the anger the bully would feel if he knew for sure he was being mocked. (If he is also after the thrill of arousing in his victim at least the suspicion

[22] See Quint. *Inst.* 9. 2. 46.

of mockery, while still maintaining plausible deniability, the thrill would derive from flirting with that same danger—it would still depend on what the victim might do if he were an audience in the know.) The fun that Melvyn's mother derives or that dog-owners derive from ironic banter with their charges depends at least implicitly on what it would be like if child or dog came back at them with a knowing response. Not so with Uriah Heep: the value that his deceptive utterances bear for him at the time that he makes them is exhausted in their success as a deception.

While it is true, then, that Socratic irony is a game of solitaire, there is after all a sense in which it involves a second player, an equal partner; but that player is a ghost who exists only in Socrates' imagination—the properly self-aware person whom he never quite gets to meet. What makes his amiable self-effacement irony rather than just politeness is its dependence on the contrast between his victims as they are and how they would be if instead they could provide his irony with an audience.[23] It is a contrast confirmed by the habitual outcome of the aporetic dialogues, when the interlocutor is compelled to acknowledge ignorance of what he had previously thought he knew. Such a person may be more alive to Socrates' irony on a second encounter, as Nicias is; but he will never be granted banter on equal terms.

Socrates' irony differs from common-or-garden solipsistic irony, then, by its constancy and by its centrality to his demeanour, and it differs from the equally constant pretence of a Uriah Heep just by virtue of being ironic; but does it not resemble, through this combination of factors, quite another type of irony: the dramatic?[24]

---

[23] Jonathan Lear's study of Socratic irony also emphasizes this contrast, which he describes as that between an interlocutor's 'pretense' and his 'aspiration'—meaning by 'pretense' only what an interlocutor claims ('pretends') to know, not pretence as it is used in the pretence-theoretical account of irony. The contrast is one that he takes from Kierkegaard's powerful but idiosyncratic discussion of irony rather than, as here, from a theory that preserves the connection between Socratic irony and everyday uses of irony.

[24] This question prompts another: Is the pretence theory of irony applicable to dramatic and, more generally, to 'situational' irony, which would include non-fictional 'ironies of fate'? Pretence-theorists compare these to communicative irony only in terms of the contrast between ignorant victim and audience in the know (Clark and Gerrig, 124), or in terms of violated expectation (Nakamura *et al.*, 3), but not in terms of pretence. The truth may be that situational irony subsumes irony as pretence, rather than vice versa. In a dramatic irony or in an irony of fate, the situation either has indeed been scripted or at least seems to have been scripted by a higher power, whether author or god. The communicative ironist, for his part,

Dramatic irony, like solipsistic irony, depends on a contrast between an ignorant victim and an audience that is in the know. The ignorant victim of dramatic irony is a fictional character within the drama; the audience in the know is the author of the fiction and those for whom he is writing. A person using solipsistic irony in a one-off conversational exchange could metaphorically be described as acting out a little scene which includes the victim as an unwitting performer; but one who uses solipsistic irony as Socrates does, as his permanent stance in society and as what gives his philosophic discussions their characteristic shape, would better be compared to a playwright deploying dramatic irony as a character in his own drama. While it is true that the more casual ironic solipsists, too, could be compared to dramatists who appears in their own dramas (Melvyn's mother, for example, scripts her own repartee), they could not be compared to dramatists using dramatic irony. Certainly, the victim must be ignorant if a solipsistic irony is to remain solipsistic and not tip over into communication; but the victim's ignorance is not constitutive of the irony itself, which is instead a matter of the kind of pretence the ironist is engaging in. Dramatic irony, by contrast, applies to a situation; and the situation includes the victim's ignorance as a constitutive element, for the plot will turn upon it.

Socrates deploys his victims' ignorance in just this way; he scripts an entire dramatic plot around their being lulled by his solipsistic irony into an innocuous-seeming conversation that will lead to an unexpected revelation. The totality of his control over events as they unfold, a manipulation that is hidden from his victims, makes his relation to them resemble that of a playwright to the victims of his dramatic irony. (To describe Socrates as having total control over events as they unfold does not exclude the possibility of deft improvisation on his part, as appears to occur at e.g. *Rep.* 348 E.) Nevertheless, because no barrier of fiction separates Socrates from his interlocutors—for we are to imagine him a flesh-and-blood participant in the discussion, as they are—his interlocutors could well be expected to resent his treating them as if they were toys of his fiction, should they become fully cognizant of his manipulation.

Hence Socrates never drops his ironic mask; he is to that extent

stages a little scene for his audience's benefit. He brings this off by pretending—by acting in his own drama. The whole issue is a fascinating one and would merit an article of its own.

like a dramatic ironist who never disabuses his fictional victims of the ignorance under which they labour. The revelation in an aporetic dialogue, when it comes, is not like that which comes to King Oedipus when he finally understands where the events of the play and of his earlier life have conspired to lead him. The revelation conceded to Socrates' partners in conversation is at most that of their own ignorance concerning the philosophic issue at hand, when it is not merely puzzlement at their inability to make their views stick. Socrates does not reveal to them the ironic ploy that helped bring them to this pass, nor does he confirm any suspicions they might harbour on that score.

Socrates does not even reveal to them how the more evident cause of their discomfiture, the relentless line of questioning to which he subjected them, brought them to this pass. They realize that they have failed to sustain their views, but they do not understand the path by which Socrates brought them step by step to failure; as a result, they do not regard their defeat as final, and feel mostly confusion rather than a sense of discovery—if they are not indeed quite unpersuaded and feel they have been tricked. (This type of reaction is made the topic of explicit comment at *Gorg.* 513 c and *Rep.* 487 c.)

The chess game of question and answer that Socrates plays is distinct from his solipsistic irony; for although many of Socrates' questions or of the statements he includes in a line of questioning may individually be ironic, they can perfectly well also be free of irony. But the practice of Socratic questioning has this much in common with the practice of Socratic irony: it too seeks to conceal from the interlocutor the moves, as they are made, by which Socrates achieves the result at which he is aiming all along; it too seeks a control resembling that which dramatic irony exerts over its victim.

Concealment would in fact be part of the question-and-answer game even if Socrates practised it on the basis of agreed rules and in a completely open fashion, as the 'dialectic' first codified by Aristotle in the *Topics* seems to have been practised in the schools.[25] In an actual game of chess, after all, each player conceals his winning

---

[25] For discussion of the connection between Socratic questioning and Aristotelian dialectic see M. Frede, 'Plato's Arguments and the Dialogue Form', in J. C. Klagge and N. D. Smith (eds.), *Methods of Interpreting Plato and his Dialogues* (*OSAP* suppl.; Oxford, 1992), 201–19.

strategy from the other and aims to be first in giving his opponent—who knows what is planned, but not how it will arrive—a nasty surprise. As Socrates in fact practises the question-and-answer game in the dialogues, however, its 'rules' typically emerge only when Socrates thinks them violated. It is not the formal practice that it later became.[26]

Given this connection between Socratic irony and Socratic questioning, it is fitting that the two interlocutors who suppose themselves immune to Socrates' irony and are happy to expose it, Thrasymachus and Callicles, should also openly rebel at the concealed manipulativeness of his questioning. Being bad sports, they resort to this rebellion only when they seem to themselves to be losing the game. At that point they withdraw their co-operation and subsequently answer Socrates with a considerable show of being manipulated, like surly puppets (*Rep.* 350 D ff.; *Gorg.* 505 C ff.). Their responses become openly ironical, and Callicles goes so far as to reduce Socrates for a while to providing the responses to his own questions (*Gorg.* 506 C–507 C). Perhaps only so can the solitary Socrates meet his equal in philosophic conversation.

3. Socratic irony vs. Platonic irony

If the character Socrates finds it expedient to cover his traces as a kind of dramatic ironist within his own drama and to remain an ironic solipsist, Plato himself, as a dramatic ironist in the usual sense of the term, is under no such restrictions. He offers his readers full-blown dramatic irony, both when he makes them privy to Socrates' manipulations of victims and when he scripts ironies that exceed what any character within the fiction could know, including Socrates.[27]

---

[26] The Platonic dialogues in which dialectic is at its most scholastic and formal and in which open reference is made to how it diverges not only from ordinary conversation but also from spontaneous philosophic discussion are notable for not involving Socrates as a participant: the *Sophist*, *Statesman*, and *Parmenides*. See esp. *Soph.* 217 D; *Polit.* 275 C; *Parm* 137 B.

[27] The *Laches*—as fertile a dialogue for our purposes as Plato ever wrote—contains a famous example of the latter, when Socrates remarks to Nicias at 195 E–196 A that a general should not cede authority in military decisions to seers. The remark is itself prophetic, but unconsciously so, of the undue influence that seers were going to have on Nicias' conduct of the Sicilian expedition—a fact notorious to Plato's readers. The example is fully discussed in Gifford, 48–52.

That Plato as author is willing to make Socrates too a victim of dramatic irony ought to give pause to those who would equate his goals as writer with those of Socrates as speaker. Admittedly, Socrates is a 'victim' of Plato's dramatic irony only in the technical sense, not in the metaphorical sense of being shown in a bad light. Nevertheless, the mere fact that Plato puts ironic allusions in Socrates' mouth of which Socrates himself could not be conscious opens a distance between author and character that Plato could have chosen to avoid. Furthermore, even the conscious irony that Plato scripts for his character and that the foregoing pages have dwelt upon contrasts in a crucial respect with the irony that Plato as author brings off in the process. Whereas Socrates' irony intends no audience but himself, Plato writes not only for himself but for any reader who can appreciate the Socratic ironies he invents. If his Socrates is forever in the public eye and forever alone, Plato, whom we are at liberty to imagine alone in his study, composing dialogues by night while others are out in society, comes across (ironically!) as writing, by virtue of his irony, for a company of his equals—for all who tread the same track as he.[28]

But what one encounters instead in discussions of Plato's reasons for deploying Socratic irony is most commonly a parallel between, on the one hand, the character Socrates' project of urging his interlocutors to greater self-awareness by engaging them in discussions that compel them to acknowledge their inability to justify their beliefs and, on the other hand, Plato's project of awakening a similar awareness in his readers by writing philosophy in the form of fictional arguments that end without resolution and must be resolved, if at all, by the readers themselves. So Mark Gifford, for example, argues that Plato's dramatic ironies prompt us to take evasive action against the fate of the interlocutors to whom ironies at their expense have allowed us to feel superior. Fearing a similar fate for ourselves, even the philosophically sophisticated among us, claims Gifford, are made anxious over our vulnerability to challenges framed at the appropriate level of attack.[29]

---

[28] This image of Plato is conjured by a passage that reads very much as a self-description along these lines, at *Phdr.* 276 D. It is in the *Phaedrus* too that Socrates himself explicitly declares the ambition of finding his philosophic equal (266 B, 278 A)—a declaration untypical of him.

[29] See Gifford, 102–5. Gifford's focus is on the particular contribution made to the reader's fear by those dramatic ironies that exceed even Socrates' awareness. That some of Socrates' interlocutors come to a sticky end in subsequent history can

The problem with any argument of this type is that dramatic irony works by making the audience feel that they know more than the victim knows. Why, then, should their reaction to the victim's fate be fearful and humble? Why should their reaction not be the very opposite: superior and complacent? Perhaps, if the audience felt itself sufficiently like the victim in other respects, such a reaction would be blocked. Greek tragedy, after all, is never more sententious than when it warns its audience of the vulnerability to which all mortals, not only the tragic hero, are subject. But the aporetic dialogues do not as a rule invite their readers to identify with the victim of the dramatic irony—too many of those victims are obviously unsympathetic characters, obvious tiros, obvious buffoons. (And notice that only if such identification were indeed the rule could it be adduced in support of the claim that Platonic irony in general seeks to arouse the reader's contagious anxiety.)

Alexander Nehamas has made this point very forcefully using the example of the *Euthyphro*. This dialogue is written in a way that makes it well-nigh inevitable that we shall feel we know better than the blindly self-assured Euthyphro. 'And knowing better, what do we do? Mostly, we read this little dialogue and then we close the book, in a gesture that is the exact replica of Euthyphro's sudden remembering of the appointment that ends his conversation with Socrates.' In making this gesture we would be demonstrating that we share Euthyphro's self-delusion, a demonstration that '*is really the aim of this whole mechanism*. Socrates' irony is directed at Euthyphro only as a means; its real goal are the readers of Plato's dialogue' (*Art*, 41).

Indeed, Gifford's own discussion inadvertently illustrates the danger of which Nehamas warns. Despite its claim that Plato's dramatic ironies have an unsettling effect on even the philosophically experienced reader, his article (which, let it be said, is both closely argued and sensitive to detail) issues unswervingly confident condemnation of the victims of Plato's irony in book 1 of the *Republic*, Cephalus and his son Polemarchus, as a family of con-

be connected with the blindness they demonstrate in discussion with him—perhaps even seen as a consequence of it. But similar views of Plato's goal as ironist are held too by those whose focus is rather on the fictional Socrates' own ironic handling of his conversation partners: e.g. Griswold, 100 ('I suggest that we understand "the point" of irony as connected to Plato's wish to invite the reader into a life of self-examination'); Boder, 166–7, citing M. J. O'Brien, *The Socratic Paradoxes and the Greek Mind* (Chapel Hill, 1967), 109.

temptible war-profiteers. It leaves no ambiguity at all about Plato's views on war, nor about the urgency with which he seeks to impress those views on his readers.

When applied to the deliberate ironies of the character Socrates, this tendency among Plato's readers leads to their saddling Socrates with dogmatic claims. Nehamas makes this point against Vlastos's 'complex irony': the complex ironist, provided his words are taken in the complex sense, is making a strong and positive claim—e.g. 'I am indeed a teacher'.[30] Jonathan Lear's Kierkegaardian approach to Socratic irony has Plato making similarly strong claims on Socrates' behalf. What lies behind Socratic practice, on this account, are Plato's answers to a series of ironic questions such as 'Among all the sophists, is there a sophist (one who knows)?' To which Plato's implied answer would be: 'Yes, there is one, Socrates—for he is the one who knows that he doesn't know' (450).

It is one thing, however, to agree with Nehamas that an appreciation of Socratic irony—which is by the same token an appreciation of the dramatic irony that results when Plato makes his leading man an ironist—could all too easily encourage either philosophic complacency or a tendency to turn Plato into a dogmatist; quite another to see this as evidence of Plato's intention to make the reader an additional victim of his irony, indeed the principal victim. For Nehamas, 'Plato's irony is more disturbing than Socrates' . . . It is deep, dark, and disdainful'; his writing amounts to a 'scornful display of the weakness of readers who assume they are morally superior to various characters while they are in fact revealing that they are made of the same stuff as those they deride'.[31]

Against our taking this further step—from foreseeing the danger of complacency to detecting outright Platonic disdain—stands the very fact that made the initial step plausible: the fact that it is impossible to appreciate a dramatic irony without feeling superior to its victim. For the reason why this is impossible has nothing to do with the reader's moral character, nor does it involve the reader in moral hypocrisy. All the reader need understand, that the victim does not, is that Socrates is ironizing at the victim's expense. This much of a sense of superiority is essential; but no more than this. In order to appreciate that Socrates is mocking Euthyphro I do not need to suppose either that I know better than does Euthyphro what

---

[30] See 'Silence', 180; *Art*, 67.
[31] The quotations are from *Art*, respectively at pp. 44 and 32.

piety really is or that I know what Socrates believes true piety to be. And even if I think that I do know what Socrates believes true piety to be, I do not need to agree with him in order to appreciate his irony; I am free to agree instead with his victim; or to hold a view quite different from both. My appreciation of the irony evinces only my competence as a reader; it says nothing about my soul.

It may be thought that this point goes some way towards redressing the balance in favour of those who believe that Plato is out to awaken his readers and stiffen their resolve for philosophy rather than to mock them. Instead of attempting to settle this dispute, let us consider its common premiss. For although Nehamas's view seems the polar opposite of Gifford's, the two share a foundational belief: that Plato aims to have an effect on his readers much like that which Socrates aims to produce in his conversation partners.[32]

Gifford offers an explicit justification for this belief. Since Plato's dialogues are a fictional representation of Socratic questioning, and since the point of that questioning within the fiction is to prompt its audience to evaluate their lives, 'it is natural to think' that Plato's reason for writing the fiction was the same as that which his character Socrates had for conducting his interrogations (46). I would call this a species of 'mimetic fallacy' if I were more confident that it must be wrong. Instead, it merely seems to be an assumption that one may quite as naturally avoid making; and certainly it misses the distinction drawn above between Socrates' and Plato's relation as ironists to their respective audiences—how Plato does and Socrates does not want his partners in discourse to penetrate his pretence.

The contrast between Plato and his character Socrates is not merely a contrast of media—Plato employing the written, Socrates the spoken word. It is a contrast of ends. Socrates does indeed, as Nehamas put it, direct his irony at victims within the dialogues only as a means; but his goal is not somehow to reach the readers of Plato's dialogues, it is to give his victims within the dialogues their intellectual come-uppance. Socrates has a job to do, and that job is to shake up his interlocutors. Plato's job, by contrast, is to write philosophic fiction; what effect his fictions have on his readership is not something he can control with anything like the manipulativeness of the fictional Socrates, who operates face to face with

---

[32] 'Much like', because both distinguish Platonic irony from its Socratic counterpart by its intensity. They do not, however, distinguish the two in kind. See Gifford, 102; Nehamas, *Art*, 44.

one interlocutor at a time. (On this issue, see *Phdr.* 275 E.) But this apparent handicap is one that a philosophic writer, particularly if he is a philosopher of a more contemplative and scholastic, less missionary bent than the character Socrates, can turn to his advantage. Platonic irony—his making a solipsistic ironist the hero of his fictions—is not a means to some ulterior end; it is among the matters that he gives his readers to ponder. Unlike Socratic irony, which works undetected, Platonic irony cannot do its work unless it finds an appreciative audience; and that is because its work is no more than to make itself understood.

My claim, in other words, is this. Given a correct analysis of Socratic irony, a contrast between Platonic and Socratic irony emerges; and what that contrast suggests is that Plato does not aim to unsettle or disturb his readers, as Socrates aims to unsettle and disturb his interlocutors; he does not aim to bring his readers to account; he is not mocking them, whether secretly or openly; he is not playing on their emotions; he is not urging them towards the philosophic life; he is not in fact out to persuade them of anything, if 'persuasion' means adapting a presentation to the needs and tastes of its audience rather than allowing it to follow internal constraints of thought and form. In short, he is not out to 'operate' on his readers in any way; he is only trying to get them to understand what he is at. If he thereby attracts precisely the type of reader who prefers not to be operated on, that (we may presume) would be no bad thing, in his eyes; but it would not constitute his reason for writing as he does.

If this is right, then Platonic irony should be understood as a kind of self-assertion. By making it a hallmark of his writing, Plato asserts himself as a writer of fiction. And in doing so he would not only be drawing a contrast with the ironic pretences of the speaker Socrates but also placing himself in relation to other writers of other types of fiction.

The fact that ignorance unexpectedly revealed is central to the action of the aporetic dialogues evokes one type of fiction for comparison more transparently than others: the tragic. The readers of these dialogues watch knowingly as Plato's dramatic irony unfolds and the interlocutor falls victim to Socratic enticement and Socratic questioning. But the revelation of ignorance in an aporetic dialogue falls well short, as we saw, of the full-dress tragic reversal experienced by an Oedipus. The scales do not fall from the interlocutor's eyes. He may be left puzzled, or suspicious, or otherwise unsatisfied, at least if he does not simply make his escape, but in any case he fails to look back with clarity, as a tragic hero does, over the plot that has enmeshed him.

In this contrast a Platonic contention is not far to seek. In tragic drama of a certain sort (the type exemplified by *Oedipus the King*) the hero's discovery of his own ignorance goes hand in hand, to all appearance, with his acquisition of knowledge and with the resolution of the dramatic plot. In seeing how he has been deceived he sees also how fate has been toying with him; he sees what has been going on. While the play may raise any number of philosophic issues, whether by means of explicit debate between its characters or by what its action implies, and while it may well leave those issues unresolved, at least its dramatic action is resolved with clarity.

These contrasts form a system, in which Plato seeks to mediate the extremes represented by the ironic practice of his character Socrates, at one pole, and the dramatic irony employed by tragedians, at the other. Socrates does not share his irony with anyone; his irony has only victims, but no audience (other than himself). What makes his irony necessary is his interlocutors' ignorance of their own ignorance about the most important matters in life. Although this recursive type of ignorance is at least partly dispelled as the dialogue unfolds, with the interlocutors being made aware, in various degrees, of their inadequacy, it leaves behind the simple ignorance that has come into view—for the dialogue ends without finding the answer to its question. The interlocutors remain puzzled both about what has happened and about the issue under discussion. Socratic irony does its work, then, by not making itself known; and when its work is done, no character in the drama claims enlightenment.

The dramatic irony of a tragedy such as *Oedipus the King* works in the opposite way. It cannot function without making itself clear, first to the audience, and eventually, as irony of fate, to the characters in the play. And when the action of the plot has resolved itself, both the characters of the play and the audience are completely clear about what has transpired.

Platonic irony straddles this divide. Like the tragedian's dramatic irony, it makes itself clear to its audience, the readers, and would be pointless otherwise. We know what is likely to happen, and watch to see how it will happen. But like Socratic irony it does not accompany the resolution of its strategem with a resolution of the fog that hangs over the dramatic action. To understand what has happened to Oedipus, at least at the level of the dramatic action, it suffices to know his life history. This will have equipped us not only to anticipate what is going to happen but to appreciate the turns in the plot by which the playwright makes it happen. But to understand what has happened in an aporetic dialogue, even at the level of the dramatic action—which is to say, to understand why the characters are unable to arrive at a satisfactory answer to their question—we need to ponder, for example, what courage is, or what self-control or piety or justice are. In every case we will be required to ponder what wisdom is. And it is a good deal harder for us to get to the bottom of *those* issues than it is to penetrate the dramatic irony in Socrates' self-effacement or in an interlocutor's bluster. Although we know what is likely to happen, we cannot be sure exactly how it happened even after it has.

Does this imply that the 'mimetic fallacy' is no fallacy after all? That in writing the aporetic dialogues Plato thinks of himself as leaving his readers in perplexity in just the way Socrates does his interlocutors? No; because in Plato's procedure, in contrast to Socrates', no deception is involved. Plato makes his fictional moves out in the open, as does the chess player; we the readers understand that our task is to interpret a fiction. We may find that fiction no easier to interpret than if Plato were our opponent at chess and we were attempting to penetrate his strategy; but we do not feel that Plato is deceiving us. Socrates does not play his dialectical chess game with an equivalent formality and openness, nor does he drop his ironic mask. His 'fictions'—his pretences—are deceptions. As such, they require justification by their salutary effects—effects that are duly noted at various places in the dialogues.[33] Plato's open fictions, however, do not require such justification; understanding them is its own reward.

On this view, our motivation for pondering, say, what courage is as we read the *Laches* need not stem from a desire to do better than Socrates' interlocutors, or from a fear that we might suffer their fate, or from a disturbing sense that Plato is mocking us. It need

---

[33] We saw Nicias offer one such justification at *La.* 188 A–B. Socrates himself provides another in the course of giving the slave boy in the *Meno* a geometry lesson (see 84 A–C); and his sentiments are echoed by the Eleatic Stranger in the *Sophist* (230 B–D).

only arise from our desire to understand what is going on in the drama.

University of California, Berkeley

BIBLIOGRAPHY

Boder, B., *Die Sokratische Ironie in den Platonischen Frühdialogen* (Amsterdam, 1973).

Brickhouse, T. C., and Smith, N. D., *The Philosophy of Socrates* (Boulder, 2002).

Clark, H. H., *Using Language [Using]* (Cambridge, 1996).

—— and Gerrig, R. J., 'On the Pretense Theory of Irony', *Journal of Experimental Psychology: General*, 113/1 (1984), 121–6.

Frede, M., 'Plato's Arguments and the Dialogue Form', in J. C. Klagge and N. D. Smith (eds.), *Methods of Interpreting Plato and his Dialogues* (*OSAP* suppl.; Oxford, 1992), 201–19.

Gifford, M., 'Dramatic Dialectic in *Republic* Book 1', *Oxford Studies in Ancient Philosophy*, 20 (2001), 35–106.

Gordon, J., 'Against Vlastos on Complex Irony', *Classical Quarterly*, NS 46 (1996), 131–7.

Gottlieb, P., 'The Complexity of Socratic Irony: A Note on Professor Vlastos' Account', *Classical Quarterly*, NS 42 (1992), 278–9.

Griswold, C. L., Jr., 'Irony in the Platonic Dialogues', *Philosophy and Literature*, 26 (2001), 84–106.

Kreuz, R. J., and Glucksberg, S., 'How to be Sarcastic', *Journal of Experimental Psychology: General*, 118/4 (1989), 375–86.

Kumon-Nakamura, S., Glucksberg, S., and Brown, M., 'How about another piece of pie: The Allusional-Pretence Theory of Discourse Irony', *Journal of Experimental Psychology: General*, 124/1 (1995), 3–21.

Lane, M., 'The Evolution of *Eirōneia* in Classical Greek Texts: Why Socratic *Eirōneia* is Not Socratic Irony', *Oxford Studies in Ancient Philosophy*, 31 (2006), 49–83.

Lear, J., 'The Socratic Method and Psychoanalysis', in S. A. Rappe and R. Kamtekar (eds.), *A Companion to Socrates* (Oxford, 2006), 442–62.

Nehamas, A., 'Voices of Silence: On Gregory Vlastos' Socrates' ['Silence'], *Arion*, 2/1 (1992), 157–86.

—— *The Art of Living: Socratic Reflections from Plato to Foucault [Art]* (Sather Classical Lectures, 61; Berkeley, 1998).

O'Brien, M. J., *The Socratic Paradoxes and the Greek Mind* (Chapel Hill, 1967).

Sperber, D., 'Verbal Irony: Pretense or Echoic Mention?' ['Verbal Irony'], *Journal of Experimental Psychology: General*, 113/1 (1984), 130–6.

—— and Wilson, D., *Relevance: Communication and Cognition* [*Relevance*] (Cambridge, Mass., 1988).

———— 'Irony and the Use–Mention Distinction', in S. Davis (ed.), *Pragmatics: A Reader* (Oxford, 1991), 550–63.

Stokes, M. C. (ed.), *Plato:* Apology (Warminster, 1997).

Utsumi, A., 'Verbal Irony as Implicit Display of Ironic Environment: Distinguishing Ironic Utterances from Nonirony', *Journal of Pragmatics*, 32 (2000), 1777–1806.

Vlastos, G., 'Socratic Irony', in G. Vlastos, *Socrates, Ironist and Moral Philosopher* (Cambridge, 1991), 21–44.

Williams, J., 'Does Mention (or Pretense) Exhaust the Concept of Irony?', *Journal of Experimental Psychology: General*, 113/1 (1984), 127–9.

APPEARANCES AND CALCULATIONS: PLATO'S DIVISION OF THE SOUL

JESSICA MOSS

WHY does Plato divide up the soul in just the way he does? The question is complicated by the fact that it is not quite clear how he does divide it. *Republic* 4 famously uses cases of motivational conflict to show that the soul has three parts: the rational part, which desires truth and the overall good of the soul, the spirited part, source of anger and ambition, and the appetitive part, which desires food, drink, sex, and other pleasures. In book 10, however, Socrates twice more argues for a divide between the rational part and some other part of the soul, without stating how these divisions relate to the one already established. At 602 C–603 A he gives an argument based on the cognitive dissonance that sometimes occurs when we experience optical illusions: the rational part calculates the truth and believes in accordance with its calculations, while an inferior part believes that things are as they appear. Then at 603 E–605 C he gives a third argument, based on what we might call emotional conflict: the rational part wishes to follow calm deliberation, while a non-rational part longs to indulge in violent emotion.

This last division maps onto the book 4 division fairly easily: most commentators assume that the emotional part is appetite, perhaps in combination with spirit, and I shall argue below that they are right to do so. The division based on optical illusions, however, is much harder to accommodate. The argument is concerned with cognitive instead of motivational conflict; worse, the kind of cognition in question bears no obvious relation to motivation at all. Thus interpreters tend to downplay the significance of this psychic division, and many hold either that it deals with different parts of

I have benefited greatly from discussion of this material with many people; I am particularly indebted to Rachel Barney, Cian Dorr, Matt Evans, Allan Silverman, Damien Storey, and audiences at Columbia and Rutgers.

the soul from that of book 4 or that the relationship between the two divisions is indeterminate.[1]

There is a serious problem for this widespread interpretation, however. As I shall argue, a fair reading of *Republic* 10—that is, a reading not specifically constructed to avoid the conclusion that the illusion-believing part is appetite or spirit—shows that the illusion-believing part *is* (or includes) appetite and spirit. The only reason anyone has wished to resist this conclusion, I surmise, is its strangeness. And indeed it is strange. Why should appetite or spirit see the submerged stick as bent? Surely doing so satisfies no craving for pleasure, or ambition for honour. One might well agree with Annas's diagnosis: Plato 'fails to see that his argument will not work, that desire has nothing to do with optical illusions, because he thinks of the lower part of the soul as being *merely* the trashy and reason-resisting part'.[2]

The project of this paper is to take the book 10 arguments not as embarrassments to be explained away, but instead as providing the key to Plato's division of the soul. I shall argue that they illuminate a distinction that is absolutely central to Platonic psychology, but opaque and much misunderstood: the distinction between rationality and non-rationality.

What all three of the *Republic*'s arguments for psychic division have in common is the claim that one part is rational while its opponent is not. More precisely, one part is guided by *logismos*—reasoning, or most literally calculation, in the narrow arithmetical

---

[1] It has been argued that the nature of the non-rational part is here left indeterminate (M. F. Burnyeat, 'Plato on the Grammar of Perceiving', *Classical Quarterly*, NS 26 (1976), 29–51 at 34), and that book 10 posits a division within reason itself (N. R. Murphy, *The Interpretation of Plato's* Republic (Oxford, 1951), 239–40; A. Nehamas, 'Plato on Imitation and Poetry', in J. M. E. Moravcsik and P. Temko (eds.), *Plato on Beauty, Wisdom and the Arts* (Totowa, NJ, 1982), 47–78; M. F. Burnyeat, 'Culture and Society in Plato's *Republic*', *Tanner Lectures on Human Values*, 20 (1999), 215–324 at 223; and D. Sedley, *The Midwife of Platonism: Text and Subtext in Plato's* Theaetetus (Oxford, 2004), 113 n.). Some, however, hold that Plato is referring to both appetite and spirit, if imprecisely (J. Adam, *The Republic of Plato* (2 vols.; Cambridge, 1902), ii. 406; T. Penner, 'Thought and Desire in Plato', in G. Vlastos (ed.), *Plato: A Collection of Critical Essays*, ii. *Ethics, Politics, and Philosophy of Art and Religion* (New York, 1971), 96–118), or to appetite alone (I. Murdoch, *The Fire and the Sun: Why Plato Banished the Artists* (Oxford, 1977), 5; J. Annas, *An Introduction to Plato's* Republic (Oxford, 1981), 131; C. D. C. Reeve, *Philosopher-Kings: The Argument of Plato's* Republic (Princeton, 1988), 127, 139). An analysis close to the one I give below is offered by H. Lorenz, *The Brute Within: Appetitive Desire in Plato and Aristotle* (Oxford, 2006), ch. 5.   [2] *An Introduction to Plato's* Republic, 339.

sense or in the wider sense of reckoning and accounting—while its opponent is not. The best part of the soul's desires arise 'out of calculation' in the first division (439 D), it measures and calculates and 'trusts in measurement and calculation' in the second (603 A), and it 'wishes to follow calculation' in the third (604 D); Plato's standard name for this part is *to logistikon*, usually translated 'the rational part', but literally that which can or tends to calculate.[3] Meanwhile, appetite is *alogiston*—unreasoning, non-rational, or most literally uncalculating—(439 D), spirit gets angry without calculation (*alogistōs*, 441 C), the part that believes optical illusions forms its belief without regard to calculation (*logismos*, 602 E–603 A), and the emotional part is uncalculating (*alogiston*, 604 D).

This distinction between rational and non-rational parts of soul is obviously of paramount importance to Plato: it is because one part has the capacity for *logismos*, a special capacity which the others lack, that this part is by nature superior and must rule the others if the agent is to be virtuous and happy. But just what is this special capacity? The question is much harder than it might seem. For, on a face-value reading of the dialogue, Plato grants the appetitive and spirited parts all sorts of states and abilities we might think paradigmatically rational: beliefs, including normative and evaluative ones,[4] the ability to be persuaded by argument,[5] and even the ability to recognize means towards given ends.[6] Hence the complaint that Plato simply contradicts himself:

[T]he appetitive element is purely appetitive and, as Plato himself says

---

[3] Translations are mine throughout except where otherwise noted.

[4] The characterization of these parts' desires implies that they must have fairly sophisticated beliefs about what is the case, e.g. that *x* is drink, that *y* is an insult. 571 C makes this explicit: the dreamer's appetitive part supposes (οἴεται) that he is trying to have sex with his mother. As further evidence that appetite and spirit must be capable of something at least very like belief, Socrates seems to endorse Glaucon's claim at 441 A–B that all children and many adults utterly lack *logismos*. Meanwhile, a number of passages dealing with the political equivalents of appetite and spirit, in books 8 and 9, appear to attribute beliefs about what is good to these parts of the soul (see e.g. 555 B); 574 D very strongly implies that the appetitive part has beliefs about what is fine and shameful. Most unambiguous is the claim that in a temperate soul, the appetitive and spirited parts 'believe in accord' (ὁμοδοξῶσι) that reason 'should' (δεῖν) rule (442 D).   [5] Implied at 554 D.

[6] Implied by the characterization of appetite as a lover of money (580 E). It is worth noting that the *Phaedrus*'s description of the non-rational parts makes all of these attributions completely explicit (see especially 253 D–254 E), and while the *Phaedrus*'s tale of horses and charioteer is allegory, unless Plato conceives of the lower parts as capable of fairly sophisticated cognition it is very misleading and unilluminating allegory indeed.

(439 D 7), has no reason in it . . . [Thus] it makes no sense at all to say that reason controls appetite with the agreement of appetite that reason should be in control [442 C–D]. That would be to assign to appetite some degree of reason which by definition it cannot possess . . . If he had not been so brief and hasty in his account of virtues in the individual, he might have detected the inconsistency himself.[7]

Of course we are not bound to take the text at face value, and many, wishing to be charitable to Plato, do not. Some dismiss the apparent attributions of beliefs and the like to appetite and spirit as metaphorical; others insist that, despite Plato's misleading silence on the matter, most of the activities he attributes to the lower parts are mediated by the rational part.[8] But these indirect readings, like the accusations of self-contradiction, are simply unmotivated unless we have a clear account of what abilities Plato means to deny these parts in calling them non-rational, an account grounded solely in Plato's texts rather than in any assumptions about the meaning of 'rational'.[9]

The fact is that Plato has a good claim to have invented the idea of rationality, and with it the rational/non-rational distinction. Although he doubtless drew on the Presocratics in important ways, he

[7] R. C. Cross and A. D. Woozley, *Plato's* Republic (New York, 1964), 124.

[8] Some scholars hold that the non-rational parts cannot have beliefs and the like because they are purely conative (and the rational part purely cognitive, explicit claims that it has its own desires notwithstanding (see e.g. 580 D)); for the classic rejection of this 'faculty psychology' reading, see J. Moline, 'Plato on the Complexity of the Psyche', *Archiv für Geschichte der Philosophie*, 60 (1978), 1–26. Others allow that each part is agent-like, with its own cognition and conation, but think that non-rational cognition must, to qualify as non-rational, be much more primitive than these passages imply. For a recent example of the metaphor strategy for downplaying these passages see R. F. Stalley, 'Persuasion and the Tripartite Soul in Plato's *Republic*', *Oxford Studies in Ancient Philosophy*, 32 (2007), 63–89; of the rational mediation strategy, see M. Anagnostopoulos, 'The Divided Soul and the Desire for Good in Plato's *Republic*', in G. Santas (ed.), *The Blackwell Guide to Plato's* Republic (Oxford, 2006), 166–88.

[9] Much is made of 437 E–438 A, which argues that 'thirst itself is for drink itself' rather than for drink of a particular sort: the passage is often taken to show that appetites are 'bare urges' or 'simple desires', involving no cognition of any kind. But (*a*) the point of the passage is not nearly as clear as is often assumed, and Socrates' analogy between 'thirst itself' and 'knowledge itself' should make us hesitate to conclude that he has in mind any claim about cognitive impoverishment (see also my brief discussion in sect. 5); and (*b*) as we have seen above, the *Republic* also applies the term *alogiston* (non-rational) to a wide range of cognitively complex desires, emotions, and other phenomena. I thus suspect that assumptions about rationality play a role both in the preference for the 'bare urge' reading of the passage and in the insistence that this one passage reveals the core meaning of *alogiston* while all the many others are misleading.

was the first to press into service the term *logismos* to characterize a
broad range of mental activity and to set it off from the rest.[10] Notably, the word he chose suggests not the common human capacity
for thought, language, and belief, but some ability over and above
these: in ordinary Greek usage a *logistikos* person is one particularly skilled in the more difficult forms of thinking (see e.g. *Rep.*
526 B), while an *alogistos* one is no subhuman, but simply foolish
or unreasonable (see e.g. *Ap.* 37 C; cf. *Rep.* 441 A–B).

Rather than accusing Plato of muddling his own distinction, then,
and rather than trying to explain away the evidence, we would do
better to examine his various characterizations of the parts of the
soul in search of a substantive concept of rationality that explains
his carving up psychic phenomena the way he does. The best place
to start, I submit, is with the mystery with which we began: the
relation between the *Republic*'s three arguments for the division
of the soul. For if we can find something common to the beliefs,
desires, and emotions classified as rational, and something common
to those classified as non-rational, we will have an excellent basis
for an account of what rationality amounts to on Plato's view.

That is what I undertake here. I begin by giving a reading of *Republic* 10 that shows that appetite and spirit believe optical illusions.
I then develop an explanation for this, as follows.

First, in the optical illusion argument Plato is redescribing the
parts of the soul with an emphasis not on their motivational but
rather on their cognitive aspects. The characterization relies on a
distinction between how things really are and how they *appear*,
where appearances are often false and always ontologically deficient. The non-rational parts are those that unreflectively accept
appearances; the rational part is that which can calculate, where
calculation involves reflecting on and when necessary resisting the
way things appear.

Second, these cognitive qualities entail and explain the parts' motivational characters. As the *Republic*'s third division emphasizes,
the category of appearances includes not only straightforward sensory appearances such as that a stick is straight or bent, but also
what I shall call evaluative appearances, such as that pastries are
good or an insult bad. All passions (desires, emotions, pleasures,

---

[10] I am here strongly influenced by M. Frede's arguments about the emergence
of the concept of rationality in his introduction to M. Frede and G. Striker (eds.),
Rationality in Greek Thought (Oxford, 1996).

and pains)[11] are responses to things *qua* valuable, but only calculation can grasp what is truly good or bad, as opposed to what merely
appears so. Thus the rational part desires what is best overall because it can calculate, and the appetitive and spirited parts have
inferior passions because they unreflectively accept appearances.
To say that (for example) the appetitive part sees the stick as bent
does not, then, mean that we see the stick as bent because doing
so satisfies some craving; it means rather that one and the same
susceptibility to appearances explains both our perception of the
stick and our appetites for pleasure.

To put the point more strongly: we discover in book 10 that what
it is for a part of the soul to be non-rational, with all that that entails
for its ethical status, is for it to accept unreflectively that things are
just as they appear to be, while what it is for the rational part to be
rational, with all that that entails for its ethical status, is for it to be
able to transcend appearances by calculating how things really are.
These are the defining features of rationality and non-rationality,
which unify and explain the various traits of the parts of the soul
and their various characterizations throughout the dialogue.

One note before I begin: my focus is on the parts of the soul as
presented in the *Republic*, but I draw on other dialogues—especially
the *Protagoras* and *Timaeus*—in developing and defending my view.
Some might object to my doing so, on the grounds that there are
significant differences between the psychological theories of these
three dialogues.[12] If we can find continuities across the dialogues,
however—such as the explanation of certain emotions and desires
as responses to quasi-perceptual appearances of things as good or
bad—then we should welcome this fact as evidence that, differences
notwithstanding, there is something common to them that can il-

[11] Unlike Aristotle, Plato does not officially introduce the term 'passions' (*pathē*
or *pathēmata*) to pick out emotions, desires, pleasures, and pains as a class, but he
frequently uses these words to refer to these states (as e.g. at *Tim.* 69 c, quoted
below). The theory I shall go on to attribute to Plato should explain why he groups
these states together.

[12] The *Protagoras* denies the possibility of the kind of motivational conflict on
which the *Republic*'s tripartition is based, while the *Timaeus* denies *doxa*, belief, to
the appetitive part of the soul (77 B, quoted below). C. Bobonich, *Plato's Utopia
Recast* (Oxford, 2002), argues that the *Timaeus* represents a change in Plato's view
of the cognitive capacities of the lower parts of the soul, while Lorenz, *The Brute
Within*, argues that it reflects instead a revision of Plato's concept of belief. My
arguments should provide indirect support for seeing the *Timaeus*'s psychology as
continuous with the *Republic*'s, despite the change in terminology.

luminate the difference between rationality and non-rationality as Plato conceived it.

1. Parts of the soul in *Republic* 10

As part of book 10's attack on imitative poetry, Socrates appeals to a division in the soul in order to identify the part over which visual imitation (painting) exerts it power (602 C–603 B).[13] First, he claims that when we experience optical illusion we often simultaneously believe both that things are as they appear and that things are as measurement and reasoning prove them to be.[14] Second, he reminds us of a principle he used in book 4's argument for psychic division (436 B–C): that no one thing can do or undergo opposites regarding the same thing at the same time—the 'principle of opposites', as it is often called. He even makes explicit reference to that earlier argument ('Didn't we say . . . ?', 602 E), a sign that we are at the very least meant to bear book 4's division in mind at this point. Next, he uses the principle of opposites to show that there must be two distinct parts of the soul, one that believes in accordance with measurements and calculation, and one that believes against them in accordance with the *phainomenon*, appearance (602 D). Since measuring, calculating, and weighing are the work of the *logistikon*, and since this is the best part of the soul, it must be an inferior (φαῦλον) part of the soul that believes in accordance with appearances (603 A). When all goes well, the rational part 'rules in us' (602 C–D). Just as, according to book 4, a person is ethically virtuous when reason rules in her and appetite and spirit are ruled

---

[13] For a detailed defence of conclusions similar to those I reach in this section, see Lorenz, *The Brute Within*, ch. 5.

[14] Aristotle denied that we believe the false appearance, insisting on a distinction between how things appear to us and how we believe them to be (*DA* 3. 3, 428ᵃ17 ff.), and most contemporary philosophers would take his side. Did Plato ignore the possibility that one might experience an appearance without assenting to it, a possibility that would have barred the application of the principle of opposites here, allowing him to attribute the experience of the appearance and the disbelief in it to the same part of the soul? I suspect that he is instead expressing the view that there is real conflict in these cases: we are compelled by the false appearance even though we do not all things considered believe it. None the less, Plato nowhere explicitly distinguishes between awareness of and assent to appearances within the lower parts of the soul; on the view I attribute to him, this might be explained by the view that for these parts assent is automatic.

(441 E ff.), here a person is cognitively virtuous when the calculating part rules and the appearance-believing part is ruled.

Socrates takes the argument to establish that art that trades in visual images 'consorts with' an inferior part of the soul. But visual art was all along of merely illustrative interest, book 10's real target being imitative poetry. Does it, too, target an inferior part of the soul? This is Socrates' question as he launches a direct discussion of the psychology of imitative poetry (603 B–C). Now we get an investigation of human behaviour, both as the subject of tragedy (what sort of behaviour tragedies represent) and as the effect of tragedy (what sort of behaviour tragedy induces in its audience). It is in this context that Plato offers his third argument for a division in the soul.

The argument centres on cases of conflict between an impulse to yield to strong emotion and a wish to follow 'reason [*logos*] and law' (604 A). Once again, the principle of opposites is used to infer the presence of two parts (604 B). On one side there is the *logistikon* again, now described as the part that resists emotion, follows calculation (*logismos*, 604 D), and deliberates about what to do. Opposed to this is an unreasoning (*alogiston*, 604 D) part which 'leads us towards memories of suffering and towards lamentation and is insatiable for these things' (604 D), feels pity (606 B), prompts laughter (606 C), and is also the source of 'lusts and spirit and all the appetitive desires and pains and pleasures in the soul' (606 D). This part is inferior (605 A–B) and 'thoughtless' (ἀνόητον) (605 B). It is this part that tragedy 'nurtures' and empowers (606 D); thus, Socrates concludes, it is right to bar such poetry from the ideal city.

I want to show (*a*) that the emotional part involved in this last division is identical to or includes appetite and spirit, and (*b*) that this emotional part is also identical to the illusion-believing part involved in book 10's earlier division of the soul. The consequence, of course, is the claim people find so bizarre: that the illusion-believing part is or includes appetite and spirit.[15]

(a) *The emotional part includes appetite and spirit*

Plato does not outright identify the part of the soul targeted by tragedy with appetite and spirit, but he comes very close. Consider a passage I quoted in part above:

[15] It should be clear that I am using 'part' in a loose sense; I take this to be justified by Plato's purposes in book 10. See below, and compare Lorenz, *The Brute Within*, 65.

Concerning lusts and spirit [θυμοῦ] and all the appetitive desires [ἐπι-θυμητικῶν] and pains and pleasures in the soul . . . poetic imitation . . . nurtures these things, watering them although they should wither, and sets them up to rule in us although they should be ruled. (606 D)

Here we have unmistakable allusions to the spirited and appetitive parts of the soul (θυμός or τὸ θυμοειδές, and the ἐπιθυμητικόν). (Even if we choose to translate θυμός here as 'anger', this emotion has been attributed to spirit throughout.) If poetic imitation nurtures appetitive and spirited desires by influencing some unreasoning part of the soul, it must be that this unreasoning part of the soul is or includes both appetite and spirit.

Moreover, the general characterization of this part of the soul is strongly reminiscent of Plato's characterization of the appetitive and spirited parts earlier in the dialogue. It is 'insatiable' for grief and lamentation (ἀπλήστως ἔχον, 604 D): variations of ἄπληστος have frequently been used in connection with the appetites.[16] It *hungers* for the satisfaction of weeping and sufficiently lamenting, being by nature such as to have an *appetite* [ἐπιθυμεῖν] for these things' (606 A, emphasis added). And the type of character that gives in to excessive emotions—that is, the type ruled by this un-reasoning part of the soul—is 'irritable and multicoloured' (ἀγανακ-τητικόν τε καὶ ποικίλον, 605 A): 'multicoloured' has earlier been used to describe the democratic character, who is ruled by his appetites (561 E; cf. 557 C, 558 C, 559 D), and to describe the appetites them-selves (588 C; see also 404 E), while ἀγανακτητικόν (which occurs in a similar context also at 604 E) strongly suggests spirit, the source of anger.

Furthermore—and this consideration seems to me decisive—the *Republic*'s earlier discussion of poetry and art, in books 2 and 3, makes it clear that poetry is important in education precisely be-cause it strongly influences both appetite and spirit, for better or worse. The 'musical' education prescribed in books 2 and 3 is de-signed to harmonize spirit with reason (411 E–412 A); it can do so because poetry affects spirit by presenting certain things as worthy of honour and admiration, or of outrage and disdain. Meanwhile, dangerous poetry offers great pleasures, but makes people intem-perate:[17] given book 4's characterization of the appetitive part as

---

[16] At 442 A, 555 B, 562 B, 562 C, 578 A, 586 B, and 590 B. (Plato also uses the word once to characterize the rational part's love for wisdom, at 475 C.)

[17] 390 A, 390 B, 397 D, 399 E.

pleasure-seeking, and of temperance as involving appetite mastery, this implies that it strengthens people's appetites. Precisely this concern is echoed at the conclusion of book 10's discussion of poetry: 'If you let in the pleasurable muse in lyric or epic poetry, pleasure and pain will be kings in your city' (607 A). Book 10's complaint that imitative poetry strengthens and nurtures an inferior part of the soul to the point that it will usurp the rational part is, then, a reiteration of the complaint in books 2 and 3 that this kind of poetry fosters vice by encouraging unruly appetites and leading spirit astray.

Some protest that neither appetite nor spirit is at issue, on the grounds that book 10 is concerned with emotions (such as grief) not explicitly included in the earlier characterization of these parts.[18] But the allusions to appetitive and spirited desire are so strong that it is more likely that Plato is here expanding his characterization of these parts. Alternatively, and perhaps most plausibly, we may take it that in book 10 Plato is simply not concerned with the distinction between the various non-rational elements in the soul—not interested in ascribing certain motivations to the appetitive part in contrast with the spirited, nor in the question of whether there are other non-rational parts besides.[19] Instead, he is here concerned with the distinction between the rational part of the soul and the rest of the soul taken as a whole, so that the differences between appetite, spirit, and any other non-rational parts matter far less than their common feature of non-rationality. (This indeterminacy between the non-rational parts will be less problematic if we can demonstrate that there is some feature shared both by appetitive and spirited desire as we know them from the earlier books and by the impulse to yield to strong emotions, a feature that justifies characterizing them all as non-rational. A main claim of this paper will be that the illusion argument reveals such a feature.)

---

[18] See e.g. A. W. Price, *Mental Conflict* (London, 1995), 68–9.

[19] In *Republic* 4 Plato says that virtue is a matter of 'harmonizing the three [parts of soul], just like the three notes in a musical scale, lowest and highest and middle, *and any others there may be in between*' (443 D, emphasis added). If this last phrase refers to the parts of the soul, it indicates that the book 4 division is not exhaustive (and even if it refers to musical notes, it arguably suggests the same point, by analogy); if so, however, it also indicates that Plato is happy to leave the matter indeterminate.

(b) The emotional part is the illusion-believing part

Recall the argumentative structure of book 10. The optical illusion argument establishes that visual imitative art appeals to a non-rational part of the soul; then Socrates enquires whether imitative poetry does as well, and addresses the question by examining the psychology of tragedy. Now look at how he phrases the result of that enquiry: imitative poetry appeals to a part that is not merely similar in its non-rationality to that appealed to by visual art, but is in fact *the very same part of the soul*:

[T]he imitative poet . . ., by making images [εἴδωλα] far removed from the truth, gratifies the part of the soul that is thoughtless and doesn't distinguish greater things from lesser, but thinks that the same things are at one time large and another time small. (605 B–C)

This is an unmistakable reference to one of the optical illusions discussed in book 10's first division argument: 'The same magnitude viewed from nearby and from afar does not appear equal to us' (602 C). Thus 605 B–C states that the imitative poet appeals to the part of the soul that believes that a person standing at a distance is smaller than he was when standing closer—that is, to the part of the soul that perceives and believes optical illusions.[20] Moreover, this is just what we should expect from book 10 (although the argument could certainly be clearer). Socrates has argued that the imitative poet, like the painter, produces mere images, things far removed from the truth. The assumption underlying the conclusion at 605 B–C seems to be that images, whether visual or poetic, all appeal to the same inferior, unreasoning part of the soul. (On the nature of poetic images, see Section 3.)

Our reading has shown, then, that it is the appetitive and spirited parts that believe the appearances in optical illusions.[21] In the next section I show that this result is far from anomalous: elsewhere in

[20] Most of those who argue that the inferior part identified in the optical illusion passage is not the same as that targeted by imitative poetry ignore 605 B–C; Burnyeat dismisses it as a misleading overstatement of an analogy ('Culture and Society in Plato's *Republic*', 224–6).

[21] There is an important but inconclusive textual objection to this reading: 602 E 4–6 reads, on the usual translation, 'But often when this [the *logistikon*] has measured and has indicated that some things are larger or smaller or the same size as others, the opposites appear *to it* [τούτῳ] at the same time' (based on the translation of G. M. A Grube, revised by C. D. C. Reeve (henceforth Grube/Reeve), in J. M. Cooper (ed.), *Plato: Complete Works* (Indianapolis, 1997); emphasis added). This implies that it is a subpart of the *logistikon* that receives and believes the illusion. (See n. 1 above

the *Republic* and in other dialogues, Plato contrasts appetite and spirit with the rational part by characterizing them as responsive to, and unable to transcend, perceptual appearances.

2. The non-rational soul as the seat of perception

A passage from the *Timaeus*, evidently ignored by those who find incredible the suggestion that appetite or spirit see the stick as bent, explicitly and unambiguously associates illusion-perception with the appetitive part of the soul:

> The part of the soul that has appetites for food and drink and whatever else it feels a need for, given the body's nature . . . [does not] understand reason [*logos*] . . . [or] have an innate regard for any arguments [*logoi*], but . . . [is] much more enticed by images and phantoms night and day. Hence the god conspired with this very tendency by constructing a liver [as the bodily seat of the appetites] . . . .so that the force of its thoughts sent down from the mind might be stamped upon it as upon a mirror that receives the stamps and returns images. (*Tim.* 70 D–71 B)[22]

The appetitive part responds not to reasoning, but instead to 'images and phantoms' (εἴδωλα καὶ φαντάσματα): that is, to the kind of shadowy appearances that occupy the lowest rung of the *Republic*'s ontology.[23] This is strong confirmation of our reading of *Republic* 10. But the *Timaeus* goes further: it attributes to the appetitive part—arguably along with spirit—not just illusory perception, but sense-perception in general:

> Within the body [the gods] built another kind of soul as well, the mortal kind, which contains within it those terrible but necessary passions [παθήματα]: pleasure . . . pains . . . daring and fear . . .; also *thumos* [anger or

for a list of those who accept this reading.) Natural as this translation may be, the weight of the evidence given here is against it. (Additional arguments are provided by Lorenz, *The Brute Within*.) A promising alternative translation of the sentence is suggested by Adam, *The Republic of Plato*, ii. 408 and 466–7 (revived with slight revision by Lorenz, *The Brute Within*, 68); others are proposed by B. Jowett and L. Campbell, *Plato's Republic* (Oxford, 1894), 451, and R. Barney, 'Appearances and Impressions', *Phronesis*, 37 (1992), 283–313 at 286–7 n.

[22] Quotations from the *Timaeus* are based on the translation of D. J. Zeyl in Cooper (ed.), *Plato: Complete Works*.

[23] Plato uses the term φαντάσματα for the shadows and reflections that are at the lowest level of the divided line (510 A), εἴδωλα for the shadows in the cave (520 C), and both terms for the products of imitative art (599 A, 599 D, 601 B, and 605 C).

spirit] . . . and hope. These they fused with unreasoning sense-perception [αἰσθήσει δὲ ἀλόγῳ] and all-venturing *erōs*, and so, as was necessary, they constructed the mortal type of soul. (*Tim.* 69 C–D)

Plato reiterates the point, and also emphasizes the contrast between perception and calculation, in commenting on the appetitive part at *Tim.* 77 B: this part 'has no share at all of belief or calculation [λογισμοῦ] or understanding [νοῦ], but instead of perception, pleasant and painful, with appetites'. Thus the *Timaeus* explicitly attributes sensory perception to the appetitive part, and at least suggests, at 69 C–D, that spirit shares in perception as well.[24]

When we turn back to the *Republic* with the *Timaeus*'s claim in mind, we notice strong associations between perception and the non-rational parts of the soul. Consider book 5's contrast between true philosophers and the 'lovers of sights and sounds', who have no awareness of the imperceptible Form of Beauty but are devoted to the beauty they perceive through sight and hearing (475 D ff.).[25] Philosophers are ruled by the rational parts of their souls. Although Plato does not emphasize the point, clearly the lovers of sights and sounds are not: if their rational parts are not free to contemplate the Forms, it must be because they are enslaved to appetite or spirit. If those ruled by appetite or spirit are also wedded to perception, the implication is that appetite and spirit themselves are confined to perception-based thought.[26]

The attribution of perception to appetite and spirit further confirms our reading of *Republic* 10. This may seem obvious: it is

[24] The *Timaeus*'s 'mortal soul' is clearly to be identified with the *Republic*'s appetitive and spirited parts: see e.g. the characterizations at *Tim.* 70 A–B. 69 C–D could be read as listing perception as an ingredient that will be housed in one or the other division of the mortal soul, with 77 B settling the question of which part by assigning it to appetite, but the description of perception and *erōs* as 'fused' (συγκερασάμενοι) with all the rest implies that each of these two features belongs to both parts of the mortal soul. This is supported by 61 C–D.

[25] Commentators point out that the 'sights and sounds' in question are theatrical spectacles, but in the context of book 5–7's metaphysical and epistemological divide between the perceptible and imperceptible the literal interpretation is clearly intended as well. See Adam's note ad loc.: 'σοφία in φιλο-σοφία is presently defined so as to exclude sense-perception: hence "lovers of sights and sounds" are not "lovers of knowledge"' (*The* Republic *of Plato*, i. 334).

[26] Bobonich puts it well: 'Although the *Republic* does not make fully clear the relation between perception and the lower parts of the soul, the lower parts do have access to perception and the beliefs that are a part of perception, while they lack higher sorts of cognitive abilities' (*Plato's Utopia Recast*, 322). Lorenz, *The Brute Within*, also argues that appetite and spirit exercise and are limited to perception-based cognition.

unsurprising that a part of the soul responsible for ordinary perception would be responsive to illusory perceptual appearances as
well. But Plato also has a deeper reason for treating ordinary perception as importantly similar to illusory perception, and for assigning
both to the non-calculating parts of the soul: perception, in sharp
contrast with calculation, has access only to mere appearances.

It will be easiest to put this point in the terms of *Republic* 6's
divided line (509 D–511 E). The lower half of the line is the 'visible' realm, and more generally the perceptible, and while Plato
certainly distinguishes between ordinary perceptible objects (the
second level) and things like shadows and reflections (the lowest
level), he also assimilates the two, most explicitly in the *Timaeus*,
where he calls the whole physical world a picture (εἰκών) and phan-
tom (φάντασμα) of the intelligible (52 c; cf. 49). Thus Plato uses the
lowest section of the line as a metaphor for the perceptible world as a
whole, and the reason for this is clear: on his view, everything we can
perceive is but a shadow and image of what is real, the Forms. 'As the
opinable is to the knowable'—that is, as the whole perceptible realm
is to the intelligible—'so the likeness is to the thing that it is like'
(510 A). What most of us take to be the real world is a mere shadow
of reality, and what most of us take to be true merely apparent.

While not all perception is illusory in the same way as the perception of the submerged stick, then, perception never captures the
truth in the full Platonic sense: never gets beyond appearances to
capture being, for this is imperceptible. This is the view that underlies *Republic* 5's denigration of the perceptible world as opinable but
unknowable, the *Phaedo*'s similar argument about the cognitive un-
reliability and ontological deficiency of the perceptible world, and
the view that the Forms, which wholly *are* and are knowable, are
inaccessible to perception. Thus, just as in the metaphysical case,
Plato uses the lowest epistemological section of the divided line as
a metaphor for the whole lower half. 'What about someone who
believes in beautiful things, but doesn't believe in the Beautiful itself?' (that is, someone who recognizes only what can be perceived):
'Isn't this dreaming?' (476 c).

If perception can never get us beyond the dream-world of mere
appearances, however, another kind of cognition has just that task:
logismos. *Logismos* in the narrow sense—a branch of mathematics
closely related to arithmetic—joins arithmetic as the first subject
of study prescribed in the education designed to turn souls away

from the perceptible world of becoming and towards the intelligible realm of being (522 C). Relying on perception keeps us in the cave, but counting and calculating about what we perceive can lead us out. Plato also uses *logismos* and its verbal variants in their more general senses to describe the kind of cognition whereby we can transcend the perceptible world:

Do sight or hearing offer people any truth? . . . And if those bodily senses are not precise or clear, our other senses can hardly be so . . . When, then, does the soul grasp the truth? . . . Is it not in reasoning [ἐν τῷ λογίζεσθαι] if anywhere that any of the things that *are* become clear to the soul? (*Phaedo* 65 B–C)

The famous finger passage of *Republic* 7 (523 A ff.) makes the same claim: when contradictions make us realize the limits of perception, 'the soul, summoning calculation [*logismos*] and understanding [νόησιν]' (524 B), searches for the truth in the imperceptible, purely intelligible realm.

These passages show that calculation, in both its narrow and broad senses, stands to perception in general just as it stands to illusory perception in the *Republic* 10 passage. Even veridical perception grasps only inadequate appearances, and thus needs supervision and correction by *logismos*.

Thus Plato provides a clear principle for characterizing perception as *alogiston*: it is sharply opposed to calculation, in being limited to appearances. As we have seen, he also assigns perception to the appetitive and spirited parts of the soul, the parts whose desires and emotions he calls *alogiston*. We may still worry that this move is unprincipled: here Plato is simply using *alogiston* as a catch-all term, and carelessly lumping inferior cognition together with inferior passions in the same part of the soul. In the next section I show that the *Republic*'s third argument for the division of the soul provides a much better rationale. Appetitive and spirited passions belong to the non-rational, perceiving part of the soul—the part that is unable to calculate, and thus limited to mere appearances—because they are unreflective acceptances of appearances: not now of ordinary sensory appearances, but of appearances of things as good and bad.

3. Evaluative appearances

Republic 10's account of the passions will be easier to recognize if we start with another passage in which Plato compares the experience of optical illusions to moral error, one that makes clearer what analogy he sees between the two: the 'art of measurement' passage from the *Protagoras*. This passage famously offers a revisionist account of practical error; in doing so, it also implies a revisionist account of the passions that motivate it.

Most people, says Socrates, maintain that they sometimes act badly because their knowledge of what is best is overpowered by some other psychic force: 'sometimes anger [*thumos*], sometimes pleasure, sometimes pain, at other times *erōs*, often fear' (352 B–C)— that is, by precisely those passions that the *Republic* and *Timaeus* will assign to the non-rational parts of the soul. In his argument against this claim, Socrates gives his own account of these passions: they are (or include) evaluations of their objects, which may be dangerously false.[27] Fear, for example, is 'an expectation [προσδοκία] of something bad' (358 D): in being afraid of something, we are taking that thing to be bad. What is wrong with the coward is not that he acts on fear, but that his fear involves an evaluative mistake: he is ignorant about what is truly to be feared (360 C), and so expects as bad—fears—something that is not. Likewise, the argument implies, what is wrong with the self-indulgent person is not that she acts on her appetite for pleasure, but that this appetite involves an evaluative mistake: she is wrong about what is truly pleasant, and so desires as most pleasant something that is not.

Socrates explains these mistakes by analogy with optical illusions. Just as the same thing appears larger when near at hand and smaller when far away (356 C—the same example we find in *Republic* 10), something near in time may appear more pleasant or painful than it is, and something remote in time less so. In matters practical, then, just as in matters visual, we are led astray by false appearances. Moreover, we can ensure that our actions are correct, just as we can

---

[27] The definition of fear as a προσδοκία, advance-belief (see next sentence), certainly implies that this passion *is* an evaluative belief or belief-like state; *Laws* 644 C–D defines fear and also confidence as *doxai*, beliefs. It may, however, be going beyond what Plato had worked out to insist that he means to equate passions with evaluations rather than holding that they are, for example, partly constituted by evaluations and partly constituted by physical feelings.

ensure that our visual beliefs are true, only by using *measurement* to determine how things really are:

> While the power of appearance [τοῦ φαινομένου] makes us wander all over the place in confusion, often changing our minds about the same things and regretting our actions and choices, . . . the art of measurement, in contrast, would make the appearance [φάντασμα] lose its power by showing us the truth . . . and would save our life . . . People who make mistakes concerning the choice of pleasures and pains—that is, goods and bads— make these mistakes through a lack of knowledge . . . of measurement. (*Prot.* 356 D–357 D)[28]

These last lines remind us of what is most fundamentally at issue in this part of the *Protagoras*: mistakes about 'goods and bads'.[29] The appearances that lead us astray in matters of action are value-appearances: appearances of things as good or bad, worthy of pursuit or of avoidance. Virtue consists in overcoming 'the power of appearance' via the 'art of measurement'—in rationally evaluating different alternatives to see which is truly best. Through the scrutiny, comparison, criticism, and sometimes rejection of appearances we reach the truth about value, and desires and emotions that result from these measurements lead us aright: the courageous person is safe in acting on his fears, because his fear is based on knowledge of what is truly bad (360 A–D). The passions that motivate wrong action, meanwhile, are (or include) the unreflective acceptance of false value-appearances. The intemperate person who craves excessive bodily pleasures does so because these appear to be better than they really are; the coward who cannot stand his ground in battle fears death because it appears to be worse than it really is.

It is worth noting briefly that this view has much in common with the theories of the passions developed explicitly by Aristotle and the Stoics. Aristotle's *Rhetoric* defines various passions as responses to quasi-perceptual appearances of things as good or bad.[30]

---

[28] Based on the translation by S. Lombardo and K. Bell in Cooper (ed.), *Plato: Complete Works*.

[29] I here bracket the question of why Socrates in this part of the *Protagoras* equates the good with the pleasant.

[30] For this interpretation of the passions in the *Rhetoric*, see among others A. Nehamas, 'Pity and Fear in the *Rhetoric* and the *Poetics*', in A. Nehamas and D. Furley (eds.), *Essays on Aristotle's* Rhetoric (Princeton, 1994), 257–82, and G. Striker, 'Emotions in Context: Aristotle's Treatment of the Passions in the *Rhetoric* and his Moral Psychology', in A. O. Rorty (ed.), *Essays on Aristotle's* Rhetoric (Berkeley, 1996), 286–302.

To give the most striking examples, fear is 'a pain or disturbance
arising from the appearance of a destructive or painful future evil
[ἐκ φαντασίας μέλλοντος κακοῦ]' (*Rhet.* 1382ᵃ21–2), pity 'a pain taken
in an apparent evil [ἐπὶ φαινομένῳ κακῷ], destructive or painful, be-
falling one who does not deserve it' (1385ᵇ13–14).[31] Despite a radi-
cally different underlying psychological theory, the Stoic definition
is strikingly similar: passions are (false) appearance-based value
judgements, beliefs that what merely appears good or bad really is
so. Appetite is for what appears good (τὸ φαινόμενον ἀγαθόν), fear is
of what appears bad.[32] Pleasure and pain, meanwhile, result from
the presence of these apparently good or bad things:[33] pleasure is
'a fresh belief that something good is present', pain or distress 'a
fresh belief that something bad is present',[34] where such beliefs are
assents to false appearances (or 'impressions': φαντασίαι, *species*).[35]
This is not the place for a careful investigation of the continuities and differences between Plato, Aristotle, and the Stoics on the
passions, but the similarities are worth noting, and, given Plato's
enormous influence on his successors, should I think count as confirmation that some version of the view of passions as responses to
evaluative appearances is there to be found in Plato.

   If we could find evidence of this view in the *Republic*, we would
have an explanation for book 10's equation of the passionate and
illusion-believing parts of the soul. The project may seem doubtful, because the *Republic*'s psychological theory is notoriously different from the one implicit in the *Protagoras*: the *Protagoras* denies
the possibility of motivational conflict, treats all desire as reason-
sensitive, and makes no distinction between better and worse parts
of the soul.[36] None the less, the continuities are stronger than generally recognized. In the *Protagoras*, the virtuous are those whose
passions arise from the art of measurement; in the *Republic*, they

---

[31] Other relevant definitions include those of anger (*Rhet.* 1378ᵃ31), hope (1383ᵃ
17), shame (1383ᵇ13), indignation (*nemesis*, 1387ᵃ8), envy (1387ᵇ23), and emulation
(1388ᵃ32).

[32] e.g. Stob. ii. 88. 8–90.   [33] Ibid.

[34] Ps.-Andron. *On Passions* 1; also attributed to Chrysippus by Galen, *On Hippocrates' and Plato's Doctrines*, 4. 2. 1–6.

[35] See e.g. Sen. *De ira* 2. 1–3.

[36] I give my own account of the differences between the *Protagoras* and the *Republic* on this topic, and argue that it is Plato's changing views about the 'power of
appearance' that motivate the shift from the *Protagoras*'s psychology to that of the
Republic, in my 'Pleasure and Illusion in Plato', *Philosophy and Phenomenological
Research*, 72 (2006), 503–35.

are those whose souls are ruled by the passions of the rational part of the soul, the *logistikon*. As we have seen, both in his name for this best part of the soul and in his descriptions of it Plato emphasizes the centrality of calculation to all its doings. Calculation is obviously similar to measurement, and *Republic* 10's optical illusion passage not only groups them together (along with weighing and counting) as belonging to the rational part of the soul (602 D–E), but characterizes both as countering the rule of appearance, τὸ φαινόμενον—a striking echo of the *Protagoras*'s contrast between 'the art of measurement and the power of appearance' (*Prot.* 356 D). Given that *Republic* 10, like the *Protagoras*, uses resistance to illusory perceptual appearances as an analogy for ethical virtue, could it be that the *Republic* too construes non-virtuous passions as responses to deceptive evaluative appearances? We find evidence that it does in *Republic* 10's discussion of the parts of soul in connection with tragedy.

Socrates' main complaint against tragedy is that it corrupts the soul by strengthening the non-rational part(s). He puts this charge in two ways. First: tragedy is dangerous because it produces 'images that are far removed from truth' (605 B–C, quoted in Section 2 above). Second: tragedy is dangerous because it induces strong emotions (see especially 606 A and 606 D). The obvious inference is that tragedy induces emotions *by* producing images: that is, that the emotions in question are responses to images.

But what sort of images are at issue? As many have noted, Socrates thinks tragedy dangerous not because it presents fiction as fact, but rather because it reinforces and exploits widespread but false judgements of value.[37] It presents certain things as good—glory, revenge, the daring and passion of an Achilles—and other things as terrible: death, disgrace, the loss of one's child. In Socrates' view these values are badly mistaken: as he is about to reiterate in the remainder of book 10, what is truly good for us is being just, and what is truly bad is being unjust. But most people have false value-

---

[37] See e.g. E. Belfiore, 'Plato's Greatest Accusation against Poetry', in F. J. Pelletier and J. King-Farlow (eds.), *New Essays on Plato* (*Canadian Journal of Philosophy*, suppl. 9; Guelph, Ont., 1983), 39–62; Burnyeat, 'Culture and Society in Plato's *Republic*', esp. pp. 313 ff.; C. Janaway, *Images of Excellence* (Oxford, 1995); Nehamas, 'Plato on Imitation and Poetry'. See also my 'What is Imitative Poetry and Why is it Bad?', in G. R. F. Ferrari (ed.), *The Cambridge Companion to Plato's* Republic (Cambridge, 2007), 415–44, for fuller argument than I can offer here that tragedy copies and presents evaluative appearances.

beliefs, and it is to these that tragedy panders. Thus the tragedian's images are evaluative images. The tragedian knows how to make Achilles' revenge appear glorious, Oedipus' fate horrible, and so on. Therefore the passions that tragedy provokes, like the non-virtuous passions of the *Protagoras*, are responses to vivid but false appearances of things as good and bad.

Moreover, Plato says that the imitator's images and appearances are themselves copies not of things as they are, but of mere images and appearances (598 A–B, 600 E, 601 B); in particular, the imitator

will imitate, not knowing in what way each thing is worthless or worthy [πονηρὸν ἢ χρηστόν]; but the sort of things that *appear* to be fine or beautiful [οἶον φαίνεται καλὸν εἶναι] to the ignorant many—this, it seems, he will imitate. (602 B, emphasis added)

The implication is that even out of the theatre most of us are aware not of genuine value but only of appearances. It is natural to suppose that these appearances form the basis for our everyday passions.

This suggestion is confirmed by *Republic* 10's characterization of the rational person's resistance to emotion. He is 'measured'[38] in his grief (603 E); he holds back from lamentation because he 'follows calculation' (604 D). This recalls the rational part's role in optical illusions, where it resists false appearances by measuring and calculating (602 D–603 A). Of course, 'calculation' in the earlier passage is naturally read in its narrow sense, as referring to a mathematical operation related to weighing and measuring, while here Plato uses the term interchangeably with 'deliberation' (τὸ βουλεύεσθαι, 604 C), but the overlap in vocabulary suggests that deliberation is somehow similar to the kind of calculation one uses to determine the relative sizes of two objects, or the true shape of a submerged stick. The idea that the tragedian copies (and produces) evaluative images, the mention of things that 'appear fine' to the many at 602 B, and a later reference to poverty, illness, and the like as 'seeming evils' (δοκοῦντα κακά, 613 A),[39] fill in the analogy. The death of a son appears terrible, just as the stick in water appears bent. In each case, to calculate is to question and scrutinize the appearance. Grieving and lamenting, meanwhile, like believing that the stick

---

[38] μετριάσει, from μετριάζειν. The word means 'to be moderate', but the context might encourage us to note the etymological connection with μετρεῖν 'to measure'.

[39] Unlike Aristotle, Plato draws no sharp distinction between appearing and seeming.

is bent, means accepting without reflection that things are as they appear.[40]

For further evidence that the *Protagoras*'s appearance-based non-virtuous passions survive tripartition as the passions of the non-rational parts, let us return to the *Timaeus*'s description of the appetitive part of the soul (71 A ff.). Knowing that appetite would be more influenced by 'images and phantoms' than by *logoi*,

> the god conspired with this very tendency by constructing a liver, a structure which he situated in the dwelling-place of [the appetitive] part of the soul. He made it into something dense, smooth, bright, and sweet, though also having a bitter quality, so that the force of the thoughts sent down from the mind might be stamped upon it as upon a mirror that receives the stamps and returns images [εἴδωλα]. So whenever the force of the mind's thoughts could avail itself of a congenial portion of the liver's bitterness and threaten it with severe command, it could then frighten this part of the soul. And by infusing the bitterness all over the liver, it could project bilious colours onto it and shrink the whole liver . . . causing pains and bouts of nausea. And again, whenever thought's gentle inspiration should paint quite opposite pictures [φαντάσματα] . . . it would . . . make that portion of the soul that inhabits the region around the liver gracious and agreeable. (*Tim.* 71 A–D)

The passage dwells more on the physiology of appetitive passions than on their psychology, but we can extract from it the following account.[41] Sometimes the rational part of a person's soul can induce passions in the appetitive part, frightening or soothing it.[42] This happens when the rational part has certain thoughts which it wants to communicate to the appetitive part in order to ensure its co-operation in action. The content of these thoughts is prescriptive and evaluative: the *logoi*—arguments or accounts—that would naturally express them would be threats, commands, reassurances,

[40] Compare Barney, 'Appearances and Impressions', 287, and G. R. F. Ferrari, 'Plato and Poetry', in G. Kennedy (ed.), *The Cambridge History of Literary Criticism* vol. i (Cambridge, 1989), 92–148 at 133.

[41] Compare Lorenz, *The Brute Within*, 98 ff. Here as elsewhere I differ from Lorenz mainly in emphasizing that the 'perception' exercised by the non-rational soul must include awareness of appearances of a special kind, evaluative appearances.

[42] Presumably appetite often responds directly to external objects and events with feelings such as hunger, lust, pleasure, pain, and the like; this passage details a way in which the rational part can gain control over the appetitive by countering these ordinary passions with rationally induced ones. It would stand to reason for the *Timaeus* also to characterize ordinary appetitive passions as responses to images and phantoms, these ones produced not by the rational soul but by the impress of external objects, but this goes beyond what we find in the text.

and the like. More particularly, because the thoughts belong to the rational part of the soul, they are concerned with good and bad, benefit and harm:[43] 'Doing this tempting but unjust act is bad'; 'Making this painful but noble sacrifice is good'. The rational part cannot deliver its thoughts to the appetitive part directly, however; instead it reflects them off the shiny surface of the liver, yielding images.[44] It is to these images that the appetitive part responds with fright, pain, calm, and other passions.

Two points in this account are crucial for us. First, these rationally induced appetitive passions are responses to things *qua* valuable. They are responses to images of thoughts about what is good and bad, and while the images do not preserve the full content of these thoughts any more than a mirror reflection preserves the full character of its original, they clearly preserve enough of it to threaten or reassure, frighten or soothe: they do not simply present scenarios, but present them as desirable or fearful, pleasant or painful. Second, the rational part does not try to explain why the agent should pursue or refrain from some course of action, but instead simply brings it about that that course of action *looks* good or bad, the way something can look good or bad in a picture. As in the *Protagoras* and *Republic* 10, then, here too passions are responses to evaluative appearances. (Here the appearances are inner states, what we might call mental images. While there is no hint of such inner states in the *Protagoras* and *Republic* 10 discussions of evaluative appearances, we might conjecture that the *Timaeus* develops the earlier view with the thesis that for x to appear F to S is for S to have an inner appearance (image, phantasm) of x as F.[45])

Taking this *Timaeus* passage as confirmation of our reading of *Republic* 10, we can now conclude that the fundamental difference between calculated and uncalculated passions in the *Republic*— that is, between the passions of the rational part and those of the non-rational parts—precisely parallels the difference between measurement-ruled and appearance-based passions in the *Protagoras*. Finally, then, we have our explanation for *Republic* 10's equa-

---

[43] See *Tim.* 71 A; cf. *Rep.* 441 C, 442 C.

[44] Note that the constitution of the liver—smooth and dense—is just like that of the eyes, as described at 45 B–C; this encourages us to take it that what the liver reflects are literal images closely analogous to those that play a role in sight.

[45] The *Philebus*'s account of hopes and other passions as involving 'painted images' (40 A) of states of affairs that cause one pleasure (or pain) indicates a similar view of appearances, and of passions.

tion of the passionate part of the soul with the part that believes optical illusion (605 B–C). Passionate emotions such as those provoked by imitative poetry are unreflective responses to vivid appearances of things as having positive or negative value, and thus they are non-rational in precisely the same sense as is the belief that the submerged stick is bent. The non-rational part of the soul is the part that fails to question appearances, with respect to value just as with respect to shape or size.

4. Calculated and uncalculated passions

We have seen evidence that Plato construes non-rational passions as the unreflective acceptance of something broadly akin to perceptual appearances; in this section I want to say something about why that view might have attracted him.

When we look at Plato's descriptions of appetite and spirit, we see that he generally characterizes them as pursuing what simply strikes them as manifestly worth having. A full defence of this claim would require detailed case studies of his presentation of the non-rational parts of the soul and of their passions, but a few examples should suffice here.[46] First, consider what we learn about the spirited part of the soul through *Republic* 2–3's discussion of childhood 'musical' education. (Plato makes it clear that this education targets the spirited part of the soul, most explicitly at 411 E.) The goal of such education is love of the fine or beautiful (τὸ καλόν, 403 C), and hatred of its opposite:

> Anyone who has been properly educated in music and poetry . . . [will] praise τὰ καλά [what is fine, admirable or beautiful] . . . [and will] rightly object to τὰ αἰσχρά [what is shameful or ugly], hating it while he's still young and unable to grasp the reason [*logos*], but, having been educated in this way, he will welcome the reason when it comes and recognize it easily because of its kinship with himself. (401 E–402 A)[47]

Children—in whose souls reasoning is not yet present, but spirit

[46] For more evidence and discussion, see my 'Pleasure and Illusion in Plato' on appetitive desire, and my 'Shame, Pleasure, and the Divided Soul', *Oxford Studies in Ancient Philosophy*, 29 (2005), 137–70, where I argue that the *Gorgias* presents the pleasant and the fine (*kalon*)—the respective objects of the *Republic*'s appetitive and spirited parts' desires—as reason-independent, potentially conflicting apparent goods.

[47] Translation based on Grube/Reeve.

is already strong (441 A–B)—cannot yet understand what is good and bad, or why; they can, however, be trained to form judgements and passions regarding the fine and the shameful. Why are they able to do so without the aid of reasoning? Surely because such qualities seem simply manifest, as ordinary sensory qualities are. In listening to music or myths, or looking at paintings or architecture, we feel ourselves simply struck by the beauty or ugliness of the sounds and sights, and just as simply struck by the fineness or shamefulness of the acts and people represented.

As to appetitive desires, consider the *Gorgias*'s treatment of appetitive pleasure as what *seems* good to foolish people, and its corresponding implication that appetitively driven people fail to distinguish pretence from authenticity, the way things appear from the way things are. Rhetoric and pastry-baking are powerful because they provide pleasure and gratification (462 C–E), and in doing so provide the 'seeming good condition' (δοκοῦσα εὐεξία) of soul and body (464 A). That is, because pastries taste pleasant foolish people think them beneficial (and hence trust the pastry-chef more than the doctor), and because the orator's speeches are pleasing they think the orator knows what is good for them (and hence are persuaded by orators more readily than by Socrates). Like seeing something with one's own eyes, taking pleasure in a thing is a vivid experience, strong and compelling—and hence authoritative for those not inclined to question how things appear.

These passages make Plato's view look much like one that has explicit defenders today: there is a special mode of perception, evaluative perception, distinct from but in the same psychological category as seeing and smelling.[48] Consider the objects most prominently associated with the non-rational parts of soul in the *Republic*: pleasure for appetite, and honour and beauty or fineness (τὸ καλόν) for spirit.[49] It takes no abstract reasoning, no calculation to be at-

---

[48] Compare J. Prinz, *Gut Reactions* (Oxford, 2004), esp. 225–7. For a related but more doxastic view of the passions, see M. C. Nussbaum, *Upheavals of Thought: The Intelligence of Emotions* (Cambridge, 2001). There is one passage in the dialogues where Plato seems to say that passions are themselves perceptions of this sort, although the statement is too indirect, and its context too convoluted, for it to bear much weight: 'For perceptions we have such names as sight, hearing, smelling, feeling cold, and feeling hot; also what are called pleasures and pains, appetites [ἐπιθυμίαι] and fears; and there are others besides, a great number which have names, an infinite number which have not' (*Theaet*. 156 B, based on the translation by M. J. Levett).

[49] See e.g. 436 A, 439 D, and 561 A ff. for appetite as pleasure-loving, 548 C, 550 B,

tracted or repelled by such things, and their appeal or repulsion often persists in the face of reasoning that impugns it. This makes it compelling to speak of desires for pleasure and honour and aversions to pain and disgrace as based on something similar to ordinary perception.[50] Plato, if my interpretation of him is right, may have been the first philosopher to take this to be more than metaphor, but he is certainly not the last. Epicurus, according to Cicero,

denies that any reason or argument is necessary to show why pleasure is to be pursued, pain to be avoided. He holds that we perceive these things, as we perceive that fire is hot, snow white, honey sweet; it is unnecessary to prove any of these things with sophisticated reasoning; it is enough just to point them out. (*Fin.* I. 30)[51]

And contemporary philosophers who speak of passions as involving value-perception emphasize the same considerations: that in feeling a passion for a thing its value seems to us manifest and compelling—

[I]n desire, one is somehow *struck* by, affected by, the merits of the thing wanted, or the prospect of having it, in a way one needn't be if one merely

and 553 D for spirit as honour-loving. Plato also characterizes appetite as desirous of wealth, and spirit as desirous of victory, but wealth is desired as a source of pleasures (580 E–581 A), and arguably victory is desired as a source of honour. What I say should, however, be consistent with these being values in their own right.

[50] Bobonich also argues that the non-rational parts of the soul and the people ruled by them base their passions on perceptible value—and that their ethical limitations derive from this cognitive one—but he means by this that they detect or ascribe values only on the basis of sensible properties such as colour or sound: 'Non-philosophers [in the *Phaedo*] . . . think that what makes things fine or good is the possession of various sensible properties. What makes something fine is, for example, its bright colour or shape (*Phd.* 100 C–D); what makes something good, for example, is its being a bodily pleasure' (Bobonich, *Plato's Utopia Recast*, 28–9; cf. 64 on the *Republic*'s lovers of sights and sounds). This may well capture part of Plato's view, but it cannot cover all cases of non-rational passion. As Bobonich himself concedes, 'honor is not obviously a sensible property' (i.e. not perceptible by any one of the five senses) (ibid. 31). (The same can be said of many objects of appetitive and spirited desire, such as victory, or some of the pleasures the democratic soul pursues in book 8.) Why then should those who value only what they can perceive value honour? The problem disappears if we grant that the appeal of honour is manifest and vivid, and that in desiring honour one is having an unreflective, unreasoned response to that appeal.

[51] The idea that on Plato's view pleasure in particular is or involves the perception of value has gained footing in recent work on the true and false pleasures of the *Philebus*. V. Harte, 'The *Philebus* on Pleasure: The Good, the Bad and the False', *Proceedings of the Aristotelian Society*, 104 (2004), 113–30, and M. Evans, 'Plato on the Possibility of Hedonic Error', MS) both argue for an interpretation of the dialogue on which a pleasure is true if its object is genuinely valuable, and otherwise false, for pleasures in general are modes of awareness of the value of their objects.

knows it would be good . . . [I]f one wants a thing it *seems* to one as if the
thing wanted would be good. This is not necessarily the case when one
merely believes (or knows) that it would be a good thing . . . [This shows
that] to desire something is to be in a kind of perceptual state, in which
that thing seems good.[52]

[W]e desire other things and other people, we are struck by their appeal, we
are taken with them. This is part of how things are manifest to us: part of
their appearing or presenting is their presenting to us in determinate ways
and to various degrees appealing or repulsive. On the face of it, appeal is
as much a manifest quality as shape, size, color and motion.[53]

—and that we seem to detect value in a way that neither requires
nor is sensitive to rational reflection:

[Affect] can have authority in the matter of what we should desire and do
[i.e. in matters of value] . . . [It] silences any demand for justification. In
this way affect is akin to perceptual experience considered more generally.[54]

By contrast, consider the passions of the rational part: its love of
wisdom and *erōs* for the Forms; its wish to abstain from drink when
drinking is harmful, and in general to do what is best; its desire
for and pleasure in knowledge. Such passions are not unreflective
acceptances of appearances of value; instead, they arise 'out of calculation' (439 D). The *logistikon* goes for what it reasons to be good
on the basis of complicated considerations about what is best in the
long run, or overall, or given the nature of the soul, and despite
one's immediate cravings, and so on.[55] In matters ethical as in matters visual it takes into account the appearances—the fact that the
stick looks bent to one's eyes, the fact that the drink appeals to one's
thirst—but only as material for its calculations about the truth.

5. Good-dependence

Before closing, we must consider an important objection. The account of the passions for which I have argued runs counter to the

[52] D. W. Stampe, 'The Authority of Desire', *Philosophical Review*, 96 (1987),
335–81 at 356, 359.
[53] M. Johnston, 'The Authority of Affect', *Philosophy and Phenomenological Research*, 63 (2001), 181–214 at 188.
[54] Ibid. 189.
[55] This part 'calculates about the better and worse' (441 C), knows 'what is advantageous for each part and for the whole' (442 C), and exercises 'foresight on behalf
of the whole soul' (441 E).

widely held view that the passions of the non-rational parts are what Terence Irwin calls 'good-independent': they in no way involve or depend on apprehension of their objects as good.[56]

I will not pretend to settle the issue of good-dependence here, but will note that it is by no means clear that the burden of proof is on my side. Indeed, although Irwin's view remains the orthodox one, there is a growing movement against it. Many recent writings argue that the *Republic* is consistent with the 'Socratic' dialogues in holding that all desire is for things *qua* good.[57] The case for this view is straightforward. In dialogues thought to precede the *Republic* Socrates claims that everyone always desires the good.[58] In dialogues thought to post-date the *Republic* Socrates claims that everyone always desires the good.[59] And in the *Republic* itself Socrates certainly seems to claim that everyone always desires the good:

Every soul [or 'the whole soul', ἅπασα ψυχή] pursues the good and does everything [πάντα πράττει] for its sake, divining that it is something but being in confusion and unable to grasp adequately what it is. (505 D–E)

It is possible (and common) to read this passage as consistent with the view that only the rational part desires the good.[60] But surely the

---

[56] T. Irwin, *Plato's Moral Theory* (Oxford, 1977), 78, 117, 192, and *Plato's Ethics* (Oxford, 1995), 208–9. Irwin in fact allows that spirited desires are 'partly good-dependent' (*Plato's Moral Theory*, 192), but the view is often proposed in a stronger form on which only rational desire is good-dependent: see e.g. M. Woods, 'Plato's Division of the Soul', *Proceedings of the British Academy*, 73 (1987), 23–47, and C. Kahn, 'Plato's Theory of Desire', *Review of Metaphysics*, 41 (1987), 77–103.

[57] See among others G. Lesses, 'Weakness, Reason, and the Divided Soul in Plato's *Republic*', *History of Philosophy Quarterly*, 4 (1987), 147–61; G. R. Carone, 'Akrasia in the *Republic*: Does Plato Change his Mind?' *Oxford Studies in Ancient Philosophy*, 20 (2001), 107–48; Price, *Mental Conflict* (esp. 49–52); Bobonich, *Plato's Utopia Recast*; and R. Weiss, *The Socratic Paradox and its Enemies* (Chicago, 2006), ch. 6. I argue against the good-independence view in my 'Pleasure and Illusion in Plato'.

[58] See *Gorg.* 468 B–C, *Prot.* 352 C ff., *Meno* 77 C–78 B, 87 E–89 A, and *Sym.* 205 A ff.

[59] '[E]verything that recognizes the good hunts for it and longs for it, wishing to capture it and possess it for itself, and caring nothing for anything except what brings about good things' (*Phileb.* 20 D). For the related claim that no one willingly chooses things other than the good, or willingly does wrong, see *Phileb.* 22 B, *Tim.* 86 D–E, and *Laws* 731 C. Each of these passages could in principle be interpreted as consistent with the existence of good-independent desires, but in each case such a reading relies on attributing to Plato implicit psychological theses for which we have no other evidence.

[60] On one version of this reading, the rational part regards as good the objects desired by whichever part rules the soul, and no one ever acts on any desire of a

straightforward interpretation is this: each part of the soul desires
what it takes to be good, and therefore each person, no matter
which part of her soul rules her, pursues things under the guise of
the good in all her actions. Only a well-educated rational part ruling
a harmonious soul, however, can 'adequately grasp what the good
is'; souls ruled by appetite or spirit err on account of their confused
notions of the good. This reading is supported, moreover, by the
passages in the *Republic* that seem to ascribe evaluative thoughts
and concern for what is good (or for how things should be) to
appetite and spirit, and to the cities ruled by the corresponding
classes.[61] Only one passage has been taken to show that at least
some non-rational desires are not for things *qua* good: the argument
that 'thirst itself' is for 'drink itself', rather than for hot or cold or
wholesome (χρηστόν) drink (437 E–438 A). But the claim that drink
is the proper object of thirst is perfectly consistent with the view
that being thirsty involves taking drink to be good.[62]

Read in the straightforward way, 505 D–E invites the following
view. The appetitive part desires pleasures and gratification (436 A,
439 D), while spirit loves honour and victory (581 B), because in
their confusion these parts of the soul take these objects to be good.
'Good' here is relatively undemanding: it certainly need not mean
'morally good', nor 'beneficial', nor 'best all things considered', but
it does mean more than simply 'desired'. Plato presents each part
of the soul as finding its characteristic object worthy of pursuit.[63]
The spirited part does not merely want honour: it takes honour

---

lower soul-part without the mediation of reason. Irwin provides the defender of
good-independence with a more plausible alternative by pointing out that πάντα
πράττει can mean 'goes to all lengths' (Irwin, *Plato's Moral Theory*, 336 n. 45):
on this reading, the passage's claim applies only to actions motivated solely by the
rational part.

[61] See 442 C–D, 555 B, 562 B, 574 D.

[62] For much fuller defence see e.g. Carone, 'Akrasia in the *Republic*', Weiss, *The
Socratic Paradox and its Enemies*, and my 'Pleasure and Illusion in Plato'; another
good-dependent reading of 437 E–438 A is offered in Adam, *The Republic of Plato*,
commentary ad loc. It is worth noting that on a natural reading of 438 A Socrates
accepts (but declares irrelevant) the claim that all people have appetites for good
things, a point perhaps deliberately obscured by some translations.

[63] Compare Lesses, 'Weakness, Reason, and the Divided Soul in Plato's *Republic*',
151. Bobonich and Carone both explain a part of the soul's desiring things *qua* good
as that part's desiring something as an 'ultimate end' for the sake of which they
desire other things (*Plato's Utopia Recast*, 245; cf. 'Akrasia in the *Republic*', 129).
This is right as far as it goes, but we must add or make explicit the qualification
about worthiness.

to make life worth living, and sees it as 'to be gone for' above all else. Likewise, the appetitive part pursues gratification because it thinks gratification the thing most worthy of pursuit. Hence the democratic city, corresponding to the appetite-ruled soul, in 'defining licence [to pursue whatever one desires] as the good' does not merely aim at licence but holds 'that this is the *finest* [κάλλιστον] thing it has, so that this is the only city *worth* [ἄξιον] inhabiting' (562 B–C). Some will insist that it is the rational part of the corresponding soul that would make such a judgement, and not the ruling appetitive part, but, as with the parallel reading of 505 D–E, I think this interpretation needlessly indirect. Surely in the democratic city it is the masses themselves—the civic counterpart to the appetitive part—who make this judgement. And if appetite itself can judge that something 'should' be done (442 D), why should it not judge something worthy, fine, and good?

Finally, the good-independence view has been popular largely due to its explanatory power: the idea is that non-rational desires are inferior, dangerous, and prone to conflict with rational ones precisely because they have no concern for the good. In fact Irwin seems at times simply to equate rationality with good-dependence, and non-rationality with good-independence.[64] Our account, however, can explain the difference between rational and non-rational motivation, the superiority of the former, and the possibility of conflict between the two, without appeal to good-independent desires. A part of the soul limited to appearances may find good and thus desire some base pleasure or honour even when the rational part has calculated that it is bad, just as such a part may believe a submerged stick bent even when the rational part has calculated that it is straight. Furthermore, on Plato's view, in matters of value as in general, what genuinely *is* does not appear (is not manifest, obvious, accessible without abstruse calculation), while what appears to most people is not what is real and true. Apparent value is an inferior, deficient, shadowy copy of true value, just as (for example) perceptible equality is an inferior, deficient, shadowy copy of the Equal itself (*Phaedo* 74 D–E).[65] Corresponding to these ontologically

---

[64] The Socratic position allegedly rejected in the *Republic* 'requires all desires to be rational or good-dependent' (Irwin, *Plato's Moral Theory*, 78); 'The appetitive part . . . .[is] entirely good-independent and non-rational, uninfluenced by beliefs about goods' (ibid. 192).

[65] By 'true value' I do not mean only the Form of the Good. The supreme rational

inferior apparent values and ontologically superior imperceptible ones are ethically inferior appearance-based passions and ethically superior calculation-based ones. If appetitive and spirited passions are based on appearances, they can never get at the ultimate truth about value any more than sight can get at the ultimate truth about the Large or the Equal. This is not to say that the objects of appetitive or spirited desire are always bad. Just as not all sense-perception is illusory, not all appetitive and spirited passions are dangerously false in the same way as those encouraged by imitative poetry, or those that lead people astray in the *Protagoras*'s art of measurement passage. None of them, however, gets beyond appearances to the truth: this is a privilege reserved for reasoning. Thus the passions of the rational part alone are for what not merely appears good, but truly is so.[66]

6. Conclusion: what it is to be rational, what it is to be non-rational

I began with a promissory note: that once we came to understand them properly, we would see that the psychic division arguments of *Republic* 10 show us what it is for a part of the soul to be rational or non-rational, and thereby provide a unifying explanation for Plato's various characterizations of the parts of the soul throughout the dialogue, a rationale for his dividing things up the way he does. Along the way we have encountered what seem to be quite disparate characterizations of these parts of the soul. Appetite and spirit

- desire pleasures and honour, respectively (*Republic* 4, 8, 9);
- are subject to strong emotions such as grief (*Republic* 10);
- perceive the submerged stick as bent, and believe that it is (*Republic* 10);

desire is for this Form, but everyday rational desires are for everyday things in so far as they partake of it.

[66] Lesses' view sounds similar: '[E]ach part is the source of distinct types of motivations, precisely because each holds beliefs about what is good . . . [But the non-rational parts'] beliefs are false, partly because appetite and spirit are unable to calculate and to measure the way the rational part can' ('Weakness, Reason, and the Divided Soul in Plato's *Republic*', 152). His intended sense of 'calculation' is, however, much narrower than mine: on his view the crucial point is that the rational part alone 'can make all-things-considered judgments about how to act' (ibid. 154). Evaluative calculation as I define it includes but is not limited to this kind of judgement.

- are the seat of perception in general (*Tim.* 69 C–D, 77 B).

Meanwhile the rational part (when free to perform its proper function) desires what is best in contrast with pleasures and honour, resists strong emotions when it judges them inappropriate, calculates the true shape of the stick instead of accepting that it is as it appears, and concerns itself less with the perceptible realm than with the purely intelligible realm of Forms.

The account I have developed unifies these features. Appetite and spirit desire pleasures and honour, and feel grief or anger, for the same reason that they perceive the stick as bent and are responsive to perceptibles in general: because they are cognitively limited to the perception and acceptance of appearances. Pleasure and honour appear good; the death of a son appears bad; the stick appears bent; the same finger appears both big and small (*Rep.* 523 E ff.). The rational part's ability to calculate, meanwhile, allows it to criticize and transcend appearances both in the sensory realm and in the ethical. Moreover, because appearances are at worst outright false and at best adequate but at an ontological remove from being and truth, a part of the soul limited to appearances is crippled cognitively—and therefore ethically as well. At worst it desires and pursues things that are worthless or bad. At best— as with the harmonious soul described at *Republic* 586 D ff.—its passions can be trained to track the higher value it cannot perceive, so that it takes pleasure in or sees as beautiful and honourable only those things which the rational part calculates to be good.

This interpretation of the distinction between rationality and non-rationality thus accounts for Plato's central, ethical use of this distinction: it shows why the rational part of the soul should rule and the non-rational parts obey. It also, I submit, does better justice to Plato's texts than interpretations that impose foreign conceptions of rationality, for it allows us a straightforward and literal reading of the implications that appetite and spirit have beliefs about how things are, including beliefs about what is best or how things ought to be, that they can recognize means to ends, and that they are open to persuasion by the rational part.[67] An uncalculating part of the

[67] Plato evidently saw no contradiction in attributing the desire for wealth to a part he calls *alogiston* (the appetitive part), and we must therefore assume either that appetite does *not* engage in means–end thinking in desiring wealth (see Lorenz, *The Brute Within*, 47–8) or, more plausibly (in the light especially of the means–end claim at 580 E–581 A), that such thinking is not, on Plato's view, a form of *logismos*

soul can receive appearances as of something being drink or an insult, of something being good or as it ought to be, of wealth leading to pleasure, or of a recommended course of action being advantageous. What it cannot do is question or criticize such appearances.

University of Pittsburgh

BIBLIOGRAPHY

Adam, J., *The* Republic *of Plato* (2 vols.; Cambridge, 1902).

Anagnostopoulos, M., 'The Divided Soul and the Desire for Good in Plato's *Republic*', in G. Santas (ed.), *The Blackwell Guide to Plato's* Republic (Oxford, 2006), 166–88.

Annas, J., *An Introduction to Plato's* Republic (Oxford, 1981).

Barney, R., 'Appearances and Impressions', *Phronesis*, 37 (1992), 283–313.

Belfiore, E., 'Plato's Greatest Accusation against Poetry', in F. J. Pelletier and J. King-Farlow (eds.), *New Essays on Plato* (*Canadian Journal of Philosophy*, suppl. 9; Guelph, Ont., 1983), 39–62.

Bobonich, C., *Plato's Utopia Recast* (Oxford, 2002).

Burnyeat, M. F., 'Culture and Society in Plato's *Republic*', *Tanner Lectures on Human Values*, 20 (1999), 215–324.

—— 'Plato on the Grammar of Perceiving', *Classical Quarterly*, NS 26 (1976), 29–51.

Carone, G. R., 'Akrasia in the *Republic*: Does Plato Change his Mind?', *Oxford Studies in Ancient Philosophy*, 20 (2001), 107–48.

Cooper, J. M. (ed.), *Plato: Complete Works* (Indianapolis, 1997).

Cross, R. C., and Woozley, A. D., *Plato's* Republic (New York, 1964).

Evans, M., 'Plato on the Possibility of Hedonic Error' (unpublished).

Ferrari, G. R. F., 'Plato and Poetry', in G. Kennedy (ed.), *The Cambridge History of Literary Criticism*, vol. i (Cambridge, 1989), 92–148.

Frede, M., and Striker, G. (eds.), *Rationality in Greek Thought* (Oxford, 1996).

Harte, V., 'The *Philebus* on Pleasure: The Good, the Bad and the False', *Proceedings of the Aristotelian Society*, 104 (2004), 113–30.

Irwin, T., *Plato's Ethics* (Oxford, 1995).

—— *Plato's Moral Theory* (Oxford, 1977).

Janaway, C., *Images of Excellence* (Oxford, 1995).

proper. My own interpretation of *logismos* provides a non-arbitrary case for the latter. As for the implication that the appetitive part is open to persuasion through *logoi*, on the interpretation I offer this need not impugn its non-rationality: that Plato thinks those who never question appearances extremely open to persuasion through *logoi* is clear from his characterizations of rhetoric, sophistry, and poetry throughout the dialogues.

Johnston, M., 'The Authority of Affect', *Philosophy and Phenomenological Research*, 63 (2001), 181–214.

Jowett, B., and Campbell, L., *Plato's* Republic (Oxford, 1894).

Kahn, C., 'Plato's Theory of Desire', *Review of Metaphysics*, 41 (1987), 77–103.

Lesses, G., 'Weakness, Reason, and the Divided Soul in Plato's *Republic*', *History of Philosophy Quarterly*, 4 (1987), 147–61.

Lorenz, H., *The Brute Within: Appetitive Desire in Plato and Aristotle* (Oxford, 2006).

Moline, J., 'Plato on the Complexity of the Psyche', *Archiv für Geschichte der Philosophie*, 60 (1978), 1–26.

Moss, J., 'Pleasure and Illusion in Plato', *Philosophy and Phenomenological Research*, 72 (2006), 503–35.

—— 'Shame, Pleasure, and the Divided Soul', *Oxford Studies in Ancient Philosophy*, 29 (2005), 137–70.

—— 'What is Imitative Poetry and Why is it Bad?' in G. R. F. Ferrari (ed.), *The Cambridge Companion to Plato's* Republic (Cambridge, 2007), 415–44.

Murdoch, I., *The Fire and the Sun: Why Plato Banished the Artists* (Oxford, 1977).

Murphy, N. R., *The Interpretation of Plato's* Republic (Oxford, 1951).

Nehamas, A., 'Pity and Fear in the *Rhetoric* and the *Poetics*', in A. Nehamas and D. Furley (eds.), *Essays on Aristotle's* Rhetoric (Princeton, 1994), 257–82.

—— 'Plato on Imitation and Poetry', in J. M. E. Moravcsik and P. Temko (eds.), *Plato on Beauty, Wisdom and the Arts* (Totowa, NJ, 1982), 47–78.

Nussbaum, M. C., *The Fragility of Goodness: Luck and Ethics in Greek Tragedy and Philosophy* (Cambridge, 1986).

—— *Upheavals of Thought: The Intelligence of Emotions* (Cambridge, 2001).

Penner, T., 'Thought and Desire in Plato', in G. Vlastos (ed.), *Plato: A Collection of Critical Essays*, ii. *Ethics, Politics, and Philosophy of Art and Religion* (New York, 1971), 96–118.

Price, A. W., *Mental Conflict* (London, 1995).

Prinz, J., *Gut Reactions* (Oxford, 2004).

Reeve, C. D. C., *Philosopher-Kings: The Argument of Plato's* Republic (Princeton, 1988).

Sedley, D., *The Midwife of Platonism: Text and Subtext in Plato's* Theaetetus (Oxford, 2004).

Stalley, R. F., 'Persuasion and the Tripartite Soul in Plato's *Republic*', *Oxford Studies in Ancient Philosophy*, 32 (2007), 63–89.

Stampe, D. W., 'The Authority of Desire', *Philosophical Review*, 96 (1987), 335–81.

Striker, G., 'Emotions in Context: Aristotle's Treatment of the Passions in the *Rhetoric* and his Moral Psychology', in A. O. Rorty (ed.), *Essays on Aristotle's* Rhetoric (Berkeley, 1996), 286–302.

Weiss, R., *The Socratic Paradox and its Enemies* (Chicago, 2006).

Woods, M., 'Plato's Division of the Soul', *Proceedings of the British Academy*, 73 (1987), 23–47.

GLAUCON'S CHALLENGE
AND THRASYMACHEANISM

C. D. C. REEVE

PLATO's brothers, Glaucon and Adeimantus, spend roughly ten
Stephanus pages—which, even in a long dialogue like the *Republic*,
is a lot—trying to tell Socrates what they want him to do as regards
justice. It has proved extremely difficult, none the less, to say what
their message—'Glaucon's challenge' as it is often called—actually
is and to identify its provenance. In this paper I take up matters afresh, looking away from the text to the secondary literature
only very selectively. In Section 1 I go through what Glaucon and
Adeimantus say, distinguishing four different, but I think consistent and mutually illuminating, formulations of the challenge they
pose. In Section 2 I look more specifically at what they think is
wrong with common conceptions and defences of justice. In Section 3 I examine the relationship between their views and those
of Thrasymachus. In Sections 4 and 5 I consider Thrasymachus'
own account of justice and assess its coherence. In Section 6 I turn
to the larger question of the philosophical significance of Thrasymacheanism and the difficulty of responding successfully to it.

1. Formulating Glaucon's challenge

Glaucon, as is well known, divides goods into three classes:

[A-GOODS:] . . . a sort of good we would choose to have not because we desire
its consequences, but because we welcome it for its own sake—enjoying,

© C. D. C. Reeve 2008

I am grateful to David Sedley for his many helpful suggestions, to Jonathan Lear
and the members of his *Republic* seminar at the University of Chicago for their
hospitality and stimulating discussion, to Jim Lesher for his quick comments, and
to Drew Johnson, David Landy, and Anabella Zagura for inspiring the paper with
their questions.

for example, and all the harmless pleasures that have no consequences afterwards beyond enjoying having them. (357 B 4–8)[1]

[B-GOODS:] . . . a sort of good we love for its own sake, and also for the sake of its consequences—knowing, for example, and seeing and being healthy. For we welcome such things, I imagine, on both counts. (357 C 2–4)

[C-GOODS:] . . . a third kind of good, which includes physical training, medical treatment when sick, and both medicine itself and other ways of making money. We would say that these are burdensome but beneficial to us, and we would not choose to have them for their own sake, but for the sake of the wages and other things that are their consequences. (357 C 6–D 2)

A-goods include harmless pleasures that we enjoy while they last. But if these must have *no* further consequences, it is hard to think of clear cases. Even a pleasant sensation or moment of day-dreaming or bit of pointless play is likely to have *some* further desirable effects—it might make us feel more relaxed or give us energy for other projects (see Arist. *NE* 10. 6, 1176^{b}27–35). Probably what Glaucon has in mind is that A-goods have no further consequences that have any substantial impact on their desirability. A passage from the *Laws* speaks of harmless pleasure only as 'doing no particular harm or benefit *worth seriously talking about*'. Such pleasure, the Athenian Stranger says, should be called 'play' (667 E 5–8). Since play is not a sensation, Glaucon's pleasures are probably not sensations either, but activities that are worthy of choice simply as enjoyable.

If intrinsic goods are those that would, for example, pass G. E. Moore's isolation test of being good even if nothing else existed, A-goods are not intrinsic ones. Instead, they are things *we* welcome by themselves—things we love or choose not as a means to something else we desire, but in some sense as ends. The goods Glaucon is interested in, then, seem to be ones that are good because good for us, or worthy of desire, love, or choice by us. That they are good for us *because of themselves*, however, strongly suggests that their being so is the result of some features or properties that *are* intrinsic to them. Adeimantus' subsequent talk of things that are 'genuine goods by nature' (367 C 9–D 1) is of a piece with this idea.

According to Giovanni Ferrari, the class of C-goods 'comprises things that, taken in themselves, are painful or tiresome, and . . . not just neutral means to desirable consequences'. Glaucon's, he claims, is 'a cultured aristocrat's classification of goods', since 'pursuing ends by [non-neutral] means is demoted to the rank of a tiresome and laborious category of good'.[2] If he is right, the division is not exhaustive, since it omits neutral means to desirable consequences, and it is not general, since it is, so to speak, class-specific. Glaucon, however, signally presents the division not as his own view of goods, but as one *we*—including the demos—at least implicitly accept in assigning justice to the class of C-goods (358 A 4–6). This makes it difficult to see the division as in any interesting sense non-general. It is equally difficult, on philosophical grounds, to see it as non-exhaustive. Since the missing fourth class of goods must be neutral means to desirable consequences, we cannot welcome, love, or choose them for their own sake. But that very fact seems to make them (mildly) burdensome, since we clearly have to expend *some* time and energy, and incur some opportunity costs, in acquiring or doing them.

The existence of B-goods might be taken to suggest, as it has been by Bernard Williams in a characteristically probing paper, that the distinction between A- (his final) and C- (his instrumental) goods 'is not one between different classes of goods; it is a distinction between kinds of goodness or ways in which things can be found good, and not . . . a distinction between different things'.[3] The properties (or powers) that make something an A-good, however, are of a distinct sort—a sort that B-goods possess along with some others of a different sort that make them also good for their consequences. This explains—which it is otherwise hard to do—why Socrates thinks that B-goods, not A-goods, are 'the finest' (358 A 1): they have the good-making powers of A-goods and C-goods combined.[4]

Asked to which of these classes of goods justice belongs, Socrates

---

[2] G. R. F. Ferrari, *City and Soul in Plato's* Republic [*City*] (Sankt Augustin, 2003), 17–18.

[3] B. A. O. Williams, 'Plato's Construction of Intrinsic Goodness' ['Construction'], in M. Burnyeat (ed.), *The Sense of the Past: Essays in the History of Philosophy* (Princeton, 2006), 118–37 at 123.

[4] Neither Glaucon nor Socrates seems to be thinking of happiness as included in the classification. For if it were included, *it* would clearly be the finest good. Moreover, it would also have to be an A-good, choiceworthy solely for itself. As Diotima insists in the *Symposium*, we can explain why human beings desire good things, by pointing out that they want happiness. But there explanation stops: 'There is no need to ask further, "What is the point of wanting happiness?"' (204 E 1–8). Aristotle, who initially includes happiness among choiceworthy goods, also makes it the best one (*NE* 1. 7, 1097^{a}25–^{b}21). He also flirts with the idea, however, that it is not really something we choose. Rather we wish for it, and choose the things that promote it (3. 2, 1111^{b}28–9). This is probably how Glaucon is also thinking.

responds that it is a B-good, the sort that 'anyone who is going to be blessed with happiness must love both because of itself and because of its consequences' (358 A 1–3). The various formulations Glaucon and Adeimantus subsequently give of their challenge are their attempts to specify what they think would constitute success in justifying the 'because of itself' component of this response. The first is Glaucon's:

[FORMULATION 1:] I want to hear what justice and injustice are, and what power [δύναμιν] each has when it is simply by itself in the soul. I want to leave out of account the wages and the consequences of each of them. (358 B 4–7)

By focusing on justice as a power in the soul, Glaucon strongly suggests—if he does not simply say—that his interest is not primarily in just actions, but in justice as a psychological state, or state of character. More precisely, as Ferrari notes, his interest is in this state, considered not as a dormant capacity, but as an active or activated one: it is not health (ὑγίεια), he mentions, but being healthy (τὸ ὑγιαίνειν).[5] A state—activated or otherwise—might well be a B-good, however, even though not all the actions it causes or motivates its possessor to do are themselves B-goods. In *Politics* 7. 13 Aristotle shows himself clearly aware of this:

Happiness is a complete activation or use of virtue, and not a qualified use but an unqualified one. By 'qualified uses' I mean those that are necessary; by 'unqualified' I mean those that are noble [καλῶς]. For example, in the case of just actions, just retributions and punishments spring from virtue, but are necessary uses of it, and are noble only in a necessary way, since it would be more choiceworthy if no individual or city-state needed such things. On the other hand, just actions that aim at honours and prosperity are unqualifiedly noblest. The former involve choosing[6] something that is somehow bad, whereas the latter are the opposite: they construct and generate goods. To be sure, an excellent man will deal with poverty, disease, and other sorts of bad luck in a noble way. But blessed happiness requires their opposites. (1332ᵃ9–21)

Socrates, too, seems committed to making the same distinction:

If we had to come to an agreement about whether a man similar in nature and training to this city of ours [i.e. courageous, temperate, just, and wise]

---

[5] Ferrari, *City*, 18. Cf. Arist. *NE* 1. 8, 1098ᵇ30–1099ᵃ7.
[6] Reading αἵρεσις with the manuscripts.

would embezzle gold or silver he had accepted for deposit, who do you think would consider him *more likely to do so* than men of a different sort? (442 E 4–443 A 1)

The implication, apparently, is that being just and passing 'the everyday tests [τὰ φορτικά]' for being so (442 E 1) may be compatible with not always doing (conventionally) just actions.[7] We must be careful, in any case, as critics often are not, not to slip unwittingly into considering actions when traits of character are alone relevant.

Glaucon's next formulation is his most complex and detailed:

[FORMULATION 2:] I want to hear it [justice] praised simply by itself, and I think that I am most likely to learn this from you. That is why I am going to speak at length in praise of the unjust life: by doing so, I will be showing you the way I want to hear you denouncing injustice and praising justice. (358 D 2–7)

Putting this together with formulation 1, we have the idea of justice as having a power and of the just life as so related to it (or to that power) that praise of the one counts as the desired sort of praise of the other. It is an idea whose foundations lie in the immediately preceding pages of *Republic* 1. The definitional power of justice, Socrates and Thrasymachus finally agree there, is to enable a soul to live well or be happy (351 D 7–352 A 10). For the soul's function is to live and virtues are defined by relation to the functions they perfect (353 D 3–354 A 5). Praise of the just life counts as praise of justice itself, we may infer, because the power of justice in which Glaucon is specifically interested is this definitional power.

The remainder of formulation 2 is an attempt so to isolate justice that this power comes into clear focus:

[FORMULATION 2 (*cont.*):] As for the decision itself about the life of the two we are discussing, if we contrast the extremes of justice and injustice, we shall be able to make the decision correctly, but if we don't, we won't. What, then, is the contrast I have in mind? It is this. We will subtract nothing from the injustice of the unjust person, and nothing from the justice of the just one. On the contrary, we will take each to be perfect in his own pursuit. First, then, let the unjust person act like a clever craftsman. An eminent ship's captain or doctor, for example, knows the difference between what his craft can and cannot do. He attempts the first but lets the second go by.

---

[7] D. Sedley, 'Philosophy, the Forms and the Art of Ruling', in G. R. F. Ferrari (ed.), *The Cambridge Companion to Plato's* Republic (Cambridge, 2007), 256–83 at 279, alerted me to the significance of this important passage.

And if he happens to slip, he can put things right. In the same way, if he is to be perfectly unjust, let the unjust person correctly attempt unjust acts and remain undetected. The one who is caught should be thought inept. For the extreme of injustice is to be reputed just without actually being so. And our perfectly unjust person must be given perfect injustice—nothing must be subtracted from it. We must allow that, while doing the greatest injustice, he has none the less provided himself with the greatest reputation for justice . . . Having hypothesized such a person, let's now put the just man next to him in our argument—someone who is simple and noble and who, as Aeschylus says, does not want to be reputed good, but to be so. We must take away his reputation. For a reputation for justice would bring him honour and rewards, so that it would not be clear whether he is being just for the sake of justice, or for the sake of those honours and rewards. We must strip him of everything except justice, and make his situation the opposite of the unjust person's. Though he does no injustice, he must have the greatest reputation for it, so that he may be tested with regard to justice by seeing whether or not he can withstand a bad reputation and its consequences. Let him stay like that unchanged until he is dead—just, but all his life believed to be unjust. In this way, both will reach the extremes, the one of justice and the other of injustice, and we will be able to judge which of them is happier [εὐδαιμονέστερος]. (360 D 8–361 D 3)

The idea of stripping away from justice whatever is not part of its definitional power is explicated by reference to that of stripping away a reputation for justice and the consequences that flow from it. The motivation is plain enough: it is *justice* that is to be defended, not reputed justice. The addition to justice of a reputation for positive *in*justice is more difficult. 'It is not clear, in particular,' as Williams writes, 'whether the genuinely just man "appears" unjust because he has an unconventional notion of justice, so that the world judges unfavourably the character he really has; or because the world factually misunderstands what his character is.'[8] What is clear, though, is that when we turn to the perfectly *un*just person it is no accident that he has a reputation for justice, since it is part of his supposedly craft-like injustice to ensure that he has it. In other words, the power to provide such a reputation for himself is one of the powers injustice by itself is taken to have more or less by definition. It seems safe to suppose, then, that the reason the just person's reputation *can* be stripped away is that justice's definitional power—as what enables a soul to live well—does not

---

[8] Williams, 'Construction', 120 n. 5.

include the power to control the sort of reputation its possessor will have with other people.

A perfectly just person can enjoy a reputation for injustice his entire life, then, either because his justice is hard for people to understand, because he has been the subject of a successful smear campaign, or for some other reason altogether. If he will be happier than the unjust person even in such circumstances, justice will not merely be a B-good, it will be one much more desirable for its own sake than for its good consequences. Adeimantus supposes, indeed, that this is actually a part of what Socrates is being challenged to prove (formulation 4 below). Since neither Socrates nor Glaucon objects, he is surely right.

What Glaucon says he wants to be shown is that the just person, simply because he is just, is happi*er* than the unjust one. The comparative formulation is important, since one person can be happi*er* than another even if neither is very happy in absolute terms. A just person who is suffering all the terrible things that follow from a bad reputation, including the rack, therefore, does not have to be all that happy. It is enough that he be happi*er* than the unjust one who enjoys a good reputation. That, too, might seem an implausibly high standard for a defence of justice to be required to meet, of course.[9] But is it? We might think here of the somewhat analogous example of health. Someone with bad flu may look and feel much sicker than someone with asymptomatic heart disease, but he is healthier all the same. It is easy to be distracted by the rack, as by appearances and feelings, in other words, into giving too much weight to symptoms and not enough to underlying conditions. Socrates makes this very point himself in discussing tyrants:

> The only fit judge of them is someone who can in thought go down into a man's character and discern it—not someone who sees it from the outside, the way a child does, and is dazzled by the façade that tyrants adopt for the outside world, but someone who discerns it adequately . . . who has lived in the same house as a tyrant and witnessed his behaviour at home; who has seen how he deals with each member of his household, when he can best be observed stripped of his tragic costume; and who has also seen how

---

[9] D. Wiggins, *Ethics: Twelve Lectures on the Philosophy of Morality* (Cambridge, Mass., 2006), 18, speaks of 'the utterly peculiar and special terms under which the Platonically just man is doomed to live' and concludes that 'a sane philosophy of morality' will set Glaucon's 'thought experiment' aside on the grounds that in it 'the health of the soul itself, along with all happiness and sanity, will long since have flown out the window'.

he deals with public dangers. Isn't it the one who has seen all this that we should ask to tell us how the tyrant compares to the others with respect to happiness and wretchedness? (577 A 1–B 4)

The tragic costume, the façade, is the 'illusionist painting of virtue' (365 C 4) in which Adeimantus thinks the unjust person wraps himself in order to win himself a good reputation by hiding the pathology within. The good judge is someone who can see through it—as the doctor can through apparent health—to the true condition of the soul it cloaks. The good judge of how happy justice makes us, we might reasonably think, had better proceed in the same way—looking to our true state and not simply to how happy we look or feel.

In his next attempt to say what he wants, Adeimantus seems at first to be speaking of the belief-mediated consequences of justice itself:

[FORMULATION 3:] 'Amazing Socrates,' we said, 'of all of you who claim to praise justice, beginning from the earliest heroes of old whose accounts survive up to the men of the present day, not one has ever blamed injustice or praised justice except by mentioning the reputations, honours, and rewards that are their consequences. No one has ever adequately described what each does itself, through its own power, by its presence in the soul of the person who possesses it, even if it remains hidden from gods and humans. No one, whether in poetry or in private discussions, has adequately argued that injustice is the greatest evil a soul can have in it, and justice the greatest good.' (366 D 7–367 A 1)

In an earlier passage, however, he moves seamlessly from consequences of that sort to others that are quite different, namely, the consequences of reputed justice or of a just reputation:

When fathers speak to their sons to give them advice, they say that one must be just, as do all those who have others in their charge. But they do not praise justice itself, only the good reputation it brings: the inducement they offer is that if we are reputed to be just, then, as a result of our reputation, we will get political offices, good marriages, and all the things that Glaucon recently said that the just man would get as a result of having a good reputation. (362 E 6–363 A 5)

A person's reputation, the thought seems to be, is a consequence of what people believe about him, not of the truth, so that a good manipulator of belief—a good simulator or mimic of justice—can acquire the good reputation without being just.

Adeimantus' final formulation adds an important negative qualification.

[FORMULATION 4:] Do not merely demonstrate to us by argument that
justice is superior to injustice, but tell us what each one itself does, because
of itself, to someone who possesses it that makes the one bad and the other
good. Follow Glaucon's advice and do not take reputations into account.
For if you do not deprive justice and injustice of their true reputations and
attach false ones to them, we will say that it is not justice you are praising,
but its reputation, or injustice you are condemning, but its reputation, and
that you are encouraging us to be unjust but keep it secret . . . You agree
that justice is one of the greatest goods, the ones that are worth having for
the sake of their consequences, but much more so for their own sake—such
as seeing, hearing, knowing, being healthy, of course, and all the others
that are genuine goods by nature and not simply by repute. This is what I
want you to praise about justice. How does it—simply because of itself—
benefit its possessor, and how does injustice harm him? Leave wages and
reputations for others to praise. (367 B 3–D 3)

What Adeimantus does not want is a proof that justice is superior.
He and his brother already believe that it is (358 C 6; 368 A 5–B
3). What he wants, it seems, is something more like an *explanation*
of how justice can be superior, given Thrasymachus' argument. If
reputations are included in that explanation, he claims, 'it is not
justice you are praising but its reputation'. So he follows Glaucon
(formulation 2) in thinking that reputations must be reversed: focus
on justice in a man who is reputed unjust and you are guaranteed
to be focused on the right target for defence, something which, if
good at all, must be good 'by nature and not simply by repute'.
Though Adeimantus does not make the attachment of false reputations depend on what powers are definitional of perfect justice and
injustice, as Glaucon does, he probably has much the same point
in view. If Socrates is to succeed in defending or praising a justice
that does not include being able to ensure a good reputation for
its possessor among its definitional powers, his defence had better
succeed when its possessor in fact has a bad one. Otherwise, it may
still be only reputed justice that is being defended.

When *we* think about justice, we tend to think either conse-
quentially or deontologically. Talk about leaving wages and consequences out of the defence of justice, as a result, tends to raise
deontological thoughts in our minds. Justice must be shown to be
choiceworthy *for its own sake*. The eudaimonistic, and so appar-

ently consequentialist, nature of Glaucon's challenge is therefore puzzling to us—as, of course, is Socrates' own apparent readiness to speak of 'the good things that come from being just [τὰ ἀπὸ τοῦ εἶναι ἀγαθά]' as what are crucial to a defence of justice as choiceworthy in the requisite way (612 D 3–10). The puzzle largely disappears, however, if what Glaucon and Adeimantus mean by consequences is only such consequences as could equally well be consequences of reputed justice—*simulator-accessible* consequences as we may call them. Since the class of simulator-accessible consequences is much narrower than the class a consequentialist appeals to, excluding them from the defence of justice is compatible with wanting that defence to be a consequentialist one. And that is precisely the sort, as we have seen, Glaucon and Adeimantus do seem to want.

If defending justice as desirable for its own sake consists in showing it desirable for the sake of those of its consequences that are not simulator-accessible, however, the desirability of other B-goods—knowing, seeing, and being healthy—*for their consequences* should reside in consequences that are simulator-accessible. That they have such consequences is perhaps obvious enough: someone can fake knowledge (think of sophists, as Plato and Aristotle conceive of them), sight, or health and reap the benefits of doing so. It is very hard to believe, none the less, that this is how the masses, who are supposed to employ the division of goods in categorizing justice as a C-good, are likely to understand the matter. It is not, in fact, how we are likely to understand it ourselves.[10] The solution to this problem lies in the distinction Glaucon draws between the powers that define justice as a virtue and the other powers or effects it may have. Though his B-goods are not all virtues, they do seem to be either virtues broadly speaking or the desirable functions they perfect. The consequences for which they are desirable, therefore, are presumably effects they have other than those definitional of them as the virtues or functions they are. What gives the simulator-accessible ones among them their special pertinence in the case of justice is not that they are its only consequences, but simply that they are the only ones appealed to in the conventional defences of it. Since the broader class is still narrower than the one to which a consequentialist appeals, it remains true that excluding even it

[10] As J. Annas, *An Introduction to Plato's* Republic (Oxford, 1981), 65–70, perceptively points out.

from the defence of justice would not preclude that defence from being of his favoured sort.

2. Justice inadequately defended

While Glaucon looks at popular views about the origins and nature of justice and injustice that have the effect of praising injustice as 'naturally good' (358 E 4), Adeimantus looks at 'the arguments that . . . praise justice and disparage injustice' (362 E 3–5). His point is that what people praise is actually reputed justice, what they blame, reputed injustice. His argument thus takes the form of a survey of received opinion, especially as expressed in the works of Homer and Hesiod (the so-called Bible of the Greeks), whereas Glaucon's is more focused on opinion's—to us somewhat more pertinent—theoretical underpinnings.[11]

According to Glaucon, the story people accept about the origins and nature of justice is something like this:

People say, you see, that to do injustice is naturally good, and to suffer injustice bad. But the badness of suffering it far exceeds the goodness of doing it. Hence, those who have done and suffered injustice and who have tasted both—the ones who lack the power to do it and avoid suffering it— decide that it is profitable to come to an agreement with each other neither to do injustice nor to suffer it. As a result, they begin to make laws and covenants, and what the law commands they call lawful and just. That, they say, is the origin and very being of justice. It is in between the best and the worst. The best is to do injustice without paying the penalty; the worst is to suffer it without being able to take revenge. Justice is in the middle between these two extremes. People love it not because it is a good thing, but because they are too weak to do injustice with impunity. (358 E 4–359 B 5)

Were this a story about the absolute origins of justice, it would be plainly incoherent: if there could be no injustice prior to the making of laws and covenants, no one could possibly be led to

---

[11] It is noteworthy that the basis cited *in the text* for the 'ancient quarrel between poetry and philosophy' mentioned in *Republic* 10 (607 B 6–7) is precisely their different attitudes to justice: 'In the course of our discussion, then, did we respond to the other points, without having to invoke the rewards and reputations of justice, as you all said Homer and Hesiod did? Instead, haven't we found that justice itself is the best thing for the soul itself, and that the soul should do what is just, whether it has the ring of Gyges, or not, or even the cap of Hades as well' (612 A 8–B 4).

make them by doing or suffering it. If we read carefully, however, we see that the story's aim, though no doubt also more generally illustrative, is the circumscribed one of explaining how *democratic* justice—the sort relevant in Athens and in Piraeus, where the conversation is taking place—arose. Glaucon refers specifically to 'what the masses think' about justice (358 A 4). He explains what its origins are in a situation in which it is those who are 'too weak to do injustice with impunity' (359 B 2)—presumably the majority of ordinary people, not the privileged and powerful few—who make the laws and covenants. Finally, he refers to the effect of the laws as forcing people to 'honour equality [τοῦ ἴσου]' (359 C 5–6), which is a distinctively democratic goal: 'Democracy comes about, I suppose, when the poor are victorious, kill or expel the others, and give the rest an equal share [ἐξ ἴσου] in the constitution and ruling offices' (557 A 3–4).

What we are to imagine, then, is a group of such people, already in a non-democratic political community, who have committed injustice (broken its laws), got away with it (perhaps simply by chance or police ineptitude), and seen how naturally good that is. At the same time, they have also suffered injustice without being able to take revenge, and have seen how much worse that is. Since the only explanation on offer for their inability to take revenge is lack of power relative to the perpetrator, it follows that within this community there must have been perpetrators sufficiently powerful to inflict injustice with impunity. In order to offer protection against such perpetrators, therefore, the agreement that members of the demos subsequently make with each other must constitute *the demos itself* as a new, yet more powerful (collective) agent that is able to 'kill or expel the others'. This is what makes their subsequent legislation an effective replacement for the laws of their previous community.

It is sometimes said that this account of the origins of justice is 'the ancestor of honourable contractualist accounts'.[12] But once we see that it is not an account of radical origins, such ancestry seems more problematic. Glaucon is not explaining how we got out of a state of nature. Nor is he explaining the legitimacy of laws by appeal to anything like the general will, or what rational agents would all agree to. This is clear from what he immediately goes on to say about someone who is 'truly a man'. As someone with enough power to be unjust (to break the laws) with impunity, *he*

---

[12] Williams, 'Construction', 119.

would not make an agreement not to do injustice on the condition of
not having to suffer it—'for him that would be insanity' (359 B 4–5).
Power, then, is the only source of legitimacy countenanced. That
is why Glaucon ends the story by saying that 'this is the *nature*
[φύσις] of justice, according to the argument . . . and those are
its *natural* [πέφυκε] origins' (359 B 6–7). The origins are natural—
not conventional—because they have to do entirely with natural
differences in power. The justice is natural, not conventional, for
parallel reasons: it gains its authority, not from the fact that it is
embodied in conventions, but from the fact that those conventions
are an expression of effective natural power.

There is an element, none the less, not of ethical, but of (benign)
semantic conventionalism in what Glaucon describes. Imagine that
there are as yet no laws. Still there are lots of natural harms being
inflicted on people, sometimes with impunity. Getting killed, sexu-
ally assaulted, deprived of shelter or food—all these are among
the thousand natural shocks to which flesh is heir. When someone
or some group emerges that is strong enough to make laws, it is
these harms they will want to protect themselves against through
legislation and designate as 'unjust'. Natural harms before, they
thereby become injustices.

That a sufficiently powerful agent would not choose justice is presented as evidence that it is not an A- or B-good, but a second best,
lying between the natural good of doing injustice with impunity,
and the much worse natural evil of suffering it without recourse.
The story of the ring of Gyges is intended to reinforce this point, by
showing that all who practise justice 'do so unwillingly, as something compulsory, not as something good' (358 C 3–4; also 359 B
7–9, 359 C 4–6, 360 C 6–7). What the ring does, as we know, is enable its wearer to practise injustice—break the law—with impunity,
by making him invisible. What it is based on, however, is a view of
human nature and the human good.

A just person—someone who obeys the laws of his community—
seems quite different from an unjust one. Give him Gyges' ring,
so the story goes, and you will soon see that deep down the two
are the same:

Suppose we grant to the just and the unjust person the freedom to do
whatever he likes. We can then follow both of them and see where their
appetite would lead. And we will catch the just person red-handed travelling the same road as the unjust one. The reason for this is the desire to

do better [πλεονεξίαν]. This is what every nature naturally pursues as good [πᾶσα φύσις διώκειν πέφυκεν ὡς ἀγαθόν]. But by law and force it is made to deviate from this path and honour equality. (359 C 1–6)

What lies on that road for the just person, according to popular opinion, is stealing what he wants from the marketplace, having sex with anyone he wants, having the power of life and death over people, and doing 'all the other things that would make him the equal of a god among humans' (360 B 4–C 3). And why would he do all that? Because on his view, as allegedly on everyone's, the natural good for anything with a nature (whether god or man) consists in letting its appetites 'grow as large as possible, without restraint'—this is what *pleonexia* consists in—and, 'when these are as large as possible, having the power to serve them' (*Gorg.* 491 E 8–492 A 1). Hence if someone did not want to do injustice, given the opportunity Gyges' ring affords, he would be thought 'most wretched and most foolish by those aware of the situation. Though, of course, they would praise him in public, deceiving each other, for fear of suffering injustice' (*Rep.* 360 D 5–7).

Going back for a moment to the account of the origins and nature of justice, let us consider what it implies, in particular, about moral motivation—about where in our motivational set justice gets a grip. The person who is 'truly a man', who is strong enough so that his opportunism faces nothing but opportunity, simply does what nature, unrestrained by law, urges, and so pursues pleonectic satisfaction without let or hindrance. The perfectly unjust man, who lives under law, has the same motivational set as the one who is truly a man, but fewer opportunities to act on it without getting caught. Members of the demos, who also live under law, are opportunists too. But since they lack both power and craft, they have little or no opportunity to act as nature urges. What is constant as we move down this list is the natural desire for the natural good of pleonectic satisfaction. All that changes is the degree of constraint that law and convention impose on it. People are just, to the extent that they are, because they are compelled to be.

We have already taken an advance draft on Glaucon's argument that the life of the perfectly unjust person, who *ipso facto* enjoys a reputation for justice, is happier than that of a perfectly just person with an unjust reputation. If the human good really is Calliclean, his argument will be very hard to resist, since the perfectly unjust man does seem to do a much better job of satisfying his enlarged appetites than does the perfectly just one—especially, when the bad consequences of his reputed injustice are factored into the equation. We would expect, therefore, that Socrates' response will need to persuade us that our (and the gods') nature has been misrepresented, and with it our (and their) natural good.

From Adeimantus' archive of the sorts of conventional defences of justice to which he does not want Socrates to add, we may select just one:

As for what people say, they say that there is no advantage in my being just if I am not also reputed just; whereas the troubles and penalties of being just are apparent. On the other hand, they tell me that the unjust person, who has secured for himself a reputation for justice, lives the life of a god. Since, then, 'opinion forcibly overcomes truth', and 'controls happiness', as the wise men say, I must surely turn entirely to it. I should create an illusionist painting of virtue around me to deceive those who come near, but keep behind it the wise Archilochus' greedy and cunning fox. (365 B 4–C 6)

Here the idea of simulation and control of belief or public opinion is explicit. Being just involves troubles and penalties, but no advantages unless one is also reputed just. Simulation of justice thus becomes the wise course, since it combines the advantages of a just reputation with the absence of the troubles and penalties of being just. But that means that it is not justice, but reputed justice, that is being defended. The defences are unsatisfactory, then, because they are all couched exclusively in terms of simulator-accessible consequences.

3. The Thrasymachean provenance of the challenge

When Glaucon says that in the view of the masses justice is a C-good (358 A 4–6), Socrates responds: 'I know that is the general view. Thrasymachus has been faulting justice and praising injustice on these grounds for some time. But it seems that I am a slow learner' (358 A 7–9). Glaucon replies that he will help Socrates to understand by developing Thrasymachus' account: 'I think Thrasymachus gave up before he had to, as if he were a snake you had charmed . . . So, if you agree, I will renew the argument of Thrasymachus' (358 B 2–C 1). A few lines later, he explains that while he himself is not persuaded by that argument, his

ears are 'deafened listening to Thrasymachus and countless others'
propound it (358 c 7–D 1). Later still, as part of formulation 4,
Adeimantus says that if Socrates fails to leave reputations out of
the defence, 'we will say that you agree with Thrasymachus that
justice is the good of another, the advantage of the stronger, while
injustice is one's own advantage and profit, though not the advantage of the weaker' (367 c 2–5). In *Republic* 8 Socrates reminds us
that it is Thrasymachus' argument to which his own is opposed:
'either [we must] be persuaded by Thrasymachus to practise injustice, or, by the argument that is now coming to light, to practise
justice' (545 B 1–2). Finally, at the end of his defence of justice, it
is again Thrasymachus' position that he presents as having been
turned upside down: 'It is not to harm the slave that we say he
should be ruled, as Thrasymachus supposed was true of all subjects, but because it is better for everyone to be ruled by a divine
and wise ruler' (590 D 1–4). From early to late, then, the position
presented as in need of critical discussion is that of Thrasymachus.
Moreover, he too seems to agree that the position in question really
is his, since to these characterizations—in contrast to his reaction
to Socrates' initial ones (338 D 2–3, 340 D 2)—he offers no objection
or emendation.[13] It is possible, of course, that everyone (including
Thraymachus himself) is getting him wrong anyway. But, given
this evidence, it is surely very unlikely. Even when very perceptive
critics tell us that 'Thrasymachus' and Glaucon's accounts seem to
be opposed to one another . . .', therefore, or that the only Thrasymachean view the brothers really share is 'that the life of justice is
in some sense a *second best*',[14] we should resist.

Thrasymachus' initial account of justice, which he subsequently
emends and fills out in various ways, is this:

Each type of rule makes laws that are advantageous for itself: democracy
makes democratic ones, tyranny tyrannical ones, and so on with the others.
And by so legislating, each declares that what is just for its subjects is
what is advantageous for itself—the ruler—and it punishes anyone who
deviates from this as lawless and unjust. That, Socrates, is what I say
justice is, the same in all cities, what is advantageous for the established rule.
Since the established rule is surely stronger, anyone who does the rational
calculation correctly will conclude that the just is the same everywhere—
what is advantageous for the stronger. (338 E 1–339 A 4)

---

[13] A point made to me in conversation by Kathryn Lofton.
[14] Williams, 'Construction', 119.

In operation in the account, apparently, are the ideas: first, of power in the service of what is advantageous to its possessors; second, of that power finding expression in political rule of different constitutional sorts, depending on who or what possesses it; third, of a *nominal* definition of justice—an explanation of the meaning of the word 'justice' in a particular city—as consisting in obedience to its laws (339 C 10–11); and, fourth, of a real definition of justice as what is advantageous to the stronger, which is invariant across constitutions ('the same in all cities'). Though, as we shall see in Section 4, the nominal and real definitions are related, it is important not to confuse them, since it muddies the crucial issue of whether Thrasymachus is a conventionalist about justice or some sort of realist.

The third idea in Thrasymachus' account is a political one. It offers an explanation in terms of power of the variety of constitutional types. It is taken up by Glaucon, as we saw in Section 2, with particular reference to democratic constitutions, understood as those in which members of the demos make the laws, and 'call lawful and just . . . what the law commands' (359 A 3–4). Thus he accepts Thrasymachus' nominal definition of justice as obedience to the law.

Thrasymachus' second idea is a broadly psychological one to the effect that people pursue their advantage to the extent that their power allows. If they have the power to make laws, therefore, they will make ones advantageous to themselves. Members of the demos are no different. So, when by banding together, they constitute themselves as a new stronger Thrasymachean ruler, the laws they make will reveal as much. Thus Glaucon also accepts Thrasymachus' real definition of justice as what is advantageous to the stronger.

Thrasymachus' prize example of the truth of his views is the perfectly unjust tyrant, whom he describes as a man of 'great power [τὸν μεγάλα δυνάμενον] who does better [πλεονεκτεῖν]'. As the phraseology indicates, he is clearly the prototype for Glaucon's 'man who has the power [τὸν δυνάμενον]' to do injustice with impunity, the one who is 'truly a man' (359 B 2–4), able to 'to do better [πλεονεξίαν]' (359 C 4). But as an expert at the craft of ruling (340 D 2–341 A 4), he is also the prototype for Glaucon's perfectly unjust person, who, because he is like doctors, ship captains, or other 'clever craftsmen' (360 E 6), ensures that he has a reputation for justice.

Glaucon's Thrasymachus is not simply a realist about justice, to
be sure, but a realist of a particular sort, namely, a *naturalist*. Yet
Thrasymachus does not mention nature or natures in laying out his
views. It is only when he is being cross-examined by Socrates that
we see how much a part of his way of thinking they actually are.
He readily accepts, for example, that injustice produces in every
one of its possessors 'the very same effects which it is in its nature
[πέφυκεν] to produce' (352 A 6–7) and shows no discomfort at all
in talking about the 'natural [πέφυκεν] aim' of a craft (341 D 8–9)
or what a ruler does or does not 'naturally [πέφυκε] seek' (347 D 5)
in practising one.

The Thrasymachean provenance of the views of Glaucon and
Adeimantus seems to be assured. But if their views are Thrasymachean, Plato must think Thrasymachus a worthy opponent. Why
have Glaucon and Adeimantus claim to be his heirs otherwise? Why
have Socrates identify his opponent as Thrasymachus? Why de-
vote so long a dialogue to his views? None of this means, of course,
that Thrasymachus *is* a worthy opponent, or that the views Plato
ascribes to Glaucon and Adeimantus coincide with—or are even
consistent with—those he ascribes to Thrasymachus. Plato could
have nodded on both counts. But that he *intended* a coincidence of
views is scarcely to be doubted given what he writes. That he did
nod is, I agree, unlikely. But that is just to say that we should favour
interpretations that make him consistent.

4. Thrasymachus' definition of justice

Socrates' conversation with Cephalus and Polemarchus is explicitly
advertised as a search for a definition of what justice is: 'speaking of
that thing itself, justice [τοῦτο δ' αὐτό, τὴν δικαιοσύνην], [what] are
we to say it is . . .?' (331 C 1–2); 'the following is not the definition
[ὅρος] of justice' (331 D 2). At the end of the conversation with
Polemarchus, this point is emphasized again: 'Since it has become
apparent, then, that neither justice nor the just consists in benefiting
friends and harming enemies, what else should one say it is [τί ἂν
ἄλλο τις αὐτὸ φαίη εἶναι]?' (336 A 9–10). Thrasymachus, moreover,
is presented as understanding all this perfectly well: 'If you really
want to know what justice is [τὸ δίκαιον ὅτι ἐστί]', he says to Socrates,
'give us an answer yourself and tell us what *you* say the just is [τί

φῆς εἶναι τὸ δίκαιον]' (336 c 2–6). When Socrates proclaims himself unable to comply (336 E 9–337 A 1; cf. 354 c 1) and Thrasymachus is persuaded to answer in his place, what he says is: 'justice is no other thing than what is advantageous for the stronger [εἶναι τὸ δίκαιον οὐκ ἄλλο τι ἢ τὸ τοῦ κρείττονος συμφέρον]' (338 c 2–3). Plato seems to be doing everything, therefore, to represent this statement—JAS for short—as being Thrasymachus' definition of justice. Even if, to repeat, we had some reason to think it was an inconsistent definition, or one inconsistent with other things Thrasymachus says, or one that failed to meet our standards for definition at all, our confidence that JAS is what the text presents as his definition should not be shaken.

When Socrates responds by asking for a clarification of how, in particular, the notion of the stronger is to be understood (338 c 5–D 1), Thrasymachus tells the story we looked at in Section 3. What is stronger in each city is the ruling element—for example, the demos in a democracy. This element makes laws advantageous to itself, applying the term 'just' to those subjects who are obedient to them and 'unjust' to those who violate them, rewarding the one and punishing the other. When a subject does what justice (law) requires of him, therefore, he does what is advantageous for 'the established rule', that is, for the stronger. This claim is E (since it is often taken by taken to be *e*mpirical rather than theoretical or conceptual in nature); the rulers involved are E-rulers; they are E-stronger and make E-laws.

Justice is the advantage of the stronger. It is also what the rulers legislate, so that 'whatever laws the rulers make must be obeyed, and that is what is just' (339 c 10–11). Rulers, however, are liable to error, so that they make some laws incorrectly—that is to say, not for their own advantage. Hence it is apparently just to do the opposite of what Thrasymachus claimed, 'since the weaker are then ordered to do what is disadvantageous for the stronger' (339 B 9–E 8). When Polemarchus enthusiastically seconds this criticism (340 A 10–B 5), Cleitophon, previously silent, steps in on Thrasymachus' behalf. What Thrasymachus meant by JAS, he claims, is 'what the stronger *believes* to be advantageous for him. That is what he maintained the weaker must do, and that is what he maintained is what is just' (340 B 6–8). But Thrasymachus implicitly rejects this interpretation of his views, opting instead for an entirely different line of defence. Pointedly ignoring Cleitophon and Polemarchus altogether, he addresses himself directly to Socrates: 'Do you think', he asks, 'that I would call someone who is in error stronger at the very moment he errs?' (340 C 6–7). Socrates replies, 'I did think you meant that, when you agreed that the rulers are not infallible, but sometimes make errors' (340 C 8–D 1). But Thrasymachus angrily denies that this is what he had in mind:

> I think we express ourselves in words that, taken literally, do say that a doctor is in error, or an accountant, or a grammarian. But each of these, to the extent that he is what we call him, never makes errors, so that, according to the precise account (and you are a stickler for precise accounts), no craftsman ever makes errors. It is when his knowledge fails him that he makes an error, and in virtue of the fact that he made that error he is no craftsman. No craftsman, wise man, or ruler makes an error at the moment when [τότε] he is ruling, even though everyone will say that a physician or a ruler makes errors. It is in this loose way that you must also take the answer I gave just now. But the most precise answer is this: A ruler, to the extent that he is a ruler, never [οὐδέποτε] makes errors, and unerringly decrees what is best for himself, and that is what his subject must do. Thus, as I said from the first, it is just to do what is advantageous for the stronger. (340 D 6–341 A 4)

What Thrasymachus refers to as his most precise answer is T (since it is often taken to be *t*heoretical or conceptual rather than empirical in nature). The rulers in question are T-rulers who are T-stronger and make T-laws.

Though few critics think well of T or the argument for it, most are agreed that it shows unequivocally that Thrasymachus is not (or not *now*) a conventionalist about justice. The fact that something accords with a conventional law, made by the acknowledged ruler or legislative body, is not what makes it just for him. To be just it must accord with a *correct* law—one that is in fact advantageous for the stronger ruler. Such critics have had little trouble accepting, however, that E does embody a sort of conventionalism that is inconsistent with T. Stephen Everson is a recent case in point. 'While it is true', he writes, 'that Thrasymachus rejects conventionalism, this is actually no help to those who want to acquit him of inconsistency, since it casts no effective doubt on the attribution of conventionalism to him in virtue of the argument at 338 C–339 C [i.e. E]'.[15] He gives two reasons for this:

[15] S. Everson, 'The Incoherence of Thrasymachus' ['Incoherence'], *Oxford Studies in Ancient Philosophy*, 16 (1998), 99–131 at 123.

(1) Thrasymachus started off by appealing to the behaviour of the rulers of actual Greek states, and this would have been quite beside the point if he were already tacitly operating with the more restrictive notion of a [T-]ruler.[16]

(2) When Socrates begins to raise his problem [at 339 B 9–C 12] for Thrasymachus' claim [E], Plato makes it clear that Thrasymachus is not operating with the revised notion of a [T-]ruler which he goes on to adopt . . . [For] here . . . he must be talking about [E-]rulers and [E-]laws and not about [T-]rulers and [T-]laws, since he allows that the rulers are capable of being incorrect . . . It is not until after Socrates has begun to spring his trap that Thrasymachus moves to reject the conventionalism which has caused the problems for his opening claim [E].[17]

In constructing this trap, however, Socrates recognizes *from the beginning* that Thrasymachus has a standard of correctness for E-laws in mind, namely, that they 'prescribe what is advantageous for the rulers themselves' (339 C 7–8). This is an embarrassment for Everson's view that E is conventionalist, since if it were, there could be no such standard and we would have to wonder why Plato sends Socrates off on so wrong a foot. If E is not conventionalist, however, it is, to that extent at least, not in conflict with T. Moreover, it is simply false to say that Thrasymachus *must* be talking about E-rulers when he admits rulers make legislative errors. For part of what he does in T is to represent such talk as loose. To say that rulers make legislative errors is not to talk precisely about E-rulers, he claims, but loosely about T-rulers.

If E is about T-rulers, however, in what sense, if any, can it be an empirical claim about the behaviour of rulers in actual Greek cities? While E- and T-rulers, laws, and the rest are excellent expository devices, it is a mistake to treat E-rulers as the sort we find in actual cities and make empirical claims about, and T-rulers as creatures of Thrasymachean ideal theory or fantasy, about whom we make *a priori* or conceptual claims. For Thrasymachus makes it quite clear that T-rulers are E-rulers *at those times* when they are actually practising the craft of ruling, and so not making errors. When E-rulers are ruling *correctly*, they are T-rulers, therefore, and so— tautologically—*never* make errors. The E-rulers in an actual city are generally speaking the stronger element there. How else could they rule? But when they make a law not in their own interest,

---

[16] Ibid. 122.   [17] Ibid. 122–3 (emphasis added).

they manifest not strength but weakness in doing so, since they are allowing others to do better than they.

Properly understood, then, E is a mix of empirical observation (some cities are democracies, some aristocracies, and so on), apparently uncontroversial political interpretation (the stronger element in a city is what rules it), and a controversial normative claim to the effect that when rulers rule correctly they rule in their own interest. Socrates has no trouble, therefore, in accepting the empirical observation—or the political interpretation, for that matter (338 D 9–10).[18] In fact, he agrees with Thrasymachus that political strength consists in mastery of the craft of ruling, and that masters of a craft never make errors (342 A 2–B 7). What he disagrees about is only the normative claim (339 A 5–6), and so about how the craft of ruling is to be defined. *He* thinks it aims not at the advantage of the stronger rulers, but at that of the weaker subjects (342 E 7–11).

Where E speaks of 'each type of rule' or ruling element making laws that are 'advantageous *for itself*' (338 E 1–2), T speaks instead of 'a ruler' unerringly decreeing 'what is best *for himself*' (341 A 1–2). Thus T seems to characterize rulers as straightforwardly *self*-interested in a way that E does not. The interests, for example, of the demos need not coincide with the self-interest of individual democrats. (If any one of them were to become powerful enough to tyrannize the city, Thrasymachus thinks, we would see this plainly.) But, of course, this just raises the question of what precisely E does mean by 'what is advantageous for *X*' when *X* is a ruling entity that is not a single person. Indeed, it raises this question even when, as in a kingship, *X is* a single person, but we can legitimately draw a distinction between what is advantageous for him *qua* king and what is advantageous for him *qua* individual. The one unproblematic case, which has the advantage of being the clearest proof Thrasymachus thinks he can give of his account, is that of the tyrant (344 A 1–3). For there is simply no gap, he thinks, between someone's interests as tyrant and his interests as an individual. With that unproblematic case as our guide, however, we can safely say this much: as it is in the tyrant's interest to do what will maintain his rule, so too it must be in the interest of a demos, or any other ruling element,

---

[18] 'That the stronger rule, while the weaker are ruled' is characterized as 'a kind of rule that is necessary' and 'the one most widely spread among living things, and in accord with nature' at *Laws* 690 B 4–8.

to do the same thing. All ruling elements are, in this sense, *self*-interested.

The following text from the *Laws*, which Everson usefully brings to our attention, looks very much like a recapitulation of Thrasymachus' account:

ATHENIAN: You realize that some people maintain that there are as many different kinds of laws as there are of governing elements . . . These people take the line that legislation should not be directed to waging war or attaining the whole of virtue, but should look to what is advantageous for the established governing element, whatever it is, so that it rules in perpetuity and is never overthrown. They say that the best way to formulate the naturalistic definition of justice [τὸν φύσει ὅρον τοῦ δικαίου] is like this.[19]

CLEINIAS: How?

ATHENIAN: That it is what is advantageous for the stronger.

CLEINIAS: Could you be a bit clearer?

ATHENIAN: The point is this: 'Surely', they say, 'it is the strong element in a city that at any given moment establishes the laws.' Right?

CLEINIAS: True enough.

ATHENIAN: 'So do you imagine', they say, 'that when the demos is victorious, or some other governing element, or even a tyrant, it will intentionally establish laws aimed primarily at something other than what is advantageous for maintaining its own rule?'

CLEINIAS: Of course not.

ATHENIAN: And if someone breaks these established laws, won't their establisher, calling 'just things' what is required by them, punish him as a doer of injustice?

CLEINIAS: Likely so.

ATHENIAN: Therefore, these things would always, for this reason and in this way, be what is just.

CLEINIAS: According to this argument, at any rate.   (714 B 3–D 10)

Everson is forced to argue, however, that the doctrine expressed is not really Thrasymachean at all. First, it involves a normative component (as E, he thinks, does not), and, second, it understands advantage not as self-interest (as T, he thinks, does), but as maintenance of rule.[20] But both views, as we have seen, are mistaken. When E and T are properly interpreted, they say essentially what the *Laws* does. We are spared, therefore, from having to explain why Plato would court misunderstanding by describing a position other than Thrasymachus' in such overtly Thrasymachean terms.

[19] Cf. ὅρος at *Rep.* 331 D 2.   [20] Everson, 'Incoherence', 109–13.

The real pay-off, though, is that the *Laws* explicitly characterizes JAS both as the *definition* of justice and as *naturalistic*. It thus provides compelling additional support for the reading of E we earlier developed on the basis of the *Republic* alone.

We can reasonably proceed now to look at some criticisms of JAS considered specifically as a definition, keeping in mind that our response may be to question the notion of definition they use or presuppose. It has been objected, for example, that JAS cannot be a definition because it is not analytic.[21] But since JAS is a real definition, and real definitions need not be analytic (think of 'water is H_2O'), this is not a problem. Similarly, it has been objected that JAS cannot be a correct definition if 'we take a definition as specifying some property with which justice is to be identified'. For identical properties must have the same extensions, but it is 'highly implausible' that every act advantageous to the stronger must be just.[22] We might respond that a good real definition need not be an identity statement of the sort envisaged. When Oscar Wilde tells us that sentimentality is the bank holiday of cynicism, he is indicating the morally or psychologically most significant thing about it. He would hardly feel that his insight was undermined were it pointed out to him that not all instances of cynicism on holiday are instances of sentimentality. Thrasymachus could reasonably make the same sort of response, claiming that the politically or prudentially most significant fact about justice *is* captured by JAS.

That point aside, the criticism is also not conclusive for other reasons. Once Thrasymachus has stated JAS, he goes on to present E as the clarification of it Socrates requests. Part of what E does, therefore, is to explain how the phrase 'advantageous for the stronger' is to be understood. That is to say, using the terminology of property identity, it tells us to what property AS is identical. First, the property S of being the stronger is identified with the property R of being the ruling element, so that

$$S = R.$$

It is political strength, in other words, or strength as manifested in political rule that is at issue, and not, for example, the sort possessed by Polydamas the pancratist (338 c 8). So the property AS of being

---

[21] G. F. Hourani, 'Thrasymachus' Definition of Justice in Plato's *Republic*', *Phronesis*, 7 (1962), 110–20 at 117–20.

[22] Everson, 'Incoherence', 109.

advantageous to the stronger is identical to the property AR of being advantageous to the ruler:

$$AS = AR.$$

Next the property J of being just is identified with the property L of being obedient to the laws made correctly by the ruling element, so that

$$J = L \text{ and } L = AR.$$

To have the property AS, therefore, an act must have the property L. Not simply *any* case of being advantageous to the stronger will be just, then, any more than any case of superior strength will result in possessing S. Counter-examples to JAS of the sort that Everson constructs, therefore, seem to be excluded even when definition is understood in his preferred way.

When a strict Thrasymachen T-ruler sits down to develop a set of correct laws, moreover, we may assume that he chooses from among the various options that set, L, obedience to which will maximize the ruler's advantage. Does this mean that every time a subject obeys L, the act he performs will maximize the advantage of the ruler—that is to say, that it will better promote his advantage than any other act the subject could have done? Surely, there is no reason to think so. An enemy of the ruler may have acquired a canister of nerve gas. A friend of the ruler may be in a position to steal it, which would be to the ruler's advantage. But L forbids theft and the friend is just and law-abiding. Nevertheless, L may still be the set of laws obedience to which is most advantageous to the ruler.[23] In this regard, the advantageousness of laws is like that of states of character (Section 1): it must not be equated or confused with the advantageousness of actions.

While criticisms of Thrasymachus that presuppose his embrace of ethical conventionalism in E or anywhere else need no longer detain us,[24] his nominal definition of 'justice' as obedience to the law does still need to be properly incorporated into his account. In a democracy, for example, 'justice' will be given its semantic content (its sense or connotation) by the laws that have in fact been

---

[23] The puzzle Everson, 'Incoherence', 118, raises about 'someone who gives his life to protect someone who a tyrant was unjustly persecuting' is open to a similar rejoinder.

[24] This includes the criticisms developed by Everson, 'Incoherence', 116–20.

enacted there. If those laws are all correct (if they are advantageous for the demos), 'justice' will then unambiguously refer to (will have as its referent or denotation) what is in fact justice, namely, what is advantageous for the stronger. When some of the laws are incorrect, the situation will be more complex. What we should then say is that the nominal definition is given by the laws, but that justice is incorrectly specified by it. When people describe as 'just' what is prescribed by an incorrect law, they will be linguistically correct but factually mistaken. When our dictionaries gave 'the largest of fish' as (part of) the meaning of 'whale', we were in the same situation when we described a whale as a large fish.

5. Justice as the good of another

In a passage immediately preceding his account of the tyrant, Thrasymachus gives a further characterization of justice:

[G1:] . . . justice is really the good of another, what is advantageous to the stronger and the ruler, and harmful to the one who obeys and serves. [G2] Injustice is the opposite, it rules those simple-minded—for that is what they really are—just people, and the ones it rules do what is advantageous for the other who is stronger; and they make the one they serve happy, but they do not make themselves the least bit happy. (343 C 3–D 1)

G1 seems to be a recapitulation of E, suggesting that in the phrase 'the good of another', the other referred to is the ruler, that is, the legislating element in the city. G2, however, which seems simply to elaborate on G1, also seems broader in compass, as the examples Thrasymachus gives in apparent support of it make clear:

[G3] You must consider it as follows, Socrates, or you will be the most naïve of all: A just man must always get less than an unjust one. First, in their contracts with one another, when a just man is partner to an unjust, you will never find, when the partnership ends, that the just one gets more than the unjust, but less. Second, in matters relating to the city, when taxes are to be paid, a just man pays more on an equal amount of property, an unjust one less; but when the city is giving out refunds, a just man gets nothing, while an unjust one makes a large profit. Finally, when each of them holds political office, a just person—even if he is not penalized in other ways—finds that his private affairs deteriorate more, because he has to neglect them, that he gains no advantage from the public purse because of his justice, and that he is hated by his relatives and acquaintances, because he is unwilling to do them an unjust favour. The opposite is true of an unjust man in every respect. I mean, of course, the person I described before: the man of great power who does better. (343 D 2–344 A 2)

While justice is what is advantageous to the legislating element in a city, then, it is also advantageous to ordinary unjust (lawbreaking) people who are clever enough—stronger enough in that way—not to get caught. When Socrates asks Thrasymachus whether he considers unjust people to be 'wise and good', he responds, 'Yes, if they commit perfect injustice and can bring cities and whole nations under their power. Perhaps, you thought I meant pickpockets? Not that such crimes aren't also profitable, if they are not found out' (348 D 5–8). If the evidence Thrasymachus gives in G3 is to be so much as relevant, therefore, the 'another' referred to in G1 cannot simply be the stronger legislating element in the city.

This fact has important bearing on the apparent inconsistency critics have detected between G and JAS. If the stronger acts justly according to G, he will, they say, act for the good of another. Hence his action will not be to his own advantage. Hence it will not be to the advantage of the stronger, namely, himself. According to JAS, therefore, it will not be just. Everson refers to this as a 'strict' inconsistency.[25] But is it really an inconsistency at all? The terms 'stronger', 'another', 'ruler', and 'subject' are comparative or contrastive. As we saw, they do not always refer to legislating elements or their subjects. Hence it is always important to find the right comparison or contrast class. At the end of the passage of which G is a part, Thrasymachus says: 'as I said from the beginning, justice is what is advantageous for the stronger, while injustice is profitable and advantageous *for oneself* [ἑαυτῷ]' (344 C 7–9). It is from the viewpoint of oneself, then, that G, too, should be understood. But that means that the relevant 'another' in G1 is simply someone *other and stronger than oneself*. If one is the T-ruler, however, who unerringly makes correct laws, there is no one who fits this bill. When one obeys these laws oneself, therefore, and acts justly, one's justice is—albeit vacuously—advantageous for everyone other and stronger than oneself, since that class is empty. Justice remains what is advantageous for the stronger, therefore, and the good of another.

Though it is perhaps a bit harder to see, something similar holds when we turn to lesser unjust agents. If X can be unjust (can

---

[25] Everson, 'Incoherence', 116.

break the relevant correct laws) in his dealings with Y without being caught—that is, caught *by anyone*—then there is no one other than X that is relevantly stronger than he, not even the generally stronger legislating entity in X's city. When X acts justly towards Y, which is precisely what, as a clever craftsman, he will do when he cannot get away with acting otherwise, his *act*, since it will be in accord with correct laws, will be of a sort that is advantageous to the stronger ruler. His *state of character*, however, his disposition towards those laws, which is to disobey them when he can get away with it, is a different matter. It is advantageous only to himself— than whom, in this regard, no one is stronger, since no one catches him. But in G_3, as in Glaucon's challenge, the focus simply is states of character, not actions. It is the *unjust man* (the one disposed by his character to break the law when he can get away with it) and the *just man* (the one disposed to abide by it even when he could get away with breaking it) that are being compared. It is 'when the partnership ends' that we should see who has done best, not at each point along the way. Opportunism requires opportunity.

Though G_3 shows that G_1 and G_2 are not about stronger legislating entities alone, its continuation presents that element as simply a special case of relative power in operation. *Whenever X can get away with treating Y unjustly, X is stronger than and rules Y and Y is weaker than, serves, and is subject to X.* So when X is the stronger legislating entity, the same holds. Rule and strength are expressions of natural power, not of conventional status. It is this fact, indeed, which explains why the tyrant is an illustration of JAS at all, let alone the very clearest illustration. Here is how Thrasymachus introduces him:

[G4:] The man of great power who does better—he is the one you should consider, if you want to figure out how much more advantageous it is for the individual to be unjust rather than just. [G5] You will understand this most easily if you turn your thoughts to injustice of the most perfect sort, the sort that makes those who do injustice happiest, and those who suffer it—those who are unwilling to do injustice—most wretched. The sort I mean is tyranny, because it uses both covert means and force to appropriate the property of others—whether it is sacred or secular, public or private—not little by little, but all at once. If someone commits a part of this sort of injustice and gets caught, he is punished and greatly reproached— temple-robbers, kidnappers, housebreakers, robbers, and thieves are what these partly unjust people are called when they commit those harms. When someone appropriates the possessions of the citizens, on the other hand, and then kidnaps and enslaves the possessors as well, instead of these shameful names he is called happy and blessed, not only by the citizens themselves, but even by all who learn that he has committed the whole of injustice. For it is not the fear of doing injustice, but of suffering it, that elicits the reproaches of those who revile injustice. So you see, Socrates, injustice, if it is on a large enough scale, is stronger, freer, and more masterful than justice. And, as I said from the beginning, justice is what is advantageous for the stronger, while injustice is profitable and advantageous for oneself. (344 A 1–C 9)

G4 refers back to the masters of the craft of ruling who appears in T. These include legislators, but also—as G3 makes clear—any citizen who is able successfully to combine real injustice with reputed justice. G5 then presents the tyrant as the perfect embodiment of that sort of injustice, because, unlike such 'partly unjust people' as temple-robbers, kidnappers, housebreakers, robbers, and thieves, he commits 'the whole of injustice', and gets away with it. Temple-robbers and the rest, however, commit injustice in a straightforward manner by breaking the relevant laws of their city. (No natural harm, as we saw in Section 2, is correctly called an injustice unless it breaks a law.) The tyrant, by contrast, seems quite different. He does not so much break the laws as overthrow both them and the previously stronger legislating entity that made and enforced them. Is he really unjust, then, or the perpetrator of a successful revolutionary coup? It is by presenting him as simply a more extreme case of straightforwardly unjust people that Thrasymachus allows us to see him in the former light—as straightforwardly but also perfectly unjust.

The tyrant is the ancestor of Glaucon's perfectly unjust man, we saw in Section 3, who combines real injustice with reputed justice. We can now appreciate more fully why that is true. For the stronger, laws function as the ultimate 'illusionist painting of virtue' with which to surround himself. So effective is it, in fact, that we can typically see through it only from the outside and by dint of adopting a historical perspective, a diachronic view. It is when the tyrant—or the demos or the aristocratic element—is represented as using his new-found greater strength to break all the laws of the previous regime that he can be seen as simply a more powerful temple-robber or pickpocket. In a moment, though, he will disappear behind his legislation—really unjust but reputed just.

Thrasymachus' account is a coherent and resourceful blend, then, of ethical realism and semantic conventionalism, which identifies justice in each city with what is advantageous to its stronger ruler, and the semantic content of 'justice' with what its particular laws prescribe. Since this is the position Glaucon and Adeimantus attribute to Thrasymachus, and further defend on his behalf, the pincer movement begun in Section 1 is complete. Glaucon's challenge, which the *Republic* undertakes to answer, is Thrasymachean. It is at Thrasymacheanism, therefore, that its counter-argument is aimed.

6. The significance of Thrasymacheanism

Though Thrasymachus presents his views as original, correct, and deserving of praise (338 c 2–4), Thrasymacheanism, as Glaucon and Adeimantus are aware, is in essence simply a digest of what most people (secretly) think (358 A 4–D 2). This congruity of beliefs and values is, in Socrates' view, no accident:

None of those private wage-earners—the ones these people call sophists and consider to be their rivals in craft[26]—teaches anything other than the convictions the masses hold when they are assembled together, and this he calls wisdom. It is just as if someone were learning the passions and appetites of a huge, strong beast that he is rearing—how to approach and handle it, when it is most difficult to deal with or most docile and what makes it so, what sounds it utters in either condition, and what tones of voice soothe or anger it. Having learnt all this through associating and spending time [χρόνου τριβῇ] with the beast, he calls this wisdom, gathers his information together as if it were a craft, and starts to teach it. Knowing nothing in reality about which of these convictions or appetites is fine or shameful, good or bad, just or unjust, he uses all these terms in conformity with the great beast's beliefs—calling the things it enjoys good and the things that anger it bad. He has no other account to give of them, but calls everything he is compelled to do just and fine, never having seen how much the natures of necessity and goodness really differ, and being unable to explain it to anyone. Don't you think, by Zeus, that someone like that would make a strange educator? (493 A 6–c 8)

Like other sophists, Thrasymachus bases his account on his experience of how people in cities talk and behave. So his views neces-

---

[26] i.e. rivals in the craft of teaching virtue.

sarily reflect—even though they may also unmask—theirs (360 D 6–7). The mistake he makes is to confuse the resulting experience-based knack (*tribē*) with genuine expert or craft knowledge (*technē*) of virtue and goodness.[27] Only the latter, however, can explain in an entirely adequate way why what are nominally or conventionally virtues are in fact genuine or natural ones, and why the latter are choiceworthy not simply because they are socially legislated and backed by rewards and punishments, but because of the contributions they themseves make to their possessor's happiness.

When Socrates contrasts the argument he is giving in the *Republic* with another better sort, he acknowledges that it falls short of what such expert craft-knowledge would provide: 'it is my belief that we will never ever grasp this matter precisely by methods of enquiry of the sort we are now using in our discussions. However, there is in fact another longer and more time-consuming road that does lead there' (435 C 9–D 4; also 504 B 1–505 B 3). This is the road that dialectic, which is 'the only method of enquiry that, doing away with hypotheses, journeys to the first principle itself in order to be made secure' (533 C 8–D 1), alone provides. Since the 'unhypothetical first principle of everything' (511 B 5–6) is the form of the good, until someone knows it, secure knowledge of all other values—including justice (504 D 4–E 2)—will escape him (534 B 8–C 6).

As a general characterization of the shorter road, that given by Simmias in the discussion in the *Phaedo* would be hard to beat:

to know the plain truth about such matters is either impossible or extremely difficult in this present life, but, on the other hand, not to examine what is said about them in every possible way [τὰ λεγόμενα περὶ αὐτῶν μὴ οὐχὶ παντὶ τρόπῳ ἐλέγχειν], and not to give up until one has investigated them exhaustively from every angle, shows utter softness in a man. You see, where these matters are concerned, it seems to me that one must certainly achieve one of two things: either learn or discover how they stand; or, if that is impossible, then at least adopt the best of the things people say, and the one that stands up best to examination, and, carried on it as on a sort of raft, face the dangers of life's voyage—provided one cannot travel more safely and with less risk on the more secure vessel of some divine saying. (85 C 1–D 4)

There is, perhaps, a hint in the *Republic* that Socrates himself may have sailed on the more secure vessel (496 A 11–E 3), but for Glau-

[27] Note χρόνου τριβῇ at 438 B 6, and see *Gorg.* 465 A 2–6; *Prot.* 356 E 2–361 B 7; *Phdr.* 260 E 5, 270 B 5; Arist. *Metaph. A* 1.

con, Adeimantus, and the rest of us, there is, for now, only the raft. The counter-argument to Thrasymacheanism that the *Republic* offers is, for that reason, self-consciously less than decisive—though, of course, the same can be said for the arguments on the other side.

Thrasymacheanism—and the challenge Glaucon formulates on its basis—presupposes a version of egoistic eudaimonism that is, as we saw in Section 1, character-focused. It asks not simply why one should be just, but why, if I want happiness for myself, I should have or acquire a just character. Somewhat less emphatically, but still quite insistently, it raises the related question of the scope or motivational locus of justice (morality), suggesting, as we saw in Section 2, that only the weak have such a motive. To appreciate how deep-going this double challenge is, it is useful to begin with the second question.

In *On the Basis of Morality* Schopenhauer criticizes specifically Kantian ethics on the grounds that it cannot explain why sufficiently powerful agents should be just or benevolent:

It is perfectly clear . . . that that fundamental rule of Kant is not . . . a categorical imperative, but in fact a *hypothetical* one. For . . . if I . . ., confident perhaps of my superior strength, always think of myself as the active but never as the passive party, with the maxim that is to be chosen as universally valid, then, assuming that there is no other foundation of morality but the Kantian, I can very well will injustice and non-benevolence as a universal maxim, and accordingly rule the world 'upon the simple plan | That they should take who have the power, | And they should keep, who can'.[28]

If an agent is strong enough not to need justice or benevolence from others, the criticism goes, he can accept Wordsworth's principle as the universal—and so Kant-approved—maxim of his action. Morality will not include him in its scope, therefore, and reason cannot be morality's sole motivational locus. If it is to have such a locus in him, after all, he must also be weak enough to need other people.

Because Kant thinks of God as within morality's scope, this problem is particularly sharp for him, since, as omnipotent and omniscient, God will hardly need help from others to realize his ends. But, of course, it is also sharp for Socrates, since he thinks that the (immortal and very powerful) Olympian gods cannot be anything

---

[28] A. Schopenhauer, *Über das Fundament der Moral* [1841], trans. E. F. J. Payne as *On the Basis of Morality* (Indianapolis, 1998), 91. The quotation is from William Wordsworth, *Memorials of a Tour of Scotland*, 11, 'Rob Roy's Grave'.

other than virtuous and good (379 B 1). Because of that, and also because his ideal human life is one of maximal godlikeness (500 D 1–3; *Theaet.* 176 A 7–B 3),[29] the motivational locus of justice in divine and human souls must, it seems, be the same. That it lies in 'the rational element of the soul' (439 D 5) can scarcely be doubted, since this is the part that knows and desires the good (442 C 5–7; 490 A 8–B 7; 581 B 6–8) and alone seems to survive the death of the body (611 B 9–612 A 6; *Phaedo* 65 B 9–67 B 5; 82 D 9–84 B 7). The good it knows and desires, however, on Socrates' own conception of it, seems to be something like rational order or harmony.[30] Hence the desire in the soul's rational part for engagement with it through knowledge or contemplation, which is the chief constituent of the best or philosophical life, will apparently be an analogue of Kant's *Achtung* (respect). In other words, it will be akin to a pure rational interest in the sort of formal consistency represented by the (supposedly) categorical imperative—the sort of rational order exhibited by forms that are 'orderly and always the same' (500 C 3–4). But that will apparently leave Socrates, too, open to some version of Schopenhauer's objection.

Unlike formal consistency, of course, the good itself, as the first principle of an orderly arrangement of forms that includes the form of justice, has obvious moral content. Hence engaging with it may be incompatible, as indeed Socrates supposes it is (500 D 1–3), with being indifferent to justice or the welfare of others. If one most perfectly imitates the forms by knowing and contemplating them, however, by living as a contemplative philosopher in 'the pure realm' (520 D 9), it seems that the life in which one's justice is manifested *towards other people* can only be a second best. Socrates himself seems to admit as much. The contemplative philosophical life is 'better', he says, than the life of ruling in the best kind of city, which is the philosopher's best kind of political life (521 A 1). When he insists, in the same breath, that the philosophers are 'compelled' (521 B 7) to lead that life by the laws, it is no wonder that critics have felt the eudaimonistic sands shifting beneath their feet.[31]

---

[29] See D. Sedley, 'The Ideal of Godlikeness', in G. Fine (ed.), *Plato 2: Ethics, Politics, Religion, and the Soul* (Oxford, 1999), 309–28.

[30] See J. M. Cooper, 'The Psychology of Justice in Plato', in J. M. Cooper, *Reason and Emotion: Essays on Ancient Moral Psychology and Ethical Theory* (Princeton, 1999), 138–50, and my 'Plato's Metaphysics of Morals', *Oxford Studies in Ancient Philosophy*, 25 (2003), 39–58.

[31] See N. White, *Individual and Conflict in Greek Ethics* (Oxford, 2002), and,

At bottom, Schopenhauer's objection is straightforward. Concern for the welfare of others, which seems essential to justice, cannot have its motivational locus in something else. In particular, it cannot have it, apparently, in any sort of egoism. The ideal of godlikeness, by contrast, seems positively to exalt egoism, self-sufficiency, and such solitary activities as contemplating the good. That the stresses and strains imposed by Glaucon's challenge are immense is easy to see: the demands of justice and those of egoistic eudaimonism seem obviously opposed or in tension. But these stresses and strains are present in Socrates' own position; they are not simply imposed on him by Glaucon. They are the result, indeed, of his ultimately—and perhaps irreparably—schizophrenic picture of human beings as essentially divided creatures, part animal, part divine.

Kant rejects the question 'Why should I be moral?' on the grounds that, like the question 'Why should I be rational?', it is self-undermining. If I am not already in the business of acting on reasons, what reason could persuade or compel me to it? Socrates, however, does not reject it. He seems to think he can show that justice pays higher dividends in terms of the agent's own *eudaimonia* or happiness than does injustice. Our motivational engagement with justice is thus teleological rather that deontological: we engage with it in order to be happy—though this requires us to engage with it for its own sake. That he takes our engagement with justice to be of this sort, however, puts a pressure on his defence of justice that Kant, by eschewing eudaimonism and consequentialism more generally, is able to avoid. We might put the matter this way: whatever happiness is, whether pleonectic satisfaction, as Thrasymacheans think, or something else, pleasure or enjoyment must surely be a large and essential constituent of it. For who would want happiness if it did not involve these things? Call this constituent 'shappiness'. What a eudaimonist defence must show is that justice better promotes shappiness than does injustice. Since Socrates agrees that pleasure is crucial to happiness (583 A 1–588 A 10), he cannot reject this demand out of hand. Whether he can meet it is another question.

The end of an already long paper is not the place, obviously, to try to determine how well Socrates' own complex (though self-

as a partial antidote, my 'Goat-Stags, Philosopher-Kings, and Eudaimonism in the *Republic*', *Proceedings of the Boston Area Colloquium in Ancient Philosophy*, 22 (2006), 185–209.

consciously provisional) theory can respond to these problems—
problems that are rooted in Glaucon's challenge. My goal has been
the altogether ancillary one, first, of identifying that challenge,
second, of showing that that the defence of justice it demands
is consequentialist, and, third, of showing that it is inspired by
a Thrasymachean account that is both consistent and consistently
naturalistic.

University of North Carolina at Chapel Hill

BIBLIOGRAPHY

Annas, J., *An Introduction to Plato's* Republic (Oxford, 1981).
Cooper, J. M., 'The Psychology of Justice in Plato', in J. M. Cooper, *Reason and Emotion: Essays on Ancient Moral Psychology and Ethical Theory* (Princeton, 1999), 138–50.
Everson, S., 'The Incoherence of Thrasymachus' ['Incoherence'], *Oxford Studies in Ancient Philosophy*, 16 (1998), 99–131.
Ferrari, G. R. F., *City and Soul in Plato's* Republic [*City*] (Sankt Augustin, 2003).
Hourani, G. F., 'Thrasymachus' Definition of Justice in Plato's *Republic*', *Phronesis*, 7 (1962), 110–20.
Reeve, C. D. C., 'Goat-Stags, Philosopher-Kings, and Eudaimonism in the *Republic*', *Proceedings of the Boston Area Colloquium in Ancient Philosophy*, 22 (2006), 185–209.
—— 'Plato's Metaphysics of Morals', *Oxford Studies in Ancient Philosophy*, 25 (2003), 39–58.
—— (trans.), *Plato:* Republic (Indianapolis, 2004).
Schopenhauer, A., *Über das Fundament der Moral* [1841], trans. E. F. J. Payne as *On the Basis of Morality* (Indianapolis, 1998).
Sedley, D., 'The Ideal of Godlikeness', in G. Fine (ed.), *Plato 2: Ethics, Politics, Religion, and the Soul* (Oxford, 1999), 309–28.
—— 'Philosophy, the Forms and the Art of Ruling', in G. R. F. Ferrari (ed.), *The Cambridge Companion to Plato's* Republic (Cambridge, 2007), 256–83.
Slings, S. R. (ed.), *Platonis Rempublicam recognovit* . . . (Oxford, 2003).
White, N., *Individual and Conflict in Greek Ethics* (Oxford, 2002).
Wiggins, D., *Ethics: Twelve Lectures on the Philosophy of Morality* (Cambridge, Mass., 2006).
Williams, B. A. O., 'Plato's Construction of Intrinsic Goodness' ['Construction'], in M. Burnyeat (ed.), *The Sense of the Past: Essays in the History of Philosophy* (Princeton, 2006), 118–37.

THE COPULA AND SEMANTIC
CONTINUITY IN PLATO'S *SOPHIST*

FIONA LEIGH

LESLEY BROWN first made a radical claim about uses of the Greek verb 'to be' (*einai*) in Plato's *Sophist* some twenty years ago (1986).[1] The view has proved quite influential. It has attracted support from scholars such as Myles Burnyeat and Charles Kahn, who endorse it in works that treat of ancient texts besides the *Sophist*.[2] Brown's paper has been anthologized in a well-received and popular collection of papers on Platonic metaphysics and epistemology.[3] The proposal concerning *einai* was subsequently developed by her beyond the *Sophist*—and beyond Plato—in an essay on the verb that appeared in a collection of papers on language in ancient Greek thought.[4] And in recent papers on the *Sophist*, Job van Eck and Blake Hestir have each assumed the validity of Brown's reading without question.[5]

In brief, Brown's innovation is as follows: The verb 'to be' in

© Fiona Leigh 2008

I am grateful to David Sedley, Lesley Brown, Dirk Baltzly, Allan Silverman, John Bigelow, and an audience at the University of Melbourne for insightful criticisms and suggestions on earlier drafts.

[1] L. Brown, 'Being in the *Sophist*: A Syntactical Enquiry' ['Being'], *Oxford Studies in Ancient Philosophy*, 4 (1986), 49–70; repr. with revisions in G. Fine (ed.), *Plato 1: Metaphysics and Epistemology* (Oxford, 1999), 455–78 (all references are to the later publication).

[2] M. Burnyeat, '*Apology* 30 B 2–4: Socrates, Money, and the Grammar of γιγνέσθαι' ['Socrates'], *Journal of Hellenic Studies*, 123 (2003), 1–25; C. Kahn, 'A Return to the Theory of the Verb *be* and the Concept of Being' ['Return'], *Ancient Philosophy*, 24 (2004), 381–405; id., *The Verb 'Be' in Ancient Greek* (Indianapolis, 2003) (repr. of the first edition (Dordrecht, 1973), with a new introduction).

[3] See n. 1 above.

[4] L. Brown, 'The Verb "to be" in Greek Philosophy: Some Remarks' ['Verb'], in S. Everson (ed.), *Language* (Companions to Ancient Thought, 3; Cambridge, 1994), 212–36.

[5] J. van Eck, 'Not-Being and Difference: On Plato's *Sophist* 256 D 5–258 E 3', *Oxford Studies in Ancient Philosophy*, 23 (2002), 63–84; B. Hestir, 'A "Conception" of Truth in Plato's *Sophist*', *Journal of the History of Philosophy*, 41 (2003), 1–24.

Greek, unlike its counterpart in modern English, permits a complete and an incomplete use. Sometimes it does not take a complement, though it could, and at other times context demands a complement (whether elided or not). In the former case, the verb exhibits what Brown calls a 'C2' complete use, and in the second, an incomplete use. Brown's view is that the verb is not being used merely homonymously in these cases, but, like 'to teach' in English, exhibits a certain continuity of meaning across uses. The mistake has been to take complete uses of *estin* as C1 complete uses, i.e. as uses that will not bear further completion.

The first critical discussion (to my knowledge) of Brown's reading has recently appeared in print.[6] In it John Malcolm advances several arguments against Brown's reading. I shall argue, however, that Malcolm's textual considerations are less than decisive. More significantly, I shall suggest that his conceptual arguments miss their mark in two ways: one objection relies on a less than charitable reading of Brown, while another involves the questionable attribution of an assumption to the author of the *Sophist*. But despite my defence of Brown's view, I do not endorse it. On the contrary, I hope to show that Brown's central thesis—that there is a semantic continuity between complete and incomplete uses of *einai*—lacks the textual support it requires from the *Sophist*. Moreover, a central argument of that dialogue tells against it. We turn first to Malcolm.

1. A defence of Brown

The *Sophist* does not take centre stage in Malcolm's critical discussion of Brown's proposal concerning *einai*: his target is Brown's later paper 'Verb' (1994), in which she draws on the results of her seminal paper 'Being' (1986) on the *Sophist*. In particular, Brown argues in the later paper that an issue concerning the use and negation of *esti*, not adequately dealt with in the *Republic*, motivated Plato's treatment of that verb in the *Sophist* (229–31). Against Brown, Malcolm advances four separate complaints: (1) her interpretation of *einai* does not square with the relevant passages in *Republic* 5; (2) one of Brown's star witnesses—the paradox at *Soph.* 238 E—turns out to be poor evidence for her view; (3) the concep-

---

[6] J. Malcolm, 'Some Cautionary Remarks on the "is"/"teaches" Analogy' ['Remarks'], *Oxford Studies in Ancient Philosophy*, 31 (2006), 281–96.

tual details of her proposal do not in fact generate the notion of a semantic continuum; (4) Brown's reading has the unwanted and serious consequence that Plato would violate what Malcolm calls the UC (uncommitted copula) Condition: '*Something can have properties attributed to it without existing*' ('Remarks', 283, emphasis original). Therefore, Malcolm argues, Brown's reading should be passed over in favour of other more viable interpretations of the *Sophist* in the literature.[7]

I shall have nothing here to say about (1), Malcolm's objections to Brown's reading of the *Republic*. For I take it that even if Brown is wrong in her 1994 paper about Plato's use of *einai* at *Rep.* 476 E–477 A, she could none the less be right in the earlier paper about his use of it in the *Sophist*, whatever his motivations for that treatment. In defence of Brown's proposal, I shall argue that the remaining three complaints are not well founded. I hope to show against (2) that the paradox at 238 E can in fact be read as evidence (albeit weak evidence) for her view; against (3) that her conception of a semantic continuum is a coherent one when more charitably construed; and against (4) that it is unclear that the author of the *Sophist* would endorse Malcolm's UC condition.

Malcolm argues that the paradox at *Soph.* 238 E does not bear out Brown's reading of *einai* after all. He presents the reasoning behind the paradox as follows: what is not is unthinkable; so what is not is something (namely, unthinkable); hence we arrive at the paradox that what *is not* also *is* (293). Brown's suggestion is that since Plato moves from an '*X* is *F*'-type statement to an '*X* is'-type statement, the text counts as evidence of a C2 complete use of *einai*—a use in which it may take a complement but need not ('Verb', 231). Malcolm observes that the paradox depends for its force on the subject being 'what is not'. If instead the subject were, say, a round square, we would not finish with a formal contradiction, whereby the same thing is both affirmed and denied of the subject, but rather the odd claim that 'a round square is'. The suggestion, therefore, that Plato is concerned in this passage to illustrate two syntactically distinct but semantically continuous uses of 'is' misses the point of

---

[7] Malcolm has in mind those who follow the work of M. Frede in *Prädikation und Existenzaussage* (Hypomnemata, 18; Gottingen: 1967), and G. E. L. Owen in 'Plato on Not-Being' ['Not-Being'], in G. Vlastos (ed.), *Plato: A Collection of Critical Essays*, i. *Metaphysics and Epistemology* (Garden City, NY, 1971), 223–67, repr. in G. Fine (ed.), *Plato 1: Metaphysics and Epistemology* (Oxford, 1999), 416–54 (references are to the later publication).

the paradox according to Malcolm: Plato's sole concern is to show up a difficulty with the Parmenidean notion of not being.

But Plato need not be deliberately drawing attention to a use of *einai* for the passage to count as evidence for it. That is, his *use* of the verb can legitimately be thought to reveal something about his understanding of its meaning and grammatical function even where his main purpose in a given passage is to make some other point entirely. The point of the paradox *is* the formal contradiction in the conclusion. But one of the inferences that Plato has his character draw on the way to reaching that conclusion is that from 'not being is unthinkable' to 'not being is'. Since this inference can be read as an application of the general rule that 'X is F' implies 'X is', it can be read, with Brown, as evidence of a C2 use of *estin*. Of course, it need not be read this way (after all, Brown presents it as merely part of a cumulative case). Alternatively, the shift between the two statements can be read as evincing an inference that does not turn on the uses of 'is' being semantically continuous: we could read the inference here as the move from the idea that the subject possesses a property to the quite independent idea that it is one of the existing things. If so, the 'is' in 'X is F' is the grammatically incomplete predicative 'is' (the copula), while the 'is' in 'X is' is a grammatically complete C1 existential 'is'. So although Malcolm is wrong to claim that the paradox is not evidence for Brown's view, we ought to bear in mind that on its own it constitutes weak evidence for it, at best.

Also in connection with the paradox, Malcolm points out that the radical Parmenidean *what is not* is outlawed by the Stranger later in the dialogue at 258 E (293). Malcolm claims that the 'what is not' encountered earlier at 238 E should not therefore be read, with Brown, as a subject in a statement penned by Plato that employs a C2 use of *einai*. For, if he rejects the radical *not being* outright—so the thought goes—he would not use it as a subject in a statement that carries existential force. This is not, however, what Brown's reading requires. All she requires is that the text contain an apparently seamless shift from an incomplete to a complete use. We are then free to read the Stranger as putting forward an *ad hominem* argument that takes Parmenidean premisses and which then employs the semantically continuous uses of 'is' to show those premisses to be contradictory. The shift between these uses, on her view, betrays a belief in a certain entailment, viz. that *if* a subject has a property, then that subject is (in a clear existential sense of 'is'). Plato can of course hold that this statement of entailment is true *and* that its antecedent does not hold true for some particular value (i.e. subject). He can thus be read as quite consistently committed to the statement of entailment without at the same time committing himself to the consequent being true in the case of *this* subject, the radical Parmenidean not being.[8] In this way, both the paradox at 238 E and the later remarks on not being at 258 E can be read as consistent with Brown's proposal of a C2 use of *einai*. We turn now to (3).

Brown alleges an analogy between uses of *estin* in Greek and verbs like 'to teach' in English. Malcolm takes it that, for Brown, just as 'teaches' has the 'same semantic force in "Jane teaches French" and "Jane teaches", so "is" has the same semantic force in "Socrates is snub-nosed" and "the gods are"' (289). But then, he objects, we have semantic identity across different uses of *esti*, not a semantic continuum. The objection would be a good one against Brown if she had claimed in either 'Being' or 'Verb' that the verb *einai* itself (or the verb 'to teach' in English) did not have the same meaning in these uses, but rather took a value on a semantic continuum. But she did not. What Brown did assert was that the complete and incomplete *uses* of the verbs were on a semantic continuum ('Being', 460; 'Verb', 226). Brown's point here, it seems to me, is that the complete and incomplete uses occur in *statements* that share an underlying syntactical structure. This has the result that the *statements* in which these different uses occur—e.g. 'Jane teaches' and 'Jane teaches French'—are on a semantic continuum, though of course the statements do not mean the same thing. It is the focus on the relation between syntactical use and semantics that gives her the required contrast between *this* statement pair and statement pairs that employ C1 complete and incomplete uses of verbs (such as 'to grow' in 'Jane is growing' and 'Jane is growing tomatoes': 'Being', 459–60). For, verbs that are merely homonymous in their complete and incomplete uses occur in semantically *discontinuous* statements.

Malcolm's fourth, most serious objection to Brown's reading is that it entails 'that "is" must have minimal existential force in nominal cases of "X is F"' (289) because the complete and incomplete

---

[8] Brown contended in 'Verb' that Parmenides anticipated the semantically continuous uses of *esti* she claims to find in Plato (219–20). It is not therefore at all surprising, Brown might say, that Plato would have the Stranger from Elea employ these semantically continuous uses of the verb in constructing a paradox out of the radical Parmenidean conception of what is not.

uses of *estin* are semantically continuous, and the complete use has existential force.[9] But if the copula has minimal existential force in nominal cases of '*X* is *F*', then every subject of such statements will be asserted to exist to some degree. It is impossible, then, to ascribe or deny properties without also committing oneself to the existence of the subject, and so to make predications of a non-existent subject. Brown's proposal about *einai* therefore reads Plato as contravening the UC or uncommitted copula condition: '*Something can have properties attributed to it without existing*' (283, emphasis original). Malcolm says it is imperative to recognize that 'we, including the ancients, *must* be able to describe things that do not exist', and, as a matter of interpretative principle, the UC Condition 'should be called into question only if all else fails!' (ibid.). Plato could not, for Brown, even contemplate a non-existent subject that possesses properties. In Malcolm's view, we ought to be chary of attributing this position to Plato:

Much worse, to my mind, is the result . . . that 'is' must have minimal existential force in nominal cases of '*X* is *F*'. Brown opens the door to the possibility that whatever may be described or classified must, to some degree, exist. The UC Condition . . . is violated! We need to be shown that there are decisive advantages to adopting so dubious a doctrine . . . The burden of proof is on her! ('Remarks', 289)

For my purposes, the question is whether the *Sophist* shows Plato to be a proponent of UC or not. Good evidence that he accepted the UC condition (or would have, had it been put to him) would be a passage that unambiguously demonstrates his awareness of the distinction between possessing some property and being an existing thing, such that something could possess a property without existing. There is no such passage in the *Sophist*, nor does Malcolm cite one from the corpus. None the less, the text cannot be said on this score to contradict Malcolm's position, that Plato well knew that *being* as *existing* was strictly separated in meaning from *being something or other* (289). For Malcolm also maintains that since Plato was not interested in questions of existence in the *Sophist*, he only deployed the sense of 'is' at work in *being something* in that dialogue, i.e. in the use of 'is' as the copula.[10] But neither can the text

---

[9] 'Being', 466 n. 16: 'Plato . . . cannot distinguish non-existence from not being anything at all.'

[10] Malcolm writes: 'I do not mean to imply that the copula is merely an empty

be said on this score to contradict Brown's position, that existence was so closely tied to the possession of some property for Plato that he could not distinguish the non-existent from what possesses no property at all.

But the text is not neutral between Brown's and Malcolm's readings alone. Plato's silence on the matter renders yet a third reading possible: Plato was aware of the conceptual distinction between being as existing and possessing some property, but upon reflection rejected it as a real distinction, and so did not accept the UC Condition (or would not have). It is possible, that is, that Plato came to analyse reality or what exists in such a way that whatever possesses a property is one of the existing or real things, and that *this* is why there appears to be no text that speaks of the non-existent as possessing some property or other.[11] If Plato arrived at this position as a result of intellectual labour, then *pace* Brown, his thought was not constrained by the semantics or syntax of the verb 'to be', and *pace* Malcolm, his grasp of a conceptual distinction did not guarantee his acceptance of it as a real distinction. I conclude that it is not at all clear that we are entitled to assume, with Malcolm, Plato's endorsement of the UC Condition.

Last, Malcolm's own reading has a puzzling consequence. Malcolm says that Plato well knew the difference between *being* as *existing* and *being something or other*, but in the *Sophist* only wished to speak of the property being in terms of the latter. Plato therefore deliberately intended a narrow sense of 'being' and a narrow (predicative) use of 'is' in our dialogue—the copula—to express it. He would have done so, moreover, in full knowledge that Greek thinkers generally 'had a use of "is" which would have the usual force of "exists"' (289)—the grammatically complete use—but which he did not consider germane to the arguments of that dialogue. So while Malcolm claims that 'a rigid existence/copula distinction is a legitimate tool for the interpretation of [Plato and others]' (281), which distinction provides the basis for his efforts to exculpate Plato from the charge of violating the UC Condition, it is not a tool he thinks is required to understand the arguments of the *Sophist*. The puzzle, then, is this: why did Plato not signal somewhere to

marker joining subject to predicate and having no meaning of its own' ('Remarks', 288 n. 15).

[11] This position may well be one we wish to criticize Plato for occupying, though a proper discussion of that question will have to await another occasion.

his readers that he was evoking this narrow sense of the property being in the central arguments of the dialogue, so narrow that it excludes existence from its sense and the Form, Being, does not correspond to existence? When the Stranger says that Motion *is* as a result of participation in Being (256 A 1), or that Motion *is a being* by the same cause (256 D 10–11; E 3–4), there is no indication at all that only a narrow sense of being—being something or other—is deliberately marked off here. It seems to me that this would be very strange for a writer allegedly familiar with both senses of 'being' *and* the fact that one sense was typically expressed by way of a syntactically complete existential use of 'is', a writer we ought to feel free to interpret according to a rigid existence/copula distinction. It is so strange, I suggest, as to be highly unlikely.

2. Against Brown on *einai* in the *Sophist*

Brown claims that in some cases at least *einai* is analogous to 'teaches' in English: that is, there are some non-elided uses of it in which it may take a complement, though it need not. Moreover, there is a clear semantic continuity between the case where it turns out to take a complement and the case where it turns out not to: where it does not, it is not a solecism to ask 'is *what*?' ('Being', 460). With this C2 use of *einai* in mind, Brown suggests good sense can be made of the distinction between *kath' hauta* and *pros alla* at *Soph.* 255 C 13–14 that has greatly vexed scholars over the last fifty years or so: the Stranger is comparing expressions that occur without completion with those that do not, and goes on to say that 'being' is spoken of in *both* these ways, and on this basis must be distinct from 'difference', which is not ('Being', 474–7).

One obvious difficulty for Brown's innovative reading lies in locating passages that would be decisive for it, for Brown is not of course claiming that all copulative uses of *einai* are semantically continuous with complete C2 uses. Brown recognizes that there are many uses of the verb that are cases of the *mere* copula: that is, cases where the function of the verb appears to be to join the subject to the predicate and not to bring with it any contribution of meaning ('Verb', 213). The crucial point, upon which her case rests, is that not all cases of the copula are like this, but some cases are instances of a use which is semantically continuous with the C2 complete use of 'to be' in Greek, the existential use (as in 'Delphi is'). Brown's work draws on Charles Kahn's earlier study of the verb 'to be' in Greek. In 'Verb' Brown makes it clear that she relies upon Kahn's view that, while many instances of incomplete uses of *esti* serve as the mere copula, there are sometimes other instances that 'go beyond the mere copula in meaning' (ibid.). Therefore she concludes with Kahn that it is false to assume that in Greek 'predicative uses lack meaning and serve merely to join subject to predicate' (ibid.). But it is not obvious how one should tell, when faced with a predicative use of *einai*, whether the verb has a meaning of its own, an existential force that goes beyond the mere copula. For my purposes, the question becomes whether we have reason to suppose that any use of the copula has this meaning for Plato in the *Sophist*.

Though much of Kahn's earlier work on *estin* is far-ranging, taking in work from Homer to Aristotle and beyond, a 1981 paper explicitly focuses on uses of the verb in Plato.[12] Kahn claims that the meaning of *esti* is frequently overdetermined in the corpus, so that the context allows it to bear several senses.[13] Often, he argues, the copula in a statement of the form '*X* is *F*' in Plato should be read with a veridical emphasis—'*X* is truly *F*'—particularly in arguments of metaphysical import central to a dialogue (e.g. *Lys.* 219 C; *Phaedo* 65 C–D). But one thing Kahn does not claim there is that there is a statement in one of Plato's works that contains a use of *einai* that serves as the copula and at the same time carries its own existentially loaded meaning.[14] And though he has recently (2004) modified his official position to incorporate Brown's, he cites only two candidate passages in support of this interpretation of the copula in Plato (*Rep.* 5, 477 A–479 D; *Laws* 10, 901 C–D), neither of which is compelling, either separately or considered together.[15]

[12] 'Some Philosophical Uses of "to be" in Plato' ['Uses'], *Phronesis*, 26 (1981), 105–34.   [13] Ibid. 105.
[14] Kahn claims in 'Uses' that there are passages in Plato where the existential 'is' is 'pregnant' with the copulative 'is' (e.g. *Sym.* 211 A: 'Uses', 108, 123), and that the notion of existence can be expressed by way of a statement containing the copula ('. . . being something rather than nothing', 112), but neither of these claims amounts to the much stronger claim that the copula has a meaning of its own and that that meaning is existential.
[15] 'Return', 385. The *Republic* reference is less than compelling because it is not clear why Kahn now prefers to read the complete use of *einai* as existential, despite his earlier lengthy argument that it should be read veridically and not existentially ('Uses', 112–13; see also Malcolm's argument against reading the *Republic* 5 passage

Also absent from Kahn's 1981 paper on the verb in Plato is any significant reference to the *Sophist*. Even in the more recent paper, a summary of his introduction to the reprinting of *The Verb 'Be' in Ancient Greek*, Kahn alludes to the *Sophist* only in reporting the results of Brown's earlier studies ('Return', 382–3), which, as mentioned above, proceed on the assumption that Kahn has shown that any reading of *estin* as the mere copula is open to doubt. This is very far, however, from demonstrating what Brown claims—a semantic continuum between incomplete uses of *estin* as the copula and complete, existential uses. But without good textual evidence, we surely have little reason to accept that Plato understood the copula sometimes to have the meaning that Brown's reading requires, and no solid reason to think he viewed the copula this way in the *Sophist*.

We turn, then, to the positive textual evidence from the *Sophist* Brown adduces in support of her reading. We saw above that the paradox at 238 E ('Verb', 231–2; 'Being', 466) constitutes weak support at best.[16] But it is only part of a cumulative case: Another passage Brown cites as potentially containing a C2 use of 'is' is 259 A 6–8:

τὸ μὲν ἕτερον μετασχὸν τοῦ ὄντος ἔστι μὲν διὰ ταύτην τὴν μέθεξιν, οὐ μὴν ἐκεῖνό γε οὗ μετέσχεν ἀλλ' ἕτερον.

Brown translates: 'partaking in being, it is by virtue of that par-

according to Brown's view: 'Remarks', 286–7). The *Laws* passage (which Kahn notes was pointed out to him by Brown in private correspondence: 'Return', 385 n. 7) contains a single occurrence of the verb that is then read into two following clauses, where the syntactical use of the verb varies: in the first clause it must be a complete use, and in the other two it must be incomplete. Kahn endorses Brown's view that 'for Plato, they are one and the same verb, which can be both complete and incomplete' (ibid.). If the second and third clauses are indeed governed by the occurrence of *einai* at 901 D 1, then the question is whether the use of the verb in the three statements is semantically continuous or not, i.e. whether the author intends the same meaning in the use of the verb in each of the three statements. Another alternative is that the copulas required by the second and third clauses have been elided, as is standard practice in Greek, so that the verb for each is not provided by the earlier occurrence of *einai* but is simply absent, though understood. As Burnyeat acknowledges, the same point can be made in regard to *Theaet.* 185 A–D, where he claims to find a C2 use of *einai* ('Socrates', 11).

[16] I shall not discuss Brown's claim of a C2 use of the verb with the negative particle ('Being', 465–8), for two reasons. (1) Brown argues only that we *can* read τὸ μὴ ὄν in the way she suggests and not that the text compels it. (2) It is enough to show that there is not a C2 use of the verb without the negative particle: if there is no such use of *einai* it would hardly seem credible to suppose that a related use exists for its negation.

taking—but not the thing of which it partakes but something different' ('Being', 461). Now, Brown's interest in these lines is, in part, dialectical. Owen had argued that the verb in the second clause must be supplied from its predecessor, and since its use in the second is clearly incomplete, its use in the first must also be an incomplete one ('Not-Being', 442). Against Owen, Brown argued that even if we think that the verb in the second clause must be supplied from the first, it none the less does not follow that the use of the verb in the first clause cannot have been a complete one. For, if we suppose a C2 use of *estin* in the first clause, it is unproblematic to find it now completed in the second. 'Compare', she writes, ' "My sister is still teaching, but not French these days, only Spanish" ' (ibid.).

There are, however, three points to be made against the possible reading Brown identifies. First, the verb need not be supplied from the previous clause, but may simply be one of the frequent cases where the predicative *estin* is elided, though understood.[17] Second, this reading of 259 A 6–8 gives a sense to those lines that does not accord well with what the Stranger is doing in this part of the dialogue. At 259 A 6–8, in the course of providing a summary of the results from 254 C to 258 C, the Stranger is reviewing the conclusions of 255 E–256 E. There the Stranger repeatedly claimed that the specimen subject, Motion, was some property, F, through sharing in the Form F, while it was at the same time different from F, and thus not F. This pattern of reasoning was deployed to show that Motion both is the same and is not the same (256 A 3–B 4), is different and is not different (256 C 4–8), and was said to be sufficient to establish that Motion is both at rest and not at rest, had they not already agreed that Motion and Rest do not share in one another (256 B 6–C 2). He also reasoned that Motion *is not* because it is different from rest, though it *is* through participation in Being (255 E 11–256 A 2). Last, it was claimed that Motion is different from Being (256 D 5–7). This leads to the final, bold conclusion at 256 D 8–9 that Motion really is not being and is being, seeing that it shares in Being.[18] These results are then generalized: all the kinds share in Difference and Being (256 D 11–E 4), so that each is different and therefore not being, while each is at the same time (a) being.

Now the contrast drawn at 259 A 6–8, to which Brown refers, occurs in a statement embedded in a rather long sentence, in a

---

[17] See n. 15 above.   [18] ἡ κίνησις ὄντως οὐκ ὄν ἐστι καὶ ὄν.

passage that runs from 258 E 6 to 259 B 7. Placed in its immediate context, that statement (italicized in the translation) reads:

ὅτι συμμείγνυταί τε ἀλλήλοις τὰ γένη καὶ τό τε ὂν καὶ θάτερον διὰ πάντων καὶ δι' ἀλλήλων διεληλυθότε τὸ μὲν ἕτερον μετασχὸν τοῦ ὄντος ἔστι μὲν διὰ ταύτην τὴν μέθεξιν, οὐ μὴν ἐκεῖνό γε οὗ μετέσχεν ἀλλ' ἕτερον, ἕτερον δὲ τοῦ ὄντος ὂν ἔστι σαφέστατα ἐξ ἀνάγκης εἶναι μὴ ὄν.

[He, the critic, has to say] that the kinds blend with each other, that that which is and the different pervade all of them and each other, that *the different shares in that which is and so, because of that sharing is. But he won't say that it is that which it shares in, but that it is different,* and necessarily, because it is different from that which is, it clearly can be not being. (259 A 4–B I, trans. after White)

The point of the contrast, then, is not, as Brown's possible alternative reading implies, that Difference is being some unspecified property in so far as it is (as a result of participating in Being), which unspecified property turns out not to be being, but rather difference (just as one could turn out not to teach French, but rather Spanish). The point is rather that, since Difference shares in both Being and Difference (in relation to Being, in this case), it is both being and not being. The explicit statement here—that Difference is not that in which it shares but is different—has been foreshadowed by the earlier generalization of the results for the specimen subject Motion, and is designed to reinforce the fact that Difference, too, can be spoken of in both these ways, though not, after all, with the consequence of contradiction.

Third, given that at 259 A 4–B I the Stranger is summarizing the earlier results, both the first and second phrase in the contested lines point back to earlier conclusions. The first phrase, 'the Different, sharing in Being, is in virtue of that partaking', points back to 256 A I, while the second, 'but not what it participates in, but something different', points back to 256 D 8. There, having stated that Motion is different from Being, the Stranger boldly concluded: 'Motion is not being.' The backward references in the summary are, I submit, further reason to suppose that Plato elided the verb in the second phrase because he took it to be well understood from 256 D 8, and the general pattern of reasoning involving the negation leading up to it.

A further passage that Brown adduces to support her claim of a

C2 use of 'is' in the *Sophist* is 256 E 3–7. There she understands Plato to be drawing an inference from

(1) Each kind shares in being (256 E 3)

to

(2) There is much that each kind is (256 E 6).[19]

She claims that the 'intimate connection between (1) and (2) . . . is quite consistent with taking (1) to contain a complete, C2, use. Compare the inference from *Jane is teaching* to *Jane is teaching something*' ('Being', 473). The move is from each kind partaking in Being, as a result of which *each is*, to each kind *being something*, indeed many 'somethings'. Crucial to Brown's reading is the idea that, through participation in Being, the participant is something, but no one thing in particular. I would like to suggest, however, that the text for and immediately preceding (1) is most naturally read otherwise, as making the point that as a result of sharing in Being the participant is one property in particular, namely being. The text Brown reads as (2), moreover, is controversial, and is at least as easily taken as asserting that, considering each of the kinds, there are multiple cases of this one property, being.

Examination of 256 A–E shows that statements of the form '*X einai*' (250 A 11–12) or '*X estin*' (256 A 1–2) are being analysed by Plato as another way of saying that *X* is one of the beings—*X* is among *ta onta* (256 E 3–4 or, as in 256 D 8–9, '*X estin on*'). Significantly, statements of both forms are understood as explained by *X*'s participation in Being. Further, Plato seems to be deliberately employing the odd phrase '. . . *estin on*' in order to draw attention to the parallel between sharing in Being and sharing in each of the other kinds. For, throughout our passage, the Stranger says that Motion possesses some property or other as a result of participation in the corresponding Form. We have seen that he does this by way of declarative statements containing the copula and a nominal predicate, i.e. of the form 'Motion is *F*' (Motion is said to be the same because it shares in the Same, etc.). Towards the end of the passage, he says that Motion *estin on*, seeing that it shares in Being (256 D 8–9), even though he had earlier expressed the result of Motion's sharing in Being by simply saying that it is (256 A 1; cf. 254 D 10; 255 B 12).

[19] περὶ ἕκαστον ἄρα τῶν εἰδῶν πολὺ μέν ἐστι τὸ ὄν, ἄπειρον δὲ πλήθει τὸ μὴ ὄν.

I would like to suggest that, in using the parallel construction here, Plato is self-consciously employing the odd phrase '. . . *estin on*' to make the point emphatically that each of the kinds of the *Sophist* 'is *F*' as a result of participation in the *F*, for every case of *F* under discussion, including the case where *F* is the Form Being. That is, he is at pains to point out that the property being is a case that parallels the other properties they have just discussed: because Motion participates in Being, it possesses the property being as an attribute, just as with each of the other properties under discussion. And though the Greek is odd, it is not without precedent in the corpus. For other cases, see *Crat.* 421 A 8; *Phdr.* 247 E 2; *Tim.* 38 C 2. The statements at 256 D 8–9 and 256 E 3–4 that contain the unorthodox Greek, then, are to be read as further clarification of the result of Motion's participation in Being, and extend this result to all the kinds (*panta ta genē*, 256 D 12). This, in turn, strongly implies that the Stranger moves from statements of the form '*X estin*' to statements that bear just one completion ('*X estin on*') because the subject in each case possesses just one *particular* property, being. The move does not, then, seem to be analogous in the relevant respect to that from *Jane teaches* to *Jane teaches something*.

It must be admitted, though, that the text cannot be said to be inconsistent with that move. Even if every statement of the form '*X* is' in Greek can be completed as '*X* is (a) being', it does not follow that this is the only possible completion.[20] But for the text here to count as even weak evidence for Brown's C2 use, it ought to contain an indication of the idea that in so far as it is (or in so far as it partakes of Being), the subject is being something but no one thing in particular. The present point is that, so far, 256 A–E contains no such indication.

But what of 256 E 6–7, from which Brown derives (2): 'There is much that each kind is'? Certainly, as Brown reads it, the assertion implies that there are many properties that each kind has, though no particular property is specified. The Stranger does not reason in quite this way, however. For, as we saw, the Stranger moves from (1) participation in Being to (1*) being one of the beings. And from there he moves, at 256 E 6–7, to the conclusion (2*): 'So concerning each kind, what is is many, and what is not indefinite in number.' The interpretation of the conclusion is controversial, and a variety of options have been proposed. It could be read, with Brown, as

---

[20] I am grateful to David Sedley for drawing my attention to this point.

(2). Alternatively, following White, it could be read as the claim 'So as applied to each of the Forms, being is extensive, and not being is indefinite in quantity.'[21] A further consideration is that *to on* at 256 E 6 clearly picks up on *on* at D 9 and *onta* at E 4.[22] On Brown's interpretation of 256 E 6, the Stranger would appear to be making a claim that he is not strictly entitled to. For, in the preceding argument he has claimed only that each of the kinds discussed is (a) being as a result of participation in Being, not that each of them has many properties. On White's interpretation, by contrast, the Stranger's reasoning throughout 256 A–E appears to be that being, like the other properties discussed, is possessed by the subject as a result of participation in the corresponding Form, and since every one of the kinds shares in Being, the property being is quite extensive. Read this way, there is nothing in the text that suggests a C2 use of *estin* in (1).

I have been arguing that there is a paucity of evidence in the *Sophist* for Brown's reading. I shall now conclude the case against that reading with a consideration of one of the central arguments of the *Sophist*, which, I think, renders Brown's innovative suggestion doubtful. On her view, there are uses of the verb in nominal predicate expressions that go beyond the mere copula in meaning, and which carry existential force. This is the basis of the view that there is a semantic continuity between such statements as 'Motion is' and 'Motion is different'. Next, recall that this copulative use of the verb is significant for Plato in the *Sophist*, according to Brown, because it is this use, together with its semantically continuous C2 complete existential use, that the Stranger points to in the *kath' hauta/pros alla* distinction, in the course of his argument at 255 C–D that Being and Difference are distinct kinds.[23]

---

[21] N. White, *Plato:* Sophist (Indianapolis, 1993), 50. A further alternative, noted by Brown ('Being', 473 n. 31), is J. McDowell's 'in the case of each of the forms, what is (it) is multiple and what is not (it) is indefinite in number' ('Falsehood and Not Being', in M. Schofield and M. Nussbaum (eds.), *Language and Logos: Studies in Ancient Greek Philosophy Presented to G. E. L. Owen* (Cambridge, 1982), 115–34 at 125).

[22] Note too that the *to mē on* it contrasts with at E 7 clearly picks up on *ouk on* at D 8 and E 1, *to mē on* at D 11, and *ouk onta* at E 2.

[23] Brown reads Plato as appealing to the idea that the verb 'to be' in Greek has a complete C2 use *and* an incomplete use, where these uses are not merely homonymous but rather generate statements that exhibit semantic continuity. It is in this regard unlike the predicate expression '. . . is different . . .', which each time demands further completion, and this dissimilarity allows Plato to conclude that the corresponding Forms, Being and Difference, must be distinct ('Being', 474–7).

But we also saw above that it is a central argument of the dialogue that, for the Forms discussed, possession of a property is explained in terms of participation in the corresponding Form. For instance, the appropriate analysis of the statement 'Motion *is different* from the Same' (256 A 3)[24] is that Motion participates in the Different with respect to the Same (256 A 5; 256 B 2–4). Given this general analysis, if Plato considered *estin* in its use as the copula sometimes to possess a meaning that goes beyond the mere copula, we would expect the metaphysical state of affairs explaining statements containing the copula to include the Form Being. We would especially expect this if its use as the copula was critical to Plato's understanding of the Form Being and what sets Being apart from other Forms. But the explanations of statements containing the copula do not make reference to the Form Being. Instead, the Forms included in the various metaphysical states of affairs invoked by the Stranger to explain statements are limited each time to the Form or Forms corresponding to the predicate term in the statement (as well as the subject term), and do not extend to Being as what corresponds to the copula.[25] Of course it is true, as we have seen, that the Form Being figures in the metaphysical state of affairs that the Stranger describes as explanatory of the statements 'Motion is' and 'Motion is (a) being'. In the statement 'Motion is', however, the verb is not functioning as the copula, while in the statement 'Motion is (a) being', it appears that it is not the verb but the complement '*on*' (256 D 8–9; '*onta*' 256 E 3–4) which corresponds to the Form Being, while the copula merely connects the subject to the predicate.

I have argued that Malcolm's arguments against Brown's reading of *einai* in the *Sophist* are ultimately unconvincing. None the less, I hope to have shown that Brown's reading receives insufficient support from the relevant passages, and is even rendered doubtful by a central argument of that work. If this is right, the contention that *einai* has a C2 complete use in the *Sophist*—a use referred to in the *kath' hauta/pros alla* distinction at 255 C 14—will turn out to be at best improbable, and at worst defeated.

Monash University and King's College London

----

[24] ἡ κίνησις ἕτερον ταὐτοῦ ἐστιν.

[25] 255 E 4–5; 256 A 3–B 4; cf. 256 B 6–10, 256 C 4–5.

BIBLIOGRAPHY

Brown, L., 'Being in the *Sophist*: A Syntactical Enquiry' ['Being'], *Oxford Studies in Ancient Philosophy*, 4 (1986), 49–70; repr. with revisions in G. Fine (ed.), *Plato 1: Metaphysics and Epistemology* (Oxford, 1999), 455–78.

—— 'The Verb "to be" in Greek Philosophy: Some Remarks' ['Verb'], in S. Everson (ed.), *Language* (Companions to Ancient Thought, 3; Cambridge, 1994), 212–36.

Burnyeat, M., '*Apology* 30 B 2–4: Socrates, Money, and the Grammar of γιγνέσθαι' ['Socrates'], *Journal of Hellenic Studies*, 123 (2003), 1–25.

Frede, M., *Prädikation und Existenzaussage* (Hypomnemata, 18; Göttingen, 1967).

Hestir, B., 'A "Conception" of Truth in Plato's *Sophist*', *Journal of the History of Philosophy*, 41 (2003), 1–24.

Kahn, C., 'A Return to the Theory of the Verb *be* and the Concept of Being' ['Return'], *Ancient Philosophy*, 24 (2004), 381–405.

—— 'Some Philosophical Uses of "to be" in Plato' ['Uses'], *Phronesis*, 26 (1981), 105–34.

—— *The Verb 'Be' in Ancient Greek* (Indianapolis, 2003) (repr. of the first edition (Dordrecht, 1973), with a new introduction).

McDowell, J., 'Falsehood and Not Being', in M. Schofield and M. Nussbaum (eds.), *Language and Logos: Studies in Ancient Greek Philosophy Presented to G. E. L. Owen* (Cambridge, 1982), 115–34.

Malcolm, J., 'Some Cautionary Remarks on the 'is'/'teaches' Analogy' ['Remarks'], *Oxford Studies in Ancient Philosophy*, 31 (2006), 281–96.

Owen, G. E. L., 'Plato on Not-Being' ['Not-Being'], in G. Vlastos (ed.), *Plato: A Collection of Critical Essays*, i. *Metaphysics and Epistemology* (Garden City, NY, 1971), 223–67; repr. in G. Fine (ed.), *Plato 1: Metaphysics and Epistemology* (Oxford, 1999), 416–54.

Van Eck, J., 'Not-Being and Difference: On Plato's *Sophist* 256 D 5–258 E 3', *Oxford Studies in Ancient Philosophy*, 23 (2002), 63–84.

White, N., *Plato: Sophist* (Indianapolis, 1993).

'WHAT'S THE MATTER
WITH PRIME MATTER?'

FRANK A. LEWIS

[T]he problem of interpreting what Aristotle has to say about
'first matter' . . . takes us to the very heart of his metaphysics. A
mistake here has repercussions throughout the interpretation
of his system just as a twitch in the human heart sets the whole
body in motion.   (WILFRID SELLARS)[1]

1. Introduction

CRITICS of the notion of prime matter traditionally found in Aristotle have challenged not only its coherence, but also the very pro-
priety of the attribution to Aristotle. In this paper I argue that
prime matter has a real place in Aristotle's metaphysics, and that
much if not all of the traditional view of it is genuinely his. I place
my account in the broader context of what it means, in general, to
say of something that it counts as matter, prime or otherwise. As I
see it, Aristotle's views can best be framed in terms of what satisfies
the property of being matter, conceived as a second-level functional
property. This is admittedly a philosophical reconstruction rather
than a direct account of Aristotle's ideas; and the reconstruction
I offer does not extend to a defence of 'bare substrate' theory as
such. But I do mean to defend the 'fit' of prime matter, much as
traditionally conceived, in what I take to be its Aristotelian context.
I begin with some main features of the traditional view, along with
their apparently Aristotelian credentials.

© Frank A. Lewis 2008
I am grateful to David Charles, David Sedley, and Michael Wedin for their characteristically generous help. Thanks are due also to David Manley, Amanda Printz,
and Jeff Pryor for valuable written comments. The flaws that remain should not be
laid at the door of any of these, except possibly Wedin.

[1] 'Aristotle's Metaphysics: An Interpretation' ['Interpretation'], in id., *Philosophical Perspectives* (Springfield, Ill., 1967), 73–124 at 83.

2. The traditional view

Foremost among the components of the traditional view is *persistence*. For Aristotle, the coming to be of a thing cannot be from nothing, as Parmenides alleged, and its destruction cannot be into nothing; so we are to suppose that there is a substratum of change—in accidental change and in cases of genuine coming to be and destruction alike—that persists through the exchange of contraries. The existence of a substratum of change is one of the first principles of natural philosophy set out in *Physics* 1:

> from all things that come to be, we can gather this . . ., that there must in every case [ἀεί] be something that underlies. . . . It is clear that there must be something that underlies the opposites, and that the opposites must be two. (*Phys.* 1. 7, 190ᵃ13–15, 191ᵃ4–5)[2]

Prime matter is, supposedly, one more instance of this general principle. If, in general, the coming to be and destruction of things is analysed in terms of a substratum that persists through the exchange of contraries, then the same analysis should apply at the lowest level of the sublunary universe, in our account of the mutual transformation of the elements, in which one element is destroyed and a second comes to be.[3] What persists through changes of this last kind, on the received view, is prime matter.[4]

If prime matter persists, however, it does so without in any ordi-

---

[2] Cf. *Phys.* 1. 9, 192ᵃ3–ᵇ34, and the summaries at (for example) *GC* 1. 2, 317ᵃ23–7, and *Metaph.* Λ 1–2, 1069ᵇ3–9, and *H* 5, 1044ᵇ27–9.

[3] In addition to two varieties of one–one transformations (one easier, the other more difficult and slower), Aristotle recognizes a third set of cases, in which two elements together give way to a third. The mutual transformation of the elements is the topic of the early chapters of *GC* 2, also *De caelo* 3. 6; see also n. 9 below.

[4] Aristotle appears committed to this concept of prime matter above all in the early chapters of *GC* 2: see especially 2. 1, 329ᵃ24–ᵇ6; 2. 7, 334ᵃ16–18, 24–5, and compare the reference back at *Meteor.* 1. 3, 339ᵃ36–ᵇ3; see also *De caelo* 4. 5, 312ᵃ30–ᵇ1, quoted in sect. 6(*a*) below. Many of the relevant passages from *De generatione et corruptione* and elsewhere are conveniently collected and discussed in the appendices to W. Charlton, *Aristotle:* Physics, Books I and II [*Physics*] (Oxford, 1970)), and to C. J. F. Williams, *Aristotle's* De generatione et corruptione [*De generatione*] (Oxford, 1982). Sceptics as to whether the notion of prime matter is really present in Aristotle, in addition to Charlton, include M. Furth, *Substance, Form and Psyche: An Aristotelian Metaphysics* [*Aristotelian*] (Cambridge, 1988), and M. L. Gill, *Aristotle on Substance: The Paradox of Unity* [*Paradox*] (Princeton, 1989). Believers, in addition to Williams, include H. H. Joachim, *Aristotle:* On Coming-to-Be and Passing-Away [*Coming-to-Be*] (Oxford, 1922), H. M. Robinson, 'Prime Matter in Aristotle', *Phronesis*, 19 (1974), 168–98, and, most

nary sense a qualitative nature of its own. According to Aristotle, prime matter is something that is 'matter for the perceptible bodies', but is itself only 'perceptible body in potentiality' (*GC* 2. 1, 329^{a}24–5, 33). More generally, it is not anything in itself, and *a fortiori*, it does not fall under any of the categories (*Metaph. Z* 3, 1029^{a}20–3, 24–6). But like matter in general, it has the capacity for being and for not being (*GC* 2. 9, 335^{a}32–^{b}6; *Metaph. Z* 15, 1039^{b}27–31)—in particular, it is receptive of the elemental contraries, hot, cold, wet, dry, as the so-called elements, earth, air, fire, water, come to be and are destroyed in the course of their mutual transformation.

The various elemental contraries, hot, cold, and the rest, are occurrent properties of prime matter, and are all accidental to it. Meanwhile, its essential properties include the corresponding dispositional properties: it essentially has the capacity to receive this or that elemental contrary.[5]

At the same time, prime matter by definition itself *has no matter*— as *prime* matter, it is not itself a compound of form and matter—so it cannot be subject to generation or destruction. These various ideas are summed up in the traditional account of prime matter, championed famously by Zeller, as the eternal substratum for all change: prime matter is 'that which is nothing, but can become everything—the Subject, namely, or substratum, to which no one

recently, D. Bostock, 'Aristotle's Theory of Matter' ['Theory'], in D. Sfendoni-Mentzou, J. Hattiangadi, and D. Johnson (eds.), *Aristotle and Contemporary Science*, ii (New York, 2001), 3–22, repr. in Bostock, *Space, Time, Matter, and Form* (Oxford, 2006), 30–47, and D. Charles, 'Simple Genesis and Prime Matter' ['Genesis'], in F. de Haas and J. Mansfeld (eds.), *Aristotle: On Generation and Corruption, Book II* (Oxford, 2004), 151–69. K. Fine, 'Aristotle on Matter' ['Matter'], *Mind*, NS 101 (1992), 35–57 at 40–2, recognizes an Aristotelian notion of *ultimate matter*, resting on his Foundation and Transitivity Axioms, but he declines to speculate whether ultimate matter should be identified with prime matter as traditionally conceived.

[5] Sellars, 'Interpretation', 87–8, is helpful here, and answers in advance Williams's worry (*De generatione*, 219), that if Aristotle's prime matter is 'nothing in actuality', then 'what is actually nothing is nothing'. Much the same puzzle has been set (in correspondence) by Michael Wedin. If prime matter is mere potentiality, how can it ever be actually anything? How can the prime matter that is the matter of a quantity of fire (say) be both actually hot, and also mere potentiality? To say that prime matter is mere potentiality, I take it, is to say that its essential properties are all dispositional—that it has no occurrent essential properties. So the potentialities of prime matter can be realized; but the occurrent properties that realize them will be accidental rather than essential to the underlying prime matter. For further essential properties of prime matter, some of them not dispositional, see n. 19 below.

of all the thinkable predicates belongs, but which precisely on that account is equally receptive of them all'.[6]

One correction to Zeller's formulation is by now standard: Aristotle's concept of prime matter does not commit him to a 'featureless bearer of properties', but to something that is a bearer of properties but (with certain exceptions) has no *occurrent* features *of its own*.[7] But the idea that prime matter is the substratum of *all* change is also open to question (it is, arguably, the controversial result of a polemical argument in *Metaphysics Z* 3).[8] I shall ignore this broader claim about prime matter in favour of the following, more restrictive view about its role as the substratum of elemental change. For clarity, take a case of the transformation of a given amount, E, of earth into an amount, F, of fire. Suppose that E is a compound of matter, m_1, and a form, cd, composed of the two contraries cold and dry: where '+' is the sign for the application of form to matter,

$$E = m_1 + (cd).$$

Similarly, suppose that the resulting amount of fire, F, is a compound of matter, m_2, and the contraries hot and dry, hd:

$$F = m_2 + (hd).$$

The transformation of E into F results from the 'flipping' of the contrary, c, as it is replaced by its contrary, h. The remaining contrary, d, meanwhile, 'jumps', and is present in both E and F. On the traditional view of the persistence of prime matter, finally, we are to suppose that $m_1 = m_2$. And if all cases of transformation among the elements follow a similar pattern, we can generalize from this single example to suppose that in every case where one element transforms into some new element, the matter of the beginning element is *identical* with the matter of the element that results.[9]

---

[6] E. Zeller, *Aristotle and the Earlier Peripatetics* [*Peripatetics*] (2 vols; London, 1897), i. 247, quoted in Charlton, *Physics*, 129.

[7] For qualifications to the claim that prime matter has no essential properties, see two paragraphs above in the main text, and n. 19 below.

[8] In sect. 6(*b*) below I argue that key elements in *Z* 3 are strictly in the service of the *reductio* under way in the chapter, and not a part of Aristotle's official theory. This (to my mind overblown) conception of prime matter is firmly embedded in the later tradition, however (Charlton *Physics*, 141–5).

[9] We should leave room also for the case where two elements together are transformed into one, *GC* 2. 4, 331^{b}11–26; here, presumably, the matters of the two be-

Prime matter is not, then, the subject of *all* change, as Zeller claimed. It is properly subject only to the different elemental contraries (and only indirectly to the higher-level forms in the constitution of a thing; and not at all to its accidents: see Section 6(*b*) below). But if we can imagine a given portion of one element transforming into a portion of another, and from here on and then back through the cycle of transformations, in isolation from the elemental transformations and changes going on around it, *one and the same* amount of prime matter will underlie all the transformations in the history of the elemental portion we began with.[10]

Finally, the traditional concept of prime matter fits within a broader picture of matter and form, and of their place in the Aristotelian 'scale of being'. Prime matter is the limiting case of the notion of matter, which applies throughout the sublunary sphere, and is absent only outside the sublunary world altogether, in the case of the Unmoved Mover, which is itself the limiting case of the

ginning elements merge. Among the one–one elemental transformations, meanwhile, there are the 'slow' as well as the 'quick' cases to consider; the slow, 'leapfrogging' cases will be important in sect. 3 below.

[10] Our main theme here is persistence, but other worries concerning prime matter as traditionally conceived warrant mention. We have seen that prime matter cannot in the ordinary way be perceived; more broadly, it has no qualitative nature of its own, so that it resists any material specification in its own right—what, then, could count as empirical evidence in its favour? Prime matter as traditionally conceived can in a way be materially specified, and can in a way be perceived, if we suppose that the specification and the perception are both *indirect*. Thus, we perceive the matter, m_1, of E indirectly when we perceive E ($= m_1 + (cd)$). Although the parallel is hardly exact, it is worth recalling that when we perceive something that is neither the special object of a single sense—a colour or a sound, for example—nor a common sensible—motion, rest, number, figure, size—our perception of it is 'accidental' or 'indirect', as when the white thing we perceive is Diares' son (*DA* 2. 6, 418^{a}9, 20–5; cf. 3. 1, 425^{a}24–7). Similarly, m_1 is a constituent in the form–matter compound, E (say), and like E itself, m_1 can be materially specified by way of the contraries c and d, that along with m_1 enter into the composition of E.

At the same time, Aristotle may think that there is some empirical basis—even if at one remove—for a theory of prime matter as conventionally conceived. He works hard to establish an empirical basis for the mutual transformation of the elements, and in particular, for the view about the tangible contraries that shapes his account of the constitution and transformability of the (in his view) inappropriately named elements or simple bodies. For appeals to empirical evidence, see e.g. *GC* 2. 3, 330^{b}1–7, with Joachim's note (*Coming-to-Be*, 213); 2. 4, 331^{b}24–6; and *De caelo* 3. 6, 304^{b}26–7 ('we see fire and water and each of the simple bodies being dissolved'). If we can observe the elements transforming, as Aristotle supposes we can, and if prime matter is required as a constituent in the elements if transformation is to take place, as on the conventional view he also supposes, then to this extent prime matter too has, albeit indirectly, a basis in empirically supported fact. For difficulties involving persistence, see n. 15 below.

correlative notion of form.[11] The Unmoved Mover is the *limiting* case of form, on the usual view, because all engagement with matter is absent from it. Just so, prime matter is the limiting case of matter, because all engagement with form is absent—of all the cases of matter, prime matter alone is not itself a compound of form and matter.

At the same time, because the Unmoved Mover has no constitutive matter, it has no shred of potentiality, but as Aristotle describes it, it is pure actuality: the activity of thinking, engaged in thinking its own activity of thinking. And because prime matter has no constitutive form, in a certain sense it exhibits the maximum degree of potentiality: the potentiality for one or other of the four elements, each of which in turn has the potentiality for elemental transformation, and beyond that, indirectly, for being mixed with the other elements into one or other uniform stuff; and so on all the way up to the living substances of nature (Section 6(*a*) below).

3. Persistence and Parmenides: 'jumping' and 'flipping', and the varieties of continuity

Behind issues of persistence, as we have seen, there lurks the figure of Parmenides. In our example of the transformation of E to F, where $E = m_1 + cd$, the contrary, d, is part of both the initial E and the resultant, F, while c that helped characterize E is now replaced in F by h. On the traditional account, $F = m_2 + hd$, and $m_1 = m_2$. Suppose, however, that $m_1 \neq m_2$, or even that there is no such thing as m_1 or m_2—that there is no material substrate at all. How, in the absence of a single persisting material substrate, can d 'jump' from E to F? And there is an equal difficulty with 'flipping', when the contrary, c, is replaced by its contrary, h.[12] Without the notion of constituent-continuity offered by a persisting material substrate, what sense is there to the claim that c (from E) is replaced by h (in F)? As Aristotle supposedly concludes in *Physics* 1, in part in response to Parmenides, an exchange of contraries requires a persisting substratum, on pain of genesis from, or destruction into, nothing.

On some accounts, the difficulty is lessened if we note that the

---

[11] This view too has been controverted: see, most recently, M. Burnyeat, *A Map of* Metaphysics *Zeta* (Pittsburgh, 2001), 130.

[12] The difficulties of 'jumping' are discussed in Charles, 'Genesis', 163. 'Flipping' and 'leapfrogging' (n. 14 below) are my contributions to the debate.

contraries in E, F, and the rest come in pairs, so that the switching of powers from c to h (say) can be stepwise, while the remaining contrary stays put. This is the thought that motivates the property-continuity version of constituent-continuity put forward by Furth and Gill, for example, who reject the version of constituent-continuity embodied in the traditional view of prime matter. In place of the traditional view, that $E = m_1 + (cd)$, we are to suppose that, instead, $E = (cd)$.[13] If, then, the switching of powers is always stepwise, does this give sufficient continuity for us to make sense of both jumping (where a contrary carries over from E to F) and flipping (where a contrary present in E is replaced in F), even in the absence of a persisting material substrate?

I am doubtful that the stepwise assumption meets the difficulty. But the merits of the stepwise hypothesis are moot, given Aristotle's view that in some cases both contraries 'flip' together, so that no contraries 'jump'. Instead, all are lost at once in the transformation of a quantity of fire into water, for example (where dry and hot give way to moist and cold), or earth into air (dry and cold, moist and hot).[14] On the Furth–Gill account, given their rejection of prime matter, constituent-continuity fails altogether in these cases, and nothing persists through the change.

Charles openly drops the commitment to constituent-continuity, while replacing it with a novel account of property-continuity. In Aristotle's view, in elemental transformation 'the whole changes, nothing perceptible remaining as the same underlier' (Charles, 'Genesis', 160–1). That is, we are to suppose, no *one* perceptible thing underlies both the destruction of E and the genesis of F: instead, there can be *two* perceptible underliers, m_1 and m_2, where

[13] Furth, *Aristotelian*, and Gill, *Paradox*. In essence, these commentators change this part of Aristotle's theory from (apparently) a version of Bare Substrate Theory to a version of Bundle Theory—on the face of it, moving Aristotle from the frying pan straight into the fire.

[14] Think of this (the slower and more difficult variety of transformation, *GC* 2. 4, 331^a20–3, $^b4$–11) as 'leapfrogging' from one element *over* an intervening element to the next-but-one element in line (from fire *over* water to air, for example) in the cycle of transformations Aristotle describes. These new cases are not merely compounds of successive steps of the simple, 'one contrary at a time' transformations already recognized—if they were, why bother mentioning them? Again, transformation among elements takes place under the influence of the contraries in surrounding elements, and there is no reason in principle why both contraries in a given element should not be simultaneously under threat from the immediate environment. But if the new transformations genuinely take place 'all at once', then no contrary 'hangs on' during the change in such a way as to give property-continuity.

$m_1 \neq m_2.$[15] At the same time, in addition to m_1 and m_2, there exists some *other* entity, call it μ, which does persist through the change from E to F, and in virtue of which m_1 and m_2 alike are capable of receiving contraries in the course of elemental change. As Charles sees it, μ—which he identifies with prime matter—is an abstract, even 'logical', object, to be construed, perhaps, along the lines of Fine's arbitrary objects, which serve as the denotation of the variables in the open sentences of quantifier logic.[16] In contrast to more conventional versions of property-continuity, what persists, the logical object, μ, is not a constituent of E or of F at all, not even in the sense in which the contraries c, h, and d are constituents of E and F, but an abstract object that is realized successively by m_1 and $m_2.$[17]

But if μ is removed to this degree from the constitution of E and of F, how does the existence of μ help with the difficulties of jumping and flipping? Contraries jump, or flip, *across elements*: but why suppose that because the matter of the first element, E, realizes the same property, μ, as does the matter of the second, F, therefore E has been *transformed* into F, rather than having been *replaced* by it? What is there about the property conferred by Charles's candidate, μ, for prime matter that supports continuity across change in the way Aristotle wants?

According to Charles, μ, the logical object, is 'that which receives

---

[15] Charles's view that $m_1 \neq m_2$ is a striking departure from the persistence requirement that is central to the traditional view. It also challenges the non-Aristotelian idea that Bare Substratum Theory provides a principle of 'numerical diversity' to meet the objection that Bundle Theory (sans substratum) is committed to the truth of the identity of indiscernibles. On some conceptions of prime matter, the challenge to a principle of numerical diversity is especially damaging. If, for example, we think of prime matter in itself as pure indeterminate extension (*Phys.* 4. 1, 209ª4–6, cf. 4. 2, 209ª9–11; cf. F. A. Lewis, *Substance and Predication in Aristotle* [*Substance*] (Cambridge, 1991), 291), how can it come in 'amounts', except in so far as it is captured by some suitable contrary-pair? For other worries about how prime matter can intelligibly be thought to persist under the conditions described, see now Bostock, 'Theory'. As Bostock suggests (p. 45), Aristotle may be in the grip of a paradigm that is blind to such difficulties.

[16] K. Fine, *Reasoning with Arbitrary Objects* [*Reasoning*] (Oxford, 1985).

[17] Properly speaking, one might think, μ and μ alone is prime matter. At the same time, however, Charles suggests that in virtue of 'realizing' μ as the matter for the destruction of E in the transformation from E into F, m_1 counts as prime matter for the destruction of E; by the same token, the matter, m_2, for the genesis of F will count as prime matter relative to this second change. Thus, different perceptible matters count as prime matters on different occasions, as they successively 'represent' or 'constitute' the logical object, μ.

genesis and destruction in material change' ('Genesis', 158). This cannot mean that μ itself receives the contraries involved in genesis and destruction: rather, this is the feature that μ confers on the various matters, m_1, m_2, and the rest, that realize μ. Does μ make it possible, *at the level of the elements*, that one and the same thing receives both the contrary responsible for the destruction of E, and the contrary responsible for the genesis of F?

In a word, no. Consider the matter, m_1, of E. For as long as E exists, m_1 exercises the capacity for exhibiting the contrary-pair, cd, distinctive of E. At the same time, m_1 is capable of losing the contrary, c, if E is transformed into F: in this way, m_1 is capable of entering into the destruction of E. Similarly, once F exists, its matter, m_2, realizes the capacity for exhibiting the contraries distinctive of F, and is capable of losing one or other of those contraries upon some further transformation—m_2 is capable of entering into the destruction of F. So we may perhaps trace to the logical object, μ, both the capacity in m_1 for constituting E and for its destruction, and the capacity in m_2 for constituting F and for the destruction of F. But if we suppose, with Charles, that $m_1 \neq m_2$, there is no route to the conclusion that m_1 also has the capacity for the generation of F, or that m_2 also has the capacity for the destruction of E. On this showing, the capacities conferred by μ are not enough to show how the destruction of E is linked to the generation of F. The threat from Parmenides remains: on the present showing, Aristotle cannot distinguish transformation among the elements from coming to be from, and perishing into, nothing.[18]

---

[18] Charles returns repeatedly to an analogy to argue his case. We are to contrast the logical, even arbitrary, object, which is individual but non-material, referred to by 'the President', with the individual material objects, Mr Clinton and Mr Bush, for example, that fall in the range associated with that arbitrary object. The President is an abstract object that is constituted by various individual material objects, Mr Clinton, Mr Bush, and the rest, at different times (for the 'constitution' language, see Charles, 'Genesis', 154). Importantly, the abstract object has all the properties common to the individuals that fall in the range associated with the abstract object. The properties are the various (constitutional rather than Aristotelian) powers of the President—the ability to sign laws, to nominate judges, and so on—and the same set of powers (or virtually the same set) is transferred in turn from Mr Clinton to Mr Bush, and so on. So it is the abstract object, with the same (or nearly the same) set of powers, that gives the continuity that binds together the different people in the one office.

Is this version of continuity sufficiently robust to explain elemental transformation in a way that keeps Parmenides at bay? The account explains the sense in which one man succeeds the other in the same office. But in the target Aristotelian case, it is not enough to say that F *succeeds* E in the cycle of elemental transformations. In the

At this point, we might be tempted to shift our ground, and suppose that the old way of answering Parmenides has been superseded in Aristotle's eyes, and that he is engaged in 'a systematic attempt to modify his *Physics*-style view' about persistence (Charles, 'Genesis', 165). Without doubt, as Charles points out, the *Physics*' view is under pressure from the account of mixing (*GC* 1. 10 and 2. 7–8), where Aristotle concedes that there is no actually persisting material substratum. But still, Aristotle insists that the earth, air, fire, and water that are the initial matter of a mixture are *present potentially* in the result of mixing. The saying here is dark, but it is arguably his attempt to preserve the *Physics*' requirement with a version of constituent-continuity, rather than the wholesale move to the property-continuity view that Charles recommends.

The *Physics*' view of a matter that persists through change is also under pressure from the idea that what serves as matter in certain cases is not independent of the form in the way that the *Physics* apparently requires. On the new view, the matter of a man is a living body, living organs and all, so that flesh and bones and the rest, without soul, are only *homonymously* a body and the like. On this view, the matter cannot exist outside the compound of body and soul in the way the *Physics* seems to require. It is controversial whether these different views of matter can be fitted together, and if so how. But in the absence of a clear resolution of this controversy, there is little warrant here for the conclusion that Aristotle has altogether abandoned the *Physics*' constraints on genesis and destruction.

4. An alternative account: the functional-property view

I shall now defend something like a traditional account of prime matter, but against the background of a fresh understanding of what it means for anything at any level, prime matter or above, to count as matter.

Prime matter, as traditionally conceived, is what underlies the

---

course of elemental transformation, E is destroyed and F comes to be. But we must show that E is not destroyed into nothing, but into F; and that F does not come to be from nothing, but from E: in short, that the one is *transformed* into the other. But ascension to, and exit from, the White House require neither the destruction of the one man nor the coming to be of the other, much less the transformation of one into the other, and as Charles himself acknowledges ('Genesis', 164), his analogy offers only the succession of otherwise persisting individuals in the same constitutional office.

elemental contraries in the cycle of generation and destruction that constitutes the mutual transformation of the elements. More broadly, concerning matter in general, 'what is most properly matter is the substratum that is receptive of generation and destruction' (*GC* 1. 4, 320^{a}2–5; cf. *Meteor.* 4. 1, 378^{b}27–379^{a}1).

As the rich world of Aristotelian biology amply shows, various stuffs and structures, at various levels of complexity, count as matter. Two questions now arise. First, what counts as matter will vary according to context: how are we to explain the variation, so that these are *different* cases of matter? Second, what stays constant, so that they are all cases of *matter*?

Above all, matter is not itself a kind of stuff, or a kind of structure, in addition to the standard stuffs and structures—fire, flesh, flesh-and-bones—found among changeable objects. Rather, we can usefully think of matter, in the standard case, in terms of *the property the standard stuffs or structures of the changeable world must have* in order to count as matter. Any number of the standard stuffs and structures of the changeable world will have the property of being matter if the right conditions are met; and we understand Aristotle's notion of matter best if we understand the special nature of this property.

Prime matter is the limiting case of matter and, hence, still matter: so prime matter too is not a kind of stuff in addition to the standard stuffs that make up the material universe. In fact, none of the stuffs or structures among changeable objects has the property of being prime matter. Instead, what counts as prime matter is not any kind of stuff or structure at all—it has no features of its own, beyond that it is matter and, hence, that it is capable of receiving contraries in generation and destruction;[19] and because this is *prime* matter, the contraries come two at a time, one from each of the two *elemental* contrary-pairs hot–cold, moist–dry. In this way

[19] As before (sect. 2 and n. 5 above), while prime matter has no features of its own, in particular if none of the elemental contraries belongs to prime matter 'in itself', still it is essential to prime matter that it be capable of receiving the elemental contraries, two at a time, and essential to it too that it have the second-level functional property of being (prime) matter, as explained later in this section. Other features too, no doubt, are essential to prime matter: for example, what is prime matter in one form–matter compound, my chair (say), cannot simultaneously be prime matter in some other discrete compound (my table). The point is adapted from M. J. Loux, *Metaphysics: A Contemporary Introduction*, 2nd edn. (London and New York, 2002), 121–3, where other examples may also be found.

every amount of each of the four elements, earth, air, fire, water, has some amount of prime matter as a constituent.

I have said that Aristotle's notion of matter is best understood by way of the single property, being matter, that applies at different levels among changeable objects. The different cases of matter count as matter in fundamentally different ways; yet in a certain way the same properties warrant the description of something as matter in each of the different cases. In part, this is a question of the same property, being matter, being realized in a variety of contexts. But the differences among the different realizations go beyond the differences among the items that count as matter. I propose that we best think of being matter as a *second-level functional* property: the (single) property of having some property or other—different in different cases—that plays a certain causal role in coming to be and destruction.

A functional property of a subject, X, is not a property of the *properties of X*; it is a second-level property of X that *it*, X, have a property or properties that satisfy a certain specified condition.[20] So there are two things to keep track of: the functional property in question, including the condition it imposes on the property or properties of X; and the property or properties of X that are constrained by the condition specified by the functional property. Thus, in the case of matter, we have:

(i) *The second-level functional property of being matter*: the property, belonging typically to a given structure or stuff, s, of s's having some property or properties that will cause s to be made to constitute a thing of a certain kind, under the appropriate realization conditions—or that will cause s to be made to cease to constitute a thing of the given kind, under suitably adverse circumstances.

(ii) *This or that capacity for receiving and losing the relevant contraries in a given case of coming to be or destruction*; the capacity in

---

[20] With J. Heil, 'Properties and Powers' ['Powers'], *Oxford Studies in Metaphysics*, 1 (2004), 223–54, I shall say that the functional property, on this view, counts as a second-*level* property of X (a property that X possesses in virtue of possessing some lower-level 'realizing' property), but not a second-*order* property (a property of some lower-level property). The view of functional properties as second-level in this sense follows the received view due to E. W. Prior, R. Pargetter, and F. Jackson, 'Three Theses about Dispositions', *American Philosophical Quarterly*, 19 (1982), 251–7. While the functional-property idea by itself in my account of Aristotelian matter is, as best as I can make it, non-negotiable, the 'higher-level' view is not; other treatments of functional properties as first-level properties are also on the market (see the discussion in Heil).

question will be a property of the structure or stuff to which the functional property belongs, and it is the property that realizes the causal role specified in the functional property.[21]

I shall suppose that a stuff or structure, s, has the second-level functional property described in (i) *in virtue of* having the relevant first-level causal properties described in (ii).[22]

The functional property in (i) and the condition it imposes on the properties of different stuffs or structures both remain the same across cases; but the capacity for receiving or losing contraries in (ii) will vary in its specifics from case to case, depending on the identity of the stuff or structure involved, and on the kind of item that comes to be or is destroyed.

The variation across cases that the notion of a functional property tolerates is a major virtue of the functional-property account.[23]

---

[21] The first-level causal properties of X are *passive* powers for being made into a thing of a given kind ('matter *qua* matter is capable of being acted on': *GC* 1. 7, 324^{b}18). Corresponding to a given passive power of X is the *active* power, lodged in the agent, for imposing the form that typifies the kind of the product that comes to be. For the two powers to be actualized, what has the active power and what has the passive power must be 'together' or otherwise in suitable proximity (*Phys.* 8. 4, 255^{a}34–^{b}1; *GC* 1. 7, 324^{b}13–18; *De long. vit.* 3, 465^{b}15–16); and the two powers must be *suited* to each other and to the product in various ways (*De caelo* 4. 3, 311^{a}4–6; *DA* 3. 5, 430^{a}10–13; *MA* 8, 702^{a}10–15, 20–1; *GA* 2. 4, 740^{b}22–6; *Metaph.* Θ 5, 1048^{a}5–7). As for the capacity for receiving or for losing a given contrary: if it is right that this is a single capacity, Aristotle will often regard receiving the form as a positive outcome, and losing it (or taking on its privation) as a degenerate exercise of the same capacity; see n. 30 below.

[22] I am indebted here to a remark by David Manley.

[23] The appeal to functional properties and the variation across cases it allows renders in a different way a significant feature of Charles's account, rooted in his comparison between Aristotle's discussion of matter and his discussion of time. According to Charles, the distinction between the logical object, μ, which he identifies with prime matter, and the different matters, m_1 and m_2, that underlie E and F respectively, can be compared with Aristotle's distinction between 'the now' *tout court*—also a logical object, according to Charles—and the now of Caesar's birth, the now of Caesar's death, and the rest (*Phys.* 4. 11 and 14). In both cases the same logical object is realized in a variety of different concrete circumstances. There is a quite different way of representing this feature of Aristotle's discussion of time, which Charles does not comment on. We may note that the term 'now' is an indexical; and while it has a lexical meaning (Aristotle's 'what divides before and after in change', for example), it does not pick out a specific time until the proper reference to context is added: 'now' uttered at the time of Caesar's death. The *indexicality* of 'now' corresponds to the variation across cases allowed for by the functional-property account in the main text. Ironically, one of the main examples Charles uses to press his 'arbitrary object' account, that of the President of the United States, is almost verbatim a textbook example of a functional property: J. Heil, *Philosophy of Mind: A Contemporary Introduction* [*Mind*], 2nd edn. (New York and London, 2004), 96–7.

Bronze, for example, and bricks and timbers, both qualify as matter[24]—both alike have the functional property that they have some capacity or other that plays a certain causal role in the coming to be or destruction of something. As for the capacity in question, this will be a *passive* power—the power to be acted on in such a way as to be made to receive or to lose the appropriate contrary or form, so that the bronze or the bricks and timbers are made to constitute a thing of a certain kind, or so that they cease to constitute the thing, under the appropriately adverse circumstances. But the passive power differs in the two cases: the passive powers of the bronze leave it open to being made into a statue; those of the bricks and timbers to their being developed into a house.

In addition to the bronze or the bricks and timbers, we will need the craftsman, with the corresponding active power for imposing the form that typifies his product. For the connections between what counts as matter, and the relevant active and passive powers, see e.g. *Metaph.* Θ 1, 1046[a]22–8 (cf. n. 21 above).

Beyond the notion of *matter*, there is that of the *proximate matter* of a thing, and finally, that of *prime matter*. Once the statue is made, for example, the result is (at least for the sake of the example) a substance:[25] it is a compound of form and matter, but it is not itself the matter for anything further. In this case, the bronze is *proximate* matter to the form of a statue as *substantial* form.[26] The passive causal powers of the bronze that bring us to think of it as being matter, let us suppose, lead directly to the statue—no intermediate matter lies in between—and those powers are exhausted when the statue is done.[27] At a lower level of complexity, by contrast, water

---

[24] For the record, not only a single item, but also a collection of parts, can count as matter; cf. the distinction between linear and non-linear constitution in Fine, 'Matter'.

[25] As an artefact, the statue is not properly a substance at all: see e.g. *Metaph.* H 2, 1043[b]4–12. But as Aristotle's own practice shows, this and similar examples can give the easiest explanation of the relationships he intends.

[26] Again, however, like all artefacts, a statue is only a quasi-substance, and has only a quasi-substantial form (see n. 25 above). For example, I may adapt my bust of Aristotle into a doorstop, when my infatuation with Aristotle wanes: the relevant forms are imposed in large part from the outside, by the user, in contrast to natural substances, whose principle of identity is internal.

[27] Two results in Fine, 'Matter', are relevant here: his Reverse Foundation, which stipulates that the sequence of coincident matters in the composition of a given object (see n. 28 below) is bounded in the upward direction (according to Aristotle, the sequence ends with the coming-to-be of the substance or quasi-substance: cf. *Metaph.* I 9, discussed briefly in sect. 6(*b*) below), and Fine's Def. 2 of proximate

has the appropriate passive powers so that it can become bronze (*Meteor.* 4. 10, 389^{a}7–9); and bronze in turn has the appropriate passive powers so that it can be turned into a statue.

Prime matter, at the beginning of the hierarchy of coincident matters, is the limiting case of this. Prime matter has the passive power for being made to constitute one or other of the four elements upon the imposition of the appropriate two contraries; but supposing the result to be water, there is room still for bronze or for any number of other products; and beyond that, room for the statue and for many other artefacts besides. If an amount of prime matter has the capacity to be made into water, where the water has the capacity to be made into bronze, the prime matter in question does not have the capacity to be made *immediately* into bronze. But it does have the capacity to be made into something that in turn can be made into bronze. In this qualified sense, there accrue to prime matter, at one or more removes, all the various powers that characterize the different matters at the different, higher levels in the composition of the finished object.[28]

The proximate matter of the statue, by contrast, has a more limited set of passive causal powers—if not for a statue, for a door, perhaps, or a bell. And in the case of the (proximate) matter of natural objects, of a human being, for example, the range of choices for the matter is the most limited of all: either it develops into a human being, or it fails to develop altogether.

Before we leave the functional-property account of the properties of being matter and of being prime matter, it may be instructive to compare this account with two rivals: the account in Fine, 'Matter', of the property of being matter as a *first*-level property; and a possible refinement of Charles's view of prime matter as an 'abstract'

---

matter. Note that the notion of proximate matter applies to the lower of *any* two adjacent matters in a given hierarchy of matters—it is not restricted to the matter at the top of the hierarchy that leads directly to the finished substance.

[28] Here as elsewhere, I take for granted the hierarchy of coincident matters in the composition of a given substance, along with the transitivity of the matter-of relation: for both assumptions, see above all Fine, 'Matter'. My remarks here and in the main text are directed to the 'vertical' story, concerning the decomposition of a given finished substance, down through the different levels of matter that enter into its composition. To this, we should add the fact of 'horizontal' complexity: at different levels of matter, regardless of how the matter at a given level in fact has been worked up, in principle it may have had the capacity for being worked up in some other way, or even for not being worked up at all.

or 'logical' object, if *not*, as Charles first suggests (Section 3 above), an arbitrary object in the sense of Fine, *Reasoning*.

Fine treats the property of being matter as a first-level property, defined in terms of what he takes to be the primitive matter-of relation. I take it that this last is a *constitutive* notion, holding only when the matter in question in fact constitutes a given thing: there can be no 'strays' ('Matter', 39)—no matter that is not the matter of anything. It may be, then, that the bronze that will later be turned into a statue is not currently matter at all, for it is not yet the matter of any statue. Or if it is matter, it is the matter of the unshaped lump. But it is hard to think that, for Aristotle, the status of the bronze as matter depends as much on the lump as it does on the statue. Instead, we may suppose that something—a stuff or structure, or even prime matter—counts as matter just in case it is the matter *for* something.

The matter-for relation is a *prospective* as well as a constitutive notion—strays are now welcome. More importantly, the relation brings to the fore the *teleological* component in Aristotle's notion of matter, which is nicely accommodated on the second-level functional property account I am proposing. On the functional property account, as before, we think of a stuff or structure or prime matter, s, as having the property of being matter *in virtue of* its having the relevant first-level powers for being made into a thing of a given kind, k. But Aristotle's view of the different passive powers of s is the opposite of egalitarian. One of the powers of s is the power to receive the form, ψ, that typifies a thing of kind k, where a thing of this kind is a desirable goal;[29] but it is only 'by way of a privation and a corruption' that, less desirably, it is the capacity to receive the privation of ψ (*Metaph. H* 5, 1044^{b}33).[30] If, then, as I suppose, a thing has the second-level property of being matter *because* it

---

[29] Aristotle expressly tells us that matter is potentially a thing of kind, k; see e.g. *DA* 3. 5, 430^{a}10–11: 'in all of nature there is on the one hand what is matter *for each kind*, and this is *potentially all those* [=all the members of the kind]'. Thus, a given passive power is defined in terms of the actuality it is the power *for*: 'It is clear that in being potentially, and in proceeding to actuality, it goes to that place, and to such a quantity and such a quality that are the place, quantity and quality that the actuality is *of*' (*De caelo* 4. 3, 311^{a}4–6). For simplicity's sake, I pretend that s is the matter for a single desirable product; in many cases, however, in the case of artifacts in particular, there may be more than one desirable product that s is for.

[30] Aristotle's discussion of wine and vinegar and their common matter, ^{b}29–34, offers a persuasive example of the differing values attaching to the different products in which a given example of matter may find itself.

possesses the relevant (first-level) capacities, then the teleology inherent in Aristotle's notion of a capacity as the capacity *for* a given product is passed on to whatever counts as matter—and hence as matter *for* the product—in virtue of possessing that capacity.

The teleological component in Aristotle's concept of matter is on display in his discussion in *Metaph.* Θ 8 of the different ways in which actuality is prior in substance. What temporally comes to be *last*, he argues, is none the less *prior in form and in substance*. As always, 'being is prior to becoming': as the matter moves from potentiality to actuality, the potentiality and the actuality alike are determined by the appropriate form—the matter 'may go to' the form, and when the process is complete, it will be 'in' the form (1050^a7–10, 15–16). Otherwise put: from the first, a stuff or structure, s, counts as matter, because it has the passive power for being made into a thing of a given kind, k, where ψ is the form that typifies a k. And if, finally, the matter 'is in the form', the passive power in s is realized, and s is actually, or actually constitutes, a k, thanks to the form, ψ. Thus, the matter is all along 'teleologically bound' to the form, and bound to it most fully when its potentiality is realized with the advent of the form. Lastly, as promised, the relevant passive powers can be in place on the functional-property account and, hence, s can count as matter, even if s does not currently constitute a k.

Next, prime matter as an 'abstract' or 'logical' object. Charles indicates that his 'arbitrary object' account (cf. Section 3 above) is not the only way to understand the claim that prime matter is an abstract, or logical, object (see e.g. Charles, 'Genesis', n. 7); in the light of this, can we see the functional-property account advanced here as a friendly amendment to his view? I suggest not, for at least three reasons. First, Charles's abstract object, if it is of utility at all, has its use only at the level of prime matter. The functional-property account, on the other hand, shows how prime matter is a limiting case of a framework that applies generally, to what counts as matter at any level: for anything to count as matter, prime or otherwise, and to be able to engage in genesis, it must possess the functional property of being matter, suitably specified for the causal context in question. Second, Charles's abstract object *is* prime matter, but it is not a constituent of any of the elements whose constitution it is invoked to explain. The functional property, being matter, by contrast, is a (second-level) property *of* whatever in a given context counts as matter, prime or otherwise; but it is not itself a matter of any kind. At the same time, what does count as (prime) matter in a given case, on the functional-property account, is not a property or (more generally) an abstract object of any sort; it is the *subject* of the relevant functional property. It is also a constituent of the compound that results (on this last account, we might even think of prime matter as *vicariously* a material object: cf. n. 10 above).

Thirdly, there is the question of persistence (cf. Section 5 immediately following). On the usual story, according to Charles, his abstract object is realized by a succession of distinct underliers, m_1, m_2, and the rest—any notion of persistence attaches to the abstract object itself, not to the underliers. In the functional-property account, by contrast, as we shall see, the property can be specified in such a way as to allow for the persistence of a single underlier in any given sequence of elemental transformations.

5. The functional-property view and Parmenides

Questions of persistence bring us once more to Parmenides, and to how the difficulties he raises are (or perhaps are not) put to rest in the functional-property account. The matter, m_1, of E, and the matter, m_2, of F both have the functional property such that each is capable of receiving (and of losing) certain elemental contraries in the course of generation and destruction. Much hangs on which contraries we take these to be. According to Charles, m_1 currently realizes the capacities of receiving cold and dry; similarly, m_2 currently realizes the capacities of receiving hot and dry. Can we say more? Once m_1 has lost the one contrary, cold, even if m_1 continues to exist, and even if it has the capacity of newly receiving the second contrary, hot, this will not be relevant to the supposed transformation from E to F. For, by hypothesis, $m_1 \neq m_2$, so that m_1 is not a constituent of F. Meanwhile, m_2 is a constituent of F, but it cannot earlier have had the capacity for being made to take on hot in a way that is relevant to the supposed transformation to F *from* E: by hypothesis, again, $m_2 \neq m_1$, so that m_2 has no connection to E. And in general, on the view that $m_1 \neq m_2$, the two have different capacities for receiving different sets of contraries (cf. Section 3 above).

On an alternative view, however, m_1 and m_2 may have the less restrictive functional property that each can receive (or lose) any one

from each of the two elemental contrary-pairs, in a certain prede-
termined order.[31] Thus, m_1, for example (the matter of E), has the
capacity for losing cold and for taking on hot, as E is transformed to
F. And once the transformation is done, m_2 ($=m_1$, we will suppose)
has realized those capacities, and has acquired the capacities for losing dry and for taking on moist in the further transformation from
F into a quantity of air. We may define the functional property by
way of a sequence of capacities along these lines, suitably extended
to allow transformations between all four kinds of elements, and to
cover the different kinds of case Aristotle describes. On the picture
given, we suppose that $m_1 = m_2$ and, generalizing from this, follow
the conventional view of the persistence of a given amount of prime
matter through all its elemental changes.

On this showing, the functional-property view of matter, in itself,
is neutral with respect to persistence. Depending on how we define
the functional property in question, for different items to have the
same functional role may presuppose the identity of a given amount
of prime matter across different elements, or it may be indifferent to
or even preclude it. If we suppose that identity is required, to avoid
the difficulties of jumping and of flipping noted (Section 3 above),
the functional-property view will accommodate this solution to
Parmenides.

But if, with Charles, we reject the persistence of prime matter
across elemental change, can the functional-property view give us
an alternative means of answering Parmenides? If the functional
property is defined as Charles's account would require (two paragraphs above), I see no answer to Parmenides. For, if the functional-
property view, in itself, is neutral with respect to persistence, it is
not neutral with respect to Parmenides. Without the further assumption of persistence across elemental change, and without a
definition of the functional property that incorporates the assumption of persistence, Parmenides will remain unanswered.

Parmenides is by no means the only predecessor Aristotle has
in mind as he puts together his account of matter and elemental
transformation. As Charles portrays him ('Genesis', 66–9), Aristotle's views in *De generatione et corruptione* position him midway
between the pluralism of his Presocratic predecessors and monism:

---

[31] The rules for which contraries or contrary-pairs can give way to which are laid
out in *GC* 2. 4.

how these two '-isms' play out in Aristotle's account will be our topic in the final section.

6. Neither a monist nor pluralist be

(a) The elements and their matter

Aristotle avoids what we might think of as the pluralism of Empedocles, for whom the four 'roots', earth, air, fire, and water, are ungenerated and indestructible, by insisting on the mutual transformation among the (unfortunately named) elements. So these are not both many and basic in the way the pluralist thinks.

Aristotle's views about mutual transformation go along with an analysis of the so-called elements into a pair of contraries and an underlying matter. Are his views about the matter for the transformation among the elements monist, or pluralist? Suppose that m_1 is the matter of a given quantity of earth, E, and m_2 the matter of some fire, F, and that E is transformed into F. Even if $m_1 \neq m_2$ (the usual case, according to Charles), by resorting to the 'logical object', μ, Aristotle finds 'a way to accommodate the idea of common matter without representing it as a mysterious, indeterminate, eternal substrate (in the style of his monist predecessors)'.[32] So the device gives Aristotle an alternative to pluralism that also avoids the perils of traditional monism.

Even if Aristotle inclines towards a non-traditional version of monism, however, his count of lowest-level matters is not unequivocal. On Charles's account, the single 'logical object', μ, is realized differently by means of four different contrary-pairs. Alternatively, on the functional-property view I am pressing, the property of being prime matter is the *same* second-level property across the board, in every case of elemental transformation; but *different* first-level causal properties or capacities are at work at different points in elemental transformation. Aristotle himself suggests that the count of

[32] The quotation is from Charles, 'Genesis', 168–9. But of the monist views Charles cites—the unbounded, atoms, fire, the cosmic mixture—only Anaximander's unbounded comes close to justifying the description 'mysterious, indeterminate'. These descriptions fit better the bare substrate of Bare Substrate Theory, discussed in sect. 6(*b*) below. Charles's phrase 'material or quasi-material substratum' ('Genesis', 166) tends to obscure the difference between the essentially materialist accounts of Aristotle's Presocratic predecessors and the very different bare substrate theory introduced in Plato's *Timaeus*. For further discussion, see sect. 6(*b*) below.

matters involved in elemental transformation varies between one and four:

> it is necessary that the matters too should be as many in number as these [=the elements], namely, four, *but in this way four, so that (on the one hand) there is one common to all, especially if they come to be from one another, but the being is different.* (*De caelo* 4. 5, 312ᵃ30–ᵇ1)

Again:

> . . . is the matter of each of these [=earth, fire] different; or ⟨if it were different,⟩[33] would they not come to be from each other or from the contraries (for the contraries belong to these, to fire, earth, water, air)? Or is it [the matter of earth, the matter of air] *in a way the same, in a way different? For what underlies, whatever it is, is the same, but the being is not the same.* (*GC* 1. 3, 319ᵃ33–ᵇ3, quoted by Charles, 'Genesis', 151)

In a way, then, there are four matters—the matter of E, the matter of F, and so on—for, different capacities are present in the different cases. At the same time, on the traditional view, the identical matter survives though the various transformations; it exhibits one and the same functional property throughout; and one and the same causal role is realized by the different capacities involved in the different cases.

On this showing, Aristotle's account of elemental transformation is not pluralist in Empedocles's sense, and perhaps not straightforwardly monist either. In fact, for all the traces of monism in his account of the elements, Aristotle finds a version of monism in his predecessors to which he himself is altogether hostile. This will be our topic in the final subsection.

(b) Matter and the rejection of 'winner takes all' monism

Aristotle's rejection of Empedoclean pluralism is relatively straightforward. Not so his distancing from monism. He sketches one route to monism in *Physics* 2. 1, where he suggests that the Presocratic tendency to explain natural objects in terms of their matter can lead to the idea that the nature of a thing and its substance can be a single, rock-bottom subject of which every other feature of the object is a modification. In the Presocratic materi-

---

[33] My translation, together with the supplement in angle-brackets, follows the account in Joachim, *Coming-to-Be*, 105; see also the translation in Williams, *De generatione*, 14.

alist reduction Aristotle describes and rejects in the *Physics*, the monists' end product is one or other single kind of material stuff.[34] In *Metaphysics Z* 3 he sketches a line of thought according to which his own theory might seem to collapse into (again) a 'winner takes all' monism, in which accidents and forms alike are all (metaphysically) predicated of a single underlying matter.[35] In this case, in contrast to the materialist picture in *Physics* 2—but in line with the traditional account of prime matter—the underlying matter has no qualitative features of its own.[36]

The bare substrate theory on display in *Metaphysics Z* 3 seriously misrepresents Aristotle's real view. Aristotle's argument in the chapter is polemical, and offers a *reductio* of the received view that substance is a subject: if *subject* is defined as in the *Categories*, perhaps also as in the *Physics*, and given certain other, probably controversial, assumptions, it seems to follow that substance is the subject for *everything*—for all the forms that enter into the constitution of a given thing, and all its accidents besides.

In the context of the *reductio*, this offers the best case the subject theorist might make for how to apply his criterion to Aristotle's theory—but it is not a case that we can reasonably expect Aristotle to endorse.[37] The scheme is similar in major ways to that on offer in Plato's *Timaeus*, where a sensible object is a collection of reflections of forms, located at a given position in the receptacle, which in itself lacks all features. On the traditional view of prime matter I have in mind, Aristotle is decidedly not a bare substrate theorist of this sort. On the traditional picture, there is no objection to seeing all the

---

[34] This brand of monism is also targeted at *GC* 1. 1, 314ᵃ8–11, ᵇ1–4: Presocratic monists cannot distinguish generation and destruction from alteration, because their single element is in itself perceptible and separate (2. 1, 328ᵇ33–329ᵃ1, 329ᵃ8–10, 24–6; 2. 5, 332ᵃ3–20, ᵃ35–ᵇ1); for them, Aristotle charges, all change is alteration, and there is no room for true generation and destruction. Evidently, the 'not perceptible and/or not separate' requirement will not serve to distinguish generation and destruction from alteration at higher levels of matter and form. I hold, but will not argue here, that when the carpenter assembles the wooden boards appropriately, a table genuinely comes to be—that this is not merely a case of alteration in the wood—for reasons that stem from the two-tier system of (metaphysical) predication described in the final two paragraphs in the main text. (When the carpenter is done, and the painter sets to work, however, that will be alteration.)

[35] For metaphysical predication, see Lewis, *Substance*, 4 and *passim*.

[36] As before, see the qualifications in n. 19 above.

[37] Further discussion in Lewis, *Substance*, ch. 10, and M. Wedin, *Aristotle's Theory of Substance: The Categories and Metaphysics Zeta* (Oxford, 2000), ch. v, sect. 4; cf. n. 8 above.

(Aristotelian) forms in the constitution of a given thing as (meta-physically) predicated at the lowest level of in-itself formless matter. But on Aristotle's view, the current condition of a thing includes its accidents, and there is no warrant for drawing accidents into the scheme of (metaphysical) predication described so far. There is a point at which the supply of forms stops, and we reach substantial form and the finished substance; and any modification beyond this point counts as accidental (cf. *Metaphysics I* 9). At this point we enter a different part of Aristotle's scheme. A thing's accidents are not (metaphysically) predicated of matter, prime or otherwise, but require an irreducibly different kind of subject, namely the finished substance, in the upper half of the scheme. The result is a two-part structure, with multiple layers of form and (coincident) matters below, and a single layer of accidents above.

On this story, Aristotle's prime matter is not subject to all the attributes, forms and accidents alike, that enter into the nature and current state of a thing. If anything, his is a 'two substrate' theory, with a core substance composed (on one analysis) of prime matter and the relevant array of forms; and a second combination of subject plus accidents *in which the core substance plays the role of subject.*[38] Accordingly, if one were to look solely at the lower half of Aristotle's scheme, he might seem, with qualifications, to be a monist in his views; but his scheme as a whole is a very emphatic rejection of the 'winner takes all' monism he finds in Plato.

University of Southern California

BIBLIOGRAPHY

Bostock, D., 'Aristotle's Theory of Matter' ['Theory'], in D. Sfendoni-Mentzou, J. Hattiangadi, and D. Johnson (eds.), *Aristotle and Contem-*

---

[38] His theory is then comparable in certain ways to the theory of 'two subbundles' —core bundle and peripheral bundle—in contemporary Bundle Theory: J. Van Cleve, 'Three Versions of the Bundle Theory', *Philosophical Studies*, 47 (1985), 95–107 at 99–100. Arguably (n. 15 above), the addition of prime matter (along with the higher levels of matter), so that the core bundle is converted into an instance of bare substrate theory, differentiates the core of essential properties associated with Socrates from the core associated with Callias (say), even though the two men have exactly the same essential properties; so we will not have the difficulty Van Cleve describes of a single core surrounded by incompatible accidental properties (Socrates' snubnosedness, Callias' concave nose) at the periphery.

porary Science, ii (New York, 2001), 3–22; repr. in Bostock, *Space, Time, Matter, and Form* (Oxford, 2006), 30–47.

Burnyeat, M., *A Map of* Metaphysics *Zeta* (Pittsburgh, 2001).

Charles, D., 'Simple Genesis and Prime Matter' ['Genesis'], in F. de Haas and J. Mansfeld (eds.), *Aristotle:* On Generation and Corruption, *Book II* (Oxford, 2004), 151–69.

Charlton, W., *Aristotle:* Physics, *Books I and II* [*Physics*] (Oxford, 1970).

Fine, K., *Reasoning with Arbitrary Objects* [*Reasoning*] (Oxford, 1985).

—— 'Aristotle on Matter' ['Matter'], *Mind*, NS 101 (1992), 35–57.

Furth, M., *Substance, Form and Psyche: An Aristotelian Metaphysics* [*Aristotelian*] (Cambridge, 1988).

Gill, M. L., *Aristotle on Substance: The Paradox of Unity* [*Paradox*] (Princeton, 1989).

Heil, J., *Philosophy of Mind: A Contemporary Introduction* [*Mind*], 2nd edn. (New York and London, 2004).

—— 'Properties and Powers' ['Powers'], *Oxford Studies in Metaphysics*, 1 (2004), 223–54.

Joachim, H. H., *Aristotle:* On Coming-to-Be and Passing-Away [*Coming-to-Be*] (Oxford, 1922).

Lewis, F. A., *Substance and Predication in Aristotle* [*Substance*] (Cambridge, 1991).

Loux, M. J., *Metaphysics: A Contemporary Introduction*, 2nd edn. (London and New York, 2002).

Prior, E. W., Pargetter, R., and Jackson, F., 'Three Theses about Dispositions', *American Philosophical Quarterly*, 19 (1982), 251–7.

Robinson, H. M., 'Prime Matter in Aristotle', *Phronesis*, 19 (1974), 168–98.

Sellars, W., 'Aristotle's Metaphysics: An Interpretation' ['Interpretation'], in id., *Philosophical Perspectives* (Springfield, Ill., 1967), 73–124.

Van Cleve, J., 'Three Versions of the Bundle Theory', *Philosophical Studies*, 47 (1985), 95–107.

Wedin, M., *Aristotle's Theory of Substance:* The Categories *and* Metaphysics *Zeta* (Oxford, 2000).

Williams, C. J. F., *Aristotle's* De generatione et corruptione [*De generatione*] (Oxford, 1982).

Zeller, E., *Aristotle and the Earlier Peripatetics* [*Peripatetics*] (2 vols.; London, 1897).

ELEMENTAL TELEOLOGY IN
ARISTOTLE'S *PHYSICS* 2. 8

MARGARET SCHARLE

THE role of nature in Aristotle's account of natural teleology has been widely misunderstood, and as a result Aristotle has been interpreted with an excessively biological focus. Scholars have thought that his natural teleology applies exclusively to biological things (plants and animals) and that the elements (earth, air, fire, and water) either are not teleological or are teleological only in so far as they play a role in biological processes.

This general misunderstanding of his natural teleology is well evidenced in interpretations of the winter rain example in *Physics* 2. 8's first argument for natural teleology—one of the most vexing and important passages in Aristotle's corpus. Some interpreters think he cites rainfall as an example of a process that is *not* teleological, while others think he cites winter rainfall as a process that is teleologically directed, and teleologically directed at growing corn.[1] In this paper I show that these interpretations fail to observe the role nature plays in the argument of *Physics* 2. 8. I then offer a new interpretation of that passage which shows winter rain to be teleological on its own, quite independently of biological processes such as corn growth. My new interpretation takes root in a fresh understanding of the elemental teleology at work in *De caelo, Physics* 8. 4, and the *Meteorologica*.

© Margaret Scharle 2008

This paper improved greatly as a result of profitable discussions with and helpful comments by David Blank, István Bodnár, John Carriero, Alan Code, Marc Cohen, Calvin Normore, and Cass Weller. Sean Kelsey, Gavin Lawrence, and David Sedley deserve special thanks.

[1] Note that I use the British translation 'corn' for σῖτος since the secondary literature on the passage usually speaks of 'corn growth'.

1. The Non-Teleological Rain Interpretation

Martha Nussbaum, W. D. Ross, David Balme, Allan Gotthelf, William Charlton, Lindsay Judson, and Monte Johnson, the main proponents of the Non-Teleological Rain Interpretation (hereafter 'NTRI'), argue that Aristotle agrees with his opponents in the following passage that rain is not for the sake of anything:[2]

ἔχει δ' ἀπορίαν τί κωλύει τὴν φύσιν μὴ ἕνεκά του ποιεῖν μηδ' ὅτι βέλτιον ἀλλ' ὥσπερ ὕει ὁ Ζεύς, οὐχ ὅπως τὸν σῖτον αὐξήσῃ ἀλλ' ἐξ ἀνάγκης—τὸ γὰρ ἀναχθὲν ψυχθῆναι δεῖ καὶ τὸ ψυχθὲν ὕδωρ γενόμενον κατελθεῖν, τὸ δ' αὐξάνεσθαι τούτου γενομένου τὸν σῖτον συμβαίνει—ὁμοίως δὲ καὶ εἴ τῳ ἀπόλλυται ὁ σῖτος ἐν τῇ ἅλῳ, οὐ τούτου ἕνεκα ὕει ὅπως ἀπόληται, ἀλλὰ τοῦτο συμβέβηκεν.

[*The statement of the problem*] There is the difficulty: what prevents nature from acting neither for something nor because it is better, but as Zeus rains—not in order that the corn may grow, but of necessity. (For what was taken up must become cold, and what has become cold, having become water, must come down. When this has happened, it turns out that the corn grows.) Similarly also, if someone's corn on the threshing floor is ruined it does not rain for the sake of this, so that the corn may be ruined, but this simply results. (*Phys.* 2. 8, 198ᵇ17–23)

According to NTRI, Aristotle here implicitly concedes to his materialist opponent that rain is not for the sake of *anything*: rain clearly is not for the sake of corn growth—rain comes of necessity and, coincidentally, is followed by corn growth or corn rot—and, this interpretation assumes, there is no better candidate end for rain.

But the passage that follows the statement of the problem offers a challenge to this interpretation:

---

[2] Proponents of this view include M. C. Nussbaum, *Aristotle's De Motu Animalium. Text with Translation, Commentary, and Interpretive Essays* (Princeton, 1978), 94; W. D. Ross, *Aristotle's Physics* (Oxford, 1936), 42; D. Balme, 'Teleology and Necessity' ['Teleology'], in A. Gotthelf and J. G. Lennox (eds.), *Philosophical Issues in Aristotle's Biology* (Cambridge, 1987), 275–86 at 277; A. Gotthelf, 'Aristotle's Conception of Final Causality', *Review of Metaphysics*, 30 (1976–7), 226–54, repr. with additional notes and a Postscript in Gotthelf and Lennox (eds.), *Philosophical Issues in Aristotle's Biology*, 204–42 at 214 n. 19; W. Charlton (*Aristotle's Physics Books 1 & 2. Translated from the Greek with Introduction and Notes [Notes]* (Oxford, 1992), xvii; M. R. Johnson, *Aristotle on Teleology [Teleology]* (Oxford, 2005), 156; L. Judson, 'Aristotelian Teleology' ['Teleology'], *Oxford Studies in Ancient Philosophy*, 29 (2005), 341–66 at 350; and perhaps also T. Irwin, *Aristotle's First Principles [Principles]* (Oxford, 1988), and S. Waterlow (Broadie), *Nature, Change, and Agency in Aristotle's Physics [Nature]* (Oxford, 1982), 80.

ταῦτα μὲν γὰρ καὶ πάντα τὰ φύσει ἢ αἰεὶ οὕτω γίγνεται ἢ ὡς ἐπὶ τὸ πολύ, τῶν δ᾽
ἀπὸ τύχης καὶ τοῦ αὐτομάτου οὐδέν. οὐ γὰρ ἀπὸ τύχης οὐδ᾽ ἀπὸ συμπτώματος
δοκεῖ ὕειν πολλάκις τοῦ χειμῶνος, ἀλλ᾽ ἐὰν ὑπὸ κύνα· οὐδὲ καύματα ὑπὸ κύνα
ἀλλ᾽ ἂν χειμῶνος. εἰ οὖν ἢ ἀπὸ συμπτώματος δοκεῖ ἢ ἕνεκά του εἶναι, εἰ μὴ οἷόν
τε ταῦτ᾽ εἶναι μήτε ἀπὸ συμπτώματος μήτ᾽ ἀπὸ ταὐτομάτου, ἕνεκά του ἂν εἴη.
ἀλλὰ μὴν φύσει γ᾽ ἐστὶ τὰ τοιαῦτα πάντα, ὡς κἂν αὐτοὶ φαῖεν οἱ ταῦτα λέγοντες.
ἔστιν ἄρα τὸ ἕνεκά του ἐν τοῖς φύσει γιγνομένοις καὶ οὖσιν.

[*The argument*] For these things [i.e. animals] and all things that are by
nature, come to be in this way either always or for the most part, and
nothing from luck or chance does. For it does not seem to be from luck or
from coincidence that it rains often in winter, but if in the dog-days; nor
that there are heat waves in the dog-days, but in winter. If, then, things
seem to be either from coincidence or for the sake of something, and if these
things are not able to be from coincidence or from chance, they would be
for the sake of something. But clearly all such things are by nature, as these
speakers themselves would say. The 'for the sake of something', then, is in
things which are and come to be by nature. (*Phys.* 2. 8, 198ᵇ35–199ᵃ8)

David Furley has already offered a definitive argument against
NTRI, so let me just briefly review his rebuttal.[3] Since the passage
is clear that *winter rain* occurs regularly and thus non-coincidentally, NTRI must show how the disjunction 'either from coincidence
or for the sake of something' does not apply to winter rain. Yet the
'all such things' of the penultimate sentence includes the winter rain
and summer heat waves as well as the animals referred to in the first
sentence.[4] In fact, winter rain and summer heat waves are used as
the examples of things that occur regularly, thus non-coincidentally,
and thus teleologically. The text does not suggest that winter rain
should be excluded, and NTRI—in maintaining that rain is not for
the sake of anything—requires such exclusion.

Given that Furley's reading of the text is the most straightforward, it may seem surprising that there are so many adherents of
NTRI. I think that, in part, scholars have tried to avoid saddling
Aristotle with what they take to be an implausible view: water comes
down from the sky for the sake of something. Although we can see
why he would have thought that plants send down roots for the sake

---

[3] D. J. Furley, 'The Rainfall Example in *Physics* II 8' ['Rainfall'], in A. Gotthelf
(ed.), *Aristotle on Nature and Living Things* (Pittsburgh, 1985), 177–82 at 179–81.
[4] D. Sedley, 'Is Aristotle's Teleology Anthropocentric?' ['Anthropocentric'],
Phronesis, 36 (1991), 179–97 at 182–3, and R. Wardy, 'Aristotelian Rainfall or the
Lore of Averages' ['Rainfall'], *Phronesis*, 38 (1993), 18–30 at 19–21, both agree with
Furley on this point.

of obtaining nourishment from the ground—for biological phenomena at least *appear* to us to be teleological—we certainly would
baulk at his suggestion that meteorological phenomena are for the
sake of something. But in their attempt to fit Aristotle to contemporary sensibilities, I think commentators have run away from some
of the most central and important features of his teleology.

On the assumption, then, that Furley has shown that Aristotle
thinks winter rain is for *something*, the rest of my discussion will
attempt to discern *what* winter rain is for.

2. The Corn Growth Interpretation

Alan Code, John Cooper, David Furley, and David Sedley, the
main proponents of the Corn Growth Interpretation, take the argument passage to show that winter rain is for the sake of corn
growth—a biological process.[5] As Furley notes, this interpretation
'at first sight at least, seems to imply a much wider application of
teleology—perhaps embracing all the workings of the whole natural world'.[6] Although Furley does not pursue this line himself,
several commentators have used the Corn Growth Interpretation
as evidence of Aristotle's commitment to a cosmic teleology of the
natural world—that is, the sort of teleology supposedly endorsed by
the *Politics*' claim that plants are for the sake of animals and animals
for the sake of humans (1. 8, 1256[b]10–22). Not only has the Corn
Growth Interpretation become the dominant view of *Physics* 2. 8,
but it has also renewed interest in the supposed cosmic character
of Aristotle's natural teleology.[7]

---

[5] See Furley, 'Rainfall'; J. M. Cooper, 'Aristotle on Natural Teleology' ['Teleology'], in M. Schofield and M. C. Nussbaum (eds.), *Language and Logos: Studies in
Ancient Greek Philosophy Presented to G. E. L. Owen* (Cambridge, 1982), 197–222
at 217–18; and A. Code, 'The Priority of Final Causes over Efficient Causes in
Aristotle's *PA*' ['Priority'], in W. Kullmann and S. Follinger (eds.), *Aristotelische
Biologie: Intentionen, Methoden, Ergebnisse* (Stuttgart, 1997), 127–43 at 130. Sedley agrees that corn growth must be at issue in *Physics* 2. 8 since Aristotle focuses
on *seasonal* rainfall ('Anthropocentric', 184). A. Mansion claims that rain is for a
purpose, but does not name the purpose (*Introduction à la Physique Aristotélicienne*
(Louvain, 1945), 252 n. 2), while D. Charles lists raining as a '(possible) teleological effect' ('Teleological Causation in the *Physics*', in L. Judson (ed.), *Aristotle's*
Physics: *A Collection of Essays* (Oxford, 1991), 101–28 at 103). See also Simpl. *In
Phys.* 374. 18–22 Diels.

[6] Furley, 'Rainfall', 177.

[7] See e.g. Sedley, 'Anthropocentric' and '*Metaphysics Λ* 10' ['*Λ* 10'], in M. Frede

The proponents of the Corn Growth Interpretation point to the argument passage as the 'most convincing reason' in favour of their interpretation: 'If Aristotle suggests a teleological explanation of winter rainfall [the argument], we can hardly suppose that he joins the mechanists in denying it in the previous paragraph [in the statement of the problem].'[8] Proponents of the Corn Growth Interpretation tacitly assume that the putative end of rain is the same both in the passage that states the problem and in the argument passage. To some extent this assumption is natural, given that the argument passage does not name the end of winter rain.

However, upon closer inspection, we find textual asymmetries between the two passages. The statement of the problem does not explicitly mention the seasonal rain and summer heat waves found in the argument.[9] And with what are summer heat waves regularly, non-coincidentally, and thus teleologically connected? Some other crop?[10] Moreover, when Aristotle discusses coincidence in the *Metaphysics* he returns to the example of seasonal weather patterns but does not mention corn growth or any other such connected event:

That which is neither always nor for the most part, we say this is an accident [συμβεβηκός]. For example, if in the dog-days winter and cold come to be, we say this is an accident [συμβῆναι], but not if stifling heat and warmth come to be, because the latter is always or for the most part, but not the former. (*E* 2, 1026ᵇ31–5)[11]

These textual points suggest that we should closely examine the assumption that corn growth is the end at issue in the argument pas-

and D. Charles (eds.), *Aristotle's* Metaphysics Lambda (Oxford, 2000), 327–50, and M. Matthen, 'The Holistic Presuppositions of Aristotle's Cosmology', *Oxford Studies in Ancient Philosophy*, 20 (2001), 171–99. For a recent discussion of their views, see I. Bodnár, 'Teleology across Natures' ['Teleology'], *Rhizai*, 2 (2005), 9–29. Sect. 4 below offers my interpretation of the *Politics* 1. 8 passage.

[8] Furley, 'Rainfall', 179.

[9] As Sedley points out, the proponents of the Corn Growth Interpretation would argue that winter rain just *is* the rain that grows corn, while summer rain just *is* the rain that rots corn ('Anthropocentric', 186).

[10] Sedley suggests that the heat of summer ripens olives ('Anthropocentric', 186).

[11] And, as Furley points out, Aristotle uses plain, unadorned indicatives when presenting the opponent's view that rain is not for the sake of corn growth, thereby suggesting that he is sympathetic with their position on the case ('Rainfall', 178). Judson also argues that Aristotle's choice of words in the statement of the problem suggests that he agrees with his opponent that winter rain is not for the sake of growing corn ('Teleology', 346–7).

sage. Both NTRI and the Corn Growth Interpretation are united in assuming that corn growth is the only thing mentioned in the statement of the problem that Aristotle could think rain is for.[12] The former argues that in the statement of the problem Aristotle denies that rain is for the sake of corn growth, while the latter argues that in the argument Aristotle shows that winter rain indeed is for the sake of corn growth. In what follows I offer an interpretation that challenges their common assumption. But first I step back for a moment to consider what Aristotle aims to show in the argument passage (Section 3), and then I return to evaluate the Corn Growth Interpretation in the light of these aims (Section 4).

3. Aristotle's aim in 2. 8

The announced aim of *Physics* 2. 8 is to show that 'nature is among causes which are for the sake of something [ἕνεκά του]' (198^{b}10–11). And the chapter concludes: 'That nature is a cause, then, and a cause for the sake of something, is clear' (199^{b}32–3). In other words, 2. 8 sets out to show that *nature* aims at an end.[13] Let me call this the 'target claim'. Moreover, it is clear that this claim is Aristotle's target not only for the chapter, but also specifically for the argument passage, which directly responds to the following problem: 'What prevents nature from acting [not] . . . for something?' (198^{b}17–18).

The conclusion of the argument passage is: 'The "for the sake of something", then, is in things which are and come to be by nature' (199^{a}7). Aristotle's very definition of nature in *Physics* 2. 1 (192^{b}21–3) claims that *nature* is *in* that which is by nature. So we can understand *nature* to be the thing '*in* things which are and come to be by nature' that the conclusion claims to be for the sake of something. So understood, the conclusion repeats the target claim announced earlier: nature aims at an end.

However, proponents of the Corn Growth Interpretation have not noticed that the argument passage aims to show this connection between ends and *natures*. Now, granted, the argument's conclusion is more loosely stated than the earlier announcements of the target

---

[12] But, as Sedley notes, winter rain could also be for the sake of other plants and replenishing bodies of water ('Anthropocentric', 185).

[13] Given that nature is in the same genus as potential (*Metaph.* Θ 8, 1049^{b}8–10), the target claim is allied with his claim that actuality is prior to potentiality (1050^{a}9–10).

claim. Taken by itself—and without careful attention to the sense in which *nature* is *in* that which is by nature—the conclusion perhaps misleadingly suggests that there are no limits on which things could be taken as the end of natural phenomena such as winter rain. It may appear that Aristotle would be satisfied to have shown that they simply have some end or other. This seems to be how Alan Code interprets the conclusion. He maintains that the aim of the argument passage is to show simply that 'there are things that come to be and exist by nature and for a purpose'.[14] This way of stating the conclusion does not make perspicuous the way in which something's *nature* is connected to the ends it has. For all Code says here, one might think that it would be enough for the argument passage to have shown that the class of things that are *by nature* is coextensive with (or a subset of) the class of things that have an end. However, it cannot be just an accident that something, which is by nature, has an end. Rather, Aristotle's target claim demands that it must be *the nature of* that thing to be for that end. Furley's interpretation likewise fails to show a *connection* between natures and ends. He argues: 'There is no way out [of interpreting the passage to show winter rain aims at growing corn] by denying that the sequence of rainfall followed by growth of crops is regular, or by denying that it is natural, or by denying that it is an end-like result.'[15] On Furley's view, winter rain must have corn growth as its end since we can tick off a list of *independent* and *unconnected* criteria true of the case. Rain? Yes, it is by nature. The connection between rain and growing corn? Yes, it is regular. Corn growth? Yes, it looks like an end. On this reading, rain 'regularly produces a useful outcome; so we must say that the process is for the sake of the outcome'; ends are somehow 'useful' outcomes regularly produced by natural processes.[16]

However, Aristotle's specific purpose in the argument is to un-

---

[14] Code, 'Priority', 129. Code would probably respond that it is *Aristotle* who fails to make this connection in 2. 8 since the discussion there is only 'partial' ('Priority', 127 and 134). For others who read the target claim in this loose sense, see C. Witt, *Substance and Essence in Aristotle* (Ithaca, NY, 1989), 93, and J. M. Cooper, 'Hypothetical Necessity and Natural Teleology', in A. Gotthelf and J. G. Lennox (eds.), *Philosophical Issues in Aristotle's Biology* (Cambridge, 1987), 243–74 at 253.

[15] Furley, 'Rainfall', 180. He goes on to claim that rainfall 'regularly produces a useful outcome; so we must say the process is for the sake of the outcome' (181). This statement suggests that an end can be identified by its usefulness without making reference to the nature that aims at the end.

[16] Furley, 'Rainfall', 181.

cover the connection between *natures* and ends: that which is *by nature* has the end at which its *nature* aims.[17] In other words, to appreciate the force of the target claim is to see that one cannot point out the end at issue without making reference to the nature at issue; a given end is not just any independently identifiable good, but the good at which a given nature aims. As Simplicius (citing Alexander) puts it, 'In the products of nature there is not only an end in view, but also it is their nature to be for some end' (*In Phys.* 375. 8–10 Diels).[18] For example, Aristotle would not be satisfied to show simply that winter rain has some end-like result. Rather, he wants to show that winter rain has the end at which *its* nature aims.

Since commentators have not paid close attention to the connection *Physics* 2. 8 aims to establish between natures and ends, they (with the single exception of David Sedley) have not paid careful attention to the question of the nature at issue in the case of winter rain.[19] The next section considers the two candidates for the nature expressed in winter rain and concludes that neither of them takes growing corn as its aim.

4. Argument against the Corn Growth Interpretation

Recall that the argument passage of *Physics* 2. 8 maintains that winter rain is φύσει, or *by nature*: winter rain is in the scope of the 'all such things' that are 'by nature' (199^{a}6). Taking this claim together with the target claim—that nature aims at an end—shows that winter rain's end is the end at which its nature aims. Thus the Corn Growth Interpretation is committed to showing that winter rain's nature aims at growing corn. It turns out that determining *which* nature is at work in winter rain is a complicated matter—as we shall see, on one reading the nature at issue is the nature of water, while on another reading it is the nature of the cosmos. In this section I shall not settle the issue of *which* nature is at work in winter rain. Rather, I shall show that on *either* reading of the nature at issue, growing corn is not its aim.

---

[17] The end of *Physics* 2. 7 (198^{b}4–9) further supports this reading of the target claim.

[18] Trans. B. Fleet, *Simplicius on Aristotle on* Physics 2 (London, 1997).

[19] Sedley's answer ('Anthropocentric') is considered in the next section.

In order to uncover the candidates for the nature of winter rain, we must first get clear on what natures there are:

Of the things that are, some are by nature, others due to other causes: by nature are animals and their parts, plants and the simple bodies, for example earth, fire, air, and water (for we say these things and such things are by nature). And it is clear that all these differ from the things which have not been put together by nature. For each of these has in itself a source of movement and rest. . . . So a nature is what has been said [i.e. a source of movement and rest in that to which it belongs primarily of itself]. And things that have a source of this sort have a nature. And each of these [i.e. those which have a nature] is a substance. For it is an underlying thing, and nature is always in an underlying thing. And these are in accordance with nature, and things that belong to these of themselves, as being carried upwards [belongs] to fire—for this neither is a nature nor has a nature, but is by nature and in accordance with nature. (*Phys.* 2. 1, 192^{b}8–14; ^{b}32–193^{a}2)

In this passage Aristotle carefully marks off 'is a nature' from 'has a nature' and 'is by nature': a nature itself *is* an inner source of movement and rest, while that which *has* a nature *has* an inner source of movement and rest. Further, the locution 'by nature' is introduced as a description of that which is *by* an inner source of movement and rest. As we learn in this passage, animals and their parts, plants, and the elements are by nature in the sense of having a nature.[20] Moreover, we can say properly that fire and the activities it undergoes *qua* fire are by nature. However, it is improper to say that the fire's activity is a nature or has a nature, since the fire's activity is *by* a nature fire has.

What is winter rain's nature? Since natures are, by definition, internal to things that have them, by listing things that have a nature, *Physics* 2. 1 offers a list of natures as well. However, this list does not include winter rain explicitly. Corn (and its parts) are on the list, but I doubt that a proponent of the Corn Growth Interpretation would go so far as to argue that winter rain is by corn's nature.[21] Given this list, water's nature seems to be the only candidate nature for winter rain. Winter rain could be taken as a

[20] This claim needs some qualification. 192^{b}8–11 technically says that the elements are φύσει. But he then goes on to say that these things (ταῦτα, which refers back to the list at 192^{b}11) are φύσει in the sense of *having* (ἔχοντα, 192^{b}14) a source of motion and rest (i.e. having a φύσις) in themselves.

[21] Code cites the nature of seeds, but not as the nature of winter rain ('Priority', 134). He does not see that he needs to show how winter rain is by nature in the sense that *its* nature is for the sake of something.

downward movement of water: so understood, water's falling down as winter rain is φύσει in the same sense as fire's movement upwards is φύσει in the paradigmatic case at 192ᵇ35–193ᵃ2.

Certainly Aristotle thinks water is what falls as winter rain (*Meteor.* 1. 11, 347ᵇ13; 2. 4, 360ᵃ2–6; *GC* 2. 11, 338ᵇ6–18; *PA* 2. 7, 653ᵃ8). And if we return to the text of *Physics* 2. 8, the process of condensation and evaporation includes rain as 'water [ὕδωρ]' that 'falls down' (198ᵇ20). Given that water's nature is the only candidate nature for winter rain on the *Physics* 2. 1 list and that Aristotle thinks water is the substance that falls as winter rain, prima facie water's nature is the nature of winter rain.

However, David Sedley, the only proponent of the Corn Growth Interpretation to consider the sense in which winter rain is natural, has proposed that the nature at issue in *Physics* 2. 8 is the nature of the cosmos:

> Whose nature is exhibited in the providential winter rainfall? Surely not the nature of the rain, which as a simple elemental body, cannot possibly have an internal principle of motion beyond its tendency to move towards its natural place. . . . Consequently, the nature which is exhibited by the anthropocentric natural hierarchy must be not so much individual nature as global nature—the nature of the whole ecosystem, so to speak.[22]

Notice that it is only *after* Sedley has settled on the Corn Growth Interpretation that he asks a question about nature, a question he admits to having 'so far avoided'.[23] Sedley's question is tailored to suit the Corn Growth Interpretation: he asks whose nature is exhibited in 'providential winter rainfall' or by the 'anthropocentric hierarchy'.[24] Given the textual points I discussed in Section 2, and given that the argument passage implies that winter rain (without explicit mention of corn growth or providence or hierarchies) is φύσει, Sedley's reading is not the only one available, and, as I shall argue, not well supported by the texts he points to as evidence. The only reason Sedley rejects water's nature as the one at work in winter rain is that it does not comport with the Corn Growth Interpretation: it is implausible to claim that water's own nature has corn growth as its end.[25]

Since the cosmos is not among the items on *Physics* 2. 1's list of natural things, in order to show winter rain to be by cosmic nature, Sedley must look outside the *Physics* to *Metaphysics Λ* 10, 1075ᵃ11–25, where Aristotle refers to the 'nature of the whole'. As Sedley admits, 'The context [of *Λ* 10] is theological, and Aristotle's interest is concentrated on the roles of the Prime Mover and the heavenly bodies.'[26] In the light of this fact, Sedley is forced to say that Aristotle defends 'the anthropocentric function of rainfall in passing, as part of his strategy against the mechanists, rather than treating it in its own right. *Physics* ii is another book concerned with individual natures. Aristotle's theology is presupposed there, but not directly addressed in its own right.'[27] Not only does Sedley import the theological discussion of *Metaphysics Λ* into the interpretation of *Physics* 2. 8, but he controversially assumes that *Metaphysics Λ* shows Aristotle committed to there being a cosmic nature.[28] Recently these difficulties for the interpretation have led commentators such as Judson to revert to NTRI, despite its own set of textual intransigencies.[29] But I think commentators have been much too quick to reject Sedley's reading of *Metaphysics Λ* 10. In what follows I concede that *Λ* 10 posits a cosmic nature, but I argue that cosmic nature does not play the role Sedley thinks it plays in *Physics* 2. 8.

Let us begin by examining Sedley's translation of the passage in *Metaphysics Λ* 10 in which Aristotle refers to cosmic nature:

[1] We must consider also in which way the nature of the whole possesses the good and the best—whether as something separated and by itself, or as its arrangement. [2] Or is it in both ways, like an army? For an army's goodness is in its ordering, and is also in the general. And more the general, since he is not due to the arrangement, but the arrangement is due to him. [3] All things are in some joint-arrangement, but not in the same way— even creatures which swim, creatures which fly, and plants. [4] And the arrangement is not such that one thing has no relation to another. They do have a relation: for all things are jointly arranged in relation to one thing. [5] But it is as in a household, where the free have least licence to act as they chance to, but all or most of what they do is arranged, while the slaves and beasts can do a little towards what is communal, but act mostly as they

[26] Ibid. 193.
[27] Ibid. 195–6. In his later paper, however, Sedley argues that the end of *Physics* 2. 6 cites the nature of 'this universe' ('*Λ* 10', 330). See my discussion of this passage in n. 39.
[28] For the most recent discussion of the controversy, see Bodnár, 'Teleology'.
[29] See Judson, 'Teleology', 346.

chance to. [6] For that is the kind of principle that nature is of each of them. [7] I mean, for example, that at least each of them must necessarily come to be dissolved; and there are likewise other things in which all share towards the whole. (1075^{a}11–25)[30]

Although commentators often dismiss Aristotle's reference to 'the nature of the whole' in [1] as a mere periphrasis for 'the whole', I am persuaded by Sedley's philological argument: the previously unnoticed second reference to this nature in [6] is strong evidence that Aristotle posits a cosmic nature.[31] Sedley identifies the nature of the whole with the Prime Mover, the 'one thing' to which everything bears a relation ([4]).[32] What kind of relation does each individual bear to the Prime Mover? Clearly, it is a kind of teleological relation in which the individual is in some sense for the sake of the Prime Mover, which [1] and [2] suggest is 'the good and the best'. Aristotle distinguishes two meanings of the phrase 'for the sake of which' (οὗ ἕνεκα): it can mean 'for the sake of which', as an aim or object to be realized (οὗ ἕνεκά τινος) or 'for the sake of which', as an object of benefit (οὗ ἕνεκά τινι). Three of the five passages throughout the corpus that distinguish these two meanings make the distinction specifically in order to show that individual things— the sphere of the fixed stars (*Metaph*. Λ 7, 1072^{b}1–2), humans (*EE* 8. 3, 1249^{b}15–16), and animals and plants (*DA* 2. 4, 415^{b}2–3)—are teleologically directed towards the Prime Mover as their aim, but *not* as an object of benefit. Individuals strive to *be* the Prime Mover, which is eternal, purely noetic activity.[33] But since they can never successfully achieve this aim, the most they can do is *approximate* it through imitation. In taking the best thing as their aim, individuals do not seek to improve or benefit the *end*, but they seek to improve *their own condition*: the more closely they approximate the activity of the best thing, the better they are.[34]

Individuals approximate the activity of the Prime Mover as fol-

[30] I use Sedley's own translation and sentence numbering ('Λ 10', 328–9).

[31] My interpretation thereby diverges from that of Bodnár, 'Teleology', who argues that we should read the passage reductively. See the next section for my interpretation of the relationship between individual nature and cosmic nature.

[32] He later amends his position to claim that cosmic nature is simply 'focused' on the Prime Mover (335).

[33] On the impossibility of distinguishing the perfect substance from the perfect activity, see G. Lawrence, 'Snakes in Paradise: Problems in the Ideal Life', *Southern Journal of Philosophy*, 43 (2005), 126–65 at 154.

[34] As Johnson points out (*Teleology*, 69), Themistius, Simplicius, and Philoponus all interpret *DA* 2. 4, 415^{a}25–^{b}7, to show that the individual animal (or the animal's

lows. The heavenly spheres directly imitate the Prime Mover's activity by eternally moving in perfect circles: since each point on a circle is as much an end as any other point (*Phys.* 8. 9, 265^{a}28–^{b}9), circular motion imitates the self-ended activity of the Prime Mover. Plants and animals imitate the eternal actuality of the Prime Mover by reproducing (*DA* 2. 4, 415^{a}25–^{b}7), while humans are the only animals who can imitate the Prime Mover in actually contemplating (*NE* 10. 7, 1177^{b}26–1178^{a}8; 10. 8, 1178^{b}7–32; *EE* 1. 7, 1217^{a}26–9). By imitating the circular movements of the heavenly bodies, the rectilinear movements of sublunary elements indirectly imitate the Prime Mover's activity: 'it is by imitating circular motion that rectilinear motion too is continuous' (*GC* 2. 10, 337^{a}1–7).[35]

But what is the nature of the teleological *joint*-arrangement mentioned in the passage? Although [4] clearly states that everything is, in fact, jointly arranged with everything else, it fails to state what kind of joint-arrangement obtains among individuals. Now, I certainly would agree with Sedley that the joint-arrangement is teleological, and not merely accidental, especially given [1] and [2]'s suggestion that the good is found in the arrangement and not just in that which is separated. But even if we can assume that the joint-arrangement is teleological, what kind of teleology is at stake? Aristotle maintains that the joint-arrangement is πρὸς ἕν, found in each thing's relation to one thing, the Prime Mover. As we have seen, the Prime Mover's activity cannot be directly imitated all the way down the hierarchy. For example, the heavenly spheres directly

soul) is the beneficiary of the body's being for the sake of participating in the divine. S. Menn seems to agree ('Aristotle's Definition of Soul and the Programme of the *De anima*', *Oxford Studies in Ancient Philosophy*, 22 (2002), 83–139 at 112). G. Richardson Lear argues, more generally, that it is 'no part' of imitative teleology that the end be a beneficiary (*Happy Lives and the Highest Good* [*Highest*] (Princeton, 2004), 76).

[35] Although there is some question about whether it is the transformation or the rectilinear movement of the elements that imitates the divine, *De generatione et corruptione* 2. 10 explicitly states that rectilinear motion does so. And, as C. H. Kahn argues, *Metaphysics* Θ 8, 1050^{b}28–30, claims that the elemental activity that imitates the imperishables is the activity they have by their own natures, so this activity must be their rectilinear movement ('The Place of the Prime Mover in Aristotle's Teleology' ['Place'], in A. Gotthelf (ed.), *Aristotle on Nature and Living Things: Philosophical and Historical Studies Presented to David M. Balme on his Seventieth Birthday* (Pittsburgh and Bristol, 1985), 183–205 at 189). Bodnár agrees that it is the elemental locomotions at issue in this passage ('Movers and Elemental Motions in Aristotle' ['Movers'], *Oxford Studies in Ancient Philosophy*, 15 (1997), 81–117 at 106).

imitate the Prime Mover's activity by their eternal rotation, while the sublunary elements must imitate the Prime Mover *indirectly*, through their imitation of the circular movement of the heavenly bodies. Now this certainly is *a* sense in which the individuals in the hierarchy are jointly arranged in relation to one thing: in aiming to imitate the Prime Mover, each individual imitates (and/or is imitated by) other individuals in the hierarchy. Given that individuals' teleological direction towards the Prime Mover is the *paradigmatic* example of the sort of teleology in which the individual does not seek to benefit the end, but seeks the end only as an aim, and given that the relationship between individual and Prime Mover is mirrored in the teleology that obtains between lower and higher individuals in the hierarchy, prima facie the teleological relationship between lower and higher individuals is one in which the lower is for the sake of the higher only as an aim. And, importantly, it seems to be no part of *this* relationship for a lower to be for the sake of *benefiting* a higher thing, but, if anything, it is part of this relationship for a lower thing to improve *its own condition* by approximating the activity of a better thing, and thereby approximating the activity of the best thing, the Prime Mover.

A closer look at the *Metaphysics Λ* 10 text suggests that Aristotle has only this imitative joint-arrangement in mind, and not an arrangement in which a lower thing is for the sake of benefiting a higher thing. According to [4], the joint-arrangement is somehow found in the relationship each thing bears to one thing. However, it is not at all clear why in both *A* and *B* aiming at some *C*, *A* and *B* would be jointly arranged so that *A* is for the sake of benefiting *B*, but it is perfectly clear why, in both *A* and *B* aiming at some *C*, *A* and *B* would be jointly arranged such that *A* is for the sake of *B* as an aim (where *B* more closely approximates *C* than *A* does). This interpretation also makes sense of [3], in which Aristotle claims that 'even creatures which swim, creatures which fly, and plants' are jointly arranged.[36] These cases are supposed to serve as *examples* of the sort of joint-arrangement Aristotle has in mind. But if Aristotle had in mind the lower benefiting the higher, it is not clear why it would (as Sedley notes) '[suit] Aristotle's purposes to trace this single activity [i.e. locomotion], the fundamental species of change, all the way down from the heavenly spheres, through the characteristic motions of natural species, and down to

[36] For my interpretation of the household analogy in [5], see the end of sect. 5.

the redistribution of the simple elements'.[37] And, again, this kind of joint-arrangement is at work in [7]: each thing is dissolved into its elements, whose rectilinear movements imitate the locomotive cycles of the heavenly bodies.

On this reading, then, *Metaphysics Λ* 10 shows that winter rain and corn are jointly arranged with each other—just to the extent to which their activities approximate that of the Prime Mover by their imitating the circular motion of the heavenly bodies: winter rain imitates the circular motion of the heavenly bodies by moving rectilinearly, while corn imitates it by generating another of its kind (*GC* 2. 10, 336ᵇ27–337ᵃ8). And even though Aristotle never suggests that sublunary things imitate other sublunary things as intermediaries to imitating the divine, he does maintain that sublunary living things are closer than sublunary elements to approximating the activity of the Prime Mover (*GA* 2. 1, 731ᵇ24–732ᵃ1).

So even though nothing in *Metaphysics Λ* 10 excludes the possibility that a lower thing is for the sake of benefiting a higher thing, such a relationship is *not* part of the teleology of approximation at work in *Metaphysics Λ* 10.[38] To find explicit reference to (or even just an obvious role for) lower things' being for the sake of benefiting higher things, Sedley's *sole* source is *Politics* 1. 8:[39]

Even at the moment of childbirth, some animals generate at the same time sufficient nutriment to last until the offspring can supply itself—for example all the animals which produce larvae or lay eggs. And those which bear live young have nutriment within themselves for their offspring for a time, the substance called milk. Hence it is equally clear that we should also suppose that, after birth, plants exist for the sake of animals, and the other animals for the sake of men—domesticated animals for both usefulness and food, and most if not all wild animals for food and other assistance, as a source of clothing and other utilities. If, then, nature makes nothing

---

[37] Sedley, '*Λ* 10', 336. See also *Phys.* 4. 14, 223ᵇ24–6.

[38] Sedley wants to show that it is in the 'objective workings' of cosmic nature to direct winter rain to grow the corn, and that it is, at a more ultimate remove, 'the world as a whole whose own nature it is to bring men rain at the right times and in the right places' ('Anthropocentric', 184 and 192). However, Sedley admits that *Metaphysics Λ* 10 is 'of neutral evidential value' as to whether Aristotle thinks lower things are for the sake of benefiting higher things ('*Λ* 10', 332 n. 9).

[39] In his most recent work, Sedley points to three additional passages in support of his view of global teleology: *Phys.* 2. 4, 196ᵃ24–35; 2. 6, 198ᵃ5–13; and *PA* 1. 1, 641ᵇ10–23 (*Creationism and its Critics in Antiquity* [*Creationism*] (Berkeley and Los Angeles, 2007), 191–6). However, these arguments seem to invoke the hierarchy at work in *Metaphysics Λ* 10, and not one in which lower benefits higher.

incomplete or pointless, it is necessary that nature has made them all for the sake of men. $(1256^{b}10-22)^{40}$

Notice that the teleology at work in this passage is different from, and does not even refer to, the teleology of approximation discussed in *Metaphysics* Λ 10. Moreover, this passage does not explicitly invoke Λ 10's 'nature of the whole'. It is Sedley who must forge the connection:

Once more, the 'nature' in question can hardly be identified with the natures of the individual plants and animals, or for that matter human nature. For Aristotle certainly does not think it is any part of the nature of the plants and lower animals to serve the interests of their predators, human or other; and although it is part of human nature to exploit them, Aristotle's point is evidently not that here: for example, plants exist for the sake of animals in general, he is telling us, and that aspect of the hierarchy could hardly be part of human nature. Rather it is the complex cosmic nature that is manifested in the world's inter-species ecology.[41]

However, the following alternative interpretation is available, and as I shall show, is well supported by other texts: plants are for the sake of animals in the sense that it is part of animal nature to make use of plants, and animals are for the sake of humans in the sense that it is part of human nature to make use of animals. Sedley is correct to note that it is not part of human nature that plants exist for the sake of animals (except, I might add, in the case of humans feeding plants to domesticated animals), but the scope of 'all' in the final sentence can be understood as limited to the domestic and wild animals invoked in the immediately preceding sentence. So understood, Aristotle is not saying that plants' being for the sake of animals is governed by human nature, but only that human nature is responsible for the fact that the domestic and wild animals are for the sake of humans.[42] Then the claim that plants are for the sake of animals can be understood to have its source in animals' natures.[43]

The biological works confirm that food's being for the sake of its

---

[40] I use Sedley's translation ('Anthropocentric', 180).

[41] Sedley, *Creationism*, 202.

[42] For a similar proposal see Bodnár, 'Teleology', 25.

[43] Aristotle argues: 'And in general, art perfects some of the things which nature cannot complete, and imitates others. Therefore, if artistic things are purposive, clearly so are natural things' (*Phys.* 2. 8, 199ᵃ15–18). From this quotation Sedley concludes that 'the imposition of art does not alter the pre-existing natural aims, but adds new ways of achieving those same aims' ('Anthropocentric', 187). For example, in Sedley's paradigm cases of the arts of agriculture, butchery, and hunting, art

beneficiary's benefit has its source in the beneficiary's nature, and
do not suggest that cosmic nature or the nature of the benefiter is

completes the pre-existing aim of feeding humans. So Sedley would argue that it is
not enough for his opponent to dismiss anthropocentrism by showing that it is in
human nature to make use of plants and animals for humans' own purpose. Rather,
the art/nature analogy at work in 199ᵃ15–18 shows that in using plants and animals
for human purposes, humans merely aid in the achievement of ends that plants and
animals *already have*.

But consider again the case of agriculture: Sedley maintains that the art of agriculture completes the pre-existing aim of feeding humans. The nature that was
unsuccessful in achieving this end is *cosmic* nature, not the plant's individual nature
(for, on Sedley's view, the plant's own nature has no such aim) ('Anthropocentric',
192). But the context of the argument suggests that Aristotle is interested to show
that *individual* natures aim at ends, as Sedley recognizes when he says that the argument seeks 'to show that other natural species [i.e. other than humans] also function
teleologically' (187), and that '*Physics* ii is another book concerned with individual
natures. Aristotle's theology is presupposed there, but not directly addressed in its
own right' (195–6). However, if cosmic nature is the source of plants' and animals'
being for the sake of human nutrition, by showing the arts of agriculture, butchery,
and hunting to complete the task of *cosmic nature*, Aristotle will not be any closer
to concluding that 'other natural species' also function teleologically according to
their own natures.

Sedley seems to lose track of the fact that he is committed to claiming in these
cases that *cosmic* nature is completed by art: Sedley thinks the case of agriculture
shows that 'it is no less the *nature of crops* to provide men with food than it is the
nature of man himself to seek food' since the '*crops* are too weak to grow without the
art of farming' ('Anthropocentric', 189, emphasis added). But in keeping with what
he says later in his article, Sedley should have said that it is in the nature of the cosmos
to provide men with food since the art of agriculture achieves the ends *cosmic* nature
was too weak to complete on its own. But this cannot be the point at issue: as I have
argued, such a point would not support Aristotle's conclusion, which (according to
Sedley's own interpretation) focuses on individual natures.

Sedley also argues: 'Aristotle does not merely assert the anthropocentric teleology, but argues for it: given that the mother's milk exists by nature for the sake
of her offspring, there is no ground for denying that same natural function to external food sources, which take over the job of milk exactly where it leaves off'
('Anthropocentric', 181). The question is, however, *which nature* directs mother's
milk to be for the sake of the child? Human nature? Milk's own nature? Cosmic
nature? And is this the same nature that directs animals to take over where milk
left off?

Sedley is clear that cosmic nature directs animals to be for the sake of humans,
and although he does not say which nature is at work in the milk example, it would
be odd if he thought cosmic nature was responsible in that case as well. It seems
more plausible that it is part of human nature to produce milk to supply the child.
Notice that in *Politics* 1. 8 the reason why the parent produces milk is because at the
time of birth the child cannot 'supply itself'. Presumably, then, when the child can
'supply itself', it is part of its human nature to lay hold of animals for nourishment,
just as its parent used milk to accomplish this task. On my reading, the child takes
over where the parent left off since the child can now 'supply itself'.

In the examples from *Historia animalium* that I go on to discuss in this section, it
is part of the parent fish's nature to migrate into the Pontus, where fresh water will
'complete the nourishment' of their eggs (7. 13, 598ᵇ4–6), but once the offspring

responsible. In *De partibus animalium* Aristotle argues that animals have the morphological features they do because of the type of food they eat. Given that animal behaviour includes eating certain foods, individual animals have the appropriate parts to deal with this food. For example, 3. 1 suggests that birds have the beaks they have based on the type of food they ingest, not that the food they ingest has the consistency it has so that it can be easily picked up by the beaks of birds (662ᵃ34–ᵇ16).⁴⁴ Aristotle offers this kind of explanation not only for external parts, but also for internal ones (3. 4 665ᵇ2–5; 3. 14 675ᵇ13–14). To continue with our example, since birds have beaks instead of teeth, they take their food in without grinding it up. Consequently they must have digestive tracts to deal with such big pieces. Some birds have a broad oesophagus and others have a strong fleshy stomach to hold the food for the long time it takes to digest such big pieces. But since the water-dwelling birds' food is moist and easily ground up all they need is a long crop (3. 14, 674ᵇ17–35).⁴⁵ Thus the digestive system is tailored to the type of food ingested, not the other way round.

When Aristotle discusses breeding and migration patterns in the *Historia animalium*, he claims these patterns depend on the seasons

---

are old enough, it will be part of their nature to migrate (that is, move *themselves*) into the places in which food is plentiful.

⁴⁴ The biological works are full of such examples. Birds' wingedness is determined by the type of food they eat: flesh-eating birds as well as migratory birds need wings, but fruit-eating ones and those that live in the water do not (*PA* 4. 12, 694ᵃ1 ff.). Long-legged birds have a long neck which is useful 'for feeding off the ground', and water-dwelling birds have a long neck which is useful 'for getting nourishment from the water'. But flesh-eating birds have a short strong neck instead of a long weak neck, since they must overpower their prey (4. 12, 692ᵇ20–693ᵃ10). Since crook-taloned birds search for food from above, they have sharp vision (2. 13 657ᵇ26–7). The camel has several stomachs because its food is thorny and woody and thus hard to concoct (3. 14, 674ᵃ29–31), and since its nourishment is thorny the roof of its mouth is hard (674ᵇ2–5). Since elephants sometimes get nourishment from the water, they have a long trunk so that they can breathe while in water (2. 16, 659ᵃ2–15). Elephants and insects have odour receptors both for taking in nourishment and for strength (4. 6, 682ᵇ35–683ᵃ3). Since they obtain their food from below, sea urchins (as well as all the other spiral-shells and limpets) have a head and mouth below, where their food is (*HA* 4. 5, 530ᵇ22–4).

For a recent discussion of some of these passages, see P. Pellegrin, 'Les ruses de la nature et l'éternité du mouvement: encore quelques remarques sur la finalité chez Aristote' ['Ruses'], in M. Canto-Sperber and P. Pellegrin (eds.), *Le Style de la pensée. En Hommage à Jacques Brunschwig* (Paris, 2002), 296–323.

⁴⁵ Fish are unable to grind up their nourishment, and thus must have a crop in front of their stomach (4. 5, 679ᵃ32–ᵇ3).

and not the other way around (8. 12, 596ᵇ21–9).⁴⁶ The treatise offers several such examples: in the summer, fish migrate into the Pontus in order to take advantage of its plentiful food supply (7. 13, 598ᵃ30–ᵇ1; 7. 19, 601ᵇ16–19), and they lay their eggs there so that the fresh water can complete the nourishment of the embryos (7. 13, 598ᵇ4–6).⁴⁷ In particular, fish lay their eggs near land since food is more plentiful there (6. 13, 567ᵇ14). Just as animal bodies are tailored to the type of food they eat, their bodies are also designed to bring them into the location of their food: for example, since insects range widely in search of food, they have light bodies propelled by four wings (*PA* 4. 6, 682ᵃ7–8).⁴⁸

The point that these passages drive home is that for Aristotle animals have the morphological features they do, and they live and breed where and when they do, because of the location and type of food they eat. Given that animals take in nutrients and grow, they have the proper bodily parts and live in a proper location for taking in such nutrients. This is *not* to say that the nutrients are to be located where they are and have the consistency they do so that the animals can take them in as food.⁴⁹ *Physics* 2. 8 suggests that this is the case with plants as well: the roots of plants grow down instead of up since their food is located in the ground (199ᵃ29–30), *not* that the water is located in the ground in order to be taken in by plant roots.⁵⁰ Applying *De generatione et corruptione* 1. 5's discussion of growth to the case of plants shows that plants grow by the growth of their non-uniform parts and these non-uniform parts grow by the growth of the uniform parts. And the uniform parts grow by acting on nourishment in such a way that they assimilate the nourishment to themselves. Growing by taking in water as food is one of the ends corn has by its very nature.

Thus, I have argued that although cosmic nature plays a role in the teleological joint-arrangement among individuals, none the less it does not play the role Sedley thinks it plays in *Physics* 2. 8. On

⁴⁶ See also 7. 1, where Aristotle claims that animal lives differ according to nutrition (588ᵃ16–17).

⁴⁷ And bloodless animals are generated near the mouths of rivers since their food is there (*GA* 3. 11, 761ᵇ9).

⁴⁸ Cf. J. Lear, *Aristotle: The Desire to Understand* (Cambridge, 1988), 25.

⁴⁹ Judson, 'Teleology', 355 and n. 46, and Pellegrin, 'Ruses', also argue along these lines.

⁵⁰ Aristotle repeats this point at *PA* 6. 4, 678ᵃ11. He also denies that fire is the cause ἁπλῶς of nutrition and growth (*DA* 2. 4, 416ᵃ10–19) and that fire and earth produce the parts of animals (*GA* 2. 1, 734ᵇ27–735ᵃ4).

Sedley's reading of that passage, winter rain is by cosmic nature, which directs winter rain to make the corn grow—that is, to aim at corn's benefit. But this joint-arrangement of winter rain and corn is not the sort of joint-arrangement that cosmic nature directs individuals to bear to one another in *Metaphysics* Λ 10. Instead, Λ 10 is interested to show an imitative joint-arrangement among individuals that mirrors (and is an intermediary to) the imitative teleological relationship that each individual bears to the Prime Mover. *Politics* 1. 8 is the *only* text that suggests the sort of joint-arrangement Sedley finds in *Physics* 2. 8. However, taking *Politics* 1. 8 together with the biological works suggests that this joint-arrangement, in which a lower benefits a higher, has its source in the beneficiary's nature, and does not suggest that cosmic nature or the nature of the benefiter is responsible.

Sedley might press, however, that although the biological works show that it is part of a higher thing's nature to make use of lower things in the hierarchy for its own benefit, I have only an argument from silence to support my claim that it is *not* part of cosmic nature or of lower things' individual natures to direct lower things to be for the sake of benefiting higher things. After all, as I admitted, nothing in *Metaphysics* Λ 10 excludes the possibility that cosmic nature directs lower things to be for the sake of benefiting higher things. And neither do the texts that focus on the natures of the sublunary elements exclude the possibility that they have such an aim. In principle, it is possible that the teleology of lower benefiting higher has two sources—that it is *both* in the nature of a higher thing to make use of lower things for its own benefit *and* in the nature of the lower things (or in the nature of the cosmos) for lower things to be for the sake of benefiting higher things.

However, even though this is true *in principle*, it seems to be ruled out by Aristotle's frequent insistence that 'nature does nothing in vain' or 'superfluous'. For example, animals whose teeth serve as offensive and defensive weapons do not, in addition, have tusks. For in such animals tusks would be superfluous—they would serve the purpose that the teeth already serve (*PA* 3. 1, 661^{b}16–33). Just as Aristotle insists that animals do not need two parts to serve the purpose that a single part accomplishes on its own, so too it seems that he would resist the view that there are two natures that serve the purpose a single nature accomplishes on its own: if, as we have seen, it is written into corn's own nature to grow roots into water's

location in order to take in the water as food, why would it *also* need
to be part of water's nature or cosmic nature to bring water to that
location for the sake of being taken in by plant roots? There need
not be two natures that aim at corn's benefiting from its watery
nourishment as long as one nature—corn's nature—can explain the
phenomenon. Thus, not only is there no textual evidence that the
teleology of lower benefiting higher has two sources, but Aristotle
has a philosophical reason to resist such a view.[51]

Let us take stock. Although I have not yet answered the question
of *which* nature is expressed in winter rain, in this section I have
argued that winter rain does not take growing corn as its end. For
there is *no* nature that directs winter rain to have such an end:
neither water's own nature nor cosmic nature directs winter rain
to grow corn, and the nature that does take growing corn as its
end—corn's own nature—is not expressed in winter rain.

5. The Natural Place Interpretation

So if, as I argued (*pace* NTRI), *Physics* 2. 8 shows winter rain to
be teleological and if, as I argued (*pace* the Corn Growth Interpretation), growing corn is neither the end of water's nature nor
the end of cosmic nature (although it is true that growing by taking in water as food is an end of corn's nature), what is the end
of winter rain? The *Physics* 2. 8 argument passage itself gives us
little guidance—all it says is that winter rain is regular, and thus
teleological. But if we return to the introduction of the rain case
in the statement of the problem, Aristotle's opponent maintains
that rain occurs 'of necessity. (For what was taken up must become
cold, and what has become cold, having become water, must come
down)' (198^{b}19–20). Since the argument passage is a response to
the statement of the problem as posed by the opponent, it makes
sense to consider, first, whether Aristotle thinks water's generation

[51] The success of this argument rests on my ability to show that there is no non-
accidental phenomenon left over for cosmic nature to explain. This section showed
that corn's benefiting from winter rain can be explained by corn's nature directing
it to make use of winter rain for the sake of corn's own benefit. But it will be crucial
for my next section to show how the explanation of its raining *when it does* need not
make any reference to biological processes. Without such an account, there would
be a remaining phenomenon for cosmic nature to explain. Cf. Sedley's argument
that 'rain *per se* may fall in order to return to its natural place; but rain falls *where
and when it regularly does* in order to make plants grow' ('Anthropocentric', 191).

and movement downwards are themselves teleological and, second, whether this teleology is the one at work in the winter rain example.

Physics 2 offers at least prima facie evidence that water's own nature aims at an end. As I argued in the previous section, *Physics* 2. 1 claims that each of the elements, as well as plants, animals, and their parts, is by nature in the sense that they have a nature ($192^{b}16$). Aristotle then claims that fire's moving upwards is by nature, thereby suggesting that fire's own nature is the source of the upward motion ($193^{a}1$). Thus *Physics* 2 at least prima facie expresses a commitment to the sublunary elements having a nature and to their natures being the source of their movements.[52] Taking these claims together with the target claim of *Physics* 2. 8—that nature aims at an end—suggests that the elemental natures teleologically direct elemental movements.

Offering a more detailed account of elemental teleology, *De caelo* cites the end to which water's nature directs it—its natural place.[53] *De caelo* 1. 8 maintains that a body moves according to nature to the place in which it rests without force ($276^{a}24$), which for water is on the ground.[54] And 4. 3 describes an element's natural place as the place in which an element has being or 'is [ἔστιν]' and has reached its 'actuality [ἐντελέχειαν]' ($311^{a}3$–6). The use of ἐντελέχειαν strongly suggests that elemental movement into natural place is robustly teleological.[55]

---

[52] And *Physics* 2 is not alone. For example, *Physics* 8. 4 repeats the claim that the elemental motions are φύσει ($255^{a}4$–5; $255^{a}29$–30). 'For indeed fire and earth are moved by something by force whenever contrary to nature, and by nature whenever, being in potential, [they are moved] into their actualities [ἐνεργείας]' (*Phys.* 8. 4, $255^{a}29$–30). See also *Phys.* 4. 4, $211^{a}4$–5 and $212^{b}29$–34.

[53] *De caelo* offers further prima facie evidence of Aristotle's commitment to elemental teleology: the four sublunary elements have functions (ἔργα: 3. 8, $307^{b}22$), and 'everything which has a function [ἔργον] is for the sake of its function [ἕνεκα τοῦ ἔργου]' (2. 3, $286^{a}8$–9). And *De caelo* explicitly argues that no natural thing is purposeless (1. 4, $271^{a}35$, and 2. 11, $291^{b}14$). Although his immediate concern in these passages from *De caelo* 1 and 2 is the heavenly bodies, none the less Aristotle phrases his statements as generalizations that seem to warrant the extension to the other natural things (including the four sublunary elements) discussed in the same treatise.

[54] The elements have the potential to be in their natural places, and their natures direct them there (*De caelo* 1. 6, $273^{a}19$–22).

[55] See also *Phys.* 8. 4, $255^{a}29$–31; $255^{b}12$–17; 4. 4, $211^{a}4$–7; 4. 5, $212^{b}30$–1. The actuality is the τέλος: see e.g. *Metaph.* Θ 8, $1050^{a}9$–10. Note that the centre/periphery is not the τέλος of an element without qualification. Place, after all, is not one of the four causes (*Phys.* 4. 1, $209^{a}20$–1). So *De caelo* 1. 6 makes it clear that an element aims not at *being* the centre or periphery but *being at* the centre or the periphery: 'But the body being carried up and down has the potentiality to come to be in this

Given that Aristotle seems to think that water's downward movement is teleological, is this the teleology at work in *Physics* 2. 8? Recall that the initial challenge in the statement of the problem is to show that nature acts for something *and* because it is better. If water's downward movement were for the sake of growing corn, it would be immediately obvious that the end is somehow a 'better', but it is at least initially puzzling how water's movement into natural place would be in any sense better.

Metaphysics Λ 10 suggests a solution. As I showed in the last section, each individual is teleologically directed at the Prime Mover as its aim. Water's movement is so directed via the heavenly bodies: water's rectilinear motions imitate the circular motion of the heavenly bodies, which in turn imitates the activity of the Prime Mover.[56] In moving rectilinearly the sublunary elements cannot become the best (for they cannot become the Prime Mover, and only the Prime Mover is best), but none the less they can *approximate* the circular movement of the heavenly bodies, which approximates the activity of the Prime Mover. The sublunary element thereby can become, as *De caelo* 2. 12 explicitly states, 'better' even though not 'best' (292^b17–25).[57]

Notice now that the very movement of water that imitates the divine—water's downward rectilinear movement—just is the movement by water's *own* nature—a καθ᾽ αὑτό (*Phys.* 2. 1, 192^b35–6) movement essential to water (8. 4, 255^b15–17).[58] *Metaphysics* Θ 8 confirms that the movements by which the sublunary elements imitate the heavenly bodies are movements the sublunary elements have '*of themselves and in themselves*' (1050^b28–30, emphasis added). Likewise in the case of animals and plants: their 'most natural' activity, generation, and indeed *all* of their natural movements, just

[δύναται ἐν τούτῳ γενέσθαι], for it is by nature [πέφυκε] to be moved from the centre and to the centre' (1. 6, 273^a19–22). *De caelo* 4. 3, 311^a3–6, describes natural place as that which is *of* a thing's actuality, vs. *being* or constituting its actuality.

[56] Later in this section I offer a more refined interpretation of Aristotle's position such that not just any rectilinear movement imitates circular movement.

[57] *GA* 2. 1 claims that the divine (i.e. the Prime Mover) is the cause of the 'better' in those things that admit of being better or worse. Aristotle is clear that non-living things, although worse than living things, none the less admit of being better or worse (731^b24–732^a1). See also *De generatione et corruptione* 2. 10 and *De generatione animalium* 2. 1, where Aristotle suggests that all natural things aim at what is best.

[58] See Kahn, 'Place', 189, and Richardson Lear, *Highest*, 86. Richardson Lear should be consulted for further exploration of these issues, especially as applied to the interpretation of *Nicomachean Ethics* 10.

are the very movements that approximate the activity of the Prime Mover. Individuals *partake* of the divine in so far as they are able to do so by their own nature (*DA* 2. 4, 415^{a}25–^{b}7), and the greater and lesser extents to which individuals partake in the divine create a hierarchy of beings stretching from the heavenly bodies—which are 'more divine' (*De caelo* 1. 2, 269^{a}32–3) since they have 'a higher nature' due to their distance from the sublunary world (1. 2, 269^{b}16–17)—all the way down to even the sublunary elements, which, *De caelo* 2. 12 confirms, 'share in the divine source [τυχεῖν τῆς θειοτάτης ἀρχῆς]' (292^{b}17–25).[59] In so far as the movements that are by the individual's own nature approximate the Prime Mover's activity, the individual nature shares in the cosmic nature. In this way, the expression of an individual's own nature *just is* an expression of the cosmic nature: for, as *Metaphysics* Λ 10 [6] maintains, the '[cosmic] nature . . . [is a principle] of each of them'. We can understand water's own nature to be cosmic just to the extent to which water's natural downward movement approximates the activity of the Prime Mover.[60]

In the light of *Metaphysics* Λ 10, we can now see how water's movement into natural place is a case not only of water's nature 'acting for something', but also 'because it is better'. However, it remains to be seen whether this is the teleology at work in *Physics* 2. 8's

[59] And, more generally, *Physics* 1. 9 maintains that form is 'divine and good and desirable' (192^{a}17).

[60] Both Sedley and Bodnár are committed to the claim that each individual's teleological direction on the Prime Mover has its source *either* in cosmic nature *or* in individual nature. Sedley argues for the former: 'It is much easier to see this inclination towards everlasting recurrence as an aspiration of the overall cosmic nature—if as we have seen confirmed, there is one—than of the individual natures of cabbages, flames, or drops of water' ('Λ 10', 334); while Bodnár argues for the latter ('Teleology', 27). My view, as inspired by Richardson Lear's discussion of approximation (*Highest*, 80–5), suggests that individual nature *partakes* of or approximates cosmic nature. Thus, I am immune to Bodnár's argument against Sedley that cosmic nature is not on a par with other natures since it is not an internal principle of movement and rest ('Teleology', 19). On my view, it is such a principle internal to individual things: the natures of individual things are cosmic to the extent to which individuals' natural movements approximate the activity of the Prime Mover. In this sense the 'nature of the whole' (Λ 10 [1]) is also a 'principle . . . of each' (Λ 10 [6]). And in countenancing a role for the *cosmic* nature of each individual that Sedley reads in [6], I am also immune to Sedley's response to Bodnár's overall argument: 'I argue in particular that the second reference to "nature" [in [6]] . . . enables us to recognize a second reference to global nature. Bodnár 2005 ['Teleology'], pp. 18–19, is right, I think, to reply that the sentence *could* still be read as referring to individual nature. But it becomes much the less natural reading, because "the nature of the whole" is the already announced topic' (*Creationism*, 199 n. 59).

winter rain example. Recall that the argument passage maintains that *winter* rain is teleological and that *summer* rain is infrequent and accidental. So if water's teleology is at issue in the winter rain example, Aristotle's view must be that water moves into its natural place teleologically in the winter but not in the summer. Although many commentators acknowledge Aristotle's commitment to the teleology of elemental motion into natural place, they deny that this is the teleology at issue in *Physics* 2. 8, for how can it make sense to say that water falls to the ground teleologically in the winter but not in the summer?[61] This is the sole reason why Sedley quickly dismisses the Natural Place Interpretation: regardless of the season, Sedley argues, water moves into natural place when it rains.[62]

Although it is true that water moves into its natural place whenever it falls unobstructed (whether as rain or otherwise), I submit that Aristotle's refined view is that water moves into its natural place *naturally and teleologically only upon being generated by the sun* (*i.e. in the winter*). *Physics* 8. 4 reveals the special relationship the elements bear to their generator, the sun. There Aristotle explicitly denies that the elements are self-movers and thereby denies that their nature is an efficient cause of their movements. Unlike self-moving living things, the elements, *qua* things that have a nature, do not have a source of moving (an ἀρχὴ τοῦ κινεῖν) but a source of suffering (an ἀρχὴ τοῦ πάσχειν, 255ᵇ31). Understanding an ἀρχὴ τοῦ πάσχειν as a source of being moved (ἀρχὴ τοῦ κινεῖσθαι) is in keeping with *Physics* 2. 1's introductory definition of nature as a 'source of movement [ἀρχὴ κινήσεως]' since 'movement [κινήσεως]' is am-

---

[61] Sedley suggests, but immediately rejects, a version of a Natural Place Interpretation: 'There is something intrinsically valuable about the downward motion of water from the clouds—namely, its return to its own place' ('Anthropocentric', 184). Philoponus rejects the Corn Growth Interpretation but accepts the fact that rainfall is teleological (*In Phys.* 312. 23–313. 28 Vitelli). Wardy offers a version of a Natural Place Interpretation that attempts to make sense of winter rain as teleological and summer rain as accidental. He claims rain (whether in the winter or in the summer) is always for the sake of being in its natural place and that only the circumstances surrounding summer rain are accidental ('Rainfall', 22). On my view, however, elemental natures are fitted to the movements of the sun so that water's coming down as rain in the summer is accidental, not just that the circumstances surrounding summer rain are accidental.

[62] Sedley, 'Anthropocentric', 184. Sedley goes on to argue: 'Rain *per se* may fall in order to return to its natural place; but rain falls *where and when it regularly does* in order make plants grow' (191).

biguous between the active (κινεῖν) and passive (κινεῖσθαι) senses.[63] In so far as the elements have as their nature an ἀρχὴ τοῦ κινεῖσθαι they are such as to be moved by something else that is their efficient cause. Thus, *Physics* 8. 4 shows that water's movement by nature—that is, its movement by its ἀρχὴ τοῦ κινεῖσθαι—requires an external efficient cause.

Physics 8. 4 further maintains that the efficient cause of water's movement into natural place is the efficient cause of its generation, the sun. Aristotle arrives at this claim in the course of arguing for the conclusion that everything that moves is moved by something (256ᵃ4):

And these [i.e. those non-self movers which are moved by nature] are those that may present a difficulty: by what is it moved?—for example, the light things and the heavy things. For these are moved into opposite places by force and into their proper places by nature—the light up [by nature] and the heavy down [by nature]. But it is no longer clear [that they are moved] by something, as when they are being moved contrary to nature [παρὰ φύσιν]. (255ᵃ1–6)

Aristotle traces the confusion regarding the efficient cause of elemental movement to the failure to recognize that 'potentiality is said in various ways' (255ᵃ30). Once we distinguish the two sorts of potentiality—the second potential to move into natural place and the first potential to come to be—we see that movement is the second phase of a single two-phase process (of which coming to be is the first stage).[64] While we had trouble identifying the efficient cause of elemental movement into natural place (the second phase), it is clear that the efficient cause of the first phase is the generator of the elements. So, once we realize that the two phases compose a single process, it is clear that the generator is the efficient cause of elemental movement into natural place; the chapter concludes: 'The light and the heavy . . . [are moved] by the thing that has generated and has made them light or heavy' (256ᵃ1–3).[65] Although

---

[63] For a helpful discussion of this point, see H. Lang, *The Order of Nature in Aristotle's Physics* (Cambridge, 1998), 40 ff.

[64] *De caelo* 4. 3, the companion passage to *Physics* 8. 4, confirms that movement is a stage in the process of generation: 'So whenever air comes into being out of water, light out of heavy, it goes upwards. It is forthwith light: it no longer comes to be, but there it is [καὶ οὐκέτι γίνεται, ἀλλ' ἐκεῖ ἔστιν]' (311ᵃ2–3). The fact that an element no longer comes to be after it is in its natural place suggests that movement is part of the process of generation.

[65] The passage also mentions the hindrance-remover as a cause (256ᵃ3), but Aris-

Aristotle does not mention what this generator is (since all that matters for his purposes here is that there is one), it is clear from what he says elsewhere that it is the sun moving along the ecliptic (*Meteor.* 1. 9, 346^{b}22; *GC* 2. 10, 336^{b}6–7).

Thus, *Physics* 8. 4 shows that water's movement by nature—that is, its movement by its ἀρχὴ τοῦ κινεῖσθαι—requires an external efficient cause. And given that water's movement into natural place is part of the process of water's coming to be, the external efficient cause of water's movement into natural place is the sun, the efficient cause of water's generation. Since water's nature makes essential reference to the sun—water's nature is a source of being moved by the sun—we can now see that Aristotle's refined position is that water falls naturally and teleologically when it is moved by the sun, which is *in the winter*. Although when water comes to be in the summer it reaches its natural place, none the less its movement there is not due to its nature, which makes essential reference to its proper mover, the sun. Aristotle stresses that that which happens

totle clearly thinks it is an *accidental* efficient cause (255^{b}27). The reason many commentators claim that the generator should also be considered an *accidental* efficient cause of elemental motion is that they think (mistakenly, on my view) Aristotle's conception of natural change requires it, not that the text of *Physics* 8. 4 demands it. See e.g. S. Sauvé Meyer, 'Self-Movement and External Causation', in M. L. Gill and J. G. Lennox (eds.), *Self-Motion: From Aristotle to Newton* (Princeton, 1994), 65–80 at 77 n. 20. However, if nature can be understood as a source of *being moved*, then movements into natural place can be understood as natural changes even if their efficient cause is external. On my view, the elements are formally responsible for their own movements, the sun is the non-accidental efficient cause of these movements. *Physics* 8. 4 highlights the contribution an element makes to its own natural movement. As Bodnár notes, *Physics* 8. 4 sharply distinguishes two questions regarding elemental movement: 'By what [ὑπὸ τίνος] is it [i.e. an element] moved?' (255^{a}2), and 'Why [διὰ τί] are the light and the heavy ever moved into their place?' (255^{b}14) ('Movers', 89). While the answer to the first question cites the efficient cause of elemental movement—the generator (ὑπὸ τοῦ γεννήσαντος, 256^{a}2)—the answer to the second question cites the formal cause—'the cause is that it is by nature somewhere and this is what it is to be [εἶναι] light and heavy' (255^{b}15–17). Even though the elements have an external efficient cause, they have an internal formal cause, their nature, which determines their manner of movement. Consequently, the elements are themselves formally responsible for their movements, and their natural movements are not at the whim of their mover.

For other commentators who maintain that the generator is an accidental cause of movement, see B. Morison, *On Location: Aristotle's Concept of Place* (Oxford, 2002), 27 and 27 n. 78, and M. L. Gill, *Aristotle on Substance: The Paradox of Unity* (Princeton, 1989), 31. Furley finds the issue perplexing ('Self-Movers', in M. L. Gill and J. G. Lennox (eds.), *Self-Motion: From Aristotle to Newton* (Princeton, 1994), 3–14 at 4). See also F. Solmsen, *Aristotle's System of the Physical World* [*System*] (Ithaca, NY, 1960), 384.

by chance is that which might have come to be (ἂν γένοιτο) for the sake of something (*Phys.* 2. 5, 197ᵃ35; see also 2. 6, 198ᵃ7). Water's falling in the summer might have been for the sake of something if it were due to the sun's recession in the winter; water moves naturally and teleologically into its natural place only when the sun serves as its efficient cause in the winter.

Given this refined view of water's teleology found in the *Physics* and in *De caelo*, and given that Aristotle thinks it is water that falls as rain, we would expect the *Meteorologica* to show that water's falling to the ground as *winter rain* is teleological, while water's falling to the ground as *summer rain* is not.[66] The Arab commentary tradition on the *Meteorologica* claims that this is indeed Aristotle's view: both Avicenna's *Kitāb aš-Šifā'* and Averroes' *Short Commentary* agree with Pseudo-Olympiodorus, who claims that condensation by recoil (i.e. summer rain and hail) occurs accidentally (*bi-tarīq al-ʿarad*), whereas condensation in the cold of winter occurs essentially (*bi-ḏātihī*) or teleologically.[67] In what follows I fill out this view found in the Arab commentary tradition by reading the *Meteorologica* in the light of water's teleology as described in *De caelo* and *Physics* 8. 4.[68]

---

[66] Notice that *Physics* 8. 4 shows water's natural downward movement to be the second phase of the two-phase process caused by the sun (of which coming-to-be is the first stage). Thus, the sun must generate water above the ground, and so when water falls naturally, it falls as *rain* (or as another form of precipitation that composes one of the three cycles caused by the sun—see n. 68).

[67] See P. Lettinck, *Aristotle's* Meteorology *and its Reception in the Arab World* (Leiden, 1999), 97–119.

[68] Aristotle clearly thinks that water, by its very nature, aims to move into its natural place by the efficient causal power of the sun. Although I focus on winter rain as one such teleological, natural movement, the *Meteorologica* claims that the sun causes *three* cycles of evaporation and condensation. First, there is the yearly cycle of summer evaporation and winter rain. As we have seen, the sun's annual movement along the ecliptic accounts for this regularity. Second, there is the daily cycle of evaporation and condensation into dew/hoar frost (into dew in summer and into hoar frost in winter), which is linked to the sun's daily movement (347ᵃ13 ff.). And last, Aristotle describes the cycle of floods and drought, a cycle that returns on itself only after 'a great period of time' (352ᵃ31; see also 2. 3, 357ᵃ2), and thus escapes our notice (1. 14, 351ᵇ8). This cycle is regular (1. 14, 351ᵃ26; 352ᵃ31; 352ᵇ16; 2. 2, 355ᵃ28) and due to the sun's movement (1. 14, 352ᵃ27–35).

On my interpretation, water moves naturally into its natural place *only* when it is moved by the sun as part of one of these three cycles. However, this is not to say that it is the goal of all the water in the world to come down as precipitation. For the water found in lakes and rivers has already reached its natural place. And once water has reached its natural place it could only come down again either by (*a*) being destroyed into air, and then regenerated above the ground, or (*b*) moving upwards by force and then getting released. But neither of these processes would be due to

According to Aristotle's own introduction, the *Meteorologica* should be read in the light of these treatises. For meteorology is a continuation of the study of nature that commenced in the *Physics* and that has been carried through *De caelo* and *De generatione et corruptione*:[69]

We have discussed before the first causes of nature,[70] and all natural motion,[71] and also the stars which have been ordered according to the upper movement,[72] and the number, kinds, and mutual transformation of the elemental bodies, and coming to be and passing away in general.[73] The remaining thing that must be considered is the part of this investigation which all our predecessors called meteorology. These are the things that happen according to nature [κατὰ φύσιν], but with a regularity less [ἀτακτοτέραν] than that of the first element of bodies, and around the place that most borders the movement of the stars. (1. 1, 338ᵃ20–ᵇ4)

Thus the *Meteorologica* sets out to account for elemental movements that are according to nature (κατὰ φύσιν) and regular (albeit less regular than the motions of the heavenly bodies). And with such an aim, the *Meteorologica* claims to belong alongside a parallel study of animals and plants:

After we have gone through these things in detail let us consider if we can give some account, according to the method [τρόπον] laid down, concerning animals and plants, both in general and separately; for when these things have been specified perhaps the end of the whole plan we had from the beginning [τῆς ἐξ ἀρχῆς ἡμῖν προαιρέσεως πάσης] may have come to be. (339ᵃ6–9)

water's nature. Rather, once water has reached its natural place, it rests there due to nature (*De caelo* 1. 8, 276ᵃ24) and has reached its actuality (4. 3, 311ᵃ3–6). Just as earth's resting in its natural place is a way in which earth imitates the divine (2. 12, 292ᵇ17–25), so does water imitate the divine by resting in its natural place. Thus, water imitates the divine not only in its movement into natural place upon the sun's recession, but also in resting there once it arrives. Notice that it is only because water is generated by the sun *away from* its natural place that it has a natural downward movement that imitates the motion of the heavenly bodies; if it were generated in its natural place, it would have no natural movement, but only a natural rest.

---

[69] Throughout the *Meteorologica* Aristotle claims to use the initial assumptions and definitions as given in *De caelo* and *De generatione et corruptione* to account for meteorological phenomena. See e.g. *Meteor.* 1. 3, 339ᵃ33–ᵇ3; 339ᵇ17–19; 340ᵇ4–6.

[70] i.e. *Physics* (H. D. P. Lee, *Aristotle's* Meteorologica [*Meteorologica*] (Cambridge, 1952), 4 note a).

[71] i.e. *Physics*, especially books 5–8 (Lee, *Meteorologica*, 4 note b).

[72] i.e. *De caelo* 1 and 2 (Lee, *Meteorologica*, 4 note c).

[73] i.e. *De caelo* 3 and 4 and *De generatione et corruptione* (Lee, *Meteorologica*, 4 note d).

Just as the *Physics* 2. 8 argument passage offers parallel explanations of winter rain and the growth of teeth in animals, here Aristotle
maintains, more generally, that meteorology belongs alongside the
study of biological things: both sorts of phenomenon are part of
the science of nature commenced in the *Physics*. By arguing that
the *Meteorologica* is part of the *Physics*' natural science, which obviously offers teleological explanations of natural phenomena, and
that the *Meteorologica* belongs alongside his biological works, which
highlight the particular ways in which the natures of organisms aim
at their ends, Aristotle suggests that the kinds of explanation found
here will be teleological. Moreover, as Furley has noted, the biological works (*De somno* 1. 3, 457^{b}31 ff., and *PA* 2. 7, 653^{a}2 ff.)
actually draw on the *Meteorologica*'s account of rain to illustrate a
brain function that Aristotle considers teleological.[74] As part of the
'whole plan' laid out in the *Physics*, the *Meteorologica* can be read
as a treatise that offers teleological explanations.[75]

When we turn to the passages in which Aristotle discusses winter rain and summer rain, he offers just the kind of explanation
we would expect given the refined view of water's teleology expressed in *De caelo* and *Physics* 8. 4. He maintains that winter rain
in particular, as part of the cycle of evaporation and condensation,
is an expression of nature—φύσις (2. 2, 354^{b}34) and is regular—
κατὰ . . . τὴν τάξιν (1. 9, 347^{a}6), κατά τινα τάξιν, ὡς ἐνδέχεται μετέχειν
τὰ ἐνταῦθα τάξεως (2. 3, 358^{a}26–7), περιόδου (1. 14, 352^{a}31), and
τεταγμένως (2. 3, 358^{a}3). The sun's annual movement along the
ecliptic is the efficient cause responsible for this regularity:

Now the sun is carried in a circle, and when it approaches it lifts up by heat
the moist evaporation; when the sun is at a distance the vapour that had
been lifted up is condensed back into water by the cold. For this reason
there is more rain in winter. (2. 4, 359^{b}34–360^{a}3)[76]

---

[74] Furley, 'Rainfall', 181.

[75] Granted, much of the study focuses on accidental occurrences such as shooting
stars (1. 4), comets (1. 6–7), coast erosion (1. 14), earthquakes (2. 7–8), thunder,
lightning (2. 9), hurricanes, and typhoons (3. 1). But in so far as the *Meteorologica*
offers what we might call a 'science of the accidental', there must be a science of the
teleological on which it is parasitic: 'Chance and luck are posterior [ὕστερον] to both
mind and nature' (*Phys.* 2. 6, 198^{a}10–11). It should not be surprising to find in the
Meteorologica less discussion of the 'prior' teleological accounts of the elements and
more lengthy discussions of a wide variety of accidental phenomena, since accidental
phenomena are more numerous (*De caelo* 3. 2, 300^{a}24–7). On this point, see also my
discussion of *Metaphysics* Λ 10's household analogy at the end of sect. 5.

[76] Since the *Meteorologica*'s theory of exhalations introduces unnecessary com-

Now, at first glance one might think that Aristotle here offers no more teleological an explanation than the one we get from his *Physics* 2. 8 opponent, who claims that rain is not for the sake of corn growth, but rather that it occurs 'of necessity. (For what was taken up must become cold, and what has become cold, having become water, must come down' (198^b19–20). Indeed, the few commentators who have discussed *Meteorologica* 1–3 maintain that explanations offered in passages such as this one from 2. 4 are all mechanistic.[77] But notice that unlike his materialist predecessors, Aristotle attempts to explain why there is more rain *in winter*—that is, why it rains regularly in the winter. Interpreted in the light of Aristotle's refined view of water's teleology, we can see that this is the kind of regularity that, according to *Physics* 2. 8, calls for teleological explanation. Just as the *Meteorologica* explains winter rain by linking the seasonal evaporation and condensation cycle to the yearly movement of the sun along the ecliptic, *Physics* 8. 4 suggests that elemental natures, as sources of *being moved*, make essential reference to their efficient cause, the sun. Water is the kind of thing that moves into its natural place due to the sun's recession in the winter, and air is the kind of thing that moves into its natural place due to the sun's approach in the summer. *Meteorologica* 2. 2 confirms *De caelo*'s relevance: Aristotle explicitly draws on *De caelo*'s teleology of natural places to argue that the water generated by the sun in its circular course, i.e. water which rains down in the winter due to nature ($φύσις$, 354^b34), reaches its natural place (355^b2).

In the summer, however, the hot air sometimes concentrates the cold in such a way as to cause air to condense back into water and fall to the ground out of season. An extreme form of this 'recoil' ($ἀντιπερίστασις$) of hot and cold results in hail, while a weaker form of recoil results in summer rain (1. 12, 348^b8–10; 349^a5–9). As *De generatione et corruptione* 2. 10 observes, 'We see that coming to be is when the sun approaches, and passing away [is when the sun] recedes, and each of the two in equal time [$ἐν ἴσῳ χρόνῳ$]' (336^b16–18), but sometimes 'comings to be are irregular [$ἀνωμάλους$]—either

plications, I discuss the cycle of evaporation and condensation simply in terms of water and air instead of water and the moist exhalation vapour.

[77] Although Furley more moderately suggests that Aristotle 'accepts the mechanistic interpretation as at least part of the truth' ('Rainfall', 181), other interpreters claim that the *Meteorologica* contains only mechanistic explanations. See Cooper, 'Teleology', 218; Lee, *Meteorologica*, xvi; Charlton, *Notes*, xvii; Johnson, *Teleology*, 150.

quicker [θάττους] or slower [βραδυτέρας]' (336^{b}23–4). Although here
the immediate context seems to be that of animal generation, ex-
tending the point to the case of the elements would explain the
Meteorologica's emphasis on the speed with which recoil generates
rain: recoil conditions force air to transform into water quickly
(ταχύ at 348^{b}8 and τάχος at 348^{b}12). Arabian and Ethiopian summer rains also occur because clouds are 'cooled quickly [ταχύ] by
recoil' (349^{a}5–9).[78] Consequently, summer rain is called 'violent
rain' (ὕδατα λαβρότερα, 348^{b}11, 348^{b}23, or ῥαγδαῖα 349^{a}7).[79]

We are now in a position to see not only that water rains down
into its natural place teleologically in the winter and not in the
summer, but also that moving there in the winter is *better*. As I
have argued, Aristotle maintains that water's movement is teleologically directed towards the Prime Mover via the heavenly bodies:
water's rectilinear motions imitate the circular motion of the heavenly bodies, which in turn imitates the activity of the Prime Mover.
But given the refined view of water's teleology as found in *De caelo*,
Physics 8. 4, and now in the *Meteorologica*, it turns out that not just
any of water's downward rectilinear movements is an imitation of

[78] Aristotle gives hail a similar treatment at 1. 12, 348^{b}16–349^{a}4. Note his emphasis
on the speed with which water freezes. See also *Physics* 5. 6, 230^{a}29–^{b}4, where
Aristotle maintains that some comings to be are forced and unnatural and that
sometimes growth is forced and thereby too quick (ταχύ repeated at 230^{b}2 and
230^{b}3).

[79] *De generatione et corruptione* 2. 4 also suggests that improper timing is a symptom of improper transformation: the transformation from fire to water, for example,
can take place, but is 'slower [βραδύτερον]' and 'more difficult [χαλεπώτερον]' (331^{b}5–
7; 331^{a}23–4). As Broadie points out, χαλεπώτερον here can also be translated 'more
harsh', which suggests that nature is 'stepmotherly' (synonymous with 'harsh', e.g.
Hes. *WD* 825). Given this reading, Broadie thinks the passage 'threatens to rock the
boat of Aristotle's metaphysical optimism. A natural cycle forever repeated must not
involve struggle against the grain (cf. *Cael.* II 1)' ('*GC* I.4: Distinguishing Alteration', in F. A. J. de Haas and J. Mansfeld (eds.), *Proceedings of the XVth Symposium
Aristotelicum* (Oxford, 2004), 123–50 at 144 n. 75). But just as we can understand
the quick generation of summer rain to 'go against the grain' of natural movement,
so too can we understand the slow transformation from fire to water. Even though
the elements are able to transform into one another under various conditions and
due to various influences, the *proper* transformations are those that are part of the
regular cycles caused by the sun. Slower or quicker transformations must take place,
but these transformations are not at the appropriate speed and timing since they are
not properly caused by the sun in its circular course. Elemental transformation and
movement into natural place have their proper timing and proper season from which
these accidental transformations and movements diverge. Perhaps Broadie does not
think it is possible for elemental motions to go against the grain because she fails to
distinguish between what an element teleologically aims to do and what an element
must do (see Waterlow (Broadie), *Nature*, 89).

the circular motion of the heavenly bodies—that is, not just any is an instance of water's moving there because it is *better*—but only its downward movement that occurs due to the sun's recession in the winter. Water's falling to the ground in the summer should not count as an imitative rectilinear movement that occurs because it is *better*.

The reason why summer rain should not count as imitative is clear from the *De generatione et corruptione* 2. 10 passage in which Aristotle claims rectilinear movement imitates circular movement: there he says that it does so *because* (expressed by ὥστε 337ᵃ7) it occurs on the heels of another rectilinear movement with which it composes a cycle.[80] And only water's natural movement due to the sun comprises part of such a cycle. The very fact that water's natural movement is efficiently caused by the sun ensures that water's natural movement will occur on the heels of air's upward rectilinear movement, which takes the opposite position of the sun as its efficient cause. Only in this way does water's movement imitate circular movement, which imitates the Prime Mover. *Meteorologica* 1. 9 confirms that, in particular, rain caused by the sun's movement—*winter* rain—comprises part of such an imitative cycle (346ᵇ35–347ᵃ1).[81] Given that the water that comes down as winter rain, and not summer rain, is part of this cycle caused by the sun, it is the rectilinear movement of water as winter rain, and not summer rain, that imitates the circular motion of the heavenly bodies. Thus, it is winter rain, and not summer rain, that falls to the ground *because it is better*.

A return to the household analogy in *Metaphysics* Λ 10 confirms that we should have expected only some of water's movements to imitate the activity of the Prime Mover:

[A]ll things are jointly arranged in relation to one thing. But it is as in a

---

[80] In showing that teleological cycles can involve only two elements, I highlight a feature of the *Meteorologica*'s account that commentators find problematic. See e.g. Solmsen (*System*, 426 n. 135), who cites Joachim. However, the fact that the *Meteorologica* does not describe a single cycle that includes all four elements is a problem only if one assumes that a 'complete cycle' must include all four. Aristotle maintains that 'we say coming to be has gone round in a circle because it has been made to return again [διὰ τὸ πάλιν ἀνακάμπτειν]' (*GC* 2. 10, 337ᵃ6–7) or when one member 'will be again [πάλιν ἔσται]' (*Meteor.* 2. 3, 356ᵇ35–357ᵃ1). Thus, for Aristotle, a cycle is 'complete' not because it has gone through a certain number of elements, but because it has returned to its starting-point, and this can be true of a cycle that includes only two elements.

[81] This is not the only cycle for which the sun is the efficient cause. See n. 68.

household, where the free have least licence to act as they chance to, but all or most of what they do is arranged, while the slaves and beasts can do a little towards what is communal, but act mostly as they chance to. (1075ᵃ19–22)

If the heavenly bodies are to the sublunary elements as the freemen are to the slaves and beasts, we should expect that the heavenly bodies 'have least licence to act as they chance to, but all or most of what they do is arranged', while the sublunary elements 'can do a little towards what is communal, but act mostly as they chance to'. My interpretation makes sense of this suggestion: although the circular motion of the heavenly bodies always imitates the activity of the Prime Mover, not all sublunary elemental movements imitate the activity of the Prime Mover, but only those movements, such as winter rain, that take the sun as their efficient cause.

Thus, I have argued that Aristotle's refined view of water's teleology, as described in *De caelo* and *Physics* 8. 4, shows that water is by its very nature such as to be moved into its natural place by the sun (i.e. *in the winter*). And it is only this rectilinear movement that occurs because it is better, for only this movement imitates the circular movement of the heavenly bodies, and thereby indirectly imitates the Prime Mover. This refined view of water's teleology appears to be at work in the *Meteorologica*'s discussion of winter rain and summer rain, and thus we should interpret the winter rain example in *Physics* 2. 8 to show that winter rain, but not summer rain, is teleologically directed to reach its natural place on the ground.

6. Conclusion

The winter rain example of *Physics* 2. 8 has exercised so many scholars because on its interpretation seems to hang our understanding of the extent and character of Aristotle's natural teleology as a whole. If I am correct in my interpretation of the argument passage, and, more generally, in my account of the metaphysical commitments underlying my interpretation, we get some interesting results for the interpretation of Aristotle's natural teleology as a whole. Let me briefly mention just two.

First, we find that each individual is teleologically directed towards the Prime Mover, and as a result, individuals are teleologically arranged with one another: individuals lower in the hierarchy imitate individuals higher in the hierarchy. Although it is true, in addition, that lower entities benefit higher entities, it is no part of their imitative teleological relationship that they do so. Rather, the fact that lower things are for the sake of benefiting higher things has its source in the *beneficiary*'s nature: it is part of the nature of a higher thing to make use of lower things for its own benefit.

Second, we find that the elements are in and of themselves natural teleological subjects, *independently* of the role they play in biological processes. Contemporary commentators have focused almost exclusively on Aristotle's biological works in order to understand his natural teleology better. As a result of this exclusive focus they have thought that natural teleology is grounded in characteristics exclusive to biological natural things—being a whole of parts or a self-mover. But if the elements are teleological independently of biological things, this fact can work as a constraint on the proper account of the ontological basis of Aristotle's ascriptions of teleological causation to natural things and show that these recent interpretations of its basis are mistaken.[82]

Reed College

BIBLIOGRAPHY

Balme, D., 'Teleology and Necessity' ['Teleology'], in A. Gotthelf and J. G. Lennox (eds.), *Philosophical Issues in Aristotle's Biology* (Cambridge, 1987), 275–86.
Bodnár, I., 'Movers and Elemental Motions in Aristotle' ['Movers'], *Oxford Studies in Ancient Philosophy*, 15 (1997), 81–117.
—— 'Teleology across Natures' ['Teleology'], *Rhizai*, 2 (2005), 9–29.
Bradie, M., and Miller, F., 'Teleology and Natural Necessity in Aristotle', *History of Philosophy Quarterly*, 1 (1984), 133–45.
Broadie, S., '*GC* I.4: Distinguishing Alteration', in F. A. J. de Haas and

[82] For example, Balme, 'Teleology', and M. Bradie and F. Miller, 'Teleology and Natural Necessity in Aristotle', *History of Philosophy Quarterly*, 1 (1984), 133–45, argue that natural teleology is based on the claim that natural explanations must make reference to a program in the seed that controls and regulates development, while Irwin, *Principles*, and S. Sauvé Meyer, 'Aristotle, Teleology, and Reduction', *Philosophical Review*, 101 (1992), 791–825, repr. in T. Irwin (ed.), *Classical Philosophy: Collected Papers* (New York and London, 1995), 81–116, argue that his natural teleology is based on ineliminativism—on the claim that natural things have an intrinsic efficient cause of their coming to be. Of course, in the case of elemental teleology, there are no seeds or intrinsic efficient causes at work.

J. Mansfeld (eds.), *Proceedings of the XVth Symposium Aristotelicum* (Oxford, 2004), 123–50.

Charles, D., 'Teleological Causation in the *Physics*', in L. Judson (ed.), *Aristotle's* Physics: *A Collection of Essays* (Oxford, 1991), 101–28.

Charlton, W., *Aristotle's* Physics Books 1 & 2. *Translated from the Greek with Introduction and Notes* [*Notes*] (Oxford, 1992).

Code, A., 'The Priority of Final Causes over Efficient Causes in Aristotle's *PA*' ['Priority'], in W. Kullmann and S. Follinger (eds.), *Aristotelische Biologie: Intentionen, Methoden, Ergebnisse* (Stuttgart, 1997), 127–43.

Cooper, J. M., 'Aristotle on Natural Teleology' ['Teleology'], in M. Schofield and M. C. Nussbaum (eds.), *Language and Logos: Studies in Ancient Greek Philosophy Presented to G. E. L. Owen* (Cambridge, 1982), 197–222.

—— 'Hypothetical Necessity and Natural Teleology', in A. Gotthelf and J. G. Lennox (eds.), *Philosophical Issues in Aristotle's Biology* (Cambridge, 1987), 243–74.

Fleet, B., *Simplicius on Aristotle on* Physics 2 (London, 1997).

Furley, D. J., 'Self-Movers', in M. L. Gill and J. G. Lennox (eds.), *Self-Motion: From Aristotle to Newton* (Princeton, 1994), 3–14.

—— 'The Rainfall Example in *Physics* II 8' ['Rainfall'], in A. Gotthelf (ed.), *Aristotle on Nature and Living Things* (Pittsburgh, 1985), 177–82.

Gill, M. L., *Aristotle on Substance: The Paradox of Unity* (Princeton, 1989).

Gotthelf, A., 'Aristotle's Conception of Final Causality', *Review of Metaphysics*, 30 (1976–7), 226–54; repr. with additional notes and a Postscript in A. Gotthelf and J. G. Lennox (eds.), *Philosophical Issues in Aristotle's Biology* (Cambridge, 1987), 204–42.

Irwin, T., *Aristotle's First Principles* [*Principles*] (Oxford, 1988).

Johnson, M. R., *Aristotle on Teleology* [*Teleology*] (Oxford, 2005).

Judson, L., 'Aristotelian Teleology' ['Teleology'], *Oxford Studies in Ancient Philosophy*, 29 (2005), 341–66.

Kahn, C. H., 'The Place of the Prime Mover in Aristotle's Teleology' ['Place'], in A. Gotthelf (ed.), *Aristotle on Nature and Living Things: Philosophical and Historical Studies Presented to David M. Balme on his Seventieth Birthday* (Pittsburgh and Bristol, 1985), 183–205.

Lang, H., *The Order of Nature in Aristotle's Physics* (Cambridge, 1998).

Lawrence, G., 'Snakes in Paradise: Problems in the Ideal Life', *Southern Journal of Philosophy*, 43 (2005), 126–65.

Lear, J., *Aristotle: The Desire to Understand* (Cambridge, 1988).

Lee, H. D. P., *Aristotle's* Meteorologica [*Meteorologica*] (Cambridge, 1952).

Lettinck, P., *Aristotle's* Meteorology *and its Reception in the Arab World* (Leiden, 1999).

Mansion, A., *Introduction à la Physique Aristotélicienne* (Louvain, 1945).

Matthen, M., 'The Holistic Presuppositions of Aristotle's Cosmology', *Oxford Studies in Ancient Philosophy*, 20 (2001), 171–99.

Menn, S., 'Aristotle's Definition of Soul and the Programme of the *De anima*', *Oxford Studies in Ancient Philosophy*, 22 (2002), 83–139.

Miller, F., 'Teleology and Natural Necessity in Aristotle', *History of Philosophy Quarterly*, 1 (1984), 133–45.

Morison, B., *On Location: Aristotle's Concept of Place* (Oxford, 2002).

Nussbaum, M. C., *Aristotle's* De Motu Animalium. *Text with Translation, Commentary, and Interpretive Essays* (Princeton, 1978).

Pellegrin, P., 'Les ruses de la nature et l'éternité du mouvement: encore quelques remarques sur la finalité chez Aristote' ['Ruses'], in M. Canto-Sperber and P. Pellegrin (eds.), *Le Style de la pensée. En hommage à Jacques Brunschwig* (Paris, 2002), 296–323.

Richardson Lear, G., *Happy Lives and the Highest Good [Highest]* (Princeton, 2004).

Ross, W. D., *Aristotle's* Physics (Oxford, 1936).

Sauvé Meyer, S., 'Aristotle, Teleology, and Reduction', *Philosophical Review*, 101 (1992), 791–825; repr. in T. Irwin (ed.), *Classical Philosophy: Collected Papers* (New York and London, 1995), 81–116.

—— 'Self-Movement and External Causation', in M. L. Gill and J. G. Lennox (eds.), *Self-Motion: From Aristotle to Newton* (Princeton, 1994), 65–80.

Sedley, D., *Creationism and its Critics in Antiquity [Creationism]* (Berkeley and Los Angeles, 2007).

—— 'Is Aristotle's Teleology Anthropocentric?' ['Anthropocentric'], *Phronesis*, 36 (1991), 179–97.

—— '*Metaphysics Λ* 10' ['*Λ* 10'], in M. Frede and D. Charles (eds.), *Aristotle's* Metaphysics Lambda (Oxford, 2000), 327–50.

Solmsen, F., *Aristotle's System of the Physical World [System]* (Ithaca, NY, 1960).

Wardy, R., 'Aristotelian Rainfall or the Lore of Averages' ['Rainfall'], *Phronesis*, 38 (1993), 18–30.

Waterlow (Broadie), S., *Nature, Change, and Agency in Aristotle's* Physics *[Nature]* (Oxford, 1982).

Witt, C., *Substance and Essence in Aristotle* (Ithaca, NY, 1989).

ALTERATION AND ARISTOTLE'S THEORY OF CHANGE IN *PHYSICS* 6

DAMIAN MURPHY

IN *Physics* 5 and 6 Aristotle outlines a theory of change. A key feature of this account is the claim that every change is infinitely temporally divisible into subchanges. So, for example, suppose a billiard ball moves from one end of the table to the other in a period of time. After part of the time it will have moved part of the way down the table, and for each smaller part of the time it will have travelled a smaller portion of the length of the table. Aristotle explicitly claims that this theory applies to *all* types of change and not merely to change of place (and change of size). Many modern critics believe that this is not Aristotle's considered opinion.[1] They claim that for Aristotle changes of quality are often not infinitely temporally divisible into subchanges because there are only, for example, finitely many shades of colour.

My aim in this paper is to show that Aristotle thought that all alterations (changes in quality) were infinitely temporally divisible. In practice I shall follow Aristotle in focusing on changes of colour.

© Damian Murphy 2008

I wish to thank Nick Denyer, my Ph.D. supervisor, for all his helpful comments on earlier versions of this paper, and David Sedley for his advice on the final versions. I would also like to thank Lindsay Judson and other members of an interview panel at Brasenose College, Oxford, for their questions on an earlier version. I am grateful to the AHRC for providing funding for my Ph.D., and to Trinity College, Cambridge, for providing a further year's funding, during which I worked the paper into its current form.

[1] In this paper I explicitly discuss certain arguments of S. Waterlow, *Nature, Change, and Agency in Aristotle's Physics* [*Nature*] (Oxford, 1982), ch. III, pt. II. This interpretation is also advocated by R. Wardy, *The Chain of Change* [*Chain*] (Oxford, 1990), 329–31; W. D. Ross, *Aristotelis Physica* (Oxford, 1967), 650–1; D. Sherry, 'On Instantaneous Velocity' ['Instantaneous'], *History of Philosophy Quarterly*, 3/4 (1986), 391–406 at 395–6; E. Hussey, *Aristotle's* Physics*: Books III and IV* (Oxford, 1983), 143; R. Heinaman, 'Alteration and Aristotle's Activity–Change Distinction' ['Alteration'], *Oxford Studies in Ancient Philosophy*, 16 (1998), 227–58; and R. Sorabji, *Time, Creation and the Continuum: Theories in Antiquity and the Early Middle Ages* [*Time*] (London, 1983).

My positive strategy in doing this is twofold. First, I show that even if there were only finitely many shades of colour, Aristotle has a way of maintaining that changes of colour are infinitely temporally divisible. Secondly, I argue that Aristotle thought that there were infinitely many shades of colour. My positive argument is relatively brief (Section 3); the bulk of the paper (Sections 4–8) argues that passages taken to undermine my view do not in fact do so. In addition to defending my main thesis, in discussing these passages I hope to provide a better understanding of many of Aristotle's claims about change in *Physics* 6.

In this paper I:

(1) explain Aristotle's claim that all changes are infinitely temporally divisible;

(2) show why modern interpreters have thought that this cannot hold for alterations;

(3) (*a*) show how alterations can be infinitely temporally divisible even if there are only finitely many qualitative degrees, and

    (*b*) argue that Aristotle thought that there were infinitely many qualitative degrees in a given range and thus that he had the conceptual apparatus for 'all-together' alterations to be infinitely temporally divisible;[2]

(4) explain what Aristotle means by saying that the very thing according to which an object changes is only coincidentally divisible;

(5) distinguish between dividing the change and dividing the path of the change, and show how this explains certain passages which have been taken to tell against my position;

(6) discuss why Aristotle does not explicitly consider all-together alteration in *Physics* 6;

(7) show that Aristotle elsewhere considers all-together alteration, and that this takes time;

(8) consider Waterlow's main objection.

---

[2] I describe a change as 'all-together' when at any division of time any bit of the object is in the same state as any other bit. The contrast is with part-by-part alteration, in which the new colour spreads gradually over the surface of the object so that some parts acquire the new colour before others. In practice many altering objects will alter in both ways at once.

1. All changes are infinitely temporally divisible

Aristotle claims that all changes take time. At *Phys.* 236[b]18–22 and 239[a]23–6 he says that we should specify the precise time taken for the change. That Aristotle thinks of *all* changes as being in time is also clear in many other places, e.g. *Phys.* 227[b]26 and 236[b]19–32. Before claiming that a change is infinitely temporally divisible, I first outline what it means to divide a change according to the time (e.g. *Phys.* 235[a]9–33, 236[a]35–6, 237[a]25–8). In particular, we should note *Phys.* 235[a]11–13:

> For since every change is in time, and every time is divisible, and in the lesser time the change will be less, it is necessary that every change is temporally divisible [διαιρεῖσθαι κατὰ τὸν χρόνον].

In this passage Aristotle explains what temporally dividing a change is. Since *every* interval of time, however small, is divisible, it follows that every change, however small, is also divisible. Thus, change is infinitely divisible.[3]

Initial place	AC	A	B	C	D	E
First phase time taken	t_1t_2					
Intermediate place	BD	A	B	C	D	E
Second phase time taken	t_2t_3					
End place	CE	A	B	C	D	E

FIGURE 1. Temporal division of locomotion

Let us consider the change of object O moving from AC to CE in the interval of time t_1t_3.[4] In Figure 1 the thick line represents the object; the thin line its path.[5] So O's change from AC to CE in time t_1t_3 is divisible into the subchanges from AC to BD in time

---

[3] For assurance that Aristotle means to put as much weight on the 'every' as I do, we may note *Phys.* 220[a]29–32, where he says that lines and time are always divisible, and there is no smallest number of the magnitude of a line or of time. That Aristotle thinks change is infinitely divisible is clear throughout *Physics* 6, e.g. 237[a]25–8.

[4] t_1t_2 denotes the *interval* of time whose initial limit is t_1 and whose end limit is t_2. I shall use (as both Aristotle and modern mathematicians do), e.g. 'AB' to indicate the length whose left-hand limit is A and whose right-hand limit is B.

[5] That Aristotle is willing to abstract from the three-dimensional objects that strictly speaking undergo change to one-dimensional lines is clear throughout *Physics* 5 and 6, e.g. at 236[b]5–10.

t_1t_2 and from BD to CE in time t_2t_3. Aristotle clearly thinks that any change can be divided into proper subchanges according to divisions of time.

1.1. *Infinite temporal divisibility (ITD)*[6]

- Suppose object O changes from initial state S_1 to end state S_2 in a period of time t_1t_2.
- Suppose, as Aristotle does, that time is infinitely divisible.
- Suppose that S_1 and S_2 belong to an array of possible states that come in some natural order (e.g. from dark to pale, cold to hot, or north to south).
- Suppose a change from S_1 to S_i is a lesser change than the change from S_1 to S_j, just in case S_i comes before S_j in the natural ordering of possible states between S_1 and S_2.
- Then O's change over t_1t_2 is infinitely temporally divisible iff

    for any pair of divisions of time in t_1t_2, at the earlier division of time O has accomplished a lesser change than it has at the later division of time.

The aim of this paper is to defend Aristotle's claim that ITD holds for all changes, and, in particular, to show that it is applicable to alterations as well as locomotions.

1.2. *Distinguishing complete changes from subchanges*

Before going on, it will be helpful to introduce a distinction between complete changes and subchanges.[7] A complete change is bounded by two periods of rest; a subchange need not be. ITD claims that all complete changes and all subchanges are divisible into subchanges. However, no change is ever divisible into further complete changes.

---

[6] The most intricate argument for infinite temporal divisibility is given at *Physics* 6. 2. M. White, *The Continuous and the Discrete: Ancient Physical Theories from a Contemporary Perspective* [*Continuous*] (Oxford, 1992), 39–46, gives a detailed discussion of this argument. It is clear that ITD as stated does not apply to the circular motion of the heavenly bodies as Aristotle understands it, since each heavenly body covers the same ground infinitely many times. However, they do not straightforwardly exemplify much of what Aristotle says about change, for example that change is the actuality of the potentiality *qua* potentiality, or that it is between contraries. Thus, in this paper I shall ignore the locomotions of the heavenly bodies and concentrate on the sublunar bodies.

[7] White, *Continuous*, e.g. 35, prefers 'kinetic segments'.

If it were it would not be a single change. This is in effect stated at *Phys.* 228^{b}1–7:

That is why for a change to be continuous and one without qualification, it must be specifically the same, and be a change of one object and in one period of time. It must happen in one period of time so that there would not be a period of lack of change in between, since when change is interrupted there is bound to be rest. Therefore, there is not one but many changes, between which there is rest, so that if some change involves rest it is neither one nor continuous. And these intervals occur if there is time in between. (Cf. 234^{b}10–13, 261^{b}13–14.)

When, e.g. at *Phys.* 237^{a}15–17, Aristotle says that a changing object must already have completed an infinite number of changes, he must, strictly speaking, mean subchanges. While Aristotle does not make this explicit, it is clear that he has the resources available to do so.[8] Failure to allow Aristotle to avail himself of this distinction leads Waterlow, *Nature*, 144–8, to claim that his account of change in *Physics* 6 fails to give adequate grounds for individuating single changes.

Whether or not this criticism by Waterlow of the *Physics* 5 and 6 account of change is correct, this question is independent from the question of whether the account of books 5 and 6 is equally applicable to alterations as well as locomotions. Strictly speaking ITD should be restated in terms of subchanges. However, having alerted the reader to this difficulty, for convenience I shall follow Aristotle's somewhat lax usage of *Physics* 6 and talk simply of dividing a change into changes.[9] Let us now consider the significance of ITD.

---

[8] D. Furley, 'Review of *Nature, Change, and Agency in Aristotle's Physics: A Philosophical Study* by Sarah Waterlow', *Ancient Philosophy*, 4 (1984), 108–10, suggests that there is scope for defending Aristotle's account of change in *Physics* 6 along these lines.

[9] Unfortunately, in *Physics* 6 Aristotle is not sufficiently careful to distinguish between complete changes and the subchanges, but it is clear from his response to Zeno in *Physics* 8. 8 that we should do this. He says that the intermediate divisions of the distance are not actual divisions but potential divisions, unless the object rests there for any period of time (262^{a}21–5). When we say that at a division of time an object is at a particular position, it is only there for an instant of time. (For the permissibility of speaking of the object as being at a particular position at an instant of time see Sorabji, *Time*, 412–14. In support he cites *Phys.* 239^{a}35–^{b}3, 262^{a}30, 262^{b}20.) In our terminology of subchanges and complete changes we might say that a complete change is bounded by two actual divisions, whereas a proper subchange is bounded only by potential divisions. In response to Zeno Aristotle argues that the infinitely many subdistances which Zeno claimed had to be traversed in order for the whole to be traversed (263^{a}4–10) are only potential distances (263^{b}3–9).

1.3. *The significance of ITD*

ITD rules out periods of rest. For suppose a single change contained a period of rest (i.e. a period of time for the whole of which the whole object is in the same state). Then there would be some pair of divisions of time such that the object's state at the earlier division did not come prior in the natural ordering to the object's state at the later division, but was the same. As we have just seen from *Phys.* 228^b1–7, if it is interrupted by periods of rest then a purported single change is not in fact a single change. At *Phys.* 239^a14–18 Aristotle says that an object is at rest if it is in the same state for a period of time.[10]

2. The application to alteration

The examples that I have given so far have focused upon locomotion. This is the intuitively easiest case to understand and the one upon which Aristotle focuses in his examples. However, he frequently claims that what he says applies to *all* changes. The places where he says that *all* changes take time, are divisible according to the time, or have no first time segment are numerous.[11] At *Phys.* 226^a26–9 he explicitly states that quality is a category in respect of which there can be change, and that such change is alteration. However, it is sometimes thought that ITD cannot apply to alterations (e.g. to changes of colour) because there are only finitely many qualitative degrees through which a change can take place (e.g. only finitely many shades of colour). The problem for ITD that occurs if there are only finitely many shades of colour (or more precisely if there is not a dense ordering of shades of colour) is as follows.[12] Suppose a tomato gradually changes all-together from being green all over to being red all over. Obviously this change will be temporally divisible to some extent, but it will not be infinitely temporally divisible. For the change from one shade to the *next* shade will not

---

[10] ITD as I have stated it is also sufficient to rule out a reversal of direction within a single change. However, Aristotle rules out reversals at *Physics* 8. 8 by arguing that in between two periods of changing in opposite directions there must be a period of rest, and thus periods of changing in opposite directions cannot constitute a single change.

[11] e.g. *Phys.* 227^b26; 232^b20–1; 235^a9–15; 235^a18–24; 236^a13–27; 236^a35–6; 237^a17–28; 237^a34–$^b8$. Some of these passages will be discussed in detail.

[12] An ordering is dense iff between any two members of the ordering there is a third distinct member.

be divisible any further. Furthermore, the tomato will be the same shade all over for an interval of time. Thus, it will be at rest for an interval of time during which it was presumed to be changing. The 'change' from green to red will not be a single change but a series of several changes interspersed with periods of rest.

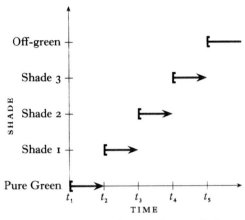

FIGURE 2. Non-continuous change of colour

However, worse is to follow. Not only must we jettison ITD, we must jettison the claim that all changes take time. For on this model the change from one shade to the next does not take any time but rather takes place at an instant. So, if Aristotle thought that there were only finitely many shades of colour and that tomatoes (or anything else) changed gradually as a whole (or indeed that any finite part changed colour all-together), he should have rejected the account of change in *Physics* 5 and 6, or at least excluded alterations from its scope.[13] The difficulties of discrete change of colour are illustrated in Figure 2. Let us assume that there are only three shades between pure green and off-green. To use modern mathematical terminology, the intervals of time for which the object is each shade are semi-open. That is, we assume that there is a first instant of the object being the new shade but no last instant of the object being the old shade.[14] Between the old and new shade there is a jump.

---

[13] Waterlow, for example, thinks that in *Physics* 8 Aristotle rejects the account of change of *Physics* 6 (*Nature*, 144–58).

[14] That the asymmetry should be this way round is justified by *Phys.* 263^{b}9–15 and 264^{a}2–3. See Sorabji, *Time*, 414.

3. In defence of ITD for changes of colour

I shall now examine two ways in which Aristotle can defend his claim that changes of colour are subject to ITD. The first works even if there are only finitely many shades of colour; the second is an argument that Aristotle thought that there was a dense array of shades of colour.

3.1. *Part-by-part change of colour*

I suggest that Aristotle often thinks in the following terms. An object can change colour part by part. For example, if I lower a piece of litmus paper into a test tube of acid, initially the whole strip is orange and finally the whole strip is red. After a part of that interval half of the strip is red and half of the strip is orange. After a smaller part of the whole interval, a quarter of the strip is red and three-quarters of the strip is orange. This sort of change satisfies ITD. The relevant ordering of states will be in terms of the total fraction of the strip that is red. Having seen how this can happen in some cases, we can easily drop the idea of the object literally moving and think instead of the new colour spreading across the object while the object itself remains in one place. At *Phys.* 240ᵃ19–29 (see Section 8.2) Aristotle clearly has in mind part-by-part change of colour.

Clearly some changes of colour do take place like this. However, it is implausible to think that they all do (or to attribute to Aristotle the belief that they all do). I now argue that Aristotle thought that there was a dense array of shades of colour and thus that all-together change of colour could satisfy ITD.

3.2. *Aristotle thought that there were infinitely many shades of colour*

My evidence comes from Aristotle's discussion of how intermediate colours come about from mixing pale and dark in *De sensu* 3. Here are some claims made by Aristotle concerning the mixing of colours:

There will be many colours on account of the fact that the ingredients may be combined with one another in many ratios; some will be based on numerical ratios [ἐν ἀριθμοῖς], but others will be based on excess only [καθ' ὑπεροχὴν μόνον]. (*De sensu* 440ᵇ18–21)

This suggests that if the ratio of pale to dark in two mixtures is different, then the resulting shade in each case is different.[15] For Aristotle offers the fact that there are many ratios as explaining *why* there are many shades. If the same shade could be produced by different ratios, then that there are many ratios need not entail that there are many shades. Thus, since there are infinitely many (and indeed a dense ordering of) ratios of the form $n : m$, we should expect that there is also a dense ordering of shades of colour. However, before we can jump to this conclusion, it is necessary to determine that there is a dense set of ratios *in which the ingredients can combine*. Clearly there is a dense set of ratios (considered in the abstract), but it could be the case that pale and dark fail to combine in certain ratios. I now wish to examine more of the text and argue that there is a dense set of ratios in which the ingredients combine:

[The product of dark and pale] could appear neither [extreme] pale nor [extreme] dark. And, as it must have some colour, and can have neither of these, this colour must be of a mixed character, in fact a kind of colour different from either. It is thus possible to believe there are more colours than [extreme] pale and [extreme] dark, and that they are many in ratio. For they may lie beside one another in the ratio of 3 to 2, or of 3 to 4, or according to other numbers, and others [may lie beside one another] according to no ratio whatever [κατὰ μὲν λόγον μηδένα] but according to some incommensurable excess and deficiency, so that these [the colours in ratios] are in the same situation as the musical concords. For the colours that are in the well-proportioned numbers [ἐν ἀριθμοῖς εὐλογίστοις], like the concords in the other case, appear to be the pleasantest of the colours, purple [ἀλουργόν] and red [φοινικοῦν], for example, and a few others like them—few for the same reason as the concords are few—whereas those that are not in numbers are the other colours. (*De sensu* 439ᵇ22–440ᵃ3)[16]

While the exegesis of this passage is complicated to say the least, the gist is tolerably clear. The ratios of the musical concords produce the

[15] While to settle the issue of what Greek colour terms mean is beyond the scope of this paper, assuming that the primary distinction is that of brightness, I shall translate μέλαν and λευκόν as 'dark' and 'pale' respectively. However, for convenience, I shall allow myself to employ English hue terms such as 'red' and 'green' in discussion.

[16] With minor alterations, this translation follows A. Barker, 'Colours, Concords and Ratios in *De sensu* 3' (paper presented to the B Club in Cambridge, 2004).

most beautiful colours, and there are only finitely many of these.[17]
However, it is abundantly clear that colours, albeit less beautiful
ones, come about in ways which are not ἐν ἀριθμοῖς εὐλογίστοις. In
order to argue that Aristotle thought that there were only finitely
many colours, it would be necessary to show why he thought that
there was only a finite number of ways of generating the other
[less beautiful] colours. For this to be plausible there ought to
be some principled means by which Aristotle distinguishes those
non-musical ratios which produce shades and those which do not.
Without such a principled means the most natural interpretation
of the *De sensu* passages is that Aristotle thought that pale and
dark mixed in infinitely many ratios, resulting in a dense array of
shades. In the remainder of Section 3.2 I defend my position in
more technical detail. Those who are happy to accept my claim
might prefer to skip to Section 3.3.

3.2.1. *The distinction between better and worse ratios*   It is debatable
what exactly the contrast is. Barker argues that the better ratios (e.g.
ἐν ἀριθμοῖς εὐλογίστοις, 439^b32) are just the ratios of the musical
concords; while the worse ratios are *all* other ratios. Alternatively
one might think that the worse class includes 'irrational ratios' such
as √2 : 1. Language such as κατὰ μὲν λόγον μηδένα (439^b29) might
be taken to suggest this. However, on either interpretation the set
of less beautiful colours is dense, and this is all that is needed for
my argument.[18]

---

[17] R. Sorabji, 'Aristotle, Mathematics and Colour', *Classical Quarterly*, NS 22
(1972), 293–308, argues that in making these claims Aristotle appears to have been
over-impressed by the analogy to the case of ratios in musical concords. Sorabji
gives an excellent account of the disanalogy between music and colour.

[18] Sorabji, *Time*, 411, argues on the basis of *De sensu* 445^b21–9 and 446^a16–20 that
Aristotle holds that there is only a finite number of discriminable shades. However,
De sensu 445^b20–9 and 446^a16–20 do not say that there are only finitely many shades,
or finitely many discriminable shades; they say rather that there are finitely many
species of colour. *De sensu* 445^b20–2 says: 'The solution of these questions will at the
same time make it clear why the species [τὰ εἴδη] of colour and flavour and sounds and
the other sensibles are limited.' Aristotle is asking why the species are limited. He is
not saying that the shades of colour themselves are limited. The same term is used
in *De sensu* 442^a19–25: 'The species of flavours and colours are roughly equal. For
there are seven species of each, if, as is reasonable, one regards grey as a sort of dark
[τὸ φαιὸν μέλαν τι εἶναι]. For the alternative is to class yellow with pale [τὸ ξανθὸν . . .
τοῦ λευκοῦ εἶναι], as rich with sweet. Red, purple, green, and blue are between pale
and dark, but others are mixtures of these.' Clearly Aristotle realized that there are
more than seven discriminable shades of colour. For purposes of classification it is
helpful to group the individual shades into species whose members are similar to

3.2.2. *The objection from quantum leaps*   What Aristotle says about mixing in *De generatione et corruptione* might be used as an objection to my position. We are told at 328^a23–31 that one drop of wine does not mix with 10,000 gallons of water, but is transformed into water. Perhaps this is also the case with mixing pale and dark. One drop of pale to 10,000 gallons of dark might simply leave us with dark. Assume for the sake of argument that this is so. However, this assumption does not force the conclusion that there is not a dense array of colours. Suppose there is a threshold of unsuccessful mixing. Suppose mixing pale and dark in a ratio of 1:10 or less results simply in an increase in the amount of the predominant colour, with no qualitative moderation. This is consistent with all ratios in between but excluding 1:10 and 10:1 producing distinct intermediate colours.[19] If the set of ratios that result in successful mixing were open-ended, then there is no first shade after extreme dark and no last shade before extreme pale. Thus, ITD can be maintained.

3.2.3. *The objection from what we can perceive straight-off*   In response to the claim that sometimes during a supposedly continuous change of colour we cannot notice any difference between the colour at one time and the colour at a subsequent time, and that thus we have no independent method of verifying that there are infinitely many shades passed through in this change, we might wonder how different this case is from that of locomotion.[20] If we take any object moving at a constant speed, then if we take two divisions of time sufficiently close to each other, we are not going to be able to perceive that the object occupies a different place at each of these

each other, but this is perfectly consistent with there being infinitely many shades in each species. The very fact that Aristotle is *debating* whether to count grey as dark or yellow as pale shows that he allows discriminable shades to be grouped together for purposes of classification. Thus, we can interpret Aristotle as being consistent through the *De sensu* and allow that he thought there was a dense array of shades of colour. Another small piece of evidence to note is that in commenting on *De sensu* 442^a25 Alexander of Aphrodisias (*On Sense Perception*, 82. 3–7 Wendland), notes that in a way the ability to mix, not only pale and dark, but also colours which have themselves been produced by mixing, results in infinitely many colours.

[19] In addition to the specific examples of 3 : 2 and 3 : 4 given in the passages under discussion, at *GC* 334^b13–15 Aristotle implies that mixing takes place in any moderate proportions, giving as examples 2 : 1 and 3 : 1.

[20] Cf. Waterlow, *Nature*, 138, who says: 'A perceptible change of quality may involve a *perceptible* gradation between termini, but perception cannot discern a shade between every pair of perceptibly distinguishable shades.'

divisions. Observation tells us only that change of place is gradual; not that it is continuous.

One might also object that we cannot distinguish straight-off with our eyes the shade that results from mixing, for example, three parts pale and two parts dark from the shade which results from mixing 3001 parts pale with 2000 parts dark. In addition to the comments of the previous paragraph, I note that just because we cannot perceive the difference straight-off does not mean that we cannot tell the difference through perceptual means. For it might be that we can tell the difference with reference to a third shade. For instance, it might be that the shade which came about from mixing 3002 parts pale to 2000 parts dark seems straight-off to be the same as the 3001 : 2000 shade, but is perceived straight-off as paler than the 3 : 2 shade. Thus, by appeal to perception, we can discriminate all three shades and place them in the correct order in terms of their ratios.

3.3. *How all-together colour change satisfies ITD*

De sensu 439^{b}22–440^{a}3 and 440^{b}18–21 provide important evidence for how many shades there are according to Aristotle. They suggest that there is a dense set of ratios (and possibly even 'irrational ratios') all of which result in some distinct shade. Non-musical ratios result in shades that are less beautiful, but shades none the less.

We are now in a position to see how a gradual all-together change of colour satisfies ITD. There will be a dense ordering of shades between the initial shade and the end shade according to the ordering of the ratios. So for any two distinct divisions of time there will be two distinct shades that the object can possess. For example, suppose the tomato changes from green to red over the period of a week. Suppose green has the ratio (of pale to dark) of 2 : 3 while red has the ratio 3 : 2. Perhaps at some intermediate stage of its ripening the tomato will have the shade whose ratio is 1 : 1, at an earlier stage the shade whose ratio is 4 : 5, at an even earlier stage the shade whose ratio is 39 : 50, etc.[21]

In a way I have given the positive argument of this paper. I have

---

[21] If, influenced by *GC* 328^{a}23–31, we might claim that ratios, let us say, greater than 10 : 1 or less than 1 : 10 produce nothing but extreme dark or extreme pale, this does nothing to refute ITD. First, this is consistent with there being no first shade after extreme dark or before extreme pale. Secondly, despite there being a gap in

defended Aristotle's claim that all changes satisfy ITD by showing two ways in which alterations can do this. However, if I were to stop here I would be unlikely to persuade any interpreters who take the opposing view. So I now turn to explain various passages in which Aristotle has been understood to imply that ITD does not hold for alterations.

4. The claim that the very thing according to which the object changes is only coincidentally divisible

4.1. Physics 236ª35–ᵇ18

It is clear from what we have said that there is not a first bit of the changing object or of the time in which it changes. But matters will no longer be the same with regard to the very thing which changes or that according to which it changes [αὐτὸ ... ὃ μεταβάλλει ἢ καθ' ὃ μεταβάλλει]. For there are three factors that we consider about change: that which changes, and that in which it changes, and that into which it changes [εἰς ὃ μεταβάλλει], for example the man and the time and the pale. So the man and the time are divisible, but concerning the pale there is another account. Except all such things are divisible coincidentally [κατὰ συμβεβηκός]. For that of which the pale or the quality is a coincidental attribute is divisible. For in those things [the very things which change or that according to which they change] which are said to be divisible in their own right and not coincidentally there will not be a first bit. For example, in magnitudes [ἐν τοῖς μεγέθεσιν]. Let AB be a magnitude and let it have been moved from B to C first. So if BC is indivisible something partless will be consecutive with something partless. But if [BC] is divisible, there will be some prior [part] of C into which AB has changed, and another before that and so on always on account of there being no end to the division. The result is that there will be no first bit into which the object has changed. And similarly in the case of change of quantity. For this is also change in something continuous. It is clear therefore that in change of quality alone can the [very thing which changes or that according to which it changes] be indivisible in its own right [φανερὸν οὖν ὅτι ἐν μόνῃ τῶν κινήσεων τῇ κατὰ τὸ ποιὸν ἐνδέχεται ἀδιαίρετον καθ' αὐτὸ εἶναι].

This is the central passage for the claim of Waterlow that Aristotle did not think that ITD holds for all alterations:

We have now to consider the merits of the analysis in *Physics* 6. Its best illustration is, of course, locomotion. But Aristotle intends it to cover

the ratios that produce distinct shades, no shades are 'missed out'. For there are no shades produced by mixing in such ratios.

change of whatever kind. Infinite temporal variegation is, in his present view, the distinguishing mark of change as such (see 6. 6, 237ᵃ34 ff.). If so, all types of change must be mathematically continuous. But there is a difficulty which he himself notes: not all properties in respect of which there is change belong to continuous ranges. Qualities, he says, are 'indivisible' (6. 5, 236ᵇ1–6), by which he means that it is not the case that between any pair of a kind there is necessarily another. (Waterlow, *Nature*, 138)[22]

I have three main criticisms of this argument by Waterlow:

(1) Saying that the αὐτὸ . . . ὃ μεταβάλλει ἢ καθ' ὃ μεταβάλλει of a change of quality can be indivisible in its own right is not the same as saying that there is not a dense array of qualities in a range.

(2) That there is not a dense array of qualities does not prevent the change between those qualities from obeying ITD, if it is a part-by-part change.

(3) That an all-together change satisfies ITD does not require there to be a path that is continuous in Aristotle's sense.

In Sections 4.2, 4.3, and 4.4 I consider the first criticism and in section 4.5 the second criticism. I save discussion of my third criticism until Section 5.4.

4.2. *Exposition of* Physics *236ᵃ35–ᵇ18*

I propose now to show why claiming that the αὐτὸ . . . ὃ μεταβάλλει ἢ καθ' ὃ μεταβάλλει can be indivisible in its own right is not the same as claiming that there are only finitely many distinct qualities on the path of a qualitative change. First, I explain 236ᵃ35–ᵇ18. At ᵃ35–6 Aristotle summarizes the argument of the previous section. There is no first bit of time in which there is change because for any candidate we might put forward there will turn out to be a better one. Suppose a complete change takes 10 seconds and I suggest that the first temporal bit should be the first second. In this case the first ½ second would be a better candidate, and the first ¼ second a better candidate than that, and so on *ad infinitum*. Hence there is no *first* temporal bit.

---

[22] In a similar vein Ross, *Aristotelis Physica*, 651 on 236ᵇ17–18, says: 'Aristotle's doctrine with regard to qualitative change is that so far as the αὐτὸ ὃ μεταβάλλει (e.g. the colour) is concerned there are indivisible instalments of change.' Cf. Heinaman, 'Alteration', 231; Sorabji, *Time*, 410–11; Sherry, 'Instantaneous', 395–6.

The argument for there being no first spatial part of the object to have changed is the same. The easiest way to think of this is to think of locomotion from one area to an adjoining area. Suppose an object is one unit long and moves its own length to the right. There will be no first part to have entered the new region. Suppose I suggest the right half of the object, then the rightmost quarter will be a better candidate. Suppose I take the rightmost quarter, the rightmost eighth will be a better candidate . . .

We have learnt that there is no first bit of the time in which there is change, and that there is no first bit of the changing object to change; but what is the third factor that Aristotle says we must consider in a change, of which it seems that sometimes there is a first bit? To clarify, let us consider *Phys.* 262ᵃ2–5:

> For there are three things [involved in a change]—the changing object (for instance, a man or a god), when (i.e. the time), and thirdly that in which there is change [τὸ ἐν ᾧ], i.e. a place or an affection or a form or a magnitude.

Clearly Aristotle has the same idea in mind. The advantage of the book 8 passage is that we get a clearer idea of what the third feature is. In locomotion it is place, in alteration an affection or form, and in growth a magnitude. But this also allows us to see the ambiguity. These could all be end states—in locomotion the final position, in growth the final size, in change of colour the final colour—or they could be the ranges or paths over which change takes place—in locomotion, the starting position, the end position, and all the space in between; in growth, the starting size, the final size, and all the sizes in between; in change of colour, the starting colour, the final colour, and the range of colours in between. I shall label these interpretations the 'end state interpretation' and the 'path interpretation'.

In order for *Phys.* 236ᵃ35–ᵇ18 to support Waterlow's claim that Aristotle denies that there is a dense range of shades, it must be subject to the path interpretation. However, the end state interpretation appears preferable.

4.3. *The end state interpretation*

At 236ᵇ1 Aristotle says that we cannot say the same thing (i.e. that there is no first bit in a change) about αὐτὸ . . . ὃ μεταβάλλει ἦ καθ᾽ ὃ μεταβάλλει. Plausibly this could be either the end state or the path. However, he goes on to describe the third feature as εἰς ὃ μεταβάλλει.

This is strongly supportive of the end state interpretation. His example of the man, the time, and the pale confirms this. The pale is not the path of the change but the end state of the change.

Thus, at 236^{b}10–16 he offers an argument for there being no first bit of the final position into which an object undergoing locomotion has moved. Suppose a line of length one unit moves in a straight line along the *x*-axis from having its leftmost limit at 0 and its rightmost limit at 1 to having its leftmost limit at 1 and its rightmost limit at 2 (henceforth denoted as moving from ⌈0, 1⌉ to ⌈1, 2⌉). Suppose I said that the first bit of the end state reached was ⌈1, $\frac{3}{2}$⌉, then ⌈1, $\frac{5}{4}$⌉ is a better candidate, and ⌈1, $\frac{9}{8}$⌉ a better candidate still, and so on . . . Thus, when the end state is a place, the same argument works as worked in the case of the object and the time.

We are then told (^{b}16–19) that the same holds for change of quantity, before concluding that the only change in which the end state of change can be indivisible in its own right is quality. Aristotle does not mean that there sometimes is a first bit of the end state that is achieved: he simply realizes that it does not even make sense to talk of some bits of the end state being reached before others. The end state does not have bits. Whereas the end position can be divided into smaller units of place and thus some are reached before others, the end colour cannot be so divided; it is simply white. On the end state interpretation, this passage is completely irrelevant to whether or not Aristotle thought that there was a dense range of shades. This is my preferred interpretation of this passage.

4.4. *The path interpretation*

However, it would be unfair simply to dismiss the path interpretation. First, 236^{b}10–16 also shows that there is no first bit of the path between and including starting position and end position in the case of locomotion. Secondly, it is difficult categorically to rule out vacillation between the two interpretations, especially as elsewhere (e.g. *Phys.* 235^{a}13–18, discussed in Section 5.1, and 237^{b}2, discussed in Section 5.4) Aristotle does seem to consider the path over which change takes place.

However, on this path interpretation insufficient weight is given to the 'in its own right'/'coincidental' distinction. In the case of change of place the path of the change is divisible in its own right. Now let us suppose that Aristotle (*a*) has in mind gradual, all-together change of colour, such as when a tomato changes from being green all over to being red all over, and (*b*) thinks that there are only finitely many shades of colour between green and red. In this case he should say that the path of the change is divisible, but not infinitely divisible, or that there is a first thing to which the altering object alters. He says neither of these things. Instead he says that the path of the change is not divisible in its own right but only coincidentally divisible. This passage provides no evidence for the claim that Aristotle denied that between any two distinct qualities in a range there is a third distinct quality. Furthermore, nowhere in *Physics* does Aristotle expressly claim that qualitative change takes place in discrete instalments.

I should note that positing a dense array of shades does not directly make it any easier to explain Aristotle's comment that change of colour is divisible only *coincidentally*, if he has in mind all-together change of colour. For in this case the path, one would think, should be subject to the same divisions as time *in its own right*. Thus, on the path interpretation, a key aspect of the passage is unexplained regardless of whether or not there is a dense range of shades. This is a further reason for favouring the end state interpretation.

4.5. *Part-by-part change of colour*

I suggest that in this passage Aristotle has in mind part-by-part alteration (as explained in Section 3.1). In terms of the very thing according to which there is change, colour, this change is not divisible at all (not merely not infinitely divisible). Returning to the example of the litmus paper, there are no colours, apart from orange and red, involved in the change at any time. However, it makes good sense to say that the end state or range is divisible coincidentally because the object is divisible. For the red spreads gradually over the object. ITD still holds. At earlier divisions of time less of the paper is red. Therefore, the end state (or the path) is divisible in terms of how much of the paper is red. This is what Aristotle means by saying that it is coincidentally divisible. It is important to understand that such part-by-part alteration provides a method for Aristotle to maintain, *pace* Waterlow, that alterations satisfy ITD even if there are only finitely many shades of colour, but that some alterations are like this does not, of course, rule out that there is still a dense array of shades.

However, even if advocates of the claim that Aristotle thought that there were only finitely many shades of colour are willing to grant that 236^{a}35–^{b}18 does not explicitly show that Aristotle thought there were only finitely many shades, they might respond as follows. 'Why should Aristotle think that changes of colour have to take place part by part when this is contrary to observational evidence? Isn't the reason for this that he was committed to ITD but also thought that there were only finitely many shades?' In Section 6 I argue that Aristotle's predilection in *Physics* 6 for the part-by-part model of alteration is not because of a belief that there were only finitely many shades of colour but because of failure always to make the necessary distinctions between different methods of dividing a change of place. Now I introduce some preliminary distinctions before addressing my third criticism of Waterlow, that for an all-together change of colour to satisfy ITD requires a range that is continuous in Aristotle's sense.

5. The distinction between dividing the change and dividing the path of the change

In this section I argue that although, for reasons I shall explain, Aristotle does not think there is a *path* that is divisible in its own right in a change of colour, he does think that the change itself satisfies ITD. To see how this is possible we need to examine Aristotle's discussion of the different divisions that can be performed.

5.1. *The five features of change whose divisions correspond*

Since everything that changes changes in some respect and in some time, and there is a change of everything [that changes], it is necessary that there are the same divisions of the time, of the change, of the changing, of that which changes [καὶ τοῦ κινουμένου], and of that in which there is change [ἐν ᾧ ἡ κίνησις]—except not in the same way of all those things in which there is change; but of place in itself, and of quality coincidentally [πλὴν οὐ πάντων ὁμοίως ἐν οἷς ἡ κίνησις, ἀλλὰ τοῦ μὲν τόπου καθ᾽ αὐτό, τοῦ δὲ ποιοῦ κατὰ συμβεβηκός].[23] (*Phys.* 235^{a}13–18)

---

[23] In reading τόπου rather than πόσου I follow Ross, *Aristotelis Physica*, against the majority of manuscripts.

And the same argument will show also that the distance [τὸ μῆκος] is divisible and generally every thing in which there is change [καὶ ὅλως πᾶν ἐν ᾧ ἐστιν ἡ μεταβολή] (except some [things in which there is change] are only divisible coincidentally, because the changing object is divisible). (*Phys.* 235ᵃ33–5)

Here Aristotle identifies the following five features, and claims that there are the same divisions of all of them:

(1) the changing object (τὸ κινούμενον);
(2) that in which there is change (ἔν τινι);
(3) time (χρόνον τινα);
(4) change (κίνησις);
(5) the changing (τοῦ κινεῖσθαι).[24]

5.2. *The divisions of the time, change, and path*

At first glance it might appear attractive for my argument to take the ἔν τινι as the end state and rerun the arguments of Section 4. However, ἔν τινι is distinct from εἰς ὃ μεταβάλλει. Thus, we must consider the path interpretation, which is the standard interpretation of the passages. These passages therefore pose a very real threat to my position.

A feature of 235ᵃ13–18 is that there are the *same* divisions of the precise interval of time, of the change, and of that in which there is change. I take this to mean not only that there are the same number of divisions of the time as of the change, but that these divisions *correspond*. For example, suppose I make a division of the time, then corresponding to this division of the time there is a division of the change, and of that in which there is change.[25]

Think of the example in Figure 1. We can describe this as the movement of the object *from* AC *to* CE during the interval of time t_1t_3, or alternatively we can describe it as the movement of the object *over a distance* of AC (or CE) during t_1t_3. Let us call the 'from . . .

---

[24] A confusing feature of this passage is what the distinction between κίνησις and τοῦ κινεῖσθαι is meant to be. Ross, *Aristotelis Physica*, 647, thinks that κίνησις refers to a certain change capable of being undergone by a variety of subjects, and τοῦ κινεῖσθαι to the historical undergoing of the change by some individual subject. White, *Continuous*, 35–6, takes the distinction to be between change as a count noun (κίνησις) and change as a mass noun (τοῦ κινεῖσθαι), as indicated by the imperfective nature of the articular infinitive. Thankfully, for present purposes it is not necessary to resolve this issue.

[25] The nature of these correspondences is noted by Hussey, *Aristotle's Physics: Books III and IV*, 142–6.

to' description 'Method A' and the distance description 'Method B'. If we divide the change using Method A, we say that at the end of the interval $t_1 t_2$ the object has moved from AC to BD. If we divide the change using Method B we say that at the end of the interval $t_1 t_2$ the object has covered the distance AB (or, since the two lengths are equal, CD). Examples of Method A include $236^b 10$–16 and $237^a 28$–34. Method B is employed at $232^b 26$–$233^a 12$.

This distinction between changes (from one position to another) and their paths (the intervening distance) is vital. It is important to note that in the case of locomotion we can think of the distance independently of the change, and (at least in the case of complete changes) the change independently of the distance. However, when we turn our attention to changes of colour, this breaks down.

I deliberately stated ITD in terms of divisions of the change, not divisions of the path. This is vital to my argument. For, while we could successfully restate ITD in terms of divisions of the path for locomotion, we cannot successfully restate it in these terms for colour.

5.3. *Changes of colour: dividing the change and dividing the path*

Let us consider a tomato that ripens. Over a period of time it changes from being green all-over to being red all-over. Further-more, it passes through an array of intermediate states, such as being orange all-over, or off-green all-over. Thus, we can easily show how divisions of the time and the change correspond (Table 1).

The view I am opposing might be as follows. Assuming that we can clearly make divisions to this extent, but that Aristotle says that the path is not (infinitely) divisible in its own right, then the reason for this must be that there are only finitely many intermediate shades in the path. However, I argue that we should, along with Aristotle, distinguish between dividing the path and dividing the change. We can divide the change as shown in Table 1, and, as I argued in Section 3.3, this process can go on *ad infinitum*. How-ever, we cannot divide the path, because, I argue, there is nothing corresponding to *distance* in the case of change of colour.

5.4. *The metrical reason why there is no path to divide according to Method B*

Distance is a general metric between *any* two positions (or states) in a range. There is no general metric with which to compare shades.

TABLE 1. *Method A: divisions of change*

Interval of time (e.g. weeks)	Changes (from initial shade to end shade)
1	from green to red (complete change)
$\frac{1}{2}$	from green to orange
$\frac{1}{4}$	from green to off-green

There is something crucially similar between any two changes over, for example, one metre, even if they have different start and end positions. However, in the case of colour we do not have a natural metric. There is no sense in which changing from pale to dark is twice as great a change as changing from pale to grey.

We should note that we have only a very weak notion (if any) of intrinsic distance between shades of colour based on immediate perception. For example, if we think of three shades of colour c_1, c_2, c_3, such that c_1 is paler than c_2 and c_2 is paler than c_3, we can (sometimes) say 'c_1 is paler than c_3 by a greater amount than c_1 is paler than c_2', but we cannot straightforwardly say 'c_1 is paler than c_3 by twice as much as c_1 is paler than c_2'. Similarly, we can say that c_2 is closer to extreme pale than c_3 but cannot say 'c_3 is twice as far away from extreme pale as c_2'. *A fortiori*, there is even less sense in claiming that one shade is, for example, twice as pale as another.

That we can assign numbers does not improve this. We can say that two metres is twice the distance of one metre. However, we cannot say that the shade whose ratio is 4 : 1 is twice as pale as the shade assigned the value 2 : 1. Nor can we say that it is paler by any specific ratio. For perception enables us to order the shades and sometimes to say that the difference between one pair of shades is greater than the difference between another pair of shades, but perception does not provide anything more fine-grained than this.

Of course, sometimes we can make sense of saying that one change of colour is greater than another change of colour. We can do this whenever one change is a proper subchange of the other change. To establish ITD we require simply that there is an ordering, not that there is a metric. So, suppose an object changes all-together from pale to dark, we can say that the following subchanges are ordered correctly: extreme-pale to pale-ish, extreme-pale to grey, extreme-pale to extreme-dark. However, this is simply Method A.

By distinguishing between dividing the change and dividing the path of the change, we can understand Aristotle's seemingly puzzling remark at *Phys.* 237^{b}2 that in the case of changes which do not have continuous paths, we can still show that the change is infinitely divisible by taking divisions of the time. Aristotle argues (237^{a}17–28) that what has changed was changing before. At 237^{a}28–30 he says that this is more clear in the case of distance on account of the distance in which the changing object changes being continuous but adds (237^{a}35–^{b}2) that the same demonstration holds also in the case of non-continuous things, for example in changes involving contraries and contradictories.[26] This would be a very strange thing to say if he thought that it failed to hold at all in the other cases. The explanation of these remarks is that in the case of locomotion we can show that the change is infinitely divisible by dividing the time, but we can make the same point more clearly by dividing the distance. However, with alteration, since there is no continuous distance to divide, we must rely on dividing the time.

Failing to distinguish between dividing the change and dividing the path leads Waterlow, *Nature*, 139, into a mistake. Commenting on 237^{a}35–^{b}3, she says:

Thus (granting for the moment that time does elapse) we are meant to say that in half the time X has completed a change to half-way being red and so on. But apart from reducing qualities in the Aristotelian sense to primary qualities in the Lockean, there is no independent method for identifying infinitely many degrees of qualitative change. It is meaningless to say that at t_n X was one thousandth more red than at t_m and millionths more for every thousandth part of the interval.

Waterlow is right to claim that it is meaningless to say that X is one-thousandth more red. However, ITD does not require this. The ratio of pale to dark in a given shade provides an independent method of identifying infinitely many shades, but this does not allow for measurement beyond ordering.

Let me take this opportunity to summarize the argument of this section. I have explained how Aristotle thinks that there is no path (in its own right) in a change of colour, and hence there is no path that is divisible, and hence no path that is infinitely divisible. But in the case of the tomato that changes from green all-over to red all-over nor is there a path that is coincidentally divisible. Why,

---

[26] In sect. 8.1 I discuss Waterlow's criticism of this passage.

then, does Aristotle focus in *Physics* 6 upon part-by-part changes of colour where at least there is a path coincidentally? I argue in the next section that his predilection rests on a mistake that is quite general and not specific to alteration. This mistake concerns the division of a change according to division of the changing object into parts.

6. Division of the change according to parts of the object

Let us now return to *Physics* 235ᵃ13–18 and Aristotle's claim that there are the same divisions of the change, the time, the path, and the object. I have considered how the divisions of the change, the time, and the path correspond; it is now time to turn to divisions of the object.[27]

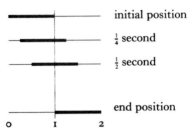

initial position

¼ second

½ second

end position

F I G U R E 3. Locomotion to an adjacent region

To see how Aristotle reached his views about divisibility of the object into parts, we must consider that it is usually possible to describe a locomotion (or more often a sublocomotion) in terms of

[27] At first sight there is no useful correspondence between the divisions of the change, the time, and the parts of the object, at least in the case of locomotion in a straight line, which is Aristotle's focus in *Physics* 6. When an object travels, it travels all-together. For example, it is not the case that when I walk from A to B in 10 seconds, after one second my head has reached B, after two seconds my neck has joined it, and finally my whole body has reached B. Thankfully, there is no reason to attribute such a position to Aristotle. I take it that when Aristotle talks about dividing a change according to the parts of the object at 234ᵇ21–235ᵃ8, he has in mind that if we divide the object into parts in thought, we can also divide the change in thought. So suppose an object moves from ┌0, 2┐ to ┌3, 5┐, then one half of the object moves from ┌0, 1┐ to ┌3, 4┐ and the other half moves from ┌1, 2┐ to ┌4, 5┐. However, these subchanges take place at the same time as each other. Thus, to these divisions of the object and the change there are no corresponding divisions in the time. So it would be a mistake if Aristotle had this sort of division in mind at 235ᵃ13–18 when he claims that there are the same divisions of the object, the path, the time, the change, and the changing.

an initial region and an end region that are adjacent. If a line starts by occupying the whole of AB and ends up occupying the whole of BC, at each division of the time in which it is moving some of the line is in the region AB and some in the region BC. Consider my previous example of a locomotion: the change from ⌐0, 1⌐ to ⌐1, 2⌐. Aristotle uses this method at *Phys.* 234^{b}10–20 (discussed in Section 6.2), 236^{a}27–35, and 240^{b}17–241^{a}5 (discussed in Section 6.1). Thus, we can show how the divisions of the time, change, path, and object all correspond.

TABLE 2. *The three methods of dividing a change*

	Method		
	A: divisions of change	B: divisions of path	C: divisions of the object
Interval of time (e.g. seconds)	Changes (from initial position to end position)	Distance traversed by (e.g.) leftmost point of line	Fraction of object in end region
1	From ⌐0, 1⌐ to ⌐1, 2⌐ (complete change)	1	1
$\frac{1}{2}$	From ⌐0, 1⌐ to ⌐$\frac{1}{2}$, $\frac{3}{2}$⌐	$\frac{1}{2}$	$\frac{1}{2}$
$\frac{1}{4}$	From ⌐0, 1⌐ to ⌐$\frac{1}{5}$, $\frac{6}{5}$⌐	$\frac{1}{5}$	$\frac{1}{5}$
$\frac{1}{8}$	From ⌐0, 1⌐ to ⌐$\frac{1}{12}$, $\frac{13}{12}$⌐	$\frac{1}{12}$	$\frac{1}{12}$

As shown in Table 2, the pattern of correspondence between Methods A and B exists for any locomotions. However, the divisions according to Method C only correspond to the other divisions when we choose the special case of locomotion from one region of the same length as the object to an adjacent region. We should note that uniform velocity is not required.

It is my conjecture that Aristotle has overestimated the general significance of the correspondence between Method C and the other methods, and it is this which explains many of his remarks about colour change. Since a colour change has no path in its own right, and Aristotle has fallen into the trap of thinking that division of the object according to Method C *always* corresponds to divisions of the change and path, in the case of colour change he appeals to Method C to do duty for Method B. This gives the unfortunate appearance that he thought all changes of colour were part by part.

On my interpretation Aristotle makes something of a mistake in the passages that we are currently considering, but it is not the mistake of generalizing from locomotion to alteration. Rather, it is the mistake of generalizing from a particular way of describing locomotion, where methods A, B, and C correspond, to thinking that there is always such a correspondence.

6.1. *The argument that all changing objects are divisible*

I now turn to consider Aristotle's arguments for the claim that all changing objects are divisible. While in Aristotelian physics the conclusion is no doubt true, these arguments rely on Method C. Indeed, my justification for introducing Method C is the text below. Thus, where this method is inapplicable, Aristotle's argument fails. Importantly, this failure is independent of whether or not there are finitely many shades.

As we said, therefore, in this way that which is without parts can change, as the man sitting in a ship changes when the ship moves, but it is not possible for something partless to change in its own right. For let it be changing from AB to BC, whether from a magnitude to a magnitude or from a form to a form or according to contradictories. Let D be the immediate time in which it changes. Therefore, it must through the time when it is changing be either in AB or in BC, or some part of it be in one and another part in the other. For every changing object is like this. It will not be the case that some of it is in each. For then it would have parts. But nor can it be in BC. For then it will have completed its change, when *ex hypothesi* it is changing. So it remains that it is in AB at the time when it is changing. So it will be at rest. For to be in the same state for a period of time was to be at rest. The result is that it is not possible for something without parts to change, nor generally to vary. (*Phys.* 240ᵇ17–241ᵃ5)

This is the clearest example of Aristotle's argument that anything which undergoes change must have parts. The basis of the argument is that a single and indivisible object cannot possess contradictory properties. The model of division being appealed to is that of dividing an object that is moving from one region to an adjacent region according to the region occupied, i.e. Method C. Aristotle argues by *reductio* of the assumption that a partless object can move from one region to an adjacent region.

We must understand the applicability of the argument. Clearly many locomotions are over distances greater than the length of the

moving object. However, there is always a subchange of the following kind: the subchange from the object's precise initial position to
the precise position immediately adjacent to it but not overlapping
with it. Any locomotion over a greater distance will contain such
a sublocomotion.[28]

So far as locomotion goes, the argument is a good one. A version
of it would also be applicable to part-by-part change of colour.
However, it is not applicable to all changes of colour, and hence
the overall argument is not valid. Nevertheless, the invalidity has
nothing to do with alteration or colour as such. As we shall see in
Section 6.2, growth and diminution also provide counter-examples.
We may note that Aristotle's use of the notation AB and BC is
inappropriate if, as he suggests, AB and BC might be forms or
contradictories. In the case of locomotion 'A' refers to the leftmost
limit of the initial position and 'B' to the rightmost limit of the
initial position, thus 'AB' refers to a distance. However, in the case
of a colour we should typically wish to say that an object is red, or
green, or pale, or whatever. It will not be a range of colours.[29] In
a schematic description of colour change, Aristotle should denote
the starting state as 'A' rather than 'AB'.

Aristotle offers a similar argument to that of *Phys.* 240^{b}17–241^{a}5
at 234^{b}10–20. Unfortunately, here he makes another mistake, but
one which is an error both on my reading and on the reading of
those who attribute to him the view that there were only finitely
many shades of colour.

6.2. Physics *234^{b}10–20: proof that every object which changes must be divisible*

Everything which changes must be divisible. Since every change is from
something into something, and whenever something is in that into which
it was changing, it is no longer changing, but whenever it is in that from

---

[28] Clearly some locomotions are over less distance than the length of the object,
e.g. when a train shunts along by just a few metres.

[29] That Aristotle is not clear on this matter suggests another reason why he did
not think of the path of a change of colour as *continuous*, even though there is a
dense range of colours. When an object starts moving from AB to CD, most of it is
still in AB and then a little less, and a little less, and so on. A series of overlapping
distances makes up the total distance AD over which the object moves. Thus, there
is an intuitive sense in which the path of the locomotion is continuous, which is not
shared by even a continuous (in the modern sense) array of shades. There is no such
overlapping chain of shades for a change of colour. In all-together change of colour,
once the object is no longer its initial shade, it is entirely a different shade.

which it was changing, both itself and all its parts, it is not yet changing (for anything which remains the same both in itself and in its parts is not changing), then it is necessary that of the changing thing, part is in this and part in that. For it is not possible for it to be in both or in neither. And I mean the first thing into which it changes according to the change, for example from pale grey, rather than dark. For the changing object need not be in either of the extremes. Therefore, it is clear that every changing object is divisible.

By a first end state of change we should understand the region of the same size as the object that shares a limit with the precise initial region but does not overlap with it. Thus, the claim here does not contradict 237^a28–34. I agree that there is no first place to which an object in motion moves according to Method A, but there is a first region of the same length as the object, between which and the initial region there is no overlap.[30]

However, Aristotle illustrates this in an inappropriate fashion. The problem is not that there is no first colour after pale. The real problem is that if the change of colour is part by part, then the object must indeed be divisible, but in this case it is irrelevant to say that the first stage of change is to being grey rather than to being dark. If, on the other hand, the crucial aspect of the change is that it should be qualitatively gradual, that the first stage of the change is to the object being grey is relevant. However, such a gradual change, if all-together, does not guarantee that the object is divisible. Even if there are only finitely many shades of colour and grey is the first shade after dark, Aristotle still makes a mistake here.[31]

As Simplicius points out, Aristotle's argument that the object of change must be divisible does not work for growth. Yet, all accept that Aristotle claims that growth is a continuous and infinitely temporally divisible change.

It is worth remarking that it is necessary that for things that change place one part be in the region from which [the object is moving], and another part be in that into which [the object is moving]. For in the case of these

---

[30] Thus, Aristotle is not committing the sort of error which Bostock attributes to him. For he says at 234^b17 '*the first end-point*: that there always is a first endpoint should be noted. The assumption must be false, if the change in question is genuinely continuous (as motion is), and this observation destroys the argument' (trans. R. Waterfield, *Aristotle's Physics* (Oxford, 1996), 276).

[31] Additionally, even if, *pace* my position, Aristotle thought there were only finitely many shades of colour, grey would not be the first colour after pale. See *De sensu* 442^a19–25, quoted in n. 18 above.

objects the 'whither whence' is this way, but in the case of alteration and increase and decrease it does not seem necessary for things to be this way, but it is possible in these cases for alteration to happen all-together [ἀθρόα] and for [an object] to increase all-together. For the addition seems to happen simultaneously to every part of the increasing object, and similarly decrease happens all-together. (Simpl. *In Phys.* 967. 31–968. 5 Diels)

Clearly we should think of growing objects as having parts; it is just that there is no *argument* from the fact that an object grows to its having parts based on the laws of the excluded middle and non-contradiction, as there was for locomotion. Aristotle's argument that every object of change is divisible into parts is certainly problematic, but the problem does not lie in the special nature of qualities.

So far I have defended the claim that ITD holds for alterations, and suggested why Aristotle is so attracted to the part-by-part model, even if his attraction is the result of an error. However, at times it looks as if he thought that alterations necessarily took place part by part. This is not a problem in terms of the defence of ITD, but it is somewhat implausible. Many changes of colour do not take place part by part. For example, suppose I spend the summer acquiring a suntan and then lock myself in a library reading room.[32] My left cheek does not become pale before my right one. Rather, the whole of my face together gradually becomes pale. I have already argued that Aristotle has the means to explain how such changes obey ITD, but let us now consider the direct textual evidence that he considers such changes.

7. Does Aristotle consider all-together alteration?

At *De sensu* 446ᵇ28–447ᵃ6 Aristotle says:

In general, it is not the same for alteration as it is for locomotion. For locomotions naturally first reach the intermediate position (and it seems that sound is a change of something being conveyed [in locomotion]) but those things which alter do not behave likewise. For it is possible for the whole body to be altered, and not one half first. For example, water freezes all at the same time. Yet, when there is a large body being warmed or being frozen, each part undergoes change at the hands of the next, and the first

---

[32] Simpl. *In Phys.* 968. 25–6 Diels gives the example of acquiring a suntan as one which occurs all-together rather than part by part.

part changes at the hands of the agent of alteration itself and it does not necessarily undergo alteration all together at the same time.

In the case of a large body of water freezing we can apply the part-by-part model of alteration. However, apparently a small body of water can freeze ἅμα and ἀθρόον. Wardy takes *Phys.* 253ᵇ23–6 together with *De sensu* 446ᵇ28–447ᵃ6 as evidence that Aristotle allowed for *instantaneous* alteration.[33] I argue that these passages are irrelevant to this assertion.

Aristotle is in fact noting that some alterations take place all-together. That is, rather than taking place part by part, at any division of the time any bit of the object is in the same state as any other bit. The distinction between instantaneous alteration and all-together alteration over time is noted by Simplicius. Furthermore, he takes Aristotle's example of a small amount of water freezing to illustrate all-together alteration over time, not instantaneous alteration. Thus, if we follow Simplicius we should not take *Phys.* 253ᵇ23–6 or *De sensu* 446ᵇ28–447ᵃ6 as evidence that Aristotle allowed for *instantaneous* alteration:

But if certain changes occur all-together [ἀθρόως], then perhaps one ought no longer to admit this. (By 'all-together [ἀθρόως]' I mean not only as in general the parts of a thing may change all-together [οὐχ ὡς καθόλου τὰ μόρια μόνον], as in the case of freezing, but rather all of the change occurring as not in time [ἀλλ' οὐχ ὡς ἐν χρόνῳ].) For in these cases changing and having changed do not precede each other, because there is no changing at all in the case of them. (Simpl. *In Phys.* 998. 9–13 Diels, on *Phys.* 237ᵇ9–22)[34]

I take *De sensu* 446ᵇ28–447ᵃ6 to be saying that while an object undergoing locomotion necessarily passes over the intermediate parts of its path, alteration *need not be* divisible part by part. In making this contradistinction Aristotle is slipping between method A of dividing a locomotion and method C of dividing an alteration. None the less, what he is saying is tolerably clear. He is not saying that alteration *cannot* be divisible part by part. (Such a claim would clearly be at odds with passages of *Physics* 6 discussed above.) Furthermore, this passage is not saying that freezing of a small amount of water is instantaneous but that it is all-together.

This passage has nothing to say in itself about whether all-together change satisfies ITD. The point is simply that each bit

---

[33] Wardy, *Chain*, 330–1. Waterlow, *Nature*, 155, is also sympathetic to this line.

[34] See also Simpl. *In Phys.* 968. 5–15 Diels, on *Phys.* 234ᵇ10–20.

is at any given time during the period of this alteration in the same state as every other bit. For example, at the initial time each bit is liquid, after one minute each bit is squishy, after two minutes each bit is rigid but not yet hard, at the end the whole is fully frozen.[35] Because of Aristotle's claims in *Physics* 6 that all changes satisfy ITD, I assume this change does also. That we do not have a *metric* of squishiness does not matter. All that is needed is that we can order states in terms of being more or less squishy.

8. Waterlow's main objection

I now turn to an objection by Waterlow. I argue that this is in fact not specific to alteration and is susceptible of a different solution.

8.1. Physics 237^a17–28: that which has changed was changing before

Not only is it necessary that what is changing has changed, but also that that which has changed was changing before. For everything which has changed from something into something has changed in time. For suppose that something has changed in the now from A into B. Then it has not changed in the same now in which it was in A (for it would have been in A and in B at the same time). For it was shown before that that which has changed, when it has changed, is not in the same state. But if [it has changed] in a different now, there will be time in between. For nows were not consecutive. Therefore, since it has changed in time, and every time is divisible, in half the time it will have completed another change, and another still in a quarter of the time, and so on always, so that it would have been changing previously.

Waterlow argues that 'the argument proves too much. On the same principle an interval can be demonstrated between a state and its contradictory. But no interval is possible between not-Q and Q, at any rate not for Aristotle who holds the Law of the Excluded Middle'[36]

On Waterlow's interpretation Aristotle's argument can be used to prove that there must be an intermediate state between *contradictories*, and clearly there can be nothing between pale and not-pale.

---

[35] We may note that at *Meteor.* 348^b22 Aristotle talks about freezing taking time. Thus in the case of a small amount of water when the freezing does not take place part by part there must be a range of intermediate states through which the whole of the object passes.

[36] Waterlow, *Nature*, 141.

However, that does not entail that any change from pale to not-pale is instantaneous (and hence not divisible according to the time). For similarly there is nothing in between being completely in the region ⌜0, 1⌝ and not-being completely in the region ⌜0, 1⌝, yet the change between these two states is a locomotion, and no party in the debate wishes to suggest that Aristotle also thought that there is instantaneous locomotion!

Let us consider an example. Suppose a football changes from not-being completely inside the goal to being completely inside the goal. A better description would be to say that it changes from being, for example, on the penalty spot to being in the back of the net. For it rests on the penalty spot for a period of time, and rests in the back of the net for a period of time, but does not rest in between.

So the mere fact that we can (misleadingly) describe a change as instantaneous does not entail that it really is so. The problem with 237ᵃ17–28 that Waterlow cites is a problem about how we describe changes in any category. The general solution is that we should strictly speaking describe changes as being from some definite state to another definite state. To say that a change takes place from not-F to F is acceptable only if we understand that 'not-F' is shorthand for some definite state. Aristotle indicates how we should cash out 'not-F' in such descriptions at *Phys.* 188ᵃ36–ᵇ3.[37]

8.2. *Aristotle's own explanation as to how change between contradictories can satisfy ITD*

While Aristotle makes it clear that in specifying a change we should specify the initial state and the end state in a precise manner, when explicitly addressing the question of how change between contradictories is possible he offers a different solution. His response is that the object can change part by part. This solution will also apply to other problems, for example an object changing from being dark to being pale. We can say that although the object is either dark or pale at any time, it is not dark as a whole, or pale as a whole, at any time while it is changing.

And nor will there be anything impossible for us in the change that involves contradictories, for example if something changes from not-pale to pale and is in neither state, so that it will be neither pale nor not-pale. And

[37] A similar solution is offered by D. Bostock, 'Aristotle on Continuity', in L. Judson, *Aristotle's Physics: a Collection of Essays* (Oxford, 1991), 179–212 at 199.

it is not the case that, if it is not as a whole in whatever state, it will not be called pale or not-pale. For we call it pale or not-pale not by it being such as a whole, but by most of its parts or the most important parts being pale. For it is not the same thing not to be in this state and not to be in this state as a whole. And similarly for being and not-being and all the other contradictories. For of necessity the object will always be in either of the contradictory states but in neither as a whole. (*Phys.* 240ᵃ19–29)

Unfortunately, Aristotle's solution to the problem of how there can be intermediates between being pale and being not-pale is unsatisfactory. He appeals to parts being pale and parts not-pale, but in fact the problem can be reformulated. How can a change from being not pale-as-a-whole to being pale-as-a-whole satisfy ITD? Such a change really should not take time. There would be a parallel in the case of locomotion: the change from being not completely within some region to being completely within that region. The only general solution is to insist that we specify the change as from some specific state or place to some specific state or place. For example, in the case of the ball undergoing a transition from being not completely over the goal line to being completely over the goal line, we should redescribe it as being a locomotion from the penalty spot to a particular position at the back of the goal.

9. Final thoughts

I have now completed the defence of my claim that ITD holds for all changes of colour and that there are two ways in which it can hold: either if the change is part by part, or if it is all-together. However, I might still be vulnerable to the following sort of criticism. 'I accept that you have shown that ITD holds for changes of colour, and probably for a few other alterations such as changes of temperature, but Aristotle's category of quality is much broader than this. How can a change from being ignorant to being knowledgeable or from being cowardly to being brave satisfy ITD?' A full answer is beyond the scope of this paper, but I shall briefly throw out some considerations which at least make it plausible that such changes might satisfy ITD.

Suppose I change from being cowardly to being brave over the period of one year. Such a change cannot be part by part. It is absurd to suggest that my foot becomes brave and then my leg and then my groin . . . The change must be all-together and thus requires a dense array of degrees of braveness. We might seriously doubt that there is such an array or that Aristotle thought that there was.

I have three comments to make in response. First, we must distinguish between a strict and loose mode of speaking. Loosely speaking, I am moving from Cambridge to London even when the train has stopped at Royston. Strictly speaking, I am not moving from Cambridge to London at this time, but rather there are (at least) two separate locomotions: one from Cambridge to Royston and one from Royston to London with a period of rest in between. Similarly, while I might not strictly speaking be in the process of becoming brave when I am asleep, in ordinary talk we are permitted to say this.

Secondly, we should doubt that there are easily and independently identifiable degrees of braveness. Aristotle's move in the case of colour does not seem plausible here. There is no sense in which an intermediate degree of braveness is a mixture of the brave and the cowardly. However, it is not essential that we are able to assign numerical values to degrees. All that matters is that there is an ordering in terms of more and less. Even in the case of locomotion we do not need numerical measurement in order to show that ITD holds.

Thirdly, we might object that in moral development there can be quantum leaps. I do not need to pass through *every* intermediate degree. In the case of locomotion, Aristotle has independent reasons for ruling out the possibility of quantum leaps. However, ITD does not rule out quantum leaps. So long as for any two divisions of time in my moral development I am braver (by however little) at the later division, it does not matter for ITD that I might 'jump over' some degrees.

I do not intend these final remarks to act as categorical proof that Aristotle thought ITD held for all alterations, merely to show that it is not obviously false. I make no apologies for concentrating on change of colour, since that is just what Aristotle does in *Physics* 6, and in this paper I have shown that he believed that all changes of colour were infinitely temporally divisible.

BIBLIOGRAPHY

Barker, A. 'Colours, Concords and Ratios in *De sensu* 3' (paper presented to the B Club in Cambridge, 2004).

Bostock, D., 'Aristotle on Continuity', in L. Judson, (ed.), *Aristotle's Physics: A Collection of Essays* (Oxford, 1991), 179–212.

Furley, D., 'Review of *Nature, Change, and Agency in Aristotle's Physics: A Philosophical Study* by Sarah Waterlow', *Ancient Philosophy*, 4 (1984), 108–10.

Heinaman, R., 'Alteration and Aristotle's Activity–Change Distinction' ['Alteration'], *Oxford Studies in Ancient Philosophy*, 16 (1998), 227–58.

Hussey, E., *Aristotle's* Physics: *Books III and IV* (Oxford, 1983).

Ross, W. D., *Aristotelis Physica* (Oxford, 1967).

Sherry, D., 'On Instantaneous Velocity' ['Instantaneous'], *History of Philosophy Quarterly*, 3/4 (1986), 391–406.

Sorabji, R., 'Aristotle, Mathematics and Colour', *Classical Quarterly*, NS 22 (1972), 293–308.

—— *Time, Creation and the Continuum: Theories in Antiquity and the Early Middle Ages* [*Time*] (London, 1983).

Wardy, R., *The Chain of Change* [*Chain*] (Oxford, 1990).

Waterfield, R. (trans.), *Aristotle's* Physics (Oxford, 1996).

Waterlow, S., *Nature, Change, and Agency in Aristotle's Physics* [*Nature*] (Oxford, 1982).

White, M., *The Continuous and the Discrete: Ancient Physical Theories from a Contemporary Perspective* [*Continuous*] (Oxford, 1992).

KINĒSIS VS. ENERGEIA:
A MUCH-READ PASSAGE IN (BUT NOT
OF) ARISTOTLE'S METAPHYSICS

M. F. BURNYEAT

In memoriam Michael Frede

WE are to discuss what is now one of the most famous passages in Aristotle: *Metaphysics* Θ 6, 1048^{b}18–35, on the distinction between κίνησις and ἐνέργεια. The Passage, as I shall capitalize it, has been endlessly analysed by philosophical enthusiasts. It is a particular favourite with those trained in analytic philosophy.[1] But

© M. F. Burnyeat 2008

This paper began as a contribution to a seminar on *Metaphysics* Θ held in Cambridge during the Spring Term of 1995. Acknowledgements for critical comments and many other kinds of help are owed to Peter Adamson, Gwenaëlle Aubry, David Charles, Alan Code, Michel Crubellier, Sten Ebbesen, Doug Hutchinson, Stephen Makin, Wolfgang Mann, Terumasa Okhusa, Jan Saif, Anna-Maria Schiaparelli, Bob Sharples. Very special acknowledgements are due to Michael Frede and David Sedley for their continuing support over the long period of gestation and for the important substantive contributions their expertise has made to its eventual outcome. To Francesco Ademollo I owe thanks for help (both philological and administrative) in connection with the manuscript in Florence, plus comments at various stages in the growth of the paper. In addition, I thank audiences in Berlin, Florence, Lille, Munich, Oxford, and Toronto for their sympathetically critical discussions.

[1] In part because of the use made of it in modern discussion by Ryle (cited and criticized by Ackrill) and Kenny. Thus Penner: 'It was Ryle who first showed analytical philosophers the gold mine there was in Aristotle.' On the other side of the Channel, the view can be rather different: 'C'est à lui [the Passage] que je m'attacherai, à cause de sa valeur philosophique considérable, et aussi — l'avouerai-je? — par ce souci sportif de venir en aide au passages quelque peu laissés-pour-compte, et relégués dans les notes et les subordonnés concessives des ouvrages savants . . .'. So wrote Brague (the 'points de suspension' are his), twenty-three years after Ackrill's seminal paper on the Passage. In the sequel Brague cites Ackrill, but none of the articles that poured out in the lively controversy he prompted. I am grateful for Brague's unanalytic discussion, despite numerous textual disagreements signalled below. The anti-analytic discussion of Dufour, by contrast, is a thicket of confusion. (References: J. L. Ackrill, 'Aristotle's Distinction between *Energeia* and *Kinesis*' ['Distinction'], in R. Bambrough (ed.), *New Essays on Plato and Aristotle* [*New Essays*] (London and New York, 1965), 121–41 at 123, 125–6 (repr. in J. L.

few of these enthusiasts have attempted to explain how it fits into the overall programme of Θ.[2] Ignoring context is usually a fault. But not here, for the good reason that the Passage does not fit into the overall programme of Θ, was not written for Θ, and should not be printed in the place we read it today. So I shall argue.

If I am right, the analysts can legitimately keep analysing the Passage on its own, as an isolated fragment of uncertain origin. I will join in myself. For nothing I say here is meant to impugn the philosophical interest and importance of the Passage, or to deny that it is authentic Aristotle. But I will suggest that its focus is rather different from what it is usually taken to be. I will also argue, controversially, that the Θ 6 distinction is unique in the corpus and should not be imported into other Aristotelian contexts such as *Nicomachean Ethics* 10 or *De anima* 2. 5.

To speak, as I have just done, of 'the overall programme of Θ' is to take a lot for granted. This is not the place to elaborate a detailed interpretation of Θ. Let me simply acknowledge that my thinking about Θ has been much influenced by Michael Frede's 1994 paper on potentiality in *Metaphysics* Θ.[3] So far as I am concerned, that is the starting-point for all future discussion of Θ's contribution to the Aristotelian philosophy.[4]

Ackrill, *Essays on Plato and Aristotle* (Oxford, 1997), 142–62); R. Brague, *Aristote et la question du monde: essai sur le contexte cosmologique et anthropologique de l'ontologie* [*Monde*] (Paris, 1988), 454; M. Dufour, 'La distinction ἐνέργεια–κίνησις en *Métaph.* Θ, 6: deux manières d'être dans le temps', *Revue de philosophie ancienne*, 19 (2001), 3–43; A. Kenny, *Action, Emotion and Will* (London, 1963), ch. 8; T. Penner, 'Verbs and the Identity of Actions: A Philosophical Exercise in the Interpretation of Aristotle' ['Verbs'], in O. P. Wood and G. Pitcher (eds.), *Ryle* (London and Basingstoke, 1971), 393–460 at 395; G. Ryle, *Dilemmas* (Cambridge, 1966), 102–3.)

[2] An honourable, even heroic, exception is L. A. Kosman, 'Substance, Being, and Energeia' ['Substance'], *Oxford Studies in Ancient Philosophy*, 2 (1984), 121–49.

[3] M. Frede, 'Aristotle's Notion of Potentiality in *Metaphysics* Θ' ['Potentiality'], in T. Scaltsas, D. Charles, and M. L. Gill (eds.), *Unity, Identity and Explanation in Aristotle's Metaphysics* (Oxford, 1994), 173–93. In M. F. Burnyeat, *A Map of Metaphysics Zeta* [*Map*] (Pittsburgh, 2001), esp. ch. 6, I do have things to say about the role of Θ in the larger context of the *Metaphysics*.

[4] This sentence was written years before Frede's sudden death at Delphi in August 2007.

PART I: TEXT

1. To motivate the textual enquiry that follows, I begin with a philosophical complaint. The main business of Θ 6 is to contrive an analogical extension. Θ began by studying the contrast between δύναμις and ἐνέργεια in the sphere of change. But Aristotle made it clear from the outset that for his current project, which is to explain potential and actual *being*, change is not the most useful sphere to consider (Θ 1, 1045^{b}27–1046^{a}4). We begin there in order to arrive somewhere else, where the contrast is between δύναμις as ὕλη and ἐνέργεια as οὐσία. That transition is the task of Θ 6, as Aristotle explains both at the start of the chapter (Θ 6, 1048^{a}25–30) and when the extension has been completed (1048^{b}6–9). I use C to mark cases of change, S for the cases of substantial being that Aristotle wants to reach:

Since we have discussed the kind of potentiality which is spoken of in connection with change, let us determine what, and what sort of thing, actuality is. In the course of our analysis it will become clear, with regard to the potential, that besides ascribing potentiality to that whose nature it is to change something else or to be changed by something else, either without qualification or in a certain manner, we also use the term in another sense, which is what we have been after in discussing these previous senses.

Actuality [ἐνέργεια] is the thing being present [ὑπάρχειν], but not in the way we speak of when we say it is potentially present; (S) we say that potentially, for instance, a Hermes is in the block of wood and the half-line in the whole, because it might be separated out, and (C) even someone who is not exercising knowledge [μὴ θεωροῦντα] we call knowledgeable [ἐπιστήμονα] if they are capable of exercising knowledge. The other case [sc. when they are exercising it] is ⟨knowledge⟩ in actuality.

Our meaning can be seen by induction from particular cases. We should not seek to capture everything in a definition, but some things we should comprehend [συνορᾶν] by analogy. Thus as (C) that which is building is to that which is capable of building, so is the waking to the sleeping, and that which sees ⟨something⟩[5] to a sighted thing with its eyes shut, and (S) that

---

[5] Throughout this paper I am faced with translation difficulties arising from the fact that the morphology of ancient Greek verbs does not distinguish, as English morphology does, between the continuous and the non-continuous present. Since I am translating, I write whichever form strikes me as the most natural way, in the given context, to put Aristotle's verbs into *English*. Consequently, I feel no obligation to follow Ross and other English translators who write 'is seeing' here to match the previous 'is building'. I write 'sees', with the accusative 'something'

which has been shaped out of the matter to the matter, and that which has been wrought to the unwrought. Let actuality [ἐνέργεια] be distinguished as one part of this antithesis, the potential [τὸ δυνατόν] as the other. Not everything is said to be in actuality [ἐνεργείᾳ] in the same sense, but only by analogy—as *A* is in *B* or to *B*, so is *Γ* in *Δ* or to *Δ*; for (C) some are related as change [κίνησις] to capacity [δύναμις], while (S) others are related as substance to some matter. (*Θ* 6, 1048^{a}25–^{b}9)[6]

Notice that in this text building is listed, alongside exercising knowledge, being awake, and seeing, as an example of ἐνέργεια, while all four are classed as κίνησις in relation to δύναμις. In the Passage, by contrast, building is not ἐνέργεια, but κίνησις (1048^{b}29–31), while seeing is not κίνησις, but ἐνέργεια (1048^{b}23, 33–4).

No problem yet. The Passage introduces a new distinction. Some actions (πράξεις) have an external goal, some do not, because the goal is the action itself. Building aims at the production of a house, which will last for years to come. Seeing, by contrast, does not aim at a further product. Its goal is internal to itself, to see what is there to be seen.[7] The new distinction divides the previous list of C-type ἐνέργειαι into two groups: those like seeing which are ἐνέργειαι in the new, more tightly defined sense that they aim at nothing beyond themselves, and those like building which aim at a further product. The latter become κινήσεις in a sense of the word more specific than

inserted to stop 'sees' being equivalent to 'has sight'. The fact is that 'is seeing' is relatively rare in English, for reasons not unconnected with the philosophical content of the Passage. It is in part because Greek morphology lacks an equivalent to our distinction between two forms of the present that Aristotle has a phenomenon to analyse. Read on.

[6] My translation here borrows freely from Ross–Barnes and Irwin–Fine, but I decline to follow them in translating ἀφωρισμένη (1048^{b}5) as if it referred to the definition Aristotle has just said we should not seek. For reasons given by the 'Londinenses' I agree with Jaeger's decision to read τῷ with EJ at 1048^{a}37, rather than A^b's accusative, and θάτερον μόριον with Alexander at 1048^{b}5–6 rather than the manuscripts' datives, but I reject Jaeger's supplement ⟨ἡ⟩ (from Al^c) at 1048^{b}5. (References: W. Jaeger (ed.), *Aristotelis Metaphysica*, recognovit brevique adnotatione critica instruxit ['Jaeger'] (Oxford, 1957); 'Londinenses', *Notes on Eta and Theta of Aristotle's* Metaphysics [*Notes*], recorded by Myles Burnyeat and others (Oxford, 1984), 125–6; W. D. Ross and J. Barnes, *Metaphysics*, in J. Barnes (ed.), *The Complete Works of Aristotle: The Revised Oxford Translation*, vol. ii ['Ross–Barnes'] (Princeton, 1984).)

[7] This should not mean that seeing is not useful to us, or that it cannot be valued as a means as well as an end. That would be inconsistent with e.g. *Metaph. A* 1, 980^{a}21–6, and *NE* 1. 6, 1096^{b}16–19 (cf. 3. 10, 1118^{a}22–3). *Protrepticus* B70 D says: 'One would choose to have sight *even if* nothing other than sight itself were to result from it.' The means–end relation extends further than the relation of action to product.

Kinēsis *vs.* Energeia   223

at 1048ᵇ8, where it covered seeing and the exercise of knowledge as well as building.

But now move on to Θ 8, 1050ᵃ23–ᵇ2:

And while in some cases the exercise [χρῆσις] is the ultimate thing (e.g. in sight the ultimate thing is seeing, and no further product besides this results from sight), but from some things a product follows (e.g. from the art of building there results a house over and above the act of building), yet none the less in the former type of case the exercise is the end [τέλος], and in the latter more of an end than the potentiality [δύναμις] is. This is because⁸ the act of building is in what is being built, and it comes to be, and is, simultaneously with the house.

Where, then, what comes to be is something apart from the exercise, the actuality [ἐνέργεια] is in the object being produced, e.g. the actuality of building is in what is being built and that of weaving in what is being woven, and similarly in other cases, and in general the change [κίνησις] is in what is being changed;⁹ but where there is no further product apart from the actuality [ἐνέργεια], the actuality is in the subjects themselves, e.g. the seeing is in the one who sees and the theorizing [θεωρεῖν] in the one who theorizes, and life is in the soul (which is why happiness is too; for it is a certain sort of life). (1050ᵃ23–ᵇ2, trans. after Ross–Barnes)

This text develops a distinction like that drawn in the Passage between seeing, which is its own end, and building, which aims at a further product, but the distinction is presented as a distinction between two kinds of ἐνέργεια. *Not* as a distinction between ἐνέργεια and κίνησις. In Θ 8 ἐνέργεια contrasts with δύναμις, not with κίνησις.

Similarly, ἐνέργεια contrasted with δύναμις before the Passage, when Θ 1 opened the enquiry by announcing that the first topic to consider would be potentiality and actuality (δύναμις and ἐνέργεια) in the sphere of change (κίνησις), where the relevant potentialities are (first and primarily) the capacity to bring about change (μεταβολή) in another or in oneself *qua* other, and (second and derivatively) the correlative capacity to undergo change by the agency of another or oneself *qua* other (1045ᵇ35–1046ᵃ13). The corresponding actuality (ἐνέργεια) is the change (μεταβολή or κίνησις)¹⁰ taking place.

⁸ The γάρ explains why the house being built is *more* of an end than the building of it; cf. W. D. Ross, *Aristotle's* Metaphysics: *A Revised Text with Introduction and Commentary* ['Ross'] (2 vols.; Oxford, 1924), ad loc., and the translation of M. Furth, *Aristotle:* Metaphysics Books Zeta, Eta, Theta, Iota (VII–X) ['Furth'] (Indianapolis, 1985).

⁹ 'Change' here includes substantial change.

¹⁰ μεταβολή is the word used in Θ 1, but κίνησις takes over from Θ 2, 1046ᵇ17.

(As *Physics* 3. 1–3 explains, the two potentialities issue in a single actuality, which is active change when viewed from the side of the agent, a passive undergoing when viewed from the side of the patient.) Editors who print the Passage in its usual place owe us an account of why, when he makes his all-important distinction, Aristotle does not alert us to the difference between his present and his previous use of ἐνέργεια. In his previous use ἐνέργεια does not contrast with κίνησις, but includes it. Indeed, Θ 3, 1047ᵃ30–2, tells us that, historically, κίνησις is the primary case of ἐνέργεια, the case from which the term ἐνέργεια was extended to cover the actuality of being as well as the actuality of change.

The text quoted from Θ 8 is another challenge for editors to explain. Why, having introduced the distinction between ἐνέργεια and κίνησις, should Aristotle proceed to ignore it? Not only Θ 8, but all the rest of Θ is written without the slightest regard for the terminological innovation which is the main burden of the Passage.

Time for philology.

2. Let me start with three different presentations of the manuscript evidence for the Passage:

(*a*) Christ (1885)   18 ἐπεὶ–35 κίνησιν om E Alex. . . . 28 τούτων–35 κίνησιν linea perducta delenda significat Aᵇ.

(*b*) Ross (1924)   18 ἐπεὶ–35 κίνησιν Aᵇ, codd. plerique, Philop., cod. F Alexandri: om EJΓ, codd. ceteri Alexandri . . . 28 τούτων–35 κίνησιν expunxit Aᵇ.

(*c*) Jaeger (1957)   18 ἐπεὶ–35 κίνησιν Aᵇ et recc. plerique: om. Π Al (add. unus Alexandri cod. F); additamentum ut vid. ab ipso Ar. ortum (cf. 35 λέγω), oratio est admodum dura et obscura et in libris corrupta; verba 35 τὸ μὲν οὖν . . . 36 ἔστω recapitulatio sunt, sed eorum quae hoc additamentum praecedunt (!) . . . 28 τούτων–35 κίνησιν delenda notat Aᵇ.

The three versions send rather different signals to the reader.

It is well known that the *Metaphysics* is an open tradition, going back to two different ancient editions of the text. It survives in two independent branches, which in Harlfinger's ground-breaking study are dubbed α and β.[11] Plate 1 gives the overall picture. You can see, very clearly, the double pattern of transmission.

[11] D. Harlfinger, 'Zur Überlieferungsgeschichte der *Metaphysik*' ['Harlfinger'], in P. Aubenque (ed.), *Études sur la Métaphysique d'Aristote* [*Études*] (Actes du vɪᵉ Symposium Aristotelicum; Paris, 1979), 7–36, introduces the idea of two different

The primary manuscripts for α are E (tenth century) and J (ninth century); Jaeger's Π denotes their consensus. For β the primary manuscript is A^b, written in the twelfth century, although from Λ 7, 1073^{a}1, to the end a fourteenth-century hand takes over and follows the EJ tradition. The Passage is found in A^b, not in EJ. Should the apparatus criticus start from the absence, as Christ does (J was unknown to him),[12] or, with Ross and Jaeger, from the presence?

I believe it is the *absence* of the Passage from one entire branch that should be underlined. Ross gives a table of the main lacunae (his word) in E, of which the Passage is by far the longest. He estimates that around 750 letters are missing (the precise number depends on how one emends a badly damaged text). The next largest omission is only 61 letters.[13] (The largest lacuna in A^b, which editors say is highly lacunose by comparison with EJ, is 169 letters.)[14] Such an exceptionally large lacuna is hard to explain by mechanical damage or the usual types of scribal error. The Passage appears to be a coherent textual unit, with beginning, middle, and end, so one possibility is a learned excision from the α branch; in due course we will be looking at evidence of an attempted excision in A^b. But a more economical suggestion is that A^b preserves what Jaeger calls an 'additamentum' of considerable length.

Jaeger had a keen nose for detecting additions made by Aristotle himself when revising or updating a treatise. In his OCT of the *Metaphysics* he uses double square brackets to mark (what he judges to be) additions of this nature, additions by Aristotle himself. Since he prints the Passage within double square brackets, we must suppose that by 'additamentum' he means an addition by Aristotle himself, which was subsequently lost or excised from the

ancient editions (Ausgaben) in his very first paragraph, with acknowledgement to W. Christ, *Aristotelis Metaphysica*, recognovit, nova editio correctior ['Christ'] (Leipzig, 1895 [1st edn. 1886]), and Jaeger. The section on 'The Text of the *Metaphysics*' in Ross, vol. i, pp. clv–clxvi, contains further useful information.

[12] Gerke was the first announcement of the importance of J, Ross the first edition to use it for constituting the text. Both Bekker and Schwegler side with Christ in highlighting the absence of the Passage from the α tradition as they knew it from E. (References: I. Bekker, *Aristoteles Graece*, edidit Academia Regia Borussica ['Bekker'] (2 vols.; Berlin, 1831); A. Gercke, 'Aristoteleum', *Wiener Studien*, 14 (1892), 146–8; A. Schwegler, *Die Metaphysik des Aristoteles*, Grundtext, Übersetzung und Commentar nebst erläuternden Abhandlungen ['Schwegler'] (4 vols.; Tübingen, 1847–8; repr. Frankfurt a.M., 1960).)

[13] Ross, vol. i, p. clx.   [14] Ibid., p. clix.

EJ tradition.[15] But Jaeger's expression 'additamentum ut vid. ab Ar. ipso ortum' could equally well suggest that the addition stems from someone *other* than Aristotle, reproducing words written by Aristotle for some *other* context. That is the line I shall eventually pursue.

For the moment, however, let me stress that 'additamentum' is the *mot juste*, for the reason Jaeger gives when in his apparatus he says of lines 1048^{b}35–6, 'recapitulatio sunt, sed eorum, quae hoc additamentum praecedunt (!)'. Θ 6 began by proposing to determine 'what, and what sort of thing, actuality is' (1048^{a}26–7: τί τέ ἐστιν ἡ ἐνέργεια καὶ ποῖόν τι). It ends, echoing these very words, by saying that the job is now done: 'What, and what sort of thing, "in actuality" is may be taken as explained by these and similar considerations' (1048^{b}35–6: τὸ μὲν οὖν ἐνεργείᾳ τί τέ ἐστι καὶ ποῖον, ἐκ τούτων καὶ τοιούτων δῆλον ἡμῖν ἔστω). The main body of Θ 6 wants to know what it is for something to be *in actuality* (note the dative ἐνεργείᾳ at 1048^{a}35, ^{b}6, 10–11, 15), i.e. to be something actually, as contrasted with what it is for something to be *in potentiality* (δυνάμει, 1048^{a}32, ^{b}10, 14, 16), i.e. to be something potentially. The Passage is about what it is to be *an actuality* (ἐνέργεια in the nominative), as opposed to a mere change (κίνησις): an entirely different question. As Jaeger remarked, the last sentence of Θ 6 ignores this second question and links back to the topic proposed at the beginning of the chapter; note EJ's dative ἐνεργείᾳ again at 1048^{b}35.[16] What is more, ἐκ τούτων in the last sentence (1048^{b}36) can hardly refer to the Passage immediately preceding, because that is on the second question, not the first.[17]

[15] See his explanation of the brackets at p. xviii. Jaeger's hypothesis about the origin of the Passage was anticipated by A. Smeets, *Act en potentie in de Metaphysica van Aristoteles: historisch-philologisch onderzoek van boek IX en boek V der Metaphysica*, avec un résumé en français ['Smeets'] (Leuven, 1952), 56–7.

[16] A^b has ἐνεργεῖν here: unsatisfactory, since the verb has not featured in the chapter so far, but it too links better with the opening question than with the narrower question of the Passage.

[17] Christ, Ross Tr. (but not his edition), and Tricot print the last sentence of Θ 6 as the first of Θ 7. The chapter divisions have no ancient authority, of course (they derive from Bessarion's Latin translation, which did not have the Passage, and first appear with a Greek text in Michael Isingrin's 1550 reissue of Erasmus' edition), but for that very reason ancient readers would expect ἐκ τούτων to refer to what immediately precedes. The move cures nothing. (References: Bessarion: see Bibliography (1), s.n. Argyropylos; D. Erasmus, *Aristotelis . . . opera . . . omnia* (Basel, 1531, 1539, 1550); W. D. Ross, *Metaphysica* ['Ross Tr.'] (The Works of Aristotle Translated into English: (1) under the Editorship of J. A. Smith and

So far, then, I agree with Jaeger that the Passage is an addition which interrupts the main argument of Θ 6. And I am inclined to agree also that the Passage is authentic Aristotle, both in style—Jaeger cites the first-person verb λέγω (1048ᵇ35), which is indeed a feature of Aristotle's prose[18]—and in thought. Who else would have such thoughts? More on that later.

Let me also make it clear that I do not take the fact that the Passage interrupts the argument of Θ 6 as a reason for doubting that the addition was made *by Aristotle*. Such awkwardness is fairly common in other places where Jaeger and others find reason to diagnose additions from Aristotle's own hand.[19] My argument for someone else's intervention will come later, on different grounds.

3. Meanwhile, a brief word about the infinite in 1048ᵇ9–17. This section is a supplement to what precedes. It applies the main question of the chapter, 'What is it to be in actuality?', to a case that does not fall under either of the headings '(C) as change [κίνησις] to capacity [δύναμις]' or '(S) as substance to some matter'. The infinite has a different way (ἄλλως) of being in potentiality and actuality. It does not have the potentiality to be actual as an infinite magnitude existing on its own (χωριστόν). Rather, it has the potentiality to be actual *for knowledge* (1048ᵇ15: γνώσει). This is difficult—difficult both to translate and to interpret.

First, the problem of translation: how much to supply with γνώσει from the preceding clause? Ross Tr.² supplies the minimum: 'It exists potentially only for knowledge'. Barnes restored Ross Tr.¹: 'its separateness is only in knowledge'. (Similarly Furth.) My para-

W. D. Ross, Oxford, 1908 = 'Ross Tr.¹', done from Christ's edition; (2) under the Editorship of W. D. Ross, Oxford, 1928 = 'Ross Tr.²', done from his own edition); J. Tricot, *Aristote: Métaphysiques*, traduction nouvelle et notes ['Tricot'] (2 vols.; Paris, 1933).)

[18] 465 hits in the *TLG*, including one just a couple of pages back at Θ 5, 1048ᵃ 10–11.

[19] Two cases which I endorse are (i) the hypothesis of Ross and others that *Metaph.* Z 7–9 began as a separate essay which Aristotle later incorporated into its present context (I discuss the resulting awkwardnesses in Burnyeat, *Map*, 29–38), and (ii) the Solmsen–Barnes hypothesis that Aristotle added two sections of syllogistic analysis to the otherwise topic-based treatment of argument in his *Rhetoric* (this too creates awkwardness, which I discuss in M. F. Burnyeat, 'Enthymeme: Aristotle on the Logic of Persuasion', in D. J. Furley and A. Nehamas (eds.), *Aristotle's Rhetoric: Philosophical Essays* (Proceedings of the XIIth Symposium Aristotelicum; Princeton, 1994), 3–55 at 35–8.

phrase of the received text, 'it has the potentiality to be actual for knowledge', is motivated by $1048^{b}10-11$, which leads us to expect an account covering *both* what it is for the infinite to be in potentiality *and* what is it for it to be in actuality.

But none of these versions is easy to understand. Certainly, we know that, however many divisions are made, more are possible.[20] But how can that knowledge of ours ensure the potential *being* of the infinite? Or its separateness? Or its actuality? The reality of the infinite ought to be prior to knowledge, not posterior. And how to square this text with *Phys.* 3. 6, $207^{a}25-6$ (cf. 1. 6, $189^{a}12-13$; *Post. An.* 1. 22, $82^{b}-83^{a}1$), where Aristotle claims that the infinite *qua* infinite is unknowable? I offer a simple emendation to remove the difficulty.

At *Metaph.* Z 13, $1038^{b}28$, there is much to be said for Lord's emendation of γενέσει to γνώσει to bring the text into line with what was said about the priority of substance in Z 1, $1028^{a}32-3$.[21] The converse emendation here (γνώσει→γενέσει) would bring Θ 6 into line with *Phys.* 3. 6, $206^{a}21-5$, where the infinite is said to be in actuality in the same way as a day or a contest, τῷ ἀεὶ ἄλλο καὶ ἄλλο γίγνεσθαι. As one hour or one race succeeds another, so a magnitude's potential for continuous division is actualized by successive cuts, one after another. The infinite has a potentiality to be actual not as a separate entity but γενέσει, in a process which may go on and on without limit.[22]

4. Now let me turn to Ross and his account of the positive testimony in favour of the Passage in the direct and indirect traditions. His commentary ad loc. is even more gung-ho than his apparatus:

This passage occurs in most of the manuscripts (including A^{b}), and a paraphrase of it occurs in a good manuscript of Alexander (F). It is omitted by EJTΓ and Bessarion, and is very corrupt in the other manuscripts. But it contains sound Aristotelian doctrine and terminology, and is quite appro-

---

[20] Such is the explanation offered by the 'Londinenses', 127, and (if I understand him) Ross ad loc. H. Bonitz, *Aristotelis Metaphysica*, recognovit et enarravit ['Bonitz'] (2 vols.; Bonn, 1848–9), is surprised at the almost frivolous way ('mira levitas') Aristotle tackles the question of how the infinite is in potentiality and actuality.

[21] In their recent edition, *Aristoteles: Metaphysik Z*, Text, Übersetzung und Kommentar (Munich 1988), M. Frede and G. Patzig print γνώσει and give convincing reasons in their note ad loc.

[22] This proposal has already been accepted by S. Makin, *Aristotle: Metaphysics, Book Θ*, translated with an introduction and commentary ['Makin'] (Oxford, 2006), ad loc.

priate to its context, and there is no apparent motive for its introduction, so that on the whole it seems safe to treat it as genuine.[23]

Clarifications: T, a fourteenth-century manuscript, is one of just two 'codices recentiores' listed among Ross's sigla.[24] Γ is the Latin translation of Aristotle's *Metaphysics* by William of Moerbeke (*c.* 1265–72), which was based on J and another manuscript from the α tradition.[25] A version of Cardinal Bessarion's Latin translation of *c.*1452 may be found in volume iii of the Berlin Academy's classic edition of the works of Aristotle.[26] None of these antedates A^b. That said by way of clarification, I take up Ross's several points in order:

(i) 'This passage occurs in most of the manuscripts (including A^b)'. Understandable at the time it was written, long before Harlfinger's stemma gave us a clear picture of how the recentiores relate to the primary manuscripts and to each other. This stemma was based on a collation of four stretches of text (book *A* 980ª21–982ª3, all of *a*, *K* 1059ª18–1060ª20, *N* 1092ª9–1093^b28), followed by a collation of *H* 1045ª1–Θ 1045^b36 for some fourteen manuscripts which the first collation had revealed to be wholly or partly independent of each other. In none of this was the Passage included. But Christian Brockmann kindly looked on my behalf at the photographic collection in the Aristoteles-Archiv in Berlin and discovered that the important manuscripts containing the Passage are all ones which Harlfinger had independently shown to belong to the β tradition or to have been contaminated by it. Thus the Passage confirms the correctness of Harlfinger's stemma.

In a letter dated 26 June 1995 Brockmann writes:

Nach Prüfung der wichtigsten Handschriften läßt sich die Frage 'Wie ist der Passus *Met.* Θ 6, 1048b 18–35, überliefert?' zunächst einmal klar

---

[23] Ross, ii. 253.   [24] For its affiliations (pretty mixed), see Harlfinger.
[25] G. Vuillemin-Diem, *Metaphysica Lib. I–XIV*, recensio et translatio Guillelmi de Moerbeka, edidit (Aristoteles Latinus, XXV 3.1–2; Leiden, New York, and Cologne, 1995), 165–99. G. Vuillemin-Diem, *Metaphysica Lib. I–X, XII–XIV*, Translatio Anonyma sive 'Media' (Aristoteles Latinus, XXV.2; Leiden, 1976), lxii–lxvii, suggests that the Translatio Anonyma sive 'Media', dating from before the start of the 13th cent., is based on a manuscript with affinities to both the α and the β traditions; nevertheless, the Passage is missing there too.
[26] The Latin version of the Passage at 513^b17–34 is in square brackets, because it is not the work of Bessarion but an addition to cater for Bekker's Greek text in volume ii of the Berlin edition. No name is attached to the translation, which differs markedly from Strozza's version (n. 44 below).

beantworten und hier bestätigt sich eindeutig das Stemma von Dieter Harlfinger.

Der Passus fehlt im Überlieferungszweig α: fehlt in Vind. phil. 100 (J), Par. 1853 (E), Esc. Y 3. 18 (E^s), Vat. 255 (V^d), Laur. 87, 18 (B^b). In Vat. 255 (V^d) ist der Text von einem zweiten Schreiber, einem Korrektor, am Ende der *Metaphysik* ergänzt worden, wobei er an der Stelle, wo der Text fehlt, einen Hinweis auf die Ergänzung eingetragen hat: ζήτει τὸ τοιοῦτον [ ]χ[ ]α ἐν τῷ τέλει τοῦ βιβλίου (wahrscheinlich σχῆμα).²⁷

Der Passus ist vorhanden im Zweig β: vorhanden in Laur. 87, 12 (A^b), Ambr. F 113 sup. (M), Taur. B VII 23 (C), Marc. 205 (D^m). Der Text ist außerdem vorhanden in Par. 1850 (D) und Oxon. N.C. 230 (O^b). Wenn man in Harlfingers Stemma schaut, erklärt sich dieser Befund: Vermittler ist der Marc. 205 (D^m), der auf A^b zurückgeht. Diese Handschriften sind also in diesem Punkt nicht unabhängig von A^b.²⁸ Im Marc. 205 (D^m) gibt es zur Stelle einen Hinweis von jüngerer Hand, daß dieser Passus sich in manchen Büchern nicht finde, und dass es mit dem Text τὸ μὲν οὖν ἐνεργείᾳ τί τέ ἐστι bei dem Zeichen weitergehe.

Jaeger's annotation 'A^b et recc. plerique' was wiser than Ross's bold 'codd. plerique', though 'plerique' is false in either case.

What is most interesting about these findings is that the Passage occurs in M (fourteenth century) and C (fifteenth century), the two recentiores which Harlfinger singled out as worthy of attention from future editors of the *Metaphysics*, because they witness to the β tradition independently of A^b.²⁹ We may thus conclude that the Passage was already in the β branch before A^b, in some common ancestor it shared with M and C. Brockmann's collation of the Passage in M and C is printed for the record as Appendix 1 below.

The next step was taken during my time as Fellow of the Wissenschaftskolleg zu Berlin in 2004/5, when over a number of visits to the Aristoteles-Archiv Brockmann kindly took me through a survey of the remaining recentiores. The results, which confirm and strengthen the findings of his original letter, are best seen in Plate 1, where my red circle marks a manuscript we found to contain

---

²⁷ The σχῆμα is a plain circle, which duly reappears right at the end of the manuscript, where the Passage is written out.

²⁸ In a later letter Brockmann reported that the Passage is also present in the 15th-cent. Taur. C I2. 5 (Z), *as was to be expected* given that Harlfinger's stemma places it between D and O^b.

²⁹ Harlfinger, 32–3. In response, C. Luna, 'Observations sur le texte des livres M–N de la Métaphysique d'Aristote', *Documenti e studi sulla tradizione filosofica medievale*, 16 (2005), 553–93, has shown what can be gleaned from collating M and C for *Metaphysics* M–N, where A^b no longer represents the β tradition.

the Passage, my blue square a manuscript which does not include book Θ. I put a dotted red circle around Marc. 211 (E^b) to indicate that the Passage is absent from the main text but a fourteenth-century hand has written it in the margin.[30] The dotted red circle around Vat. 255 (V^d) also indicates a corrector's activity, as explained in Brockmann's letter. The majority of the manuscripts have no mark from me because they transmit Θ without the Passage.

Before continuing my response to Ross, let me note that the investigation summarized in Plate 1 amounts to a complete collation of the relevant manuscripts for a passage of the *Metaphysics* which did not figure in Harlfinger's original project. The results of this independent research uniformly confirm his stemma. All the more reason for me to express my deep gratitude to Christian Brockmann for help over many hours staring at microfilm in the Aristoteles-Archiv: time and again his trained eyes understood what mine could only see.

(ii) 'and a paraphrase of it occurs in a good manuscript of Alexander (F)'. True, but the situation is more complicated than Ross reveals. In Hayduck's Berlin Academy edition of Alexander, which Ross is using, the siglum F denotes a copy of the so-called Alexander commentary written in the margins of one of the recentiores just mentioned, Ambr. F 113 sup. (M). I say 'so-called' because by the time the commentary gets to Θ—in fact from book E onwards—we are no longer reading Alexander of Aphrodisias (second century AD), but a Pseudo-Alexander who can safely be identified as Michael of Ephesus, who wrote early in the twelfth century.[31] Now another good text of the Alexander commentary, Hayduck's L, is found in the margins of A^b itself (thus $L = A^b$ as $F = M$)—and here the paraphrase is missing. Furthermore, F's paraphrase begins by

[30] On this hand, which made extensive corrections in E^b and may have affiliations with C, see Harlfinger, 14.

[31] The identity of Pseudo-Alexander with Michael, proposed by S. Ebbesen, *Commentators and Commentaries on Aristotle's* Sophistici Elenchi: *A Study of Post-Aristotelian Ancient and Medieval Writings on Fallacies* [*Commentators*] (Corpus Latinum Commentariorum in Aristotelem Graecorum, 7; 3 vols.; Leiden, 1981), is now thoroughly confirmed by C. Luna, *Trois études sur la tradition des commentaires anciens à la Métaphysique d'Aristote* [*Trois études*] (Leiden, Boston, and Cologne, 2001). Michael's commentaries were convincingly redated by R. Browning, 'An Unpublished Funeral Oration for Anna Comnena', *Proceedings of the Cambridge Philological Society*, NS 8 (1962), 1–12, repr. in R. Sorabji (ed.), *Aristotle Transformed: The Ancient Commentators and their Influence* (London, 1990), 393–406, to the period 1118–38; previously, his date was standardly given as *c.*1070.

saying τοῦτο τὸ κεφάλαιον ἐν πολλοῖς λείπει: 'this chapter is missing in many copies'. Hayduck prints the feeble paraphrase that follows in a footnote, not in his main text, which implies that in his judgement (to be confirmed below) its author is not even Pseudo-Alexander. It is someone else's addition to the commentary, a supplement designed to make up for the fact that Pseudo-Alexander himself said nothing about the Passage, because he did not know of its existence. Hence the absence of the paraphrase in L, despite the presence of the Passage in A^b where L is written. The paraphrase is an anxious response to the presence of the Passage in M, not independent evidence in favour of reading it there.

(iii) 'But it [the Passage] contains sound Aristotelian doctrine and terminology'. Where exactly does Ross find his proof of soundness? The issue is important enough to claim our attention later. I will argue that Ross is right about the *doctrine* (witness Θ 8 as just quoted, or *NE* I. 1), but that the *terminology* is unique to the Passage. Even *NE* 10. 3–5, often cited as parallel, will not serve.

(iv) 'and is quite appropriate to its context'. Not really, as Jaeger helped us see. Readers from the USA please note that 'quite' here does not mean 'very'. That would be an absurd claim.

(v) 'and there is no apparent motive for its introduction'. I agree. The motive remains to be discovered.

One further item, from Ross's apparatus: 'Philop.' An unwary reader could easily be reassured by this: at least the Passage was known to Philoponus in the sixth century AD. Not at all. The commentary in question was wrongly ascribed to Philoponus, as is proved by its containing references to Michael of Ephesus.[32]

Two further facts about Pseudo-Philoponus are relevant here. The first is that it was he who composed the paraphrase added in F. The Greek text of his commentary remains unpublished; for a long time it was known only through a sixteenth-century Latin translation by Francesco Patrizzi (=Frane Petrić, the founding father of Croatian philosophy).[33] But Michael Frede showed me pho-

---

[32] See Ebbesen, *Commentators*, appendix 8: 'Ps.-Philoponus, in Metaphysicam'.

[33] Now reprinted with an introduction by Lohr. Already Bonitz in his 1847 edition of the Alexander commentary was led by the Latin to suspect that Pseudo-Philoponus might be the author of the paraphrase, which Bonitz knew in the incomplete citation of Brandis's collected scholia. (References: Alexander of Aphrodisias, *In Aristotelis Metaphysica commentaria*, ed. H. Bonitz (Berlin, 1847), 551; C. A. Brandis (ed.), *Scholia in Aristotelem*, collegit Christianus Augustus Brandis, edidit

Stemma Codicum

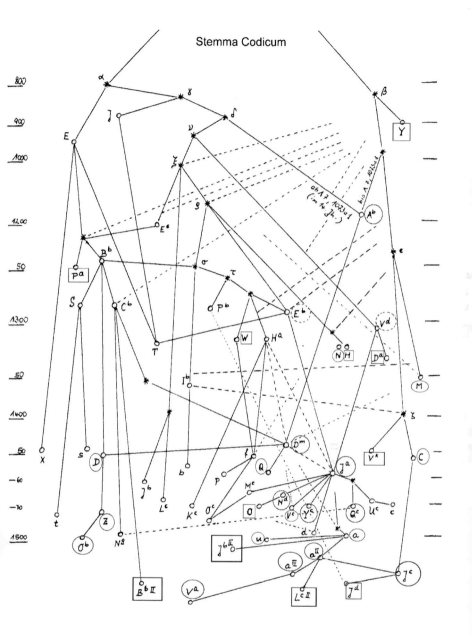

PLATE 1. Distribution of the Passage in the Stemma Codicum. Red circles mark the presence of the Passage, blue squares the omission of Θ

Reproduced by kind permission of the author and publisher from D. Harlfinger, 'Zur Überlieferungsgeschichte der *Metaphysik*', in P. Aubenque (ed.), *Études sur la Métaphysique d'Aristote* (Actes du vi^e Symposium Aristotelicum; Paris, 1979), 7–36 at 27. © Librairie Philosophique J. Vrin, 1979. http://www.vrin.fr

PLATE 2. Line of deletion on fo. 361ʳ of Aᵇ = Florence,
Biblioteca Medicea Laurenziana, MS Laur. Plut. 87.12

Photograph supplied by the Biblioteca Medicea Laurenziana and reproduced by
kind permission of the Ministero per i Beni e le Attività Culturali

tographs of the two known complete Greek manuscripts of this commentary: the paraphrase occurs on fos. 105^v–106^r of cod. Vat. Urb. gr. 49 (fourteenth century) and fo. 150^v of cod. Vind. gr. Phil. 189 (sixteenth century).[34] In both the paraphrase is plain to see. The second relevant fact is that it has recently been revealed that what Ross called 'a good MS of Alexander (F)' is not all by Alexander and Pseudo-Alexander. From book *K* onwards it is Pseudo-Philoponus, and the manuscript ascribes this portion of the commentary to George Pachymeres (1242–*c*.1310).[35] There can be little doubt that the scribe who wrote F in Ambr. F 113 sup. (M) had access in the Bibliotheca Ambrosiana to the commentary of Pseudo-Philoponus, i.e. Pachymeres, who is a century later than A^b. For the end of the Pseudo-Philoponus commentary is also found at fos. 27^v–30^r of Ambr. I 117 inf. (sixteenth century).[36] When the scribe noticed that Pseudo-Alexander had nothing to say about the Passage, he compensated by borrowing the paraphrase from a nearby copy of Pseudo-Philoponus.

5. Finally, the curious and highly unusual line drawn through the latter part of the Passage in A^b, most clearly described by Christ: '28 τούτων–35 κίνησιν linea perducta delenda significat A^b'. Plate 2 shows a thin vertical line starting just above the middle of τούτων, near the centre of the first line of fo. 361^r, which then proceeds downwards to the fourteenth line of writing. The last words of the fourteenth line are ἐκείνην δὲ κίνησιν. The line stops under the ε

Academia Regia Borussica [vol. iv of the Academy's edition of Aristotle] (Berlin, 1836), 781^{a}47–^{b}12; Pseudo-Philoponus, *Expositiones in omnes XIV Aristotelis libros Metaphysicos*, übersetzt von Franciscus Patritius, Neudruck der ersten Ausgabe Ferrara 1583 mit einer Einleitung von Charles Lohr (Commentaria in Aristotelem Graeca: Versiones Latinae temporis resuscitatarum litterarum, herausgegeben von Charles Lohr, 2; Stuttgart-Bad Cannstatt, 1991).)

[34] These two manuscripts are, respectively, nos. 1999 and 2214 in A. Wartelle, *Inventaire des manuscripts grecs d'Aristote et de ses commentateurs: contribution à l'histoire du texte d'Aristote* ['Wartelle'] (Paris, 1963).

[35] S. Alexandru, 'A New Manuscript of Pseudo-Philoponus' Commentary on Aristotle's *Metaphysics* Containing a Hitherto Unknown Ascription of the Work', *Phronesis*, 44 (1999), 347–52 at 350 n. 11, and 351. E. Pappa, *Georgios Pachymeres, Philosofia Buch 10: Kommentar zur Metaphysik des Aristoteles, Editio Princeps. Einleitung, Text, Indices* (Corpus Philosophorum Medii Aevi, Commentaria in Aristotelem Byzantina, 2; Athens, 2002), 21–2 n. 74, is puzzled and sees numerous similarities with Pseudo-Alexander, but this cannot hold for the paraphrase of the Passage now under discussion. Pachymeres' own *Metaphysics* ignores Θ (Pappa, 30).

[36] See Wartelle no. 1022 with annotation.

of ἐκείνην, where it meets the circumflex accent over ἐνεργεῖν (A^b's variant for ἐνεργείᾳ at 1048^{b}35)[37]—again roughly in the centre of the line of writing. This the editors interpret as marking for deletion all of 1048^{b}28–34 plus the first four words of 35.

Now the reddish-brown ink used for the line is the same colour as the ink used for L, the version of the Alexander commentary written in the margin of A^b. The Aristotelian text in A^b is also reddish-brown but noticeably darker, often almost black. This is clear evidence that the line was drawn by the scribe who wrote L, not by some later corrector. There was no such line in the ἀντίγραφον, otherwise it would have been copied (if copied at all) in the darker ink of the main text. This is confirmed by the fact that there is no such line in either M or C.[38]

But the scribe who wrote the bulk of L, including the part under discussion, also wrote the corresponding part of the main text of A^b up to Λ 7, 1073^{a}1.[39] The two inks flow from two pens (the letters in the text are thicker than those in the margin) held in turn by a single hand.[40] As one page succeeds another, you see each ink oscillating independently between darker and lighter, as each pen is dipped into the ink or its ink bottle is refilled. But what matters here is that the Passage is a different tint from the surrounding commentary and the line of deletion. This suggests that the scribe would first write a chunk of Aristotle, leaving space for the commentary above, below and alongside the main text, and only later go back to enter the relevant portion of commentary. One can almost see it happening.

Across the top of fo. 361^r, above the first line of the main text (1048^{b}18, where the vertical line begins), run two lines of the commentary (581. 16–19 in Hayduck's edition: καὶ εἰπὼν τὸ μὲν οὖν ἐνεργείᾳ τί ἐστι καὶ ποῖον . . . νῦν λέγει, ὅτι πότε δυνάμει), which belong to the transition that Pseudo-Alexander is now making from Θ 6 to Θ 7. He has finished with Θ 6. Not so the main text below,

---

[37] n. 16 above.

[38] Which puts paid to the fantastic suggestion of P. Gohlke, *Übersetzung der Metaphysik des Aristoteles*, 2nd edn. (Paderborn, 1951), 455 n. 77, that the line was drawn by Aristotle, once he had committed himself to the *Physics* 3 doctrine that κίνησις is after all a kind of ἐνέργεια, and faithfully transmitted in the A^b tradition.

[39] Harlfinger, 32 with n. 62, hesitates over whether to assign responsibility for *Metaph.* A–Λ 7 to one scribe or two contemporary ones. That is irrelevant here since, if they are two, the change-over comes at fo. 456^v, nearly a hundred pages after Θ 6.

[40] The same situation in M: both text and commentary are one and the same hand throughout.

in which Θ 7 only starts near the bottom of the page at the seventeenth of nineteen lines of writing, because the Passage is still in full flow. Whether or not the scribe noticed this extra material earlier, he cannot help noticing it now. And that puts him in exactly the situation that led to the paraphrase from Pseudo-Philoponus being added to F in the margin of M. What to do about a large chunk of Aristotelian text to which nothing in the commentary corresponds? The same situation but a different response. Instead of adding to the commentary, the scribe of L pauses to subtract some of the Aristotelian text. At least, that is what he does if editors are right to interpret the line as a mark of deletion.

I shall assume that they are right, because the result of deleting exactly the words τούτων . . . κίνησιν would be to restore the balance between the main text and the accompanying commentary. The last sentence of Θ 6 would begin on the first line of the main text, just below the last line of the upper portion of commentary where ὅτι πότε δυνάμει starts elucidating Θ 7. Delete the first part of the Passage as well and the commentary would run a full page ahead of the Aristotelian text. Keeping text and commentary in step with each other is something any scribe might care about, but this one more than most—because he got it so disastrously wrong before.

All through the first five books of the *Metaphysics* A^b is full of blank white spaces. Evidently, the scribe began what was meant to be an *édition de luxe* by copying out the whole of books *A–Δ* on their own, often only a few lines per page, leaving much more space than would turn out to be needed for the Alexander commentary in the margin. Perhaps he did not have the Alexander commentary to hand and assumed it would be more expansive than it is.[41] When he did get hold of the commentary, all he could do was trail it down the margin in lines of irregular length, at times writing as few as two or three words in a space that could take many more. The effect is pretty, like a cascade of pink water each side of the page, but wasteful of expensive parchment. By contrast, from book *E* onwards the layout is efficiency itself. The white margin separating commentary and text can stay reasonably constant, because text and commentary keep more or less in step with each other—until we reach the Passage on fo. 361^r. At which point the scribe signals the need to take action.

---

[41] In that case Harlfinger, 32, would not be right to suggest that the ἀντίγραφον of A^b included both main text and commentary.

The action is twofold. First, the deletion of exactly the words τούτων . . . κίνησιν, no more. Second, adjusting the balance of text and commentary in the following pages in order to restore correspondence between the two. This takes a while. When chapter 8 begins on fo. 363ᵛ the main text (a smaller chunk than usual) is still running some 10 cm. ahead of the commentary. But by the beginning of chapter 9 on fo. 371ᵛ exact parity has been achieved, allowing Θ to end as neatly as it began. Iota then begins a new page of its own.

This is a thoroughly 'physical' explanation of the line of deletion.[42] There is simply no need to wonder why the scribe did not turn back a page to delete the earlier part of the Passage (1048ᵇ18–27) as well. He is not objecting to the content, but dismayed to find his text and commentary out of sync again.

6. To sum up: the Passage is well attested in branch β, not at all in α. Harlfinger's investigations, which postdate the editions of Ross and Jaeger, underline the difficulties that both confronted. The Passage is better confirmed than before in β, eliminated entirely from α. What is an editor to do?

We are so familiar with the Passage that most of us find it hard to imagine a *Metaphysics* which simply leaves it out. But there have been such versions. As already noted (Section 4 above), it was not in Cardinal Bessarion's Latin translation (*c.*1452), done from Hᵃ,[43] which Plate 1 shows as lacking the Passage. It was neither in the Latin translation/paraphrase of the first twelve books of the *Metaphysics* by Argyropoulos (*c.*1415–87) nor among the lemmata Latinized by Sepúlveda for his translation of the Alexander commentary (1527). Tracking back further, none of the medieval Latin translations includes the Passage. In particular, its absence from the Moerbeke translation used by Aquinas ensured that we have no comment on its subtleties from the Angelic Doctor. No comment from Averroes either: the Passage did not get into Arabic.[44]

---

[42] In reaching which I have been helped by discussion with Michel Crubellier.

[43] So E. Mioni, 'Bessarione bibliofilo e filologo', *Rivista di studi bizantini e neoellenici*, NS 5 (1968), 61–83 at 78.

[44] In the Venice 1562 edition of the *Metaphysics* in Bessarion's Latin translation, accompanied by a Latin text of Averroes' commentary, although not in the earlier edition of 1552, the Passage is presented (without comment from Averroes of course!) in a Latin version which, the reader is told, was prepared for teaching purposes by Kyriacos Strozza.

The ancient commentators on Aristotle speak frequently enough of τελεία ἐνέργεια or of ἐνέργεια κυρίως, contrasting this with ἐνέργεια ἀτελής,[45] but to my knowledge not one of them uses the single word ἐνέργεια in the sense of the Passage, as equivalent to τελεία ἐνέργεια. The only clear echo of the Passage I have been able to discover comes from medieval Byzantium. Michael of Ephesus, commenting on Aristotle's account of pleasure in *NE* 10. 2, obviously knows the Passage, and uses it to good effect. But given that Michael is the same person as Pseudo-Alexander, we have just seen both A[b] and M = F testifying that he did not find it in the copy of the *Metaphysics* he used when writing his commentary! I shall return to Michael in a final Postscript (Section 16 below).

Meanwhile, let me simply mention here that there is scholarly dispute about whether, when Plotinus in *Enneads* 6. 1 [42]. 16 ff. criticizes the Aristotelian account of change as ἐνέργεια ἀτελής, he has the Passage in view as well as *Physics* 3. 1–3, from which he quotes.[46] The issue is best reserved for Appendix 2 below, where I argue, controversially, that Plotinus' remarks and the discussion they inspired among later Platonists show a striking *absence* of acquaintance with the Passage. There is certainly no sign of the Passage in *Enneads* 2. 5 [25], a treatise which starts from the question

---

[45] Samples, all of them commenting on passages where modern scholars are tempted to invoke the narrow meaning given to ἐνέργεια in the Passage: Them. *In DA* 55. 6–12, 112. 25–33 Heinze; Philop. *In DA* 296. 20–297. 37 Hayduck; Simpl. (?) *In DA* 126. 2–3, 264. 25–265. 16 Hayduck. A particularly clear account of the difference between τελεία ἐνέργεια and κίνησις, which is ἀτελὴς ἐνέργεια, is Philop. *Aet.* 64. 22–65. 26 Rabe. In a work that long-windedly dots every possible I and crosses every possible T, it is hard to believe that the author would not have drawn on, or at least mentioned, the Passage—had he known of its existence. I infer that he did not.

[46] P. Henry and H.-R. Schwyzer (eds.), *Plotini Opera* (3 vols.; Paris and Brussels, 1951–73) ['Henry–Schwyzer'], ad loc. cite the Passage, but A. H. Armstrong, *Plotinus with an English Translation* (7 vols.; Cambridge, Mass., and London, 1966–88), vi. Enneads *VI 1–5* ['Armstrong'], does not. Brague, *Monde*, 454 with n. 2, is sceptical. I agree with him that ch. 16 can be understood without reference to the Passage. If ch. 18 seems to operate with some sort of contrast between κίνησις and ἐνέργεια, that can be explained as the product of Plotinus' own dialectic in chs. 16 and 17. The recent discussion of this dialectic in R. Chiaradonna, *Sostanza movimento analogia: Plotino critico di Aristotele* ['Chiaradonna'] (Naples, 2002), ch. 2, does appeal to the Passage. So too I. Croese, *Simplicius on Continuous and Instantaneous Change: NeoPlatonic Elements in Simplicius' Interpretation of Aristotelian Physics* ['Croese'] (Utrecht, 1998), ch. 4, entitled 'The Late NeoPlatonic interpretation of the motion–energeia distinction'. Yet Damascius is a late Neoplatonist who can write as if it is a matter of course that ἐνέργειαι are either τέλειαι or ἀτελεῖς (*In Phileb.* 191 Westerink). Returning to 6. 1. 16 ff., Gwenaëlle Aubry points out to me that the absence of the term πρᾶξις, in a Plotinian text which is bent on distinguishing ἐνέργεια from ποίησις, makes it doubtful that its author has the Passage in mind.

whether τὸ ἐνεργείᾳ εἶναι is the same as, or different from, ἡ ἐνέργεια. Nor in two treatises on happiness, 1. 4 [46] and 1. 5 [36].

A good way to appreciate how contingent were the factors that brought the Passage into our editions is to study the route by which it got into the Aldine. Sicherl has shown that the 'Druckvorlage' of the Aldine was Par. 1848 (Q^c, c.1470).[47] Q^c is a descendant of Vind. Phil. 64 (J^a), and J^a has the Passage, presumably by 'contamination' from D^m, which was one of Brockmann's positive results. Now J^a is one of the most copied manuscripts of all time,[48] as can be seen from the stemma. What is interesting is that, while four of its descendants have the Passage, three of them do not. Why the difference?

Go back to D^m (written for Bessarion around 1443) and the annotation by a later hand mentioned at the end of Brockmann's letter (above, p. 230). Attached to the beginning of the Passage, the annotation reads: σ(ημείωσ)αι ὅτι ἔν τισι βιβλίοις οὐκ εὑρίσκεται ἕως τὸ μὲν οὖν ἐνεργείᾳ ('Note that up to τὸ μὲν οὖν ἐνεργείᾳ is missing in some books'). The identical annotation, with the identical sign ≏ linking annotation to the relevant part of the text, is found not only in D^m's direct descendant Marc. 200 (Q), but also in J^a.[49] In J^a, moreover, the annotation is in the same hand as the main text and there is a line drawn in the left vertical margin to clarify the reference of the annotation. This line has been mistaken in modern times for a mark of deletion.[50] It is presumably a similar mistake that leads Ambr. L 117 sup. (M^c), Salm. M 45 (d), and Paris. Suppl. 204 (U^c) to omit the Passage without indicating the fact. By contrast, Paris. Suppl. 332 (Y^c) at fos. 313–14 neatly copies Passage, sign, and annotation exactly as it appears in J^a but without the marginal line; Vat. 257 (V^c) inserts ζηαι at the beginning and end of the Passage without specifying what is to be noted; while Neap. III D 35 (N^d) includes the Passage in its main text with no trace of annotation. Had the scribe of Q^c thought along the same lines as the scribe of U^c, the Passage would not have appeared in the Aldine and the

[47] M. Sicherl, 'Handschriftliche Vorlagen der editio princeps des Aristoteles', *Akademie der Wissenschaften und der Literatur, Mainz*, Abhandlungen der Geistes- und Sozialwissenschaftlichen Klasse, 8 (1976), 1–90; acknowledged by Harlfinger at p. 26 n. 56 *bis*, too late to redraw the lower right-hand quarter of his stemma (Plate 1), where a, a^{II}, a^{III} designate successive editions of the Aldine.

[48] Harlfinger, 25.

[49] Thereby providing yet another independent confirmation of Harlfinger's stemma.

[50] S. Bernadinello, *'Eliminatio codicum' della Metafisica di Aristotele* (Padua, 1970), 70.

world might well not have known what it was missing until Brandis collated A^b for his school edition of the *Metaphysics* (1823) and for Bekker's Berlin Academy edition of 1831.[51] As it is, Q^c is like N^d in that it simply transmits the Passage as part of the main text with no indication that it has ever been questioned. Aldus would have seen no reason to worry.

Let us dwell a moment on contingency. The manuscript tradition now before you in Plate 1 shows that not all ancient readers of Aristotle's *Metaphysics* (I suspect, rather few) would meet the Passage. Its quiet entry via Q^c into the tradition of modern publication ensured that lots of us would come to find it familiar, hard to think away, hence hard to suppose it might have been unavailable to many ancient students of Aristotle. None the less, not all moderns have succumbed.

Once the Passage was included in the first Aldine (1498), it was printed in the Greek text of editions by Erasmus (1531, 1539; reissued 1550), Turrisanus (1552), and Sylburg (1585).[52] But not in the Basel Latin translation of 1542. In 1590 Isaac Casaubon put the Passage in square brackets, on the grounds that, although it is in the manuscripts (sc. the manuscripts he knows or knows of), it was unknown to the old Latin translators and to Alexander; his brackets and note reappear in a series of editions by W. du Val (1619, 1629, 1654), the brackets alone in Mauro's Latin version with commentary (1658) and in Weise's edition of the Greek (1843). The Passage is completely omitted in Thomas Taylor's English translation of 1801.[53] Barthélemy-Saint-Hilaire (1879), having had the benefit

[51] C. A. Brandis (ed.), *Aristotelis et Theophrasti Metaphysica*, ad veterum codicum manuscriptorum fidem recensita indicibusque instructa in usum scholarum edidit ['Brandis ed.'] (Berlin, 1823), vii, looks forward to Bekker's big edition, the preface to which (Bekker, vol. i, p. iii) makes it clear that they shared the task of travelling around Europe to inspect the 101 manuscripts there listed (Bekker, vol. i, pp. iii–vi) and divided the responsibilities of preparing the final product on behalf of the Berlin Academy. Both note in their apparatus criticus that the Passage is omitted in certain manuscripts, although only Bekker specifies these as ET and only he records the crossing out in A^b; both note A^b's ἐνέργειν for ἐνέργεια at 1048^{b}35. Brandis's apparatus ascribes F's τοῦτο τὸ κεφάλαιον ἐν πολλοῖς λείπεται to 'Alex.'!

[52] Schwegler, vol. i, pp. xv–xx, gives a helpful history of *Metaphysics* editions since the Aldine, brought up to date by M. Hecquet-Devienne, 'Les mains du *Parisinus Graecus* 1853: une nouvelle collation des quatre premiers livres de la *Métaphysique* d'Aristote (folios 225^v–247^v)', *Scrittura e civiltà*, 24 (2000), 103–71 at 105–33 (repr. with slight alterations in R. Goulet (ed.), *Dictionnaire des philosophes antiques*, supplément (Paris, 2003), 245–9).

[53] T. Taylor, *The Metaphysics of Aristotle*, translated from the Greek (London, 1801), 210 n.: 'Several lines follow this word [γνώσει] in the printed text which are

of Bonitz's emendations when translating the Passage, still found the result so unsatisfactory that he complained in his note ad loc., 'peut-être eût-il mieux valu le passer tout à fait sous silence, comme l'ont fait Alexandre d'Aphrodise et Bessarion'. We should prepare to think the unthinkable.

Ross writes:

> It is perfectly clear that neither EJ nor A^b should be followed exclusively. But the weight of the Greek commentators and of the medieval translation is decidedly on the side of EJ, and I have accordingly followed this group of manuscripts, except where the evidence of the Greek commentators, or the sense, or grammar, or Aristotelian usage . . . turns the scale in favour of A^b.[54]

For the particular case of book Z, this judgement has recently been strengthened by Michael Frede and Günther Patzig. They have produced a Greek text of Z which aims to follow the α tradition of EJ, not exclusively, but wherever possible. The result, in my view, is a triumph. The text is harder to read than Jaeger's, to be sure, but that is the point. For A^b, as they put it, systematically smoothes out the crabbiness of Aristotle's treatise style, sometimes as the result of misunderstanding.[55]

Z is only one book of the *Metaphysics*. We may not infer from one book to the rest. But we should, none the less, take note of a possibility: in $\varTheta$ too the balance in favour of the α branch may be even stronger than Ross described. Let this be the cue for my alternative to Jaeger's suggestion that the Passage originated as an addition by Aristotle himself, which must therefore have been lost or excised from the EJ tradition (branch α) at a fairly early stage.

Look at the emendations all over the Passage in your Greek text. As Bonitz said, before he applied his magic touch,

> Sed librariorum error, ex quo omissus est in quibusdam exemplaribus universus hic locus, idem ad singula videtur verba pertinuisse; ea enim tot scatent corruptelis, ut non alia Metaphysicorum pars cum iis possit comparari.[56]

not to be found in the Commentary of Alexander, and are not translated either by Bessarion or Argyropylus, the most antient translators of Aristotle. I have, therefore, omitted them in my version, as undoubtedly spurious.'

[54] Ross, vol. i, pp. clxiv–clxv.
[55] Consult their introduction, vol. i, ch. 1, 'Zum griechischen Text'.
[56] Bonitz, 397. Brague, *Monde*, 456–7, would minimize the extent of corruption

As Ross said afterwards, 'The text has been vastly improved by Bonitz.'[57] An obvious hypothesis to explain the extent of corruption is that the Passage began as an annotation in the β tradition, written in a margin where it was cramped for space or liable to damage (fraying, finger wear, moisture, etc.).[58] That is why so many vitally important words now appear as supplements, in angled brackets. They were missed out when, at some later point in the β tradition, the annotation was mistakenly copied into the main text.

On this hypothesis, the Passage is a fragment of Aristotelian philosophy from some work now lost to us.[59] The annotator could be quite late, as late as such works were still around to be consulted. There is no need at all to think of ancient editors, let alone of an addition signalled somehow by Aristotle himself for inclusion in the next copying out of Θ. Aristotle is the last person to have reason for writing the aberrant terminology of the Passage into the main text of Θ.

7. This brings us to the question of motive. What was the annotation meant to explain or illuminate? Several possibilities come to mind:

(i) The text it best explains is Θ 8, $1050^a23–^b2$, already quoted. The distinction there between ἐνέργειαι which aim at a further product and those which are their own end is parallel to the distinction drawn in the Passage between πράξεις which aim at a further product and those which are their own end. The motive for a marginal note would be to tell readers of Θ that elsewhere Aristotle marks the distinction with special terminology.

The snag is that Θ 8 is over two Bekker pages on from Θ 6. How

by hypothesizing that the Passage began as a hastily scribbled note from Aristotle to himself. But then why was it not transmitted in the α tradition?

[57] Ross, ii. 253. To verify this observation, try making sense of the Passage as printed in Bekker. Schwegler made a noble effort with both text and translation, but the strain is evident on nearly every line. Yet it should be added that in Bonitz's apparatus every single emendation is marked 'fort.', i.e. 'perhaps'; his commentary is similarly modest and hesitant about restoring the Passage.

[58] An important, well-known case of this kind is A 5, $986^a29–30$, where a marginal note about the relative dates of Pythagoras and Alcmaeon has been written into the text of E, but is unknown both to Alexander and to the A^b tradition.

[59] Cf. J. H. von Kirchmann, *Die Metaphysik des Aristoteles*, übersetzt, erläutert und mit einer Lebensbeschreibung des Aristoteles versehen (2 vols.; Berlin, 1871), ii. 50–1 n. 815, who rightly finds the Passage so irrelevant to its context in Θ that he suggests it may have been interpolated into the text 'aus einem anderen Werke des Aristoteles'.

would a note on Θ 8 get written into the text of Θ 6? Either (*a*) by carelessness or (*b*) by design. (*a*) is not impossible. For example, a learned reader thinks the Passage should be in the main text of Θ 8, but his copyist misunderstands the directions he has been given. (*b*) supposes a learned reader who thinks that the Passage is genuinely relevant to Θ 6 and has it written there. Why not, if an outstanding scholar like Ross finds it 'quite appropriate to its context'?

(ii) Alternatively, the annotation was a comment on Θ 6. Either (*a*) by someone who failed to see, as have many others since, that the Passage addresses a different question from the rest of Θ 6, or (*b*) by someone who knew that very well and wished only to point out that elsewhere Aristotle takes a different tack from the one he follows in the earlier part of Θ 6.

A different tack on what? On a sentence in Θ 6 that might well disturb a reader who knows the Passage, or *NE* 10, or *Metaphysics Λ*. The sentence, quoted above, p. 222, is 1048ᵇ8–9:

τὰ μὲν γὰρ ὡς κίνησις πρὸς δύναμιν, τὰ δ' ὡς οὐσία πρός τινα ὕλην.

Some are related as change to capacity, while others are related as substance to some matter.

Once the analogical extension is completed, these are the two headings under which all instances of the contrast between δύναμις and ἐνέργεια are subsumed: some are contrasted (C) as δύναμις to κίνησις, others (S) as ὕλη to οὐσία. Examples under the second heading, the one Θ is really interested in, are the Hermes in the wood, the half-line in the whole (1048ᵇ32–3), the matter as opposed to what is separated out of it, and the unworked up as opposed to what it is worked up into (1048ᵇ3–4). The disturbing bit is the examples Aristotle cites under the first head, as δύναμις to κίνησις: knowledge vs. contemplation, the craft of building vs. building, sleeping vs. waking, sight vs. seeing (1048ᵃ34–ᵇ2). Subtract building, and in each case the second term is the sort of item which the Passage calls ἐνέργεια in *contrast* to κίνησις. Subtract waking and seeing, and what remains is an activity that Aristotle in *NE* 10 and *Metaphysics Λ* ascribes to God: contemplation, theorizing, the exercise of knowledge.

Now in Θ 6, 1048ᵇ8, the noun κίνησις is used broadly to cover a builder's active agency as well as the passive change undergone by the bricks: it picks up both κινεῖν and κινεῖσθαι from 1048ᵃ28–9. We know that Aristotle's God κινεῖ ὡς ἐρώμενον. But that describes God's relation to the rest of the cosmos. Contemplation is what he is, his οὐσία (Λ 6, 1071ᵇ19–20), his life (Λ 7, 1072ᵇ26–8), his pleasure (1072ᵇ16). Contemplation is what makes him the most excellent of all beings (Λ 9, 1074ᵃ18–21). Any student of Aristotle could think it misleading to say that God is κίνησις or that his contemplating is κίνησις. Especially since κίνησις usually refers to passive change (κινεῖσθαι), which would imply that God, the great Contemplator, undergoes change. A Byzantine cleric might well agree with Philoponus (*Aet.* 4. 4) that the very thought is blasphemous. Someone who knew the Passage might well think to write a marginal note to show that Aristotle knew better, that elsewhere νόησις is not κίνησις but ἐνέργεια.⁶⁰

This last suggestion, (ii*b*), would be my preferred choice for a story about how the Passage began its journey into the text of Θ 6. But let imagination be reined in here. It is enough that once the marginal note hypothesis is accepted, to account for extreme textual disrepair in the Passage, plausible stories can be told about how it got into the main text. The next question is what to say about our newly discovered fragment of Aristotle.

8. The style is that of the treatises rather than the published 'exoteric' works: no connecting particle in 1048ᵇ25, neither verbs nor connectives in 29–30. As Jaeger says, 'oratio est admodum dura et obscura'. The best clue as to its original context is the word πρᾶξις, which does not occur elsewhere in Θ. This has a wide spread of meanings, but not endlessly wide. In biology almost any function

---

⁶⁰ Indeed, C. Natali, 'Movimenti ed attività: l'interpretazione di Aristotele, *Metaph.* Θ 6', *Elenchos*, 12 (1991), 67–90 at 70 and 76 (repr. in C. Natali, *L'Action efficace: études sur la philosophie de l'action d'Aristote* (Louvain-la-Neuve, Paris, and Dudley, Mass., 2004), 31–52), suggests that the Passage is 'una glossa di Aristotele a 1048ᵃ34–5': Aristotle wanted to clarify the status of θεωρῆσαι in those lines. But I suspect that by 'glossa' Natali means 'explanation', not a marginal note, in which case my previous objection stands: why does Aristotle in the sequel continue to use ἐνέργεια in the same broad sense as it had before the Passage? The same objection tells against two other attempts to make the Passage fit into Θ 6: (i) S. Menn, 'The Origins of Aristotle's Concept of ἐνέργεια: ἐνέργεια and δύναμις', *Ancient Philosophy*, 14 (1994), 73–114 at 106–7, has it 'repair the damage' done by the broad (and, he claims, chronologically early) use of κίνησις at 1048ᵇ8; (ii) T. H. Irwin, *Aristotle's First Principles* (Oxford, 1988), 565 n. 19, suggests that the actualitites that Aristotle identifies with forms also meet the present-perfect test, e.g. '*x* is a statue' and '*x* has been a statue' are both true if either is.

of living things, from heavenly bodies down through animals to plants, may count as a πρᾶξις: *De caelo* 2. 12, 292^{b}1–2; *DA* 2. 4, 415^{a}18–22; *De sensu* 1, 436^{a}4; *HA* 8. 1, 589^{a}3; 10, 596^{b}20–1; *PA* 1. 5, 645^{b}14–35; *GA* 1. 23, 731^{a}25; cf. *NE* 7. 14, 1154^{b}20.[61] But the word does not consort easily with inanimate things. When we turn to the first chapter of the *Nicomachean Ethics*, we find that some πράξεις aim at an end beyond themselves, others just at the ἐνέργεια, the doing of the action itself. But the *Ethics* also has a narrower use of πρᾶξις, confined (as the Passage confines it) to things done for their own sake: 6. 2, 1139^{a}35–^{b}4; 6. 5, 1140^{b}6–7; cf. 1. 8, 1098^{b}18–20; *Pol.* 7. 3, 1325^{b}16–21. A good example is the second of the passages just listed:

τῆς μὲν γὰρ ποιήσεως ἕτερον τὸ τέλος, τῆς δὲ πράξεως οὐκ ἂν εἴη· ἔστι γὰρ αὐτὴ ἡ εὐπραξία τέλος.

For while making has an end other than itself, action cannot; for good action itself is its end. (trans. Ross)

If Aristotle is going to restrict πρᾶξις, or πρᾶξις τελεία, or the more general term ἐνέργεια, to things done for their own sake, the most likely context is an ethical one. That would fit the inclusion of εὖ ζῆν and εὐδαιμονεῖν among the examples in Θ 6 (their perfects, not previously attested, may have been dreamt up by Aristotle for the purpose) and give relevance to the statement that with these you don't have to stop, as you do when you are slimming someone (1048^{b}26–7). I shall reinforce this suggestion later with an argument to show that the Passage *cannot* have started life in a physical treatise.

But of course there may be ethical stretches, long or short, in

---

[61] The inclusion of plants in the *De caelo* and of recuperation in the *Nicomachean Ethics* passage respectively should alleviate the concern of M.-T. Liske, 'Kinesis und Energeia bei Aristoteles', *Phronesis*, 36 (1991), 161–78 at 161, that Aristotle would hardly count recuperation and becoming something as 'Handlungen'. R. Polansky, 'Energeia in Aristotle's *Metaphysics* IX', *Ancient Philosophy*, 3 (1983), 160–70 (repr. in A. Preus and J. P. Anton (eds.), *Aristotle's Ontology* (Albany, NY, 1992), 211–25), correctly points out that all the ἐνέργειαι exemplified in the Passage are psychical, since all involve soul, but incorrectly (n. 18) allows this to be equivalent to P. S. Mamo's claim in his 'Energeia and Kinesis in Metaphysics Θ. 6', *Apeiron*, 4 (1970), 24–34, that they are all mental processes, which living is not. Polansky's exclusion of plant life (pp. 165, 168), which would narrow the range of ἐνέργειαι yet further, is a non sequitur from the premiss that nutrition and reproduction are not themselves ἐνέργειαι in the narrow sense. To his credit he does, however, point out (p. 164) that most of the κινήσεις mentioned (being slimmed, learning, being cured, walking, building) are equally 'psychical', being confined to animate things. Only coming to be and movement have wider scope.

non-ethical writings. One remarkable example is *De caelo* 2. 12, 292ᵃ22–ᵇ25, where value theory is brought in to solve problems about the motion of the heavenly bodies. A small-scale example is Θ 8, 1050ᵇ1–2, the parenthesis about happiness at the end of the passage quoted earlier, which Ross wrongly describes as a 'digression'.[62] Even the *Physics* finds it relevant at one point to say that happiness is a sort of πρᾶξις.[63] Ethical considerations are seldom far from Aristotle's mind, whatever he is writing on. All we can say at this stage is that the Passage looks ethical in character, and leave future editors of *Aristotelis Fragmenta* to decide where to print it. I will propose a more positive location later.

PART II: MEANING

9. Now for the philosophical content. The discussion in the scholarly literature is largely focused on the so-called 'tense test': φ-ing is an ἐνέργεια if, and only if, from the present tense (whether Englished as '*x* φs' or as '*x* is φing') we may infer '*x* has φed'. If we may not infer the perfect from the present, φing is a κίνησις. Thus seeing is an ἐνέργεια because 'Theaetetus sees Socrates' implies 'Theaetetus has seen Socrates', but building is a κίνησις because 'Ictinus is building a temple' does not imply 'Ictinus has built a temple'; on the contrary, it implies that the temple he is presently building (which may be his first) is not yet built. There is much to say, much has been said, about this test as a criterion for distinguishing ἐνέργειαι from κινήσεις. But why suppose that *inferences* are what Aristotle has in view?

On the face of it, all we find in the Passage is a string of conjunctions:

At the same time we see *and* have seen, understand *and* have understood, . . . while it is not true that at the same time we are learning *and* have learnt, or are being cured *and* have been cured. (1048ᵇ23–5; trans. after Ross)

It takes argument to show that these and other expressions of the form 'at the same time *p* and *q*' indicate entailments from *p* to *q*.

So far as I know, the first to appreciate this point was J. L. Ackrill

---

[62] Ross ad loc.: 'The reference to εὐδαιμονία is a digression.'
[63] *Phys.* 2. 5, 197ᵇ5: ἡ δ' εὐδαιμονία πρᾶξίς τις· εὐπραξία γάρ; cf. *Pol.* 7. 3, 1325ᵃ32.

in his pioneering article on the Passage.[64] The argument he provided was convincing (see below), with the result that the main focus of subsequent debate has been on inference from the present to the perfect. What few[65] have remarked upon is this. In nearly all Aristotle's instantiations of 'at the same time p and q', p is present and q perfect. But just once it is the other way round:

ἑώρακε δὲ καὶ ὁρᾷ ἅμα τὸ αὐτό, καὶ νοεῖ καὶ νενόηκεν.

One has seen and sees the same thing at the same time, understands and has understood ⟨the same thing at the same time⟩.[66] (1048ᵇ33–4)

If the second limb of this chiasmus is treated as licence to infer 'x has understood' from 'x understands', by parity of reasoning the first should license inferring from 'x has seen' to 'x sees'.

This suggestion has one advantage. If 'at the same time p and q' asserts a biconditional, not just a one-way entailment, then Aristotle's putting the point as a conjunction is logically less sloppy than it would otherwise appear. If he has a two-way connection in mind, it no longer matters that he does not spell out whether it is p that entails q or vice versa. His thought could be put as follows: 'For all times t, p and q are true together at t or false together at t.'

A second advantage is that it helps to explain why Aristotle should make a point of saying that, where κινήσεις are concerned, present and perfect are different (1048ᵇ30–3: ἕτερον).[67] If in the case of ἐνέργειαι, by contrast, present and perfect are the same, they had better be mutually entailing.

The obvious objection is that from Theaetetus' *having* seen Soc-

---

[64] The alternative interpretation he was arguing against has it that 'at the same time p and q' expresses the logical *compatibility* of p and q. This idea is taken up by S. Waterlow, *Nature, Change, and Agency in Aristotle's* Physics ['Waterlow'] (Oxford 1982), 183 ff., and endorsed by T. Potts, 'States, Activities and Performances' ['Potts'], *Proceedings of the Aristotelian Society*, suppl. 39 (1965), 65–84 at 66–7, while Russo actually *translates* 'è possibile nello stesso tempo vedere e aver già visto' (A. Russo, *Aristotele: opere*, vol. vi. *Metafisica* (Rome and Bari, 1973)), etc. But surely 'at the same time p and q' asserts actual joint truth, not just the possibility of joint truth. When Aristotle, in a related context, does want to speak of the possibility of joint truth, he uses the modal verb ἐνδέχεσθαι (*SE* 2, 178ᵃ9–28, discussed below).

[65] The one exception I have noted is Potts, 66.

[66] I take τὸ αὐτό as the object of the verbs in this sentence, not their subject. All the other illustrative examples in the Passage are verbs with no subject expressed, this being an idiom Aristotle often uses (especially in *Topics* and *Rhetoric*) to indicate that it does not matter what the subject is; in the felicitous terminology of J. Brunschwig, *Aristote: Topiques*, texte établi et traduit (Paris, 1967), pp. lxxxix and 138 n. 2, the absence of a subject may be regarded as 'un variable en blanc'.

[67] On construing ἕτερον as predicate, not with Ross as subject, see n. 89 below.

rates it does not follow that he sees him now. This objection assumes that the perfect refers to the past, either directly or indirectly. Direct reference to the past is characteristic for the perfect in Latin ('Veni, vidi, vici'), and in spoken French or spoken Italian, where the perfect is often a simple past tense (like the past definite in literary French and Italian) which would go over into English as an aorist of the form '*x* φed': '[Hier] j'ai lu votre livre et puis . . .', 'Io sono arrivato [due mesi fa] e dopo . . .'. In spoken German too the perfect is a past tense: '[Gestern] habe ich Brot gekauft'.[68] But English preserves a distinction between '*x* φed' and '*x* has φed', the perfect being a tense of *present* time. Consider the difference between 'I lost my passport' and 'I have lost my passport'. The second implies, as the first does not, that at the time of speaking the passport is still lost. This is *indirect* reference to the past. Rather than referring directly to a past event, the perfect in English commonly expresses the continuing present relevance of some past event. 'I have come, I have seen, I have conquered' would sound bizarre unless we imagine Caesar still in Britain. And it is now much too late for you or me to say, in the third person, 'Caesar has invaded Britain'.[69] As Goodwin's *Syntax of Greek Moods and Tenses* put it long ago in 1897, 'The perfect, although it implies the performance of the action in past time, yet states only that it *stands completed* at the *present* time. This explains why the perfect is classed with the present as a primary tense, that is, as a tense of *present* time.'[70]

In ancient Greek the so-called resultative perfect behaves very

[68] The bracketed time-references are of course optional.

[69] Here I am indebted to Stephen Makin. Interestingly, the Stoics reported by Sextus Empiricus, *M.* 8. 254–6, treat constructions with the verb μέλλειν (not as future but) as present tense with indirect reference to the future, in parallel to their analysis of the Greek perfect as, like the English, present tense with indirect reference to a past event. Were it to be correct, as claimed by M. J. White, 'Aristotle's Concept of θεωρία and the ἐνέργεια–κίνησις Distinction' ['White'], *Journal of the History of Philosophy*, 18 (1980), 253–63 at 254, that '*x* has φed' is true if, and only if, at some earlier time '*x* φ's' or '*x* is φing' was true, English would lose the difference between perfect and aorist. We could say, both truly and appositely, 'Caesar has invaded Britain'. The fact is, we can't.

[70] W. W. Goodwin, *Syntax of the Moods and Tenses of the Greek Verb* ['Goodwin'] (London, 1897), 13–14. Plato, *Parm.* 141 D–E, lists γέγονε as a verb *both* of past (when coupled with ποτέ) *and* of present time (coupled with νῦν, as e.g. at Plato, *Rep.* 354 C). Ignored by philosophical commentators on the *Parmenides*, this interesting feature is discussed by P. Chantraine, *Histoire du parfait grec* ['Chantraine'] (Paris, 1927), 159–62, following the seminal contribution of A. Meillet, 'Le sens de γενήσομαι: à propos de *Parménide* 141', *Revue de philologie, de littérature et d'histoire anciennes*, 48 (1924), 44–9. Proclus, *In Tim.* i. 290. 23–6 Diehl, combines past and present

much like the perfect in English.[71] But there is also another, more ancient type of perfect which survives into the fourth century BC and beyond. Consider the following: γέγονα, δέδοικα, εἴωθα, ἔοικα, ἕστηκα, λέληθα, μέμνημαι, οἶδα, πέφυκα, πέπονθα, συμβέβηκα, τέθνηκα. They are or can be wholly present, with no past reference at all. They are best analysed in terms of aspect rather than tense. Or consider a famous line of Empedocles: γαίῃ μὲν γὰρ γαῖαν ὀπώπαμεν, ὕδατι δ᾽ ὕδωρ, 'With earth do we see earth, with water water' (fr. 109. 1). ὀπώπαμεν is a perfect formation, but it functions as the sort of timeless present one finds in 'The Sun sets in the West', 'Lions are mammals'; no competent translator would render 'With earth have we seen earth . . .'.[72] Occasionally, English has a form to match: 'I *am* persuaded', 'I *am* called' could in a given context translate πέποιθα and κέκλημαι better than 'I have been persuaded', 'I was called', while the Tailor of Gloucester's 'Alack, I am undone!' might on occasion do justice to the Greek οἴμοι.

Tense locates an event or situation in time: past, present, or future. (Pluperfect and future perfect are no exception, since they locate an event or situation before a previously specified past, or after a previously specified future.) Aspect, by contrast, views an event or situation as complete or incomplete.[73] Past, present, and future

when, to explain πῶς γενητὸν τὸ πᾶν, he writes of the cosmos as ἀεὶ γιγνόμενον ἅμα καὶ γεγενημένον.

[71] For a nice trio of examples see Plato, *Gorg.* 508 E 6–509 A 7. At least in English the resultative perfect should be treated in terms of tense, not aspect, since it has both imperfective and perfective forms, e.g. 'I have been reading *War and Peace*' vs. 'I have read *War and Peace*', the first of which is true rather more often than the second. This tells against Bauer's counsel of despair (G. Bauer, 'The English "Perfect" Reconsidered', *Journal of Linguistics*, 6 (1970), 189–98 at 196): 'the English perfect can neither be regarded as a tense nor as an aspect, but is a category in its own right'.

[72] Many more examples of the two types of perfect, and a wonderful discussion of the evolution of the Greek perfect from aspect into tense, in Chantraine, ch. 7.

[73] B. Comrie, *Aspect: An Introduction to the Study of Verbal Aspect and Related Problems* (Cambridge, 1976), is a helpful general introduction to this subject; Y. Duhoux, *Le Verbe grec ancien: éléments de morphologie et de syntaxe historiques* (Louvain-la-Neuve, 1992), 138 ff., is nice and clear on aspect in ancient Greek. For a monograph devoted to ways in which aspect is expressed in English, see L. J. Brinton, *The Development of English Aspectual Systems: Aspectualizers and Post-Verbal Particles* (Cambridge, 1988). One scholar of the Passage who has seen that the issue is aspect, not tense, is Kosman, 'Substance', 123–7. He too infers the sameness of present and perfect in the case of ἐνέργειαι, but he misses his best evidence by translating 1048[b]33–4 the wrong way round: 'At the same moment one sees and has seen' (similarly H. Tredennick, *Aristotle: The Metaphysics*, with an English

may each be expressed in two different ways: an imperfective way that talks of an ongoing process, divisible into stages, or a perfective way that presents something whole and complete, without regard for internal temporal divisions. For an English example, contrast the imperfective 'Next year I will be writing a book on Aristotle' with the perfective 'Next year I will write a book on Aristotle': same tense, different aspect.[74] It could matter a lot which form you used on your grant application.

For a Greek example, we may turn to Plato's *Protagoras*, 316 B 3–4, where Protagoras asks whether Socrates and Hippocrates would like to hold their discussion with him (διαλεχθῆναι) in private or in company. Socrates replies that it makes no difference to him. Let Protagoras decide how he wishes to discuss (διαλέγεσθαι) the matter of young Hippocrates' education (316 C 3–4). In Greek, the

translation (2 vols.; Cambridge, Mass., and London, 1933–5)). And he persists in trying to make the English perfect convey the purely aspectual meaning he wants, without even indirect reference to the past. Others who have shifted attention from tense to aspect are Potts, Penner, 'Verbs', A. D. P. Mourelatos, 'Events, Processes, and States' ['Mourelatos'], *Linguistics and Philosophy*, 2 (1978), 415–34, repr. in P. J. Tedeschi and A. Zaenen (eds.), *Tense and Aspect* (New York and London, *c.*1981), 191–212, D. W. Graham, 'States and Performances: Aristotle's Test' ['Graham'], *Philosophical Quarterly*, 30 (1980), 117–30, Furth, L. Jansen, *Tun und Können: Ein systematischer Kommentar zur Aristoteles' Theorie der Vermögen im neunten Buch der Metaphysik* ['Jansen'] (Frankfurt a.M., 2003), A. Linguiti, *La felicità e il tempo: Plotino, Enneadi, I 4–I 5*, con testo greco, introduzione, traduzione e commento ['Linguiti'] (Milan, 2000), White, and M. Frede, 'The Stoic Doctrine of the Tenses of the Verb' ['Tenses'], in K. Döring and T. Ebert (eds.), *Dialektiker und Stoiker: Zur Logik der Stoa und ihrer Vorläufer* (Stuttgart, 1993), 141–54, this last being a paper in which the Passage is seen as the stimulus (direct or indirect) for discussions of aspect in Diodorus Cronus, the Stoics, and later grammarians. While hailing all these, especially Frede for his demonstration that the ancients themselves distinguished between tense and aspect, I maintain that, apart from R. Hope, *Aristotle: Metaphysics*, translated (New York, 1952), and Graham, no one has appreciated what drastic measures are required (see below) to produce an English version that highlights aspect rather than tense.

[74] Recall n. 71 above. Faced with Aristotle's statement at *Metaph. Δ* 7, 1017^{a}27–30 (cf. *De int.* 12, 21^{b}9–10), that there is no difference between τὸ ἄνθρωπος ὑγιαίνων ἐστί and τὸ ἄνθρωπος ὑγιαίνει, or between τὸ ἄνθρωπος βαδίζων ἐστί ἢ τέμνων and τὸ ἄνθρωπος βαδίζει ἢ τέμνει, R. A. Cobb, 'The Present Progressive Periphrasis and the Metaphysics of Aristotle', *Phronesis*, 18 (1973), 80–90, supposes that it puts all *Greek* present-tense statements on a par with the *English* present-progressive periphrasis '*x* is φing'. This would require English translators to go in for nonsensical locutions such as 'He is knowing . . .', 'We are believing . . .', not to mention that Cobb has to follow Ross in rendering ὑγιαίνων ἐστί by 'He is recovering' rather than 'He is in good health', for which the only parallel offered by LSJ comes from the Book of Ezekiel! On the contrary, Aristotle's message is that, while being is involved in every category, it is a *different* kind of being in each.

M. F. Burnyeat

dependent moods of the verb (subjunctive, optative, infinitive, imperative) generally differ in aspect, not tense,[75] and this enables Plato to mark a subtle difference between Socrates and the sophist. Protagoras' aorist infinitive already envisages a definite end to the discussion, which he eventually declares at 361 E 6: 'Now it is time to turn to something else'. Socrates' present infinitive is characteristically open-ended: he will go on for as long as the interlocutor is willing.[76] A less 'studied' Platonic example[77] is the contrast between the imperfect and the aorist of one and the same verb at *Ion* 530 A 8: 'Were you competing [ἠγωνίζου] and how did the competition go for you [ἠγωνίσω]?'

True, Aristotle is not interested in verbs as such, but what they stand for; if he was interested in the verbs themselves, he would hardly treat living well and living as distinct examples (1048[b]25–7). But if we do translate into linguistic terms, to help our own understanding, then Aristotle's contrast between κινήσεις and ἐνέργειαι comes out as a contrast between verbs whose present tense has imperfective meaning, e.g. 'to slim' or 'to build', and verbs whose present tense has perfective meaning, e.g. 'to see'.[78] We shall later (pp. 259–60) find Aristotle remarking on the fact that the difference is purely semantic, not a difference which is grammaticalized in the morphology of the relevant Greek verbs.

All this makes it difficult to translate the Passage into English. In English we cannot eliminate the perfect's (indirect) reference to the past. Therefore we must insert a counteracting phrase.[79]

---

[75] The exceptions involve indirect discourse or the presence of ἄν. For a full elucidation, see Goodwin, 22–47. Although he does not use the term 'aspect', that is what he is describing.

[76] The dramatic difference between the two infinitives was first brought to my attention by Heda Segvic. I discuss this and other character-revealing aspectual contrasts in the *Protagoras* in M. F. Burnyeat, 'The Dramatic Aspects of Plato's *Protagoras*' ['Aspects'], forthcoming.

[77] Borrowed from Mourelatos, 195.

[78] With Ackrill, 'Distinction', 127: 'The perfect [sc. of an ἐνέργεια verb] can always be used of the period preceding a moment at which the present can be used', and the phrasing 'X has (just) φed Y' in Waterlow, 188–9, compare Frede, 'Tenses', 146: 'Aristotle clearly does not think that the fact that somebody who grasps something has grasped it, shows that somebody who grasps something must have grasped it at some previous time.' While agreeing with Frede, I add that, equally clearly, as Ackrill stresses, Aristotle thinks that, in the case of κίνησις, someone who is moving something *has* moved it earlier! This is his thesis that there is no first moment of motion, set out in *Physics* 5. 6.

[79] Compare Brague *Monde*, 460–1, 468–9, 471–2, on the 'acrobaties' required when translating the Passage into French.

Two of Aristotle's examples may help: εὖ ζῆ καὶ εὖ ἔζηκε ἅμα, καὶ
εὐδαιμονεῖ καὶ εὐδαιμόνηκε. Translate: 'at the same time *x* lives well
and has achieved the good life',[80] '*x* is happy and has achieved
happiness'. For these cases at least, the objection is overcome. The
entailment runs both ways: not only from '*x* lives well' to '*x* has
achieved the good life', and from '*x* is happy' to '*x* has achieved
happiness', but also from '*x has* achieved happiness/the good life'
to '*x is* happy/living well'. The counteracting phrase 'has achieved'
enforces perfective meaning and makes the past irrelevant. It does
not matter when happiness/the good life started. The assertion is
that it is going on now,[81] complete at every moment. That is, there
is no moment at which its goal is not (yet) achieved. Happiness,
the good life, is continuing success. And so indeed is life itself
(1048ᵇ27). Living things for Aristotle are self-maintaining systems.
It is thanks to the threptic soul, whose function is nutrition and
reproduction, that throughout life, be it long or short, they succeed
in staying alive. A splendid example of perfective meaning. Present
and perfect are indeed the same.

   So much for the examples of ἐνέργειαι expressed by intransitive
verbs. The other examples of ἐνέργειαι in the Passage involve transitive verbs,[82] for which we must supply, not only an object, as we
did for slimming—the same object for both the present and the
perfect—but also a phrase to counteract the English perfect's reference to the past. Here goes: '*x* sees *y*' implies, and is implied by,
'*x* has got sight of *y*' or '*x* has (got) *y* in view'; '*x* understands *y*'
implies, and is implied by, '*x* has understood *y*'; '*x* knows *y*' implies,
and is implied by, '*x* has achieved knowledge of *y*'.

   I now offer a rendering of the whole Passage which attempts to
convey its full meaning in plausible English. At this stage I keep to
Jaeger's text, except that at 1048ᵇ33 I prefer Ross's solution: ἕτερον,
καὶ κινεῖ καὶ κεκίνηκεν.

Since of actions which have a limit none is an end, but all belong to the class
of means to an end, e.g. slimming, and since the things themselves, when
one is slimming them,[83] are in process of changing in this sense, that what

---

[80] Modern readers are at liberty to substitute 'a good life' for 'the good life'.

[81] Note the impropriety of coupling '*x* has achieved happiness' with '*x* died last
month', which goes quite properly with '*x* achieved happiness'.

[82] Similarly, the κίνησις verbs include both transitive examples (learning, building)
and intransitive ones (being cured, walking).

[83] In taking αὐτά as the object of some agent's slimming, I follow Ross and the

is aimed at in the change is not yet present, these[84] are not cases of action, or not at any rate of complete action. For none of them is an end. Action properly speaking[85] is one in which the end is present. For example, at the same time one sees ⟨a thing⟩ and has ⟨it⟩ in view, and one is wise and has achieved wisdom, and one understands ⟨something⟩ and has understood ⟨it⟩, but it is not the case that ⟨at the same time⟩ one is learning ⟨something⟩ and has learned ⟨it⟩, or that ⟨at the same time⟩ one is being cured and has been cured. One lives well and has achieved the good life at the same time, and one is happy and has achieved happiness ⟨at the same time⟩. If that were not so, the action would at some time have to cease,[86] as when one is slimming ⟨someone⟩. But as it is, this is not the case: one lives and ⟨at the same time⟩ has stayed alive.

Of these ⟨actions⟩, then, we should call one set changes, the other actualities. For every process of change is incomplete: slimming, learning, walking, building. These are changes, and they are certainly[87] incomplete. For it is not the case that at the same time one is walking and has taken a walk,[88] nor that one is building ⟨something⟩ and has built ⟨it⟩, nor again that one is becoming ⟨something⟩ and has become ⟨it⟩ or is being changed

communis opinio against Brague, *Monde*, 458, who construes αὐτά as the means of slimming and translates, 'ces moyens, chaque fois que l'on fait maigrir, sont en mouvement de façon telle [οὕτως referring forwards] qu'ils ne sont pas en eux-mêmes [ὑπάρχοντα in its copulative use] les résultats en vue de quoi le mouvement (se produit)'. If this makes sense at all, it seems to be tautological. On the other hand, for translating αὐτά I prefer Ross Tr.¹, 'the things themselves when one is making them thin', to Ross Tr.², 'the bodily parts themselves when one is making them thin', which forgets that the target of a slimming course may be the whole person, not just their tummy.

[84] ταῦτα must pick up 'actions which have a limit', not the nearer αὐτά.

[85] 'Properly speaking' renders the intensifying καί before πρᾶξις in 1048ᵇ23; Penner, 'Verbs', 454, uses italics to the same effect: 'that in which the end inheres *is* an action'.

[86] Ross translates 'would have *had* sometime to cease', followed by 'as it is, it *does* not cease' (emphasis added); likewise Furth and Makin. But ἔδει ἄν is the sole main verb in the sentence, which continues in the present tense. For this reason I take the unfulfilled condition to be present, not past. 'Does not cease' comes dangerously close to implying that happiness and life never cease at all. I take it that Aristotle means living to be an obvious example to buttress the less obvious claim about living well. The point is well put by Makin, 142 (despite his translation): 'It would not make sense to ask whether Candy has *finished* living, seeing, or understanding the theorem (as opposed to having *stopped* doing those things).'

[87] Emphatic γε (Tricot: 'certes'), to be contrasted with the limitative γε of 1048ᵇ22: J. D. Denniston, *The Greek Particles*, 2nd edn. ['Denniston'] (Oxford, 1954), 114–16 and 157.

[88] Or: 'has walked ⟨to where one is going⟩'. Scholars commonly feel the need to supply a destination, as found at *NE* 10. 4, 1174ᵃ29–ᵇ2. But 'has taken a walk' has perfective meaning even if the walking was merely a postprandial stroll.

⟨in some way⟩ and has been changed ⟨in that way⟩, but they are different;[89] as are one's changing and one's having changed ⟨something⟩. But one has got in view, and one sees, the same thing at the same time, and one understands ⟨something⟩ and has understood ⟨it⟩. The latter type ⟨of action⟩ I call actuality, the former change.

Call this Version A. Its sole purpose is to give readers a sense of how the Passage runs when the focus shifts from tense to aspect.

PART III: A REVISED TEXT

10. But prior to translation is establishing the text. Version A sticks closely to the printed text we are all familiar with. That text needs to be re-examined in the light of the hypothesis that the Passage began as a marginal annotation. For the hypothesis changes the ground rules for resolving difficulties of text and translation. The two recommendations that follow are a gift from David Sedley, very gladly received.

(i) When writing the Passage into the main text from a cramped margin, a scribe might well lose words, even important words, but it is much less likely that he would make additions. Additions, if any, would be due to subsequent attempts to clarify the obscurities of the Passage once it had entered the main text of branch β, as attested by A^b, M, and C. Conclusion: let us try to eliminate as many editorial square brackets from the printed text as is feasible, on the grounds that they presume to diagnose an unwanted addition to the original text as it stood in the margin. (*a*) Jaeger's bracketing of καὶ κινεῖ καὶ κεκίνηκεν at 1048^b33 is plainly unnecessary. I have already chosen to read, with Ross, ἕτερον, καὶ κινεῖ καὶ κεκίνηκεν. (*b*) In Version B below, an annotated rendering of the first few sentences of the Passage (1048^b18–23), I insist on retaining the 'abstraction operator' αὐτό, deleted by Christ on the grounds, hardly compelling, that 'αὐτό et αὐτά variae lectiones esse videntur'. This decision was accepted by Ross without further explanation, and by Jaeger, who said 'vel οὕτως abundat', which I simply do not

---

[89] Taking ἕτερον, with most translators, as predicate, not subject to the verbs. By contrast, in his note ad loc. Ross renders, 'It is not the case that a thing at the same time is being moved and has been moved; that which has been moved is different from that which is being moved, and that which has moved from that which is moving': three falsehoods in a row! The versions in his Tr.¹, Tr.², and Ross–Barnes hardly fare much better. Casting ἕτερον as subject only makes for trouble.

understand. One might alternatively diagnose dittography. I shall defend αὐτό.[90] Finally, only one, easily explicable pair of square brackets will remain.

(ii) An inserted portion of text may contain anaphoric pronouns whose reference in the original context was to something no longer visible in the new environment. A nice illustration is the masculine pronoun οὗτοι at *Metaph.* Λ 8, 1074ᵇ3, usually taken to pick up the neuter θείων σωμάτων at 1074ᵃ30–1. Elsewhere I have argued that 1074ᵃ38–ᵇ14 was originally written as the immediate sequel to 1073ᵃ3–ᵇ38, so that οὗτοι picks up the planets (Venus, Mercury, Jupiter, etc.) named at 1073ᵇ31–8. This is a case where the context preceding the pronoun has not vanished. It has merely been separated so that Aristotle can stop to do his calculation of the number of intelligences needed to move the spheres postulated by the astronomical systems of Eudoxus and Callippus; for which purpose he reverts to his usual staccato style, in striking contrast to the literariness of the preceding and following sections.[91] A rare glimpse of a process we cannot usually observe.

No wonder the most serious difficulties of text and translation are located in the first portion of the Passage. That is the portion most likely to become obscure as the result of being separated from an earlier discussion we can no longer read. Accordingly, I now offer Version B, an annotated rendering of the first few sentences, to try out the possibilities opened up by the conclusions reached under (i) and (ii). As with those conclusions, so too much of the detail to follow is owed to David Sedley. All of it should be read as tentative exploration, not a set of firm proposals. Changes to Jaeger's text

[90] Brague, *Monde*, 457–8, too would keep αὐτό, but in predicate position: 'la cure d'amaigrissement est, par rapport au fait de faire maigrir, justement cela'. This is his translation of the manuscripts' text τοῦ ἰσχναίνειν ἡ ἰσχνασία αὐτό, ignoring Bywater's emendation τό for τοῦ and citing Δ 2, 1013ᵃ35–ᵇ1 (the only other occurrence of ἰσχνασία in Aristotle), as warrant for taking ἡ ἰσχνασία to cover all the means—instruments as well as activities—to the completed action ἰσχναίνειν; αὐτό he construes as a reference to τῶν περὶ τὸ τέλος, so that 'justement cela' means 'is a member of the class of means to an end'. That strikes me as an awfully long-winded way to secure the same result as Jaeger gets by simply deleting ἡ ἰσχνασία αὐτό, and Δ 2 hardly justifies so distinguishing ἰσχνασία from ἰσχναίνειν, since the verb does not appear in the chapter.

[91] Burnyeat, *Map*, 141–5. The argument takes off from Friedrich Blass's suggestion ('Aristotelisches', *Rheinisches Museum*, 30 (1875), 481–505) that, since both stretches of text (1073ᵃ3–ᵇ38, 1074ᵃ38–ᵇ14) avoid hiatus (a mark of literary style), they were copied out by Aristotle from his lost *De philosophia*. That they were not originally written for Λ is further confirmed by the backwards-referring δέδεικται of 1073ᵃ5, for no such proof has preceded in the text of Λ as we have it.

are marked with an asterisk. Bold type marks a phrase discussed in the relevant numbered annotation.

Since of actions which have a limit **none** is an end, but all **belong to the class of means to an end** (1), e.g. slimming in the sense of the slimming process considered in itself [οἷον τὸ ἰσχναίνειν [ἡ ἰσχνασία] αὐτό*] (2), and since the things themselves one is slimming, when one is slimming them, are in process of changing **in this sense, that** the results aimed at in the change are not yet present (3), these are not cases of action, or not at any rate of complete action. For none of them is **in itself** (4) an end. It is in that former thing [ἐκείνῃ* without ⟨ἦ⟩*] (5) that the end and **the** [retaining ἦ*] **action are present** (6).

(1) The partitive genitive τῶν is appropriate because κινήσεις are not the sole members of that class; if they were, nothing could be both an end and means to some further end. On the other hand, the emphatic 'none' excludes from present consideration actions which are both means and ends, in accordance with what appears to be a semi-technical meaning of πέρας, exemplified at *DA* I. 3, 407[a]23–5: τῶν μὲν γὰρ πραγματικῶν νοήσεων ἔστι πέρατα (πᾶσαι γὰρ ἑτέρου χάριν), αἱ δὲ θεωρητικαί . . ., 'Practical thoughts have limits, for they are all *for the sake of something else*, whereas theoretical thoughts . . .'.

(2) One could remove the square brackets by printing ἦ *if*, but *only* if, ἦ ἰσχνασία αὐτό is a plausible Aristotelian phrase. On this, see below. Bonitz made αὐτό pick up τέλος, so that ἡ ἰσχνασία is the τέλος of τὸ ἰσχναίνειν: 'So ist z. B. das Ziel des Abmagerns die Magerkeit'. Ross Tr.[1] proposed to read just οἷον ἡ ἰσχνασία αὐτό: ' "the process of making thin" is of this sort', which reappears (without the inner quotation marks) in Ross–Barnes, but in his edition and Tr.[2] he favours τὸ ἰσχναίνειν ἦ ἰσχνασία [αὐτό], αὐτά . . ., crediting τό and ἦ to Bywater.

(3) With Ross Tr. I take the accusative absolute μὴ ὑπάρχοντα . . . κίνησις to elucidate οὕτως, the way they are changing. To Ross's note, 'αὐτά is curious, and some corruption may be suspected', I respond that the word is curious, but might cease to be so if we could access its original context. Alternatively, it emphasizes the transition from the slimming process considered in itself to the items under treatment.

(4) Line 20's αὐτό is still in force.

(5) ἐκείνῃ was printed in the Aldine and every subsequent edition

until Bonitz emended,[92] as well as by Christ after him; iota subscript, often omitted in papyri and manuscripts, scarcely counts as
an emendation.[93] I propose that the pronoun picks up an earlier but
now lost designation of the kind of thing that will soon be dubbed
ἐνέργεια. The Berlin Academy's bracketed Latin version (on which
see n. 26 above) renders the sentence thus: 'nec enim ea finis est, sed
in illa inest finis et actio', where 'ea' corresponds to ταῦτα but 'illa'
has no visible reference at all. Full marks to the unnamed translator!

(6) Since Bonitz this sentence has been doubly emended to yield
the meaning 'that movement in which the end is present is an
action' (Ross), with πρᾶξις in predicative position. Version B puts
ἡ πρᾶξις in subject position alongside τὸ τέλος, in line with the
transmitted text. The idea of the action itself being present when the
end is[94] may be compared with *NE* 10. 4, 1174[a]19–21: an instance
of building is complete either at the moment it is finished or in
the whole time *up to and including* that finish. In the Passage αὐτό
abstracts from the finish, so that τὸ ἰσχναίνειν cannot count as action,
or at any rate not as a complete action; cf. αὐτῇ τῇ βαδίσει at *NE*
10. 4, 1174[a]32. Aristotle shifts from speaking of the act as *being* or
not being the *telos* (1048[b]18 and 22) to saying that it *contains* the
telos (1048[b]22).

In Version B the key to the whole passage is the retention of what I
would call the 'abstraction operator' αὐτό at line 20. The manuscript
text, found in M and C as well as A[b], is τοῦ ἰσχναίνειν ἡ ἰσχνασία
αὐτό. Bekker, Schwegler, and Christ all print the transmitted τοῦ,[95]
but Bywater's τό for τοῦ is accepted by both Ross and Jaeger. As
a result, they have a problem with ἡ ἰσχνασία αὐτό. Ross opts to
follow Bywater in printing ᾗ for ἡ at 1048[b]19, while Jaeger brackets

---

[92] Both Ross and Jaeger cite Bonitz as proposing ἐκείνῃ ᾖ (misprinted in Jaeger's
apparatus as ἐκείνη ᾖ). True enough for Bonitz's apparatus, but in the commentary
ad loc. he prints ἐκείνη ἐν ᾖ.

[93] Ross's apparatus does in fact report 'ἐκείνῃ codd.', and Jaeger probably means
to do the same (the iota subscript in his apparatus has mistakenly migrated to
the immediately preceding ἐκείνη), but this has to be (correct) inference from the
grammar of ἐνυπάρχει, not autopsy, for no subscript is visible in A[b]. Christ, pp. vii–
viii, reports that E is punctilious in writing iota subscript, whereas A[b] hardly bothers.
Brockmann's collation of the Passage in M and C (Appendix 1 below) found no iota
subscript in either.

[94] Similarly Brague, *Monde*, 459, on both text and meaning.

[95] Which Schwegler, ii. 155 (cf. iv. 383), equates with τὸ τέλος: 'so ist die Magerkeit
Zweck des sich Abmagerns'. A similar rendering in A. Lasson, *Aristoteles: Metaphysik*, ins Deutsche übertragen (Jena, 1907), who would print οἷον τοῦ ἰσχναίνειν ἡ
ἰσχνασία, αὐτὸ δε ὅταν . . . (p. xv).

ἡ ἰσχνασία as a reader's gloss on τὸ ἰσχναίνειν. Restoring αὐτό, as I propose to do, makes it essential to delete the two preceding words. Let me explain why.

Plato frequently couples the neuter αὐτό with a feminine or masculine noun, and not just in contexts involving the Theory of Forms. At *Rep.* 363 A Adeimantus complains that the poets do not praise δικαιοσύνην αὐτό, but the consequences of a reputation for it; he does not mean they fail to praise the Platonic Form of Justice. At *Sym.* 199 D a question about αὐτὸ τοῦτο πατέρα is a question about a father—any father—in so far as he is a father.[96] But the only Aristotelian examples of this usage recorded in Bonitz's *Index Aristotelicus* s.v. αὐτό are references to Platonic Forms. My *TLG* search through the corpus under αὐτό, αὐτοῦ, αὐτῷ confirmed his finding: several thousand examples, but the only relevant ones are semi-quotes from Plato. On the other hand, it is Aristotelian usage to couple αὐτό with article plus infinitive:

GA 5. 8, 789ᵃ4–6: Suckling as such [τὸ θηλάζειν αὐτό] contributes nothing to the growth of teeth.
NE 9. 11, 1171ᵃ35–ᵇ1: The very act of seeing one's friends is pleasant [αὐτὸ . . . τὸ ὁρᾶν τοὺς φίλους ἡδύ].
EE 7. 12, 1244ᵇ29–30: If one were to cut off and abstract mere knowledge and its opposite [εἰ . . . τις ἀποτέμοι καὶ ποιήσειε τὸ γινώσκειν αὐτὸ καθ᾽ αὑτὸ καὶ μή].
Pol. 8. 3, 1338ᵃ1–3: Leisure of itself [τὸ σχολάζειν . . . αὐτό] is thought to give pleasure and happiness and a blessed life.

I conclude that the phrase τὸ ἰσχναίνειν αὐτό is well chosen to concentrate our minds on the slimming process as such, excluding its end and completion.

If this is accepted, ἡ ἰσχνασία becomes a reader's gloss—a correct gloss guided by ἰσχνασία at 1048ᵇ29—not, as Jaeger supposed, on τὸ ἰσχναίνειν, but on the full phrase τὸ ἰσχναίνειν αὐτό. Without much preceding context to clarify the point of the phrase, it was understandably found obscure. And once the gloss got copied into the main text between ἰσχναίνειν and αὐτό, the two successive nominatives led a scribe or reader who decided for η as ἡ, not ᾗ or ἥ, to change τὸ to τοῦ.

[96] For a more general discussion, with examples, of the 'abstraction operator' αὐτό in Plato, see M. F. Burnyeat, 'Plato on Why Mathematics is Good for the Soul' ['Mathematics'], in T. Smiley (ed.), *Mathematics and Necessity: Essays in the History of Philosophy* (Proceedings of the British Academy, 103; Oxford, 2000), 1–81 at 35–7.

So much for the square brackets. Doug Hutchinson has urged in correspondence that two pairs of angled brackets could go as well if we adopt Fonseca's emendation of 1048ᵇ23: ὁρᾷ ἅμα καὶ ἑώρακε καὶ νοεῖ καὶ νενόηκεν.⁹⁷ Reducing Bonitz's three verb pairs to two leaves a neat parallel with the pairs of contrasting pairs that follow in lines 24–6. I am mildly favourable to this idea.

Someone may say I have now cut the ground from under my feet, in that, if Version B is accepted, and Fonseca's restoration of 1048ᵇ23 preferred to Bonitz's, the Passage is no longer so corrupt as it was when I argued from its extreme textual disrepair to the marginal annotation hypothesis (pp. 240–1 above). Certainly, it is less corrupt. But removing a quantity of brackets leaves plenty of emending still to do. Bonitz's emendation ἅμα for ἄλλα at lines 23 and 25 must certainly stand; in the manuscripts only lines 30 and 33 have ἅμα. Whatever the fate of φρονεῖ in line 23, we must supply ἑώρακε to twin with ὁρᾷ. Bonitz's ⟨δεῖ⟩ after δή at 1048ᵇ28 is extremely plausible too, rather more so than Schwegler's λέγω/λέγομεν—unless it is thought sufficient to follow Brague in attributing imperatival force to the bare infinitive λέγειν.⁹⁸ Then there is Bywater's crucially important τό for τοῦ at 1048ᵇ19, not to mention the iota subscript for ἐκείνῃ at 1048ᵇ22. Further doubts, worries, and improvements are recorded in the apparatus of Ross and Jaeger, but not endorsed by them.⁹⁹ The Passage is still a highly damaged stretch of the *Metaphysics*.

---

⁹⁷ Petrus da Fonseca, *Commentaria in Metaphysicorum Aristotelis Stagiritae libros* (4 vols.; Cologne, 1615–29 [1st edn. of Θ: 1604]), ad loc. Fonseca does not explain how he arrives at this proposal, but Hutchinson's suggestion is that 1048ᵇ23's φρονεῖ originated when the ἑώρακε needed after ὁρᾷ got corrupted into φρονε and was later 'corrected' into φρονεῖ. Alternatively, φρονεῖ might have originated as a gloss on νοεῖ.

⁹⁸ Brague, *Monde*, 456 n. 9. While Plato quite often uses the infinitive that way, Bonitz, *Index*, 343ᵃ22–5, cites for such usage only the inauthentic *Rhet. ad Alex.* 23, 1434ᵇ18–19. Yet then he proceeds to a row of impeccably Aristotelian infinitives which have, he says, the force of a verbal noun in -τέον. Nearly all are from logical works, which will be relevant in sect. 14 below. A striking example, given the subject-matter of this paper, is *Top.* 6. 8, 146ᵇ13–16: σκοπεῖν δὲ καὶ εἰ γένεσίς ἐστι πρὸς ὃ ἀποδέδωκεν, ἢ ἐνέργεια· οὐδὲν γὰρ τῶν τοιούτων τέλος· μᾶλλον γὰρ τὸ ἐνηργηκέναι καὶ γεγενῆσθαι τέλος ἢ τὸ γίνεσθαι καὶ ἐνεργεῖν.

⁹⁹ Although Jaeger speaks *in propria persona* when his apparatus says that the sentence ἀλλ' οὐ μανθάνει . . . ὑγίασται at 1048ᵇ24–5 belongs after εὐδαιμόνηκεν in line 26.

PART IV: UNIQUENESS

11. Let me now return to Ross and his confidence that the Passage 'contains sound Aristotelian doctrine *and terminology*' (p. 228 above). Ross offers no proof of this assertion, but he always had Bonitz's commentary in front of him as he wrote, and Bonitz does offer proof. He lists parallels in other works from which, he claims, the Passage 'cum placitis Aristotelicis optime concinere . . . apparet'. I shall take his proof texts one by one, to show that, while each features some element also found in the Passage, none of them contains everything we find there. Most importantly, none of them contains or requires the *terminological* distinction between κίνησις and ἐνέργεια. Nor, to be fair, does Bonitz, unlike Ross, assert that they do.

What is at stake in this section of the enquiry is whether the distinction drawn in the Passage between κίνησις and ἐνέργεια occurs anywhere else in the corpus. If, as I shall argue, it does not, scholars should stop treating it as a central theme of Aristotle's philosophy and stop importing it into their exposition of his other works. It is a unique, problematic intrusion into the text of the *Metaphysics*.

(*a*) We begin with one of Aristotle's logical treatises. *SE* 22 is a study of a type of fallacy which depends on the fact that linguistically similar expressions can stand for categorially different things. The example I am interested in is developed at 178ᵃ9–28. You are asked, 'Is it possible to act and to have acted on the same thing at the same time [ἆρ' ἐνδέχεται τὸ αὐτὸ ἅμα ποιεῖν τε καὶ πεποιηκέναι]?'[100] 'No.' 'But it is possible surely to see and to have seen the same thing at the same time and in the same respect/at the same angle [ἀλλὰ

---

[100] W. A. Pickard-Cambridge, *The Works of Aristotle Translated into English*, i. Topica *and* De sophisticis elenchis (Oxford, 1928), writes, 'Is it possible to be doing and to have done the same thing at the same time?', which makes τὸ αὐτό an internal accusative. But the follow-up question demands that it be an external accusative, as does the solution in terms of categories. Of course, the ambiguity of ποιεῖν can give rise to fallacy (Plato, *Euthd.* 284 B–C), but that is not the sort of fallacy Aristotle wants to illustrate here. E. Poste, *Aristotle on Fallacies or the* Sophistici Elenchi, with a translation and notes (London, 1866), translates, 'Can we be making and have made one and the same thing?' (similarly Ackrill, 'Distinction', 123, and L.-A. Dorion's French translation: *Les Réfutations sophistiques*, introduction, traduction et commentaire (Paris, 1995)), but no one would be tempted to class seeing something as a case of making something, whereas Platonic accounts of vision do involve the perceiver's acting on the object: *Theaet.* 153 E–154 A; *Tim.* 45 B–D.

μὴν ὁρᾶν γέ τι ἅμα καὶ ἑωρακέναι τὸ αὐτὸ καὶ κατὰ ταὐτὸ ἐνδέχεται].'[101]
You can accept that, without being refuted, provided you insist that seeing belongs in the category of undergoing (πάσχειν), not the category of action (ποιεῖν).

Now this is about the *possibility* of seeing and having seen, not about the *necessary* conjoint truth of present and perfect, but it is still interesting that the argument under discussion presupposes respondents who will find themselves inclined both to answer 'No' to the opening question and to accept the apparent counter-example. Despite the linguistic similarity between the verbs ποιεῖν and ὁρᾶν, there is a difference to which a native speaker of Greek will be sensitive, even though it may take a sophism to jolt them into thinking about it and a philosopher to provide a theory of categories which can explain it.

Aristotle provides the theory, but he writes in terms which suggest that anyone might propound the sophism in an attempt to trick their opponent.[102] The scenario envisaged is a dialectical exchange. He treats the simultaneity of seeing and having seen as a commonplace of dialectical debate, not his own discovery.[103]

(*b*) In *De sensu* 6, 446[b]2–6, Aristotle comes closer to asserting the necessary conjoint truth of present and perfect for verbs of perception:

Now, even though it is always the case that at the same time one hears a thing and has heard it,[104] and in general perceives and has perceived,

[101] 'At the same angle' is a nice suggestion by Brague, *Monde*, 462.

[102] Michael of Ephesus [alias Pseudo-Alexander], *In SE* 149. 29 Wallies, is explicit that it is sophists who put the questions. V. Goldschmidt, *Temps physique et temps tragique chez Aristote: commentaire sur le quatrième livre de la Physique (10–14) et sur la Poétique* ['Goldschmidt'] (Paris, 1982), 172, agrees.

[103] Brague, *Monde*, 462–3, agrees, as does Graham, 121. If the point is indeed a commonplace, we can reject outright the claim of A. Rijksbaron, *Aristotle, Verb Meaning and Functional Grammar: Towards a New Typology of States of Affairs*, with an appendix on Aristotle's distinction between *kinesis* and *energeia* (Amsterdam, 1989), 45, that it 'cannot possibly be seen as reflecting actual Greek usage', in which ἑώρακε always involves a past reference. Of course ἑώρακε does often have past reference (Plato, *Soph.* 239 E 1, is a nice example signalled to me by Lesley Brown), but Chantraine's message is that the perfect evolved over time with successive forms continuing to coexist.

[104] ἅπαν can be taken either as the subject of the verbs (Ackrill, 'Distinction') or as their object. I prefer the latter, in line with n. 100 above. But either way, a universal generalization results, which can equally well be conveyed by the 'always' I have borrowed from Barnes's revision of the Oxford translation. As for καὶ εἰ, it suits the context well to take it as 'even though', introducing an admitted fact: Denniston, 301–2.

and they [perceptions] involve no becoming, but exist [sc. when they do] without undergoing a process of coming to be, nevertheless, just as, when the blow has been struck, the sound is not yet at the ear . . .

There is little point to this (incomplete) sentence unless Aristotle wants to affirm the antecedent of its opening conditional 'even though . . . nevertheless . . .'. The antecedent presents a 'logical' truth which might seem hard to reconcile with the evident physical truth that sound and smell take time to travel to the perceiver. It was the quantifier 'always' that Ackrill adduced as evidence that in this text, and so also in the Passage, the form 'at the same time *p* and *q*' is meant to indicate an inference from *p* to *q*, not just a conjunction.[105] I agree, but add that the quantifier serves even better as evidence for an inference going both ways at once.

(*c*) We now move fully into physics. At *Phys.* 3. 2, 201ᵇ31–3, we find this:

ἥ τε κίνησις ἐνέργεια μὲν εἶναί τις δοκεῖ, ἀτελὴς δέ· αἴτιον δ' ὅτι ἀτελὲς τὸ δυνατόν, οὗ ἐστιν ἐνέργεια.

Change is thought to be a sort of actuality, but an incomplete one; the explanation is that the potential thing whose actuality it is is incomplete.

The thesis that change is a sort of actuality, but an incomplete one, is no passing remark. It is part of Aristotle's definition of change, which has a foundational role in his physics. In the wider argumentative context of *Physics* 3. 2, to deny that change is incomplete actuality would be to reduce it to not-being, the status the Platonists assign it. In effect, Aristotelian physics, which is the study of things with an internal principle of change and stability, would have no real subject-matter to investigate.[106] The thesis that change is incomplete actuality reappears in *DA* 2. 5, 417ᵃ16–17, this time without the qualification 'is thought to be' and with a back-reference to *Physics* 3. 1–3 as the place where the thesis was explained (καὶ γὰρ ἔστιν ἡ κίνησις ἐνέργειά τις, ἀτελὴς μέντοι, καθάπερ ἐν ἑτέροις εἴρηται). Another comparable text is *DA* 3. 7, 431ᵃ6–7:

---

[105] Ackrill, 'Distinction', 124, except that in his translation the quantifier is 'everything' taken as subject of the verbs: 'everything at the same time hears and has heard'.

[106] This is one of the places where Frede, 'Potentiality', is especially relevant to my discussion.

ἡ γὰρ κίνησις τοῦ ἀτελοῦς ἐνέργεια,[107] ἡ δ' ἁπλῶς ἐνέργεια ἑτέρα, ἡ τοῦ τετελεσμένου.

For change is the actuality of the incomplete; actuality unqualified, the actuality of what is complete, is different.

Here Aristotle makes explicit what the other two physical texts imply, that incomplete actuality contrasts with another sort of actuality: actuality unqualified, actuality *simpliciter*, or, as he might equally well have said, complete actuality.

But this is still not the doctrine of the Passage. ἐνέργεια still contrasts with potentiality (as it does in the rest of *Metaphysics* Θ), not with κίνησις. On the contrary, κίνησις is explained as ἐνέργεια: ἐνέργεια which is incomplete. I conclude that the original home of the Passage was not a physical treatise. For its exclusive distinction between κίνησις and ἐνέργεια runs counter to a foundational thesis of Aristotelian physics. In the Passage being a κίνησις entails not being ἐνέργεια at all.

12. To say this is not to deny the Aristotelian provenance of the distinction. The Passage shows how easy it is to pass from '*x* is only qualifiedly *F*' to '*x* is not *F* at all, but something else'. Thus, by way of preparing for its terminological innovation, the Passage says that actions (πράξεις) which are not their own end *either* do not count as action, *or* at any rate they are not complete action (1048ᵇ21–2: οὐκ ἔστι ταῦτα πρᾶξις ἢ οὐ τελεία γε). In the sequel the first disjunct is chosen, with ἐνέργεια substituted for πρᾶξις. κινήσεις, because they are incomplete, are not ἐνέργειαι at all. It is the second disjunct that prevails in the physical treatises. Yes, κινήσεις are ἐνέργειαι, subject to the qualification that they are incomplete ἐνέργειαι. To motivate the terminological innovation of the Passage, we should look for a (non-physical) context where the first disjunct would be philosophically more appropriate than the second, where there are grounds for saying that a πρᾶξις or ἐνέργεια which is not its own end is not πρᾶξις or ἐνέργεια at all.

Which brings me, of course, to the *Nicomachean Ethics* and to Aristotle's critique of the theory put forward in Plato's *Philebus* that pleasure is a process of becoming (γένεσις). *NE* 10. 3–5 is the text most often, and most confidently, cited as parallel for the κίνησις–

---

[107] Some editors add C's ἦν here.

ἐνέργεια distinction in the Passage.[108] Before tackling it, it will be helpful to review our findings so far.

Go back to *Metaph.* Θ 6, 1048^{b}8–9: τὰ μὲν γὰρ ὡς κίνησις πρὸς δύναμιν, τὰ δ' ὡς οὐσία πρός τινα ὕλην ('some are related as change to capacity, while others are related as substance to some matter'). In his note ad loc. Ross writes:

> At one time Aristotle includes ἐνέργεια in κίνησις (*Rhet.* 1412a 9); at another he includes κίνησις in ἐνέργεια (*Phys.* 201b 31, *De An.* 431a 6, *E.N.* 1154b 27); at another he speaks of the two as mutually exclusive (1048b 28). κίνησις is said to be an ἐνέργεια but ἀτελής (*Phys.* 201b 31), or to differ from ἐνέργεια because it is ἀτελής (1048b 29). The variations of language need not disturb us. κίνησις and ἐνέργεια are species of something wider for which Aristotle has no name, and for which he uses now the name of one species, now that of the other. The difference is brought out as well in ll. 18–35 [i.e. the Passage] as anywhere in Aristotle.[109]

It is correct that both κίνησις and ἐνέργεια have what one may call a generic use; in Section 1 above we noted generic κίνησις in Θ 6, generic ἐνέργεια in Θ 8. It is correct also that κίνησις has a specific use for processes directed towards an end-state external to themselves, as laid down in *Physics* 3. 1–3. Such variety should not surprise. κίνησις and its parent verb had already had a long history in ordinary Greek. But ἐνέργεια and the associated verb ἐνεργεῖν are first attested in Aristotle himself. Probably his invention, they start off as terms of art.[110] Furthermore, while it is correct—I emphasized the point earlier (above, p. 222)—that at Θ 6, 1048^{b}8–9, κίνησις is generic in that it covers both building and seeing, nowhere does Aristotle expressly divide κινήσεις into those which are their own goal and those that aim at a further product. He does so divide ἐνέργεια, as in *NE* 1. 1, 1094^{a}16–17, and in Θ 8 as quoted above, but the nearest he gets to a parallel division of κίνησις is *NE* 10. 3, 1174^{b}4: '*Most* κινήσεις are incomplete' (αἱ πολλαὶ ἀτελεῖς). Nor does he ever ack-

---

[108] In dealing with book 10 I have been helped by testing discussion with David Charles.

[109] Quoted with approval by Smeets, 108 n. 37, Goldschmidt, 176, and Linguiti, 59 n. 149. Contrast J. B. Skemp, 'The Activity of Immobility', in Aubenque (ed.), *Études*, 229–45 at 244: 'we are all dissatisfied with the complacent remark of Ross in his note on *Metaph.*, 1048^{b}8 that "the variations of language need not disturb us"'.

[110] At *NE* 7. 12, 1153^{a}15–17, the persons who wrongly think that ἐνέργεια is γένεσις are clearly philosophers. On Aristotelian word formation, K. Von Fritz, *Philosophie und sprachlicher Ausdruck bei Demokrit, Plato und Aristoteles* (New York, Leipzig, Paris, and London 1938; repr. Darmstadt, 1966), esp. 66–9 on ἐνέργεια and ἐντελέχεια, is most interesting.

nowledge the idea of κίνησις unqualified, or complete κίνησις.[111] In the philosophical language of the time that would sound bizarre.[112]

I conclude that the generic uses of κίνησις and ἐνέργεια are not on a par. They should not be regarded as alternative extensions to the generic level of the terminology for two parallel species. Ross's account is not only too simple. He goes wrong at the start by making the Passage his point of departure. The Passage is the only text he cites—I have been arguing it is the only text he can cite—for κίνησις and ἐνέργεια as parallel species of a wider but nameless genus.[113] But even here he ignores two important facts. First, in the Passage the genus does have a name: πρᾶξις. Second, its subdivision into κινήσεις and ἐνέργειαι is presented as a terminological innovation. Ross's procedure is methodologically back to front.

The truth is that, when Aristotle says in *DA* 2. 5 that κίνησις is ἐνέργειά τις, ἀτελὴς μέντοι ('change is a sort of actuality, but an incomplete one'), he is not locating specific κίνησις in a wider class. 'Change is a sort of actuality' does not mean 'Change is one species of actuality alongside others', but 'Change is an actuality of a sort, not a mere nothing'. Aristotle is reminding us of how in *Physics* 3. 1–3 he rescued κίνησις from the oblivion of unreality and not-being to which the Platonists would consign it. The τις in ἐνέργειά τις has an *alienans* function. The difference between ἡ ἁπλῶς ἐνέργεια and ἐνέργειά ἀτελής is not the difference between two species of a genus (like the ἐνεργείας διαφερούσας τῷ εἴδει at *NE* 10. 5, 1175ᵃ25–6), but the difference between an ἐνέργεια in the full sense of the term and one from which you cannot expect everything you would normally expect from an ἐνέργεια.[114]

Thus the relation of specific κίνησις to generic ἐνέργεια is not a species–genus relation like that of deer to animal. Only in the Passage do κίνησις and ἐνέργεια appear as parallel species of a common genus, πρᾶξις. That requires a change in the meaning of the term ἐνέργεια, such that being an ἐνέργεια entails not being a κίνησις, which

---

[111] The phrase κίνησιν τελείαν at *NE* 10. 3, 1174ᵃ28, denotes a thing you cannot find at any time prior to arrival at the (external) goal: a comple*ted* change rather than one that is intrinsically comple*te*.

[112] Contrast Proclus, much later, on τελεία κίνησις at *In Parm.* 797. 32–8 Cousin. Ross's use of the phrase in his note on *Metaph.* Θ 6, 1048ᵇ18–21, is illicit.

[113] Similarly, in his *Physics* commentary (W. D. Ross, *Aristotle's* Physics*: A Revised Text with Introduction and Commentary* (Oxford, 1936)), ad 201ᵇ31–2, Ross refers to the Passage as a fuller statement of the doctrine of *Physics* 3. 2!

[114] See Appendix 2 for an exemplary ancient explanation of this point by Iamblichus.

is enough to make it the case that, by contraposition, being a κίνησις entails not being (in the new, narrowed sense) an ἐνέργεια. To produce the exclusive contrast between κίνησις and ἐνέργεια there is no need for the term κίνησις to change meaning as well. κίνησις in the Passage keeps to the specific use it has elsewhere, for changes (active or passive) intrinsically directed at an end-state outside themselves. In that case it can still be called ἐνέργειά τις in the *Physics* sense of that phrase. In view of what the Passage does with the generic term πρᾶξις, one might say that κίνησις is now not ἐνέργεια, *because* it is only ἐνέργειά τις in the old sense.

I conclude that what we should look for in the *Nicomachean Ethics* is evidence that the term ἐνέργεια is being used in the exclusive sense of the Passage. Then, provided κίνησις has its standard specific sense, each term will exclude the other.

13. The place to start is Aristotle's report of the *Philebus* account of pleasure:

τέλειόν τι τἀγαθὸν τιθέντες, τὰς δὲ κινήσεις καὶ τὰς γενέσεις ἀτελεῖς, τὴν ἡδονὴν κίνησιν καὶ γένεσιν ἀποφαίνειν πειρῶνται, οὐ καλῶς δ' ἐοίκασι λέγειν οὐδ' εἶναι κίνησιν. (*NE* 10. 3, 1173ᵃ29–31)

Postulating that the good is something complete, whereas changes and becomings are incomplete, they try to show that pleasure is change and becoming. But they seem to be wrong when they say this. Pleasure seems not to be change at all.

The word Plato used is γένεσις, not κίνησις.[115] γένεσις, not κίνησις, is the word Aristotle himself uses when criticizing the *Philebus* theory in *NE* 7. 12, 1153ᵃ7–17. If the book 10 discussion brings in κίνησις as well, Aristotle must have a purpose in mind. I suggest that the purpose is to translate what Plato means by γένεσις into his own terminology.[116]

After all, γένεσις in Aristotle standardly refers to the coming to be of a new substance, in contrast to the alteration, growth, or spatial movement of an existing substance. The *Philebus* announces a compendious, exclusive dichotomy between γένεσις and οὐσία, where γένεσις covers, not only the building of ships (54 B), but also

---

[115] So far as I know, the only place where Plato uses κίνησις of pleasure and pain themselves is *Rep.* 583 E 9–10, where the point is to contrast them with the ἡσυχία of the intermediate state in which one feels neither pleasure nor pain.

[116] Cf. *Top.* 6. 8, 146ᵇ13–19, a curious passage where γένεσις is glossed by ἐνέργεια (broad sense).

the body's being restored to its natural state by food and drink (54 E). When Aristotle needs a compendious noun to cover all types of change, he chooses κίνησις or μεταβολή.[117] So what more natural than to gloss Platonic γένεσις as Aristotelian κίνησις? In its standard specific sense κίνησις is directed towards an end-state outside itself, and this fits the *Philebus* characterization of γένεσις as always 'for the sake of' the οὐσία that results.

Problem: the *Philebus* understands 'for the sake of' in an *exclusively* instrumental sense. Goodness is confined to the οὐσία for the sake of which any particular γένεσις occurs (54 C–D). Then, if pleasure is γένεσις, it is altogether excluded from the class of things that are good. If Aristotelian κίνησις does duty for Platonic γένεσις, it too must be completely severed from the class of things that are good. This is not Aristotle's normal view: the text from *Metaphysics* Θ 8 quoted earlier (p. 223) has it that the exercise of a capacity to build is *more* of an end than the capacity, although it is less of an end than the ultimate thing, the resulting house (1050ᵃ23–8).[118] In the *Philebus* the activity of shipbuilding is not an end at all, because it is *entirely* for the sake of the resulting ship.

To see how this could lead to an exclusive contrast between κίνησις and ἐνέργεια, as in the Passage, turn to the other place where the *Philebus* account of pleasure comes under fire, *Nicomachean Ethics* 7. 12:[119]

ἔτι οὐκ ἀνάγκη ἕτερόν τι εἶναι βέλτιον τῆς ἡδονῆς ὥσπερ τινές φασι τὸ τέλος τῆς γενέσεως· οὐ γὰρ γενέσεις εἰσὶν οὐδὲ μετὰ γενέσεως πᾶσαι, ἀλλ' ἐνέργειαι καὶ τέλος. οὐδὲ γινομένων συμβαίνουσιν, ἀλλὰ χρωμένων· καὶ τέλος οὐ πασῶν ἕτερόν τι, ἀλλὰ τῶν εἰς τὴν τελέωσιν ἀγομένων τῆς φύσεως.

Again, it is not necessary that there should be something else better than pleasure, as some say the end is something better than becoming; for pleasures are not in fact becomings, nor even do they all accompany some becoming. *On the contrary, they are actualities and themselves each an end.* Nor do they occur when we are becoming something, but when we are exercising a capacity already possessed. And not all have an end distinct from themselves, only the pleasures of people who are being led to the perfection of their nature. (1153ᵃ7–12)

---

[117] *Cat.* 14; *Phys.* 3. 1, 200ᵇ33–201ᵃ9; 5. 1, 224ᵇ35–225ᵃ20; and n. 10 above. But for a strikingly compendious use of the verb γίγνεσθαι, see *Metaph. Z* 7, 1032ᵃ13–15.

[118] Cf. ὧν κίνησις τὸ τέλος at 1050ᵃ17 and the comparative formulation at *NE* 1. 1, 1094ᵃ5–6. Remember that, besides producing a house, the exercise of the builder's art helps to preserve it for future use (*DA* 2. 5, 417ᵇ3–5).

[119] In studying which I have been greatly helped by discussion with Christof Rapp.

The last sentence quoted is proof that ἐνέργεια in this text does not have the exclusive sense of the Passage. It speaks of pleasurable ἐνέργειαι directed towards a further, external goal, the perfecting of our nature: these will be, or at least they will include, the pleasures of learning in theoretical, ethical, or practical domains (cf. *Phys.* 7. 3, 246ᵃ12–ᵇ3, 247ᵃ2–3). The pleasures of learning are expressly mentioned at 1153ᵃ22–3; the pleasures of κινήσεις more generally feature in the next chapter, alongside those of ἕξεις, at 1154ᵃ13–15. In *Physics* 3. 1–3 learning was both κίνησις and thereby ἀτελὴς ἐνέργεια, and so it must be here if, however delightful in itself, it is an ἐνέργεια in pursuit of an external goal. But in the Passage learning is a paradigm example of κίνησις as *opposed* to ἐνέργεια. QED. More on the pleasures of learning and progress below.

Meanwhile, pursuing his polemic with Plato Aristotle here puts γένεσις and ἐνέργεια in exclusive contrast, as again at 1153ᵃ15–17, although the penultimate sentence in the quotation just given (οὐδέ . . . χρωμένων) implies that ἐνέργεια retains its standard contrast with δύναμις or ἕξις (cf. 1153ᵃ24–5). Still, once γένεσις is glossed as κίνησις, which does not happen in the book 7 discussion, we might expect a corresponding exclusive contrast between κίνησις and ἐνέργεια.

Many scholars find that expectation fulfilled in book 10, where γένεσις is indeed glossed as κίνησις (10. 3, quoted above; cf. 4, 1174ᵇ10 and 13) in the initial statement of the *Philebus* theory.[120] But so far as I can see, the critique that follows nowhere forces us to abandon Aristotle's usual understanding of κίνησις and ἐνέργεια. He does not take up the opportunity to make ἐνέργεια incompatible with κίνησις. Let me track through the arguments one by one.

(*a*) 10. 3, 1173ᵃ32–ᵇ4: It is a feature of all κίνησις that it can be qualified by the adverbs 'quickly' and 'slowly'. We can walk quickly or slowly, but we cannot enjoy something quickly or slowly. True enough, and an effective argument against the *Philebus* account of pleasure as κίνησις. But since the term ἐνέργεια does not occur, the argument cannot help our enquiry.

The next argument (1173ᵇ4–7) is couched in terms of γένεσις, not κίνησις. In the string of arguments that rounds off the chapter

---

[120] Ackrill, 'Distinction', set the pattern and many followed suit. A rare sign of caution is D. Bostock, 'Pleasure and Activity in Aristotle's Ethics' ['Bostock'], *Phronesis*, 33 (1988), 251–72 at 260–1: *NE* 10 argues 'at least roughly' along the same lines of thought as the Passage.

γένεσις comes up once more (1173ᵇ19), κίνησις not at all. κίνησις does not return until 10. 4.

(b) 10. 4, 1174ᵃ14–ᵇ14: all κίνησις takes time to reach its form and completion, whereas pleasure, like seeing, is complete at any moment. Aristotle does not say that κίνησις is incomplete ἐνέργεια, but he insists that it is incomplete (1174ᵃ22, 27–8, ᵇ4), and he refers us elsewhere for an accurate, scientific account of κίνησις (1174ᵇ2–3). If, as some think, the reference is to *Physics* 5. 1–4, note this remark at 5. 1, 224ᵇ10: 'We have defined κίνησις previously', which presupposes 3. 1–3. So the term κίνησις retains its standard specific sense, as defined in those crucial chapters. Other scholars (beginning with Michael of Ephesus, *In EN* 10. 4, 552. 17 Heylbut) suppose the reference is to *Physics* 6–8, but this changes nothing since 8. 1, 251ᵃ8–10, also draws on 3. 1–3. As for ἐνέργεια, it simply does not occur in the lines we are discussing. Once more, the enquiry draws a blank.

Some may protest that even if the word ἐνέργεια does not occur, Aristotle is presupposing the narrow use defined in the Passage when he contrasts the idea that pleasure is κίνησις or γένεσις with his own view that it is a whole and wholly present at every instant (1174ᵃ17–19, ᵇ9).[121] I reply that what this contrast shows is that Aristotle can make his point in other words, without calling on the term ἐνέργεια in either the broad or the narrow sense. To say that pleasure does not require a stretch of time, because it is a complete whole in the present now, is enough to refute the claim that pleasure is γένεσις or κίνησις, which do require a stretch of time, but it does not impose the narrow meaning of the Passage on the word ἐνέργεια for the simple reason (to repeat) that that word is neither used nor mentioned.

(c) 10. 4, 1174ᵇ14–17, launching Aristotle's own account of pleasure, does use ἐνέργεια, but qualifies it as τελεία, which would be redundant if the term had the narrow sense defined in the Passage:

αἰσθήσεως δὲ πάσης πρὸς τὸ αἰσθητὸν ἐνεργούσης, τελείως δὲ τῆς εὖ διακειμένης πρὸς τὸ κάλλιστον τῶν ὑπὸ τὴν αἴσθησιν (τοιοῦτον γὰρ μάλιστ᾽ εἶναι δοκεῖ ἡ τελεία ἐνέργεια . . .) . . .

Since every sense is active in relation to its object, and a sense which is

---

[121] Liske, after acknowledging (p. 161) that the Passage is the sole explicit presentation of the distinction, goes on to describe *NE* 10. 4 as the text where 'Aristoteles die κίνησις–ἐνέργεια-Unterscheidung *zwar nicht explizit* thematisiert, aber doch eine genauste Charakterisierung von ihr gibt, die sich in seinem Werk findet' (p. 166).

in good condition acts completely in relation to the most beautiful of its objects (for complete activity seems to be especially of this nature . . .) . . . (trans. Ross–Urmson)

Even those like myself who would prefer to translate τελεία ἐνέργεια here as 'perfect activity' should acknowledge that Aristotle begins in a way which positively discourages taking ἐνέργεια in the narrow meaning of the Passage. Compare τελειοτάτη ἐνέργεια at 1074ᵇ20 and 22.

(*d*) From 10. 4, 1174ᵇ14, to the end of 10. 5 Aristotle expounds his own theory that pleasure completes an ἐνέργεια as a supervenient end. Since he states that there is no pleasure without ἐνέργεια (1175ᵃ20–1), it is not surprising that the words ἐνέργεια and ἐνεργεῖν occur again and again. The main examples often remind scholars of the Passage: perceiving, thinking, contemplating, living.[122] But there is nothing to show that ἐνέργεια is being used in the exclusive sense defined in the Passage, and at least one of Aristotle's examples should give us pause. This is 10. 5, 1175ᵃ30–5:

The pleasure proper to a given ἐνέργεια helps it forward. For those who enjoy that ἐνέργεια do it with more discernment and with greater accuracy. Thus those who are fond of geometry become proficient in it, and grasp its problems better, and similarly those who are fond of music *or of building* or of other arts make progress towards their proper function [ἐπιδιδόασιν εἰς τὸ οἰκεῖον ἔργον], because they enjoy it.[123]

Building, as we have seen, is a standard example of incomplete ἐνέργεια. What are these lovers of building (φιλοικοδόμοι) doing here if Aristotle means to confine ἐνέργεια to the restrictive meaning

---

[122] So, influentially, Ackrill, 'Distinction', 128: 'Aristotle does not say that he is here talking of the distinction between energeiai and kineseis. But he likens pleasure or enjoyment (ἡδονή) to seeing, and contrasts both with kineseis, using as examples of kineseis house-building and walking—which were also used as examples of kineseis in the *Metaphysics* passage. Both the choice of examples and the general account of the contrast leave no doubt that it *is* the energeia–kinesis distinction that he is using.' As if building and (if not walking) rolling and jumping were not both κινήσεις and ἀτελεῖς ἐνέργειαι in the *Physics* (3. 1, 201ᵃ16–19; ᵇ8–13). As if Θ 8 (quoted above) does not contrast seeing with building while counting both as ἐνέργειαι. Only Croese, 122 n. 3, has the grace to say that she accepts Ackrill's conclusion because 'To our knowledge this claim has not been questioned.' Others just follow suit, although I. M. Crombie, in his review of Bambrough (ed.), *New Essays*, in *Classical Review*, NS 17 (1967), 30–3 at 32, was an early dissenting voice, spot on: '[Ackrill] says that Aristotle "classifies enjoying on the energeia side of the energeia–kinesis distinction". But what Aristotle says is simply that enjoying is not a κίνησις.'

[123] Translation indebted to H. Rackham, *Aristotle: The Nicomachean Ethics*, with an English translation, 2nd edn. (London and Cambridge, Mass., 1934).

of the Passage?[124] Sophisticated answers have been offered, to the
effect that a κίνησις such as building may be looked upon as an
ἐνέργεια in so far as at each and every moment the builder can be
said to exercise, and to have exercised, the art of building.[125] But
in the absence of any positive indication that in book 10 ἐνέργεια
and κίνησις exclude each other, it seems better to suppose they do
not.[126] We then have to admit that the Passage is the sole place
in the corpus where Aristotle's now famous distinction between
κίνησις and ἐνέργεια can be found.

And it is not just lovers of building who make difficulty for the
view I am opposing. All the people in this text are learners. The
ἐνέργεια helped forward by their keen enjoyment is that of learning
some knowledge or skill, not the exercise of finished expertise.
Certainly one learns to build by building, though not in the fully
skilled way a qualified craftsman does. But this is a point made in
Metaph. Θ 8, 1049^{b}29–1050^{a}3, in the very chapter I quoted earlier
to illustrate the generic use of ἐνέργεια, which covers both seeing
and building. There Aristotle suggests that a practising apprentice
must at each stage have acquired, and be exercising, some part of the
body of knowledge (1050^{a}1: τι τῆς ἐπιστήμης) they are learning. So
we have two options for what it is that the lovers of building enjoy. It
is either (i) the (active) exercise of partial productive knowledge or
(ii) the (passive) process of acquiring more and more of the full body
of knowledge. The two are compatible, even extensionally the same,
and could each be highly enjoyable. Both are intrinsically directed
towards a product or end-state outside themselves. According to
Θ 8, (i) is an ἐνέργεια directed at a further product; according to
Physics 3. 1–3, (ii) is an incomplete ἐνέργεια. The Passage would say

---

[124] Another example most naturally taken as incomplete is writing (10. 5, 1175^b
19).

[125] G. E. L. Owen, 'Aristotelian Pleasures' ['Owen'], *Proceedings of the Aristotelian
Society*, 72 (1971–2), 135–52 at 143 (repr. with the original pagination in J. Barnes,
M. Schofield, and R. Sorabji (eds.), *Articles on Aristotle*, ii. *Ethics and Politics*
(London, 1977), 92–103; and again, with the original pagination, in G. E. L. Owen,
Logic, Science and Dialectic (London, 1986), 334–46); L. A. Kosman, 'Aristotle's
Definition of Motion' ['Motion'], *Phronesis*, 14 (1969), 40–62 at nn. 21 and 32 (cf.
Waterlow, 186–9); M.-L. Gill, 'Aristotle's Theory of Causal Action in *Physics* III 3',
Phronesis, 25 (1980), 129–47 at 136; Liske, 176–8. J. C. B. Gosling and C. C. W.
Taylor, *The Greeks on Pleasure* (Oxford, 1982), 312–14, is to my mind a crushing
critique of this solution.

[126] Owen, 147 and 150, agrees, while being equally confident (cf. 139) that in
book 7 (which Ackrill, 'Distinction', does not discuss) ἐνέργεια *does* carry the exclusive sense of the Passage; Owen's book 7 claim was refuted earlier, p. 267.

that both are κίνησις, not ἐνέργεια at all. But nothing in *Nicomachean Ethics* 10. 5 requires, or even hints, that we should understand ἐνέργεια in the exclusive sense of the Passage. Nothing requires, or even hints, that we should understand Aristotle's theory of pleasure to exclude the possibility of enjoying those ἐνέργειαι (generic) which are κινήσεις (specific) as well as those which are their own goal.[127] What he insists on is that pleasure is complete at every moment, from which it hardly follows that the activity enjoyed must itself be complete at every moment. Every child knows that making things is fun. A crossword puzzle offers adult pleasures—until you have completed it! Why shouldn't a keen apprentice delight in each and every moment of the process of slowly carving out the flutes of a column? Aristotle is undoubtedly right to say that their enjoyment will hone their skill.

This last point is worth dwelling on. A very good reason to avoid reading the narrow Passage meaning of ἐνέργεια into *NE* 10. 3–5 is that it would saddle the work with a monstrously distorted account of what we can enjoy. It would also make those chapters clash, not only with 7. 12, 1153ᵃ7–12, discussed above, but also with 7. 14, 1154ᵇ26–8:

. . . God always enjoys a single and simple pleasure; for there is not only an activity of movement [κινήσεως ἐνέργεια] but an activity of immobility [ἐνέργεια ἀκινησίας], and pleasure is found *more* in rest than in movement [μᾶλλον ἐν ἠρεμίᾳ ἐστὶν ἢ ἐν κινήσει]. (trans. Ross, emphasis added)

Which surely implies that there *can* be pleasure in κίνησις, even if it is less, or less satisfying, than pleasure in rest or pleasure in action undertaken for its own sake.[128] I propose, therefore, that in 10. 3–5 ἐνέργεια has the same generic meaning as it has in *NE* 1. 1 and *Metaphysics* Θ 8, not the narrowed meaning of the Passage.

(*e*) For confirmation, read on to the end of book 10. Aristotle twice insists that happiness involves ἐνέργειαι from which no further end is sought beside the ἐνέργεια itself (10. 6, 1176ᵃ35–ᵇ7; 7, 1177ᵇ1–26). In both cases the context makes it clear that this is a substantive requirement, not a mere tautological expansion of (in the terminology of the Passage) 'Happiness involves ἐνέργειαι'.

---

[127] Here I agree with Waterlow, 187 n. 19, and Owen, 151, against e.g. Bostock, 260.

[128] Compare Michael of Ephesus, *In EN* 10, 555. 20–9 Heylbut, for the view that τέλειαι ἐνέργειαι are the most pleasurable, but ἀτελεῖς ἐνέργειαι can be pleasurable too.

From beginning to end, *NE* 10 is innocent of the restrictive sense
of ἐνέργεια defined in the Passage.[129]

13. Finally, *DA* 2. 5 again. I have already quoted from it the statement that change is incomplete actuality (417ᵃ16). The chapter
proceeds to make distinctions 'concerning potentiality and actuality' (417ᵃ21: διαιρετέον δὲ καὶ περὶ δυνάμεως καὶ ἐντελεχείας), but
none of the distinctions involves withdrawing the statement that
change is incomplete actuality. The main distinction put before us
is the one that tradition knows as the distinction between first and
second potentiality, a distinction entirely absent from the Passage.
Conversely, throughout *DA* 2. 5 actuality contrasts with δύναμις, not
with κίνησις. Ackrill was right when he denied that the *De anima*
has any truck with the κίνησις–ἐνέργεια distinction as presented in
Metaphysics Θ 6.[130]

None the less, there are two very interesting disjunctions in *DA*
2. 5 which can illuminate the disjunction at Θ 6, 1048ᵇ21, 'either
these are not action [πρᾶξις], or at any rate they are not complete
action'. About the Θ 6 disjunction I said that it would depend on
the context of enquiry which disjunct was appropriate. The same
is true, I believe, of *DA* 2. 5, 417ᵇ6–7, '[the transition to exercising
knowledge] is either not alteration or it is a different kind of alteration', and 417ᵇ13–15, '[learning] is either not to be described
as being affected or there are two kinds of alteration'. In the case
of the transition to exercising knowledge, Aristotle immediately
opts for the first alternative: not alteration at all (417ᵇ8–9). And
this despite the fact that the transition to exercising knowledge
serves him as a model for the transition to perceiving, which he
insists on continuing to call alteration (417ᵇ29–418ᵃ3). Learning,
on the other hand, the acquisition of knowledge as opposed to

---

[129] This blocks an argument to the effect that the account in *Metaph.* Λ 7 and 9
of God's changeless activity of contemplation and its enjoyment 'provides us with
Aristotle's philosophical motivation' for the distinction drawn in the Passage (C.
Kahn, 'On the Intended Interpretation of Aristotle's *Metaphysics*', in J. Wiesner
(ed.), *Aristoteles: Werk und Wirkung* (2 vols.; Berlin and New York, 1985–7), i.
Aristoteles und seine Schule, 311–38 at 333). The claim is premissed on the assumption that *NE* 10 treats both pleasure and contemplation as ἐνέργειαι in the narrow
sense of the Passage. God is indeed changeless, but in Λ as in Θ 8 ἐνέργεια contrasts
with δύναμις, not with κίνησις.

[130] Ackrill, 'Distinction', 140–1, endorsed by M. F. Burnyeat, '*De anima* 2. 5'
['*De anima*'], *Phronesis*, 47 (2002), 1–90 at 49 n. 56. Contrast the free use made of
the Passage for the elucidation of *DA* 2. 5 by Kosman, 'Substance', and others too
many to list.

its use, he continues to treat as a special type of alteration, even while acknowledging the legitimacy of a perspective from which it too is not alteration. I have argued elsewhere[131] that his motive for treating perception and intellectual learning as special types of alteration, different from the alteration by which fire heats the surrounding air, is to keep some (but not all) psychology within the scope of Aristotelian physics, which is defined as the study of things that have an internal principle of change and stability. That enables him to use the analysis of alteration worked out in the *Physics* and *De generatione et corruptione* 1, and now refined in *De anima* 2. 5, to explain the cognitive accuracy of both perception and intellectual learning. If perception and intellectual learning did not fall within Aristotelian physics, this project would abort.

If that is correct, it confirms, I submit, my earlier claim that it cannot have been in a physical context that Aristotle opted to say that change is not actuality at all. The most likely context is ethical, and more specifically a critique of the account of pleasure in Plato's *Philebus*. Earlier it transpired that, contrary to standard expectations, *NE* 7 gets closer to the restrictive language of the Passage than *NE* 10. But book 7 still does not quite make it. That leaves the lost works. We should look for a suitable title in the ancient catalogues of Aristotle's numerous writings.

14. Diogenes Laertius twice lists a one-book work *On Pleasure* (Περὶ ἡδονῆς).[132] The first such title keeps company with a number of Aristotle's dialogues. The Passage is hardly in the polished prose for which the dialogues were known. The second, however, goes with a group of works that one would classify as 'logical': Περὶ ἡδονῆς α΄ or, more probably, Περὶ ἡδονῆς προτάσεις α΄.[133]

Nothing but the title is known of it, yet it is just possible that one fragment survives:

καὶ περὶ ἡδονῆς δ᾿ εἴρηται ποιόν τι καὶ πῶς ἀγαθόν, καὶ ὅτι τά τε ἁπλῶς ἡδέα καὶ καλὰ καὶ τὰ ἁπλῶς ἀγαθὰ ἡδέα. οὐ γίνεται δὲ ἡδονὴ μὴ ἐν πράξει· διὰ τοῦτο ὁ ἀληθῶς εὐδαίμων καὶ ἥδιστα ζήσει, καὶ τοῦτο οὐ μάτην οἱ ἄνθρωποι ἀξιοῦσιν.

Concerning pleasure, too, it has been said what sort of thing it is and how it is a good, and that the things pleasant without qualification are also fine,

---

[131] Burnyeat, '*De anima*'.

[132] D.L. 5. 22 and 24; cf. Hesych. no. 15; Ptolemy el-Garib no. 17.

[133] On text and context I follow P. Moraux, *Les Listes anciennes des ouvrages d'Aristote* ['Moraux'] (Louvain, 1951), 93–5.

and the things good without qualification are pleasant. *But pleasure does not occur except in action*; for that reason, the truly happy man will also live most pleasantly, and it is not vainly that people believe this. (*EE* 8. 3, 1249ᵃ17–21; trans. Woods)

This fragment does not fit into its wider context. It concludes a discussion ('Concerning pleasure, too, it has been said . . .') which is not in fact to be found earlier in the chapter, with the result that we have been given no means of understanding 'for that reason'.[134] But we are clearly in the presence of an Aristotle who in some ethical context wants to connect pleasure, πρᾶξις, and happiness.

Nor is Aristotle alone in having written a monograph *On Pleasure*. So too, apparently, did Speusippus (D.L. 4. 4: one book), Xenocrates (D.L. 4. 12: two books), Heracleides Ponticus (Athen. 512 A), Strato (D.L. 5. 59), and Theophrastus, who is credited (D.L. 5. 44) with one book Περὶ ἡδονῆς ὡς Ἀριστοτέλης (*On Pleasure according to Aristotle* or *On Pleasure in the Style of Aristotle*)[135] plus another entitled simply *On Pleasure*,[136] and—last, but would that we had it!—*On False Pleasure* (D.L. 5. 46: one book). It would seem that the *Philebus*, like Plato's Lecture on the Good, aroused a furore of discussion.

Ethics, however, is not the only branch of philosophy which the Aristotelian scheme of things kept apart from physics. Another is theology or first philosophy. David Sedley has urged me to consider this intriguing fragment:

ἀπαθὲς γὰρ ὁ νοῦς, φησὶν ὁ Θεόφραστος, εἰ μὴ ἄρα ἄλλως ᾖ τὸ παθητικόν, οὐχ ὡς τὸ κινητικόν (ἀτελὴς γὰρ ἡ κίνησις), ἀλλ' ὡς ἐνέργεια. ταῦτα δὲ διαφέρει, χρῆσθαι δὲ ἀναγκαῖον ἐνίοτε τοῖς αὐτοῖς ὀνόμασιν . . . (Thphr. fr. 307D FHS&G)

'For *nous* is unaffected', Theophrastus says, 'unless of course "capable of being affected" has a different sense: not "capable of being changed" (for

---

[134] See M. Woods, *Aristotle: Eudemian Ethics Books I, II, and VIII*, translated with a commentary (Oxford, 1982), ad loc. I owe thanks to Doug Hutchinson for directing my attention to the fragment.

[135] For the idiom, compare Aristotle's Πολιτικῆς ἀκροάσεως ὡς ἡ Θεοφράστου α' β' γ' δ' ε' ϛ' ζ' η' (D.L. 5. 24) and the (hardly enlightening) commentary of Moraux, 95–6 with n. 3.

[136] R. Bodéus, *Aristote: [Catégories]*, texte établi et traduit (Paris, 2001), pp. cv–cvii, proposes (i) that these two Theophrastus titles are identical with Aristotle's two Περὶ ἡδονῆς titles, while (ii) the absence of a *Politics* in the list of Theophrastus titles to correspond to ἡ Θεοφράστου in my preceding note suggests hesitation over the authorship of a single 8-book *Politics*. The first proposal is less likely than the second, given that Theophrastus did not write dialogues.

change is incomplete), but *"energeia"*. These are different, but sometimes it is necessary to use the same names . . .'

Could Theophrastus be suggesting that all would be clear if we used the language of the Passage when speaking about νοῦς, giving ἐνέργεια its exclusive sense? In which case, we might propose his crisp, Aristotelian style (which includes frequent use of the first-person verb λέγω) as a possible originator for the Passage itself.

I think not. The quoted fragment is still in the field of physics, more specifically in the triple scheme of *De anima* 2. 5 and its careful, qualified extension to νοῦς in 3. 4, especially 429ᵃ13–18.[137] Aristotle wants to say that the intellect's taking on an intelligible form is not a change so much as the fulfilment of its nature, the actualization of the inherent potentiality for knowledge which he counts as part of our biological make-up, our matter (2. 5, 417ᵃ22–8). The qualification is necessary because he too, just like Theophrastus at the end of the quoted fragment, considers it necessary to go on using the language of change when speaking of the intellect (417ᵇ28–418ᵃ3). The intellect's taking on of form is a change or, if you prefer, a switch to *first* actuality, not second. Second actuality is the using of what one has learnt.[138]

15. Now look at Jaeger's apparatus criticus to the last sentence of *Γ*. In Aᵇ the sentence is followed by a doublet of the first three words of *Δ*. The same thing happens at the transition from *E* to *Z* and from *I* to *K*. Again, Ross records that in Aᵇ the end of *H* duplicates the first words of *Θ*. Ambr. F 113 sup. (M) shows the same phenomenon at the end both of *Γ* and of *H*.[139] Such 'reclamantes', as they are called, or (less correctly) 'custodes', are designed to help readers identify with confidence which papyrus roll comes next in the edition they are studying. Evidently, each roll contained two books. Aᵇ also shows traces of uncial stichometric numerals. The β tradition must

---

[137] On this point I am in agreement with P. Huby, *Theophrastus of Eresus: Sources for his Life, Writings, Thought and Influence*, Commentary vol. iv. *Psychology* (*Texts 265–327*), with contributions on the Arabic material by D. Gutas (Leiden, Boston, and Cologne, 1999), 124–5.

[138] Further clarification in Burnyeat, '*De anima*'. I address Aristotle's theory of the intellect in my forthcoming Aquinas Lecture, 'Aristotle's Divine Intellect'.

[139] The information about M comes from S. Alexandru, 'Traces of Ancient *Reclamantes* Surviving in Further Manuscripts of Aristotle's *Metaphysics*', *Zeitschrift für Papyrologie und Epigraphik*, 131 (2000), 13–14, who also reports unspecified examples of the same phenomenon in Vat. 115 (Vᵏ, 15th cent., containing only books *A–E*).

go back to a papyrus edition from pre-codex days,[140] when lots of Aristotle was available. The Passage could have begun as a marginal annotation quite early.

But the marginal annotation hypothesis is no less compatible with a codex edition. For at least some of Aristotle's lost works survived into late antiquity. In the fifth and sixth centuries AD we find Damascius reporting from Aristotle's three-book treatise on the philosophy of Archytas,[141] Simplicius quoting verbatim from Aristotle's *On Democritus* and his Epitome of the *Timaeus*.[142] Harlfinger's stemma shows the α and the β traditions of the *Metaphysics* starting, independently, in the ninth century, the period when masses of ancient literature were lost as crucial choices were made about which uncial manuscripts should be transcribed into the new minuscule script. Often, the transcription would be made from a single uncial manuscript which was then discarded.[143] The corruption of ἅμα to the nonsense-making ἀλλά at 1048^{b}23 and 25 (common to A^b, M, and C) would have happened in an uncial manuscript: AMA can be mistaken for ΑΛΛΑ much more easily than αμα for αλλα.[144] We can safely conclude that the Passage was already present in the hyparchetype β itself.

The question I must perforce leave unanswered is this: How many copies of the *Metaphysics* circulating in antiquity would have had the Passage? How typical, in other words, was the β tradition? My failure to find a single ancient author who knows the Passage may be just that, my failure; my search was very far from exhaustive. Yet it is telling that scholars as widely read as Philoponus and Simplicius (see Appendix 2) remain ignorant of its existence, as do the medieval Arabic and Latin traditions.

A more important lesson to learn from this investigation is that present-day scholarship should stop citing the Passage as a source of standard Aristotelian doctrine. It is a freak performance.

---

[140] As Christ was the first to note. See now Harlfinger, 29.

[141] Damasc. *Pr.* 306 (ii. 172. 20 Ruelle)=Arist. fr. 207 Rose[3]. For the title, see D.L. 5. 25.

[142] *In De caelo* 294. 33–295. 22 Heiberg=Ar. fr. 208; 296. 16–18 (cf. 379. 12–17)= Arist. fr. 206. For the titles, see D.L. 5. 25 and 27.

[143] See L. D. Reynolds and N. G. Wilson, *Scribes and Scholars: A Guide to the Transmission of Greek and Latin Literature* (Oxford, 1991), 58–61. Harlfinger, 29–30, argues against Jaeger's proposal in his OCT Preface, p. viii, that E and J came from two distinct transcriptions.

[144] So Jaeger: 'idem error est frequens in script. unciali'.

Postscript on Michael of Ephesus

16. Volumes 19–20 of the Berlin Academy Commentaria in Aristotelem Graeca contain the surviving paraphrases of, and commentaries on, the *Nicomachean Ethics*. Look up the passages that deal with Aristotle's discussion of pleasure in *NE* 7 or 10. In volume 19 no one has anything of interest to say, and there is a total absence of echoes from the Passage in *Metaphysics* Θ 6. They simply talk of ἐνέργειαι as either τέλειαι or ἀτελεῖς. The same is true of volume 20 until one reaches the last commentary, by Michael of Ephesus. Suddenly, the overall intellectual quality improves and— lo and behold—at 543. 22 Heylbut, commenting on *NE* 10. 2, he writes οὐ γάρ ἐστι γένεσις, ἀλλ' ἐνέργεια . . . αἱ δ' ἐνέργειαι τέλη εἰσὶν ἀλλ' οὐχ ὁδοὶ πρὸς τέλη. The subject he is speaking of is pleasure. What follows is this:

ὅτι δὲ τέλος ἐστὶν ἡδονὴ καὶ οὐχὶ γένεσις, μάθοιμεν ἂν ἐντεῦθεν. ἐπὶ μὲν γὰρ τῶν γενέσεων οὐχ ἅμα γίνεταί τι καὶ ἔστιν ὅτε γίνεται. οὐ γὰρ ἅμα γίνεται σὰρξ καὶ σάρξ ἐστιν ὅτε γίνεται, οὐδὲ ὅτε γίνεται ἡ οἰκία τότε ὅτε γίνεται καὶ ἔστιν. ἐπὶ δὲ τῶν ἐνεργειῶν, οἷον τοῦ ὁρᾶν, ἅμα τε ὁρᾷ καὶ ἑώρακε· καὶ ἐπὶ τῶν ἡδονῶν ἅμα τε ἥδεται καὶ ἥσθη, ὥστε ἐνέργειά ἐστι καὶ οὐ γένεσις. εἰ δὲ ἐνέργεια, καὶ τέλος ἀλλ' οὐχ ὁδός τις καὶ μεταβολὴ πρὸς τέλος. (*In EN* 543. 22–30 Heylbut)

That pleasure is an end and not a becoming, we may learn from the following. In the case of becomings, it is not the case that something is at the same time both becoming ⟨something⟩ and already being ⟨that something⟩ while becoming it.[145] For it is not the case that, at one and the same time when flesh is coming to be, it both is flesh and is coming to be flesh, nor that when a house is coming to be, at the same time as it is coming to be a house it also is a house. But in the case of actualities like seeing, at the same time one sees and has seen. So too with pleasures: at the same time one enjoys ⟨something⟩ and has enjoyed ⟨it⟩,[146] so that pleasure is an

---

[145] This sentence and the next look to be indebted to Alexander's commentary on the *De sensu* passage which I quoted in sect. 11(*b*) above: Alex. *In De sensu* 125. 3–9 Wendland.

[146] Translation problem: ἥσθην is aorist, not perfect. As Owen, 150, remarked, the verb ἥδεσθαι 'had no known perfect tense'. Answer: at *In SE* 149. 31–2 Wallies, while commenting on the passage of Aristotle's *Sophistici elenchi* discussed above, pp. 259–60, Michael explicitly casts ἑώρακε as past tense, doubtless because that was what by his day the perfect had become (E. Mihevc, 'La disparition du parfait dans le grec de la basse époque', *Razaprave Slovenska akademija znanosti in umetnosti*, razred za filološke in literarne vede, 5 (1959), 93–154 at 120–30); cf. n. 103 above. Compare the way Plotinus, *Enn.* 1 [42]. 16. 13–14 (from the part of this treatise

ἐνέργεια, not a γένεσις. *And if it is an* ἐνέργεια, *it is also an end, not a journey or change towards an end.*

This is almost a *Rückübersetzung* into Byzantine Greek of Ackrill on the same Aristotelian text, with both construing the perfect as a tense with past reference. Neither Ackrill nor Michael found the equivalence of present and perfect in the *NE* passage they were commenting on. As we have seen, the equivalence is noticed in the *Sophistici elenchi* and the *De sensu* as well as Θ 6, but only Θ 6 uses it as a criterion for being an ἐνέργεια in the special narrowed sense that Michael is temporarily using here.[147] There can be little doubt that Michael knows the Passage. He is indeed the sole ancient or medieval writer I have been able to find who clearly reveals that he does know it.[148] But we also saw that Michael, alias Pseudo-Alexander, did not read the Passage in the *Metaphysics* when composing his commentary on that work. He knows it, but not from the *Metaphysics*; or at least, not from the manuscript he used when writing his *Metaphysics* commentary. He must have read it, or a text making the same or a similar point, somewhere else.

A couple of comments on Michael's methods of work are pertinent here:

Michael . . . was remarkable among Byzantine scholars for the scope of his interests. He commented on Aristotelian works which were all but ignored by other commentators as well as on those which were studied traditionally.[149]

. . . Michael vacuumed old manuscripts to find notes for his *Elenchi* commentary. Indeed his whole method of work consisted in gathering whatever ancient materials he could lay hands on, putting them together, mending them and supplementing them, so as to produce something that could be

discussed in Appendix 2 below), puts κεκίνηται parallel to ἔτεμε, a verb which also has a normally formed perfect.

[147] I say 'temporarily' because already at 545. 7 Heylbut, after the very next lemma, he has gone back to the normal broad use of ἐνέργεια, which continues in the sequel: see esp. 545. 20–30, 562. 34–6, 568. 35–569. 2 Heylbut.

[148] No sign of the Passage in, for example, Alexander's *Ethical Questions*, despite his having plenty to say about pleasure. Appendix 2 below casts doubt on the common view that the Passage was known in Neoplatonist circles.

[149] H. P. F. Mercken, 'The Greek Commentators on Aristotle's *Ethics*', introduction to *The Greek Commentaries on the* Nicomachean Ethics *of Aristotle in the Latin Translation of Robert Grosseteste*, vol. i (Corpus Latinum Commentariorum in Aristotelem Graecorum, 6.1; Leiden, 1973), 3–29, repr. in Sorabji, *Aristotle Transformed*, 407–43 at 433.

a companion to a whole work by Aristotle. He put together commentaries on the *Metaphysics* and *Ethics* in this way too.[150]

Even if in the libraries of twelfth-century Constantinople he is rather unlikely to have come across an old uncial manuscript containing Aristotle's Περὶ ἡδονῆς, Michael could well have read a report of its exclusive distinction between ἐνέργεια and κίνησις. More must have happened than that one day he stumbled upon a *Metaphysics* manuscript from the β tradition which did contain the Passage, for his remarks contain material (e.g. about the coming to be and being of flesh and house) which do not echo either the Passage or the *Nicomachean* chapter he is commenting upon.[151] The one thing we may be sure of is that he would not have used such material unless he had reason to believe it represented, directly or indirectly, the Philosopher's thoughts.

My argument has not tried to deny that they are the Philosopher's thoughts. Only to affirm that they derive from some very, very special context about which we can only speculate.

Robinson College, Cambridge

APPENDIX 1
The Passage in M and C

The collation was kindly carried out by Christian Brockman, using Jaeger's OCT as the work of reference. All differences from this edition are noted, except missing accents and differences in the use of accents in connection with enclitics; there is no iota subscript in either manuscript.

M (Ambr. F 113 sup.)

1048^{b}19–20 οἷον τοῦ ἰσχναίνειν ἡ ἰσχνανσία αὐτό·
          The words occur in the last line of fo. 151^v. The page turns after ἰσχναν. Later, in 1048^{b}29, the scribe writes ἰσχνασία and not ἰσχνανσία.
1048^{b}20   δ' ὅταν
1048^{b}22   ἐκείνη ἐνυπάρχει
1048^{b}23–4 καὶ ἡ πρᾶξις· οἷον ὁρᾷ· ἀλλὰ καὶ φρονεῖ καὶ νοεῖ
1048^{b}25   ἀλλὰ instead of ἅμα

---

[150] S. Ebbesen, 'Philoponus, "Alexander" and the Origins of Medieval Logic', in Sorabji (ed.), *Aristotle Transformed*, 445–61 at 451.

[151] Cf. n. 145 above.

1048^b27   ἔζηκε (no nu ephelkystikon)

1048^b28   no δεῖ (of course)

1048^b31   It seems that he writes ᾠκοδόμησεν, but the sigma is not clearly
               visible on the photograph

1048^b31(?) The manuscript has καὶ κινεῖ καὶ κεκίνηκεν

1048^b34   νενόηκε· (no nu ephelkystikon)

C (Taur. B VII 23)

1048^b19   ἀλλὰ τὸ περὶ (τὸ instead of τῶν)

1048^b19–20 οἷον τοῦ ἰσχναίνειν ἡ ἰσχνανσία αὐτό.

1048^b20   δ' ὅταν

1048^b21   ὑπάρχοντος οὗ ἕνεκα

1048^b21   ταύτῃ (?)

1048^b21   ἡ πρᾶξις (add ἡ)

1048^b21   Between ἡ πρᾶξις and ἦ there might something, but the photo-
               graph does not permit precise determination of whether there
               really is something meaningful and what it is.

1048^b22   ἐκείνη ἐνυπάρχει

1048^b23–4   καὶ ἡ πρᾶξις· οἷον ὁρᾶ ἀλλὰ καῖ φρονεῖ καὶ νοεῖ καὶ νενοημένα
               μανθάνει (!) <u>νενοημένα and no ἀλλ' οὐ</u>
               In the margin *varia lectio*, but the margin is damaged. The
               sign (two dots) seems to refer back to ὁρᾶ.
               First line of the note: γρ(άφεται) and the beginning of a word,
               three letters more or less visible: καλ (?)
               Second line of the note: φρονεῖ (it seems)

1048^b25   ἀλλὰ instead of ἅμα

1048^b27   omits οὗ

1048^b28   no δεῖ (of course)

1048^b28   λέγει instead of λέγειν

1048^b29   ἰσχνανσία

1048^b31   The manuscript has καὶ κινεῖ καὶ κινεῖται (!)

Postscript on C

A number of C's unusual readings (ἀλλὰ τὸ περὶ; ἡ before πρᾶξις; omission
of ἀλλ' οὐ; καὶ νενοημένα μανθάνει as an independent sentence) are shared by
N and by the fifteenth-century hand (very similar to Bessarion's) which
has written the Passage into the margin of E^b (twelfth century). Bessarion
owned E^b as well as D^m, which has the Passage, plus three more *Metaphysics*
manuscripts: H^a, f, and Q.

APPENDIX 2
Did Plotinus, *Enneads* 6. 1 [42]. 15–22,
start a debate about the Passage?

Enneads 6. 1. 16 opens an interesting critique of Aristotle's definition of κίνησις as ἐνέργεια ἀτελής. There is no doubt that Plotinus has *Physics* 3. 1–3 in mind, since he starts with an abbreviated quotation of the definition at *Physics* 3. 2, 31–2.[152] Where Aristotle writes:

ἥ τε κίνησις ἐνέργεια μὲν εἶναί τις δοκεῖ, ἀτελὴς δέ· αἴτιον δ' ὅτι ἀτελὲς τὸ δυνατόν, οὗ ἐστιν ἐνέργεια.

Change is thought to be an actuality of a sort, though incomplete, because the potential thing whose actuality it is is incomplete,

Plotinus rehearses no more than this:

εἰ δέ τις λέγοι τὴν κίνησιν ἀτελῆ ἐνέργειαν εἶναι . . .

If someone were to say that change is incomplete actuality . . .

Whether deliberately or because he is quoting from memory, he omits Aristotle's explanation of just *why* the actuality which change is is an incomplete actuality. He proceeds, as will emerge shortly, to substitute a quite different account of his own.

The critique of Aristotle's definition which then follows elicited comments and replies from Porphyry, Iamblichus, and finally Simplicius, who wrote up the debate in his commentary on Aristotle's *Categories* 303. 32 ff. Kalbfleisch. An impressive body of modern literature treats this many-sided encounter as a debate about the Passage as well as about *Physics* 3. 1–3. Both Croese chapter 4 and Chiaradonna chapter 2 are such contributions, as is Natali, 'La critica', which I recommend as a helpful guide for reading through Plotinus' text.[153] I shall argue that, on the contrary, no contestant in this ancient discussion reveals knowledge of the Passage. Since one or another of them would probably have mentioned it had they

---

[152] The definition is repeated at *DA* 2. 5, 417ª16–17, without further explanation, just a back-reference to *Physics* 3. 2.

[153] C. Natali, 'La critica di Plotino ai concetti di attualità e movimento in Aristotele', in C. Natali and S. Maso (eds.), *Antiaristotelismo* (Amsterdam, 1999), 211–29. The only justification I have found offered for coupling the Passage with *Physics* 3. 1–3 in discussion of the debate between Plotinus and his critics is Croese, 122: 'The way in which motion is described in the two passages shows that Aristotle has in mind *more or less* the same concept as in the *Physics*' (emphasis added). E. Emilsson's recent *Plotinus on Intellect* (Oxford, 2007), 56, is properly cautious about bringing in the Passage.

been aware of its existence, the debate is evidence that the Passage re-mained as little known in antiquity as it is in our manuscript tradition.

To put the issue in a nutshell: in annotating *Enneads* 6. 1. 16 Henry–Schwyzer cite the Passage alongside *Physics* 3, Armstrong mentions only the latter. I shall argue (as promised above, p. 237 n. 46) that Armstrong's choice was the canny one. The double tradition displayed by Harlfinger's *stemma codicum* guarantees that not all ancient readers of the *Metaphysics* would find the Passage in the copy before them. The Arabic and Latin translators clearly did not. The burden of proof must now be on anyone who maintains that Plotinus or his critics did know the Passage. Meanwhile, congratulations to Gwenaëlle Aubry for writing a considerable book on δύναμις and ἐνέργεια in Aristotle and Plotinus[154] which mentions the Passage only once—to set it aside. *Ab esse ad posse valet consequentia.*

Plotinus starts out by treating 'Change is incomplete actuality' as a straight-forward definition *per genus et differentiam*, the genus being ἐνέργεια and ἀτελής the differentia. The immediate result is that incompleteness be-comes a straightforward attribute of the ἐνέργεια which is κίνησις and Plo-tinus can argue, against Aristotle as thus construed, that walking, for example, is walking, in the completest possible sense, from the walker's very first steps. What remains incomplete after a step or two is not the walker's walking, but his walking a certain distance (16. 5–12).

True, but the purported criticism of Aristotle's definition is in fact an elucidation of the point Aristotle is making when he grounds the incom-pleteness of the walking on incompleteness as an attribute of the walker (τὸ δυνατόν). The walking, for Aristotle, is the actuality of the walker's poten-tial to *be* in another place (not a potential to *walk*). Accordingly, it remains an incomplete actuality throughout the period of a walker's walking right up to their arrival at the place they have the potential to be in.[155]

I conclude that, as so often, two great minds are talking past each other. Aristotle does not deny what Plotinus affirms, that walking is walking all along, from the start, or that κίνησις is already ἐνέργεια, already therefore actual κίνησις, before it reaches its goal. On the contrary, ἀτελής expresses what *sort* of ἐνέργεια it has been (actually) all along, namely, one that ma-nifests and seeks to realize the walker's potentiality for being at a certain place (which may never be reached).

Since the very concept of κίνησις as ἀτελὴς ἐνέργεια is excluded by the Pas-sage, Plotinus is most unlikely to have the Passage in view. His subsequent

---

[154] G. Aubry, *Dieu sans la puissance: dunamis et energeia chez Aristote et chez Plotin* (Paris, 2006).

[155] For clear elucidation of this point, see the now classic article Kosman, 'Mo-tion'.

argument (16. 14–39) that ἐνέργεια is no more 'in timelessness' (ἐν ἀχρόνῳ) than κίνησις is is expressly indexed to *Phys.* 1. 3, 186ᵃ15–16 (cf. 8. 3, 253ᵇ25; *Pol.* 1307ᵇ35) on ἀθρόα μεταβολή, not to *Metaphysics* Θ 6.[156] Nowhere does he allude to the relation of present and perfect tenses. Nor does anyone in the debate recorded by Simplicius, which ranges widely through the merits and demerits of the Aristotelian category ποιεῖν καὶ πάσχειν. The best contribution comes from Iamblichus (ap. Simpl. *In Cat.* 303. 35–304. 10 Kalbfleisch). He attacks Plotinus' assumption that 'Change is incomplete actuality' is a straightforward definition *per genus et differentiam*, the genus being ἐνέργεια and ἀτελής the differentia. Instead, he says we should read ἀτελής as an *alienans* qualification. Rather than placing κίνησις within the wider class of ἐνέργεια, it indicates that κίνησις barely counts as ἐνέργεια at all: 'it falls away into some altogether inferior nature' (303. 37–8 Kalbfleisch). But at least it has a nature of sorts. The definition allows Aristotle to insist that κίνησις is not the nothing, the not-being, to which some Platonists of the Academy would condemn it.[157]

This acute piece of commentary brings me back to Plotinus. If he says in 6. 1. 16. 6–7 that κίνησις is ἐνέργεια μὲν πάντως, ἔχει δὲ καὶ τὸ πάλιν καὶ πάλιν, he cannot be using ἐνέργεια in the sense defined in *Metaphysics* Θ 6, which is such that κίνησις is not ἐνέργεια at all. He casts κίνησις as a proper species of the genus ἐνέργεια, substituting ἔχει δὲ καὶ τὸ πάλιν καὶ πάλιν[158] for what he took to be Aristotle's differentia ἀτελής. Accordingly, when he

---

[156] Likewise, J. C. De Groot's very interesting article 'Philoponus on *De anima* II 5, *Physics* III 3, and the Propagation of Light', *Phronesis*, 28 (1983), 177–96, fails to show that Philoponus knows the Passage as well as the ἀθρόα μεταβολή passages in Aristotle's *Physics*. Cf. n. 45 above on the striking absence of the Passage from Philoponus, *De aeternitate mundi*.

[157] Here again, as at the very beginning of this project, I refer readers to Frede, 'Potentiality'.

[158] Whatever that means: neither Brehier's 'un acte qui recommence de nouveau à chaque instant' (E. Bréhier (ed.), *Plotin: Ennéades* (6 vols.; Paris, 1924–8)), nor Armstrong's 'has also the "over and over again"', nor Linguiti's 'si presenta come un di nuovo e poi di nuovo' (p. 73 n. 200) is helpful. M. F. Wagner, 'Plotinus on the Nature of Physical Reality', in L. P. Gerson (ed.), *The Cambridge Companion to Plotinus* (Cambridge, 1996), 130–70 at 140, is just baffling: 'embraces its completeness recursively'. MacKenna, as usual, strives for a definite meaning: 'It entails repetition (lacks finality). It repeats, not in order that it may achieve actuality—it is that already—but that it may attain a goal distinct from itself and posterior' (S. MacKenna, *Plotinus: The Enneads, Translated*, 2nd edn. (London, 1956)). A better guide, perhaps, is *Enn.* 3. 7 [45]. 8. 37–41, where the πάλιν καὶ πάλιν of κίνησις is likened to the πάλιν καὶ πάλιν of water flowing πάλιν καὶ πάλιν and the distance it is observed to cover. This rather suggests that the phrase τὸ πάλιν καὶ πάλιν simply refers to κίνησις being something that is essentially extended through time, as opposed to a thing which is complete ἐν τῷ νῦν. In other words, πάλιν καὶ πάλιν conveys the idea of going on and on. Cf. πάλιν ἐφεξῆς in the discussion of time itself at 3. 7 [45]. 11. 36–7 and the contrast with eternity at 3. 15 ff. Why can't Plotinus translators give us something that makes sense?

proceeds to say that κίνησις is already ἐνέργεια, he cannot mean ἐνέργεια in the sense of *Metaphysics* Θ 6. In general, no one who predicates ἐνέργεια of κίνησις or κίνησις of ἐνέργεια is following the exclusive distinction we find, uniquely, in the Passage.

Now to pull back the curtain. Simpl. *In Cat.* 307. 1–6 Kalbfleisch cites ἐνέργεια μὲν πάντως, ἔχει δὲ καὶ τὸ πάλιν καὶ πάλιν, plus the words that follow down to the end of Plotinus' sentence at 16. 8, as a quotation from Iamblichus recording a *Stoic* objection to Aristotle's account of κίνησις as ἐνέργεια ἀτελής. Everything I have found in Plotinus so far is borrowed from Stoics. This shows some Stoics—whether of Hellenistic or Imperial vintage we need not decide—responding to Aristotle's *Physics*. It does not and cannot show them aware of the Passage,[159] which eliminates the very possibility of ἐνέργεια ἀτελής.[160]

BIBLIOGRAPHY

(1) *Metaphysics*: modern editions; ancient, medieval, and modern commentaries; medieval and modern translations

Academia Regia Borussica, *Aristoteles Latine*, interpretibus variis edidit (Berlin, 1831); Nachdruck herausgegeben und eingeleitet von Eckhard Keßler (Munich, 1995).

Alexander of Aphrodisias. *In Aristotelis Metaphysica Commentaria*, (1) ed. H. Bonitz (Berlin, 1847); (2) ed. M. Hayduck (CAG 1; Berlin, 1891).

Aquinas, Thomas, *In duodecim libros Metaphysicorum Aristotelis expositio*, editio iam a M.-R. Cathala, O.P. exarata retractatur cura et studio P. Fr. Raymundi M. Spiazzi, O.P. (Turin and Rome, 1964).

Argyropylos, J., *Aristotelis . . . opus metaphysicum a . . . Bessarione . . . Latinitate . . . donatum . . . cum adiecto in XII. primos libros Argyropyli . . . interpretamento*, ed. J. Faber (Paris, 1515).

Averroes, *Aristotelis Metaphysicorum libri XIIII, cum Averrois Cordubensis in eosdem commentariis, et epitome, etc.* (Venice, 1562; photographic repr. Frankfurt a.M., 1962).

Barnes, J.: see Ross and Barnes.

Barthélemy-Saint-Hilaire, J., *Métaphysique d'Aristote*, traduite en français avec des notes perpétuelles (3 vols.; Paris, 1879).

---

[159] *Pace* Frede, 'Tenses', 146. The Stoic origin of Plotinus' words is not signalled by Armstrong, although Kalbfleisch as editor of Simplicius is scrupulously detailed in his source citation.

[160] In preparing this Appendix I have been helped by the knowledgeable advice of Riccardo Chiaradonna, Paul Kalligas, and Lucas Siorvanes. It is more important than usual to add that they are not responsible for my conclusions.

Bekker, I., *Aristoteles Graece*, ex recensione Immanuel Bekker, edidit Academia Regia Borussica ['Bekker'] (2 vols.; Berlin, 1831).

Bessarion: see Argyropylos.

Bonitz, H., *Aristoteles: Metaphysik*, übersetzt (ed. Eduard Wellmann, 1890), mit Gliederungen, Registern und Bibliographie herausgegeben von Héctor Carvallo und Ernesto Grassi (Munich, 1966).

——*Aristotelis Metaphysica*, recognovit et enarravit ['Bonitz'] (2 vols.; Bonn, 1848–9; vol. ii. *Commentarius* repr. Hildesheim, 1960).

Brandis, C. A., *Aristotelis et Theophrasti Metaphysica*, ad veterum codicum manuscriptorum fidem recensita indicibusque instructa in usum scholarum edidit ['Brandis ed.'] (Berlin, 1823).

Casaubon, I., *Operum Aristotelis Stagiritae philosophorum omnium longe principis, nova editio Graecè et Latinè* (Lyon, 1590).

Christ, W., *Aristotelis Metaphysica*, recognovit, nova editio correctior ['Christ'] (Leipzig, 1895 [1st edn. 1886]).

Du Val, W., *Aristotelis opera omnia, Graece et Latine* (Paris, 1629, 1654, etc.).

Erasmus, D., *Aristotelis . . . opera . . . omnia* (Basel, 1531, 1539, 1550).

Fonseca, Petrus da, *Commentaria in Metaphysicorum Aristotelis Stagiritae libros* (4 vols.; Cologne, 1615–29 [1st edn. of Θ: 1604]).

Frede, M., and Patzig, G., *Aristoteles: Metaphysik Z*, Text, Übersetzung und Kommentar (2 vols.; Munich, 1988).

Furth, M., *Aristotle:* Metaphysics *Books Zeta, Eta, Theta, Iota (VII–X)*, translated ['Furth'] (Indianapolis, 1985).

Gemusaeus, H., *Aristotelis Stagiritae, philosophorum omnium facile principis, opera quae in hunc usque diem extant omnia, Latinitate partim antea, partim nunc primum a viris doctissimis donata, et ad Graecum exemplar diligenter recognita* (Basel, 1542).

Gohlke, P., *Übersetzung der Metaphysik des Aristoteles*, 2nd edn. (Paderborn, 1951).

Hope, R., *Aristotle:* Metaphysics, translated (New York, 1952).

Irwin, T., and Fine, G., *Aristotle: Selections*, translated, with introduction, notes, and glossary ['Irwin–Fine'] (Indianapolis, 1995).

Jaeger, W., *Aristotelis Metaphysica*, recognovit brevique adnotatione critica instruxit ['Jaeger'] (Oxford, 1957).

Kirchmann, J. H. von, *Die Metaphysik des Aristoteles*, übersetzt, erläutert und mit einer Lebensbeschreibung des Aristoteles versehen (2 vols.; Berlin, 1871).

Lasson, A., *Aristoteles: Metaphysik*, ins Deutsche übertragen (Jena, 1907).

'Londinenses', *Notes on Eta and Theta of Aristotle's* Metaphysics, recorded by Myles Burnyeat and others (Oxford, 1984).

Makin, S., *Aristotle:* Metaphysics, *Book Θ*, translated with an introduction and commentary ['Makin'] (Oxford, 2006).

Mauro, S., *Aristotelis opera omnia . . . brevi paraphrasi et litterae perpetuo inhaerente expositione illustrata* (Rome, 1658; repr. Paris, 1885).

Moerbeke: see Vuillemin-Diem.

Pappa, E., *Georgios Pachymeres, Philosophia Buch 10: Kommentar zur Metaphysik des Aristoteles, Editio Princeps. Einleitung, Text, Indices* (Corpus Philosophorum Medii Aevi, Commentaria in Aristotelem Byzantina, 2; Athens, 2002).

Pseudo-Philoponus, *Expositiones in omnes XIV Aristotelis libros Metaphysicos*, übersetzt von Franciscus Patritius, Neudruck der ersten Ausgabe Ferrara 1583 mit einer Einleitung von Charles Lohr (Commentaria in Aristotelem Graeca: Versiones Latinae temporis resuscitatarum litterarum, herausgegeben von Charles Lohr, 2; Stuttgart-Bad Cannstatt, 1991).

Ross, W. D., *Aristotle's* Metaphysics: *A Revised Text with Introduction and Commentary* ['Ross'] (2 vols.; Oxford, 1924).

——*Metaphysica* (The Works of Aristotle Translated into English under the Editorship of J. A. Smith and W. D. Ross; Oxford, 1908) ['Ross Tr.¹', done from Christ's edition].

——*Metaphysica* (The Works of Aristotle Translated into English under the Editorship of W. D. Ross (Oxford, 1928) ['Ross Tr.²', done from his own edition].

——and Barnes, J., *Metaphysics*, in J. Barnes (ed.), *The Complete Works of Aristotle: The Revised Oxford Translation*, vol. ii ['Ross–Barnes'] (Princeton, 1984).

Russo, A., *Aristotele: opere*, vol. vi. *Metafisica* (Rome and Bari, 1973).

Schwegler, A., *Die Metaphysik des Aristoteles*, Grundtext, Übersetzung und Commentar nebst erläuternden Abhandlungen ['Schwegler'] (4 vols.; Tübingen, 1847–8; repr. Frankfurt a.M., 1960).

Sepúlveda, Juan Ginès de, *Alexandri Aphrodisiei commentaria in duodecim Aristotelis libros de prima philosophia*, interprete J.G.S. (Paris, 1536 [1st edn. Rome, 1527]).

Sylburg, F., *Aristotelis et Theophrasti Metaphysica* (Frankfurt a.M., 1635).

Taylor, T., *The* Metaphysics *of Aristotle*, translated from the Greek (London, 1801).

Tredennick, H., *Aristotle:* The Metaphysics, with an English translation (2 vols.; Cambridge, Mass., and London, 1933–5).

Tricot, J., *Aristote: Métaphysiques*, traduction nouvelle et notes ['Tricot'] (2 vols.; Paris, 1933).

Vuillemin-Diem, G., *Metaphysica Lib. I–X, XII–XIV*, Translatio Anonyma sive 'Media' (Aristoteles Latinus, XXV.2; Leiden, 1976).

——*Metaphysica Lib. I–XIV*, recensio et translatio Guillelmi de Moerbeka, edidit (Aristoteles Latinus, XXV 3.1–2; Leiden, New York, and Cologne, 1995).

Weise, C. H., *Aristotelis opera omnia*, editio stereotypa (Leipzig, 1843).

(2) Other works

Ackrill, J. L., 'Aristotle's Distinction between *Energeia* and *Kinesis*' ['Distinction'], in Bambrough (ed.), *New Essays*, 121–41; repr. in J. L. Ackrill, *Essays on Plato and Aristotle* (Oxford, 1997), 142–62 [cited here from the first publication].

Alexandru, S., 'A New Manuscript of Pseudo-Philoponus' Commentary on Aristotle's *Metaphysics* Containing a Hitherto Unknown Ascription of the Work', *Phronesis*, 44 (1999), 347–52.

—— 'Traces of Ancient *Reclamantes* Surviving in Further Manuscripts of Aristotle's *Metaphysics*', *Zeitschrift für Papyrologie und Epigraphik*, 131 (2000), 13–14.

Armstrong, A. H. (ed.), *Plotinus with an English Translation* ['Armstrong'] (7 vols.; Cambridge, Mass., and London, 1966–88).

Aubenque, P. (ed.), *Études sur la Métaphysique d'Aristote* [*Études*] (Actes du vie Symposium Aristotelicum; Paris, 1979).

Aubry, G., *Dieu sans la puissance:* dunamis *et* energeia *chez Aristote et chez Plotin* (Paris, 2006).

Bambrough, R. (ed.), *New Essays on Plato and Aristotle* [*New Essays*] (London and New York, 1965).

Bauer, G., 'The English "Perfect" Reconsidered', *Journal of Linguistics*, 6 (1970), 189–98.

Bernadinello, S., *'Eliminatio codicum' della Metafisica di Aristotele* (Padua, 1970).

Blass, F., 'Aristotelisches', *Rheinisches Museum*, 30 (1875), 481–505.

Bodéus, R., *Aristote: [Catégories]*, texte établi et traduit (Paris, 2001).

Bonitz, H., *Index Aristotelicus* (Berlin, 1870; repr. Darmstadt, 1960).

Bostock, D., 'Pleasure and Activity in Aristotle's Ethics' ['Bostock'], *Phronesis*, 33 (1988), 251–72.

Brague, R., *Aristote et la question du monde: essai sur le contexte cosmologique et anthropologique de l'ontologie* [*Monde*] (Paris, 1988).

Brandis, C. A. (ed.), *Scholia in Aristotelem*, collegit Christianus Augustus Brandis, edidit Academia Regia Borussica [vol. iv of the Academy's edition of Aristotle] (Berlin, 1836).

Bréhier, E. (ed.), *Plotin: Ennéades* (6 vols.; Paris, 1924–8).

Brinton, L. J., *The Development of English Aspectual Systems: Aspectualizers and Post-Verbal Particles* (Cambridge, 1988).

Browning, R., 'An Unpublished Funeral Oration for Anna Comnena', *Proceedings of the Cambridge Philological Society*, NS 8 (1962), 1–12; repr. in Sorabji (ed.), *Aristotle Transformed*, 393–406.

Brunschwig, J., *Aristote: Topiques*, texte établi et traduit (Paris, 1967).

Burnyeat, M. F., *A Map of* Metaphysics *Zeta* [*Map*] (Pittsburgh, 2001).

—— '*De anima* 2. 5' ['*De anima*'], *Phronesis*, 47 (2002), 1–90.

—— 'Enthymeme: Aristotle on the Logic of Persuasion' ['Enthymeme'], in D. J. Furley and A. Nehamas (eds.), *Aristotle's* Rhetoric*: Philosophical Essays* (Proceedings of the XIIth Symposium Aristotelicum; Princeton, 1994), 3–55.

—— 'Plato on Why Mathematics is Good for the Soul' ['Mathematics'], in T. Smiley (ed.), *Mathematics and Necessity: Essays in the History of Philosophy* (Proceedings of the British Academy, 103; Oxford, 2000), 1–81.

—— 'The Dramatic Aspects of Plato's *Protagoras*' ['Aspects'], forthcoming.

Chantraine, P., *Histoire du parfait grec* ['Chantraine'] (Paris, 1927).

Chiaradonna, R., *Sostanza movimento analogia: Plotino critico di Aristotele* ['Chiaradonna'] (Naples, 2002).

Cobb, R. A., 'The Present Progressive Periphrasis and the Metaphysics of Aristotle', *Phronesis*, 18 (1973), 80–90.

Comrie, B., *Aspect: An Introduction to the Study of Verbal Aspect and Related Problems* (Cambridge, 1976).

Croese, I., *Simplicius on Continuous and Instantaneous Change: NeoPlatonic Elements in Simplicius' Interpretation of Aristotelian Physics* ['Croese'] (Utrecht, 1998).

Crombie, I. M., review of Bambrough (ed.), *New Essays*, in *Classical Review*, NS 17 (1967), 30–3.

De Groot, J. C., 'Philoponus on *De anima* II 5, *Physics* III 3, and the Propagation of Light', *Phronesis*, 28 (1983), 177–96.

Denniston, J. D., *The Greek Particles*, 2nd edn. ['Denniston'] (Oxford, 1954).

Dorion, L.-A., *Les Réfutations sophistiques*, introduction, traduction et commentaire (Paris, 1995).

Dufour, M., 'La distinction ἐνέργεια–κίνησις en *Métaph. Θ*, 6: deux manières d'être dans le temps', *Revue de philosophie ancienne*, 19 (2001), 3–43.

Duhoux, Y., *Le Verbe grec ancien: éléments de morphologie et de syntaxe historiques* (Louvain-la-Neuve, 1992).

Ebbesen, S., *Commentators and Commentaries on Aristotle's* Sophistici Elenchi*: A Study of Post-Aristotelian Ancient and Medieval Writings on Fallacies* [*Commentators*] (Corpus Latinum Commentariorum in Aristotelem Graecorum, 7; 3 vols.; Leiden, 1981).

—— 'Philoponus, "Alexander" and the Origins of Medieval Logic', in Sorabji (ed.), *Aristotle Transformed*, 445–61.

Emilsson, E., *Plotinus on Intellect* (Oxford, 2007).

Frede, M., 'Aristotle's Notion of Potentiality in *Metaphysics Θ*' ['Potentiality'], in T. Scaltsas, D. Charles, and M. L. Gill (eds.), *Unity, Identity and Explanation in Aristotle's Metaphysics* (Oxford, 1994), 173–93.

—— 'The Stoic Doctrine of the Tenses of the Verb' ['Tenses'], in K. Döring and T. Ebert (eds.), *Dialektiker und Stoiker: Zur Logik der Stoa und ihrer Vorläufer* (Stuttgart, 1993), 141–54.

Gercke, A., 'Aristoteleum', *Wiener Studien*, 14 (1892), 146–8.

Gill, M.-L., 'Aristotle's Theory of Causal Action in *Physics* III 3', *Phronesis*, 25 (1980), 129–47.

Goldschmidt, V., *Temps physique et temps tragique chez Aristote: commentaire sur le quatrième livre de la Physique (10–14) et sur la Poétique* ['Goldschmidt'] (Paris, 1982).

Goodwin, W. W., *Syntax of the Moods and Tenses of the Greek Verb* ['Goodwin'] (London, 1897).

Gosling, J. C. B., and Taylor, C. C. W., *The Greeks on Pleasure* (Oxford, 1982).

Graham, D. W., 'States and Performances: Aristotle's Test' ['Graham'], *Philosophical Quarterly*, 30 (1980), 117–30.

Harlfinger, D., 'Zur Überlieferungsgeschichte der *Metaphysik*' ['Harlfinger'], in Aubenque (ed.), *Études*, 7–36.

Hecquet-Devienne, M., 'Les mains du *Parisinus Graecus* 1853: une nouvelle collation des quatre premiers livres de la *Métaphysique* d'Aristote (folios 225^v–247^v)', *Scrittura e civiltà*, 24 (2000), 103–71; repr. with slight alterations in R. Goulet (ed.), *Dictionnaire des philosophes antiques*, supplément (Paris, 2003), 245–9 [cited here from the first publication].

Henry, P., and Schwyzer, H.-R. (eds.), *Plotini Opera* ['Henry–Schwyzer'] (3 vols.; Paris and Brussels, 1951–73).

Huby, P., *Theophrastus of Eresus: Sources for his Life, Writings, Thought and Influence*, Commentary vol. iv. *Psychology (Texts 265–327)*, with contributions on the Arabic material by D. Gutas (Leiden, Boston, and Cologne, 1999).

Irwin, T. H., *Aristotle's First Principles* (Oxford, 1988).

Jansen, L., *Tun und Können: Ein systematischer Kommentar zur Aristoteles' Theorie der Vermögen im neunten Buch der Metaphysik* ['Jansen'] (Frankfurt a.M., 2003).

Kahn, C., 'On the Intended Interpretation of Aristotle's *Metaphysics*', in J. Wiesner (ed.), *Aristoteles: Werk und Wirkung* (2 vols.; Berlin and New York, 1985–7), i. *Aristoteles und seine Schule*, 311–38.

Kenny, A., *Action, Emotion and Will* (London, 1963).

Keßler, E.: see Academia Regia Borussica in section (1).

Kosman, L. A., 'Aristotle's Definition of Motion' ['Motion'], *Phronesis*, 14 (1969), 40–62.

—— 'Substance, Being, and *Energeia*' ['Substance'], *Oxford Studies in Ancient Philosophy*, 2 (1984), 121–49.

Linguiti, A., *La felicità e il tempo: Plotino, Enneadi, I 4–I 5*, con testo greco, introduzione, traduzione e commento ['Linguiti'] (Milan, 2000).

Liske, M.-T., '*Kinesis* und *Energeia* bei Aristoteles', *Phronesis*, 36 (1991), 161–78.

Luna, C., 'Observations sur le texte des livres *M–N* de la *Métaphysique* d'Aristote' ['Observations'], *Documenti e studi sulla tradizione filosofica medievale*, 16 (2005), 553–93.

——— *Trois études sur la tradition des commentaires anciens à la Métaphysique d'Aristote* [*Trois études*] (Leiden, Boston, and Cologne, 2001).

MacKenna, S., *Plotinus: The Enneads, Translated*, 2nd edn. (London, 1956).

Mamo, P. S., '*Energeia* and *Kinesis* in Metaphysics Θ. 6', *Apeiron*, 4 (1970), 24–34.

Meillet, A., 'Le sens de γενήσομαι: à propos de *Parménide* 141', *Revue de philologie, de littérature et d'histoire anciennes*, 48 (1924), 44–9.

Menn, S., 'The Origins of Aristotle's Concept of ἐνέργεια: ἐνέργεια and δύναμις', *Ancient Philosophy*, 14 (1994), 73–114.

Mercken, H. P. F., 'The Greek Commentators on Aristotle's *Ethics*', introduction to *The Greek Commentaries on the Nicomachean Ethics of Aristotle in the Latin Translation of Robert Grosseteste*, vol. i (Corpus Latinum Commentariorum in Aristotelem Graecorum, 6.1; Leiden, 1973), 3–29; repr. in Sorabji, *Aristotle Transformed*, 407–43 (cited here from the second publication).

Mihevc, E., 'La disparition du parfait dans le grec de la basse époque', *Razaprave Slovenska akademija znanosti in umetnosti*, razred za filološke in literarne vede, 5 (1959), 93–154.

Mioni, E., 'Bessarione bibliofilo e filologo', *Rivista di studi bizantini e neoellenici*, NS 5 (1968), 61–83.

Moraux, P., *Les Listes anciennes des ouvrages d'Aristote* ['Moraux'] (Louvain, 1951).

Mourelatos, A. D. P., 'Events, Processes, and States' ['Mourelatos'], *Linguistics and Philosophy*, 2 (1978), 415–34; repr. in P. J. Tedeschi and A. Zaenen (eds.), *Tense and Aspect* (New York and London, c.1981), 191–212 [cited here from the second publication].

Natali, C., 'La critica di Plotino ai concetti di attualità e movimento in Aristotele', in C. Natali and S. Maso (eds.), *Antiaristotelismo* (Amsterdam, 1999), 211–29.

——— 'Movimenti ed attività: l'interpretazione di Aristotele, *Metaph.* Θ 6', *Elenchos*, 12 (1991), 67–90; repr. in C. Natali, *L'Action efficace: études sur la philosophie de l'action d'Aristote* (Louvain-la-Neuve, Paris, and Dudley, Mass., 2004), 31–52 [cited here from the first publication].

Owen, G. E. L., 'Aristotelian Pleasures' ['Owen'], *Proceedings of the Aristotelian Society*, 72 (1971–2), 135–52; repr. with the original pagination in J. Barnes, M. Schofield, and R. Sorabji (eds.), *Articles on Aristotle*, ii. *Ethics and Politics* (London, 1977), 92–103; and again, with the original pagination, in G. E. L. Owen, *Logic, Science and Dialectic* (London, 1986), 334–46 [cited here by the original pagination].

Penner, T., 'Verbs and the Identity of Actions: A Philosophical Exercise in the Interpretation of Aristotle' ['Verbs'], in O. P. Wood and G. Pitcher (eds.), *Ryle* (London and Basingstoke, 1971), 393–460.

Pickard-Cambridge, W. A., *The Works of Aristotle Translated into English*, i. Topica *and* De sophisticis elenchis (Oxford, 1928).

Polansky, R., '*Energeia* in Aristotle's *Metaphysics* IX', *Ancient Philosophy*, 3 (1983), 160–70; repr. in A. Preus and J. P. Anton (eds.), *Aristotle's Ontology* (Albany, NY, 1992), 211–25 [cited here from the first publication].

Poste. E., *Aristotle on Fallacies or the* Sophistici Elenchi, with a translation and notes (London, 1866).

Potts, T., 'States, Activities and Performances' ['Potts'], *Proceedings of the Aristotelian Society*, suppl. 39 (1965), 65–84.

Rackham, H., *Aristotle:* The Nicomachean Ethics, with an English translation, 2nd edn. (London and Cambridge, Mass., 1934).

Reynolds, L. D., and Wilson, N. G., *Scribes and Scholars: A Guide to the Transmission of Greek and Latin Literature* (Oxford, 1991).

Rijksbaron, A., *Aristotle, Verb Meaning and Functional Grammar: Towards a New Typology of States of Affairs*, with an appendix on Aristotle's distinction between *kinesis* and *energeia* (Amsterdam, 1989).

Ross, W. D., *Aristotle's* Physics*: A Revised Text with Introduction and Commentary* (Oxford, 1936).

Ryle, G., *Dilemmas* (Cambridge, 1966).

Sicherl, M., 'Handschriftliche Vorlagen der editio princeps des Aristoteles', *Akademie der Wissenschaften und der Literatur, Mainz*, Abhandlungen der Geistes- und Sozialwissenschaftlichen Klasse, 8 (1976), 1–90.

Skemp, J. B., 'The Activity of Immobility', in Aubenque (ed.), *Études*, 229–45.

Smeets, A., *Act en potentie in de Metaphysica van Aristoteles: historisch-philologisch onderzoek van boek IX en boek V der Metaphysica*, avec un résumé en français ['Smeets'] (Leuven, 1952).

Sorabji, R. (ed.), *Aristotle Transformed: The Ancient Commentators and their Influence* (London, 1990).

Von Fritz, K., *Philosophie und sprachlicher Ausdruck bei Demokrit, Plato und Aristoteles* (New York, Leipzig, Paris, and London, 1938; repr. Darmstadt, 1966).

Wagner, M. F., 'Plotinus on the Nature of Physical Reality', in L. P. Gerson (ed.), *The Cambridge Companion to Plotinus* (Cambridge, 1996), 130–70.

Wartelle, A., *Inventaire des manuscripts grecs d'Aristote et de ses commentateurs: contribution à l'histoire du texte d'Aristote* ['Wartelle'] (Paris, 1963).

Waterlow, S., *Nature, Change, and Agency in Aristotle's* Physics ['Waterlow'] (Oxford, 1982).

White, M. J., 'Aristotle's Concept of θεωρία and the ἐνέργεια–κίνησις Distinction' ['White'], *Journal of the History of Philosophy*, 18 (1980), 253–63.

Woods, M., *Aristotle:* Eudemian Ethics *Books I, II, and VIII*, translated with a commentary (Oxford, 1982).

ARISTOTLE'S ARGUMENT
FOR A HUMAN FUNCTION

RACHEL BARNEY

> Practising your craft in expert fashion is noble, honorable and
> satisfying.
>> (ANTHONY BOURDAIN, *Kitchen Confidential*)

> Really, if the lower orders don't set us a good example, what
> on earth is the use of them?
>> (OSCAR WILDE, *The Importance of Being Earnest*)

IN the famous 'function argument' of *Nicomachean Ethics* 1. 7
($1097^{b}22$–$1098^{a}18$) Aristotle gives an outline account of human
virtue and happiness by relating them to our function or work
[*ergon*]. If something has a function, he argues, its function determines what counts as 'the good and the well' for that thing. Human
beings do have a function; and since the function of a thing consists
in the activity proper to or characteristic of it, the human function
must consist in rational activity. The virtue or excellence [*aretē*]
of a thing is what makes it perform its function well; so, Aristotle
concludes, the human good—that is, happiness—is activity of the
soul involving rational virtue.

The function argument is one of the most discussed and debated
arguments in all of ancient philosophy.[1] But little attention has

© Rachel Barney 2008

My thanks for helpful comments on this paper go to audiences which heard early
versions of it at Williams College, UC Davis, and the University of Western Ontario;
and in particular to Melissa Barry, Victor Caston, Joe Cruz, John Thorp, and James
Wilberding. Earlier drafts have been much improved by helpful, and deeply sceptical, comments from Sarah Broadie, Michael Green, Tom Hurka, Brad Inwood,
Monte Johnson, Richard Kraut, and Jennifer Whiting.

[1] Recent readings include: P. Destrée, 'Comment démontrer le propre de
l'homme? Pour une lecture "dialectique' de *EN* I, 6' ['Comment démontrer'], in G.
Romeyer Dherbey and G. Aubry (eds.), *L'Excellence de la vie* (Paris, 2002), 39–61; A.
Gomez-Lobo, 'The Ergon Inference', *Phronesis*, 34 (1989), 170–84; C. Korsgaard,

been paid to the opening moves of the argument, which lead up to Aristotle's claim that human beings do have a function—a claim I shall call the *function thesis*.[2] Strikingly, Aristotle introduces the function thesis in advance of any claims as to what our function might consist in:[3]

Presumably, however, to say that happiness is the chief good seems a platitude, and a clearer account of what it is is still desired. This might perhaps be given, if we could first ascertain the function of man. For just as for a flute-player, a sculptor, or any artist, and, in general, for all things that

'Aristotle on Function and Virtue', *History of Philosophy Quarterly*, 3 (1986), 259–79; G. Lawrence, 'The Function of the Function Argument' ['Function'], *Ancient Philosophy*, 21 (2001), 445–75; id., 'Human Good and Human Function' ['Good'], in R. Kraut (ed.), *The Blackwell Guide to Aristotle's* Nicomachean Ethics (Malden, Mass., 2006), 37–75; and J. Whiting, 'Aristotle's Function Argument: A Defense' ['Defense'], *Ancient Philosophy*, 8 (1988), 33–48, in addition to those offered in more general studies, such as D. Bostock, *Aristotle's Ethics [Ethics]* (Oxford, 2000), 15–21; S. Broadie, *Ethics with Aristotle [Ethics]* (Oxford, 1991), 34–41; S. Broadie and C. Rowe (trans., intro., and comm.), *Aristotle:* Nicomachean Ethics [*Commentary*] (Oxford, 2002), 276; D. S. Hutchinson, *The Virtues of Aristotle* (London, 1986); T. Irwin, *Aristotle's First Principles [Principles]* (Oxford, 1988), 363–5, 607 n. 37; M. R. Johnson, *Aristotle on Teleology [Teleology]* (Oxford, 2005), 217–22; R. Kraut, *Aristotle: Political Philosophy [Aristotle]* (Oxford, 2002), 82–4; M. C. Nussbaum, 'Aristotle, Nature, and Ethics', in J. E. Altham and R. Harrison (eds.), *World, Mind and Ethics: Essays on the Ethical Philosophy of Bernard Williams* (Cambridge, 1995), 86–131 at 112–13; M. Pakaluk, *Aristotle's* Nicomachean Ethics*: An Introduction [Ethics]* (Cambridge, 2005), 74–7; C. D. C. Reeve, *Practices of Reason [Practices]* (Oxford, 1995), 123–8; G. Santas, *Goodness and Justice* (Oxford, 2001), 236–50; and F. Sparshott, *Taking Life Seriously: A Study of the Argument of the* Nicomachean Ethics *[Life]* (Toronto, 1994), 40–5.

[2] The only studies I know of which focus on the argument for the function thesis are B. Suits, 'Aristotle on the Function of Man: Fallacies, Heresies and other Entertainments' ['Fallacies'], *Canadian Journal of Philosophy*, 4 (1974), 23–40; and T. Tuozzo, 'The Function of Human Beings and the Rationality of the Universe: Aristotle and Zeno on Parts and Wholes' ['Function'], *Phoenix*, 50 (1996), 146–61 (cf. n. 22). Other particularly helpful discussions include those in Broadie, *Ethics*, Destrée, 'Comment démontrer', Kraut, *Aristotle*, Pakaluk, *Ethics*, and Sparshott, *Life*, as well as that of Thomas Aquinas, *Commentary on Aristotle's* Nicomachean Ethics, trans. C. Litzinger (Notre Dame, 1993), sects. 119–22, 40–1.

[3] A question this raises is what work the function thesis does in the function argument as a whole. If we take 1097^{b}33–1098^{a}3 as establishing *independently* the more precise claim that the human function is rational activity, then the thesis may serve only a propaedeutic, formally dispensable role. Alternatively, the specification of the human function as rational activity could be read as *depending* on the prior claim that there is such a function. I am inclined towards the latter reading, but to argue for this would require a fuller discussion of the argument as a whole than I can here undertake. My understanding of the agenda of the function argument as a whole largely follows the 'formal' reading of Lawrence, 'Function', but this leaves the status of 1097^{b}28–33 underdetermined (cf. his 454 n. 17).

have a function [*ergon*] and action [*praxis*], the good and the 'well' are thought to reside in the function, so would it seem to be for man, if[4] he has a function. Have the carpenter, then, and the shoemaker certain functions [*erga*] and actions, and man none—is he by nature idle [*argon*]? Or as eye, hand, foot, and in general each of the parts evidently has a function, may one lay it down that man similarly has a function apart from all these? What then can this be?[5]

The proliferation of conditionals and rhetorical questions here suggests an acknowledgement on Aristotle's part that his reasoning is quick, sketchy, and less than demonstrative. Still, it seems clear that the conditions are supposed to hold; that his rhetorical questions are to be answered no and yes respectively; and that lines 1097^{b}25–33 are supposed to add up to an argument for the conclusion that human beings have a function. My purpose in this paper is to figure out what that argument is.

1. Preliminaries

At a first glance, Aristotle's argument for the function thesis has the look of an induction (*epagōgē*) or argument by analogy: a survey of ostensibly analogous cases leading up to either a general rule or, as here, a conclusion about a target case.[6] Carpenters and shoemakers (standing in for all practitioners of the crafts) have functions; so do eyes, hands, and feet (standing in for all the organic parts of the body); therefore human beings have functions too. So read, the passage has a claim to be—among stiff competition—Aristotle's very

---

[4] εἴπερ is marked in comparison to simple εἰ, but ambiguously so; it can mean either 'if/since in fact' (i.e. given that it is so) or 'if indeed' (but I am sceptical that it is so) (cf. LSJ s.v.). My translation is intended as neutral; but given Aristotle's soon-to-be-announced position on the question, the former connotations are more likely to be in play.

[5] *NE* 1. 7, 1097^{b}22–33. Quotations from *Nicomachean Ethics* are from the revised Ross translation, with further revisions in some cases; other quotations from Aristotle are from the Revised Oxford Translation, sometimes with revisions, except as noted (W. D. Ross (trans.), *Aristotle:* The Nicomachean Ethics, rev. J. L. Ackrill and J. O. Urmson (Oxford, 1980); J. Barnes (ed.), *Aristotle: The Revised Oxford Translation* (2 vols.; Princeton, 1984)).

[6] For readings of the argument as inductive, see e.g. J. Burnet (ed. with intro. and notes), *The* Ethics *of Aristotle* [*Ethics*] (London, 1900), ad loc.; J. M. Cooper, *Reason and Human Good in Aristotle* (Cambridge, Mass., 1975), 70. *Epagōgē* is a standard mode of non-demonstrative, dialectical argument in Aristotle, discussed in the *Topics* (1. 12; cf. 108^{b}7 ff. and *Post. An.* 71^{a-b}, 80^{a}40 ff., 100^{b}4) and mentioned in the *Metaphysics* as a distinctively Socratic innovation (*M* 4, 1078^{b}27–9).

worst induction ever. From the fact that five other not-very-similar things have functions, why would it follow that human beings must as well?[7]

But on closer examination, it seems unlikely that an induction is really intended here at all.[8] If it were, we would expect Aristotle to cite uncontroversially function-bearing objects, such as tools and other artefacts; or perhaps beings relevantly *like* human beings, such as other animals and natural substances. In fact he does neither.

Some sympathetic interpreters conclude that there is no argument here at all, but merely an exercise in clarification. According to Sarah Broadie, 'An inductive argument from these examples to the case of man would be weak, but perhaps the examples are meant rather to illustrate the concept of *characteristic function (ergon)*.'[9] Likewise Terence Irwin suggests that Aristotle's first examples are simply 'one of his normal expository devices, an appeal to crafts'; the passage as a whole is an 'analogical exposition, to show what Aristotle has in mind, but is not in itself an argument to show that a human being has a function'.[10]

---

[7] As David Bostock puts it (*Ethics*, 16): 'Aristotle makes little attempt to argue for this . . .. Clearly one can admit that the various special skills he cites . . . do have functions . . . without supposing that the same applies to man as such. For being a man does not appear to be a similar and special kind of skill. Similarly, it would seem that we could admit that the various parts of the human body . . . have functions, without supposing that this applies to the human being as a whole.'

[8] The corresponding passage in the *Eudemian Ethics* does include an induction, but in support of a different step in the argument: '⟨Let it be assumed of⟩ excellence, that it is the best disposition, state, or capacity of anything that has some employment or function. This is evident from induction: in all cases this is what we suppose. For example, a cloak has an excellence—and a certain function and employment also; and the best state of the cloak is its excellence. Similarly too with a boat, a house, and other things. So the same is true also of the soul; for there is something which is its function' (*EE* 2. 1, 1218^{b}37–1219^{a}5: translations from the *Eudemian Ethics* are from M. Woods (trans. and comm.), *Aristotle:* Eudemian Ethics Books *I, II and VIII* (Oxford, 1992)). Here what requires inductive support is the claim that an excellence always presupposes a function—a claim not in play in the *NE* version of the argument (though it comes up later, at *NE* 2. 2, 1106^{a}14–20, and 6. 2, 1139^{a}16–17). The *NE* version is sufficiently different in structure that it seems best to read it independently—if we take the *NE* to be the later work, as an attempt to come up with a new and more perspicuous line of argument.

[9] Broadie and Rowe, *Commentary*, 276; in *Ethics* Broadie notes that the argument taken inductively is 'dismally weak', but defends the underlying thought (34–5).

[10] Irwin, *Principles*, 607 n. 37. Cf. also Lawrence, 'Function', 454 n. 17: 'it seems doubtful to what extent Aristotle would suppose it possible to argue *that* humans have a nature—and thus that talk of function is in place—as against arguing about *what* it is (cf. perhaps *Phys.* ii 1. 193^{a}3–9). If so, the lines are more an orientation of

It is hard to imagine a more undemanding reading than this. But so read, Aristotle still bungles the job. His examples serve him only awkwardly, since the functioning of a craftsman, unlike that of a human being, is not essential to him. The parts of animals 'are better examples', as Irwin says, but still not quite right; for their function is a matter of their usefulness as instruments.[11] And a natural substance as a whole, such as a human being, is not an instrument at all.

Now we have reason to suspect that Aristotle's text is both more careful and more ambitious than this. For while the instances of function he gives are not induction-supporting, neither are they random. Rather, they are closely related to the case of human beings, in two different ways. The builder and the shoemaker *are* human beings, identified *qua* practitioners of a particular craft [*technē*]: they are socially constructed *kinds* of human being, or *roles* or *identities* which a human being may take on. Eye, hand, and foot are organic *parts* of an animal's body. In fact, the hand is, as Aristotle emphasizes elsewhere, a distinctively human part (*PA* 4. 10, 687ᵃ3–ᵇ22); so the argument here is not just from natural functioning in general but from the parts of a *human* body to the whole of a human being. Likewise, the carpenter and shoemaker are here said to have *praxeis*, 'actions', as well as *erga*: and *praxeis*, since they require *prohaireseis*, deliberate choice, are a distinctively human form of behaviour (*NE* 6. 2, 1139ᵃ31–ᵇ5; *EE* 2. 10, 1225ᵇ26–7).

So Aristotle seems to be offering two distinct lines of argument for the function thesis, neither inductive and both appealing to the distinctively human. First, *the argument from the crafts* claims that if the practitioners of the crafts (such as carpenters and shoemakers) have functions, a human being as such must have a function. Second, *the argument from the organic parts* claims that if parts such as the eyes, the hands, and the feet of a human being have functions, a human being as such should be taken to have a function over and above them.

the reader, than strict argument'; and Reeve, *Practices*, 124: the argument is 'not so much a direct argument that human beings have a function as an indirect one, which relies on the implausibility of the view that they lack a function. For the alternative to having a function is being by nature inactive, and it is no more credible that human beings are by nature inactive than it is that they might be *eudaimōn* while asleep (1095ᵇ31–1096ᵃ2)'. Reeve thus rightly brings out the dialectical significance of Aristotle's invocation of 'inactivity' as the alternative; I have something to say about this in sect. 3.   [11] Ibid.

Of course, this preliminary sketch presses anew the question
of why the all-important inferences here are to be accepted. We
may also wonder just how the two arguments are supposed to fit
together, whether as independent or complementary. In this paper,
I shall focus on the question of how the argument from the crafts
is supposed to work; but my reading will also suggest a role for
Aristotle's second argument.

2. Platonic and Aristotelian functions

If a shoemaker has a function, then a human being as such must have
a function. Why would Aristotle believe that? Obviously the answer
will turn on what it means for Aristotle to attribute a function (*ergon*) to anything: if the claim that a shoemaker has a function were
merely the uncontroversial descriptive claim that shoemaking is a
socially recognized job, it is hard to see how any pertinent inference
could get off the ground. Now to many modern readers, Aristotle's
concept of function is the great stumbling-block presented by the
function argument as a whole. For instance, W. F. R. Hardie answers Aristotle's rhetorical question 'May one lay it down that man
similarly has a function?' with a resounding No: 'The obvious answer is that one may not, unless one is prepared to say that a man
is an instrument designed for some use.'[12] Hardie assumes that a
thing can have a function only if it is a tool or instrument, with a de-
signer and a user (or 'customer'). But, rightly or wrongly, Aristotle
simply does not accept this contemporary conception of function
as instrumentality.[13] And this is not because there is anything exclusively modern about that conception: rather, I believe we can see
Aristotle deliberately *rejecting* it in the function argument itself. To
see this, we need to view the function argument in relation to an
important predecessor passage in book 1 of Plato's *Republic*. Here
Socrates introduces the concept of a function in order to argue that
justice is necessary for human happiness. He asks:

---

[12] W. F. R. Hardie, *Aristotle's Ethical Theory* [*Theory*] (Oxford, 1968), 23.
[13] That is: the contemporary intuitive conception relied on by Hardie, and by
those of my students who find the function argument obviously fallacious. I shall not
be concerned here with ideas of function in contemporary biology and philosophy
of science.

SOCRATES. Tell me, do you think there is such a thing as the function [*ergon*] of a horse?

THRASYMACHUS. I do.

SOCR. And would you define the function of a horse or of anything else as that which someone can do only with it or best with it?'

(*Rep.* 352 D 9–E 4)[14]

Socrates explains what he means using examples of bodily organs and man-made instruments. You can prune a vine with a dagger or a carving knife; but you can do a better job with a pruning knife than with anything else, which is why pruning is its function. And each thing which has a function also has an *aretē*, a virtue or excellence (such as the power of sight in an eye), by means of which it performs its function well. We use our souls to deliberate, make decisions, and generally manage our lives; and the proper excellence of the soul is justice. So, Socrates concludes, a just man will live well and happily, and an unjust one badly and wretchedly (353 E 4–354 A 5).

This conception of function as instrumentality—that is, as necessarily connected to *use* and a user—is evidently an important point for Plato.[15] He reaffirms the principle in book 10 of the *Republic*: 'Then aren't the virtue or excellence, the beauty and correctness of each manufactured item, living creature, and action related to nothing but the use [χρεία] for which each is made or naturally adapted?' (601 D 4–6).[16]

As has long been recognized, Aristotle's function argument

---

[14] Translations from the *Republic* are by G. M. A. Grube, revised by C. D. C. Reeve, in some cases with some further revisions (Plato, *Complete Works*, ed. J. M. Cooper with D. S. Hutchinson (Indianapolis, 1997)).

[15] Sufficiently important to warrant Plato's treating the soul as distinct from the person who uses it, which not only sounds odd but very likely conflicts with his own considered view: cf. *Alc. I* 129 B 5–130 E 6. The *Alc. I* identification of the self with the soul seems to me likely to represent Plato's position accurately, whatever the authorship of the dialogue, since this identity provides the necessary basis for two central Platonic principles: that the goods and evils of the soul are far more important than those of the body or one's external possessions; and that *I* am immortal by virtue of the immortality of my soul (or at any rate its rational part). Cf. L. Gerson, *Knowing Persons* (Oxford, 2003), ch. 1, esp. 22 ff.; but cf. n. 16 below.

[16] Perhaps this text helps to explain the puzzling fact that Plato nowhere (excluding the *Alcibiades*) explicitly states that the self and the soul are identical, though the *Alcibiades* seems likely to be accurate in presenting this as the Platonic view (cf. n. 15). If only what has a function can have an excellence, and only instruments can have functions, then in order for the soul to be capable of virtue Plato must hold that it is distinct from the self which uses it (unless he is prepared to hold, more oddly still, that we ourselves are somehow instruments with users).

closely recalls the function argument of *Republic* 1.[17] Its basic
agenda is identical: to prove that the happy person, one who lives
well, does so by having the proper virtues of the soul. It reiterates
Socrates' two crucial claims: that the soul has a function, and that
its successful functioning depends on virtue (1098[a]7 ff.). It repeats
the canonical examples of eyes and other bodily organs. But (and
this is not so often recognized)[18] Aristotle departs from Plato—
and, I suggest, consciously corrects him—in one crucial respect.
There are no references to tools in Aristotle's version; nor to other
organisms *used as* tools, like Plato's instance of the horse; nor to
any user. There is nothing in Aristotle's argument comparable to
Plato's phrase 'that which someone [τις] can do only with it or best
with it' (352 E 2–3). In short, Aristotle avoids anything which would
suggest the Platonic conception of function as instrumentality.

It is worth briefly noting that there are at least two good reasons—
and I shall later note a third—for Aristotle to reject this Platonic
conception of function. (I do not intend to claim that these reasons are actively deployed in *NE* 1. 7, only that they shed light
on Aristotle's assumptions about function there.) Function is a
concept with an important role to play in Aristotle's teleological
physics and metaphysics; and in that context, the function (*ergon*)
of a thing is closely tied to its final cause (*hou heneka*) or end (*telos*).
Indeed, Aristotle tells us that 'everything that has a function is for
the sake of [*heneka*] its function' (*De caelo* 2. 3, 286[a]8–9; cf. *Metaph.*

---

[17] See e.g. Burnet, *Ethics*; A. Grant, *Aristotle's Ethics* [*Ethics*], 4th edn. (2 vols.;
London, 1885), vol. i; and H. Joachim, *Aristotle: The Nicomachean Ethics* (Oxford,
1951), ad loc.

[18] With the exception of Sparshott (*Life*, 42), who notes how different Aristotle's
analogues are, and a brief mention in Lawrence ('Function', 449 n. 10). The power
of the Platonic precursor can be seen from the fact that it often leaches into reports
of Aristotle's version. For instance Irwin, in the context of an otherwise accurate
and helpful account of Aristotle's passage, says: 'Having illustrated his concept of
function from artifacts and organs Aristotle asks if a human being has a function in
the same way' (*Principles*, 607 n. 37). Likewise Santas, in what otherwise looks to
be a discussion of our passage: 'Both Plato and Aristotle illustrate their definitions
of function with artifacts, roles and occupations, organs of animals and animals'
(Santas, *Goodness and Justice*, 238). And Grant reports the argument as one 'by
which, from the analogy of the different trades, of the different animals, and of the
separate parts of the body, the existence of a proper function for man is proved',
and says that it 'comes almost *verbatim* from Plato's *Republic*'—a claim which would
be more accurate if the 'different animals' were indeed in Aristotle's text (*Ethics*, i.
449). Whiting ('Defense') rightly points out that an argument from artefacts would
be a significant departure from what we have in the text (46 n. 4); but, by taking
Aristotle's reasoning to be restricted to natural kinds, her reading ends up excluding
some of the examples he *does* give—namely, the craftspeople.

B 2, 996ᵇ7); and that 'the function of each thing is its end' (*telos,*
EE 2. 1, 1219ᵃ8). He associates both function and end with activity
(*energeia*): 'the function is an end, and the activity is the function,
hence also the word '*energeia*' is based on '*ergon*' and points towards
the "actuality" [*entelecheia*]' (*Metaph.* Θ 8, 1050ᵃ21–3). Thus function determines identity: as Aristotle says in the *Politics*, 'all things
are defined by their function [*ergon*] and power [*dunamis*]' (1. 2,
1253ᵃ24). This relation to end and identity makes *ergon* a powerful normative concept, closely linked to the good of a thing and
determining what counts as its excellence or virtue (*aretē*).[19] The
upshot is that for Aristotle as a biologist, the end of an organism
is to lead a good life for organisms of that kind, one constituted
by a certain kind of successful activity. And so the function of a
horse is *not*, as it is for Plato, to serve human needs, but to lead a
flourishing equine existence, doing well the things that horses are
by nature such as to do.

Second, Aristotle must also reject Plato's account of how functions are to be attributed. For he will eventually, at *NE* 10. 6–8,
identify our function with contemplative activity. And contemplation is something which the gods also do, and do better than us—for
one thing, they can do it continuously and eternally. So for Aristotle, unlike Plato, the human function *cannot* be *idion*, 'peculiar
to' us, in the sense that it is something we do better than anything
else does—let alone what some mysterious user does *with* us better
than could be done with any other tool.[20] Rather, it must be what
is distinctive of or proper to us, in the sense that it best realizes our
nature: we do it best and most characteristically of the things *we* do.

So Aristotle does not and should not grant the Platonist assumption that all function is instrumental. Rather, for Aristotle, to say
that a human being has a function is to say that a human being has
a nature, an end, a characteristic activity, and so also a distinctive

---

[19] To us, it might sound odd to ascribe a good to some of the subjects to which
Aristotle attributes functions. But for Aristotle every natural substance has its own
distinctive good, teleologically construed (*NE* 1141ᵃ20–33; *EE* 1217ᵃ25–9: cf. Johnson, *Teleology*, 222–9). And at least on occasion he is willing to ascribe a good to
tools: 'the latter in each case ⟨craftsman and tool, soul and body, master and slave⟩
is benefited by that which uses it, but there is no friendship or justice towards lifeless
things' (*NE* 8. 12, 1161ᵃ34–ᵇ2, emphasis added).

[20] The problem of reconciling this with the *idion* criterion is discussed by R.
Kraut, 'The Peculiar Function of Human Beings', *Canadian Journal of Philosophy*,
9 (1979), 467–78, and *Aristotle on the Human Good* [*Good*] (Princeton, 1989), 312–
19 at 313; and Whiting, 'Defense', 37–8.

excellence and good. No doubt in the special case of tools or instruments Aristotle will agree with Plato that function consists in
being correctly used; for natural substances such as animals and
humans, however, functioning consists in an activity which has its
value *not* instrumentally but intrinsically, as a realization of the
subject's own end.

Now the extent to which these (meta)physical principles are actually brought to bear in the function argument is another question.
Scholars often do present the argument as if it were just a device
for wheeling in the fundamental principles of Aristotle's natural
teleology. On this line of interpretation, whatever Aristotle may say
here, the *real* basis for presuming that human beings have a function is simply that, like the members of any other biological kind,
our natures are constituted by a set of capacities exercised in a characteristic mode of activity. I shall call this the 'biological' reading
of the function argument.[21] Though fair enough as a presentation
of general Aristotelian doctrine, such readings operate at an unsa-
tisfying remove from the text of the *Ethics*: this line of argument
cannot be one that Aristotle expects his readers to extract from the
reasoning he presents. And it threatens to wreck the reasoning he
does present. For in so far as function is assumed to be a strictly
biological concept, uniform across members of a species, being a
shoemaker is not a function at all. (I shall argue in Section 4 that
this tension can be resolved; but it still tells against any assumption
that we are expected here simply to read in principles from Aristotle's natural science.[22])

[21] Cf. Irwin, *Principles*, and 'The Metaphysical and Psychological Basis of Aristotle's Ethics', in A. O. Rorty (ed.), *Essays on Aristotle's Ethics [Essays]* (Berkeley,
1980), 35–53; also Whiting, 'Defense', and Kraut, *Aristotle*, 83–5 (but note sect. 3
and nn. 27 and 29 below); against such readings cf. T. Roche, 'On the Alleged
Metaphysical Foundation of Aristotle's *Ethics*' ['Foundation'], *Ancient Philosophy*,
8 (1988), 49–62.

[22] A broadly 'biological' or metaphysical reading on which Aristotle's text does
present an argument for the function thesis is provided by Tuozzo, 'Function'.
Tuozzo makes a powerful case for reading both the argument from the crafts and
the argument from the organic parts as arguments from the parts to the whole. As
he notes, for Aristotle, 'the function of a bodily part, or of a trade, is only fully
intelligible when its role in a larger, complex functional whole is understood' (148).
Tuozzo carefully notes that this does not entail what would be false for Aristotle,
namely that the function of the whole is simply *composed* of the functions of the
parts: rather, the relation is a teleological one, and 'the function of the whole is also
the function of some one pre-eminent part' (148 n. 7). As with the bodily organs,
so too in the case of the crafts: 'the functions of the various craftsmen are not fully
intelligible independently of the one activity to which they contribute and which

The biological reading becomes even more unsatisfactory if we ask what sort of argument we might expect from Aristotle at this point, given his well-known claims to begin his arguments from the reputable opinions (*endoxa*) or appearances (*phainomena*), and from 'what is better known to us' (γνωριμώτερον ἡμῖν).[23] Of course, exactly how these claims should be interpreted, and what they can tell us about Aristotelian practice, is enormously controversial.[24] Still, it seems fair to say that nothing at 1097^{b}24 ff., or earlier in the *Ethics*, looks much like a cue to the reader to import wholesale the teleological framework of Aristotelian natural science. We should prefer a reading on which, without introducing anything *incompatible* with his physics and metaphysics, Aristotle's reasoning can get some traction by doing what it seems to do: appealing to obvious facts about carpenters and shoemakers, eyes, hands, and feet. I shall call this strategy of interpretation 'dialectical',[25] and in the rest of the paper will attempt to offer such a reading.

The challenge for the dialectical reading is to identify some argumentative support for the function thesis which avoids both the Scylla of dubious induction and the Charybdis of surreptitious natural science. This paper will locate that support in a conception of function which is more robust than the merely descriptive but falls well short of assuming the full framework of Aristotelian natural teleology. I shall argue that, for Aristotle, the claim that shoemaking is a function is offered as shorthand for a set of *normative* claims.

they subserve' (150). As a claim about intelligibility this may seem far-fetched; but Tuozzo is right that the opening of the *Nicomachean Ethics* establishes a hierarachical and teleological relation between the crafts and the human good (as pursued by the city) which may well match the relation between the organs and the human good (as pursued by the individual). In effect, Tuozzo's reading offers to bolster the architectonic reading (cf. sect. 3) with the teleological principle that if the parts of a whole have a function, the whole must have one as well. Aristotle may well believe this: Tuozzo argues plausibly for its being entailed by his conception of part–whole relations (147–51; cf. Johnson, *Teleology*, 218–19 with n. 8). On the other hand, the principle is controversial to say the least, and needs to be very carefully articulated to avoid the 'fallacy of composition'; and I see no evidence that Aristotle invokes it here.

[23] *NE* 7. 1–3; *Phys.* 1. 1; *NE* 1. 4, 1095^{b}2–4; *Metaph. B* 1 and *H* 3, 1029^{b}1–12. Cf. also the argument of Roche, 'Foundation', from the 'autonomy of the sciences' (53–5).

[24] On these methodological issues, cf. J. Barnes, 'Aristotle and the Methods of Ethics', *Revue internationale de philosophie*, 34 (1981), 490–511; Roche, 'Foundation'; Destrée, 'Comment démontrer'; and M. C. Nussbaum, *Aristotle's De motu animalium* (Princeton, 1978; rev. edn. 1985), 103–6.

[25] Cf. Destrée, 'Comment démontrer'.

There is nothing peculiarly Aristotelian about this: *ergon* is often a normative concept, for the work appropriate to and incumbent on a particular person or kind of person.[26] In the *Iliad* Hector tells Andromache to busy herself with her own *erga* (6. 490), and the two Aiantes urge that there is work (*ergon*) for everyone to do (12. 271). In Aeschylus' *Eumenides* Athena says that it is her *ergon* to cast the final vote, as she does to acquit Orestes (734, cf. also *PV* 635; *Cho.* 673). Likewise for Aristotle, to say that shoemaking is a function is not (or not merely) to make the descriptive point that some people pay other people to do it: it is to say something about what it is incumbent upon certain people to do, and what norms are rightly applicable to them. Read along these lines, Aristotle's reasoning here does not assume natural teleology but argues towards it, as being presupposed by what we might call *social* teleology. His claim is that the normativity of social functions must derive from their relation to a function embedded in human nature.

3. The hierarchy of crafts and the architectonic reading

There are two very different ways in which a reading along these lines may be spelt out. One takes Aristotle's point to be that shoemaking must contribute to a functional good on the part of the broader shoe-wearing community. As Richard Kraut puts it:

This train of thought rests on the assumption that when one finds a nested series of functions, they ultimately serve one highest function. The various functions of craftsmen must ultimately serve some higher function—and what else could that be but our functioning as human beings?[27]

We may call this the *architectonic* reading of the argument: if a shoemaker as such has a function, the end of shoemaking must contribute to some further end which is functional in nature, and ultimately to the functioning of human beings as such.

Aristotle might well expect the argument to be read in this way. For the *Ethics* opens, in 1. 1, with a vision of the crafts and sciences as ordered into a hierarchy, corresponding to the ends or goods which they serve. Every craft serves some useful end, but some crafts are subordinate to others: for instance, 'bridle-making

---

[26] Cf. LSJ s.v., esp. IV.1 for *ergon* as 'proper work'; cf. Lawrence, 'Good', for function as normative.

[27] *Aristotle*, 82.

and the other crafts concerned with the equipment of horses fall under the craft of riding, and this and every military action under generalship' (1094ᵃ10–13). To avoid an infinite regress, these hierarchies must culminate in a single architectonic craft which directs the whole system. This is political science (*politikē*), which supervises all the others; and 'the end of this science must encompass [περιέχοι] those of the others, so that this end must be the human good' (1094ᵇ6–7). This ideal of politics or practical wisdom as an architectonic science is inherited from Plato, and the *Republic* and *Charmides* in particular. It builds on traditional Greek conceptions of the crafts (*technai*) as serving specialized ends or goods, conjoined with Platonic worries about the need for their rational ordering and philosophical supervision.[28]

Now in the earlier part of 1. 7, by way of leading up to the function argument, Aristotle recalls this passage at length (1097ᵃ15–34). He emphasizes that in each sphere the good consists in an end achievable by action—in medicine health, in strategy victory—and notes that some ends (e.g. the making of a flute) are clearly chosen for the sake of others. Happiness is then identified as the highest good, the end of action which is always choiceworthy for its own sake: 'something final and self-sufficient, and . . . the end of action' (1097ᵇ20–1). Aristotle then launches the function argument by noting that it is something of a platitude to say that happiness is the chief good (or more literally the 'best', τὸ ἄριστον); he proposes to give the platitude content by recourse to our function (1097ᵇ22–5).

The architectonic reading of the argument from the crafts takes it, plausibly, as putting this argumentative context to work. The conception of a human community as organized in terms of functional activities is used to suggest that the highest good to which they are oriented is the same in kind. However, this suggestion falls well short of a conclusive argument.[29] Indeed it opens the way for a threatening objection: perhaps the functional nature of the subordinate goods is actually a symptom of their subordinate status.

---

[28] I have discussed this architectonic conception more fully in 'The Carpenter and the Good' ['Carpenter'], in D. Cairns, F.-G. Herrmann, and T. Penner (eds.) *Pursuing the Good: Ethics and Metaphysics in Plato's* Republic (Edinburgh, forthcoming). It is perhaps worth noting that builder and shoemaker are two of the first five members of the First City in *Republic* 2 (369 D): these are the most primordial and necessary of the crafts, and thus are paradigmatic for *technē* as such.

[29] Accordingly Kraut, as it seems to me, eventually throws in the towel and shifts to a version of the biological reading (*Aristotle*, 83–5).

This objection might go with a range of alternative, non-functional conceptions of the ultimate good.[30] Perhaps the good is pleasure, and shoemaking contributes to it by providing shoe-based hedonic units. Perhaps it consists in a life of leisurely amusement, *paidia*— a possibility that still worries Aristotle near the end of the *Ethics* (10. 6)—and shoes serve it in so far as they amuse. Perhaps the good for you is whatever you happen to think it is, so that shoes contribute to your good if you think they do. On any of these accounts, shoemaking turns out to be of strictly instrumental value to the shoemaker and society alike; and the activities or states in which our good consists (pleasure, leisure, mindless amusement, subjective satisfaction, etc.) do not themselves have the structure of a function.

I shall call this loose cluster of hedonist and subjectivist objections the *instrumentalist objection*. This way of putting it should recall Plato's conception of function as instrumentality; and we can now see another reason, perhaps the most important, why Aristotle must reject that conception. For it provides a natural grounding for the instrumentalist objection. Instrumental goods are conditional goods: if function is understood as instrumentality, the hierarchy of functional goods provided by the crafts must, on pain of infinite regress, ultimately serve some unconditional and non-functional end, both for society (if the craft is have any value) and for the individual practitioner (if he is to be motivated to practise it). (And we cannot assume that these two ends will converge: there is no *necessary* relation between the satisfactions of the shoemaker and of the shoe-wearer.)

The instrumentalist conception of function thus threatens to ground a conception of human society and functioning which was recognized by Plato and Aristotle as a dangerous alternative to their own—a kind of evil twin to the hierarchical vision of Platonic–Aristotelian *politikē*. As Aristotle complains in the *Politics*, many people take the value of crafts and even virtues to be purely instrumental, with money (presumably as a proxy for pleasure) as the end:

And even those who do aim at living well seek what serves bodily enjoy-

---

[30] I here discuss just one prominent ancient version of anti-functionalism about the good. Obviously, as Tom Hurka has emphasized to me, there are many other ways to reject Aristotelian functionalism, even within the framework of a broadly perfectionist or teleological ethics; I do not claim that Aristotle even attempts to exclude them all.

ments, so that since this too seems to be found in the possession of property, they spend all their time on making money . . . using each of the abilities, but not in accordance with its nature. For courage is for the creation not of wealth, but daring; nor is generalship or medicine ⟨for wealth⟩, but rather ⟨for⟩ victory and health respectively. But these people turn everything into a form of moneymaking, taking it that this is the end [*telos*] and that everything must contribute to the end. (1258ª2–13, my translation)

The view recalls that of Thrasymachus in book 1 of the *Republic* (340 D–344 C): the shepherd fattens his flocks not for any distinctive end intrinsic to the practice of shepherding, but as an instrument of his own self-interest—just like the practitioner of every other craft, including the expert ruler. All the crafts thus serve the *same* end, a point emphasized when this stance is articulated in Aristophanes' play *Wealth*. Here Chremulos and Karion sing the praises of their new-found friend, personified Wealth himself; their speech deliberately recalls Prometheus' great speech in *Prometheus Bound* (441–506), probably the most deeply influential text for Greek thinking about the *technai*.[31] The canonical examples of craft are once again the shoemaker and the carpenter:

CHREMULOS. All crafts and clever inventions of the human race have been
   discovered because of you. For one of us sits making shoes—
KARION. Another works metal, or as a carpenter—
CHREM. Or is a goldsmith, taking gold from you—
KAR. Another steals clothes, or breaks into houses—
                              (Ar. *Plut.* 160–5, my translation)

And so on through wool-making, clothes-washing, hide-tanning, onion-selling, political bribery, mercenary warfare, story-writing, and love, to the resounding conclusion that *all* things done in the world are done for the sake of Wealth (182–3)—as if in a parodic anticipation of Plato's claim that we do all things for the good, or Aristotle's claim that all activities aim at happiness. Aristophanes here presents the instrumentalist conception carried to its logical conclusion: carpentry and burglary are the same sort of enterprise, since there is no salient dividing line between the *technai* and other strategies for obtaining profit.

This instrumentalist vision of crafts and the good represents a prominent contemporary alternative to that of Plato and Aristotle.

---

[31] As noted ad loc. by J. Van Leeuwen (ed. and notes), *Aristophanes: Plutus*, 2nd edn. (Leiden, 1968).

But on the architectonic reading, the argument from the crafts offers nothing to convince anyone inclined towards this rival view. Indeed, by raising the question of what occupies the 'top' of the hierarchy of crafts, it is likely to *provoke* the instrumentalist objection; and that objection is not easily answered. It recurs in the *Ethics* like a toothache, a peripheral irritant which Aristotle can neither get rid of nor entirely ignore (e.g. *NE* 1. 5; 10. 6). His habit is to dismiss it with a rhetorical appeal to the reader's shame and self-respect, as expressing a vulgar, slavish, and childish point of view (1. 5, 1095^{b}19–23; 10. 6, 1176^{b}16–1177^{a}11).[32]

Does this show that the architectonic reading of the argument should be rejected? Should we suppose that Aristotle must have known better than to lay himself open to the instrumentalist objection here? Not necessarily. For Aristotle seems to acknowledge the objection, and to try to stare it down, immediately following his invocation of the crafts, when he asks, in what registers as an incredulous tone of voice, whether it can be that a human being as such has *no* function: 'is he by nature idle [*argon*]?' (1097^{b}29–30).[33] The key term *argos* here is by origin *a-ergos*, literally *ergon*-less. And this is no coinage or technical term, but rather a standard term for idle, lazy, or unemployed (LSJ s.v.). So the question operates simultaneously, and rather sneakily, on two levels. On the one hand Aristotle is simply specifying the logical alternative to his proposal that human beings have a natural function; but on the other he is using the pejorative connotations of *argos* to suggest, with a strong hint of *reductio*, that this would amount to claiming that human beings are by nature *lazy* or *unemployed*. That is, he suggests that the rival view is committed to a degrading conception of human nature—just the sort of shaming move Aristotle offers against instrumentalism in 1. 5 and 10. 6.

Moreover, Aristotle's argument for the function thesis is far from over. For his rhetorical question is immediately followed by the

---

[32] Indeed, Aristotle never seems to offer a systematic argument against the instrumentalist objection, though such an argument could be provided by his analysis of the nature of pleasure (*NE* 7. 11–14 and especially 10. 1–5). Since pleasures are not fungible, and are epiphenomenal on activities, 'pleasure' as such is not really an independent and homogeneous candidate for the human good; and the life of amusement is in any case not the most pleasant life. It seems to me debatable whether the rejection of the life of amusement in 10. 6 should be read as a (rather sketchy) deployment of these results, or as just another rhetorical sideswipe.

[33] Cf. Suits, 'Fallacies', 27; Sparshott, *Life*, 43–4.

argument from the organic parts; and we are now, I think, in a position to see where this can do some work. The organs of the body are, as always for Aristotle, the most uncontroversial instances of function in nature. He expects us to find it intuitively plausible, even obvious, that the eye and hand have functions. Eyes are for seeing, and good eyes are ones which see well—claims which are not reducible to facts about what I happen to like to do with mine. If we assent to this much, we thereby assent to the general point that there *are* functions to be found in nature (and human nature in particular), and that they impose normative standards independent of our contingent desires.

If this is the point of the argument from the organic parts, there is no need to read it as an attempt to evoke Aristotle's full account of natural teleology from elsewhere, or as sketching a (rather tricky) deductive argument from the parts of the human body to the whole of a human being. Rather, I would suggest, we may take it as aiming only to defuse the instrumentalist objection, by showing that we have no good reason to assume that recognized social functions can *only* be a matter of social construction.

To sum up: on the architectonic reading, Aristotle's argument for a human function involves three moves. The argument from the crafts recalls the nested hierarchy of human functions and goods to suggest that all the crafts ultimately serve a human function as such. Aristotle then meets the obvious instrumentalist objection with the insinuation that the alternative view involves a degrading conception of human nature (as 'lazy'). His invocation of the organic parts then offers reassurance that functions *can* belong to the realm of nature, and to human nature in particular. This does not add up to a deductive argument for the function thesis, but it might reasonably be taken to shift the burden of argument against an instrumentalist opponent; more important, it might reasonably carry along a reader who has received the right preliminary moral education and is thus predisposed to Aristotle's side of the argument.

4. Social teleology and human nature: the realization reading

There is also a very different way to read the argument from the crafts: as imputing a human function, not to the community served by shoemaking, but to the shoemaker himself. On this reading, Aristotle's reasoning is that if shoemaking is the function of any particular shoemaker—Simon, say, the well-known follower of Socrates and author of Socratic dialogues—it must be because of some connection between that function and a function naturally belonging to Simon as a human being.[34] My general hypothesis, again, is that Aristotle's argument depends on taking the crafts to have, as functions, a certain normative standing. On the architectonic reading, Aristotle takes this standing to depend on Simon's work subserving a human good, realized by his *polis* as a whole, which is likewise functional in nature. On the *realization reading*, as I shall call it, Aristotle holds that Simon's functioning as a shoemaker can have normative standing only if it realizes or instantiates Simon's own function as a human being.

The realization reading is suggested by the initial invocation of the crafts—the 'good and the well' claim, as I shall call it—with which Aristotle introduces the idea of function at 1097^{b}25–8:

For just as for a flute-player, a sculptor, or any artist [τεχνίτης], and, in general, for all things that have a function and action, the good and the 'well' are thought to reside in the function [ἐν τῷ ἔργῳ δοκεῖ τἀγαθὸν εἶναι καὶ τὸ εὖ], so would it seem to be for man, if he has a function.

Now scholars have noted an ambiguity here in the phrase 'the good and the well', as regards 'good' in particular.[35] Aristotle might be making either or both of two claims:

If an *x qua x* has as its function to φ, then *a good x qua x* is one which φ's well.

or:

---

[34] Simon was also a character in Socratic dialogues written by others, including Phaedo's *Simon*: cf. D.L. 2. 122–4, and C. Kahn, *Plato and the Socratic Dialogue* (Cambridge, 1996), 9–11.

[35] Cf. P. Glassen, 'A Fallacy in Aristotle's Argument About the Good', *Philosophical Quarterly*, 7 (1957), 319–22, and the more sympathetic K. Wilkes, 'The Good Man and the Good for Man in Aristotle's Ethics', *Mind*, 87 (1978), 553–71, repr. in Rorty (ed.), *Essays*, 341–57. If Aristotle simply equivocates between 'the human good' and 'goodness in a human being', then the charge of fallacy is hard to avoid. But as I understand it, Aristotle's claim that a human being has a function is intended precisely as a substantive claim that these two kinds of good are inseparable. The human good is happiness, which consists in living well; and well is the way the excellent person lives.

If an *x qua x* has as its function to φ, then the good *of* an *x qua x*—its flourishing as an *x*—consists in φ'ing well.[36]

I shall call the first of these the 'weak' claim, the latter the 'strong' one. The weak claim seems to be an analytic truth, though perhaps it does not quite go without saying: we do sometimes need to be reminded that fame, income, and worldly success are simply irrelevant to the evaluation of professionals, unless they are somehow part of the end of the profession in question. The weak claim also paves the way for Aristotle to say, as he will, that, given a human function, the good or excellent person will be one who performs that function well. The strong claim involves the more controversial idea that the extent to which one flourishes in relation to some role is dependent on one's functioning in that role. It paves the way for Aristotle to claim, as he will, that given a human function, human *happiness* is constituted by functioning well.

The two claims are not exclusive: they are combined in the claim that the good *of* a functional entity consists in its being active *as* a good entity of that kind. And while the weak claim is obvious, the context clearly requires the strong claim as well. For Aristotle has just identified the human good with happiness; he can hardly expect the reader to take 'the good' here (1097^b27) as referring back to anything other than the 'best' which he has just undertaken to explain, i.e. happiness (1097^b22). (Note too that 'the good' here is *tagathon*, neuter, which is more easily read as the abstraction 'the good [of an *x*]' than as a placeholder for 'good [masc.] flute-player' *et al*.) Moreover, as I have noted, it is the strong claim that Aristotle will need when he comes to apply the 'good and the well' claim to the case of human functioning. So Aristotle is best read as here asserting a three-place relation connecting functioning well, excellence, and flourishing.

The upshot so far is that if shoemaking is a function, and the function of Simon in particular, then the good of Simon *qua* shoemaker is to be active as a good shoemaker. Now this idea of the good of the craftsperson—to stick with Aristotle's example here, the sculptor *qua* sculptor—should be a familiar one. We also rely

---

[36] Karen Nielsen has pointed out to me that this is a problematic general principle: an axe presumably has an *ergon* but no 'good of'. But since Aristotle specifies at 1097^b26 (as at $^b29$) that he is talking about things with an *ergon* and a *praxis* (taking καί as 'and' rather than Ross's 'or'), we can take the context here to be restricted to human beings. Cf. also *NE* 8. 12, $1161^a34–^b2$, quoted in n. 19 above.

on it whenever we speak of what is good *for* someone as a sculptor, since the good *for* x is (typically) what promotes the good *of* x.[37] Plant food is good *for* plants because it promotes the good *of* plants, namely healthy growth. It might seem that the 'good of' a sculptor *qua* sculptor is ambiguous, between excellence as a sculptor and flourishing or success as one. But on reflection, if we are careful to bracket irrelevant considerations of 'wage-earning', there is plausibly no real gap between the two: to flourish as a sculptor, strictly speaking, *just is* to excel in one's artistic activity. And that is why the sculptor is introduced here: this is precisely the pattern of connection between excellence and the good which Aristotle wants to establish for human beings as such.

Of course, this is not yet sufficient for the function thesis. For the sculptor *qua* sculptor might be dismissed as a metaphysical abstraction, and one of dubious relevance to what Aristotle needs to establish.[38] If Simon is a shoemaker, then 'Simon the shoemaker' is what Aristotle would class as an 'accidental unity', since being a shoemaker is not essential to him. And the attributes of an accidental unity cannot automatically be predicated of the underlying substance (cf. *SE* 177^{b}14–15; *De int.* 20^{b}33–5).[39] So what Aristotle needs to get to the function thesis is a stronger claim still, which I shall call the *transitivity* claim:

> If an *x qua x* has as its function to φ, then the good of the substance which is *x* consists (at least in part)[40] in φ'ing well.

---

[37] Sometimes the 'good for *x*' picks out what serves to make an *x* a good *x*: sharpening is good for knives because it makes them good (as) knives. This ambiguity dovetails nicely with the Aristotelian view that doing well and faring well are not fundamentally separable. (For a fuller discussion of 'good of', 'good as', and 'good for', cf. my 'Carpenter'.)

[38] Cf. Hardie, *Theory*, 23–4; and likewise Irwin, *Principles*, 607 n. 37: 'The usefulness of this appeal to function, however, depends on the character of the description under which the function is ascribed to the subject; if Socrates is a tailor, and idler, and a gourmand, we can find what is good for him qua each of these, and be none the wiser about what is good for Socrates. If the description identifies an essential property of the subject, then the description of the function will be useful.' I take the range of relevant descriptions to be broader than the explicitly essential; but they must pick out identities which help to realize the individual's good, which is dictated by his essence.

[39] This is brought out by the fact that *some* claims we can make about the '*x qua x*' lead nowhere normatively. A good hit man *qua* hit man is one who always carries out his assignment; but nothing follows from this about what Martin Blank, who is a hit man, ought to do, since being a hit man is *not* properly an *ergon*.

[40] Nothing so far rules out the possibility that a number of different activities

Applied to the case at hand: if shoemaking is a function, and the function of Simon in particular,[41] then it is (at least part of) the good of *Simon* to be a good shoemaker, and to make shoes well.

The transitivity claim gives Aristotle an attractive and even elegant basis for the function thesis. And we might well think that transitivity is entailed by Aristotle's metaphysical commitments: for the connections among function, end, and identity which I outlined in Section 2 would seem to entail that Aristotelian functions can belong to their bearers only essentially, not under a *per accidens* description. (That is, Simon can have a function *qua* shoemaker only if it is also Simon's function *simpliciter—qua* Simon, or *qua* human being.[42]) However, as a line of argument for the function thesis this begs the question of why we should suppose that shoemaking *is* a function in the metaphysically loaded Aristotelian sense. And it might be objected that for Aristotle craftspeople *cannot* in fact count as exercising the human function.[43] After all, in the *Politics* Aristotle repeatedly denounces the 'banausic' or menial occupations as degraded and corrupting: since banausic labour

might all be expressions of the human function for Simon; whether Aristotle would want to reject this sort of pluralism or inclusivism is a complicated question. Simon's functioning is second-rate anyway, relative to the exercise of perfect virtue available only in the life of *theōria*; so it is not clear that shoemaking would have to be the sole locus of his functional activity even if *theōria* has that status in the *best* life. To explore this issue would require entering much more fully into the later stages of the argument of the *Nicomachean Ethics*.

[41] I take it that this is a distinct condition, over and above (1) shoemaking is a function and (2) Simon is a shoemaker. For presumably it is a condition of the normativity of a function that it be appropriate to one's nature: shoemaking would not be the *ergon* of Socrates even if hard times forced him to the bench. Aristotle has little to say about the fundamental Platonic thesis, central to *Republic* 2–7, that occupations should be allocated in accordance with the nature of the worker; but his discussion of the 'natural slave' shows that he accepts the basic principle (*Pol.* 1. 1–2). It might be objected that the cases are different, since as Aristotle says, 'a slave is among the things by nature, but no one is by nature a shoemaker or any of the other craftsmen' (*Pol.* 1. 12, 1260^{b}1–2). But his point here is only, reasonably enough, that by and large our natures underdetermine which functions are appropriate to us, not that they do not determine their range at all.

[42] For the identity of what Simon is essentially, what he is *qua* human being, and what he is as Simon, cf. *Categories* 5 and *Metaphysics Z* 6; cf. Broadie, *Ethics*, 38.

[43] Another objection would be, more simply, that in the *Ethics* itself the human good will turn out to consist in *theōria*, of which shoemaking is pretty obviously not a species. But Aristotle's interest in the *Ethics* seems to be in the best human life, and the good for Simon does not necessarily coincide with *that*: what matters for our purposes is whether his work can instantiate the human function of rational activity *at all*.

precludes leisure, free thought, and virtuous action (and with it happiness), Aristotle argues, its practitioners cannot really be capable of citizenship (*Pol.* 1264^{b}22–4, 1277^{b}33–1278^{a}21, 1319^{a}24–30, 1328^{b}33–41, 1329^{a}19–29). The principal criterion for the banausic is hand-work; the category is clearly one to which most of the *technai* belong to some extent, shoemaking included. And, as with his discussion of slavery, Aristotle is shockingly ready to assume that the actual occupants of these roles are naturally suited to them.

Still, this cannot quite be the whole Aristotelian story. If the shoemaker could not to any degree at all attain the good independently, so that the value of his life were purely instrumental, he would be a natural slave; and this is in fact a distinct and much more restricted category (cf. *Pol.* 1260^{b}1–2: 'independently' because even the slave can attain a good of sorts, coinciding with that of his master (*Pol.* 1252^{a}34–5)). Moreover, in *NE* 6. 4 *technē* is said to be one of the intellectual virtues, with *logos* as a defining feature (1140^{a}1–23). A *technē* properly speaking is a rational practice, correlative with *epistēmē* rather than mere experience (*Metaph.* A 1, 981^{a}12–^{b}24); to exercise *technē* must therefore count as an exercise (however imperfect) of rational virtue, which the function argument itself will identify with the human good (*NE* 1098^{a}7–18). So it would be a mistake to take Aristotle's deprecations of the lower *technai* in the *Politics* as entailing an identity of the technical and the banausic, and as excluding Simon altogether from the human good.[44]

A difficulty in the argument which I have so far ignored points in the same direction. As noted above and in Section 2, within the structure of Aristotelian teleological (meta)physics, an object's function is correlated with its nature or essence; so there should strictly speaking be no non-essential functions. Moreover, Aristotle holds that functions are common to the members of a species: 'Every animal is thought to have a proper pleasure, as it has a proper function; viz. that which corresponds to its activity' (*NE* 10. 5, 1176^{a}3–5). This suggests, disastrously, that *on any reading* the argument from the crafts depends on a premiss Aristotle considers false: shoemaking is not in fact a function. But on the realization reading this difficulty is resolved: for shoemaking *can* be Simon's

[44] And though their voices are not much heard in our surviving texts, there can be little doubt that in the Greek world as now, professional identities were an enormous source of meaning and value for ordinary people, and the practice of a craft (even a 'banausic' one) often a source of pride. Cf. G. E. M. de Ste. Croix, *The Class Struggle in the Ancient Greek World* (Ithaca, NY, 1981), 274–5.

function if it coincides with or instantiates his function as a member of the human species.

I conclude that, his contempt for the lower orders notwithstanding, Aristotle is committed to allowing that a range of ways of life may attain the good in different degrees, ordered by the degree to which they express rational activity.[45] Within its limitations, shoe-making must constitute a realization of the human function and the human good for those who can aspire to no better. So read, the argument from the crafts is reminiscent of a very odd passage of *Republic* 3. The context is Socrates' denunciation of decadent modern medicine, which will be banned from the *kallipolis*:

SOCRATES. Everyone in a well-regulated city has his own work [*ergon*] to do and . . . no one has the leisure to be ill and under treatment all his life. It is absurd that we recognize this to be true of craftsmen while failing to recognize that it is equally true of those who are wealthy and supposedly happy.

GLAUCON. How is that?

SOCR. When a carpenter is ill, he expects to receive an emetic or a purge from his doctor or to get rid of his disease through surgery or cautery. If anyone prescribed a lengthy regimen to him, telling him that he should rest with his head bandaged and so on, he'd soon reply that he had no leisure to be ill and that life is no use to him if he has to neglect his work [*ergasia*] and always be concerned with his illness.   (406 C 3–D 7)

Socrates suggests that this is 'because his life is no profit to him if he doesn't do his work [*ergon*]' (407 A 1–2). The rich person, by contrast, is generally assumed to have no work without which his life is not worth living: but this assumption ignores the all-important truth that 'once you have the means of life, you must practise virtue' (407 A 7–8). Socrates' point seems to be that the person of leisure should consider life not worth living except in so far as it enables him to live *well*, i.e. in the pursuit of virtue.

On the face of it, this passage has the air of a creepy aristocratic joke. Socrates purports to suggest that the carpenter's life is 'un-liveable' without his work because of a dedication which the rich person should emulate, when the sense is rather, as Socrates knows perfectly well, that without it he will starve to death. Yet the idea

---

[45] This point has often been made, more thoroughly than I can do here, in relation to Aristotle's higher-level candidates for the good, i.e. the lives of contemplation and politics, and on the basis of more general considerations about the argument of the *Nicomachean Ethics*: cf. Kraut, *Good*.

being introduced is a deeply serious one, and normative rather than descriptive. The lowly craftsperson provides a humble small-scale model of what should be expected from his betters—a favourite Platonic move we might call *argument from the lowly* (cf. e.g. *Rep.* 374 B–E; 467 A). This shaming trope can be traced back to Socrates, who in the *Apology* insists that only among the craftsmen, not the politicians and not the poets, did he encounter any real knowledge at all (22 A–E). The reader is presumed to look down on shoemakers and carpenters, as incapable of pursuing the highest human good. And yet—having no alternative—they are getting something important right.

This account of the sickly carpenter expresses one of the central themes of the *Republic*, the idea that happiness is to be found in the way of life for which one is naturally suited. The principle comes out most clearly when Socrates mounts a defence against Adeimantus' charge that, lacking wealth and property, the Guardians will not be happy (419 A 1–420 A 2). Part of his response is that he has to consider the happiness of the whole city: this means supplying its citizens with only an appropriate, politically sustainable happiness, of a sort compatible with their roles. Neither the Guardians nor the productive class, Socrates affirms, will be 'happy as at some festival but not in a city' (421 B 2–3). Rather, 'as the whole city grows and is well governed, we must leave it to nature to provide each group with its share of happiness' (421 C 3–6). But Socrates also hints heavily that the Guardians will indeed be very happy in their way of life (420 B), a suggestion he later claims has been proven true (465 E–466 C). What the sickly carpenter brings out is that, as we would expect, the same principle applies to the members of the other classes: their good is realized not in holiday-making or skiving off but in doing their appropriate work. And since craftspeople themselves tend to recognize this fact even in existing societies (albeit for lack of any alternative), they have something to teach their ostensible betters. Aristotle, it seems to me, inherits and assumes this perspective on the good of the craftsperson. The transitivity claim puts it to work, identifying Simon's good as a shoemaker with Simon's good *simpliciter*.

This line of argument might prompt a kind of aristocratic variant on the instrumentalist objection. Perhaps the good of *Simon*, such as it is, is realized by his function; the highest good of the highest sort of person might still be of a very different order. Strikingly,

Aristotle moves to block just this possibility later in the function argument, when he specifies that a good *x* and an *x simpliciter* have the same function:

> we say 'a so-and-so' and 'a good so-and-so' have a function which is the same in kind, e.g. a lyre-player and a good lyre-player, and so without qualification in all cases . . . (for the function of a lyre-player is to play the lyre and that of a good lyre-player is to do so well). (*NE* 1. 7, 1098ᵃ8–12; cf. *EE* 2. 1, 1219ᵃ19–24)

This passage seems at first oddly gratuitous, differing only in emphasis from the weak version of the 'good and the well' claim already stated: for any craft or function, the good practitioner is the one who performs well. It is worth Aristotle's while to repeat the point here because the application to human beings as such might well encounter resistance. For we might see ourselves as better than Simon precisely in having some nobler function or, aristocratically, none at all. Aristotle insists that, on the contrary, what goes for Simon goes for all of us: a good human being has the same function as a human being, together with the responsibility of performing it better.

On the realization reading, Aristotle's argument seems to me to touch on some important truths implicit in our everyday ways of thinking about social functioning and the ends of action. Our agency is almost always embedded in some social role which we accept as normative, and which involves just the unity of doing well and faring well to which Aristotle draws our attention. The good doctor typically enters the consulting room aiming not to maximize utility, nor to obey the categorical imperative, nor for that matter to maximally serve her own interests, but simply *to do a good job*[46]—that is, to act successfully as a good doctor, just as she might at other times of the day aim to act as a good friend, sister, dog-owner, party member, and so on for every description she takes as contributing to her identity. In ancient ethical theory, it is the Stoics who most fully work out this way of thinking about

---

[46] Tom Hurka has objected to me that this sounds inappropriately self-referential: the aim is rather to bring about the patient's health using the medical art. But these are two ways of saying the same thing; and which thought we should ascribe to the doctor may well depend on context and emphasis. I discuss the alleged problem of inappropriate self-reference in the virtuous person's thoughts in 'Comments on Sarah Broadie, "Virtue and Beyond in Plato and Aristotle"', *Southern Journal of Philosophy*, 43, suppl. (2005), 115–25.

the ethical life: as Epictetus puts it, we can discover what actions are appropriate to or incumbent on us, *ta kathēkonta*, from looking at the names we bear.[47] But the basic principles here (notably the conception of crafts as paradigmatic functions, and of functions as norm-giving) go back to Plato; indeed what interests Aristotle is not this picture in its own right, which he largely takes for granted, but the pathway it offers to his conception of human nature. His point, surely a plausible one, is that it would be perverse for us to look for the human good in some distinct 'lazy' way of being, different in kind from the activities of the doctor, party member, etc. in which our everyday social ends are realized. The human good is not some extra, specially structured business to be worked awkwardly into our spare moments: it is just like what the doctor experiences when she is working well; it *is* what the doctor experiences when she is working well. Or rather, it is the common denominator which gives value to all such activities, but is far more fully present in some than others: the exercise of human rationality.

As on the architectonic reading, Aristotle's appeal to the organic parts of the human body can serve to reassure us that such functions are a natural phenomenon. The instrumentalist looks at the shoe-maker, hunched over and slaving away in his shop, and construes *ergon* as mere work: a social construct of strictly instrumental value to practitioner and society alike. The shoemaker's good, he infers, would be to close up shop for ever, if only he could: what would suit him best, or any of us, is the life of leisure and amusement. Aristotle's appeal to the organic parts is a sharp reminder that this inference is invalid, and rests on a misconception. *Erga* are not just social roles serving extrinsic ends: nature is pullulating with them, human nature included. What suits my eyes best is not an endless holiday from the labour of seeing, but to be active in the way best suited to their capacities. So why assume that my own case—or the shoemaker's—will be any different?

5. Conclusions

The architectonic and the realization readings are complementary. Each brings out one dimension of a plausible understanding of crafts as functions and functions as normative: the architectonic

---

[47] Epict. *Diss.*, 2. 10.

reading notes the value of the crafts as contributions to an architectonic hierarchy of social goods, while the realization reading
points to the norms of excellence and flourishing they enable their
practitioners to realize. Taking both readings together, we can see
Aristotle proposing that to make sense of these normative features
of craft (or, presumably, of any social function), we need to see them
as deriving their standing from natural teleology.

In a famous passage of the *Parts of Animals*, Aristotle complains
about students who, by the sound of it, protested at having to study
the parts of animals. He insists, with unusual warmth:

We must avoid childish complaints about examining the less honourable
animals; for in all natural things there is something wonderful. The story
goes that when some strangers wanted to see Heraclitus, they stopped on
their way in, since they saw him warming himself at the oven; but he
kept urging them, saying, 'Come in, and don't worry; for here too there are
gods.'[48] In the same way, then, we must go forward without embarrassment
with our search into each type of animal, assuming that there is something
natural and fine in each of them. For what is for something and not a
matter of luck is most characteristic of the products of nature; and the
end for which these things are constituted or have come to be counts as
something beautiful. (*PA* 1. 5, 645^{a}15–26)[49]

Crafts too are 'for something': as Aristotle emphasizes, they imitate
and complete the workings of nature (*Phys* 2. 3, 194^{a}20–1; *Meteor.*
4. 3, 381^{b}4–6). And Aristotle's appeals to the crafts, like those of
Socrates and Plato before him, are in the same spirit as this appeal
to the beauty of frogs and bugs. Such arguments from the lowly are
not just a shaming trope, but a species of reasoning from what is
better known to us to what is better known by nature. They use a
lower object to make visible features which are more fully present
in some higher one, but less obviously and uncontroversially so.
And in the social version of the argument as in the zoological,
what we are directed to observe is, above all, the pervasiveness and
importance of teleology. Unfortunately, Aristotle was less interested
in shoemakers and carpenters than in frogs and bugs: he has much
less to say about them, and what he does say is often distorted by
class prejudice. But it is still enough to convey a vision—largely

---

[48] For the significance of this anecdote, see P. Gregoric, 'The Heraclitus Anecdote:
De partibus animalium i 5. 645^{a}17–23', *Ancient Philosophy*, 21 (2001), 73–85.

[49] The translation is from T. Irwin and G. Fine (trans., intro., and notes), *Aristotle: Selections* (Indianapolis, 1995), with revisions.

inherited from Plato's *Republic*—of our ethical lives as structured around activities which at once express our natures, realize our good, and contribute to our communities. If this is a way of thinking about work and success which continues to deserve attention, so too does Aristotle's claim that it presupposes a conception of human nature as functional already.

University of Toronto

BIBLIOGRAPHY

Aquinas, Thomas, *Commentary on Aristotle's* Nicomachean Ethics, trans. C. Litzinger (Notre Dame, 1993).

Barnes, J., 'Aristotle and the Methods of Ethics', *Revue internationale de philosophie*, 34 (1981), 490–511.

—— (ed.), *Aristotle: The Revised Oxford Translation* (2 vols.; Princeton, 1984).

Barney, R., 'Comments on Sarah Broadie, "Virtue and Beyond in Plato and Aristotle"', *Southern Journal of Philosophy*, 43, suppl. (2005), 115–25.

—— 'The Carpenter and the Good' ['Carpenter'], in D. Cairns, F.-G. Herrmann, and T. Penner (eds.), *Pursuing the Good: Ethics and Metaphysics in Plato's* Republic (Edinburgh, forthcoming).

Bostock, D., *Aristotle's Ethics* [*Ethics*] (Oxford, 2000).

Broadie, S., *Ethics with Aristotle* [*Ethics*] (Oxford, 1991).

—— and Rowe, C. (trans., intro., and comm.), *Aristotle:* Nicomachean Ethics [*Commentary*] (Oxford, 2002).

Burnet, J. (ed. with intro. and notes), *The* Ethics *of Aristotle* [*Ethics*] (London, 1900).

Clark, S., *Aristotle's Man* (Oxford, 1975).

Cooper, J. M., *Reason and Human Good in Aristotle* (Cambridge, Mass., 1975).

—— with D. S. Hutchinson (eds.), *Plato: Complete Works* (Indianapolis, 1997).

de Ste. Croix, G. E. M., *The Class Struggle in the Ancient Greek World* (Ithaca, NY, 1981).

Destrée, P., 'Comment démontrer le propre de l'homme? Pour une lecture "dialectique" de *EN* I, 6' ['Comment démontrer'], in G. Romeyer Dherbey and G. Aubry (eds.), *L'Excellence de la vie* (Paris, 2002), 39–61.

Gerson, L., *Knowing Persons* (Oxford, 2003).

Glassen, P., 'A Fallacy in Aristotle's Argument about the Good', *Philosophical Quarterly*, 7 (1957), 319–22.

Gomez-Lobo, A., 'The Ergon Inference', *Phronesis*, 34 (1989), 170–84.

Grant, A., *Aristotle's Ethics* [*Ethics*], 4th edn. (2 vols.; London, 1885).

Gregoric, P., 'The Heraclitus Anecdote: *De partibus animalium* i 5. 645ᵃ17–23', *Ancient Philosophy*, 21 (2001), 73–85.

Hardie, W. F. R., *Aristotle's Ethical Theory* [*Theory*] (Oxford, 1968).

Hutchinson, D. S., *The Virtues of Aristotle* (London, 1986).

Irwin, T., *Aristotle's First Principles* [*Principles*] (Oxford, 1988).

—— 'The Metaphysical and Psychological Basis of Aristotle's Ethics', in Rorty (ed.), *Essays*, 35–53.

—— and Fine, G. (trans., intro., and notes), *Aristotle: Selections* (Indianapolis, 1995).

Joachim, H., *Aristotle:* The Nicomachean Ethics (Oxford, 1951).

Johnson, M. R., *Aristotle on Teleology* [*Teleology*] (Oxford, 2005).

Kahn, C., *Plato and the Socratic Dialogue* (Cambridge, 1996).

Korsgaard, C., 'Aristotle on Function and Virtue', *History of Philosophy Quarterly*, 3 (1986), 259–79.

Kraut, R., *Aristotle on the Human Good* [*Good*] (Princeton, 1989).

—— *Aristotle: Political Philosophy* [*Aristotle*] (Oxford, 2002).

—— 'The Peculiar Function of Human Beings', *Canadian Journal of Philosophy*, 9 (1979), 467–78.

Lawrence, G., 'Human Good and Human Function' ['Good'], in R. Kraut (ed.), *The Blackwell Guide to Aristotle's* Nicomachean Ethics (Malden, Mass., 2006), 37–75.

—— 'The Function of the Function Argument' ['Function'], *Ancient Philosophy*, 21 (2001), 445–75.

Nussbaum, M. C., 'Aristotle, Nature, and Ethics', in J. E. Altham and R. Harrison (eds.), *World, Mind and Ethics: Essays on the Ethical Philosophy of Bernard Williams* (Cambridge, 1995), 86–131.

—— *Aristotle's* De motu animalium (Princeton, 1978; rev. edn. 1985).

Pakaluk, M., *Aristotle's* Nicomachean Ethics*: An Introduction* [*Ethics*] (Cambridge, 2005).

Reeve, C. D. C., *Practices of Reason* [*Practices*] (Oxford, 1995).

Roche, T., 'On the Alleged Metaphysical Foundation of Aristotle's *Ethics*' ['Foundation'], *Ancient Philosophy*, 8 (1988), 49–62.

Rorty, A. O. (ed.), *Essays on Aristotle's Ethics* [*Essays*] (Berkeley, 1980).

Ross, W. D. (trans.), *Aristotle:* The Nicomachean Ethics, rev. J. L. Ackrill and J. O. Urmson (Oxford, 1980).

Santas, G., *Goodness and Justice* (Oxford, 2001).

Sparshott, F., *Taking Life Seriously: A Study of the Argument of the* Nicomachean Ethics [*Life*] (Toronto, 1994).

Suits, B., 'Aristotle on the Function of Man: Fallacies, Heresies and other Entertainments' ['Fallacies'], *Canadian Journal of Philosophy*, 4 (1974), 23–40.

Tuozzo, T., 'The Function of Human Beings and the Rationality of the Universe: Aristotle and Zeno on Parts and Wholes' ['Function'], *Phoenix*, 50 (1996), 146–61.

Van Leeuwen, J. (ed. and notes), *Aristophanes:* Plutus, 2nd edn. (Leiden, 1968).

Whiting, J., 'Aristotle's Function Argument: A Defense' ['Defense'], *Ancient Philosophy*, 8 (1988), 33–48.

Wilkes, K., 'The Good Man and the Good for Man in Aristotle's Ethics', *Mind*, 87 (1978), 553–71; repr. in Rorty (ed.), *Essays*, 341–57.

Woods, M. (trans. and comm.), *Aristotle:* Eudemian Ethics *Books I, II and VIII* (Oxford, 1992).

NICOMACHEAN ETHICS 7. 3
ON AKRATIC IGNORANCE

MARTIN PICKAVÉ AND JENNIFER WHITING

NE 7. 3 (=*EE* 6. 3) is generally agreed to be the foundational chapter in Aristotle's account of akrasia.[1] It is also agreed to involve extreme difficulties, not only about how to interpret particular lines but even about what lines to read. Some difficulties are so great that commentators have proposed radical emendations without manuscript support, such as Ramsauer's proposal to read 'particular' for 'universal' in 1147ª4. Others raise questions about the structure of the whole: there is enough at least apparent repetition for some commentators to hypothesize that 7. 3 is a patchwork containing redundant bits of what were originally two separate treatments. Cook Wilson, for example, takes the four central sections and treats the second and fourth more or less as alternative versions of the first and third.[2] But we believe that each section introduces an important ingredient in Aristotle's eventual account, which is presented in stages: each seems to resolve an issue left unresolved in the earlier

© Martin Pickavé and Jennifer Whiting 2008

We would like to thank David Sedley for the exemplary, but for him customary, editorial help he provided. We also want to thank those who participated in the workshop we held in Toronto in May 2006—especially Charles Brittain, David Bronstein, David Charles, Brad Inwood, Marta Jimenez, Henrik Lorenz, Jessica Moss, and Jozef Müller. And we have benefited from comments by Myles Burnyeat and above all Sarah Broadie.

[1] 'Akrasia' is frequently rendered 'incontinence', 'weakness of will', or 'lack of self-control'; but we leave it untranslated so as to avoid controversial questions about, for example, whether Aristotle had notions of what later came to be called 'the will' or 'the self'. The main idea is that of acting because of passion against one's knowledge (or belief) about what one ought to do.

[2] On Ramsauer's proposal, see sect. 4. The idea of two redactions was suggested by H. Rassow in *Forschungen über die Nikomachische Ethik des Aristoteles* [*Forschungen*] (Weimar, 1874), 20 ff., and developed by J. Cook Wilson in *Aristotelian Studies*, i. *On the Structure of the Seventh Book of the* Nicomachean Ethics *Chapter I–X* [*Aristotelian Studies*] (Oxford, 1879). For a modern commentator sympathetic to a double-redaction view, see H. Lorenz, '*Nicomachean Ethics* 7. 4: Plain and Qualified Lack of Control', in Acts of the XVIIth Symposium Aristotelicum (forthcoming).

sections. We also believe that radical emendations are unnecessary and have been motivated largely by failure to appreciate the 'progressive articulation' by which we think this chapter can be read as a coherent whole. Our aim is thus to elucidate and defend this 'progressive articulation', which, however, requires us to give up one assumption on which otherwise divergent commentators seem to agree—namely, that Aristotle seeks to explain akratic behaviour by appeal to a failure either to have or to use knowledge of some *particular*.

1. Preliminaries: the voluntary but
non-vicious character of akratic behaviour

In interpreting 7. 3, we take as our guide the general summary provided in 7. 10:

[1] *NE* 7. 10, 1152ᵃ6–19

(*a*) Nor is the same person able to be simultaneously *phronimos* and akratic. For character has been shown to be simultaneously *phronimos* and excellent. Further, ⟨one is⟩ *phronimos* not by knowing only but also by being *praktikos*; and the *akratēs* is not *praktikos*. (But nothing prevents someone who is clever being akratic; whence it also seems that people are sometimes *phronimoi* but akratic, because cleverness differs from *phronēsis* in the way mentioned in the first arguments, being close ⟨to *phronēsis*⟩ with respect to the *logos* ⟨involved⟩ but different with respect to the *prohairesis* ⟨involved⟩.)[3]

(*b*) Nor ⟨is the *akratēs*⟩ like one knowing and contemplating, but rather like one asleep or drunk.

(*c*) And ⟨the *akratēs* acts⟩ voluntarily (for he knows in some way both what he does and for the sake of what), but is not bad. For ⟨his⟩ *prohairesis* is decent with the result that he is ⟨only⟩ half-bad . . . One ⟨sort of *akratēs*⟩ does not stick by the results of his deliberations, while the other, melancholic ⟨sort⟩ does not deliberate at all.

(*a*) alludes to the conclusion of *NE* 6. 12–13 (namely, that one cannot be *phronimos* without being fully virtuous) and then states a

---

[3] προαίρεσις is a technical term for Aristotle. It has become common to render it 'decision' (as distinct from 'choice', which is used for the non-technical αἵρεσις), but we shall simply transliterate so as to signal its technical status and to avoid taking a stand on how exactly Aristotle conceives of it. The same rationale applies to our transliteration of φρόνησις (often rendered 'practical wisdom') and its cognates.

corollary developed in *NE* 7 (namely, that one cannot be simultaneously *phronimos* and akratic). (*b*) and (*c*) then explicate the condition of the *akratēs*. According to (*b*), the *akratēs* knows what she knows not in the way that someone contemplating what she knows knows it, but rather in something like the way in which someone who is asleep or drunk knows it. According to (*c*), she acts voluntarily in the sense that she in some sense knows what she is doing.

The requirement that the *akratēs* act voluntarily plays a crucial role in our account, so it is worth noting how Aristotle explains the voluntary in *NE* 3. 1. An action will be voluntary only if it satisfies two conditions. The first, that the source be in the agent herself, is irrelevant to the discussion of akrasia. What matters is the second condition—namely, that she act 'knowing the particulars [εἰδότι τὰ καθ' ἕκαστα] involved in the action' (1111ᵃ22–3). The following passage (whose references to drunkenness and madness show its relevance to 7. 3) indicates the sorts of particulars in question and reveals an important distinction between ignorance of *these*, which often constitutes a kind of excuse, and the sort of ignorance that is involved in vice and does not constitute any excuse—namely, ignorance in one's *prohairesis* or of some *universal*.

[2] *NE* 3. 1, 1110ᵇ24–1111ᵃ26

(*a*) Acting because of ignorance [δι' ἄγνοιαν] seems to be different from ⟨acting⟩ in ignorance [τοῦ ἀγνοοῦντα]; for the one drunk or angry seems to act not because of ignorance but because of some one of the things mentioned [e.g. drunkenness or anger], not ⟨however⟩ knowing but being ignorant. Every wicked agent is ignorant of the things which he ought to do and from which he ought to refrain, and because of such error ⟨people⟩ come to be unjust and generally vicious. But the ⟨term⟩ 'involuntary' [τὸ δ' ἀκούσιον] is not meant ⟨to apply⟩ if someone is ignorant of the sorts of things that are ⟨generally⟩ advantageous. For ignorance in the *prohairesis* is not the cause of the involuntary but of wickedness; nor is it ⟨ignorance⟩ of the universal ⟨that is the cause of the involuntary⟩ (for people are blamed because of this), but rather ignorance of the particulars in which and concerning which the action occurs . . .

(*b*) Perhaps, then, it is not a bad idea to define these, what and how many they are: who, what, concerning what, and in what someone acts, and sometimes also with what (for example, with ⟨what⟩ instrument) and for the sake of what (for example, ⟨for the sake⟩ of safety), and how (for example, gently or excessively). *No one could be ignorant of all of these unless he were mad.* It is plain that he could not be ignorant of the one acting. For how at any rate ⟨could he fail to know that it is⟩ himself? But one might be ignorant of *what* he does, as for example those saying that the things just slipped out while they were speaking . . . And someone might think his son to be an enemy (just as Merope ⟨did⟩), or the pointed spear to be covered with a button, or the stone to be a pumice ⟨stone⟩ . . .

(*c*) Since what is involuntary is what is by force or because of ignorance, the voluntary would seem to be that of which the source is in the ⟨agent⟩ himself, knowing the particulars involved in the action. For things ⟨done⟩ because of *thumos* or *epithumia* are presumably not rightly called involuntary, first of all because ⟨on this account⟩ none of the other animals will act voluntarily; nor will children . . .

The reference to *thumos* or *epithumia* points to the distinction, articulated in 7. 4–6, between the qualified forms of akrasia associated with *thumos* and the unqualified form associated with *epithumia*. And the passage reflects Aristotle's general view that, although the *akratēs* is capable of *prohairesis*, she acts—like beasts and children—voluntarily but not from *prohairesis* (1148ᵃ13–17, 1150ᵃ19–31, 1151ᵃ 1–14).[4]

Yet it is not to beasts or children that 7. 3 compares the *akratēs*: it is rather to those asleep, drunk, and mad. But assimilating the *akratēs* to those who are mad, drunk, and asleep threatens the claim that the *akratēs* acts voluntarily. For [2(*b*)] explicitly associates madness with the sort of ignorance of particulars that renders an action involuntary. And [2(*a*)] suggests that the ignorance *in* which (if not *because of* which) the drunk acts differs from the wicked agent's ignorance precisely in being ignorance of some particular rather than ignorance in the *prohairesis* or of some universal. This suggests that Aristotle takes drunken actions of the relevant sort to be *involuntary* (but still perhaps culpable). But he clearly takes akratic actions to be *voluntary*. So there remains a question about the point of [1(*b*)]'s comparison between the *akratēs* and those who are asleep or drunk.

Moreover, the more one takes the *akratēs* to be characterized by ignorance of the relevant particulars, the less puzzling it becomes how she can act against her knowledge of what she ought or ought not do. It is only to the extent that the *akratēs* acts knowing both what she does *and* that she ought not do it, that there is a real problem explaining how akratic action is possible. And Aristotle

---

[4] On beasts and children see 1111ᵇ6–10, 1149ᵇ31–1150ᵃ1.

seems to share Socrates' sense that there *is* a real problem here, one associated with the idea that knowledge is especially powerful.

[3] *NE* 7. 2, 1145ᵇ22–31

> . . . some deny that it is *possible* for someone who knows ⟨to act akratically⟩. For, as Socrates believed, it would be *deinon* if, when knowledge [ἐπιστήμη] is in ⟨someone⟩, something else should rule and drag it about like a slave. For Socrates generally fought against the account ⟨according to which knowledge is dragged about⟩, maintaining that there is no ⟨such thing as⟩ akrasia. For no one acts against what is best while supposing ⟨that he does so⟩; but ⟨it is⟩ because of ignorance ⟨that such actions occur⟩. This [viz. Socrates'] argument, then, is clearly opposed to the phenomena, and it is necessary to enquire about the condition [τὸ πάθος] ⟨of the *akratēs*⟩: if it *is* because of ignorance, then what sort of ignorance does this turn out to be? For it is clear that the one who acts akratically does not believe ⟨he should do what he actually does⟩ before he comes to be in this condition.⁵

Given that Aristotle takes knowledge of particulars to be required for voluntary action, it is easy to conclude that the kind of ignorance involved in akratic action (if ignorance is in fact involved) is ignorance of something universal. But this is problematic given [2(*a*)]'s association of such ignorance with vice. Although *Socrates* may diagnose so-called akratic behaviour as due to ignorance about what in general ought to be done, *Aristotle* seems to rule this out: he thinks the *akratēs* must know generally the sorts of things she ought and ought not do, and must in some sense reach the right *prohairesis* about what to do yet act against her knowledge. So if Aristotle is to include ignorance among the causes or conditions of akrasia, he must toe a narrow line: he must avoid the kind of ignorance of universals that would render the agent vicious, without, however, appealing to the sort of ignorance of particulars that would undermine the claim that she acts voluntarily.

2. Setting up the main question of 7. 3

The question whether the *akratēs* acts knowingly, and if so in what way she knows, heads the list of questions with which 7. 3 opens,

---

⁵ We choose 'condition', which often connotes a temporary abnormality, to render πάθος, so as to reserve 'state', which lacks this connotation, for ἕξις.

and it remains the focus throughout. The other questions are taken up in the chapters that follow.

[4] *NE* 7. 3, 1146^{b}8–24^6

(a) First, then, we must enquire (1) whether ⟨akratic agents act⟩ knowing or not; and ⟨if they know⟩ in what way they know. Next we must set down (2) the sorts of things with which the *akratēs* and the *enkratēs* are concerned, I mean whether ⟨they are⟩ concerned with every pleasure and pain or with some definite ones [taken up in *NE* 7. 4–6]; and (3) whether the *enkratēs* and the tough are the same or different [taken up in *NE* 7. 7]; and similarly (4) concerning the other ⟨problems⟩ whatever ones are akin to this enquiry [presumably those discussed in *NE* 7. 8–10].

(b) The starting-point of our enquiry is whether the *enkratēs* and the *akratēs* are differentiated by the *things* with which ⟨each is concerned⟩ or by the *way* in which ⟨each is concerned with the relevant things⟩. I mean, whether the *akratēs* is *akratēs* merely by being concerned with these things, or rather by the way ⟨in which he is concerned with these⟩ or not ⟨simply by one⟩ but by both. [And then whether akrasia and enkrateia are concerned with all things or not.] For the *haplōs akratēs* is not concerned with all things, but with the things with which the intemperate agent [ὁ ἀκόλαστος] is concerned. Nor ⟨is he *akratēs*⟩ simply by being concerned with these things—for then ⟨akrasia⟩ would be the same as intemperance—but ⟨he is *akratēs* by being concerned with them⟩ in the following way: the one [viz. the *akolastos*] *prohairoumenos* is led ⟨to act⟩ thinking that he should always pursue the present pleasure; while the other [viz. the *akratēs*] thinks he should not ⟨pursue the present pleasure⟩ but pursues it anyway.

The point of (b) is that the intemperate agent and the *akratēs* pursue the same object but in different ways: the intemperate agent thinks she *should* pursue the present pleasure, while the *akratēs* thinks she *should not*.[7] But many commentators are puzzled about how exactly (b) is supposed to follow on (a). Some worry because they think it obvious that (b) addresses question (2) and they take Aristotle to return to question (1) only in the lines immediately following this passage (viz. in [5]).[8] Others have a more general worry about what

---

[6] Passages [4]–[10] provide a continuous translation of the whole of *NE* 7. 3.

[7] For this construction of οὐκ οἴεται, see H. W. Smyth, *Greek Grammar* (Cambridge, Mass., 1920), 2692a.

[8] Irwin reads (b) as taking up in chiastic order the questions raised in (a). See T. Irwin, *Aristotle:* Nicomachean Ethics [*Nicomachean Ethics*], 2nd edn. (Indianapolis, 1999), 257. But this does not fully address the problem. For (b) does not address (2): it simply assumes, largely by way of returning to question (1), points made in later chapters.

they see as (*b*)'s repetition of points made in (*a*).[9] But both worries assume that the question bracketed in (*b*) corresponds to question (2). If, as some editors suggest, this question does not belong where it appears, there is no problem.[10] Aristotle first asks whether akratic agents *in general* are to be distinguished from others by the objects with which they are concerned, by their attitudes towards these objects, or by both. He then explains why this question arises in spite of what might seem to be the presumption in favour of distinguishing them by their objects—namely, because there is one sort of *akratēs* who seems to be concerned with precisely the *same objects* with which the intemperate agent is concerned. So in order to explain how *this* sort of *akratēs* differs from the *akolastos*, Aristotle must appeal to some difference in their *attitudes*.

Aristotle thus turns to an idea mentioned back in *NE* 7. 2: the idea that the *akratēs* does *not know but only believes* that she should not do what she does. He dismisses this quickly, apparently because it rests on the false assumption that belief tends to be associated with lesser confidence in its objects than knowledge is:

[5] *NE* 7. 3, 1146^{b}24–31

Concerning ⟨the suggestion⟩ that it is true belief and not knowledge by which people act akratically, this *makes no difference* [οὐδὲν διαφέρει] to the account. For some of those who ⟨merely⟩ believe are not at all divided ⟨in their beliefs⟩ but take themselves to know exactly. If, then, it is because of their trusting only weakly ⟨in what they believe⟩ that

---

[9] Cook Wilson suggests that (*b*) was originally an alternative version of the material covered in (*a*), and he proposes to bracket or excise one or other of these paragraphs. See his *Aristotelian Studies*, 19. Broadie is sympathetic: see S. Broadie and C. Rowe, *Aristotle:* Nicomachean Ethics [*Nicomachean Ethics*] (Oxford, 2002), 388.

[10] See G. Ramsauer, *Aristotelis Ethica Nicomachea* [*Ethica Nicomachea*] (Leipzig, 1878), ad loc.; and R. A. Gauthier and J. Y. Jolif, *Aristote: L'Éthique à Nicomaque* [*L'Éthique*], 2nd edn. (2 vols.; Louvain and Paris, 1970), ad loc. One can easily see how the bracketed question might have been introduced by an editor or copyist who had difficulty in its absence understanding the connection between (i) the original question about how the *akratēs* and *enkratēs* differ from other characters and (ii) the γάρ that introduces the subsequent claim that the *haplōs akratēs* is not concerned with all things but only with the things with which the intemperate agent is concerned. For this claim seems simply to answer the original question, while the γάρ suggests that something is being argued or explained. But this is perfectly intelligible once we see that the original question (like most of what precedes) speaks of the *akratēs* in *general*, while the γάρ sentence refers to a *specific sort* of *akratēs*, the *haplōs akratēs*, whom Aristotle takes to be concerned with precisely those pleasures with which the *akolastos* is concerned. Given this shift, the paragraph makes perfect sense without the bracketed question, which was perhaps introduced by an editor or copyist who failed to appreciate the shift.

those who believe act against their supposition more than those who know, knowledge will differ in no way from belief. For some are no less confident in the things they ⟨merely⟩ believe than others are in the things they know. Heraclitus makes this clear.

One might object that the difference between knowledge and belief is in fact relevant for reasons having nothing to do with any differences in degree of confidence. One might allow, for example, that knowers and mere believers may be equally confident, and then argue that knowers (unlike mere believers) can give proper accounts of what they know. But even if Aristotle *is* overlooking this possibility, that is irrelevant here: he clearly thinks, whether correctly or not, that this distinction makes 'no difference'.

3. The generic solution: the first step in Aristotle's 'progressive articulation'

Aristotle moves on immediately to a distinction that he says '*will* make a difference'.

[6] *NE* 7. 3, 1146ᵇ31–5

> But since we speak of knowing [τὸ ἐπίστασθαι] in two ways—for both the one having but not using his knowledge and the one using it are said to know—it *will make a difference* [διοίσει] whether ⟨we talk⟩ about having but not contemplating the things one ought not do or about contemplating ⟨these things⟩.[11] For this [viz. acting akratically while contemplating the things one ought not do] seems *deinon*, but ⟨it does⟩ not ⟨seem *deinon* to act akratically⟩ if one is not contemplating ⟨these things⟩.

Here Aristotle invokes a distinction, familiar from Plato's *Theaetetus*, between the state of someone who has acquired knowledge but is not at the moment using it and the state of someone who is actively using previously acquired knowledge.[12] Aristotle treats this distinction, in *De anima* 2. 1, as involving two kinds of actuality

---

[11] Following I. Bywater, *Aristotelis Ethica Nicomachea* (Oxford, 1894), we omit τοῦ ἔχοντα καὶ θεωροῦντα.

[12] The *Theaetetus* (see 197 B–198 D), however, puts the point somewhat differently, distinguishing τὸ κεκτῆσθαι (viz. having acquired and so possessing something) from τὸ ἔχειν (which is a stronger form of having, a kind of having something actually 'in hand'). So Socrates uses τὸ ἔχειν to refer specifically to what Aristotle calls 'using' or 'contemplating' what one knows.

(ἐντελέχεια): the kind involved when someone who has acquired knowledge is *not actively using* that knowledge and the kind involved when someone who has acquired knowledge *is actively using* her knowledge (412^a21-8). Because Aristotle refers to the former as 'first' actuality, commentators typically speak here of 'first' and 'second' actuality knowledge. First actuality knowledge is itself a kind of potentiality or capacity (δύναμις), to be distinguished from the mere capacity *to acquire* knowledge that is characteristic of someone who has not yet learnt some subject; it is a capacity *to use* (already acquired) knowledge in situations where such use is called for (see 417^a21-^b2).

Aristotle says that the distinction will make *some* difference to the account of akrasia. The question is *how far* it actually takes us. What is Aristotle's point when he says that it seems *deinon* if someone does what she ought not do while actively contemplating and so *using* her knowledge of what she ought not do, but not *deinon* if someone does what she ought not do while she is not actively contemplating but merely *has* (first actuality) knowledge of what she ought not do? Does *deinon* mean something like 'absolutely amazing', in which case Aristotle would seem to be ruling out what is sometimes called 'clear-eyed' akrasia—viz. cases where someone who knows she should not φ nevertheless φ's while actively thinking she should not? Or does *deinon* mean simply 'strange', in which case Aristotle may or may not be allowing that 'clear-eyed' akrasia sometimes occurs? Is the idea that clear-eyed akrasia is, as we might say, 'strange but true'?[13]

Note, however, that nothing much is to be gained by specifying the sense of *deinon*, since even if we read Aristotle as rejecting 'clear-eyed' akrasia there remain questions about the spirit in which he proceeds. He may be assuming that his readers will agree that there is nothing strange about acting against knowledge one is not actively using, and simply trotting out standard distinctions that he takes to illuminate this phenomenon. But it is not clear that Aristotle would be entitled to this assumption. As he himself recognizes, those who *have* knowledge typically *use* it in situations where it is called for

---

[13] The same question arises in [3]. Because this recalls *Prot.* 352 B–C, many commentators take [3]'s use of *deinon* to connote the sort of impossibility of akrasia defended by Socrates in the *Protagoras*. Note, however, that, although Plato sometimes uses *deinon* to refer to something especially paradoxical (as, for example, at *H. Mi.* 375 D 3 and *Theaet.* 203 D), this term does not appear in the *Protagoras* argument.

(see *Phys.* 8. 4, 255ᵃ33–ᵇ5). So he himself should be puzzled by the idea that someone can act against knowledge she *has*, provided only that she is *not using* this knowledge. Perhaps, then, we should read what follows as seeking to *justify* his claim that there is nothing strange in this.

What follows [6] are three sections of text each introduced by *eti*, which clearly signals some further point. There is, however, controversy about how each additional point is related to the preceding points. For example, does the first *eti* signal the first in a series of *mere additions* to the fundamental account, whose essentials are *already present* in [6]? Or does it perhaps signal the second in a series of steps that lead *only eventually* to an adequate characterization of akratic failure?

Some commentators speak of several different 'solutions' to the problem of explaining how the *akratēs* can act against her knowledge. Of these, some see the 'real' solution as coming only in the fourth stage.[14] Others see the essence of Aristotle's solution as more or less fully present in [6], whose distinction between merely having and actively using reappears in somewhat different guises in each of the remaining 'solutions'.[15] But many commentators see each of the earlier stages as preparing in some way for the account reached in the last stage or stages. Some think we do not get a proper characterization of akratic failure—as distinct from examples of *other* sorts of failure that shed light on it—until the third or fourth stage. Irwin, for example, claims that in the first three stages Aristotle 'discusses different cases that do not completely fit incontinents, but eventually help us to understand some aspects of incontinents' state of mind' (characterized in the fourth stage).[16] Others see Aristotle as reaching one sort of *akratēs* (namely, the

---

[14] See e.g. J. Burnet, *The Ethics of Aristotle* (London, 1900), 299: 'the first three are dialectical . . . The fourth is the real *lusis* and is of a strictly psychological character. We need not expect to find the three first quite consistent with each other or with the fourth.'

[15] See e.g. R. Robinson, 'Aristotle on Akrasia' ['Akrasia'], in id., *Essays in Greek Philosophy* (London, 1969), repr. in J. Barnes, M. Schofield, and R. Sorabji (eds.), *Articles on Aristotle*, ii. *Ethics and Politics* (London, 1977), 139–60 at 141: 'I hold that Aristotle accepts this solution [viz. the one given in [6]] and believes it to contain virtually everything necessary for the explanation of akrasia, since it shows how the akratic both knows and does not know that his act is wrong . . . However, Aristotle adds three more solutions.'

[16] Irwin, *Nicomachean Ethics*, 258; and A. Kenny, 'The Practical Syllogism and Incontinence' ['Practical Syllogism'], *Phronesis*, 10 (1966), 163–84 at 173–6.

impetuous) in the third stage, and another (namely, the weak) only in the fourth.[17]

We agree with those who see the earlier stages as preparing for the proper account, which is given only in the fourth stage. But we do not think the early stages introduce examples only of *other* sorts of failure that shed light on the failure of the *akratēs*. We see instead a progression in which the first stage describes a generic sort of failure of which the *akratēs'* failure is eventually shown to be a species. Each subsequent stage is required because the previous stage does not yet capture the sort of failure *distinctive* of the *akratēs*. In this sense, each stage takes us 'further' along a continuous route.

4. The first *eti* passage (and second step): a difference in the universal

The progressive articulation is perhaps clearest in the transition from the first to the second stage—viz. from [6] to the first *eti* passage:

[7] *NE* 7. 3, 1146^{b}35–1147^{a}10

(a) Further [ἔτι] since there are two *tropoi* of *protaseis*, nothing prevents someone who has both ⟨*protaseis*⟩ from acting against ⟨his⟩ knowledge if he is using the universal ⟨*protasis*⟩ but not the particular one [χρώμενον μέντοι τῇ καθόλου, ἀλλὰ μὴ τῇ κατὰ μέρος].[18] For it is the particulars [τὰ καθ' ἕκαστα] that are to be acted on.

(b) There is a difference *also* with respect to the universal [διαφέρει δὲ καὶ τὸ καθόλου]: for one ⟨universal⟩ applies to oneself and the other to the object. For example, that dry ⟨foods⟩ benefit every man, and that one

---

[17] See e.g. Rassow, *Forschungen*, 128; J. A. Stewart, *Notes on the* Nicomachean Ethics [*Notes*] (2 vols.; Oxford, 1892), ii. 146; G. Hughes, *Aristotle on Ethics* (London, 2001), 148–59.

[18] We render both κατὰ μέρος (in this line) and καθ' ἕκαστα (in what follows) as 'particular' because Aristotle often uses these terms interchangeably, as he seems to do here. (For the reverse move in another practical context, see *NE* 1107^{a}28–32.) Either term can of course be applied both at the level of a particular kind (e.g. to chicken as a particular kind of dry food) and to a particular token (e.g. to a particular piece of chicken). Aristotle may use κατὰ μέρος here because he wants to allow (especially in 1147^{a}4–7) that some universal terms such as 'dry food' (as compared with 'man') are applied in a series of steps, first from a whole kind (e.g. dry food) to a part of that kind (e.g. chicken), then to a particular instance of that part (e.g. this piece of chicken here). And καθ' ἕκαστα is perhaps more strongly associated than κατὰ μέρος with particular instances.

is ⟨oneself⟩ a man or that such ⟨food⟩ is dry. But whether this ⟨food⟩ is such, either he does not have or does not exercise.

(c) With respect to *these tropoi* there will be an enormous difference [κατά τε δὴ τούτους διοίσει τοὺς τρόπους ἀμήχανον ὅσον], so that it seems that to know in this way ⟨yet act against one's knowledge⟩ is in no way strange, while ⟨acting against one's knowledge⟩ is otherwise amazing.

Aristotle builds here on the suggestion in [6] that the *akratēs* might have knowledge without actively using it. But even if [6] provides a generic solution, its account is still incomplete. Since there are two kinds of proposition knowledge of which someone might have but fail to use, there is a further question about whether it is knowledge of one rather than the other kind of proposition that the *akratēs* fails to use, and if so which one: knowledge of a *universal* proposition or knowledge of a *particular* one.[19]

Aristotle thinks this distinction important because he sees no difficulty—at least in the sense that there is no contradiction involved—in someone's acting against knowledge where it is only knowledge of a *universal* proposition that is active or 'used'. He elsewhere describes cases of theoretical knowledge where someone has and uses only knowledge of a universal proposition—for example, the case where someone knows that all triangles have angles equal to two right angles but does not recognize that some particular figure which is in fact a triangle has angles equal to two right angles, either because she is not (yet) aware of its existence or because she does not (yet) recognize it *as* a triangle (*Prior Analytics* 2. 21; *Posterior Analytics* 1. 1). And just as he sees no contradiction in such theoretical cases, he may see no contradiction in practical ones.

We must, however, caution against assuming too quickly, as many commentators assume, that Aristotle's appeal to cases like those in the *Analytics* shows that he takes the failure of the *akratēs* to lie likewise in a failure either to have or to use knowledge of some *particular*.[20] For it may be that we are intended to carry only some and

---

[19] We follow David Charles in taking *protasis* to mean 'proposition' while recognizing that Aristotle often uses it to refer specifically to premises in an argument. See D. Charles, *Aristotle's Philosophy of Action* [*Action*] (London, 1984), 120 n. 13; and 'Acrasia in Venice: VII. 3 Reconsidered' ['Venice'], in Acts of the XVIIth Symposium Aristotelicum (forthcoming). We thus remain neutral on the question of whether Aristotle means to refer to the premises of some syllogism.

[20] Commentators who refer to the *Analytics* passages, and then proceed to identify the failure of the *akratēs* as a failure to have or to use some *particular* proposition, include: H. H. Joachim, *Aristotle: The Nicomachean Ethics* (Oxford, 1951), 223–29;

not all of the features of theoretical cases over to the practical case. This is especially plausible since theoretical knowledge is primarily of universals in a way that practical knowledge is not. Moreover, it is more obvious in theoretical than in practical contexts how one might use a universal without applying it to particulars: for this is how universals are in fact used in demonstrations. But the idea that one can actively use universal knowledge without applying it to particulars may not transfer readily to practical contexts, where competent use of a universal *consists* largely in applying it to particulars. In such contexts, there is a question how one *could* use a universal proposition without thereby (or at least also) using one's knowledge of particular propositions.

More importantly, there is a special problem with taking it to be knowledge of *particular* propositions that the *akratēs* fails to use: this threatens the claim that she does voluntarily what she thinks she ought not do. For an action must be voluntary if it is to count as akratic; but according to Aristotle, ignorance of particulars renders actions involuntary (or at least non-voluntary: see *NE* 1110ᵇ18–1111ᵃ2). This suggests that the practical case may differ from the theoretical one with respect to which sort of proposition fails to get used. If so, [7(*a*)] may not diagnose the failure of the *akratēs* as lying in her failure to use some *particular* proposition; it may seek to establish, by appeal to a familiar case, only that the *akratēs* fails to use *one or other* of these two sorts of proposition without yet telling us *which*.[21]

Indeed, the fact that Aristotle focuses in [7(*b*)] on a 'difference

---

Gauthier and Jolif, *L'Éthique*, ii. 606; F. Grgić, 'Aristotle on the Akratic's Knowledge', *Phronesis*, 47 (2002), 344–55; and A. W. Price, 'Acrasia and Self-Control' ['Acrasia'], in R. Kraut (ed.), *The Blackwell Guide to the* Nicomachean Ethics [*Guide*] (Oxford, 2006), 234–54.

[21] Sarah Broadie has objected (in discussion) that because *NE* 3. 1 (quoted in [2] above) has not yet introduced the distinction between merely having and actually using knowledge, it may claim only that voluntary action requires *having* knowledge of the relevant particulars, whereas our appeal to *NE* 3. 1 tends to assume that *actual use* is required. Note, however, that many of [2(*b*)]'s examples of ignorance of particulars are of highly context-specific facts, such as whether the spear in one's hand at a particular place and time has a button on it, or whether the individual approaching at a particular place and time is one's son. With knowledge of such propositions, whose contents tend to be partly demonstrative, there is not generally the sort of dispositional knowledge that might or might not be actualized in particular situations that there is with knowledge of universal propositions. In other words, there seems to be less room here for the sort of gap required to make sense of the distinction between merely having and actually using the relevant knowledge. Moreover, as we

with respect to the *universal'* suggests that he may well be looking for a way to diagnose the *akratēs'* failure at least partly in terms of her failure to use some universal proposition. But this possibility tends to be overlooked because most commentators focus primarily on Aristotle's claim that an agent might fail either to have or to use knowledge of the proposition 'this food is such', but neglect to situate this claim in its proper context, which concerns a difference in the universal. Aristotle's point turns on the fact that universal propositions have two terms, either of which the *akratēs* might fail to use properly. Some of these terms are such that their application is relatively straightforward in ways that the application of others is not. Consider Aristotle's example: 'dry ⟨foods⟩ are good for every human'. Any *practical* use of this universal requires the application of both of its terms: the agent must recognize *both* that she herself is human *and* that such and such food (viz. the kind before her) is dry. It goes without saying that the agent will use her knowledge that she herself is human, even if she does not stop to give it explicit thought.[22] So Aristotle points instead to the possibility that she either does not know or does not use her knowledge that *this* food (viz. the food before her) is such and such. And in this sense she fails to use her knowledge of various *universal* propositions, including the propositions that such-and-such food is dry, and that such-and-such food is beneficial for every human (herself included).

Reading Aristotle as shifting our attention to failure to use knowledge of a *universal* proposition suggests a way of explaining [7(*c*)] that makes better sense than commentators usually make of what [7(*b*)] is doing here in the first place. Commentators have been uniformly troubled by the question of how to take 'these *tropoi*' in [7(*c*)]. For the only references to *tropoi* in the vicinity are to the two *tropoi* of *protasis* back in [7(*a*)] and to 'another *tropos* of having *epistēmē*' that Aristotle has yet to introduce in [8(*a*)]. It would be highly unnatural to take τούτους τοὺς τρόπους to refer forward. And while it might seem natural to connect the occurrence of τρόπους in [7(*c*)] to its occurrence in [7(*a*)], this too is problematic: for it ren-

shall see in [9(*b*)], Aristotle's positive account explicitly says that the *akratēs* actively uses knowledge of the relevant particular.

[22] As Aristotle notes in *MA* 7, some propositions are so obvious that thought does not stop to consider them; and his example is precisely that one is oneself human (701ᵃ26–9; see 701ᵃ13–16). Moreover, in listing the particulars knowledge of which is required for voluntary action, Aristotle says in [2(*b*)] that no sane agent could fail to know the fact that she herself is the one acting.

ders [7(*b*)] largely parenthetical and makes it hard to see why [7(*b*)] is here at all. Moreover, the use of τούτους (rather than ἐκείνους) encourages us to seek a more immediate referent somewhere in [7(*b*)].

Two possibilities are salient. One is to take τούτους τοὺς τρόπους to refer to the difference in [7(*b*)] between *not having* the particular knowledge that this food is such and such and *having but not exercising* such knowledge.[23] The point of [7(*c*)] would then be that there is so great a difference between merely having *particular* knowledge without exercising it and both having and exercising *particular* knowledge, that it would seem in no way strange for someone who has such knowledge without using it to act against that knowledge, while it would be absolutely amazing for someone who both has and uses such knowledge to act against it. But this makes the point of [7(*c*)] virtually indistinguishable from the point of [6], and so makes it harder to see what [7] adds to [6].[24] It is of course true that [7(*a*)] focuses in a way that [6] does not on knowledge of particular propositions. Many take this to show that [7] *as a whole* diagnoses the *akratēs'* failure as a failure to use knowledge of some particular proposition. But this makes it difficult not only (as we have seen) to claim that the *akratēs* acts voluntarily but also (as we now maintain) to understand the point of [7(*b*)].

There is, however, another way to take τούτους τοὺς τρόπους as referring to something in [7(*b*)]: we can take it as referring to the 'difference with respect to the universal' introduced in [7(*b*)]. In this case, the point in [7(*c*)] may be that there is so great a difference between failing to recognize that a term like 'human' applies to oneself and failing to recognize that a term like 'dry' applies to a certain sort of food, that it would be in no way strange for someone to act against her knowledge that 'dry foods are good for every human' because she fails to apply a term like 'dry' to a certain

---

[23] Commentators and translators tend, understandably, not to be explicit about what is going on here, so it is sometimes (as in Irwin's case) difficult to be sure how they take τούτους τοὺς τρόπους. For a relatively clear example of this first way of taking it, see Rowe's translation of 1147ᵃ7–8: 'whether this is such-and-such—this is what the agent either does not "have", or does not activate; and which of *these* ways we mean will make an immense difference, with the result that his knowing seems, in one way, not at all strange, and in another way amazing.' Note, however, that the scare-quotes with 'have' seem to anticipate the different *tropoi* of having introduced in [8(*a*)], so Rowe's position is not entirely clear.

[24] This might, of course, seem grist for Cook Wilson's mill. But if there is a way to interpret [7] as part of a coherent progression that adds to the point of [6], then we should reject his view. So the jury on our reading of [7] should be out until we show how it fits into the overall progression.

sort of food (which happens to be in front of her), though it would
be amazing for someone to act against this knowledge because she
fails to apply a term like 'human' to herself.[25] This way of taking
'these *tropoi*' allows us to explain why Aristotle introduces [7(*b*)]
in the first place. There would be little point to adding that there
is difference *also* in the *universal* if his diagnosis of the *akratēs'*
failure rested entirely in her failure to have or to use knowledge of
particular propositions. But introducing this difference makes good
sense if Aristotle is seeking a way to trace the *akratēs'* failure at least
partly to her failure to use knowledge of some *universal* proposition.

It is worth pausing here to note that one commentator, namely
Ramsauer, was so puzzled by Aristotle's claim that 'there is a difference also with respect to the universal' that he proposed to substitute κατὰ μέρος for καθόλου in 1147[a]4: he wanted to read 'there is
a difference also with respect to the *particular*'![26] But given the lack
of any manuscript support, this is clearly the counsel of despair.
So most commentators settle instead for reading Aristotle's remark
about the 'difference with respect to the universal' as merely parenthetical. But the weakness of this becomes clear when we consider
two things: the emphatic position of διαφέρει and the overall context. Aristotle began, back in [5], by rejecting a distinction alleged
to make a difference to the account of akrasia: he says in 1146[b]25
that this distinction will make *no difference* [οὐδὲν διαφέρει]. He then
turns in [6] to a distinction that he says *will* make a difference
[διοίσει in [b]33] and follows up in [7] and in [8] with talk of further
differences: the one in question here and the difference in *hexis* to
be introduced in [8]. In this context, any talk of difference must

---

[25] It may be that Aristotle's main point is to distinguish terms whose application
is obvious from terms whose application is not so obvious, and that the example
he uses to illustrate this point simply happens to be one in which it is the *subject*
term rather than the *object* term whose application is obvious. His way of putting
the point admittedly suggests that he thinks that it is for the most part *subject* terms
whose application is obvious. And he might have thought this (whether correctly or
not) if he thought it difficult (though not perhaps impossible) to overlook the fact,
once one knows it, that some relevant term (such as 'married' or 'diabetic') applies to
oneself. See also n. 47. The objection that one might easily fail to know that some
practically relevant term (such as 'diabetic') applies to oneself is irrelevant here,
since that would not yield a case in which the agent acts *voluntarily* against what
she in some sense *knows*.

[26] Ramsauer, *Ethica Nicomachea*, ad loc. This is a far more radical emendation
than the one proposed by Stewart and discussed in sect. 8. But the stimulus is largely
the same—namely, failure to understand how Aristotle could be tracing the failure
of the *akratēs* to some defect in her knowledge of *universals*.

be taken as talk of a difference that *matters*. And the position of διαφέρει in διαφέρει δὲ καὶ τὸ καθόλου is not just ordinarily emphatic: it is highly emphatic. The sentence it introduces would be extraordinary coming from someone who viewed his remark about the 'difference with respect to the universal' as merely parenthetical.

Aristotle is no doubt concerned with the application of universals to particulars. For this plays a crucial role in the practical sphere, where, however, failure to have or to use knowledge of some particular proposition is not easily separated from failure to use knowledge of some universal proposition. In fact, an agent may sometimes fail to use knowledge of some universal proposition precisely because she either lacks or does not use knowledge of some particular proposition whose use would in fact *constitute* her use of the relevant universal. But given this, it might seem that the failure of those who act against knowledge can be described in *either way*—as failure to use knowledge of some particular or as failure to use knowledge of some universal. Why, then, should [7(*b*)] flag a 'difference with respect to the *universal*'?

Our hypothesis is that Aristotle redirects attention to a difference in the universal because he thinks this is required in order to say that the akratic action is voluntary. In [7(*b*)] he considers a case where an agent fails to use her knowledge of some universal *because* she fails either to have or to use knowledge of some particular. But in this case her action (or omission) is not voluntary. That is not a problem if (as we think) the point of [7(*b*)] is not to capture the failure distinctive of the *akratēs*, but rather to redirect our attention generally to failures to use universal knowledge so as to prepare the way for the account of akratic failure to come in [9], where (as we shall see) failure to use knowledge of some universal proposition is explained by something other than the sort of ignorance of particulars that would undermine the claim that the agent acts voluntarily.

5. The second *eti* passage (and third step): sleep, drunkness, and madness

Whichever sort of knowledge the *akratēs* is supposed to have but not use, Aristotle suggests that there is a *further* question about the sense in which the *akratēs has* this knowledge.

[8] *NE* 7. 3, 1147ᵃ10–24

Further [ἔτι], 'having knowledge' applies to human beings in another way [ἄλλον τρόπον] from those just mentioned.

(*a*) For ⟨among cases of⟩ having-but-not-using we see the *hexis* ⟨itself⟩ differing, with the result that ⟨there is⟩ also having in a way [πως] and not having ⟨the relevant knowledge⟩, for example, one sleeping or mad or drunk ⟨both has in a way and does not have the relevant knowledge⟩. And surely those at any rate who are in passionate conditions [οἵ γε ἐν τοῖς πάθεσιν ὄντες] are so disposed. For *thumoi* and sexual appetites and some ⟨other⟩ such things clearly change the body too, and in some folk even produce madness. It is plain, then, that we should say that akratic agents are disposed similarly to these ⟨folk⟩.

(*b*) Uttering the formulae [τὸ δὲ λέγειν τοὺς λόγους] that stem from knowledge is no sign ⟨of having knowledge⟩. For even those in such passionate conditions utter proofs and the verses of Empedocles, and those first learning string together the ⟨relevant⟩ formulae, but they do not yet know. For it is necessary for ⟨the relevant contents⟩ to become part of one's nature, and this takes time. So just as actors ⟨utter the formulae⟩, we must suppose that akratic agents ⟨do the same⟩.

Here Aristotle introduces a new sort of *hexis* to be included among the ways of having knowledge—viz. having in a way [πως] and not having. Talk of 'having knowledge' has hitherto been talk of the sort of *dunamis* whose possession Aristotle takes to constitute first actuality knowledge. And the subject of such a *dunamis* is ordinarily able to actualize it more or less at will—viz. to contemplate the relevant objects whenever she wishes, provided that nothing external is preventing her (see *DA* 417ᵃ27–8). But if we take this ability (viz. to actualize at will) as a *criterion* for having knowledge, then it may appear that those who are mad, drunk, or asleep do not even *have* the sorts of knowledge it seems clear (when they are sane, sober, and awake) they do have.

Aristotle, however, recognizes cases where a subject who clearly has a kind of knowledge is temporarily in a condition such that she is not able to exercise her knowledge at will—for example, the sleeping geometer mentioned at *GA* 735ᵃ9–11. There is no suggestion here that the sleeping geometer *lacks* knowledge. And this makes sense since, as Aristotle explains at *Phys.* 247ᵇ13–16, we would otherwise have to treat the geometer's waking as involving the reacquisition of knowledge. Moreover, Aristotle's general account of sleeping and waking helps to explain what is going on here. He regards sleep as a *pathos*, not itself involving any external impediment, in which its subject cannot activate or use her capacities in the ways she ordinarily can when she is awake.[27]

[8(*a*)] compares the *akratēs* not only to those who are asleep, but also to those who are mad and drunk. Note that this is the first place, since Aristotle started introducing distinctions that do 'make a difference', where he explicitly likens the condition of the *akratēs* to any of the states or conditions he describes. Though one might (and some commentators do) at various points take him to be assimilating the condition of the *akratēs* to one of the states or conditions previously mentioned—for example, the state of someone having but not using knowledge of *particular* propositions—Aristotle does not himself do so, at least not explicitly. So it is crucial to understand the point of these comparisons, especially since he returns in *NE* 7. 10's final summary (viz. in [1(*b*)]) to the comparison with those asleep and drunk.

One common feature of these conditions is the fact that they (like madness) involve changes in the subject's body. Aristotle elsewhere explains some of these changes and the mechanisms underlying them in ways indicating that he thinks such changes can interfere with the normal functioning of perception and the other mechanisms involved in belief-formation. In the case of normal sleep, he thinks there are physical changes (associated with heating and cooling, and required for proper digestive functioning) that result in a seizing up of the primary sense organ so that it is not able to act—at least not in the ways it acts when the subject is awake (*De somno* 458ᵃ28–9). Similar changes occur in drunkenness, where heating and cooling may move the bodily elements around in similar ways (456ᵇ16–457ᵃ20). Moreover, though Aristotle thinks we do not generally perceive during sleep, he allows that it is nevertheless possible for sight and the other senses to be affected (*De insomniis* 459ᵃ1–9). Dreams, for example, occur because one and the same faculty is involved both in normal perception and in the operations of imagination (459ᵃ15–23); because the normal operations of the senses set up motions that can persist and cause other motions when the objects themselves are no longer present (459ᵃ23–ᵇ23); and because some of these motions can be so like those caused by the actual presence of the relevant

[27] For references to sleep as a *pathos* of the perceptive faculty, see *De insomniis* 459ᵃ26 (cf. 460ᵇ31).

objects as to make it appear as if the objects were present when they are not.

Aristotle clearly allows that the doxastic faculty is at least sometimes active in sleep: 'sometimes *doxa* says, as if the person were awake, that the thing seen ⟨in a dream⟩ is false; but sometimes ⟨*doxa*⟩ is taken in and follows the appearance' (459ᵃ6–8). Aristotle makes the same point about the doxastic faculties of those who suffer various forms of illness. It may appear to those with fevers that there are animals dancing on the wall, and those whose fever is severe may be taken in by this appearance in ways that those whose fever is less severe are not: the latter may realize that the appearance is false and act accordingly, while the former act in ways suggesting that they take the appearance at face value (460ᵇ12–16). We might, however, hesitate—and so might Aristotle—to say that the former *really believe* what their actions suggest they do: for nothing prevents the contents of these appearances being such that the subject ordinarily denies them, in some cases denying even their possibility. Take, for example, a case where someone who would ordinarily deny the very existence of pink elephants is taken in by the appearance, in the sense that she acts *as if* she accepts the appearance, that pink elephants are dancing on barstools. Here we seem forced to choose between saying on the one hand that she *now* believes something that contradicts what she *ordinarily* believes, and saying on the other that she does not really believe what she now *appears* to believe even though she acts *as if* she did believe it. If we say the former, the question then arises whether she now *also* believes what she ordinarily believes and so now has contradictory beliefs, or whether she has temporarily lost her ordinary belief. We cannot resolve these questions here. But Aristotle himself seems reluctant to ascribe pairs of contradictory beliefs to an agent, perhaps because he realizes that doing so threatens the coherence of ascribing either belief. So it seems likely that he takes the agent simply to act *as if* she believed something she does not really believe. Moreover, it seems open to him to do so, given the way in which he allows that *phantasia*, without belief in its contents, can sometimes (as in non-rational animals) play the role ordinarily played by belief in the generation of action.

We emphasize the ways in which the material and efficient causal conditions associated with sleep, drunkenness, and madness can interfere with the normal mechanisms of perception and belief-formation because Aristotle clearly sees similar conditions and disturbances accompanying the *pathē* characteristic of the *akratēs*, e.g. excessive anger and inordinate sexual desire. Such *pathē* are partly constituted by and can themselves give rise to bodily conditions like those associated with sleep, drunkenness, and certain forms of illness. Even thoughts can produce bodily changes, at least where their objects are also objects of emotion. As Aristotle says in *De anima* 3. 9, the thought of something fearful or pleasant, even when it does not lead to action, sometimes produces bodily changes: if the object is fearful, the heart is moved; if the object is pleasant, some other part (432^b29–433^a1). And such changes can interfere with the normal operations of perception and belief-formation. This is no surprise, since Aristotle takes perception itself to involve certain bodily conditions and perhaps also bodily changes.

Our account takes seriously Aristotle's explicit assimilation of the *akratēs'* condition to the conditions of those asleep, mad, and drunk. And it takes the central paradigm to be that of the sleeping geometer. It is assumed that the *akratēs generally has* the sort of knowledge she acts against (in the sense that she has already acquired first actuality knowledge, which she can *ordinarily* actualize at will); but she is in a *temporary condition* that resembles sleep in that it prevents her from moving at will from first to second actuality knowledge. So, in so far as *having* knowledge involves the ability to actualize it at will, there is an important sense in which, when she is in this condition, she does *not have* the knowledge: that is why Aristotle says she both 'has it in a way and does not have it'.

Here, however, one might wonder whether this *can* be what Aristotle has in mind, given that at least some akratics seem to be well aware of what they are doing. In fact Aristotle himself seems to imagine someone asking how he can say this, given that some even say while they are acting that they should not be doing what they do. Aristotle accepts this appearance: he allows that some akratics 'utter the formulae' that would *normally* indicate not only that they possess but are in fact actualizing the sort of knowledge they act against. Yet he denies that it follows from this that they are really actualizing the relevant knowledge. He cites three examples of people who may 'utter the formulae that stem from knowledge' without, however, actualizing the knowledge that such formulae typically express: those who, in passionate conditions such as anger and sexual desire, utter proofs and the verses of Empedocles; those first learning a subject; and actors. And whereas actors may or may not know whereof they speak, it is clear in the case of those '*first learning*' a subject that the agents do not yet possess the sort of knowledge their utterances ordinarily express. So *their* utterances *cannot* be taken as any sign that *they* are actualizing the relevant knowledge, which *ex hypothesi* they do not even possess.

The fact that some of the subjects mentioned do not even *have* the knowledge that their utterances seem to express is overlooked by those commentators who take Aristotle to assimilate the condition of the *akratēs* to that of the learner.[28] Such commentators aim to explain the sense in which the *akratēs* both 'has in a way and does not have' the relevant knowledge by saying that she has only a *partial* grasp of it. And they seek to justify this partly by connecting [8(*b*)] with passages where Aristotle emphasizes the crucial role played by experience of particulars in the acquisition of practical knowledge (as distinct from knowledge of subjects such as mathematics). One such passage is indeed similar to [8(*b*)]: Aristotle says that in areas where experience of particulars is crucial, 'young people lack conviction but simply speak' (1142^a19–20).

But if one assimilates akratic agents generally to learners, one moves away from the idea that the *akratēs* is, like the sleeping geometer, someone who has already reached first actuality knowledge but in a condition such that she cannot, while in that condition, access it at will. Moreover, [8(*b*)] does *not* say that the condition of the *akratēs* is *generally* like that of the learner: it is aimed primarily at disarming the previously mentioned objection by showing that it does *not follow* from the fact that someone 'utters the formulae that stem from knowledge' that she is *using* the knowledge. Aristotle is not adding the learner to [8(*a*)]'s list of paradigms. He simply appeals, in order to answer the objection, to a limited respect in which at least some akratic agents are like those first learning a subject.[29]

If one were to read [8(*b*)] as adding to (*a*)'s list of paradigms, one should read it as adding the actor rather than the learner. For [8(*b*)] concludes by saying that we should take the utterances of the *akratēs* as we take those of actors. But here again the point of the comparison is limited. It concerns only what we can *infer* from

[28] See e.g. N. O. Dahl, *Practical Reason, Aristotle, and Weakness of the Will* [*Practical Reason*] (Minneapolis, 1984), 208–10; Charles, 'Venice'.

[29] See also G. Lawrence, 'Akrasia and Clear-Eyed Akrasia', *Revue de philosophie ancienne*, 6 (1988), 77–106 at 90–101.

the utterances of those *akrateis* who 'utter the formulae that stem from knowledge'; it is not meant to provide a positive account of the disposition of such agents, let alone of akratic agents in general. Aristotle does not say here, as in [8(*a*)], that akratic agents are in a condition similar to that of those to whom they are compared (in this case actors). His paradigm remains that of someone who has reached first actuality but is in a condition (like sleep, madness, and drunkenness) such that she cannot (or cannot readily) access it at will.

Some commentators may be reluctant to allow that this *is* Aristotle's paradigm because they underestimate the capacities of those asleep, mad, and drunk. They may worry that those who are asleep do not act at all, and that those who are mad and drunk do not know what they are doing in the way required for their actions to count as voluntary. But Aristotle himself allows even sleepers some fairly sophisticated activities: some, for example, can answer questions when asked (see *De insomniis* 462ª19–28). Commentators who overlook this and moreover assimilate Aristotle's drunken subjects to those who are asleep are likely to take his drunken subjects, if not as literally passed out, at least as quite far gone. But drunkenness, as Aristotle might himself put it, 'admits of the more and the less'.[30] It is not every drunk who can recite the verses of Empedocles; it is only the drunk who already in some sense knows them. And while it seems possible for someone to memorize these verses without any comprehension of their contents, those who have some grasp of their contents are surely more likely to succeed in memorizing them. A similar point applies to the person who can utter proofs while in a condition of sexual passion: if you find yourself in bed with someone who does this, it is a good bet that she is someone who, when in her senses, actually has some understanding of these proofs. But the crucial point remains: it does *not follow* from this that her utterance of these proofs while she is in a passionate condition counts as an *expression* or *actualization* of that understanding.

[30] See e.g. *Prob.* 3. 2: 'Why is it that it is not those who are very drunk that are most troublesome in their cups, but those who are only half blotto? Is it because they have neither drunk so little that they still resemble the sober nor so much that they are in the incapacitated state of those who have drunk deep? Further, those who are sober have more power of judgment, while those who are very drunk make no attempt to exercise their judgment; but those who are only half blotto can still exercise their judgment because they are not very drunk, but they exercise it badly . . .' (translation by E. S. Forster, in J. Barnes (ed.), *The Complete Works of Aristotle: The Revised Oxford Translation* [*Complete Works*] (2 vols.; Princeton, 1984)).

Even if her utterances of the very same formulae on *other* occasions
are in fact expressions or actualizations of the relevant knowledge,
we need not treat her utterances of these formulae while she is in a
passionate condition as themselves expression or actualizations of
that knowledge.

   This is important because one might be tempted in cases where
the agent *does* have the relevant first actuality knowledge to assume
that the utterances that would normally express such knowledge
must *always* involve the agent's moving from first to second actualization. But there is an important difference between an utterance
being an *expression of* knowledge and an utterance being somehow
facilitated by the subject's possession of the relevant knowledge.
And the fact that only an agent with first actuality knowledge of
proofs is likely to be capable of uttering such proofs in passionate
conditions does *not* show that any utterance of them in passionate
conditions involves the sort of comprehension that is essential to
the move from first to second actuality. This is the point of [8(*b*)],
whose examples include both those who have and those who do not
even have the sort of knowledge their utterances might be taken to
express: such utterances cannot be taken as any sign that the agent
in question is in fact *actualizing* the relevant knowledge, not even
in cases (such as that of the sleeping geometer) where she in fact
has the relevant (first actuality) knowledge.

6. The third *eti* passage (and fourth step): the failure distinctive of the *akratēs*

One problem with assimilating the condition of the *akratēs* to the
conditions of those asleep, drunk, and mad is that these conditions
involve relatively indiscriminate impairment of their subjects: they
interfere not just with practical reasoning but also with theoretical
reasoning and many other activities. This, we think, is why Aristotle
adds the final *eti* section. Although this section is sometimes taken
simply as explaining what he has already said, but from a different
more scientific point of view, we take the section to be crucial to
completing Aristotle's account.[31] Its task is largely to identify and

---

[31] For a radical example of someone who fails to see any new point in the *phusikōs*
passage, see Robinson, 'Akrasia', 151: 'Aristotle adds a *phusikōs* explanation, not in
order to get down at last to the question, but rather to set aside those unfortunate

explain the relatively local impairment characteristic of the *akratēs*, an impairment compatible with her being proficient, even during akratic episodes, in doing many things that those who are asleep or drunk are typically impaired in doing.

This, we think, is part of the point of examining the cause of the *akratēs'* failure, as Aristotle puts it, *phusikōs*. He often distinguishes investigating something *phusikōs* from investigating it *logikōs* or *katholou*. The latter seems to involve examining something at a relatively high level of abstraction (often in a way to do with the meanings of terms), while the former seems to involve examining something according to principles proper to the specific nature of the phenomenon in question.[32] But the distinction is not always between investigations that appeal to principles within natural science and those that appeal to purely logical considerations. For, as *De generatione animalium* 2. 8 makes clear, even within natural science, a proof can be more or less *logikos*. Here, Aristotle criticizes the more *logikos* proof of those who seek to explain the sterility of mules by appeal to principles that apply to the products of *all* interspecies unions, because (as he says) their argument is 'too universal and empty'. He goes on to say that we are more likely to grasp the true cause of the mule's sterility if we start the investigation from specific facts about the horse and the ass ($747^b27–748^a16$).

Though Aristotle tends to use *phusikōs* and its cognates primarily in connection with the objects of natural sciences, he draws similar distinctions in his ethical works between investigations that are carried out more and less *phusikōs*. But his usage is complicated, since what is more *phusikōs* is sometimes treated as being at what is in some sense a *higher* level of explanation than that to which it is compared. Whether or not this is a good thing is determined by the primary consideration of whether the enquiry is at the level *appropriate* to the explanandum. So although Aristotle dismisses

persons who cannot distinguish philosophy from psychology . . . Though Aristotle does not say so, I think I hear him adding under his breath: "But this pretty psychological story has nothing to do with our question, the answer to which still resides in the logical distinctions I have drawn between the different kinds of knowing." We note that a little later he refer us to "the physiologers", if we wish to know "how the ignorance is dissipated and the acratic resumes his knowledge" (1147b6–9). That is physics, not ethics.'

[32] See *De caelo* $280^a32–4$ ($\phi\upsilon\sigma\iota\kappa\tilde{\omega}\varsigma$ vs. $\kappa\alpha\theta\acute{o}\lambda\upsilon$); $283^b17–18$ ($\phi\upsilon\sigma\iota\kappa\tilde{\omega}\varsigma$ $\delta\grave{\epsilon}$ $\kappa\alpha\grave{\iota}$ $\mu\grave{\eta}$ $\kappa\alpha\theta\acute{o}\lambda\upsilon$); *GC* $316^a5–14$. For useful discussion of this contrast, see M. Burnyeat, *A Map of* Metaphysics *Zeta* (Pittsburgh, 2001), 19–24.

the *phusikōteron* approach of those who seek to explain friendship by appeal to fundamental principles of matter on the ground that this sort of approach is 'higher' than it should be (ἀνώτερον, *NE* 1155ᵇ2) and 'too universal' (λίαν καθόλου, *EE* 1235ᵃ29–31), he elsewhere rejects attempts to explain why benefactors love their beneficiaries more than their beneficiaries love them by appeal to the psychology of creditors and debtors, apparently because their explanation is *too specific*. In this case, Aristotle prefers what he calls the *phusikōteron* approach of those who appeal to general principles of human nature rather than principles peculiar to the psychologies of creditors and debtors (*NE* 1167ᵇ17–1168ᵃ9). In sum, the issue is not so much the level of specificity as whether the principles invoked are appropriate to the nature of the explanandum.[33]

So when the explanandum is *akratic* behaviour, the move to considering the cause *phusikōs* must involve appeal to principles proper to the behaviour of *rational* animals. It is a move to a distinctive kind of psychological investigation, one in which the explanation of behaviour by appeal to interactions among the subject's beliefs (or belief-like states) and desires is complicated by the subject's degree of appreciation of logical relations, especially among the propositions that serve as both possible and actual contents of her beliefs. This is why, as we shall see, Aristotle takes the trouble in [9(*b*)] to explain how the *akratēs'* appetitive action differs from the appetitive actions of *non-rational* animals. Aristotle attends here to the ways in which psychological states (such as beliefs and desires) tend to interact in rational animals, not just where things go *right*, but also where things go *wrong*. And, as appropriate in a teleological framework, he begins in [9(*a*)] with an account of 'normal' or 'default' cases, where things go as they are supposed to go, and then turns in (*b*) to analysing cases where things go wrong by appealing to ways in which they depart from the norm.

[9] *NE* 7. 3, 1147ᵃ24–ᵇ12

   Further [ἔτι], one might also look at the cause ⟨of the *akratēs'* failure⟩ in the following way, according to the point of view proper to its nature [φυσικῶς].

(*a*) For the one ⟨?⟩ is *katholou doxa*, while the other ⟨?⟩ is about the particulars, concerning which perception is in fact authoritative. And whenever

---

[33] On this use of *phusikōteron* see J. Whiting, 'The Nicomachean Account of Philia', in Kraut (ed.), *Guide*, 276–304, esp. 288. Note that we differ here from David Charles, who actually translates *phusikōs* as 'more specifically' (see *Action*, 128).

one ⟨?⟩ comes to be from these, it is necessary with respect to what results [τὸ συμπερανθέν], in other cases [ἔνθα μέν] for the soul to affirm it,
but in the productive cases ⟨for the soul⟩ to act ⟨on it⟩ straightaway.[34]
For example, if one should taste everything sweet, and this is sweet
⟨counts⟩ as one of the particulars, it is necessary for one who is able
and not prevented, at the same time as this [viz. τὸ συμπερανθέν] ⟨comes
to be⟩, also to act.

(b) Whenever, then, the universal ⟨*doxa*⟩ *preventing* tasting is present, ⟨and
also⟩ the ⟨universal *doxa*⟩ that everything sweet is pleasant, and this
is sweet[35] (and this ⟨*doxa*⟩ is active), and *epithumia* happens also to be
present, then the one ⟨*doxa*⟩ says in fact to avoid this [ἡ μὲν οὖν λέγει
φεύγειν τοῦτο], but *epithumia* leads ⟨the way⟩. For each of the parts ⟨of
soul⟩ is able to move ⟨the animal⟩.[36] So it happens by *logos* in a way
and by *doxa* that he acts akratically, not ⟨by *doxa*⟩ opposed in itself to
right reason but ⟨*doxa* opposed⟩ accidentally; for it is *epithumia* and not
doxa that is opposed ⟨to right reason⟩. And it is also because of this that
beasts are not akratic, because they do not have universal supposition,
but ⟨only⟩ *phantasia* and memory of particulars.

(c) How the ignorance [ἡ ἄγνοια] is dissolved, and the *akratēs* again comes
to be ⟨in the condition of⟩ one who knows, the same account ⟨holds
as⟩ in the case of one who is drunk or asleep, and not ⟨one⟩ proper to
this ⟨particular sort of⟩ *pathos*, ⟨but⟩ one which we must hear from the
phusiologoi. And since the last *protasis* is both a *doxa* about something

---

[34] We stop short of introducing explicit reference to theoretical reasoning into our
translation (as is done both by Irwin and by Gauthier and Jolif); but we follow the
common view that the contrast signalled in ἔνθα μέν . . . ἐν δὲ ταῖς ποιητικαῖς is one
between theoretical reasoning and productive reasoning construed broadly enough
to include the sort of *praxis* that Aristotle sometimes distinguishes from *poiēsis*. We
are not persuaded by what we take to be the most plausible alternative—namely, John
McDowell's suggestion that the clause is meant to contrast *praxis* proper with *poiēsis*
proper. See his 'Incontinence and Practical Wisdom in Aristotle' ['Incontinence'],
in S. Lovibond and S. G. Williams (eds.), *Identity, Truth and Value: Essays for
David Wiggins* (Oxford, 1996), 95–112, esp. 98–9.

[35] Although 'this is sweet' might seem simply to report a fact and not actually
to express the content of some further *doxa*, that would make it difficult to explain
the agent's acting in accord with *either* universal. So we take 'this is sweet', along
with the immediately following claim that 'this is active', to indicate that the agent
actively thinks, of some particular, '*this* is sweet'. See n. 49.

[36] Most translators take this as making the point (similar to one made in 1110ᵃ15–
17) that *epithumia* can move each of the parts of the body. But we follow David
Charles ('Venice') in thinking it more relevant here that each of the parts of soul can
move the animal, than that *epithumia* can move each of the parts of the body. The
idea here is pretty clearly that either reason or appetite might move the agent, one
leading to enkratic and the other to akratic behaviour. Ramsauer (*Ethica Nicomachea*,
ad loc.) also adopts this view.

perceptible and authoritative over actions,³⁷ it is this that ⟨the *akratēs*⟩ either does not have while he is in this *pathos* or has ⟨only⟩ in the sense that he does not know but ⟨simply⟩ utters ⟨the words⟩, like the drunk ⟨uttering⟩ the ⟨verses⟩ of Empedocles.³⁸

There is some question straightaway about what Aristotle takes himself to be talking about in the first sentence of (*a*). What are the unexpressed subjects that are said to be either 'universal *doxa*' or 'about the particulars', and from which something further is said to result? Aristotle's reference to what results as τὸ συμπερανθέν leads many commentators to read him as speaking here of syllogisms, in which some conclusion results in the sense that some proposition follows logically from a pair of premisses (προτάσεις)—one a universal proposition and the other a proposition about particulars. And some translators actually supply '*protasis*' here in 1147ᵃ25 in spite of the fact that the term last appeared at 1147ᵃ1 (viz. 25 lines and two '*eti*'s ago): they read Aristotle as saying 'since the one *protasis* is a universal *doxa* and the other *protasis* is about the particulars'.³⁹

It is, however, pretty clear from Aristotle's talk about what results when 'nothing impedes' that he is thinking primarily about psychological states and not (or at least not primarily) about the contents of such states.⁴⁰ He is, for example, more concerned with actual beliefs than with the propositions that serve as their contents. The two are of course linked in so far as the psychological states of *rational* subjects tend to respect the logical relations among their contents. But the two need to be distinguished precisely in order to allow for cases where the subject's actual psychological states fail to mirror the logical relations—cases, for example, where a subject fails to draw from her actual beliefs logical consequences that would normally be transparent to her or fails to act in accordance with her beliefs and any consequences she draws (or at least seems to draw) from them. This appeal to beliefs and other psychological

---

³⁷ On the proper way to read this, see sect. 7.

³⁸ The text continues with [10] below, which can be treated as completing the third *eti* passage. But it may simply clarify the relation between Aristotle's ultimate account (viz. the one culminating in the third *eti* passage) and the Socratic view with which Aristotle began. So we treat it separately in sect. 8.

³⁹ See Rowe's translation; and Charles, 'Venice', who argues in detail for supplying *protasis*.

⁴⁰ This is also emphasized by J. Bogen and J. Moravcsik, 'Aristotle's Forbidden Sweets' ['Forbidden Sweets'], *Journal of the History of Philosophy*, 20 (1982), 111–27 at 113–14.

states is, in our view, part of what is involved in considering the matter *phusikōs*.[41]

Aristotle begins with normal or default cases: those where someone has both a universal belief and a belief about particulars, as a result of which some further state comes about. He shows no signs here of thinking that he needs to explain how this further state comes about: when things are working as they should, it *just does*. That is part of what it is for their subject to be a *rational* animal. And this holds both in the theoretical sphere and in the practical and productive spheres. But matters are more complicated in the practical and productive spheres, where there is a potential gap between belief and action, and one might reach the proper conclusion (either about how one ought to act or about how to produce some result) but fail to act accordingly. Yet here, where Aristotle is discussing normal or default cases, he shows no sign of thinking he needs to introduce anything else, once the further state results, to explain the action's occurrence. This may be because (as he elsewhere suggests) 'what results' *is* the action. Or it may be simply that he treats 'what results' as a belief in some proposition and thinks of the appropriate action as following with a kind of necessity from this belief, at least in cases where things go as they are supposed to go.[42]

Aristotle turns in (*b*) to cases where things go wrong. Here again we lack an explicit subject. What is 'the universal preventing tasting'? Is it (as some translations suggest) a universal *premiss*? Or is

---

[41] We offer the following hypothesis about why Aristotle does not supply a definite subject in (*a*): he lacks a term that would allow him to straddle, in the requisite way, the *contents* of the psychological states and the *states themselves*. In the case where things go right and these contents are affirmed, *doxa* is actually required to explain the agent's behaviour. But in cases where things go wrong and the relevant beliefs do not result, *doxa* is neither appropriate nor explanatorily relevant. Nor is *protasis*, since the question is not primarily about logical relations but about the *actual* psychological states whose presence (or rather absence) explains what the agent does.

[42] Some commentators see here the view (explicitly expressed at *MA* 701ᵃ19–20) that the conclusion is an action. See e.g. G. E. M. Anscombe, *Intention* (Oxford, 1957), 60; and M. C. Nussbaum, *Aristotle's* De motu animalium (Princeton, 1978), 201–4 (also 184–6). Nussbaum seems to take the kind of necessity involved to be logical, but we want to leave open the possibility that it is psychological, in which case the action may (when nothing impedes) follow necessarily without, however, being *identified* with the conclusion. So we propose to remain neutral on this issue. But for defence of the controversial view that the conclusion of practical reasoning is an action—though not of Aristotle's commitment to it—see P. Clark, 'The Action as Conclusion', *Canadian Journal of Philosophy*, 31 (2001), 481–506.

it perhaps (taking '*protasis*' in its more general sense) a universal *proposition*? We take Aristotle's claim to consider the cause *phusikōs* to suggest that he means *neither*: here, where things go wrong, what matters is what the subject *actually* believes and desires, and how exactly she does so. Aristotle considers a case in which a subject has (in some sense of 'have') two universal *doxai*, one preventing tasting (presumably of sweet things) and the other affirming the proposition 'everything sweet is pleasant'. Note that we differ here from those commentators who take the second *doxa* to be or to involve some *particular* proposition. We take it to be universal for two (related) reasons: first, it is natural to take the ἡ δέ clause that answers ἡ μέν καθόλου as introducing another example of the sort of thing explicitly introduced in the ἡ μέν clause (viz. another universal *doxa*); and second, what follows the ἡ δέ (namely, 'that everything sweet is pleasant') is as clearly universal as the next claim (namely 'that this is sweet') is particular. In this case, 'this is active' seems to refer simply to the particular belief 'this is sweet', and the immediately following reference to *epithumia* seems intended somehow to explain why the agent acts akratically in spite of the fact that the universal *doxa* preventing tasting is in some sense in the agent.[43]

Our account assumes what is in some sense uncontroversial—namely, that the *universal doxa* preventing tasting, however it is to be formulated, is *not used*. This is just the sort of diagnosis that our reading of the first *eti* passage led us to expect, one in which some failure to use knowledge of a *universal* is implicated. Note, however, that there is an important difference between the sort of case described in the first *eti* passage and the sort described here. In the first case, what explained an epistemic subject's failure to use a relevant bit of universal knowledge was the fact, cited in [7(*b*)], that she either did not have or did not exercise some *particular* item of knowledge such as '*this* food is such'. But in the present case, Aristotle goes out of his way to say that the analogous item—namely 'this is sweet'—*is* active.[44] If so, we cannot in *this* case appeal (as

---

[43] Irwin, *Nicomachean Ethics*, 260, takes the second *doxa* to be the conjunction 'everything sweet is pleasant *and* this is sweet', and he takes 'this is active' to refer to this conjunctive belief. Price, 'Acrasia', 237 and 241, and Kenny, 'Practical Syllogism', 178–81, adopt a similar view.

[44] Note that even commentators who see the second belief or premiss as conjunctive agree that 'this is sweet' is (*qua* part of the conjunctive belief or premiss) active. So they accept the difference, crucial to our account, between the case described here and the case described in the first *eti* passage.

most commentators do) to the absence or inactivity of the *particular doxa* in order to explain why the relevant universal is not used. Nor would appealing to the absence or inactivity of the particular help, since that would (as we have seen) undermine the claim that the akratic agent acts voluntarily. So the present case requires a *different sort of explanation* (from the one given in the first *eti* passage) of why the relevant universal fails to get used.

Moreover, we take it to be part of the point of the second *eti* passage to prepare the way for the different sort of explanation, given here, of the *akratēs'* failure to use her knowledge of the relevant universal. The second *eti* passage points to physical states, associated with conditions like sleep and drunkenness, that interfere with the mechanisms by which an agent normally moves from first to second actuality knowledge: when the agent is in one of these states, moves that are normally more or less automatic fail to occur and moves that are normally performed at will are no longer subject (or readily subject) to the agent's will. But conditions like sleep and drunkenness involve relatively *global* impairment, whereas the sort of impairment involved in akrasia seems *local*. The *akratēs* may be able, while in the akratic condition, to move from first to second actuality knowledge in many domains, both theoretical and practical; her incapacity prevails primarily in areas where she is vulnerable to temptation.[45] We think it is precisely in order to account for this that the third *eti* passage introduces *epithumia*, whose presence may help to explain why it is the *akratēs'* knowledge only of certain universal propositions that fails to get actualized—why it tends to be only her knowledge of universals that *prohibit* pursuing the objects of *epithumia* that fails to get actualized and *not* her knowledge of universals that do *not prohibit* the pursuit of these objects.

The *akratēs'* problem is that her *epithumia* encourages the 'wrong' beliefs to be activated.[46] By 'wrong' beliefs we do *not* mean *false* beliefs. Given the nature or strength of her desire, her perception of some particular as (for example) sweet leads her more or less immediately to think, truly enough, 'this is pleasant'.[47] But whether

---

[45] This point is emphasized by J. Gosling in 'Mad, Drunk or Asleep? Aristotle's Akratic', *Phronesis*, 38 (1993), 98–104.

[46] Note that we generally oppose Irwin's view that deliberation itself excites the desire. See T. Irwin, 'Some Rational Aspects of Incontinence' ['Rational Aspects'], *Southern Journal of Philosophy*, 27, suppl. (1988), 49–88 at 70.

[47] Here we have an example of a universal term whose application to a particular is so obvious that the agent can scarcely fail to apply it. This is like the case where

or not she has previously deliberated and reached the conclusion that she should not taste this (or this sort of thing), it happens that when *epithumia* is active in the relevant way she thinks 'this is pleasant' at the expense of thinking 'this is fattening' or 'this should not be tasted'. And when this belief results, it is natural for her to act straightaway, provided she is able and nothing interferes. So what happens here is not unlike what happens in the normal case where things go as they are supposed to go. And here, as there, *epithumia* does not simply co-operate with belief to produce action; by facilitating the move from perception to some rather than other beliefs, *epithumia* actually helps to explain *which* universal beliefs get activated.[48]

Note that the point here is simply that the *akratēs* fails to actualize any universal that would prohibit her action, and not that there must be some universal that recommends or even prescribes her action. Though many commentators see two syllogisms here, one 'good' and one 'bad', and some even imagine that there must be a prescriptive major for the 'bad' syllogism corresponding to the prohibitive major of the 'good' one, Aristotle's example suggests that a merely descriptive universal, such as 'everything sweet is pleasant', may be more or less automatically activated and acted on *before* the agent has a chance to activate any knowledge she might have of prohibiting universals.[49] The relatively automatic nature of the processes involved and the lack of any need for a prescriptive major are closely tied to the fundamentally animal nature of the

---

she cannot fail to realize she is human; only here it is the *object* term in the universal, rather than the *subject* term, whose application is more or less automatic. See n. 25.

[48] *Epithumia* can play other roles as well: it can colour perception, sometimes even to the point of distorting it.

[49] Although some commentators who see two syllogisms here take the major of the so-called 'bad' syllogism to be prescriptive (e.g. Gauthier and Jolif, *L'Éthique*, ii. 612; Broadie and Rowe, *Nicomachean Ethics*, 392), Irwin sees that this is not required and takes the two syllogisms to share a minor premiss, such as 'this is sweet'. On his account, the agent has deliberated in a way such that she at some point connects 'this is sweet' to the 'good' major, which prohibits tasting such sweets, and so at some point draws the conclusion that she should not taste this; but the activity of the minor premiss later leads (in conjunction with *epithumia*) to the minor premiss becoming 'detached' from the 'good' major and being conjoined instead with the 'bad' major (viz. with 'everything sweet is pleasant'), thus producing action. See Irwin, *Nicomachean Ethics*, 260–1, and 'Rational Aspects', 67. For versions of the two-syllogism view that take each syllogism to have a different minor premiss, see J. Cooper, *Reason and Human Good in Aristotle* (Cambridge, Mass., 1975), 49–50, and Robinson, 'Akrasia', 145.

epithumiai involved in 'unqualified' akrasia, viz. the sort of *epithumiai* on which non-rational animals can act in the absence of *any* sort of belief (whether prescriptive or not). And while some commentators take the relatively automatic nature of these processes to show that Aristotle assimilates the *akratēs'* behaviour to that of non-rational animals, we would not ourselves go this far. We allow, of course, that he takes akratic action to follow, when *epithumia* is present, relatively automatically upon the perception of something as (for example) sweet. But we think that taking him to assimilate the *akratēs'* behaviour to that of non-rational animals fails to do justice to [9(*b*)]'s claims that the *akratēs* acts 'by *logos* in a way and by *doxa*' and that she has a kind of universal *hupolēpsis* that non-rational animals lack.[50]

It is, however, important not to over-interpret Aristotle's claim that the *akratēs* acts ὑπὸ λόγου by taking it to mean that she relies on some sort of prescriptive premiss.[51] For this is neither necessary nor helpful. It is not necessary, since (as we have seen) his point is that a universal *doxa* like 'everything sweet is pleasant' can, together with the relevant desire, produce action in the absence of anything further.[52] Nor is it helpful: for introducing a prescriptive universal would seem *either* to undermine the claim that the agent knows that she should not do what she does *or* to involve ascribing contradictory beliefs to her (which would itself undermine the claim that she knows the proper universal). This may be why Aristotle says that the relevant belief is not in itself, but only coincidentally, opposed to her admittedly correct reason: his point is that the relevant belief

---

[50] For a strong assimilation of akratic behaviour to that of non-rational animals, see J. Müller, 'Tug of War: Aristotle on Akrasia' (unpublished paper), and H. Lorenz, *The Brute Within: Appetitive Desire in Plato and Aristotle* (Oxford, 2006), ch. 13, who explicitly accepts (197 n. 27) the idea we reject, that Aristotle posits a global (albeit temporary) impairment of the *akratēs'* reason.

[51] It is important not to forget the πως in ὑπὸ λόγου πως.

[52] For this point, see 1149ᵃ32–ᵇ2, where Aristotle is contrasting qualified akrasia, involving anger, with unqualified akrasia. He says 'when on the one hand [μέν] *logos* or *phantasia* has revealed that there is hubris or a slight, the agent, as if having syllogized [ὥσπερ συλλογισάμενος] that it is necessary to fight such a thing, gets angry straightaway. But when on the other hand [δ᾽] *logos* or *aisthēsis* simply says that something is pleasant, *epithumia* has an impulse [ὁρμᾷ] towards the enjoyment. So *thumos* follows reason in a way, but *epithumia* does not.' The idea seems to be that *epithumia* does not require the sort of prescription that seems to be operative in the case of *thumos*, where the agent thinks 'one must [or should, δεῖ] fight such a thing'. And even in the case of *thumos*, Aristotle says only that the agent becomes angry 'as if having syllogized'.

tends, when it coincides with certain *epithumiai*, to encourage only *action* (and not also *belief*) that is contrary to correct reason. For there is no *logical* conflict between the universal prohibiting tasting (however exactly it is to be formulated) and the merely descriptive universal 'everything sweet is pleasant'. So Aristotle can explain how the agent acts in a way that involves *doxa* (and not simply the sort of *phantasia* involved in the behaviour of non-rational animals) but without having to introduce any beliefs that would conflict with the agent's knowledge of the so-called 'good' universal.

This is crucial because the *akratēs must* in some sense share the virtuous agent's knowledge of what she ought to do. So she *cannot believe* when she acts that she *ought* to be doing what she is supposed to *know* she *ought not* do. For that would undermine her claim to *know* what she ought to do. It would also involve the sort of corruption of belief that Aristotle explicitly takes to characterize vicious as distinct from akratic agents. As he explains in 7. 8, the *akratēs* still in some sense has the right principle: her *pathos* masters her to the extent that she does not act in accordance with the right principle (ὥστε μὲν μὴ πράττειν κατὰ τὸν ὀρθὸν λόγον), but not to the extent that she becomes such as to be *persuaded* (τοιοῦτον οἷον πεπεῖσθαι) that she *ought* to act on some other principle (1151ᵃ11–26). This, we argue, explains why Aristotle focuses on her failure to use or activate some sort of *universal* knowledge. Since her action must be voluntary, he cannot allow (as he did in the theoretical case) that she fails to use or activate her knowledge of the relevant *particular*. And since he cannot say that her belief in the relevant universal propositions is *corrupted*, he concludes that her access to these universal beliefs must be temporarily *impeded*.

The temporary impediment is of course due to *epithumia*, which renders the subject vulnerable to bodily disturbances like those involved in sleep and drunkenness. Like those who are drunk or asleep, the *akratēs* is temporarily unable to actualize her knowledge in situations in which its use is called for. So it is not surprising that [9(c)] refers to the temporary inability of the *akratēs* as a kind of ignorance [ἄγνοια], and concludes with a few remarks about how 'this ignorance is dissolved and the *akratēs* comes again to be ⟨in the condition of⟩ one who knows'. The point here is that there is no special sort of explanation peculiar to the recovery of the *akratēs*; the same sort of explanation applies here as in the case of those asleep and drunk, the sort for which we must turn to the so-called

physiologoi. Aristotle must have in mind the sort of explanation
given in the *Parva Naturalia*, where (for example) sleep is said to
occur as a result of certain material and efficient causal processes
(such as heating, evaporation, and settling) that are associated with
the digestion of food, and waking is said to occur when these processes are complete and the heat that has been occupied in digestion
returns to its normal position (*De somno* 457^{b}20–458^{a}26).[53] His idea
seems to be that because the sort of desires and emotions involved
in akratic episodes are associated with the body, and so with the
sort of processes of heating and cooling that control bodily functions, akratic episodes too can pass as a result of similar material
and efficient causal processes having run their course.

Aristotle's reference to the *phusiologoi* is sometimes read simply
as a consequence of the *phusikōs* approach adopted in the third *eti*
passage.[54] But we think this misguided. The point is clearly that
the explanation of the *akratēs'* recovery from her temporary ignorance is *not proper* to the *akratēs*, but the same as the explanation
of the drunk's and the sleeper's recoveries from their temporary
ignorance: when the body has returned to its 'normal' state, the
subject is in each case able once again to actualize her knowledge
readily in situations where such actualization is called for. This is
not a phusikōs explanation, which would be (as explained above)
one *proper* to the nature of the phenomenon in question. Such an
explanation would presumably mention psychological causes, such

---

[53] The *Problemata*, which may or may not be by Aristotle, suggests (in book 3)
that drunkenness, which is also associated with processes of heating and
cooling, subsides when the relevant processes have run their course. For, as book 30 explains,
those who are drunk are often temporarily in conditions (such as talkativeness or
boldness) that are characteristic of the permanent character of others, which happens because both wine and nature produce these characteristics by the same (no
doubt material and efficient causal) means since 'the whole body functions under
the control of heat' (953^{a}33–^{b}23).

[54] Many translations do not clearly signal the distinction between (*a*) φυσικῶς
investigations and (*b*) investigations characteristic of τῶν φυσιολόγων: Irwin pairs
(*a*) 'referring to [human] nature' with (*b*) 'the natural scientists'; Ross (in Barnes,
Complete Works, 1812) is similar, pairing (*a*) 'with reference to the facts of nature'
with (*b*) 'the students of natural science'; Rowe pairs (*a*) 'scientifically' with (*b*) 'natural scientists'; and Price ('Acrasia', 237) pairs (*a*) 'scientifically' with (*b*) 'scientists'.
Rackham signals a distinction and gets it nearly right with (*a*) 'scientifically' (to
which he adds the note 'i.e., in this case, psychologically: literally with reference to
its nature') and (*b*) 'to physiology'. The point is that Aristotle tends to associate the
phusiologoi with explanations in terms of material principles. Such explanations will
sometimes (viz. where they are in fact proper to the nature of the explananda) be
phusikōs. But they should not be conflated with *phusikōs* explanations as such.

as satisfaction of the akratic desire or redirection of the agent's attention to other objects. It may of course be true that some such psychological causes supervene on some of the same sort of material and efficient causal processes as those involved in waking up. But it is one thing to explain the *akratēs'* recovery of knowledge by appeal to such psychological causes and another to explain it by appeal to the sort of material and efficient causal processes mentioned (for example) in *De somno*.

It is clear from the *Eudemian* discussion of friendship that Aristotle distinguishes the sort of explanations of friendship given by the *phusiologoi* from those 'nearer and proper to the *phainomena*' in question: the *phusiologoi* tend to appeal to general principles such as 'like tends towards like' or 'opposites attract', rather than to principles specific to the behaviour of animals, such as their tendency to love their offspring (1235ᵃ10–35). It is also clear that Aristotle himself prefers to appeal to *phusikos* principles, such as the principle that those who have produced something (like a poem or child) tend to love it (1240ᵇ40–1241ᵃ9). And however odd it may seem to *us* to explain the onset of the akratic episode by appeal to psychological mechanisms and the passing of the akratic episode by appeal to material and efficient causal ones, this does seem to be what *Aristotle* proposes, perhaps in part because of the sort of explanatory asymmetries afforded by his teleological framework. But we cannot discuss these here.[55] For present purposes, the lesson of (*c*) is simply that Aristotle takes some sort of ignorance—however it happens to be resolved—to be implicated in akratic behaviour.

Aristotle speaks here of *agnoia* because he thinks the *akratēs* temporarily unable to make the sort of move from first to second actuality that is characteristic of those who have knowledge: her condition is thus a kind of temporary ignorance not unlike the 'temporary insanity' of modern legal counsel. It is, more specifically, knowledge of some *universal* that the *akratēs* is temporarily unable to use. But this is not (as in the first *eti* passage) because she lacks the sort of knowledge of a particular that is required for the actualization of the universal. She has the requisite knowledge of particulars, but her *epithumia* somehow prevents her from applying her universal knowledge to the relevant particulars. In her present condition she

---

[55] For more on these explanatory asymmetries, see J. Whiting, 'Hylomorphic Virtue: Cosmology, Embryology, and Moral Development in Aristotle' (forthcoming).

does not actualize the universal she should actualize and would in fact actualize if the disturbances associated with *epithumia* did not prevail.

7. Digression on the different types of *akratēs*: the 'weak' and the 'impetuous'

Some commentators will object that our account cannot be right. For they take Aristotle's use of τοῦτο in [9(*b*)]'s claim that 'the one ⟨*doxa*⟩ says in fact to avoid *this*' to show that he thinks the *akratēs* actually reaches the conclusion that follows from the prohibiting universal taken together with 'this is sweet'. Such commentators assume that Aristotle pictures the *akratēs* as at some point thinking, with respect to some particular, 'I should not taste *this*'. They read Aristotle as concerned in this passage primarily (and perhaps even exclusively) with what he later calls the 'weak'—as distinct from the 'impetuous'—*akratēs* (see 1150ᵇ19–28). Their idea is that the paradigmatic *akratēs* initially reaches the right conclusion but then manages to lose her grip on it at some point before the time when she acts against it.[56] Such commentators are likely to object to our account on the ground that it applies primarily, and perhaps even exclusively, to the impetuous *akratēs*. And this will appear especially problematic if, as John McDowell suggests, the weak *akratēs* is the only interesting variety.[57]

But given that Aristotle does not introduce the distinction between the impetuous and the weak *akratēs* until 7. 7, it seems preferable (if possible) to interpret 7. 3 as giving a generic account meant to cover both. So just as we think it problematic for these commentators to claim that Aristotle means to speak here only about the weak *akratēs*, we agree that it would be a problem for our interpretation *if* we had to read him as speaking here only about the impetuous.[58] But we do not think our interpretation requires this. Nor do we think it necessary to concede that [9(*b*)] should be read as referring primarily, or even exclusively, to the weak *akratēs*. Note in connection with this second point that Aristotle's use of τοῦτο

[56] See e.g. Irwin, *Nicomachean Ethics*, ad loc., and 'Rational Aspects', 52–6 and 67–71; and Charles's account of the 'weak' *akratēs* (*Action*, 127–8).

[57] McDowell, 'Incontinence', 100.

[58] See D. Bostock, *Aristotle's Ethics* (Oxford, 2000), 133, who thinks the passage applies only to the impetuous *akratēs*, and cannot accommodate the weak.

does *not* require us to read him as taking the *akratēs* to reach the conclusion 'do not taste *this*', where 'this' refers to some determinate particular. The point may simply be that the prohibiting *doxa* 'says' that this should not be tasted *only* in the sense that the prohibiting *doxa* entails that this should not be tasted.[59] Note also how Aristotle formulates the particular proposition 'this is sweet' in the immediately preceding line: he uses τουτί, presumably to indicate that he is talking about a concrete particular to which one can point here and now.[60] So he clearly *had*—and was even in the immediate context *using*—a device that would have allowed him to make it clear, had he wanted to, that what the agent was to avoid was not simply 'this' as in this *sort* of thing, but 'this here' *particular* thing.

The point about how to understand τοῦτο is closely connected to the vexed question of the meaning and reference of 'the last *protasis*' (τελευταία πρότασις) in [9(*c*)]'s claim that the last *protasis* is what the *akratēs* 'either does not have while he is in this *pathos* or has ⟨only⟩ in the sense that he does not know but ⟨simply⟩ utters ⟨the words⟩'. We take 'last *protasis*' to refer to the conclusion. But many commentators resist this on the ground that in contexts where Aristotle is discussing arguments, he typically uses the term *protasis* to refer to a premiss as distinct from the conclusion of an argument. This is one reason why so many commentators are convinced that the failure of the *akratēs must* be the sort of failure (familiar from the *Analytics* examples) either to have or to use the *minor* (or some *particular*) premiss. But saying this threatens, as we have seen, to compromise the claim that akratic action must be done voluntarily.

Fortunately, we need not take τελευταία πρότασις as referring to a premiss as such.[61] Although Aristotle often uses πρότασις specifically (to refer to premisses as such), nothing prevents us from taking it here in its general sense (to refer simply to some proposition)—

---

[59] For this way of taking λέγει, see W. F. R. Hardie, *Aristotle's Ethical Theory*, 2nd edn. (Oxford, 1980), 283; and Robinson, 'Akrasia', 145. Note also that David Charles has suggested (in conversation) that οὖν in ᾗ μὲν οὖν λέγει φεύγειν τοῦτο is a sign that some conclusion is being drawn. But even if οὖν signals a conclusion, it need not be the one reached by the *akratēs*; it may be a conclusion Aristotle is priming his reader to draw. Moreover, οὖν need not be inferential; it may signal either a *new stage* in some non-inferential sequence or (as we render it) that something is *in fact* the case.

[60] We are indebted to Brad Inwood for calling our attention to the relevance of Aristotle's use of the deictic suffix -ι. See Smyth, *Greek Grammar*, 333g.

[61] See n. 19. The view that πρότασις here means 'proposition' rather than 'premiss' has also been defended by Kenny, 'Practical Syllogism', 183 n. 36, and Bogen and Moravcsik, 'Forbidden Fruits', 125–6.

not even its conjunction with τελευταία, which may indicate only that he is talking about the last in some series of propositions, possibly even (as we think) about a conclusion. In our view, Aristotle's point is that the *akratēs either* lacks the conclusion 'don't taste this' *or* has this conclusion only in the way in which the drunk uttering the verses of Empedocles may be said to have knowledge of what he utters: either way, of course, the *akratēs* does not really have this conclusion.[62] Moreover, the fact that Aristotle mentions both possibilities here is probably intended (as many commentators think) to allow him to capture both the impetuous (who does not have it at all) and the weak (who has it only in the way the drunk who utters the verses of Empedocles 'has' them).[63]

Note that the *akratēs'* failure is supposed to be due to the fact that the physical changes associated with the presence of *epithumia* have put her in a condition such that she is temporarily prevented from actualizing her knowledge of the universal that prohibits tasting: for drawing the conclusion is precisely what would be involved in actualizing her knowledge of that universal in these circumstances. Our account can easily explain how this applies to the case of the impetuous *akratēs*: she acts straightaway on the upshot of her perception of something as sweet and the 'good' universal never gets properly activated. But more is required to explain how we can accommodate the case of the weak *akratēs*, who has deliberated but fails (because of her *epithumia*) to abide by the results of her deliberation (1150ᵇ19–21). For this suggests that she reaches the right conclusion, and so that her knowledge of the universal premiss *is* actualized.

The standard way of accommodating the weak *akratēs* is to say that she reaches the right conclusion but then somehow loses it before the time when she fails to act accordingly. And there is nothing in our account that prevents us from adopting this line, provided we can read [9(*b*)] as pointing to some mechanism capable of explaining not only how someone can be prevented from reaching

---

[62] Joseph Owens, somewhat surprisingly, takes 'Don't taste this' as the *akratēs'* τελευταία πρότασις but regards it as a *premiss* (rather than a conclusion). See 'The Acratic's "Ultimate Premise" in Aristotle', in J. Wiesner (ed.), *Aristoteles: Werk und Wirkung*, vol. i (Berlin, 1985), 376–92.

[63] See e.g. Charles, *Action*, 127; Dahl, *Practical Reason*, 207; J. Timmermann, 'Impulsivität und Schwäche: Die Argumentation des Abschnitts Eth. Nic. 1146b31–1147b19 im Lichte der beiden Formen des Phänomens "Akrasia"', *Zeitschrift für philosophische Forschung*, 54 (2000), 47–66.

the proper conclusion but also how someone might lose her grip on the proper conclusion after having reached it. And *epithumia* seems equally capable of playing both roles: even in cases where the agent has deliberated and reached the proper conclusion, the presence of *epithumia*—at least where it is strong—can lead an agent more or less automatically from her perception of something as sweet and therefore pleasant, to tasting that thing, in spite of the fact that she has previously deliberated and reached the conclusion that she should not taste sweets, perhaps even the conclusion that she should not taste this *particular* sweet. In such cases, she no longer properly grasps this conclusion at the time when she acts.[64]

The idea that the *akratēs* lacks the conclusion when she acts, either because she never reached it or because she has lost her grip on it, may help to explain Aristotle's use of ἡ τελευταία πρότασις. He may be reluctant to use τὸ συμπέρασμα or any other term indicating a conclusion as such because his point is that the agent *lacks* the relevant conclusion in the sense that she does not believe it, at least not at the time when she acts. Similar reasoning might explain why Aristotle does not speak instead of 'the last *doxa*': the *akratēs* does not have the relevant *belief*, except in the sense that she believes things from which it follows—namely, the particular proposition 'this is sweet' (which is currently active) and the universal proposition prohibiting tasting (which is not currently active and which something about her *epithumia* renders her temporarily unable to activate in the normal way). Note that ἡ τελευταία πρότασις is a unique phrase: Aristotle is apparently struggling for the right words to make his point. And neither τὸ συμπέρασμα nor ἡ τελευταία δόξα will do: either might mislead the reader into thinking that the akratic agent actively has the *particular* belief that she should not be doing what she now does.

One might object here that [9(c)] explicitly refers to the last *protasis* as a *doxa*. But note what Aristotle says: 'since the last *protasis* is both a *doxa* about something perceptible and authoritative [κυρία] over actions, it is this that ⟨the *akratēs*⟩ either does not have . . . or has ⟨only⟩ in the sense that he does not know but ⟨simply⟩ utters ⟨the words⟩ . . .'. Clearly Aristotle does *not* think that the *akratēs*

---

[64] Aristotle may in fact think that the weak *akratēs*, although she deliberates and *seems* to reach the right conclusion, does not *really* reach it. But our aim here is to show how we can handle what might seem the most difficult case for our view, the case in which Aristotle thinks that the weak *akratēs* really draws the right conclusion.

acts on the last *protasis*. So in this case, where things go wrong, he *cannot* be saying that the last *protasis* is *in fact kuria* over action. Thus, he may not be saying that it is *in fact a doxa* either. This makes perfect sense if—as we maintain—Aristotle is contrasting the case of the *akratēs* with normal cases such as those discussed in (*a*). If this is right, then we should perhaps read the point in (*c*) as follows: since the last *protasis* is *normally* a *doxa* and *kuria* of actions, this (either the *protasis* or the corresponding *doxa*) is what the *akratēs* either does not have or has only in the way the drunk uttering the verses of Empedocles might be said to have the propositions or beliefs those words normally express. Even if she 'says the words', whatever they are—possibly even 'I should not taste *this*'—she is not thereby expressing the *belief* those words normally express: at this point she grasps the relevant proposition (if at all) only in the way the drunk reciting the verses of Empedocles grasps the propositions these verses are normally taken to express.

This explains how we can take Aristotle to be giving a generic account, intended to cover both the weak and the impetuous *akratēs*. Though neither strictly speaking *has* the conclusion she is said to act against, at least not when she acts, some weak akratics nevertheless *appear* to have this conclusion even when they act. They deliberate and can even when they act 'say the words' normally used to express belief in this conclusion. But as we argued in our discussion of the second *eti* passage, the fact that someone 'says the words' does not show that she is then actualizing the knowledge that utterances of those words ordinarily express—not even in cases where the speaker *has* the relevant (first actuality) knowledge.

Some might worry that this way of accommodating the weak *akratēs* does not leave room for the sort of struggle or psychic conflict that many commentators take to distinguish the weak from the impetuous *akratēs*. Such commentators tend to emphasize passages such as the following from *NE* 1. 13 (1102^{b}13–25):

There seems to be also some other kind of non-rational soul, which, however, participates in a way in reason. For we praise the reason of the *enkratēs* and *akratēs*, and the ⟨part⟩ of ⟨their⟩ soul that has reason because it correctly exhorts ⟨them⟩ towards what is best. But there seems also to reside naturally in them something else besides reason, which fights and opposes reason [ὃ μάχεται καὶ ἀντιτείνει τῷ λόγῳ]. For just as when someone has decided to move the parts of the body affected by paralysis to the right, they are carried off to the left, something similar happens in the soul; for the impulses of akratic subjects are towards opposite things. But while we see the thing carried off in these bodies, we do not see ⟨it⟩ in the case of the soul. None the less, we should presumably say also that there is in the soul something besides reason, opposing this and resisting ⟨it⟩ [ἐναντιούμενον τούτῳ καὶ ἀντιβαῖνον].

Cook Wilson cites this passage, along with others, as evidence that Aristotle took 'mental struggle' to characterize the *akratēs* in a way such that Aristotle would have rejected any solution premissed on any kind of ignorance (even temporary ignorance) that would obviate the element of struggle. Because he finds talk of such struggle prominent in other Aristotelian texts, Cook Wilson claims on the basis of 7. 3's appeal to ignorance that:

The theory [of 7. 3] appears quite unworthy of Aristotle . . . Clearly the answer given in this chapter is worse than no answer: if in the *akratēs* knowledge of right and wrong is not realised but dormant (μὴ θεωροῦντα ἃ μὴ δεῖ πράττειν, 1146b33); if, though he knows the general principle (the major premiss) which would condemn his action, he has not realised the particular circumstances (the minor premiss) in his act which make the principle applicable to it;—then he does not know that what he is doing is wrong, and therefore is not *akratēs* at all. A mental struggle is impossible, since there is no actual knowledge for appetite to struggle with. Aristotle could scarcely have acquiesced in a mistake like this.[65]

Cook Wilson concludes that 7. 3 was probably not by Aristotle— nor by the author of the *Eudemian Ethics*, nor even the author of the most important parts of the rest of *NE* 7/*EE* 6!

Note that many of the problems Cook Wilson sees are eliminated by our interpretation, especially the problems posed by assuming ignorance of the minor premiss. But what can we say about the room left for psychic struggle by the sort of appeal to ignorance we see in 7. 3? Whether or not struggle is in fact excluded depends, of course, on what Aristotle takes to be involved in the relevant sort(s) of struggle. And the answer to this question seems to us to some extent indeterminate. First, the phenomenology of akratic experience seems to allow for a range of possibilities, running from the case of one who deliberates and later simply neglects her decision doing (without any struggle) something else instead, to the case of someone who is constantly vacillating and anguished over each of

---

[65] Cook Wilson, *Aristotelian Studies*, 48–9; he then refers (p. 50) to *DA* 433ᵃ1–3 and 433ᵇ5–10 as further evidence of Aristotle's conception of the *akratēs* as characterized by 'mental struggle'.

the alternatives from the point of view of the other. Second, Aristotle's texts do not make it clear what sorts of cases (if any) he takes to be paradigmatic: he himself seems to leave open a range of possibilities. Moreover, we need not take Aristotle's talk of ignorance as incompatible with the idea of struggle, for the *akratēs'* moments of ignorance may simply be phases of a cycle whose various stages together constitute a kind of struggle.[66] And though Aristotle often speaks as if the *akratēs* is simultaneously aware of (for example) the pleasures presently afforded by some pursuit and the prospective pains attendant on it, even his talk of such awareness need not indicate that he thinks of its subject as feeling especially torn at the time of action: she may happily pursue the present pleasure while paying lip-service to the belief that she will regret it later. But in this sort of case she must be saying what she says in something like the way in which the drunk recites the verses of Empedocles: her utterance is not at present a genuine expression of the relevant belief.[67]

8. Aristotle's solution and its relation to Socrates' view

Let us return to the remainder of 7. 3. Aristotle concludes by explaining how his own view is related to the Socratic denial that required him, given his commitment to the endoxic method, to undertake the present investigation. And he allows that it follows from his own account that there is a sense in which Socrates was right.

[10] *NE* 7. 3, 1147ᵇ13–19

> And because ⟨the proposition containing⟩ the last *horos* is not universal, nor scientifically knowable [ἐπιστημονικόν] in a way similar to the universal, it seems that what Socrates sought also results. For the *pathos* does not occur when what seems to be *epistēmē* in the strict sense is

[66] J. J. Walsh, *Aristotle's Conception of Moral Weakness* (New York, 1963), 187, adopts something like this view when he suggests that the *akratēs'* ignorance is the 'outcome of struggle' and says that 'Aristotle might not have considered struggle and ignorance to be two contradictory descriptions of akrasia, but successive phases in it' (188).

[67] Note also that it does not follow from the fact that Aristotle speaks of the impulses of the *akratēs* as being opposed to one another, and of a part of the soul that opposes reason and resists it, that he thinks of the subject as necessarily *conscious* of the opposition. The claim in *NE* 1. 13 that 'we do not see in the case of the soul' (as we do in the case of bodies) 'the thing that is carried off' in the wrong direction suggests that he may even allow for a kind of unconscious opposition that counts as a form of struggle.

present [οὐ γὰρ τῆς κυρίως ἐπιστήμης εἶναι δοκούσης παρούσης γίνεται τὸ πάθος][68]—nor is this [αὕτη] dragged about because of the *pathos*—but ⟨only when⟩ perceptual ⟨*epistēmē* is present⟩. Concerning, then, the one who knows and ⟨the one who does⟩ not, and how it is possible for one knowing to act akratically, let so much be said.

In saying that the *pathos* of akrasia occurs not when what seems to be *epistēmē* proper is present but when a kind of perceptual knowledge is present (by which he seems to mean 'active'), Aristotle seems to be saying that akratic behaviour occurs when it is only the perceptual knowledge (which is of particulars), and not also the relevant universal knowledge, that gets used. In other words, he seems to be assuming that if the agent *did* use her universal knowledge by bringing her belief in the prohibiting universal to second actuality, then the proper conclusion *would* result and she would act more or less immediately in accordance with it. This makes good sense if (as we suggested in Section 4) he takes using a *practical* universal to consist largely in applying it to the relevant particulars, which is scarcely distinguishable from reaching the proper conclusion. And given that Aristotle takes the conclusion to be either the action or something that in the absence of preventing factors leads to the action, his view looks highly Socratic.

Aristotle may, however, be reluctant to express his agreement with Socrates by speaking (as Socrates spoke) of a kind of *epistēmē* such that one *cannot* act against it. For at least some of the resistance to Socrates' view stems from a conception of *epistēmē* as purely theoretical and in itself inert. If one conceives of *epistēmē* in this way, then it will seem obvious that one *can* act against it, and Socrates' view (at least as formulated in terms of *epistēmē*) will seem a complete non-starter. This is presumably why Aristotle insists in *EE* 7. 13 (or 8. 1) that Socrates was right to say that nothing is stronger than *phronēsis*, but wrong to say that nothing is stronger than *epistēmē*, since *phronēsis* is not *epistēmē* but a different kind of cognition (ἀλλὰ γένος ἄλλο γνώσ⟨εως⟩, 1246[b]34–6). It may also explain why Aristotle speaks in [10] not simply of *epistēmē*, but of 'what *seems* to be *epistēmē* in the strict sense' (τῆς κυρίως ἐπιστήμης εἶναι δοκούσης). He is talking about what most people (including Socrates) would call *epistēmē*; but it is not *epistēmē* in the strict

---

[68] Stewart, *Notes*, ii. 163, mentions that a few manuscripts read τῆς κυρίως εἶναι δοκούσης ἐπιστήμης παρούσης, but this change in word order does not affect our interpretation.

sense explained in *NE* 6, where he distinguishes *epistēmē* strictly
so called from various cognitive states (including *phronēsis*) that resemble it in certain ways.[69]

Many commentators miss this point and so are puzzled about
why Aristotle speaks only of 'what *seems* to be knowledge in the
strict sense'. Such commentators tend to assume that the object
of the relevant knowledge is something like the prohibiting universal. And because they take *epistēmē* proper to be of universals,
they think that knowledge of the prohibiting universal *is* a form of
epistēmē proper. So they cannot understand what Aristotle seems to
be saying here—namely, that akrasia does *not* occur in the presence
of *epistēmē* proper. 'The difficulty', as Broadie puts it, 'is that nothing in the account so far suggests that the affective state [viz. akrasia
or the affective state involved in it] does not occur *in the presence of*
the universal.'[70] But the difficulty appears largely because Broadie,
like most commentators, identifies the *akratēs'* failure as a failure to
use knowledge of some *particular*. So in her view, which is shared
by many, what Aristotle *should* be saying is that akrasia does not
occur in the presence of *particular* knowledge.

This explains why many, including Broadie and Rowe, adopt
Stewart's proposal to emend the text by reading περιγίνεται in place
of παρούσης γίνεται.[71] This allows them to read Aristotle as saying
that it is not *epistēmē* proper, but only perceptual *epistēmē* (which is
of particulars), that *pathos overcomes*.[72] But this emendation is not
only (as Bostock admits) 'paleographically improbable'; it is also
unnecessary.[73] Moreover, the motivation for it is largely ideological,
being grounded in the questionable (albeit common) view that it is
particular (rather than universal) knowledge that the *akratēs* fails

[69] On the question whether Socrates himself conceived of what he called *epistēmē*
as purely theoretical and so inert, on which we here remain neutral, see H. Segvic,
'No One Errs Willingly: The Meaning of Socratic Intellectualism', *Oxford Studies
in Ancient Philosophy*, 19 (2000), 1–45.

[70] Broadie and Rowe, *Nicomachean Ethics*, 393. Robinson ('Akrasia', 152–3) is
puzzled for similar reasons.

[71] See Stewart, *Notes*, ii. 161–4.

[72] Here is Rowe's translation: 'For it is not what seems to be knowledge in the
primary sense that the affective state in question overcomes (nor is it this kind of
knowledge that is "dragged about" because of the state), but the perceptual kind.'
Others who follow Stewart's proposal include Ross (in Barnes (ed.), *Complete Works*)
and Gauthier and Jolif. Note that Broadie herself suggests an alternative emendation
in her *Ethics with Aristotle* (New York and Oxford, 1991), 311 n. 38.

[73] Bostock, *Aristotle's Ethics*, 130 n. 21.

to use. So if our account is right, much of the motivation for the emendation falls away.[74]

Note that we do not mean to say that the original text provides any *independent* argument for our thesis that it is knowledge of some *universal* that the *akratēs* fails to use. The argument for this thesis lies in our overall defence of the interpretation according to which Aristotle progressively articulates the failure of the *akratēs* in the sequence discussed above. Given this interpretation, the original text makes perfectly good sense: if (as we suggest) Aristotle uses the phrase 'what *seems* to be *epistēmē* in the strict sense' to indicate that he is referring to *phronēsis* and not to what he himself calls *epistēmē proper*, then the original text simply states a corollary of the view (defended in *NE* 6. 13) that one cannot be *phronimos* without being fully virtuous, a corollary he spells out in *NE* 7. 10, when he says in [1(*a*)] 'nor is the same person able to be simultaneously *phronimos* and *akratēs*'.

Aristotle's reasons for thinking that there is a form of practical cognition that cannot be overruled or dragged about like a slave are complicated, and the interpretative issues involved in unpacking them are highly controversial. They are partly a function of his view that (correct) desire is involved in *phronēsis* itself.[75] This constitutes an important difference between *phronēsis* on the one hand and theoretical knowledge on the other, a difference explained in *NE* 6, which we take to set the stage for book 7's discussion of akrasia. A proper study of the organizing role played in *NE* 7 by the distinctions between theoretical and practical forms of cognition set up in *NE* 6 would require at least another paper as long as

---

[74] Stewart offers an additional reason for emending the text: that the original requires us to take πάθος in two different senses (viz. as referring first to the *pathos* of ἀκρατεύεσθαι itself and then to the *epithumia* whose presence is responsible for the agent's ἀκρατεύεσθαι). But this is not obvious. If we are right that 'what seems to be *epistēmē* in the proper sense' refers to *phronēsis*, then Aristotle could well be using τὸ πάθος to refer to *epithumia* in both places: he could be saying that 'it is not when *phronēsis* is present that the *pathos* [viz. the disruptive *epithumia*] comes about, nor is it *phronēsis* that is dragged about because of this *pathos*'. And even if the first occurrence of τὸ πάθος does refer (as seems plausible) to the akratic condition itself, Aristotle might nevertheless proceed to use it to refer to the *epithumia* responsible for the agent's being in that condition: using τὸ πάθος in these two senses is not sufficiently problematic to warrant the emendation.

[75] It is clear from [1(*a*)] that Aristotle takes *phronēsis* to involve *prohairesis*, which he describes in *NE* 6 as 'deliberative desire' (ὄρεξις βουλευτική, 1139ᵃ23; see 1113ᵃ9–11) and as (apparently indifferently) 'either desiderative thought or thinking desire' (ἢ ὀρεκτικὸς νοῦς ἡ προαίρεσις ἢ ὄρεξις διανοητική, 1139ᵇ4–5).

this.[76] Obviously we can at present only recommend and not begin this eminently worthwhile project. Our point here is simply that the account of *phronēsis* presented in *NE* 6 has remarkably Socratic implications, to which Aristotle owns up in *NE* 7. 3.

University of Toronto

BIBLIOGRAPHY

Anscombe, G. E. M., *Intention* (Oxford, 1957).

Barnes, J. (ed.), *The Complete Works of Aristotle: The Revised Oxford Translation* [*Complete Works*] (2 vols.; Princeton, 1984).

Bogen, J., and Moravcsik, J., 'Aristotle's Forbidden Sweets' ['Forbidden Sweets'], *Journal of the History of Philosophy*, 20 (1982), 111–27.

Bostock, D., *Aristotle's Ethics* (Oxford, 2000).

Broadie, S., *Ethics with Aristotle* (New York and Oxford, 1991).

—— and Rowe, C., *Aristotle:* Nicomachean Ethics [*Nicomachean Ethics*] (Oxford, 2002).

Burnet, J., *The* Ethics *of Aristotle* (London, 1900).

Burnyeat, M., *A Map of* Metaphysics *Zeta* (Pittsburgh, 2001).

Bywater, I., *Aristotelis Ethica Nicomachea* (Oxford, 1894).

Charles, D., 'Acrasia in Venice: VII. 3 Reconsidered' ['Venice'], in Acts of the XVIIth Symposium Aristotelicum (forthcoming).

—— *Aristotle's Philosophy of Action* [*Action*] (London, 1984).

Clark, P., 'The Action as Conclusion', *Canadian Journal of Philosophy*, 31 (2001), 481–506.

Cook Wilson, J., *Aristotelian Studies*, i. *On the Structure of the Seventh Book of the* Nicomachean Ethics *Chapter I–X* [*Aristotelian Studies*] (Oxford, 1879).

Cooper, J., *Reason and Human Good in Aristotle* (Cambridge, Mass., 1975).

Dahl, N. O., *Practical Reason, Aristotle, and Weakness of the Will* [*Practical Reason*] (Minneapolis, 1984).

Gauthier, R. A., and Jolif, J. Y., *Aristote: L'Éthique à Nicomaque* [*L'Éthique*], 2nd edn. (2 vols.; Louvain and Paris, 1970).

---

[76] Commentators often miss the organizing role played in the final chapters of *NE* 6 by the distinction between theoretical and practical forms of cognition, as in the following passage, where the fourth sentence is routinely misinterpreted as saying that *nous* is of last things 'in both [viz. *both universal and particular*] directions': 'All *ta prakta* are among the last and particular things. For it is necessary for the *phronimos* to recognize these things. And *sunesis* and *gnōmē* are about *ta prakta*, and these are last. *Nous* is of last things in both ⟨viz. *theoretical and practical spheres*⟩' (1143ᵃ32–6; cf. 1142ᵃ23–30).

Gosling, J., 'Mad, Drunk or Asleep? Aristotle's Akratic', *Phronesis*, 38 (1993), 98–104.

Grgić, F., 'Aristotle on the Akratic's Knowledge', *Phronesis*, 47 (2002), 344–55.

Hardie, W. F. R., *Aristotle's Ethical Theory*, 2nd edn. (Oxford, 1980).

Hughes, G., *Aristotle on Ethics* (London, 2001).

Irwin, T., *Aristotle:* Nicomachean Ethics [*Nicomachean Ethics*], 2nd edn. (Indianapolis, 1999).

—— 'Some Rational Aspects of Incontinence' ['Rational Aspects'], *Southern Journal of Philosophy*, 27, suppl. (1988), 49–88.

Joachim, H. H., *Aristotle:* The Nicomachean Ethics (Oxford, 1951).

Kenny, A., 'The Practical Syllogism and Incontinence' ['Practical Syllogism'], *Phronesis*, 10 (1966), 163–84.

Kraut, R. (ed.), *The Blackwell Guide to the* Nicomachean Ethics [*Guide*] (Oxford, 2006).

Lawrence, G., 'Akrasia and Clear-Eyed Akrasia', *Revue de philosophie ancienne*, 6 (1988), 77–106.

Lorenz, H., '*Nicomachean Ethics* 7. 4: Plain and Qualified Lack of Control', in Acts of the XVIIth Symposium Aristotelicum (forthcoming).

—— *The Brute Within: Appetitive Desire in Plato and Aristotle* (Oxford, 2006).

McDowell, J., 'Incontinence and Practical Wisdom in Aristotle' ['Incontinence'], in S. Lovibond and S. G. Williams (eds.), *Identity, Truth and Value: Essays for David Wiggins* (Oxford, 1996), 95–112.

Müller, J., 'Tug of War: Aristotle on Akrasia' (unpublished paper).

Nussbaum, M. C., *Aristotle's* De motu animalium (Princeton, 1978).

Owens, J., 'The Acratic's "Ultimate Premise" in Aristotle', in J. Wiesner (ed.), *Aristoteles: Werk und Wirkung*, vol. i (Berlin, 1985), 376–92.

Price, A. W., 'Acrasia and Self-Control' ['Acrasia'], in Kraut (ed.), *Guide*, 234–54.

Ramsauer, G., *Aristotelis Ethica Nicomachea* [*Ethica Nicomachea*] (Leipzig, 1878).

Rassow, H., *Forschungen über die Nikomachische Ethik des Aristoteles* [*Forschungen*] (Weimar, 1874).

Robinson, R., 'Aristotle on Akrasia' ['Akrasia'], in id., *Essays in Greek Philosophy* (London, 1969); repr. in J. Barnes, M. Schofield, and R. Sorabji (eds.), *Articles on Aristotle*, ii. *Ethics and Politics* (London, 1977), 139–60.

Segvic, H., 'No One Errs Willingly: The Meaning of Socratic Intellectualism', *Oxford Studies in Ancient Philosophy*, 19 (2000), 1–45.

Smyth, H. W., *Greek Grammar* (Cambridge, Mass., 1920).

Stewart, J. A., *Notes on the* Nicomachean Ethics [*Notes*] (2 vols.; Oxford, 1892).

Timmermann, J., 'Impulsivität und Schwäche: Die Argumentation des Abschnitts Eth. Nic. 1146b31–1147b19 im Lichte der beiden Formen des Phänomens "Akrasia"', *Zeitschrift für philosophische Forschung*, 54 (2000), 47–66.

Walsh, J. J., *Aristotle's Conception of Moral Weakness* (New York, 1963).

Whiting, J., 'Hylomorphic Virtue: Cosmology, Embryology, and Moral Development in Aristotle' (forthcoming).

—— 'The Nicomachean Account of Philia', in Kraut (ed.), *Guide*, 276–304.

AUTOMATIC ACTION IN PLOTINUS

JAMES WILBERDING

1. Introduction

SEVERAL Plotinus scholars have recently called attention to a kind of action in the sensible world, which one could call 'spontaneous' or 'automatic' action, that is supposed to result automatically from the contemplation of the intelligible.[1] Such action is meant to be opposed to actions that result from reason, calculation, and planning, and has been put to work to provide a way for Plotinus' sage to act, and in particular to act *morally*, without compromising his

© James Wilberding 2008

A version of this paper was presented at the Katholieke Universiteit Leuven in 2006, where it received a helpful discussion. For comments and suggestions I am particularly indebted to Peter Adamson, Julie Cassiday, Christoph Helmig, Christoph Horn, Jan Opsomer, David Sedley, and Carlos Steel. I have also profited greatly from a reading group held in autumn 2005 at King's College London on *Ennead* 3. 8 with Peter Adamson, Verity Harte, M. M. McCabe, and others. I would like to thank Williams College and the Humboldt-Stiftung for funding the research leave during which this paper was written, and Andreas Speer for welcoming me into the Thomas-Institut for this period.

[1] e.g. A. Schniewind, *L'Éthique du sage chez Plotin* [*L'Éthique*] (Paris, 2003), 190 with n. 7: 'les actions du sage sont l'expression (παρακολούθημα) de sa propre contemplation . . . Plotin évoque deux possibilités: d'une part, les actions par faiblesse (ἀσθένεια) de contemplation, pour ceux qui ne parviennent pas à l'Un; d'autre part — et c'est là ce qui correspond au sage — les actions en tant qu'activités secondaires (παρακολούθημα), issues de la contemplation'; D. O'Meara, *Platonopolis* (Oxford, 2003), 75: 'As regards humans, this means that human action and production can result as by-products, secondary effects, of knowledge, or, if not, as inferior substitutes for knowledge'; A. H. Armstrong, 'Platonic Eros and Christian Agape', *Downside Review*, 75 (1961), 105–21 at 114–15 (repr. in A. H. Armstrong, *Plotinian and Christian Studies* (London, 1979), ch. IX): 'A man, in his opinion, will act more virtuously if, instead of thinking "I propose to perform the following virtuous actions", he simply concentrates his mind on virtue so intensely that the virtuous actions follow naturally and spontaneously as occasion requires.' Cf. J. R. Bussanich, 'The Invulnerability of Goodness: The Ethical and Psychological Theory of Plotinus', *Proceedings of the Boston Area Colloqium in Ancient Philosophy*, 6 (1990) 151–84 at 180–4.

contemplation.[2] This opposition is found most markedly when he compares the non-deliberative manner in which the World-Soul (as well as Nature and the heavenly bodies) acts with the deliberative manner in which we normally act. 'Automatic action' is thus a term I am using to describe this kind of spontaneous and non-deliberative action. A theory of automatic action can easily close the gap between the contemplative man and the practical man by allowing for action without deliberation. This is helpful because it is the deliberative element in action that would seem to be incompatible with contemplation. Deliberating about the world—and deliberation is always about the world, since it is about what can be otherwise[3]—forces one's rational soul to look away from the intelligible to the sensible.

Since this theory has so far been introduced only in a rather cursory manner, I would like to investigate it more closely. What is needed is a more detailed examination of the evidence in favour of the theory and a psychological account that would explain how such action would arise. In addition, the scope of the thesis needs to be determined: just which kinds of action can be performed automatically? Moreover, we need to consider the possibility that deliberation and attention to the sensible world might be in some sense compatible with contemplation after all. As I shall argue in what follows, the metaphysics of Plotinus' psychology commits him to something like a theory of automatic action, and this is corroborated by his views both on the employment of craft knowledge and on the motion of the heavenly bodies. Yet there also seems to be considerable evidence for denying that the sage's actions are always performed in such an automatic manner. Sometimes it appears that he must deliberate, but this is mitigated by the fact that there seems to be a sense in which deliberation about the sensible world *is* compatible with contemplation after all. In short, the automatic execution of practical actions is the ideal but the deliberative execution of them is often a necessity. The extent to which this necessity asserts itself in the sage's life is uncertain.

---

[2] Not all scholars, however, are in agreement on this. J. M. Rist, *Plotinus: The Road to Reality* [*Road*] (Cambridge, 1967), for example, insists 'the brave man is not an automaton whose reflexes simply cause him to act bravely. That is certainly not how Plotinus understands any virtue' (132).

[3] This derives from Aristotle: *NE* 3. 3 and 1139^{a}13–14.

2. *Praxis* in *Ennead* 3. 8

Before turning to the positive grounds for attributing a theory of automatic action to Plotinus, it is necessary to clear the table a bit by dispelling a piece of spurious evidence. It has been claimed that in 3. 8 Plotinus says that practical action (*praxis*) can be either an automatic by-product of contemplation or else a mere substitute for it for those who cannot contemplate effectively.[4] However, nowhere in 3. 8 does Plotinus give the former positive and automatic account of *praxis*.

Ennead 3. 8 is Plotinus' most in-depth discussion of contemplation and action, and central to this discussion is a distinction between productive action (*poēsis, poiein*) and practical action (*praxis, prattein*), a distinction that Plotinus maintains consistently throughout 3. 8. Right at the start of this section Plotinus underlines the negative aspect of practical action:

Every practical action is eager to arrive at contemplation, the necessary practical actions more so [ἡ μὲν ἀναγκαία [καὶ] ἐπὶ πλέον],[5] even though they draw contemplation towards the outer world, and the so-called voluntary practical actions less so, but nevertheless even these [viz. voluntary] practical actions arise by a desire for contemplation. (3. 8. 1. 15–18)

As Plotinus says here and repeats several times throughout 3. 8, all practical action is due to a desire for contemplation. Far from being a by-product of contemplation, these actions all result from an inability to contemplate on account of the feebleness of one's soul.[6] Contrasted with this practical action is productive action, or what one might call 'automatic action', which is described as

---

[4] O'Meara, *Platonopolis*, 133. O'Meara then refers back to an earlier section of his book in order to support this claim, but in this earlier section (p. 75) he supports it entirely by 3. 8. 4. 39–47, which I shall discuss below.

[5] This is Theiler's emendation. Although it is not adopted by Henry–Schwyzer (who print the manuscripts' καὶ ἐπιπλέον), Theiler's reasons are compelling and have mostly to do with the parallels between this passage and 4. 4. 44 and 6. 3. 16 (to which he refers): 'der Zwang entschuldigt, nicht die willentliche Wahl'. What is puzzling about the received text is the way that voluntary action is described. It is first said to be *less* directed at the outer world than necessary action, from which we should expect it *more than* necessary action to result from a desire for contemplation. But Plotinus defies this expectation when he says that *'nevertheless [ὅμως] even this'* voluntary action springs from a desire for contemplation. Why would anyone think otherwise, if voluntary action really is less directed at the outer world? It might even be possible to retain the καί in the sense of 'even'.

[6] Cf. 3. 8. 4. 31–6 (cited below) and 3. 8. 6. 1–4.

an action that flows from contemplation as its natural by-product. Plotinus consistently uses ποιεῖν and γεννᾶν to refer to this brand of activity.[7]

In 3. 8. 6 Plotinus narrows down his conception of *praxis* even further through an inventive exegesis of Plato's divided line. The goal of the ascent is *noēsis*, i.e. the contemplation of *Nous* in the best way possible, which is the contemplation of it as *Nous* itself contemplates, namely without any division between subject and object. Yet as long as one is still below *Nous*, it is not *Nous* itself but the *logos* of it that forms the object of one's intellectual activity. Plotinus' account begins at the level of belief (*pistis*). The man of practical action is at this level. Owing to the feebleness of his soul, the only way he can understand the *logos* of *Nous* is through practical actions. These actions create a *logos* in his soul that gives him at least some conception of the intelligible. To the extent that he now has this, he can refrain from practical action. Importantly, there are degrees of *pistis*, which means that the *logos* that the practical man receives in his soul can vary in clarity. Plotinus seems to be suggesting that the first stage of one's epistemic journey is practical, and that if one is successful at this stage the *logos* created by practical action will become clearer and clearer until the soul finally appropriates it as its own (*oikeion*, 3. 8. 6. 1–21). Once the *logos* has been appropriated, one is at the level of discursive thought (*dianoia*)—an intermediate stage between *pistis* and proper contemplation (*noēsis*). As before, one's epistemic relation to *Nous* is still deficient, and as before this deficiency leads to a specific kind of activity. At this level, however, the activity is no longer practical

---

[7] ποιεῖν and γεννᾶν are used synonymously in 3. 8. 1. 20–1. Throughout 3. 8. 2, which is devoted to Nature, Plotinus never uses πράττειν. Rather, Nature is said to ποιεῖν a γέννημα (3. 8. 2. 29, cf. 3. 8. 4. 29–31). Likewise, the higher Soul and the *logoi* in it are said to γεννᾶν and are explicitly said not to πράττειν (3. 8. 4. 10–14). Hence, γέννημα (3. 8. 4. 16) and γεννηθέν (3. 8. 4. 29) are used to describe the automatic outflowings of higher principles. In 3. 8. 7. 4–6 Plotinus contrasts the πράξεις which are aimed *at* contemplation with the γεννήσεις which proceed *from* contemplation. This is further confirmed in 3. 8. 5. 22–5. Here again γεννώμενον is used in opposition to πρᾶξις. Plotinus' point is that Nature's action only *looks* like a πρᾶξις (πρᾶξιν δοκοῦσαν εἶναι; in fact, it is a γεννώμενον of contemplation and itself contemplation in a weaker form (Nature does not engage in practical action, only humans do (3. 8. 4. 31–2)). This is not to say that Plotinus always uses ποιεῖν in this positive sense (though he might do this with γεννᾶν); it is too generic for that (for example, in 3. 8. 2. 6–9 he describes craftsmen in terms of ποιεῖν, and cf. 3. 8. 4. 32 and 37). Rather, when automatic action is under discussion, Plotinus must resort to these terms, since πράττειν invariably signals a contemplative deficiency.

action but discursive action (προφέρειν, προχειρίζεσθαι): that is to say, now one ascends by linguistically working through what one does not yet understand. This points to an important difference between the methods of advancing through each of these two sections. In practical action the soul advances by responding to external needs, whereas at this level the soul's action responds to its own needs.[8] Needless to say, here too there are degrees. To progress through this section of the line involves eliminating the gaps in one's understanding, and by doing this one ensures not merely that the *logos* is one's own (*oikeion*) but that it is no longer even distinct from oneself (*allo*). At this point one has achieved proper contemplation (3. 8. 6. 21–34).

Hence, there seem to be both wider and narrower conceptions of *praxis* in 3. 8. According to the wider conception found throughout 3. 8. 1–5, a *praxis* seems to be any action that results from a feeble soul's desire to contemplate, regardless of whether it is a physical action performed with one's hands or a linguistic one performed with one's head. In 3. 8. 6 we find it used in a narrower sense that refers only to the former. Yet in both cases a practical action is one that occurs in the absence of contemplation and not as its by-product. This also holds for the passage that is sometimes cited[9] as support for the claim that the sage will perform virtuous *praxeis* as by-products of his contemplative activity:

Everywhere we shall see that productive and practical action [τὴν ποίησιν καὶ τὴν πρᾶξιν] are either a feebleness of contemplation or a by-product of it. It is a feebleness if one has nothing after the practical action [μετὰ τὸ πραχθέν], and a by-product if someone has something else to contemplate that is prior to and better than the result of the productive action [τοῦ ποιηθέντος].[10] For who, being able to contemplate what is authentic, would prefer to go to the authentic thing's image? And slower children also illustrate this point: being incapable with respect to academic subjects and contemplation, they turn to the arts and crafts. (3. 8. 4. 39–47)

---

[8] ἃ μὲν γὰρ εὖ προήνεγκεν, οὐκέτι προφέρει, ἃ δὲ προφέρει, τῷ ἐλλιπεῖ προφέρει εἰς ἐπίσκεψιν καταμανθάνουσα ὃ ἔχει. ἐν δὲ τοῖς πρακτικοῖς ἐφαρμόττει ἃ ἔχει τοῖς ἔξω (3. 8. 6. 27–30).

[9] O'Meara, *Platonopolis*, 75; Schniewind, *L'Éthique*, 190.

[10] Here Plotinus might be drawing on Aristotle's distinction between *praxis* and *poiēsis* as described in *MM* 1197[a]3–13 (putting aside for now the question of the *MM*'s authenticity—the work was in any case known to Atticus (fr. 2. 9 Des Places)), though if he is, he reverses Aristotle's verdict regarding the relative importance of each. For Aristotle *praxis* is superior since it contains its end, and for Plotinus *poiēsis* is superior because it, as it were, follows from the true end of contemplation.

The central contrast between productive and practical action, however, is clearly at work in this passage. Plotinus describes the case
of feebleness in terms of practical action (τὸ πραχθέν), and the by-
product in terms of productive action (τοῦ ποιηθέντος). Hence, he
is not saying that both *poiēseis* and *praxeis* can be either feeble substitutes or by-products; rather he is reiterating what he has said all
along, namely that although *praxeis* are by definition feeble substitutes aimed at contemplation, there are some actions, namely
poiēseis, which are by-products of contemplation.

3. Some evidence in favour of automatic action

This does not necessarily mean that virtuous actions cannot proceed automatically from contemplation, as some scholars have
claimed that they do. Rather, it means only that what we have
seen so far does not show this. What would be needed is some reason to believe that virtuous action is not necessarily a *praxis* in this
technical sense but can rather be a *poiēsis*, and I believe several such
reasons can be provided. The first of these is drawn from the metaphysical psychology that emerges from some of Plotinus' remarks
elsewhere in 3. 8, while the others relate to his discussion of *technai*
and of celestial motion.

Plotinus' example of the geometer in 3. 8. 4 sheds some interesting light on his psychology. Recall Plato's short discussion of
mathematics in the passage of *Republic* 6 on the divided line. There
the student of mathematics is described as beginning his study by
'using what were previously originals as images [τοῖς τότε μιμηθεῖσιν
ὡς εἰκόσιν χρωμένη]' (510 B 4), and this is spelt out a little more fully
in the sequel: 'the things which they mould and draw . . . they
use as images in their search to apprehend those things which one
can apprehend only by thought [*dianoia*]' (510 E 1–511 A 2). Of
course, the method, role, and objects of mathematics in the line
are all subjects of much debate, but what is important here is that
Plato presents the physical activity of drawing geometrical figures
as what Plotinus would describe as a *practical* activity. The student
of mathematics draws figures because he is *seeking* to understand
something more intelligible. Hence, this is an activity that aims to
correct a contemplative deficiency. It would be difficult to maintain
that Plotinus disagreed with Plato here by denying that drawing

geometrical figures is an activity that can help one—at least at some stage—ascend to contemplation, and this is why what Plotinus says about geometers in the course of Nature's speech in 3. 8. 4 is so striking: 'My contemplating produces what is contemplated, *just as geometers draw by contemplating.*'[11] Nature likens her production to that of geometers, but since throughout 3. 8 Nature is described in terms of productive activity and is denied any practical activity,[12] what we have here is a description of actual geometers engaged in productive activity: their drawings are by-products of their contemplation. This strongly suggests that the same activities, namely drawing figures, that were performed as practical actions in order to achieve a contemplative state will continue to be performed in the contemplative state, only this time as productive actions.

This view is so remarkable that one might wonder why Plotinus even held it. It surely seems reasonable to say that a student who is striving to understand geometry in a purely intellectual manner will require some kind of visual aid to help him or her conceptualize the subject-matter. But why would an accomplished geometer who is actually conceptualizing the subject-matter produce the same or similar visual aids as an, as it were, automatic consequence of his or her contemplation? I suspect an answer to this question can be found in Plotinus' understanding of the relation of the parts of one's soul to one another. For the sake of simplicity, let us restrict our attention to three parts or powers of soul, as Plotinus often does himself, namely the soul proper—by which I mean the higher soul including reason—the sensitive soul, and the growth soul. We are told that just as soul itself is the offspring of Intellect and receives form (εἰδοποιεῖσθαι) by turning to and, as it were, looking at Intellect,[13] so too are each of the lower parts of soul offspring that are formed by turning to their respective generators. Hence, the sensitive and generative parts or powers of soul, being offspring of soul proper, are themselves informed by turning to this soul and receiving form from it.[14] Each of these three parts of soul,

---

[11] 3. 8. 4. 7–8: καὶ τὸ θεωροῦν μου θεώρημα ποιεῖ, ὥσπερ οἱ γεωμέτραι θεωροῦντες γράφουσιν.   [12] See n. 7.

[13] Cf. 5. 1. 7. 35–49, and M. Atkinson, *Plotinus:* Ennead *V. 1* (Oxford, 1983), ad loc.

[14] This pattern continues all the way to matter, which is itself the product of *phusis* and informed by *phusis*, though in this one case we get an exception to the rule. Matter cannot turn back to *phusis* and so *phusis* must itself turn to matter a second time in order to give it form (see D. O'Brien, 'La matière chez Plotin:

then, is essentially interested in contemplating. Moreover, since at every ontological level turning to and contemplating what is above are essence-determining activities, we should expect the successful execution of these activities at one level to have consequences for the subsequent ontological levels. More specifically, if one is successful at turning his or her rational soul to the intelligible and maintaining a contemplative state, then this should have some effect on the sensitive and generative parts of soul in so far as they are themselves essentially determined by their focus on this soul.

The student of geometry has trouble contemplating the intelligible all by itself because his or her rational soul is still caught up in the lower activities of soul. To this extent, this epistemological ascent seems to run parallel to the ascent in virtue as described in *Ennead* I. 2. There Plotinus distinguishes between two types of virtue, which he labels 'political' (πολιτικαί) and 'higher' (μείζους), such that all four cardinal virtues are found in each type.[15] The point of this distinction is to reconcile two competing conceptions of virtue in the Platonic corpus. In the *Republic* Plato describes the four virtues in terms of the relationship among the appetitive, spirited, and rational parts of soul such that the two non-rational parts are made obedient to and harmonious with the rational part. In the *Phaedo*, by contrast, the same four virtues are described in a much different manner. Rather than emphasizing the concord between the rational and irrational parts of soul, the *Phaedo*'s account demands the separation of the soul from the body, which is understood to mean that the rational part of soul must be separated from the irrational,[16] and it is this latter account that seems better suited to explain the *Theaetetus*'s call to 'become like god as much as possible [ὁμοίωσις θεῷ κατὰ τὸ δυνατόν]'.[17] Plotinus' 'higher' virtues are

---

son origine, sa nature', *Phronesis*, 44 (1999), 45–71). A very clear exposition of this doctrine can be found in Porphyry's *Ad Gaurum* 6. 2–3 (42. 17–43. 5 Kalbfleisch). Here Porphyry makes the plant-like soul an offspring of the sensitive soul, and Plotinus might have intended his remarks to be understood this way. Nevertheless, he usually speaks in more general terms of the sensitive and generative powers both being the offspring of soul (e.g. 3. 4. 1. 1–3; 5. 2. 1. 19–21).

[15] πολιτικαί at I. 2. 1. 16, 21, 23; I. 2. 2. 13–14; I. 2. 3. 3, 5, 8, 10; I. 2. 7. 25. μείζους at I. 2. 1. 22, 26; I. 2. 3. 2, 4; I. 2. 6. 24; I. 2. 7. 11, 14, 21.

[16] *Phaedo* 67 B 6 ff. (cf. 82 A 10–B 3).

[17] *Theaet.* 176 B 1–2. On this tension in Plato see J. M. Dillon, 'Plotinus, Philo and Origen on the Grades of Virtue' ['Virtue'], in H.-D. Blume and F. Mann (eds.), *Platonismus und Christentum: Festschrift für Heinrich Dörrie* (Münster, 1983), 92–105 at 92–3, who also notes that the qualification κατὰ τὸ δυνατόν takes on a new sense

meant to capture these virtues of separation. There are two prominent aspects of these higher virtues corresponding in turn to the
rational soul's relation to what is below it and above it. Drawing
on the *Phaedo*'s characterization, Plotinus describes these higher
virtues in terms of purity and purification,[18] that is to say in terms
of cleansing the rational part of the lower non-rational parts of soul:

> It [the soul] will be good and possess virtue when it no longer has the
> same opinions but acts alone—this is intelligence and wisdom—and does
> not share the body's experiences—this is self-control—and is not afraid
> of departing from the body—this is courage—and is ruled by reason and
> intellect, without opposition—and this is justice. (1. 2. 3. 10–19, trans.
> Armstrong)

In 1. 2. 6. 11–26 Plotinus then redescribes them in terms of the
rational soul's turning towards Intellect. These two sides of higher
virtue are what provided the occasion for Porphyry to further distinguish between different kinds of higher virtue, calling the ones
'purificatory' and the others 'contemplative', and capping his list
with 'paradigmatic' virtues, which correspond to what Plotinus insists are not virtues at all but rather the Forms of these virtues in
the Intellect.[19]

According to this scale of virtue, the rational soul is originally
wrapped up in the affairs of the body and lower soul, and so virtue
is to be achieved by working with these lower powers—in particular on the appetites and spirit—training and habituating them to be
moderate. Once this is achieved, the ascent continues by working
to loosen the grip that the lower soul has on the rational soul, and

for some subsequent Platonists: 'in virtue of that element in us which is capable of
this' (98).

[18] *Phaedo* 67 A ff.; *Enn.* 1. 2. 3. 8, 10–11, 21; 1. 2. 4. 1–9, 16–17; 1. 2. 5. 1, 21–2;
1. 2. 7. 6 and 9.

[19] 1. 2. 6. 13–19 and 1. 2. 7. 1–6. Cf. Porph. *Sent.* 32. 15–70. To what extent
Porphyry thereby accurately captures Plotinus' meaning remains a matter of debate.
For the different degrees of acceptance of Porphyry's four degrees of virtues as a
fair interpretation of *Ennead* 1. 2, compare: Dillon, 'Virtue' 100; H.-D. Saffrey and
A.-P. Segonds, 'Introduction', in *Marinus: Proclus, ou sur le Bonheur*, ed. and trans.
H.-D. Saffrey, A.-P. Segonds, and C. Luna (Paris, 2001), pp. ix–clxiv at p. lxxv;
M. Vorwerk, 'Plato on Virtue: Definitions of Σωφροσύνη in Plato's *Charmides* and
in Plotinus *Enneads* I. 2 (19)', *American Journal of Philology*, 122 (2001), 29–47
at 40; C. Wildberg, '*Pros to telos*: Neuplatonische Ethik zwischen Religion und
Metaphysik', in T. Kobusch and M. Erler (eds.), *Metaphysik und Religion: Zur
Signatur des spätantiken Denkens. Akten des internationalen Kongresses vom 13.–17.
März 2001 in Würzburg* (Munich and Leipzig, 2002), 261–78 at 267.

although in 1. 2 Plotinus does not indicate the means by which this
is to be achieved, it is likely that he saw mathematics playing an
important role here (although probably not as important as Plato
thought). Yet here too we should expect the lower powers of soul
to play some role, in so far as the rational part is still caught up in
them, only here the emphasis will be on the sensitive power. Hence,
visual images can be used to present, albeit somewhat obscurely,
intelligible content to the rational soul, which would become less
dependent on the sensible soul the more it understood of the intelligible. This is, of course, nothing more than a crude sketch of
the psychology of the ascent, but one that emphasizes the roles that
the lower parts of soul have to play in it. This becomes important
when we look to explain the accomplished geometer's automatic
drawings. The psychological explanation of such automatic action
appears to be that this is how the lower parts of soul respond to the
contemplation of the higher part, as Plotinus' exegesis of the myth
in the *Phaedrus* makes clear:

Nor is [the object of contemplation] in every part of soul in the same way.
This is why the charioteer gives his horses some of what he sees, and they,
having received it, clearly would [still] desire what they saw. For they did
not receive all of it. And since they are desiring, if they engage in practical
action [πράττοιεν], they act [πράττουσιν] for the sake of what they desire.
And that is contemplation and the object of contemplation. (3. 8. 5. 33–7)

As we saw above, the contemplation of the rational part (the charioteer) should have an effect on the lower parts of soul. They should
receive something from it in so far as they are turned towards
it, looking to it, and determined by it. The lower parts of soul,
however, are by their very nature deficient and incapable of true
contemplation, and for this reason they have to settle for 'seeing'
what they can with the means at their disposal. Thus, in the accomplished geometer, the rational soul actually contemplates the true
objects of geometry, but this contemplation puts the sensitive soul
in a peculiar position. On the one hand the object of contemplation
does trickle down to it in some muted form, but on the other hand
this muted object of contemplation serves only to awaken or inten-
sify the sensitive soul's desire to see this object more completely.
Although it is impossible for the sensitive soul *qua* sensitive soul to
fulfil this desire by actually contemplating the intelligible directly,
it still seeks to improve its contemplation, and it does so by the very

means that originally helped the rational soul to ascend, namely by moulding and drawing. In this way Plotinus' description of practical men would also seem to apply to the lower parts of soul:

Men too, whenever they are too feeble to contemplate, create practical action [τὴν πρᾶξιν ποιοῦνται] as a shadow of contemplation and of the formative principle. For, because their [ability] to contemplate is inadequate on account of a weakness of soul, they are not able to receive the object of contemplation [i.e. the formative principle] adequately and for this reason are not filled [by it], but since they desire to see it, they are drawn to practical action, in order to see [with their eyes] what they could not see with their minds. (3. 8. 4. 31–6)[20]

If this is right, then Plotinus would seem to think that whichever actions can be performed as practical actions, i.e. that aim to correct a deficiency in contemplation, might also be performed as productive actions, i.e. as actions that arise automatically from contemplation—at least in so far as the actions in question pertain to the lower parts of soul. This also allows for saying that such a productive action of a sage is in some sense simultaneously a practical action. As far as the accomplished geometer's rational soul is concerned, the drawing of figures is productive by resulting automatically from his contemplation. But from the perspective of his sensitive part of soul, it is a practical action, since this part is still deficient and is using the act of drawing to overcome this deficiency.

Plotinus' remarks on the employment of *technai* further suggest that moral actions might be produced in an automatic manner. It might seem odd to lump actions of conventional virtue together with the actions involved in crafts, especially since we can often find Plotinus taking a rather deprecatory attitude towards the crafts. There are passages, for example, where he emphasizes the shortcomings of the *technai* when compared to Nature;[21] elsewhere he demeans craftsmen and their role in the *polis* (2. 9. 7. 5–7). Yet it is precisely in these criticisms of the *technai* that we can see why it is appropriate for us to consider them together with virtuous action. For perhaps his most damaging criticism of the arts and crafts is that they are directed at another (the bodily) rather than at the self (the higher soul) (3. 8. 6. 19–30; 6. 1. 12. 26–30), and it is this that would seem to make them off-limits to the sage, since he is conti-

---

[20] Armstrong's translation is infelicitous at certain points. This translation is closer to Theiler's.

[21] 2. 9. 12. 18; 4. 3. 10. 16–19 (and see Armstrong's note here); 4. 3. 21. 14.

nually directed to his higher self. But this is exactly the criticism that
Plotinus typically levels against the acts of conventional virtue (3. 6.
5. 15–17; 4. 4. 43. 18–22; 5. 3. 6. 35–9), and so if other-directedness
is the problem, then the sage's life will be bereft of both technical
actions *and* practical virtue. In fact, Plotinus himself underlines
their similarity in this respect. In 6. 3. 16. 13–32 he describes the
technai of *Republic* 7, namely arithmetic, geometry (presumably including stereometry), music, and astronomy, as double, with one
kind directed at the intelligible world and one kind directed at the
sensible world. From this he concludes that the lower crafts should
be considered as belonging to the sensible world. He then goes on
to make effectively the same point about virtue: the conventional
virtues belong to the sensible world, while the cathartic virtues belong more to the intelligible world. Similarly, a central objection
that Plotinus advances against virtuous action in 6. 8. 5 is that it is
intrinsically dependent on and even compelled by external circumstances. An act of conventional courage, for example, depends on
there being a war of some kind, and if there is a war, a courageous
man is compelled to act. One conclusion that Plotinus draws from
this is that there is something almost paradoxical about virtuous action. From a virtuous perspective, virtuous action is not desirable,
because there is nothing desirable about the external circumstances
that make virtuous action at once possible and necessary. And it is
in this regard that Plotinus once again likens virtue to craft:

> For certainly if someone gave virtue itself the choice of whether, in order to
> be able to act, it wants there to be wars for it to be brave in, or injustice so
> that it might define and set down what is just, and poverty so that it might
> demonstrate its generosity, or rather whether it wants to remain at rest
> with all things being well, it would choose rest from action with nothing
> requiring its services, just as any doctor, for example Hippocrates, would
> prefer that no one required his craft. (6. 8. 5. 13–20)

The employment of crafts and the actions of conventional virtue
appear, therefore, to be in the same predicament. They are other-
directed, are dependent on and necessitated by external circumstances, and cannot be proper objects of desire in so far as the
accompanying circumstances are unwelcome.[22] One might say that
this resemblance between virtuous and technical activity is due not

---

[22] This is not to say that Plotinus nowhere distinguishes between the two. He
places, for example, the acts of practical virtue higher on the scale of beauty than
works of the crafts (1. 6. 9. 2–5). The point here is rather that obstacles that appear

so much to a higher estimation of the *technai*—though, as we shall see below, he does elevate them to some extent—as to a lower estimation of the actions of conventional virtue.

Plotinus, however, also seems to think that this problem of other-directedness can be overcome. He makes it clear, in any case, that the sage will perform both technical actions and acts of conventional virtue.[23] Indeed, the performance of virtuous acts is closely tied to technical know-how. The exhibition of traditional courage requires all sorts of technical skills, e.g. swordsmanship, equestrian and archery skills, etc. If the sage is to have a leading pedagogical role,[24] then he will probably need to make use of the psychagogical *technai*, namely music and poetry, rhetoric, and suchlike.[25] Moreover, not only is it hard to imagine that the sage would abstain from practising basic skills such as reading and writing, but Plotinus even insists that he will practise more arcane skills such as magic.[26] But even if it is clear that the sage is performing such activities, it is not clear *how* this can be so given the problem of other-directedness. Plotinus' remarks on craft-knowledge and its employment suggest that his solution to this problem might involve saying that such actions flow automatically from the sage's contemplation.

The disparaging passages on *technē* briefly reviewed above are balanced by a number of passages where Plotinus is enthusiastic about the crafts and emphasizes the similarities between them and Nature. In particular, he emphasizes a handful of features of *technai* that speak for understanding the proper performance of technical activity to be automatic. First, he takes over from Aristotle the

---

to stand between the sage and technical action seem to be very much the same as those that appear to stand between him and practical virtue. Plotinus' remark about the ends of crafts not being proper objects of desire might prima facie seem limited to crafts such as medicine which aim at restoring the natural. But this should apply to all crafts. The doctor *qua* doctor might wish for sickness and disease so that he can practise his craft, but *qua* man he desires goodness and flourishing. So too, the cobbler might *qua* cobbler desire that people need shoes, but *qua* man (or at least virtuous man) he should desire that people's needs are met so that they are not in need of his services. The point of all skills is to compensate for shortcomings. But no virtuous person could desire that there be shortcomings.

[23] Regarding virtuous actions, see the discussion of 4. 4. 44 below.

[24] As emphasized by Schniewind, *L'Éthique*, 161–70.

[25] Cf. 4. 4. 31. 16 ff.

[26] Plotinus repeatedly refers to magic as a *technē* (e.g. 1. 4. 9. 2; 4. 4. 26. 3; 4. 4. 43. 22), which is reasonable given his naturalistic understanding of magic as the ability to manipulate the cosmos through the sympathy of its parts. In 4. 4. 43 ὁ σπουδαῖος is described as countering any spells put on him through his own use of magic.

thesis that *technē* does not deliberate,[27] and it is precisely such deliberate, calculated action to which automatic action is opposed. He
further describes the action of the handworker as simply flowing
from the craft itself in a manner suggestive of an automatic experience: 'Just as even in the crafts, reason [is active only] when the
craftsmen are at a loss, but whenever there is no difficulty, the craft
takes over and does the work' (4. 3. 18. 5–7). And this should be
taken hand in hand with Plotinus' observation that conscious attention to both technical activities and virtuous activities enfeebles the
activities.[28] Plotinus even explains substandard artefacts in terms
of a deficiency in contemplation (3. 8. 7. 23–6). Hence, the products of the handcrafts are called images of the intelligible and
the good (e.g. 3. 8. 4. 44), just as virtuous actions are (e.g. 4. 4.
44. 26). Moreover, crafts are described as serving, correcting, and
completing Nature by using the same *logoi* ultimately derived from
Intellect that Nature uses.[29] For this reason the crafts, like Nature,
are responsible for delivering beauty from the intelligible world to
the sensible world,[30] which is possible only through contemplation
(3. 8. 7. 23–7).

   This provides strong reason for concluding that Plotinus thought
such actions could be performed automatically, at least under some
circumstances, though for most people they would be performed
by conscious effort. Those sceptical of this conclusion might do
well to consider an example from Leo Tolstoy's *Anna Karenina*
(part III, chapters 4–5)—the famous account of Levin's mowing
experience—which is extremely suggestive of something resembling such a theory of automatic action. It would be difficult, if
not impossible, to come up with an account of automatic technical
action that is more detailed and compelling than this one.[31] Here
Konstantin Dmitrich Levin has decided to join the muzhiks in
their seasonal mowing because in the past he noticed this helped
him maintain his character. At first he does a very poor job, though

[27] 4. 8. 8. 15–16; cf. Arist. *Phys.* 199^b28–9.

[28] 1. 4. 10. 21–33. His examples include courageous action and reading, and he
adds that there are 'very many others'.

[29] 5. 8. 1 *passim*; 5. 8. 5. 1 ff.; 5. 9. 5. 39–41 (and see Armstrong's note).

[30] 1. 3. 2. 10–11; 1. 6. 2. 25–7; 2. 3. 18. 5–8; 2. 9. 16. 43–7; 5. 8. 1 *passim*.

[31] All translations to follow are from *Anna Karenina*, trans. R. Pevear and L.
Volokhonsky (New York, 2000). The mowing account (251–6) should be read in
its entirety for its parallels to be fully appreciated. This short discussion benefited
from a correspondence I had with Julie Cassiday.

he puts an enormous amount of effort and thought into it.[32] Yet at some point Levin begins to overcome this awkward start so that his swaths come out perfectly; the mowing action itself becomes effortless and transpires 'without a thought'; he has 'lost all awareness of time' and is in some sense 'unconscious' of what he is doing; the action seems to flow into him from some external source 'as if by magic'; and he is 'happy'. Note that for Levin this automatic mowing remains somewhat sporadic. Whenever he encountered a tussock, 'he had to stop this by now unconscious movement and think'. To this extent one might complain that Levin is a poor illustration of automatic activity. For automatic activity is above all to be attributed to the sage who lives in continual contemplation and is thus presumably exercising automatic action continually. Hence, one might insist that automatic action should not come in a mere sporadic manner, nor should it be endangered by obstacles as it is in Levin's case.[33] Yet, of this superior instantiation of automatic action, too, Tolstoy offers in the same passage an exemplary character in the form of an unnamed old muzhik man who constantly produces perfect swaths in an effortless manner, even when he encounters tussocks or sloping gullies. Since the account is presented from Levin's perspective, we do not learn the details of the old man's inner life, but the construction of the passage seems to encourage us to attribute to him the same interior experiences that Levin had, only in an uninterrupted manner that allows for a variety of complicated tasks.[34] For now I would like to keep it an open question whether Plotinus' sage is better captured by the old man than by Levin. What is important here is that Tolstoy's description of the psychological lives of the mowers, and in particular the aloofness with which they execute these activities, captures some of the features that Plotinus makes essential to the ideal practice of crafts, and collectively these features present an approach to phy-

[32] Levin 'swung strongly' (249) and 'had to strain all his strength' (250). He also rationally considers his technique: '"I'll swing less with my arm, more with my whole body," he thought, comparing Titus's swath, straight as an arrow, with his own rambling and unevenly laid swath' (250).

[33] Cf. 4. 3. 18. 5–7, cited above.

[34] Even the old man's jocular attitude towards the sensible world ('as if in play', 'gay', 'jocular', 'joking'; cf. the description of Titus working 'as if playing with his scythe' (249)) is reminiscent of Plotinus' view of the sensible world as an object of play (3. 2. 15. 31–62; 3. 6. 7. 21–7; 3. 8. 5. 6–8; 4. 3. 10. 17–19), in particular when compared to the old man's very reverent attitude towards God: during a single break from mowing, he offers two separate prayers (253–4).

sical activity that does not require that one's conscious attention be directed to the sensible world and would therefore seem fully compatible with contemplative activity.

Finally, Plotinus' discussion of the activities of the celestial bodies in 4. 4. 8. 48–61 would also seem to support automatic action. Here he is concerned to show that they are not even conscious of their movements, which is to say that here again we have the problem of other-directedness. In order to show this, he emphasizes that an action that is not preferred (*proēgoumenon*) does not produce a conscious perception. He illustrates this principle through a sort of psychological reflection on Zeno's paradox. When someone consciously steps a distance of one foot, one also necessarily passes through an initial distance of, say, one inch without being conscious of this passage in so far as it was not one's intended or preferred goal.[35] This is exactly how Plotinus wishes to understand the local motions of the celestial bodies. They execute these motions in such a way that they are not preferred, and this is precisely the kind of sensible activity that is compatible with their perpetual contemplation, since it does not draw their attention to the sensible world. Rather, just as the passage through the smallest fraction of a step follows automatically from the step itself, without impinging on one's conscious thought, so too do the complex local motions of the heavenly bodies[36] seem to follow automatically from their contemplation of the intelligible.[37]

The significance of this account of celestial motion grows when one bears in mind Plotinus' view that the motions of the celestial bodies—while not primarily causing sublunar events[38]—do serve as signs of coming sublunar affairs. This means that for celestial things contemplation results in actions which are in tune with the

---

[35] 4. 4. 8. 19–30; cf. 4. 4. 7. 7–9.

[36] Cf. *Rep.* 530 B 2–3 and *Enn.* 2. 1. 2. 8–10, with J. Wilberding (ed., trans., and comm.), *Plotinus' Cosmology: A Study of Ennead II. 1 (40)* (Oxford, 2006), ad loc.

[37] And cf. 4. 4. 35. 42–4.

[38] They are contributing causes of some events, however. The universe is described as a contributing cause in 2. 3. 14. 15–17; 3. 1. 5. 21–2; 4. 4. 31. 3 ff.; 4. 9. 2. 28–33; the heavenly circuit in 2. 3. 10. 7–10; 3. 1. 6. 3–5; the celestial bodies in 2. 3. 8. 6–8; 2. 3. 12. 1–11; 2. 3. 14. 4–7; 2. 9. 13, 14–18; 4. 4. 6. 15–16; 4. 4. 30. 1–16; 4. 4. 31. 8–12; 4. 4. 38. 22–3; place in 2. 3. 14. 4–7 and 16; 3. 1. 5. 24–7. The effects for which these cosmic agents are responsible include emotions and characters (2. 3. 9. 10–14), dispositions and temperaments (2. 3. 11), corporeal states (3. 1. 6. 1 ff.), and perhaps actions (4. 4. 30–1). For an excellent recent discussion, see P. Adamson, 'Plotinus on Astrology', forthcoming in *Oxford Studies in Ancient Philosophy*, 35 (2008).

goings-on in this world and of which the celestial things themselves are only remotely if at all conscious. And this is precisely how the sage would behave according to the theory of automatic action. Of course, human agents cannot be put on a par with celestial agents, but it might still be the case that some contemplation leads to some automatic action for humans as well as for celestials.[39]

4. Some evidence against automatic action

As was briefly discussed in the introduction, deliberation in action seems to be a problem because it forces the rational soul to turn its attention away from the intelligible towards the sensible. This is what gives the theory of automatic action some of its force. For in some important sense attention to the sensible world is incompatible with being directed to the intelligible. And since Plotinus and Porphyry in his *Life of Plotinus* insist that practical action is in fact compatible with 'looking or being directed to the intelligible' (βλέπειν πρὸς τὸ νοητόν),[40] one might conclude from this that practical action must proceed automatically. However, as we shall see presently there is also an equally important sense in which attention to the sensible world is compatible with 'looking at the intelligible'. It all depends on how we (and Plotinus) understand the expression 'to look or be directed at something' (*blepein pros ti*).

It is important to distinguish between the continuous state of being directed to the intelligible and the intermittent state of union with the One (cf. *VP* 8 ad fin. and 23). In the latter one actually steps outside oneself and is taken over by the One. In this state activity seems to be impossible. Plotinus makes it clear, for instance, that virtue is left behind during such moments (1. 2. 7 and 6. 9. 11). The former state, however, seems to be compatible with activity. Porphyry, for instance, describes Plotinus as being continually directed at the intelligible (πρὸς τὸν νοῦν)[41] and yet engaging in all sorts of demanding activities, such as conversations and managing

---

[39] Note too the significance of Plotinus' use of προηγούμενον here. Plotinus often contrasts προηγούμενον and ἀναγκαῖον (e.g. 6. 3. 16. 30–1), and as we shall see below, the sage too is supposed to perform his actions not as preferred but as necessary.

[40] Or sometimes ἔχειν πρός τι (e.g. 4. 4. 43. 22).

[41] *VP* 8. 23; 9. 17–18; 23. 4. For Plotinus the Intellect (ὁ νοῦς) and its intelligible object (τὸ νοητόν) are identical (*Enn.* 5. 5).

financial accounts.[42] This roughly fits with Plotinus' own remarks on contemplation and action. For as we shall see below, he clearly thinks that the sage is engaged in action while remaining directed to the intelligible. Yet he also makes it clear that at times the sage will go beyond this continuous state, abandon himself and action, and unite with the One (1. 2. 7; 4. 8. 1; 6. 9. 11). In what follows I shall restrict my focus to the former, the question of how it is psychologically possible for the sage to be *both* turned towards the intelligible world *and* engaged in practical action in the sensible world.

There are two general ways for these activities to be compatible. The first is thoroughgoing, which is to say that even when the sage is performing these sensible activities, his contemplative life goes on as usual. This full compatibility seems prima facie somewhat fantastic, since it amounts to saying that the sage can engage in contemplation just as well on the battlefield as in his armchair. The alternative would be a more moderate version of compatibility. The idea here would be that although sensible activity really does distract one's reason from contemplation and prohibits one from actively contemplating at the same time, such activity is nevertheless not incompatible with the contemplative *life* in so far as contemplation can immediately resume once these activities are completed without having to go through the motions of reascending. These two varieties of compatibility roughly correspond to two possible senses of 'looking or being directed at something' (*blepein pros ti*)— one attentive and one normative. In the former, attentive sense, *blepein pros ti* is used in a very commonplace way to refer to one's attention being directed at some thing. For example, someone who 'looks or is directed at' a colour is simply looking at the colour and taking in the impression it offers.[43] But Plotinus usually uses the expression in a much stronger and more normative sense, as in those passages where it is used to describe the successful epistemic relation to the Forms.[44] Here *blepein pros ti* means to take something as a model, as, for example, in 4. 4. 12. 29–31: 'But if [the soul] does not know the future things which it is going to make, it will not make them with knowledge or looking at any [model] but will make whatever comes to it', and in 1. 4. 6. 4–7: 'But if well-being is to

---

[42] *VP* 8. 19–20 and 9. 16–18.

[43] Cf. 4. 5. 1. 24–6 and 4. 5. 2. 50–3.

[44] Cf. the Demiurge in the *Timaeus*, who is said to βλέπειν πρὸς τὸ κατὰ ταὐτὰ ἔχον ἀεί (28 A 5–6).

be found in possession of the true good, why should we disregard this and omit to use it as a standard to which to look in judging well-being?'[45] Central to the issue of the sage's relation to action is the question of how these two senses of *blepein pros ti* are related. If Plotinus thinks that they simply collapse into one, we end up with a sage who, because he is clearly focused on the intelligible, is unaware of what is going on around him in the sensible world. On this account the sage is still capable of practical action—but only via something comparable to a theory of automatic action according to which his actions would simply fall from his contemplation without him having to direct his attention to the sensible world. If these two senses remain distinct, on the other hand, it should be possible to direct oneself to earthly matters in the harmless sense of attending to one's daily business, without directing oneself to earthly matters in the damaging sense of taking such things as one's model.

Porphyry's description of Plotinus's interaction with his students both confirms our findings that contemplation and action are compatible and strongly suggests that the compatibility at issue is of the more moderate variety. At *VP* 8. 11–15 he relates:

Even when he was talking to someone and engaged in conversation, he kept to his speculation, so that while satisfying his necessary part in the conversation he preserved his train of thought on the matters of his present investigation.

This is a clear statement of the compatibility between theoretical contemplation and other-directed action. It is *not*, however, a clear statement that both of these activities can *actively be pursued* at once, as Harder's and Bréhier's translations would suggest.[46] As the larger context makes clear, Plotinus has already thought through some issue from beginning to end before the conversation in question takes place.[47] Once the conversation is over, he resumes putting

[45] Both translations by Armstrong, who brings out well the normative sense involved. In the former passage, I put 'the soul' in brackets to make the subject clear, but the bracketed 'model' is Armstrong's.

[46] Harder: 'Er konnte sich mit jemandem unterhalten und zusammenhängende Gespräche führen, und doch bei seiner Untersuchung sein; was zum Gespräch gehörte, nahm er wahr, und *gleichzeitig führte er unausgesetzt den Gedanken seiner Untersuchung weiter*'; Bréhier: 'Il pouvait causer avec quelqu'un et entretenir une conversation, *tout en poursuivant ses réflexions*; il satisfaisait aux convenances de l'entretien, sans s'interrompre de penser aux sujets qu'il s'était proposé d'étudier'. (See the Plotinus entries in the bibliography below for these translations.)

[47] *VP* 8. 8–11.

his thoughts down on the page as if he had never been interrupted.[48]
Thus, Porphyry is far from claiming that Plotinus made active contemplative progress while chatting over tea about some unrelated
subject. He is simply paying tribute to the resilience of his master's
power of concentration. This, then, is how we should understand
his subsequent claim that Plotinus 'was simultaneously present to
both himself and to others' (*VP* 8. 19).[49] The idea here is not that
Plotinus can actively be making progress in both the human and
the noetic arenas at precisely the same moment. Rather, they are
both present to him in the sense that he never loses touch of either,
and for this reason he can alternately pursue the one without losing
track of where he is in the other. Porphyry's subsequent account
of Plotinus' attention to his charges' financial accounts should be
understood similarly. He says that 'though [Plotinus] shielded so
many from the worries and cares of ordinary life, he never, while
awake, relaxed his attention [τάσιν] towards the Intellect'.[50] Here
again it would be unreasonable to understand Porphyry to be saying
that Plotinus actively contemplated while filling out his students'
tax reports. The claim is rather that Plotinus can direct his attention to such trifling matters without cutting himself off from
the intelligible world. While his *advance* in the intelligible world
is compromised by his attention to these mundane activities, his
preservation of intelligible presence benefits him in two significant
ways. First, as we saw in the previous example from *VP* 8, any
theoretical progress he has made is preserved in such a way that
he can access it immediately when his attention is again free to do
so. Secondly, the normative sense of *blepein pros ti* is surely preserved, which is to say that even when Plotinus is obliged to engage
in financial dealings, he is not 'bewitched' by them into thinking
that these things are genuinely important.[51] It is a testament to his
preserved intelligible presence that he does not have to go through
the motions of reascending after such activities. This distinction
between attentive and normative directedness shows that the compatibility of contemplation and practical action does not necessarily

[48] Ibid. 15–19.

[49] On this see A. Smith, 'The Significance of Practical Ethics for Plotinus', in J.
Cleary (ed.), *Traditions of Platonism: Essays in Honour of John Dillon* (Aldershot,
1999), 227–36.

[50] *VP* 9. 16–18: καὶ ὅμως τοσούτοις ἐπαρκῶν τὰς εἰς τὸν βίον φροντίδας τε καὶ
ἐπιμελείας τὴν πρὸς τὸν νοῦν τάσιν οὐδέποτ' ἂν ἐγρηγορότως ἐχάλασεν (trans. Armstrong, revised).   [51] On this aspect of bewitchment, see below on 4. 4. 44.

demand a theory of automatic action. In fact, a closer examination of Plotinus' understanding of the psychology involved in both natural and moral activities reveals, at the very least, that there must be limits to any theory of automatic action.

By 'natural activities' I mean those activities that are directed towards the body and care for it. Although this sort of activity might seem trivial, the possibility of performing such activities automatically might be critical to Plotinus' understanding of the sage. Plotinus pinpoints the origins of these desires in the body itself—or more specifically the qualified body (τὸ τοιόνδε σῶμα), i.e. body plus a trace of soul—but the lower soul appropriates these desires on account of its having sunk into body.[52] Importantly, neither the body nor the lower soul seems to be in a position to satisfy these desires alone. Rather, the middle soul, reason, is said to attend to the desires of the body and decide whether and how to satisfy those needs.[53] In other words, Plotinus describes even these basic activities as requiring calculation and planning, and hence as not being automatic. The significance of this emerges through a comparison between a particular soul in its relation to its body on the one hand, and the World-Soul and stellar souls in relation to their bodies, the universe and stars respectively, on the other.[54]

The World-Soul and stellar souls are analogous to our own souls in two respects. First, each of them is responsible for a specific body, just as we are. Moreover, their souls are also divided into two parts or powers: a higher soul that remains above and contemplates and a lower soul that takes on responsibility for the body.[55] However, Plotinus emphasizes over and over again that the World-Soul and stellar souls, unlike particular souls, care for their bodies *without calculation or planning*.[56] Does this mean that an individual human being, too, can care for his or her body in this automatic way, if only he or she achieves the status of sage? There are good reasons for thinking that this is not the case. For the automatic maintenance of

---

[52] 4. 4. 20, esp. ll. 25–35, and 4. 4. 21. 19–21.

[53] 4. 3. 12. 6–8; 4. 4. 20. 16–19 and 33–6 (where τὸ μέν refers to the body, the first τὴν δέ to nature, and the second τὴν δέ to the higher soul); 4. 4. 21. 7–14; 4. 8. 5. 26–7; cf. 2. 1. 5. 21–3.

[54] This situation of stellar souls is equivalent to that of the World-Soul (4. 8. 2. 38–42—see below).

[55] 2. 3. 18. 12–13; 3. 8. 5. 9–16; 4. 3. 4. 21–9; 4. 3. 11. 8–12; 4. 8. 2. 26–33; 4. 8. 7. 26–31; 4. 8. 8. 13–16. Stars, too, are said to have lower souls or natures in 2. 3. 9. 34–5.

[56] e.g. 2. 2. 2. 26–7; 2. 3. 17. 9–11; 2. 9. 11. 8–9; 4. 4. 11. 4–5; 4. 8. 8. 15.

the universe and stars is due in large part to special features of the
bodies being maintained. The body of the universe has its parts in
their natural places: that is, earth is already at the centre and fire
at the periphery.[57] Furthermore, it suffers no loss of parts[58] and
is not attacked by other bodies outside of it,[59] and consequently
does not require nourishment in order to replace any lost parts.[60]
Likewise, the stars are made up only of a special kind of fire called
corporeal light whose natural place is in the heavens and which is
especially co-operative with their souls. Therefore, even though the
stars are parts of the universe and not wholes, they do not suffer any
(external) flux and consequently do not require any nourishment
either.[61] It is on account of all of these features that these bodies
themselves are said to have no desires or needs (4. 8. 2. 48–9), and are
therefore able to co-operate in such a way that the souls responsible
for them, i.e. their lower souls, take care of them without toil (and
hence everlastingly).[62] This in turn is the reason why the higher
parts of the World-Soul and stellar souls do not have to 'sink' into
body by applying their cognitive faculty to work at maintaining
their bodies (4. 8. 2. 46–53).[63] Rather, each of them can 'keep itself
in a place of safety' (4. 3. 6. 21–2).

By contrast, human bodies, like the bodies of all sublunar living
things, are made up of a collection of elements that are forcibly
constrained to remain in unnatural places. The fire in a human
body, for example, tries to leave the body and move up to the
periphery of the universe. Hence, our individual natures must act
as a 'second bond', trying to keep the body's constituent parts in
their place,[64] but in spite of this the constituent elements achieve
some degree of success in these attempts and for this reason we

---

[57] 2. 9. 7. 27–32; 4. 8. 2. 10–11; cf. 2. 1. 3. 5–7.

[58] 2. 1. 3. 2–4; cf. 2. 9. 7. 30.

[59] 1. 1. 2. 13 ff.; 1. 2. 1. 11–12; 2. 1. 1. 14; 2. 1. 3. 10–12.

[60] 4. 8. 2. 18–19; cf. *Tim.* 33 C 4–8 and *Enn.* 2. 1. 3. 25–6.

[61] 2. 1. 7. 27 ff., and see Wilberding, *Cosmology*, 45–62.

[62] 2. 1. 3. 10–12, where after μηδέν one should understand ῥεῖ or ἄπεισι, and not
ἐστιν as Armstrong does. See Wilberding, *Cosmology*, ad loc. and 49–50.

[63] This is why the maintenance of the universe by Nature is repeatedly said to
proceed without planning or reason (e.g. 2. 2. 2. 26–7; 2. 3. 17. 9–11; 2. 9. 11. 8–9;
4. 4. 11. 4–5; 4. 8. 8. 15). By contrast, in the case of individual bodies, it is precisely
reason that is forced to provide for the lower parts of the soul and their bodily
concerns. On this, see below. This is also the reason why Plotinus can say that the
World-Soul is not subject to enchantment (5. 1. 2. 11–14).

[64] 2. 9. 7. 28–30; cf. 2. 1. 5. 8–14; 4. 8. 8. 16–23.

require nutrition, unlike the universe and the celestial things. But as we saw above, it is the middle (rational) soul that must provide for the bodily desires of the lower parts of soul, and so, unlike the universe and the celestial things, the maintenance of a human body does require reasoning, since it is for reason to answer the lower parts' cries when our body needs attention.[65] This means that the very feature that allowed the World-Soul and stellar souls to maintain their bodies automatically and therefore to contemplate without interruption is problematically absent in our case,[66] and this absence is reflected in the status of the middle soul. There does not even seem to be a middle soul for the World-Soul and the stellar souls, since they do not operate by planning and calculation. But for us the middle soul is all-important.[67] Our higher souls are, after all, always contemplating no matter what we do,[68] and our lower souls are more or less committed to the body. It is the middle soul and its respective attention to what lies above and below it that determines the extent of one's sagacity. Hence, our relation to contemplation appears to be jeopardized by these natural activities to the extent that our middle soul provides for the needs of the body and lower soul.[69] All of this suggests that while it would be extremely helpful if our bodies could be maintained automatically, the fractional nature of our bodies precludes precisely this.

In spite of all this, the possibility of automatic natural activity might be defended up to a point. After all, animals are in a similar position to humans in so far as they, too, are parts of the universe and not the universe as a whole, being made up of elements that strive to get back to their natural places and requiring nourishment to replace them, and animals are able to maintain their bodies without the calculations of reason, since according to Plotinus animals do not possess faculties of reason.[70] This is effectively an admission that it is possible to perform these natural activities, such as keep-

---

[65] See above, n. 53, and 4. 8. 2. 11–14; 4. 8. 4. 12–21.

[66] To make matters worse, at one point Plotinus even suggests (2. 1. 5. 8–14) that it is not *just* our bodies that create problems, but that our lower souls are also deficient compared with that of the World-Soul (2. 9. 7. 7 ff.; 4. 3. 6. 10–15), and that the sublunar region is itself efficacious in some negative way.

[67] This is no doubt related to our being 'in the middle' between gods and beasts (3. 2. 8. 4–11).

[68] On this see T. Szlezák, *Platon und Aristoteles in der Nuslehre Plotins* (Basel and Stuttgart, 1979), 167–9.

[69] 4. 3. 17. 26–8; 4. 8. 3. 25–7; 4. 8. 4. 18–21.

[70] Reason, being the 'middle' soul, is between gods and animals (3. 2. 8. 4–11).

ing warm and consuming food, without the aid of planning and calculation, although Plotinus does not give details as to how such activities could be executed without them.[71] Perhaps this opens up the possibility that the sage, too, can accomplish these things without actually directing his rational attention to them. There is, however, a problem with suggesting that the sage's execution of these activities proceeds in a manner similar to that of animals. Animals simply do what comes naturally. At best, dogs eat when they are hungry, but at worst they eat whenever there is food around, and this is not the manner of bodily care that Plotinus envisages for the sage. Rather, he says that the sage needs to neglect his body, though not entirely:

There must be a sort of counterpoise on the other side, towards the best, to reduce the body and make it worse, so that it may be clear that the real man is other than his outward parts . . . He will take care of his bodily health, but will not wish to be altogether without experience of illness, nor indeed also of suffering. (1. 4. 14. 11–14, 21–3, trans. Armstrong, slightly revised)

One reason for this delicate neglect is that if the body grows too strong, the strength of its desires and their ability to attract reason's attention will likewise increase. Hence, even of health there can be too much for the sage (1. 4. 14. 8–11).[72] So the sage's care for his body will be decidedly different from that of animals for their bodies, and indeed one might say it is different from the *natural* approach to bodily maintenance. This seems to compromise the claim that the sage's bodily upkeep could proceed in the non-reflective manner that it does in animals, since reason needs to play

[71] As R. R. K. Sorabji has shown (*Animal Minds and Human Morals* (Ithaca, NY, and London, 1993), 7–29), the denial of reason in animals requires an expansion of their perceptual content, in order to account for the variety of activities in which animals engage. Some nutritive activities must find some analogous explanation, since plants, which lack even sensation, perform them (1. 4. 1. 21–3).

[72] This is drawn from Plato's account in *Republic* 9 of how to groom the tripartite soul so that reason can rule. He emphasizes that the appetitive part must be weakened so as not to be in a position to challenge reason's authority (588 E–589 B). Schniewind argues that this 'counterpoise' serves only a pedagogical role: the sage's body shows his comrades and acquaintances that the goal in life is not to be found in the bodily (161–5). But in my opinion this fails to account for ll. 8–11 and especially for ll. 17–19: περὶ δὲ σοφὸν ταῦτα ἴσως μὲν ἂν οὐδὲ τὴν ἀρχὴν γένοιτο, γενομένων δὲ ἐλαττώσει αὐτός, εἴπερ αὐτοῦ κήδεται. This passage clearly states that it is for the sage's *own* sake, i.e. for the sake of his higher soul, that he 'reduces' his body. While Schniewind is right to draw out this pedagogical function directed to others, a weak body and lower soul is also important to the sage himself, since a robust body would demand more attention.

an active role in order to achieve this kind of delicate neglect. After all, it is hard to imagine that the lower soul, when left to its own devices and desires and needs, would 'reduce the body and make it worse'.

The lower soul, however, is *not* left to its own devices. Plotinus repeatedly emphasizes the need to train and habituate the lower soul,[73] and it is reasonable to suppose that part of this training is aimed at habituating the lower soul, for example, to consume less than would be conducive to a robust body. This training is, of course, performed by reason and ultimately should allow the sage to take care of his body, to some extent at least, without turning away from the intelligible world (2. 9. 15. 15–17).[74] More importantly, according to the metaphysical psychology described above, the sage's contemplation should have a positive effect all by itself on the lower part of soul. In so far as the lower soul is constantly looking to and informed by the middle soul, all of the actions of the lower soul will in some sense flow from the middle soul even when it is not consciously directing its activity. Hence, the desires and actions of the sage's lower soul are not due merely to habituation; rather, they are the mediate result of the sage's contemplation. Porphyry's report that Plotinus's contemplation reduced the amount of sleep he needed can be viewed as an example of how contemplation can have a positive trickle-down effect on the needs and desires of the lower parts of soul.[75] So it would seem that the sage might have some chance of emulating the stars, though Plotinus indicates clearly enough at times that any such emulation has its limits, even for the sage.[76]

[73] This is political virtue—political in the psychological sense of a soul that is analogous to a city, i.e. tripartite (cf. 4. 4. 17. 23–35)—which is achieved by habituation and training (1. 1. 10. 11–14; 6. 8. 6. 22–5; 1. 3. 6. 6–7; 2. 9. 15. 15–17).

[74] It might be one's own reason that trains the lower soul, but more probably it is another's reason—e.g. that of one's parents or educators.

[75] *VP* 8. 21–3. Moreover, Porphyry reports that Plotinus had built up a certain resistance to magic: the magical assault on Plotinus backfired because of 'the great power of Plotinus' soul' (*VP* 10). This is significant because magic properly affects only the body and lower soul, so that any resistance to it that he had acquired would suggest that Plotinus' contemplative activity as a philosopher had some sort of effect on his lower soul. For an alternative view, see L. Brisson, 'Plotin et la magie', in L. Brisson *et al.* (eds.), *Porphyry: La Vie de Plotin* (2 vols.; Paris, 1992), ii. 465–75 at 465–8, who suggests that Plotinus' resistance is not automatic, but results rather from 'les efforts de la partie rationelle de l'âme' and in particular through arguments and exhortations (467).

[76] 1. 4. 15. 16–20, and see below.

These limits to any theory of automatic action seem to be made most explicit in Plotinus' discussion of moral psychology in 4. 4. 44. This chapter is part of a larger section (4. 4. 40–5) in which he examines the efficacy of magic and enchantment, which for the most part Plotinus restricts to the lower parts of soul (4. 4. 43. 3–5). For Plotinus magic loses any trace of the supernatural because it is Nature itself that is responsible for the efficacy of magic spells, which simply exploit the cosmic sympathy at work in the universe. Yet an individual's rational soul can also fall victim to enchantment if one allows it to become too attached to the lower parts of soul. This serves as a point of departure for Plotinus in 4. 4. 43–4 to examine the kind of psychological enchantment that takes place entirely within an individual soul, namely when the lower parts of soul and in particular nature 'enchant' one's rational part.[77] In this he is drawing on *Phaedo* 81 B 3–4, where the soul is said to be 'enchanted' (γοητευομένη) by the body and its pleasures and desires, and on *Rep.* 3, 413 B 1 ff., where Socrates describes how men might lose the beliefs they received through education by 'being enchanted' (γοητευθέντες) by pleasures or fears. The central question of this discussion concerns the relative susceptibility of the man of contemplation and the man of action to such internal enchantment. The main conclusion of the discussion is that the contemplative man is not subject to magic, but we also find here a discussion of what it is about practical activity that might be opposed to contemplation and in what way the contemplative man might engage in moral action. For this reason the chapter deserves close attention.

The critical point that Plotinus makes against practical activity is that it is necessarily motivated by the lower part of the soul: 'reason does not provide the impulse, rather the premises [*protaseis*] of passion are the starting-point and belong to the irrational'.[78] He supports this general claim by going through nine different categories of action and showing how in each case an irrational motivation is at work:

(1) care for (one's) children (ll. 6–7);
(2) eagerness to get married (l. 7);

---

[77] Cf. 4. 4. 43. 22–3 and 44. 29–30.
[78] ll. 5–6: οὐχ ὁ λόγος τὴν ὁρμήν, ἀλλ᾽ ἀρχὴ καὶ τοῦ ἀλόγου αἱ τοῦ πάθους προτάσεις. Note that Armstrong puts a comma after ἀλόγου and translates rather awkwardly.

(3) whatever entices humans through appetitive pleasure (ll. 8–9);

(4) actions caused by our spirit (l. 9);

(5) actions caused by our appetite (l. 10);

(6) political activity and desire for office (ll. 10–11);

(7) actions taken to avoid suffering (l. 12);

(8) actions taken to increase one's share (l. 13);

(9) actions taken on account of necessities and which seek to satisfy nature's needs (ll. 14–15).

There are several things to note about this list. First, many of these categories of action are already described in psychological terms in such a way that it becomes more or less tautologous to say that they are necessarily motivated by the lower soul, e.g. (4) or (5). Yet other categories, e.g. (1) (2), and (6), are not described psychologically, so that Plotinus' psychological claim becomes more substantive, though hardly unreasonable. After all, it is realistic to say, for example, that marriage and children are objects of the generative soul and that it therefore supplies an irrational desire for them, so that any action aimed at these ends will be at least partially irrational in its motivation, and similarly for the spirited part of soul and its desire for power.

This depreciatory account of the motivation behind actions in the sensible world might seem to make them completely off-limits to the sage who has advanced to contemplation and therefore turned his reason away from the body and lower soul, but in the sequel Plotinus suggests otherwise. This begins with an objection: 'What if someone says that the actions [*praxeis*] concerned with noble things are not subject to enchantment, or else even contemplation, since it is of noble things, must be said to be under enchantment?' (ll. 16–18). One might expect Plotinus to answer this objection by going through his distinction between contemplation and action, but instead he offers a more nuanced account of the practical man and his relation to practical actions by distinguishing two ways in which actions might be performed.

In this more nuanced account, the practical man is no longer defined simply by the fact that he performs actions. Rather, his attitude to these actions becomes all important, the distinctive feature of his attitude being that he is taken in by the mere traces of nobility that these noble actions possess, and—similar to Plato's lovers

of sights and sounds—is unaware that there is something else beyond these actions that is truly noble. And this is why he chooses to
perform these noble actions (ll. 25–7). Plotinus strikingly describes
the practical man both as 'choosing' (αἱρεῖται, l. 26) and as being
'dragged by his irrational impulses' (ἐλχθέντα ἀλόγοις ὁρμαῖς, l. 31).
As we shall see, a combination of necessity and choice is also prominent in the contemplative man's relation to action, though in a very
different way. Here the practical man chooses in the sense that this
could hardly be described as a case of weakness of will, where the
rational part of the soul is helpless in its attempt to achieve the goal
it set for itself on account of the coerciveness of the irrational parts.
Rather, this action is precisely what the rational part wants, and
so it steers the soul to action. His freedom of choice, however, has
been compromised by his ill-gotten conception of nobility, and this
is where the irrational impulses come in. Without getting into the
psychological mechanics, Plotinus acknowledges (surely correctly)
that certain desires have the power to change the way we see the
world,[79] and the problem with the practical man is that the desires
of his lower parts of soul have exercised such a power. As a result the practical man believes, for example, that suffering really is
bad and that the death of one's child is a genuine tragedy. Hence,
he comes to the conclusion that conventional human flourishing is
life's noble end (*to kalon*), and it is this that he aims to promote.
The irrational impulses, therefore, do not drag him in the akratic
sense of overpowering; rather, they do so by exercising their power
of enchantment over the rational soul.

The alternative to the practical man's approach to action is described in ll. 18–24 as the approach that the contemplative man
takes.[80] We are told that he performs these actions 'as necessary'.

---

[79] This again is in tune with Plato's remarks about how certain passions can
influence the (rational) soul (*Phaedo* 81 B and *Rep.* 413 B ff.). For Plato erotic desire
was particularly dangerous in this regard (*Phdr.* 238 E; *Rep.* 572 E–573 B).

[80] That this is a description of the contemplative man is clear from the characterization given here. We are told that (i) he is not enchanted (l. 20), (ii) he does not
look to the things in this world (ll. 20–1) and his life is not other-directed (l. 21),
(iii) he has no false illusions about his actions—he knows they are merely necessary
(ll. 18, 20), (iv) he grasps something else, namely what is truly good (ll. 19–20), and
finally (v) he nevertheless does act when necessary (ll. 18–19). These are precisely
the characteristics that mark the contemplative man: (i) he alone is not subject to
enchantment (ll. 1–2 and 33); (ii) he is self-directed rather than other-directed (l. 2)
and so does not have to pursue (ll. 34–5); (iii) his reason is not deceived by his lower
parts of soul (ll. 34–6); (iv) what is good is in his possession (l. 36); and yet he does
do what is required of him (l. 4).

The discussion leading up to this remark would suggest that the necessity in question concerns the impulses coming from the lower soul. The rational soul is in some sense required to fulfil the demands of the lower soul. This fits well with the description of the lower impulses themselves. They are described as *protaseis* (l. 6) or premisses in a syllogism, and as such one would expect some action to follow necessarily from them. Likewise, and more specifically, the ninth category above is explicitly said to deal with the necessary demands of nature. Both the practical man and the contemplative man, then, are subject to the necessity coming from the lower soul. The difference between them is that the practical man is enchanted by this necessity into believing that flourishing in the sensible world is all-important, while the contemplative man retains the appropriate perspective. He does act, but he acts out of compulsion coming from his lower soul, realizing that these actions are not what is truly noble (ll. 18–20).[81] He is not enchanted 'because he knows the necessity and does not direct his gaze to this world, and because his life is not directed to other things' (ll. 20–1). This last phrase is particularly significant, since it was precisely the other-directedness of the practical man's life that made him susceptible to enchantment:

Everything that is directed to [πρός] something else is enchanted by something else. For what it is directed to enchants it and directs it. Only what is directed to itself is not susceptible to enchantment. Therefore, both every action and the entire life of the practical man are in a state of enchantment. For he is moved to those things that charm him. (4. 4. 43. 16–20)

---

[81] Plotinus is making a distinction in these lines between being enchanted and (merely) being forced, but the text as it is punctuated by Henry–Schwyzer (and thus translated by Armstrong and others) obscures his point. I believe the text of 4. 4. 44. 16–24 should be as follows: εἰ δέ τις λέγοι τὰς πράξεις τῶν καλῶν ἀγοητεύτους εἶναι ἢ καὶ τὴν θεωρίαν καλῶν οὖσαν γοητεύεσθαι λεκτέον, εἰ μὲν ὡς ἀναγκαίας καὶ τὰς καλὰς λεγομένας πράξεις πράττοι ἄλλο τὸ ὄντως καλὸν ἔχων, οὐ γεγοήτευται. οἶδε γὰρ τὴν ἀνάγκην καὶ οὐ πρὸς τὸ τῇδε βλέπει, οὐδὲ πρὸς ἄλλα ὁ βίος. ἀλλὰ τῇ τῆς φύσεως τῆς ἀνθρωπίνης βίᾳ καὶ τῇ πρὸς τὸ ζῆν τῶν ἄλλων ἢ καὶ αὐτοῦ οἰκειώσει. δοκεῖ γὰρ εὔλογον ἴσως μὴ ἐξάγειν ἑαυτὸν διὰ τὴν οἰκείωσιν ὅτι οὕτως ἐγοητεύθη. In ll. 21–3 one should mentally supply πράττοι or something to that effect (cf. l. 4 ὃ δεῖ ποιεῖ). The idea is that the contemplative man acts by compulsion but is not enchanted. Armstrong's translation, following the punctuation of H–S², makes the contemplative man enchanted by this necessity, thereby eliminating the very distinction Plotinus is working to establish. I also believe that Theiler (and following him Henry–Schwyzer, Armstrong, *et al.*) was wrong to delete ὅτι in l. 24. I understand ll. 23–5 to be saying that even though we are all compelled by our natural concern for ourselves and others to act in certain ways, this is no reason to commit suicide (in the hope of leaving such concerns behind), because (ὅτι) by committing suicide (οὕτως) one has been enchanted (ἐγοητεύθη). On suicide see *Enn.* 1. 9.

The important question here concerns the sense in which the contemplative man is not directed to this world. As we saw above, there are two general senses possible. One involved directing his conscious attention to the goings-on in this world, while the other was more normative and amounted to setting one's moral compass by the sensible world, which is to say taking the states of physical well-being to be the *summum bonum*.

The details of 4. 4. 44 strongly suggest that Plotinus has only the latter sense in mind here. He places explicit emphasis on the sage's *life* (ὁ βίος, 4. 4. 44. 21) not being directed at other things, and on the sage's being in possession of the correct conception of what is genuinely good, this being different from the object of his practical actions. Finally, we are told that the contemplative man is 'compelled' by his lower soul to perform these actions, and that does not sound at all like automatic action.[82] So it looks as though what we have here is the more moderate version of compatibility: action is compatible with the contemplative life, but not because one is simultaneously acting and contemplating.

[82] One might fairly demand to know the sense in which the contemplative man's rational soul is compelled or necessitated by the lower soul here. Often Plotinus writes as if the sage is simply morally obliged to care for bodies and their needs as long as he is in the sensible world (e.g. 4. 3. 12. 6–8; 4. 8. 4. 31–3; 4. 8. 5. 10–14). This might suggest that the sage is obeying a categorical imperative to look after the body and lower soul, yet a categorical imperative would seem to fit rather awkwardly into a teleological philosophical system such as Plotinus'. The sense of necessity might, therefore, be more hypothetical. The actions might be necessary in the sense of constituting conditions that need to be met in order for contemplation to take place. Michael of Ephesus (*In EN* 583. 3–584. 26, esp. 583. 33–4 Heylbut) suggests something along these lines, insisting that the sage should pursue bodily health as necessary and not preferred since a sick body can obstruct contemplation, and it is contemplation which is preferred (cf. Porph. *Abst.* 53. 10–12). Plotinus might want to say something similar here about noble acts of virtue. If the lower soul really is incorrigibly concerned with the welfare of living bodies, it might be counter-productive for the rational soul to deny its urgings completely, since as Plato insisted, suppressing a necessary appetite results in that desire building up and eventually overtaking the soul (*Rep.* 571 E 1–2). Hence, the rational soul would have to perform noble acts of virtue in order to keep the lower soul at least minimally content. Yet Plotinus seems to reject the idea that disturbances in the body will inhibit one's contemplation. In 1. 4 [46]. 4. 25–32, for example, he repeats the position we have found in 4. 4 [28]. 44 that the sage will indeed take care of the body's needs with an attitude of necessity, but here Plotinus makes it clear that the necessity is not hypothetical. Even in times when the body's needs cannot be fulfilled, the sage's contemplation and thus his happiness are not diminished (and cf. 1. 4 [46]. 14. 26–31). Other senses of necessity are surely possible as well. One might, for example, say that these actions are necessary for the sage in the sense that not all the circumstances involved in them are under his control (see Rist, *Road*, 132), but note that this would not explain *why* the sage is performing these actions.

What this discussion of 4. 4. 44 has shown is that despite the arguments in favour of automatic action provided above, Plotinus seems to think that, at the very least, automatic action has its limits. For in 4. 4. 44 we find the contemplative man being *compelled* to practical action by his lower soul and remaining in contemplation only in the more moderate sense of not losing his intelligible ideals. This need not mean that the sage's action is never automatic, but it does strongly suggest that it often is not.

5. Conclusion

What has been shown is that Plotinus' psychology and in particular his account of how the lower parts of soul are formed by and respond to the achievements of the higher parts demand something like automatic action. For any improvement in one level of soul will automatically trickle down to the next level, which is turned to it and formed by it, and in so far as these lower levels of soul are intrinsically concerned with the sensible world, their response will be in the form of sensible activity. Further, Plotinus' account of both crafts and the actions of the heavenly bodies also seems to point in this direction. The contentious question that remains has to do with the extent to which the sage's acts of virtue are performed automatically. For as we have now seen, the sage does not appear to be always acting in an automatic manner, though this need not be at odds with his contemplative life.

However, one could easily raise a number of objections to any account of sagacious virtuous action regardless of the above caveats and limitations. First, according to the metaphysical psychology as described in Section 3, it would seem to be the sensitive soul rather than the rational soul that is responsible for these virtuous actions, and that seems bizarre both because the sensitive soul would turn out to be rather sophisticated and because to the extent that reason is not involved, the actions themselves would be, if not irrational, then at least non-rational. Second, the solemn struggle to determine the right course of action seems to lie close to the core of our ethical experience, and any account that disregards this pensive effort does not really seem to be an account of *ethical* action at all. As Rist remarks, 'the brave man is not an automaton whose reflexes simply cause him to act bravely'.[83] Third, it is audacious enough to say that the sage performs virtuous actions without any deliberation, but this account seems to go even further by suggesting that he is not even *conscious* of any virtuous act that he performs automatically, and surely such blind acts do not deserve to be called virtuous.

These piercing objections swiftly expose to view this account's distance from our modern moral intuitions, but perhaps they over-state the case against automatic action. Surely it must be granted that there is something bizarre about saying that the sage's virtuous actions are executed solely by the sensitive soul. Such a figure would indeed approach Rist's automaton. This characterization, however, draws its force from an oversimplification of Plotinus' psychology. The sensitive soul does not exist in a vacuum, and the sage's sensi-tive soul in particular is turned to and formed by his rational soul. This means, first of all, that the lower soul is not merely on auto-pilot nor are these actions merely the result of habituation. That would be a different and lower kind of virtue (at least according to the later discussions of levels of virtue).[84] The problem, of course, with such habitual virtue is that it lacks understanding. The little boy lets the old woman have his seat in the bus simply because he was brought up that way. He might say and even think that it is a good thing to do, but he does not understand what goodness is. This is not the case with the sage. He does understand what the Good is (or at least virtue at the intelligible level). Moreover, the sage's good actions and his understanding of the Good are not two unrelated phenomena. Even after the training and when reason is not stepping in, there is a sense in which his actions are *flowing* from his understanding. Hence, the sensitive soul is far from be-ing the sole executor of these actions. According to the theory of automatic action, reason is involved in the sage's actions, but in a unique way. Reason does not turn down and attend to the needs of the sensitive soul and body. This, after all, would come at the cost of its contemplation. Rather, the sensitive soul looks up to reason and participates in it, and in this way its activities are informed by reason without reason being distracted.[85] Does this mean that the sage is completely unconscious of his actions? Probably not. Recall how Tolstoy described Levin's mowing experience also in terms of his being unconscious of the movement. This can hardly mean

[83] *Road*, 132.
[84] e.g. Porph. *Sent.* §32.   [85] And cf. 4. 4. 12. 1 ff.

that Levin had no idea where he was or that he was mowing. His obliviousness is limited to his technique and the mechanics of his swinging the blade. Such unconsciousness is not a drawback but a consequence of real expertise, be it in craft or in moral behaviour.[86]

In order to illustrate the attractiveness of such a position, consider some case of moral action with a more or less obvious answer: for example, a wealthy man, full from a large lunch, happens to win a large bag of fresh bagels and then on his way out of the restaurant encounters a starving child on the street. Not only is it clear that the man should give some of the bagels to the starving child, but there even seems to be something monstrous about anyone who really has to deliberate about the matter. In such obvious cases—rare but perhaps not as rare as moral sceptics would have us believe—the immediacy with which one responds to the situation is a key ethical element of one's action. And it is perhaps reasonable to expect that for a sage, who really understands what it is to be good, a great part of his ethical life will consist of such obvious cases to which he can provide an immediate correct response. To bring the issue to a point, the modern moral intuition that ethical behaviour must be deliberative is at odds with the intuition (central to virtue ethics) that immediacy is itself essential to many ethical responses. A Plotinian theory of automatic action would side with the latter intuition but without rendering the action irrational in doing so, since reason would still be influential in a non-deliberative manner.

It is perhaps fitting to conclude by reiterating Plotinus' caveat regarding the extent to which human beings can give themselves over to automatic action. As we saw above in the discussion of natural activities, Plotinus underlined a number of critical differences between sublunar living things on the one hand and superlunar living things and the universe on the other, all of which went in the direction of saying that the former simply cannot live in the automatic and carefree manner of the latter. This verdict is echoed in certain other passages. In 3. 2. 14. 16–20, for example, Plotinus declares that human beings will never achieve the zenith of virtue because they are parts.[87] This is also part of his explanation of the cycle of

---

[86] This would also be comparable to the celestial things' awareness of the goings on down here (4. 4. 6–12). See A. Smith, 'Unconsciousness and Quasi-Consciousness in Plotinus', *Phronesis*, 23 (1978) 292–301.

[87] καὶ ἄνθρωπος δή, καθ' ὅσον μέρος, ἕκαστον, οὐ πᾶς. εἰ δέ που ἐν μέρεσί τισι καὶ ἄλλο τι, ὃ οὐ μέρος, τούτῳ κἀκεῖνο πᾶν. ὁ δὲ καθ' ἕκαστα, ᾗ τοῦτο, οὐκ ἀπαιτητέος τέλεος εἶναι εἰς ἀρετῆς ἄκρον· ἤδη γὰρ οὐκέτ' ἂν μέρος. This problem of being parts, again, does

life and death, since in his view only death puts us in a position to contemplate in the manner of the World-Soul and celestial things (4. 8. 4. 31–5).[88] Thus, even the sage—to the extent that the sage really exists and is not merely an ideal—will at times encounter obstacles that draw him out of his contemplative state. When such obstacles are present, the sage will maintain his normative directedness to the intelligible world while directing his attention to the sensible world. Just like Levin, when he encounters a tussock, the sage will be forced to deliberate how best to deal with certain situations. The question remains: just how many tussocks will there be in the sage's world?

Newcastle University

BIBLIOGRAPHY

Adamson, P., 'Plotinus on Astrology', forthcoming in *Oxford Studies in Ancient Philosophy*, 35 (2008).

Armstrong, A. H., 'Platonic Eros and Christian Agape', *Downside Review*, 75 (1961), 105–21; repr. in A. H. Armstrong, *Plotinian and Christian Studies* (London, 1979), ch. ix.

——(ed. and trans.), *Plotinus:* Enneads (7 vols.; Cambridge, Mass., 1966–88).

Atkinson, M., *Plotinus:* Ennead V. 1 (Oxford, 1983).

Bréhier, É. (ed. and trans.), *Plotin: Ennéades* (7 vols.; Paris, 1924–38).

Brisson, L., 'Plotin et la magie', in L. Brisson *et al.* (eds.), *Porphyry: La Vie de Plotin* (2 vols.; Paris, 1992), ii. 465–75.

Bussanich, J. R., 'The Invulnerability of Goodness: The Ethical and Psychological Theory of Plotinus', *Proceedings of the Boston Area Colloquium in Ancient Philosophy*, 6 (1990), 151–84.

Dillon, J. M., 'Plotinus, Philo and Origen on the Grades of Virtue' ['Vir-

---

not apply to the heavenly bodies on account of their superior physical constitutions (see above).

[88] And cf. Plotinus' distinction of the four kinds of 'man' in 4. 4. 17. 27–38. I agree with Schniewind (*L'Éthique*, 108) that the description of the highest kind really applies only to the World-Soul (and celestial souls): ἐν δὲ τῷ ἀρίστῳ, τῷ χωρίζοντι, ἕν τὸ ἄρχον, καὶ παρὰ τούτου εἰς τὰ ἄλλα ἡ τάξις· οἷον διττῆς πόλεως οὔσης, τῆς μὲν ἄνω, τῆς δὲ τῶν κάτω, κατὰ τὰ ἄνω κοσμουμένης. This can be understood from the lines that immediately follow: 'But it has been stated that it is in the World-Soul that unity, sameness, and likeness are found, and that in other souls things are different, and the reasons for this have been stated as well.'

tue'], in H.-D. Blume and F. Mann (eds.), *Platonismus und Christentum: Festschrift für Heinrich Dörrie* (Münster, 1983), 92–105.

Henry, P., and Schwyzer, H.-R. (eds.), *Plotini opera* (3 vols.; Oxford, 1964–82).

O'Brien, D., 'La matière chez Plotin: son origine, sa nature', *Phronesis*, 44 (1999), 45–71.

O'Meara, D., *Platonopolis* (Oxford, 2003).

Rist, J. M., *Plotinus: The Road to Reality* [*Road*] (Cambridge, 1967).

Saffrey, H.-D., and Segonds, A.-P., 'Introduction', in *Marinus: Proclus, ou sur le Bonheur*, ed. and trans. H.-D. Saffrey, A.-P. Segonds, and C. Luna (Paris, 2001), pp. ix–clxiv.

Schniewind, A., *L'Éthique du sage chez Plotin: le paradigme du* spoudaios [*L'Éthique*] (Paris, 2003).

Smith, A., 'The Significance of Practical Ethics for Plotinus', in J. Cleary (ed.), *Traditions of Platonism: Essays in Honour of John Dillon* (Aldershot, 1999), 227–36.

—— 'Unconsciousness and Quasi-Consciousness in Plotinus', *Phronesis*, 23 (1978), 292–301.

Sorabji, R. R. K., *Animal Minds and Human Morals* (Ithaca, NY, and London, 1993).

Szlezák, T., *Platon und Aristoteles in der Nuslehre Plotins* (Basel and Stuttgart, 1979).

Theiler, W., and Beutler, R. (eds.), *Plotins Schriften*, trans. R. Harder (6 vols.; Hamburg, 1956–71).

Tolstoy, L., *Anna Karenina*, trans. R. Pevear and L. Volokhonsky (New York, 2000).

Vorwerk, M., 'Plato on Virtue: Definitions of Σωφροσύνη in Plato's *Charmides* and in Plotinus *Enneads* I. 2 (19)', *American Journal of Philology*, 122 (2001), 29–47.

Wilberding, J. (ed., trans., and comm.), *Plotinus' Cosmology: A Study of Ennead II. 1 (40)* (Oxford, 2006).

Wildberg, C., '*Pros to telos*: Neuplatonische Ethik zwischen Religion und Metaphysik', in T. Kobusch and M. Erler (eds.), *Metaphysik und Religion: Zur Signatur des spätantiken Denkens. Akten des internationalen Kongresses vom 13.–17. März 2001 in Würzburg* (Munich and Leipzig, 2002), 261–78.

INDEX LOCORUM

Aeschylus
Choephori
673: 304
Eumenides
734: 304
Prometheus Vinctus
441–506: 307
635: 304

Alexander of Aphrodisias
In Aristotelis Metaphysica commentaria,
ed. Bonitz
551: 232–3 n. 33
In Aristotelis Metaphysica commentaria,
ed. Hayduck
581. 16–19: 234
[*In Aristotelis Sophisticos elenchos commentarium*], ed. Wallies
149. 29: 260 n. 102
In librum De sensu commentarium, ed. Wendland
125. 3–9: 277 n. 145
On Sense Perception, ed. Wendland
82. 3–7: 194–5 n. 18

[Andronicus]
On Passions
1: 52 n. 34

Aristophanes
Plutus
160–5: 307
182–3: 307

Aristotle
Categorires
14: 266 n. 117
De anima
407ᵃ23–5: 255
412ᵃ21–8: 331
415ᵃ18–22: 244
415ᵃ25–ᵇ7: 158–9 n. 34, 159, 170
415ᵇ2–3: 158
416ᵃ10–19: 165 n. 50
417ᵃ16–17: 261, 281
417ᵃ27–8: 340

417ᵃ21–ᵇ2: 331
417ᵃ21: 272
417ᵃ22–8: 275
417ᵇ3–5: 266 n. 118
417ᵇ6–7: 272
417ᵇ8–9: 272
417ᵇ13–15: 272
417ᵇ28–418ᵃ3: 275
417ᵇ29–418ᵃ3: 272
418ᵃ9: 127 n. 10
418ᵃ20–5: 127 n. 10
425ᵃ24–7: 127 n. 10
428ᵃ17 ff.: 41 n. 14
429ᵃ13–18: 275
430ᵃ10–13: 135 n. 21
430ᵃ10–11: 138 n. 29
431ᵃ6–7: 261–2
431ᵃ6: 263
432ᵃ29–433ᵇ1: 343
433ᵃ1–3: 364 n. 65
433ᵇ5–10: 364 n. 65
De caelo
269ᵃ32–3: 170
269ᵇ16–17: 170
269ᵇ17–25: 170
271ᵃ35: 168 n. 53
273ᵃ19–22: 168 n. 54, 168–9 n. 55
276ᵃ24: 168, 174–5 n. 68
280ᵃ32–4: 347 n. 32
283ᵇ17–18: 347 n. 32
286ᵃ8–9: 168 n. 53, 300
291ᵇ14: 168 n. 53
292ᵃ22–ᵇ25: 245
292ᵇ1–2: 244
292ᵇ17–25: 169, 174–5 n. 68
300ᵃ24–7: 176 n. 75
304ᵇ26–7: 127 n. 10
307ᵇ22: 168 n. 53
311ᵃ2–3: 172 n. 64
311ᵃ3–6: 168, 168–9 n. 55, 174–5 n. 68
311ᵃ4–6: 135 n. 21, 138 n. 29
312ᵃ30–ᵇ1: 124–5 n. 4, 143
De generatione animalium
731ᵃ25: 244
731ᵇ24–732ᵃ1: 161, 169 n. 57
734ᵃ27–735ᵃ4: 165 n. 50

410   *Index Locorum*

735ᵃ9–11: 340
740ᵇ22–6: 135 n. 21
747ᵇ27–748ᵃ16: 347
761ᵇ9: 165 n. 47
789ᵃ4–6: 257
De generatione et corruptione
314ᵃ8–11: 144 n. 34
314ᵇ1–4: 144 n. 34
316ᵃ5–14: 347 n. 32
317ᵃ23–7: 124 n. 2
319ᵃ33–ᵇ3: 143
320ᵃ2–5: 133
324ᵇ13–18: 135 n. 21
324ᵇ18: 135 n. 21
328ᵃ23–31: 195, 196–7 n. 21
328ᵇ33–329ᵃ1: 144 n. 34
329ᵃ8–10: 144 n. 34
329ᵃ24–ᵇ6: 124–5 n. 4
329ᵃ24–6: 144 n. 34
329ᵃ24–5: 125
329ᵃ33: 125
330ᵇ1–7: 127 n. 10
331ᵃ20–3: 129 n. 14
331ᵃ23–4: 178 n. 79
331ᵇ4–11: 129 n. 14
331ᵇ5–7: 178 n. 79
331ᵇ11–26: 126–7 n. 9
331ᵇ24–6: 127 n. 10
332ᵃ3–20: 144 n. 34
332ᵃ35–ᵇ1: 144 n. 34
334ᵃ16–18: 124–5 n. 4
334ᵃ24–5: 124–5 n. 4
334ᵇ13–15: 195 n. 19
335ᵃ32–ᵇ6: 125
336ᵇ6–7: 173
336ᵇ16–18: 177
336ᵇ23–4: 178
336ᵇ27–337ᵃ8: 161
337ᵃ1–7: 159
337ᵃ6–7: 179 n. 80
337ᵃ7: 179
338ᵃ20–ᵇ4: 175
338ᵇ6–18: 156
De insomniis
459ᵃ1–9: 341
459ᵃ6–8: 342
459ᵃ15–23: 341
459ᵃ23–ᵇ23: 341
459ᵃ26: 341 n. 27
460ᵇ12–16: 342
460ᵇ31: 341 n. 27
462ᵃ19–28: 345

De interpretatione
20ᵇ33–5: 312
21ᵇ9–10: 249 n. 74
De longitudine vitae
465ᵇ15–16: 135 n. 21
De motu animalium
701ᵃ13–16: 336 n. 22
701ᵃ19–20: 351 n. 42
701ᵃ26–9: 336 n. 22
702ᵃ10–15: 135 n. 21
702ᵃ20–1: 135 n. 21
De partibus animalium
641ᵇ10–23: 161 n. 39
645ᵃ15–26: 319
645ᵃ17–23: 319 n. 48
645ᵇ14–35: 244
653ᵃ8: 156
653ᵃ22 ff.: 176
657ᵇ26–7: 164 n. 44
659ᵃ2–15: 164 n. 44
661ᵇ16–33: 166
662ᵃ34–ᵇ16: 164
665ᵇ2–5: 164
674ᵃ29–31: 164 n. 44
674ᵇ2–5: 164 n. 44
674ᵇ17–35: 164
675ᵇ13–14: 164
678ᵃ11: 165 n. 50
679ᵃ32–ᵇ3: 164 n. 45
682ᵃ7–8: 165
682ᵇ35–683ᵃ3: 164 n. 44
687ᵇ3–ᵇ22: 297
692ᵇ20–693ᵃ10: 164 n. 44
694ᵃ1 ff.: 164 n. 44
De sensu
436ᵃ4: 244
439ᵃ22–440ᵃ3: 193, 196
439ᵇ29: 194
439ᵇ32: 194
440ᵇ18–21: 192–3, 196
442ᵃ19–25: 194–5 n. 18, 211 n. 31
442ᵃ25: 194–5 n. 18
445ᵇ20–2: 194–5 n. 18
445ᵇ21–9: 194–5 n. 18
446ᵃ16–20: 194–5 n. 18
446ᵇ2–6: 260
446ᵇ28–447ᵃ6: 212–13, 213
De somno
456ᵇ16–457ᵃ20: 341
457ᵇ20–458ᵃ26: 357
457ᵇ31 ff.: 176
458ᵃ28–9: 341

Eudemian Ethics
6. 3: 323 ff.
1217ᵃ25–9: 301 n. 19
1217ᵃ26–9: 159
1218ᵇ37–1219ᵃ5: 296 n. 8
1219ᵃ8: 301
1219ᵃ19–24: 317
1225ᵇ26–7: 297
1235ᵃ10–35: 358
1235ᵃ29–31: 348
1240ᵇ40–1241ᵃ9: 358
1244ᵇ29–30: 257
1246ᵇ34–6: 366
1249ᵃ17–21: 273–4
1249ᵇ15–16: 158
Fragments, ed. Rose³
206: 276 n. 142
207: 276 n. 141
208: 276 n. 142
Historia animalium
530ᵇ22–4: 164 n. 44
567ᵇ14: 165
588ᵃ16–17: 165 n. 46
589ᵃ3: 244
596ᵇ20–1: 244
596ᵇ21–9: 165
598ᵃ30–ᵇ1: 165
598ᵇ4–6: 162–4 n. 43, 165
601ᵇ16–19: 165
Magna moralia
1197ᵃ3–13: 377 n. 10
Metaphysics
B 1: 303 n. 23
980ᵃ21–982ᵃ3: 229
980ᵃ21–6: 222 n. 7
981ᵃ12–ᵇ24: 314
986ᵃ29–30: 241 n. 58
996ᵇ7: 301
1013ᵃ35–ᵇ1: 254 n. 90
1017ᵃ27–30: 249 n. 74
1026ᵇ31–5: 151
1028ᵃ32–3: 228
1029ᵃ20–3: 125
1029ᵃ24–6: 125
1029ᵇ1–12: 303 n. 23
1032ᵃ13–15: 266 n. 117
1038ᵇ28: 228
1039ᵇ27–31: 125
1043ᵇ4–12; 136 n. 25
1044ᵇ27–9: 124 n. 2
1044ᵇ29–34: 138 n. 30
1044ᵇ33: 138
1045ᵃ1–ᵇ36: 229

1045ᵇ27–1046ᵃ4: 221
1045ᵇ35–1046ᵃ13: 223
1046ᵃ22–8: 136
1046ᵇ17: 223 n. 10
1047ᵃ30–2: 224
1048ᵃ5–7: 135 n. 21
1048ᵃ10–11: 227 n. 18, 228
1048ᵃ18–27: 236
1048ᵃ25–ᵇ9: 221–2
1048ᵃ25–30: 221
1048ᵃ26–7: 226
1048ᵃ28–9: 243
1048ᵃ32: 226
1048ᵃ34–ᵇ2: 242
1048ᵃ34–5: 243 n. 60
1048ᵃ35: 226
1048ᵃ37: 222 n. 6
1048ᵇ3–4: 242
1048ᵇ5–6: 222 n. 6
1048ᵇ5: 222 n. 6
1048ᵇ6–9: 221
1048ᵇ6: 226
1048ᵇ8–9: 242, 263
1048ᵇ8: 223, 242, 243 n. 60, 263 n. 109
1048ᵇ9–17: 227
1048ᵇ10–11: 226
1048ᵇ10: 226
1048ᵇ14: 226
1048ᵇ15: 226, 227
1048ᵇ16: 226
1048ᵇ18–35: 219 ff.
1048ᵇ18–23: 253
1048ᵇ18–21: 264 n. 112
1048ᵇ18: 234, 256
1048ᵇ19–20: 279, 280
1048ᵇ19: 256, 258, 280
1048ᵇ20: 279, 280
1048ᵇ21–2: 262
1048ᵇ21: 272, 280
1048ᵇ22: 252 n. 87, 256, 258, 279, 280
1048ᵇ23–5: 245
1048ᵇ23–4: 279, 280
1048ᵇ23: 222, 252, 258, 276
1048ᵇ24–5: 258 n. 99
1048ᵇ25–7: 250
1048ᵇ25: 243, 276, 279, 280
1048ᵇ26–7: 244
1048ᵇ27: 251, 280, 280
1048ᵇ28–34: 234
1048ᵇ28: 258, 263, 280
1048ᵇ29–31: 222
1048ᵇ29–30: 243
1048ᵇ29: 257, 263, 280

1048^{b}30–3: 246
1048^{b}31: 280
1048^{b}32–3: 242
1048^{b}33–4: 222, 246
1048^{b}33: 251, 253
1048^{b}34: 280
1048^{b}35–6: 226
1048^{b}35: 226, 227, 234, 239 n. 51
1048^{b}36: 226
1049^{b}8–10: 152 n. 13
1049^{b}29–1050^{a}3: 270
1050^{a}1: 270
1050^{a}7–10: 139
1050^{a}9–10: 152 n. 13, 168–9 n. 55
1050^{a}15–16: 139
1050^{a}17: 266 n. 118
1050^{a}21–3: 301
1050^{a}23–^{b}2: 223, 241
1050^{a}23–8: 266
1050^{b}1–2: 245
1050^{b}28–30: 159 n. 35, 169
1059^{b}18–1060^{a}20: 229
1069^{b}3–9: 124 n. 2
1071^{b}19–20: 243
1072^{b}1–2: 158
1072^{b}16: 243
1072^{b}26–8: 243
1073^{a}1: 225, 234
1073^{a}3–^{b}38: 254, 254 n. 91
1073^{a}5: 254 n. 91
1073^{a}31–8: 254
1074^{a}18–21: 243
1074^{a}30–1: 254
1074^{a}38–^{b}14: 254, 254 n. 91
1074^{b}3: 254
1074^{b}20: 269
1074^{b}22: 269
1075^{a}11–25: 157, 157–8
1075^{a}19–22: 179–80
1078^{b}27–9: 295 n. 6
1092^{a}9–1093^{b}28: 229

Meteorologica
339^{a}6–9: 175
339^{a}33–^{b}3: 175 n. 69
339^{a}36–^{b}3: 124–5 n. 4
339^{b}17–19: 175 n. 69
340^{b}4–6: 175 n. 69
346^{b}22: 173
346^{b}35–347^{a}1: 179
347^{a}6: 176
347^{a}13 ff.: 174–5 n. 68
347^{b}13: 156
348^{b}8–10: 177

348^{b}11: 178
348^{b}12: 178
348^{b}16–349^{a}4: 178 n. 78
348^{b}22: 214 n. 35
348^{b}23: 178
349^{a}5–9: 177, 178
349^{a}7: 178
351^{a}26: 174–5 n. 68
351^{b}8: 174–5 n. 68
352^{a}27–35: 174–5 n. 68
352^{a}31: 174–5 n. 68, 176
352^{b}16: 174–5 n. 68
354^{b}34: 176, 177
355^{a}28: 174–5 n. 68
355^{b}2: 177
356^{b}35–357^{a}1: 179 n. 80
357^{a}2: 174–5 n. 68
358^{a}3: 176
358^{a}26–7: 176
359^{b}34–360^{a}3: 176
360^{a}2–6: 156
378^{b}27–379^{a}1: 133
381^{b}4–6: 319
389^{a}7–9: 137

Nicomachean Ethics
7. 1–3: 303 n. 23
7. 3: 323 ff.
1094^{a}5–6: 266 n. 118
1094^{a}10–13: 305
1094^{a}16–17: 263
1094^{b}6–7: 305
1095^{b}2–4: 303 n. 23
1095^{b}19–23: 308
1095^{b}31–1096^{a}2: 296–7 n. 9
1096^{a}16–19: 222 n. 7
1097^{a}15–34: 305
1097^{a}25–^{b}21: 71 n. 4
1097^{b}20–1: 305
1097^{b}22–1098^{a}18: 293
1097^{b}22–33: 294–5
1097^{b}22–5: 305
1097^{b}22: 311
1097^{b}24 ff.: 303
1097^{b}25–33: 295
1097^{b}25–8: 310
1097^{b}26: 311 n. 36
1097^{b}27: 311
1097^{b}28–33: 294 n. 3
1097^{b}29–30: 308
1097^{b}29: 311 n. 36
1097^{b}33–1098^{a}3: 294 n. 3
1098^{a}7 ff.: 300
1098^{a}7–18: 314

1098^{a}8–12: 317
1098^{b}18–20: 244
1098^{b}30–1099^{a}7: 72 n. 5
1102^{b}13–25: 363–4
1106^{a}14–20: 296 n. 8
1107^{a}28–32: 333 n. 18
1110^{a}15–17: 349 n. 36
1110^{b}18–1111^{a}2: 335
1110^{b}24–1111^{a}26: 325–6
1111^{a}22–3: 325
1111^{b}6–10: 326 n. 4
1111^{b}28–9: 71 n. 4
1118^{a}22–3: 222 n. 7
1139^{a}9–11: 368 n. 75
1139^{a}13–14: 374 n. 3
1139^{a}16–17: 296 n. 8
1139^{a}23: 368 n. 75
1139^{a}31–^{b}5: 297
1139^{a}35–^{b}4: 244
1139^{b}4–5: 368 n. 75
1140^{a}1–23: 314
1140^{b}6–7: 244
1141^{a}20–33: 301 n. 19
1142^{a}19–20: 344
1142^{a}23–30: 369 n. 76
1143^{a}32–6: 369 n. 76
1145^{b}22–31: 327
1146^{b}8–24: 328
1146^{b}24–31; 329–30
1146^{b}25: 338
1146^{b}31–1147^{b}19: 361 n. 63
1146^{b}31–5: 330
1146^{b}33: 338
1146^{b}35–1147^{a}10: 333–4
1147^{a}1: 350
1147^{a}4–7: 333 n. 18
1147^{a}4: 323, 338
1147^{a}7–8: 337 n. 23
1147^{a}10–24: 340
1147^{a}24–^{b}12: 348–50
1147^{a}25: 350
1147^{b}6–9: 346–7 n. 31
1147^{b}13–19: 365–6
1148^{a}13–17: 326
1149^{a}32–^{b}2: 355 n. 52
1149^{b}31–1150^{a}1: 326 n. 4
1150^{a}19–31: 326
1150^{b}19–28: 359
1150^{b}19–21: 361
1151^{a}1–14: 326
1151^{a}11–26: 356
1152^{a}6–19: 324
1153^{a}7–17: 265

1153^{a}7–12: 266, 271
1153^{a}15–17: 263 n. 110, 267
1153^{a}24–5: 267
1154^{a}13–15: 267
1154^{b}20: 244
1154^{b}26–8: 271
1154^{b}27: 263
1155^{b}2: 348
1161^{a}34–^{b}2: 301 n. 19, 311 n. 36
1167^{b}17–1168^{a}9: 348
1171^{a}35–^{b}1: 257
1173^{a}29–31: 265
1173^{a}32–^{b}4: 267
1173^{b}4–7: 167
1173^{b}19: 268
1174^{a}14–^{b}14: 268
1174^{a}17–19: 268
1174^{a}19–21: 256
1174^{a}22: 268
1174^{a}27–8: 268
1174^{a}28: 264 n. 111
1174^{a}29–^{b}2: 252 n. 88
1174^{a}32: 256
1174^{b}2–3: 268
1174^{b}4: 263, 268
1174^{b}9: 268
1174^{b}10: 267
1174^{b}13: 267
1174^{b}14–17: 268–9
1174^{b}14: 269
1175^{a}20–1: 269
1175^{a}25–6: 264
1175^{a}30–5: 269
1175^{b}19: 270 n. 124
1176^{a}3–5: 314
1176^{a}35–^{b}7: 271
1176^{b}16–1177^{a}11: 308
1176^{b}27–35: 70
1177^{b}1–26: 271
1177^{b}26–1178^{a}8: 159
1178^{b}7–32: 159
Physics
1. 1: 303 n. 23
2. 8: 147 ff.
183^{a}15–16: 283
188^{a}36–^{b}3: 215
189^{a}12–13: 228
190^{a}13–15: 124
191^{a}4–5: 124
192^{a}3–^{b}34: 124 n. 2
192^{a}17: 170 n. 59
192^{b}8–14: 155
192^{b}8–11: 155 n. 20

192^b11: 155 n. 20
192^b14: 155 n. 20
192^b16: 168
192^b21-3: 152
$192^b32-193^a2$: 155
$192^b35-193^a2$: 156
192^b35-6: 169
193^a1: 168
193^a3-9: 296–7 n. 9
194^a20-1: 319
196^a24-35: 161 n. 39
197^a35: 174
197^b5: 245 n. 63
198^a5-13: 161 n. 39
198^a7: 174
198^a10-11: 176 n. 75
198^b4-9: 154 n. 17
198^b10-11: 152
198^b17-23: 148
198^b17-18: 152
198^b19-20: 167, 177
198^b20: 156
$198^b35-199^a8$: 149
199^a6: 154
199^a7: 152
199^a15-18: 162–4 n. 43
199^a29-30: 165
199^b28-9: 386 n. 27
199^b32-3: 152
$200^b33-201^a5$: 266 n. 117
201^a16-19: 269 n. 122
201^b8-13: 269 n. 122
201^b31-3: 261
201^b31-2: 264 n. 113
201^b31: 263
206^a21-5: 228
207^a25-6: 228
209^a4-6: 130 n. 15
209^a9-11: 130 n. 15
209^a20-1: 168–9 n. 55
211^a4-7: 168–9 n. 55
211^a4-5: 168 n. 52
212^b29-34: 168 n. 52
212^b30-1: 168–9 n. 55
220^a29-32: 187 n. 3
223^b24-6: 161 n. 37
224^b10: 268
$224^b35-225^a20$: 266 n. 117
226^b26-9: 190
227^b26: 187, 190 n. 11
228^b1-7: 189, 190
230^a29-^b4: 178 n. 78
230^b2: 178 n. 78

230^b3: 178 n. 78
232^b20-1: 190 n. 11
$232^b26-233^a12$: 204
234^b10-20: 208, 210 ff., 213 n. 34
234^b10-13: 189
234^b17: 211 n. 30
$234^b21-235^a8$: 207 n. 27
235^a9-33: 187
235^a9-15: 190 n. 11
235^a11-13: 187
235^a13-18: 200, 202, 203, 207, 207 n. 27
235^a18-24: 190 n. 11
235^a33-5: 203
236^a13-27: 190 n. 11
236^a27-35: 208
236^a35-^b18: 197 ff.
236^a35-6: 187, 190 n. 11, 198
236^b1: 199
236^b5-10: 187 n. 5
236^b10-16: 200, 204
236^b16-19: 200
236^b17-18: 198 n. 22
236^b18-22: 187
236^b19-32: 187
237^a15-17: 189
237^a17-28: 190 n. 11, 206, 214–15
237^a25-8: 187, 187 n. 3
237^a28-34: 204, 211
237^a28-30: 206
237^a34-^b8: 190 n. 11
237^a35-^b3: 206
237^a35-^b2: 206
237^b2: 200, 206
237^b9-22: 213
239^a14-18: 190
239^a23-6: 187
239^a35-^b3: 189 n. 9
240^a19-29: 192, 215–16
$240^b17-241^a5$: 208, 209, 210
246^a12-^b3: 267
247^a2-3: 267
247^b13-16: 340
251^a8-10: 268
253^a23-6: 213
253^b25: 283:
255^a1-6: 172
255^a2: 172–3 n. 65
255^a4-5: 168 n. 52
255^a29-31: 168–9 n. 55
255^a29-30: 168 n. 52
255^a30: 172
255^a33-^b5: 332
255^a34-^b1: 135 n. 21

255^b12-17: 168–9 n. 55
255^b14: 172–3 n. 65
255^b15-17: 169, 172–3 n. 65
255^b27: 172–3 n. 65
255^b31: 171
256^a1-3: 172
256^a2: 172–3 n. 65
256^a3: 172–3 n. 65
256^a4: 172
261^b13-14: 189
262^a2-5: 199
262^a21-5: 189 n. 9
262^a30: 189 n. 9
262^b20: 189 n. 9
263^a4-10: 189 n. 9
263^b3-9: 189 n. 9
263^b9-15: 191 n. 14
264^a2-3: 191 n. 14
265^a28-^b9: 159
Politics
1252^a34-5: 314
1253^a24: 301
1256^b10-22: 150, 161–2
1258^a2-13: 307
1260^b1-2: 313 n. 41, 314
1264^b22-4: 314
$1277^b33-1278^a21$: 314
1307^b35: 283
1319^a24-30: 314
1325^a32: 245 n. 63
1325^b16-21: 244
1328^b33-41: 314
1329^a19-29: 314
1332^a9-21: 72
1338^a1-3: 257
Posterior Analytics
1. 1: 334
71^{a-b}: 295 n. 6
80^a40 ff.: 295 n. 6
82^b-83^a1: 228
100^b4: 295 n. 6
Prior Analytics
2. 21: 334
Problems
3. 2: 345 n. 30
953^a33-^b23: 357 n. 53
Protrepticus
B70 D: 222 n. 7
Rhetoric
1378^a31: 52 n. 31
1382^a21-2: 52
1383^a17: 52 n. 31
1383^b13: 52 n. 31

1385^b13-14: 52
1387^a8: 52 n. 31
1387^b23: 52 n. 31
1412^a9: 263
[*Rhetorica ad Alexandrum*]
1434^b18-19: 258 n. 98
Sophistici elenchi
177^b14-15: 312
178^a9-28: 246 n. 64, 259
Topics
1. 12: 295 n. 6
108^b7 ff.: 295 n. 6
146^b13-19: 265 n. 116
146^b13-16: 258 n. 98

Athenaeus
512 A: 274

Atticus, ed. Des Places
fr. 2. 9: 377 n. 10

Cicero
De finibus
1. 30: 59

Damascius
De principiis
306, ii. 172. 20 Ruelle: 276 n. 141

Diogenes Laertius
2. 122–4: 310 n. 34
4. 4: 274
4. 12: 274
5. 22: 273 n. 132
5. 24: 273 n. 132, 274 n. 135
5. 25: 276 n. 142
5. 27: 276 n. 142
5. 44: 274
5. 46: 274
5. 59: 274

Empedocles, 31 DK
B 109. 1: 248

Epictetus
Dissertationes
2. 10: 318 n. 47

Galen
On Hippocrates' and Plato's Doctrines
4. 2. 1–6: 52 n. 34

Hesiod
Works and Days
825: 178 n. 79

Homer
Iliad
6. 490: 304
12. 271: 304

Michael of Ephesus
In Aristotelis Sophisticos elenchos commentarium, ed. Wallies (attr. Alex. Aphr.)
149. 29: 260 n. 102
149. 31–2: 277–8 n. 146
In Ethica Nicomachea commentarium, ed. Heylbut
543. 22–30: 277
543. 22: 277
545. 7: 278 n. 147
545. 20–30: 278 n. 147
552. 17: 268
555. 20–9: 271 n. 128
562. 34–6: 278 n. 147
568. 35–569. 2: 278 n. 147
583. 3–584. 26: 402 n. 82
583. 33–4: 402 n. 82

Philoponus
De aeternitate mundi, ed. Rabe
4. 4: 243
64. 22–65. 26: 237 n. 45
In Aristotelis De anima libros commentaria, ed. Hayduck
296. 20–297. 37: 237 n. 45
In Aristotelis Physica commentaria, ed. Vitelli
312. 23–313. 28: 171 n. 61

Plato
Alcibiades I
129 B 5–130 E 6: 299 n. 15
Apology
22 A–E: 316
30 A: 17
31 B: 17
33 C: 13
37 C: 39
Charmides
169 B: 12 n. 16
175 A–end: 12 n. 16
Cratylus
421 A 8: 118

Euthydemus
273 E–274 A: 12 n. 16
276 C: 13
284 B–C: 259 n. 100
Euthyphro
5 A: 12 n. 16
15 D–end: 12 n. 16
Gorgias
447 B: 19
465 A 2–6: 99 n. 27
468 B–C: 61 n. 58
475 D: 19
482 C–E: 19
489 E: 19
491 E 8–492 A 1: 82
505 C ff.: 24
506 C–507 C: 24
508 E 6–509 A 7: 248 n. 71
509 A: 12 n. 16
513 C: 23
Hippias Major
286 D: 12 n. 16
304 D–E: 12 n. 16
Hippias Minor
369 D: 12 n. 16
375 D 3: 331 n. 13
376 C: 12 n. 16
Ion
530 A 8: 250
Laches
186 B ff.: 11
187 E–188 C: 18
188 A–B: 18, 31 n. 33
188 B: 19
195 E–196 A: 24 n. 27
199 E: 18
Laws
644 C–D: 50 n. 27
667 E 5–8: 70
690 B 4–8: 90 n. 18
714 B 3–D 10: 91
731 C: 61 n. 59
901 C–D: 113
901 D 1: 113–14 n. 15
Lysis
212 A: 12 n. 16
219 C: 113
223 B: 12 n. 16
Meno
71 B: 12 n. 16
77 C–78 B: 61 n. 58
84 A–C: 31 n. 33
87 E–89 A: 61 n. 58

94 E: 16
Parmenides
137 B: 24 n. 26
Phaedo
65 B–C: 49
65 B 9–67 B 5: 101
65 C–D: 113
67 A ff.: 381 n. 18
67 B 6 ff.: 380 n. 16
74 D–E: 63
81 B: 400 n. 79
81 B 3–4: 398
82 A 10–B 3: 380 n. 16
82 D 9–84 B 7: 101
85 C 1–D 4: 99
100 C–D: 59 n. 50
Phaedrus
238 E: 400 n. 79
247 E 2: 118
253 D–254 E: 37 n. 6
260 E 5: 99 n. 27
266 B: 25 n. 28
267 C: 18
270 B 5: 99 n. 27
275 E: 29
276 D: 25 n. 28
278 A: 25 n. 28
Philebus
20 D: 61 n. 59
40 A: 56 n. 45
54 B: 265
54 C–D: 266
54 E: 266
Politicus
275 C: 24 n. 26
Protagoras
316 B 3–4: 249
316 C 3–4: 249
352 B–C: 50, 331 n. 13
352 C ff.: 61 n. 58
356 C: 50
356 D–357 D: 51
356 D: 53
356 E 2–361 B 7: 99 n. 27
358 D: 50
360 A–D: 51
360 C: 50
361 C–D: 12 n. 16
361 E 6: 250
Republic
bk. 1: 12 n. 16
331 C 1–2: 86
331 D 2: 86, 91 n. 19

336 A 9–10: 86
336 C 2–6: 87
336 E 9–337 A 1: 87
337 A: 19
337 D: 12 n. 16
338 C 2–4: 98
338 C 2–3: 87
338 C 5–D 1: 87
338 C 8: 92
338 D 2–3: 84
338 D 9–10: 90
338 E 1–339 A 4: 84
338 E 1–2: 90
339 A 5–6: 90
339 B 9–E 8: 87
339 B 9–C 12: 89
339 C 7–8: 89
339 C 10–11: 85, 87
340 A 10–B 5: 87
340 B 6–8: 87
340 C 6–7: 88
340 C 8–D 1: 88
340 D–344 C: 307
340 D 2–341 A 4: 85
340 D 2: 84
340 D 6–341 A 4: 88
341 A–C: 19
341 A 1–2: 90
341 C: 19
341 D 8–9: 86
342 A 2–B 7: 90
342 E 7–11: 90
343 D 2–344 A 2: 94–5
343 C 3–D 1: 94
344 A 1–C 9: 96–7
344 A 1–3: 90
344 C 7–9: 95
347 D 5: 86
348 D 5–8: 95
348 E: 22
350 D ff.: 24
351 D 7–352 A 10: 73
352 A 6–7: 86
352 D 9–E 4: 299
352 E 2–3: 300
353 D 3–354 A 5: 73
353 E 4–354 A 5: 299
354 C: 247–8 n. 70
354 C 1: 87
357 B 4–8: 69–70
357 C 2–4: 70
357 C 6–D 2: 70
358 A 1–3: 72

358 A 1: 71
358 A 4–D 2: 98
358 A 4–6: 71, 83
358 A 4: 80
358 A 7–9: 83
358 B 2–C 1: 83
358 B 4–7: 72
358 C 3–4: 81
358 C 6: 77
358 C 7–D 1: 84
358 D 2–7: 73
358 E 4–359 B 5: 79
358 E 4: 79
359 A 3–4: 85
359 B 2–4: 85
359 B 2: 80
359 B 4–5: 81
359 B 6–7: 81
359 B 7–9: 81
359 C 1–6: 82
359 C 4–6: 81
359 C 4: 85
359 C 5–6: 80
360 B 4–C 3: 82
360 C 6–7: 81
360 D 5–7: 82
360 D 6–7: 99
360 D 8–361 D 3: 73–4
360 E 6: 85
362 E 3–5: 79
362 E 6–363 A 5: 76
363 A: 257
365 B 4–C 6: 83
365 C 4: 76
366 D 7–367 A 1: 76
367 B 3–D 3: 77
367 C 2–5: 84
367 C 9–D 1: 70
368 A 5–B 3: 77
374 B–E: 316
379 B 1: 101
390 A: 43 n. 17
390 B: 43 n. 17
397 D: 43 n. 17
399 E: 43 n. 17
401 E–402 A: 57
403 C: 57
404 E: 43
406 C 3–D 7: 315
407 A 1–2: 315
407 A 7–8: 315
411 E–412 A: 43
411 E: 57

413 B ff.: 400 n. 79
413 B 1 ff.: 398
419 A 1–420 A 2: 316
420 B: 316
421 B 2–3: 316
421 C 3–6: 316
435 C 9–D 4: 99
436 A: 58–9 n. 49, 62
436 B–C: 41
437 E–438 A: 38 n. 9, 62, 62 n. 62
438 B 6: 99 n. 27
439 D: 37, 58–9 n. 49, 60, 62
439 D 5: 101
439 D 7: 38
441 A–B: 37 n. 4, 39, 58
441 C: 37, 56 n. 43, 60 n. 55
441 E ff.: 42
441 E: 60 n. 55
442 A: 43 n. 16
442 C–D: 38, 62 n. 61
442 C: 56 n. 43, 60 n. 55
442 C 5–7: 101
442 D: 37 n. 4, 63
442 E 1: 73
442 E 4–443 A 1: 72–3
443 D: 44 n. 19
462 C–E: 58
464 A: 58
465 E–466 C: 316
467 A: 316
475 C: 43 n. 16
475 D ff.: 47
476 C: 48
476 E–477 A: 107
477 A–479 D: 113
487 B–D: 18 n. 21
487 C: 23
490 A 8–B 7: 101
493 A 6–C 8: 98
496 A 11–E 3: 99
500 C 3–4: 101
500 D 1–3: 101
504 B 1–505 B 3: 99
504 D 4–E 2: 99
505 D–E: 61, 63
509 D–511 E: 48
510 A: 46 n. 23, 48
510 B 4: 378
510 E 1–511 A 2: 378
511 B 5–6: 99
520 D 9: 101
521 A 1: 101
521 B 7: 101

522 C: 49
523 A ff.: 49
523 E ff.: 65
524 B: 49
526 B: 39
530 B 2–3: 388 n. 36
533 C 8–D 1: 99
534 B 8–C 6: 99
545 B 1–2: 84
548 C: 58–9 n. 49
550 B: 58–9 n. 49
553 D: 58–9 n. 49
554 D: 37 n. 5
555 B: 37 n. 4, 43 n. 16, 62 n. 61
557 A 3–4: 80
557 C: 43
558 C: 43
559 D: 43
561 A ff.: 58–9 n. 49
561 E: 43
562 B–C: 63
562 B: 43 n. 16, 62 n. 61
562 C: 43 n. 16
571 E 1–2: 402 n. 82
572 E–573 B: 400 n. 79
574 D: 37 n. 4, 62 n. 61
577 A 1–B 4: 75–6
578 A: 43 n. 16
580 D: 38 n. 8
580 E–581 A: 58–9 n. 49, 65–6 n. 67
580 E: 37 n. 6
581 B: 62
581 B 6–8: 101
583 A 1–588 A 10: 102
583 E 9–10: 265 n. 115
586 B: 43 n. 16
586 D ff.: 65
588 C: 43
588 E–589 B: 396 n. 72
590 B: 43 n. 16
590 D 1–4: 84
598 A–B: 54
599 A: 46 n. 23
599 D: 46 n. 23
600 E: 54
601 B: 46 n. 23, 54
601 D 4–6: 299
602 B: 54
602 C–603 B: 41
602 C–603 A: 35
602 C–D: 41
602 C: 45
602 D–603 A: 54

602 D–E: 53
602 D: 41
602 E–603 A: 37
602 E: 41
602 E 4–6: 45–6 n. 21
603 A: 37, 41
603 B–C: 42
603 E–605 C: 35
603 E: 54
604 A: 42
604 B: 42
604 C: 54
604 D: 37, 42, 43, 54
604 E: 43
605 A–B: 42
605 A: 43
605 B–C: 45, 45 n. 20, 53, 57
605 B: 42
605 C: 46 n. 23
606 A: 43, 53
606 B: 42
606 C: 42
606 D: 42, 53
607 A: 44
607 B 6–7: 79 n. 11
611 B 9–612 A 6: 101
612 A 8–B 4: 79
612 D 3–10: 78
613 A: 54
Sophist
217 D: 24 n. 26
230 B–D: 31 n. 33
238 E: 106, 107, 108, 109, 114
239 E 1: 260 n. 103
250 A 11–12: 117
254 C: 115
254 D 10: 117
255 B 12: 117
255 C–D: 119
255 C 13–14: 112
255 C 14: 120
255 E–256 E: 115
255 E 4–5: 120 n. 25
255 E 11–256 A 2: 115
256 A–E: 117, 118, 119
256 A 1–2: 117
256 A 1: 112, 116, 117
256 A 3–B 4: 115, 120 n. 25
256 A 3: 120
256 A 5: 120
256 B 2–4: 120
256 B 6–C 2: 115
256 B 6–10: 120 n. 25

256 C 4–8: 115
256 C 4–5: 120 n. 25
256 D 5–7: 115
256 D 8–9: 115, 117, 118, 120
256 D 8: 116, 119 n. 22
256 D 9: 119
256 D 10–11: 112
256 D 11–E 4: 115
256 D 11: 119 n. 22
256 D 12: 118
256 E 1: 119 n. 22
256 E 2: 119 n. 22
256 E 3–7: 117
256 E 3–4: 112, 117, 118, 120
256 E 3: 117
256 E 4: 119
256 E 6–7: 118
256 E 6: 117, 119
256 E 7: 119 n. 22
258 C: 115
258 E: 108, 109
258 E 6: 116
259 A 4–B 1: 116
259 A 6–8: 114, 115
259 B 7: 116
Symposium
199 D: 257
201 D: 11
204 E 1–8: 71 n. 4
205 A ff.: 61 n. 58
211 A: 113 n. 14
216 E: 18
218 C–219 D: 18
Theaetetus
153 E–154 A: 259 n. 100
156 B: 58 n. 48
176 A 7–B 3: 101
176 B 1–2: 380–1 n. 17
185 A–D: 113–14 n. 15
197 B–198 D: 330 n. 12
203 D: 331 n. 13
Timaeus
28 A 5–6: 390 n. 44
33 C 4–8: 394 n. 60
38 C 2: 118
45 B–D: 259 n. 100
45 B–C: 56 n. 44
49: 48
52 C: 48
61 C–D: 47 n. 24
69 C–D: 46–7, 47, 47 n. 24
69 C: 40 n. 11
70 A–B: 47 n. 24

70 D–71 B: 46
71 A ff.: 55
71 A–D: 55
71 A: 56 n. 43
77 B: 40 n. 12, 47, 47 n. 24

Plotinus
1. 1. 10. 11–14: 397 n. 73
1. 1. 2. 13 ff.: 394 n. 59
1. 2: 382
1. 2. 1. 11–12: 394 n. 59
1. 2. 1. 16: 380 n. 15
1. 2. 1. 21: 380 n. 15
1. 2. 1. 22: 380 n. 15
1. 2. 1. 23: 380 n. 15
1. 2. 1. 26: 380 n. 15
1. 2. 2. 13–14: 380 n. 15
1. 2. 3. 2: 380 n. 15
1. 2. 3. 3: 380 n. 15
1. 2. 3. 4: 380 n. 15
1. 2. 3. 5: 380 n. 15
1. 2. 3. 8: 380 n. 15, 381 n. 18
1. 2. 3. 10–19: 381
1. 2. 3. 10–11: 381 n. 18
1. 2. 3. 10: 380 n. 15
1. 2. 3. 21: 381 n. 18
1. 2. 4. 1–9: 381 n. 18
1. 2. 4. 16–17: 381 n. 18
1. 2. 5. 1: 381 n. 18
1. 2. 5. 21–2: 381 n. 18
1. 2. 6. 11–26: 381
1. 2. 6. 13–19: 381 n. 19
1. 2. 6. 24: 380 n. 15
1. 2. 7: 389, 390
1. 2. 7. 1–6: 381 n. 19
1. 2. 7. 6: 381 n. 18
1. 2. 7. 9: 381 n. 18
1. 2. 7. 11: 380 n. 15
1. 2. 7. 14: 380 n. 15
1. 2. 7. 21: 380 n. 15
1. 2. 7. 25: 380 n. 15
1. 3. 2. 10–11: 386 n. 30
1. 3. 6. 6–7: 397 n. 73
1. 4. 1. 21–3: 396 n. 71
1. 4. 6. 4–7: 390
1. 4. 9. 2: 385 n. 26
1. 4. 10. 21–33: 386 n. 28
1. 4. 14. 8–11: 396, 396 n. 72
1. 4. 14. 11–14: 396
1. 4. 14. 17–19: 396 n. 72
1. 4. 14. 21–3: 396
1. 4. 15. 16–20: 397 n. 76
1. 4 [46]: 238

1. 4 [46]. 4. 25–32: 402 n. 82
1. 4 [46]. 14. 26–31: 402 n. 82
1. 5 [36]: 238
1. 6. 2. 25–7: 386 n. 30
1. 6. 9. 2–5: 384–5 n. 22
1. 9: 401 n. 81
1 [42]. 16. 13–14: 277–8 n. 146
2. 1. 1. 14: 394 n. 59
2. 1. 2. 8–10: 388 n. 36
2. 1. 3. 2–4: 394 n. 58
2. 1. 3. 5–7: 394 n. 57
2. 1. 3. 10–12: 394 n. 59, 394 n. 62
2. 1. 3. 25–6: 394 n. 60
2. 1. 5. 8–14: 394 n. 64, 395 n. 66
2. 1. 5. 21–3: 393 n. 53
2. 1. 7. 27 ff.: 394 n. 61
2. 2. 2. 26–7: 393 n. 56, 394 n. 63
2. 3. 8. 6–8: 388 n. 38
2. 3. 9. 10–14: 388 n. 38
2. 3. 9. 34–5: 393 n. 55
2. 3. 10. 7–10: 388 n. 38
2. 3. 11: 388 n. 38
2. 3. 12. 1–11: 388 n. 38
2. 3. 14. 4–7: 388 n. 38
2. 3. 14. 15–17: 388 n. 38
2. 3. 14. 16: 388 n. 38
2. 3. 17. 9–11: 393 n. 56, 394 n. 63
2. 3. 18. 5–8: 386 n. 30
2. 3. 18. 12–13: 393 n. 55
2. 5 [25]: 237
2. 9. 7. 5–7: 383
2. 9. 7. 7 ff.: 395 n. 66
2. 9. 7. 27–32: 394 n. 57
2. 9. 7. 28–30: 394 n. 64
2. 9. 7. 30: 394 n. 58
2. 9. 11. 8–9: 393 n. 56, 394 n. 63
2. 9. 12. 18: 383 n. 21
2. 9. 13: 388 n. 38
2. 9. 14–18: 388 n. 38
2. 9. 15. 15–17: 397, 397 n. 73
2. 9. 16. 43–7: 386 n. 30
3. 1. 5. 21–2: 388 n. 38
3. 1. 5. 24–7: 388 n. 38
3. 1. 6. 1 ff.: 388 n. 38
3. 1. 6. 3–5: 388 n. 38
3. 2. 8. 4–11: 395 nn. 67, 70
3. 2. 14. 16–20: 405
3. 2. 15. 31–62: 387 n. 34
3. 4. 1. 1–3: 380–1 n. 14
3. 6. 5. 15–17: 384
3. 7 [45]. 8. 37–41: 283 n. 158
3. 7 [45]. 11. 36–7: 283 n. 158
3. 8: 375 ff.

3. 8. 1–5: 377
3. 8. 1. 15–18: 375
3. 8. 1. 20–1: 376 n. 7
3. 8. 2: 376 n. 7
3. 8. 2. 6–9: 376 n. 7
3. 8. 2. 29: 376 n. 7
3. 8. 4: 378, 379
3. 8. 4. 7–8: 379 n. 11
3. 8. 4. 10–14: 376 n. 7
3. 8. 4. 16: 376 n. 7
3. 8. 4. 29–31: 376 n. 7
3. 8. 4. 29: 376 n. 7
3. 8. 4. 31–6: 375 n. 6, 383
3. 8. 4. 31–2: 376 n. 7
3. 8. 4. 32: 376 n. 7
3. 8. 4. 37: 376 n. 7
3. 8. 4. 39–47: 375 n. 4, 377
3. 8. 4. 44: 386
3. 8. 5. 6–8: 387 n. 34
3. 8. 5. 9–16: 393 n. 55
3. 8. 5. 22–5: 376 n. 7
3. 8. 5. 33–7: 382
3. 8. 6: 376, 377
3. 8. 6. 1–21: 376
3. 8. 6. 1–4: 375 n. 6
3. 8. 6. 19–30: 383
3. 8. 6. 21–34: 377
3. 8. 6. 27–30: 377 n. 8
3. 8. 7. 4–6: 376 n. 7
3. 8. 7. 23–7: 386
3. 8. 7. 23–6: 386
3. 15 ff.: 283 n. 158
4. 3. 4. 21–9: 393 n. 55
4. 3. 6. 10–15: 395 n. 66
4. 3. 6. 21–2: 394
4. 3. 10. 16–19: 383 n. 21
4. 3. 10. 17–19: 387 n. 34
4. 3. 11. 8–12: 393 n. 55
4. 3. 12. 6–8: 393 n. 53, 402 n. 82
4. 3. 17. 26–8: 395 n. 69
4. 3. 18. 5–7: 386, 387 n. 33
4. 3. 21. 14: 383 n. 21
4. 4. 6–12: 405 n. 86
4. 4. 6. 15–16: 388 n. 38
4. 4. 7. 7–9: 388 n. 35
4. 4. 8. 19–30: 388 n. 35
4. 4. 8. 48–61: 388
4. 4. 11. 4–5: 393 n. 56, 394 n. 63
4. 4. 12. 1 ff.: 404 n. 84
4. 4. 12. 29–31: 390
4. 4. 17. 23–35: 397 n. 73
4. 4. 17. 27–38: 406 n. 88
4. 4. 20: 393 n. 52

4. 4. 20. 16–19: 393 n. 53
4. 4. 20. 33–6: 393 n. 53
4. 4. 21. 7–14: 393 n. 53
4. 4. 21. 19–21: 393 n. 52
4. 4. 26. 3: 385 n. 26
4. 4 [28]. 44: 402 n. 82
4. 4. 30–1: 388 n. 38
4. 4. 30. 1–16: 388 n. 38
4. 4. 31. 3 ff.: 388 n. 38
4. 4. 31. 8–12: 388 n. 38
4. 4. 31. 16 ff.: 385 n. 25
4. 4. 35. 42–5: 388 n. 37
4. 4. 38. 22–3: 388 n. 38
4. 4. 40–5: 398
4. 4. 43–4: 398
4. 4. 43: 385 n. 26
4. 4. 43. 3–5: 298
4. 4. 43. 16–20: 401
4. 4. 43. 18–22: 384
4. 4. 43. 22–3: 398 n. 77
4. 4. 43. 22: 385 n. 26, 389 n. 40
4. 4. 44: 375 n. 5, 385 n. 23, 392 n. 51,
   398, 402, 403
4. 4. 44. 1–2: 400 n. 80
4. 4. 44. 2: 400 n. 80
4. 4. 44. 4: 400 n. 80, 401 n. 81
4. 4. 44. 6–7: 398
4. 4. 44. 7: 398
4. 4. 44. 8–9: 399
4. 4. 44. 9: 399
4. 4. 44. 10–11: 399
4. 4. 44. 10: 399
4. 4. 44. 12: 399
4. 4. 44. 13: 399
4. 4. 44. 14–15: 399
4. 4. 44. 16–24: 401 n. 81
4. 4. 44. 16–18: 399
4. 4. 44. 18–24: 400
4. 4. 44. 18–20: 401
4. 4. 44. 18–19: 400 n. 80
4. 4. 44. 18: 400 n. 80
4. 4. 44. 19–20: 400 n. 80
4. 4. 44. 20–1: 400 n. 80, 401
4. 4. 44. 20: 400 n. 80
4. 4. 44. 21–3: 401 n. 81
4. 4. 44. 21: 400 n. 80, 402
4. 4. 44. 23–5: 401 n. 81
4. 4. 44. 24: 401 n. 81
4. 4. 44. 25–7: 400
4. 4. 44. 26: 386, 400
4. 4. 44. 29–30: 398 n. 77
4. 4. 44. 31: 400
4. 4. 44. 33: 400 n. 80

4. 4. 44. 34–6: 400 n. 80
4. 4. 44. 34–5: 400 n. 80
4. 4. 44. 36: 400 n. 80
4. 5. 1. 24–6: 390 n. 43
4. 5. 2. 50–3: 390 n. 43
4. 8. 1: 390
4. 8. 2. 10–11: 394 n. 57
4. 8. 2. 11–14: 395 n. 65
4. 8. 2. 18–19: 394 n. 60
4. 8. 2. 26–33: 393 n. 55
4. 8. 2. 38–42: 393 n. 54
4. 8. 2. 46–53: 394
4. 8. 2. 48–9: 394
4. 8. 3. 25–7: 395 n. 69
4. 8. 4. 12–21: 395 n. 65
4. 8. 4. 18–21: 395 n. 69
4. 8. 4. 31–5: 406
4. 8. 4. 31–3: 402 n. 82
4. 8. 5. 10–14: 402 n. 82
4. 8. 5. 26–7: 393 n. 53
4. 8. 7. 26–31: 393 n. 55
4. 8. 8. 15–16: 386 n. 27
4. 8. 8. 15: 394 n. 63
4. 8. 8. 16–23: 394 n. 64
4. 9. 2. 28–33: 388 n. 38
5. 1. 2. 11–14: 394 n. 63
5. 1. 7. 35–49: 379 n. 13
5. 2. 1. 19–21: 380–1 n. 14
5. 3. 6. 35–9: 384
5. 5: 389 n. 41
5. 8. 1: 386 n. 29, 386 n. 30
5. 8. 5. 1 ff.: 386 n. 29
5. 9. 5. 39–41: 386 n. 29
6. 1. 12. 26–30: 383
6. 1. 16: 281, 282
6. 1. 16. 6–7: 283
6. 1. 16. 14–39: 283
6. 1. 16. 5–12: 282
6. 1 [42]. 15–22: 281 ff.
6. 1 [42]. 16 ff.: 237
6. 3. 16: 375 n. 5
6. 3. 16. 13–22: 384
6. 3. 16. 30–1: 389 n. 39
6. 7. 21–7: 387 n. 34
6. 8. 5: 384
6. 8. 5. 13–20: 384
6. 8. 6. 22–5: 397 n. 73
6. 9. 11: 389, 390
8. 8. 13–16: 393 n. 55
8. 8. 15: 393 n. 56

Porphyry
Ad Gaurum
6. 2–3, 42. 17–43. 5 Kalbfleisch: 380–1
   n. 14
De abstinentia
53. 10–12: 402 n. 82
Life of Plotinus
8: 389, 392
8. 8–11: 391 n. 47
8. 11–15: 391
8. 15–19: 392 n. 48
8. 19–20: 390 n. 42
8. 19: 392
8. 21–3: 397 n. 75
8. 23: 389 n. 41
9. 16–18: 390 n. 42, 392 n. 50
9. 17–18: 389 n. 41
10: 397 n. 75
23: 389
23. 4: 389 n. 41
Sententiae
32: 404 n. 84
32. 15–70: 381 n. 19

Proclus
In Platonis Parmenidem, ed. Cousin
797. 32–8: 264 n. 112
In Platonis Timaeum commentaria, ed.
  Diehl
i. 290. 23–6: 247–8 n. 70

Ptolemy el-Garib
no. 17: 273 n. 132

Quintilian
Institutio oratoria
9. 2. 46: 20 n. 22

Scholia in Aristotelem, ed. Brandis
781ᵃ47–ᵇ12: 232–3 n. 33

Seneca
De ira
2. 1–3: 52

Sextus Empiricus
Adversus mathematicos
8. 254–6: 247 n. 69

Simplicius
In Aristotelis Categorias commentarium,
  ed. Kalbfleisch
303. 35–304. 10: 283
303. 37–8: 283
307. 1–6: 284
In Aristotelis De caelo commentaria, ed.
  Heiberg
294. 33–295. 22: 276 n. 142
296. 16–18: 276 n. 142
379. 12–17: 276 n. 142
In Aristotelis Physicorum libros commen-
  taria, ed. Diels
357. 8–10: 154
967. 31–968. 5: 211–12
968. 5–15: 213 n. 34
998. 9–13: 213
In libros Aristotelis De anima commen-
  taria, ed. Hayduck
126. 2–3: 237 n. 45
264. 25–265. 16: 237 n. 45

Stobaeus
ii. 88. 8–90: 52 nn. 32, 33

Themistius
In libros Aristotelis De anima paraphra-
  sis, ed. Heinze
55. 6–12: 237 n. 45
112. 25–33: 237 n. 45

Theophrastus
Fragments, ed. FHS&G
307D: 274–5

Notes for Contributors to Oxford Studies in Ancient Philosophy

1. Articles should be submitted with double or $1\frac{1}{2}$ line-spacing through-out. At the stage of initial (but not final) submission footnotes may be given in small type at the foot of the page. Page dimensions should be A4 or standard American quarto ($8\frac{1}{2} \times 11''$), and ample margins should be left.

2. Submissions should be made as a file in PDF format attached to an e-mail sent to the Editor. Authors are asked to supply an accurate word-count (*a*) for the main text, and (*b*) for the notes. The e-mail which serves as a covering letter should come from the address to be used for correspondence on the submission. A postal address should also be provided. If necessary, arrangements for alternative means of submission may be made with the Editor. Authors should note that the version first submitted will be the one adjudicated; unsolicited revised versions cannot be accepted during the adjudication process.

The remaining instructions apply to the final version sent for publication, and need not be rigidly adhered to in a first submission.

3. In the finalized version, the text should be double-spaced and in the same typesize throughout, **including displayed quotations and notes**. Notes should be numbered consecutively, and may be sup-plied as either footnotes or endnotes. Any acknowledgements should be placed in an unnumbered first note. Wherever possible, references to primary sources should be built into the text.

4. **Use of Greek and Latin.** Relatively familiar Greek terms such as *psychē* and *polis* (but not whole phrases and sentences) may be used in transliteration. Wherever possible, Greek and Latin should not be used in the main text of an article in ways which would impede comprehen-sion by those without knowledge of the languages; for example, where appropriate, the original texts should be accompanied by a translation. This constraint does not apply to footnotes. Greek must be supplied in an accurate form, with all diacritics in place. A note of the system employed for achieving Greek (e.g. GreekKeys, Linguist's Software) should be supplied to facilitate file conversion.

5. For citations of Greek and Latin authors, house style should be fol-lowed. This can be checked in any recent issue of *OSAP* with the help of the Index Locorum.

6. In references to books, the first time the book is referred to give the ini-tial(s) and surname of the author (first names are not usually required), and the place and date of publication; where you are abbreviating the

title in subsequent citations, give the abbreviation in square brackets, thus:

> T. Brickhouse and N. Smith, *Socrates on Trial* [*Trial*] (Princeton, 1981), 91–4.

Give the volume-number and date of periodicals, and include the full page-extent of articles (including chapters of books):

> D. W. Graham, 'Symmetry in the Empedoclean Cycle' ['Symmetry'], *Classical Quarterly*, NS 38 (1988), 297–312 at 301–4.

> G. Vlastos, 'The Unity of the Virtues in the *Protagoras*' ['Unity'], in id., *Platonic Studies*, 2nd edn. (Princeton, 1981), 221–65 at 228.

Where the same book or article is referred to on subsequent occasions, usually the most convenient style will be an abbreviated reference, thus:

> Brickhouse and Smith, *Trial*, 28–9.

Do *not* use the author-and-date style of reference:

> Brickhouse and Smith 1981: 28–9.

7. Authors are asked to supply *in addition*, at the end of the article, a full list of the bibliographical entries cited, alphabetically ordered by (first) author's surname. Except that the author's surname should come first, these entries should be identical in form to the first occurrence of each in the article, including where appropriate the indication of abbreviated title:

> Graham, D. W., 'Symmetry in the Empedoclean Cycle' ['Symmetry'], *Classical Quarterly*, NS 38 (1988), 297–312.

8. If there are any unusual conventions contributors are encouraged to include a covering note for the copy-editor and/or printer. Please say whether you are using single and double quotation marks for different purposes (otherwise the Press will employ its standard single quotation marks throughout, using double only for quotations within quotations).

9. Authors should send a copy of the final version of their paper in electronic form by attachment to an e-mail. The final version should be in a standard word-processing format, accompanied by a note of the word-processing program used and of the system (**not just the font**) used for producing Greek characters (see point 4 above). This file must be accompanied by a second file, a copy in PDF format of the submitted word-processor file; the PDF file must correspond **exactly** to the word-processor file. If necessary, arrangements for alternative means of submission may be made with the Editor.